The Future of Financial Regulation

Edited by
Iain G MacNeil
and
Justin O'Brien

·H A R T·
PUBLISHING

OXFORD AND PORTLAND, OREGON
2010

Published in North America (US and Canada) by
Hart Publishing
c/o International Specialized Book Services
920 NE 58th Avenue, Suite 300
Portland, OR 97213-3786
USA
Tel: +1-503-287-3093 or toll-free: +1-800-944-6190
Fax: +1-503-280-8832
Email: orders@isbs.com
Website: www.isbs.com

First printed in 2010, reprinted in 2011

Hart Publishing, 16C Worcester Place, Oxford, OX1 2JW
Telephone: +44 (0)1865 517530   Fax: +44 (0) 1865 510710
Email: mail@hartpub.co.uk
Website: http://www.hartpub.co.uk

British Library Cataloguing in Publication Data
Data Available

ISBN: 978-1-84113-910-4

Typeset by Forewords, Oxford
Printed and bound in Great Britain by
TJ International Ltd, Padstow, Cornwall

CONTENTS

Introduction:
The Future of Financial Regulation

IAIN MACNEIL AND JUSTIN O'BRIEN*

The global financial crisis is the latest, if most catastrophic, in a series of financial crises linked both with 'boom–bust' phases in the economic cycle and 'regulate–deregulate' swings in government policy. As the impact moves progressively and decisively from the financial into the real economy, the enormous political and socio-economic costs associated with a failure to address the question of the role of financial markets and institutions more generally in society comes into clear view. The design of effective and flexible regulatory and corporate governance rules, principles and norms to address the inter-linked and intractable problems in both dimensions of the economy at national and international levels has become a global policy imperative. Moreover, the extent of state intervention required to stabilise financial markets has fundamentally transformed conceptual and practical dynamics. The power and influence of government within the regulatory matrix has been augmented considerably. The unresolved question is: what will it do with this power? Notwithstanding the certainty of the former chairman of the Federal Reserve, Alan Greenspan, that it is impossible to have a perfect model of risk or that it is difficult to legislate for ethics, it has become essential that basic flaws in risk-based regulatory techniques be remedied and that the integrity deficit in regulatory frameworks be addressed.[1]

The G-20 Summit in London in April 2009 laid the foundations for a new international regulatory architecture covering all systemically important financial institutions and markets (including, significantly, hedge funds which, through judicious structuring, have been effectively unregulated to date) as well as systemically important financial instruments (such as securitisation and credit derivatives). The EU has proposed the establishment of a European Systemic Risk Council and a European System of Financial Supervisors. Much work needs to be done to put flesh on this skeletal framework, not least how the superstructure will integrate or subsume national regulatory priorities, particularly over the governance of the City of London. The US has also begun the process of overhauling its dysfunctional regulatory system, a process that it likely to generate turf

* Alexander Stone Professor of Commercial Law, University of Glasgow and Professor of Law, University of New South Wales, Sydney.
[1] A Greenspan, 'We Will Never Have a Perfect Model of Risk', *Financial Times*, 17 March 2008, 13; A Greenspan, 'Capitalizing Reputation', speech delivered at Financial Markets Conference, Federal Reserve Board of Georgia, 16 April 2004.

wars in Washington for some time to come. Changes in regulatory structure alone, however, are unlikely to be the answer. Moreover, a retreat to legal rules will not necessarily guarantee better ethical practice or inculcate higher standards of probity. Indeed, the passage of legal rules may itself constitute a serious problem: it creates the illusion of change. Thus, for example, it appears that the risk management procedures required by the Sarbanes-Oxley Act (2002) had the unfortunate consequence of discounting the benefits of critical thinking within financial institutions and their advisers as to the risks associated with the expansion of securitisation. While substantial progress can be achieved through better rules, it is clear that the entire regulatory framework must be underpinned by much clearer concepts of accountability and integrity applicable to individuals, entities and markets as a whole. Addressing the accountability and integrity deficit requires an expansion of focus beyond legal restraints, irrespective of whether they are formulated as generalised principles or more detailed rules. It is only through such an approach that the inevitable gaps in any regulatory framework can be resolved adequately.

Latest estimates by the International Monetary Fund put the total cost of the multi-faceted collapse at $4 trillion, the vast majority of which can be attributed to systemic failures of corporate, regulatory and political oversight in the US. Many of its leading bankers have been forced to resign, castigated for destroying their institutions through a combination of hubris, greed and technical gaming (ie compliance with but derogation from the underlying principles of regulatory rules). The crisis, however, was not just a failure of rules-based regulation. In the UK, the Financial Services Authority (FSA) has seen its vaunted principles-based approach to regulation fall into as much reputational disrepute as that country's leading banks, whose forced nationalisation has added to the humiliation of the City of London. Similar dynamics are apparent in countries as culturally, politically and economically divergent as Iceland and Ireland. Each has seen its banking system fail, with profoundly destabilising effects on the underlying economy. Ostensibly more cautious regulatory frameworks within the EU have proved equally deficient. The 'passport system', allowing banks to operate across borders with supervision vested in the home jurisdiction, was a demonstrable failure, as witnessed by the collapse of regional German banks operating in Dublin and of Icelandic banks 'passporting' into the UK. Regulatory arbitrage over the implementation of directives relating to the finance sector reinforced the problems. Much more fundamentally, however, it is important to stress that, although there has been criminal activity in the margins, the global financial crisis is the result of 'perfectly legal' if ethically questionable strategies.

After taking into account specific national factors, three interlinked global phenomena are at play: flawed governance mechanisms, including remuneration incentives skewed in favour of short-term profit-taking and leverage; flawed models of financing, including, in particular, the dominant originate-and-distribute model of securitisation, which promoted a moral hazard culture; and regulatory structures predicated on risk reduction, which created incentives for risk capital arbitrage and paid insufficient attention to credit risk. Each combined to create an architectural blueprint for economic growth in which innovation trumped security. Financial engineering, in turn, created complex mechanisms that, ultimately, lacked structural and ethical integrity. Take, for example, the collateralised debt obligation and credit default swap market, which generated enormous fee income for the investment bank that created or distributed the instruments. This raises real doubts as to whether the investment bank in question acted in an ethical manner, even where there has been formal compliance with legal obligation. Those doubts have also been raised in relation to other participants in these types of transactions, including accountants, lawyers and ratings agencies.

Asymmetric information flow and variable capacity—or willingness—to use internal management systems, market mechanisms or regulatory enforcement tools led to a profound misunderstanding of national and international risks associated with the rapid expansion of structured finance products such as securitisation. Deepening market integration ensured that risk, while diversified geographically, remained undiluted. As the Nobel Laureate Joseph Stigliz put it in excoriating testimony to Congress, 'securitisation was based on the premise that a fool was born every minute. Globalisation meant that there was a global landscape on which they could search for these fools—and they found them everywhere.'[2] From northern Norway to rural New South Wales, local councils bought complex financial products on the basis of misplaced trust in the efficacy of internal controls, the strength of independent directors to hold management to account, the attestation provided by external auditors, legal due diligence, the assurances of those providing corporate advisory services, including inherently conflicted rating agencies, and, ultimately, the robustness of the overarching regulatory system at either national or international levels. The progressive visualisation of those flaws has led to a massive loss of confidence in the accountability mechanisms designed by or demanded of key actors in the financial markets.

The critical issue facing regulatory authorities across the world is how to deal with a model of financial capitalism based on technical compliance with narrowly defined legislation and a working assumption that, unless a particular action is explicitly proscribed, it is deemed politically and socially acceptable. The unrelenting focus on the punishment of individual malefactors serves to obscure this much more fundamental problem. Corporate malfeasance and misfeasance on the scale witnessed cannot be readily explained by individual turpitude. It is essential to evaluate how epistemic communities within specific corporate, professional or regulatory practice interpret these rules and principles, and whether this is done in an emasculated or holistic manner. A necessary first step is to map more precisely the contours of the crisis across a range of institutional and professional settings. Secondly, it is important to emphasise the dynamic interplay between the culpability of individual actors and the cultural and ideational factors that not only tacitly condoned but also actively encouraged the elevation of short-term considerations over longer-term interests.

The political wrangling in the US over executive pay suggests, rhetorically at least, a much more interventionist approach. More encouragingly, perhaps, in his inaugural address, President Obama emphasised the need for the inculcation of a new 'ethics of responsibility'. This echoed earlier calls by the British Prime Minister, Gordon Brown, for moral restraint within financial centres (if only for instrumental reasons).[3] Beyond London and New York, however, the extent to which the crisis has metastasised with such ferocity has substantially strengthened calls for an integrated response to nullify what the

---

[2] J Stiglitz, 'Regulatory Restructuring and the Reform of the Financial System', Evidence to House Committee on Financial Services, Washington, DC, 21 October 2008. For discussion of 'an ideological agenda [which] has pushed excessive reliance on capital adequacy standards,' see J Stiglitz, 'Principles of Financial Regulation: A Dynamic Portfolio Approach' (2001) 16 *World Bank Research Observer* 1 (arguing that 'despite its long history, financial market regulation is poorly understood' and suggesting the need for strong regulation to address 'failures in the banking system [which] have strong spillovers, or externalities, that reach well beyond the individuals and firms directly involved', 2).

[3] G Brown, 'The Global Economy', speech delivered at the Reuters Building, London, 13 October 2008.

Australian Prime Minister, Kevin Rudd, has called 'extreme capitalism'.[4] Although many would disagree with the polemical framing, there can be no question that we have reached an inflexion point for both the theory and practice of regulation. Restoring the confidence of investors is critical to the success of the various government initiatives worldwide to address the global financial crisis. It is against this background that scholars were invited to attend a major conference at the University of Glasgow on the eve of the G-20 London summit. Its aim was to play a leading role in informing and influencing public policy and framing theoretical and empirical research into the causes and consequences of the global financial crisis. Reform cannot be achieved on a sustainable basis unless the structural changes address the ethical and governance dimensions that form the core of the research agenda advanced here.

This volume is divided into four parts. First, the credit crisis is put in context. Secondly, the impact on regulatory practice and techniques is investigated. Thirdly, we explore why the corporate governance system proved so defective, and fourthly, the trajectory of reform and suggested necessary recalibrations are examined.

A.   The Credit Crisis in Context

Now that the most severe phase of the financial crisis has receded, it is possible to view it in historical context. It is possible to identify elements that are common to previous crises and others that are defining of the age. Common features include the easy availability of credit as a result of loose monetary policy; the relaxation of lending standards associated with that process; speculative bubbles in property and financial assets driven both by excess liquidity and a herding mentality among investors; and the 'moral hazard' problem associated with central banks acting as 'lender of last resort' to banks deemed too big to fail. Features that are associated with this financial crisis much more so than those experienced in the past include the impact of financial innovation in creating difficult to value complex products; the globalisation of financial services; and the effect of regulatory arbitrage in creating a shadow banking system that was able to operate largely outside regulatory purview.

While these background influences are now acknowledged, it is much more difficult to attribute direct causality to any one of them. This carries important implications for the regulatory reform agenda. With so many interrelated causes, it is very difficult and probably not worthwhile attempting to attribute specific causality. Since it is clear that the genesis of the crisis does not rest exclusively in any single causal influence, neither will the solution. Thus, it makes more sense to focus on the significance of the interaction between the multiple failures associated with the crisis than to attempt to finesse causality. The construction of simplistic narratives focusing on corporate greed or regulatory incompetence without ascertaining how and why social norms were so eroded risks both misdiagnosing the problem and compromising the search for a solution. A second difficulty is that causality itself is inevitably a contested issue, with resolution contingent on the relative strength of individual corporate or professional actors. While it is fashionable

---

[4] K Rudd, 'The Global Financial Crisis,' *The Monthly*, February 2009, 20; see also K Rudd, 'The Children of Gordon Gekko,' *The Australian*, 1 October 2008, 12.

to defenestrate investment bankers, the failure of financial capitalism indicts a much wider range of market participants. Both dynamics are evidenced in the debates over the accountability of central banks and regulators and the turf wars that are now being fought on both sides of the Atlantic over the survival, shape and remit of regulatory authorities. At the same time, it is essential to emphasise that overarching these micro-failures is an ideational meta-failure of the terms of reference that underpinned the trajectory of corporate governance and financial regulation reform in the decades either side of the turn of the millennium.

A particularly striking feature of corporate and regulatory responses to the financial crisis has been the paucity of institutional memory. At both Congressional hearings in Washington and testimony provided to the Treasury Select Committee in Westminster, banking executives claimed that the crisis was the result of a 'perfect storm' or 'financial tsunami'; the conflation of factors beyond control. Similar defences, it will be recalled, were used during the conflicts of interest investigations that accompanied the collapse of Enron, WorldCom and Tyco in the accounting scandals at the turn of the century. The falsification of the efficient market hypothesis and the belated acceptance that the pursuit of (deluded) self-interest is not only corrosive but, when taken to its logical conclusion diminishes accountability, suggests the need to pay attention to the reinforcing and restraining power of social norms.[5] It has long been recognised that strong moral and ethical codes are required to ensure economic viability.[6] Arguably the gradual erosion of these codes was an essential contributing factor to the creation and maintenance of the latest manifestation of irrational exuberance.[7] If the social compact is to have validity, we have to design mechanisms that allow us to calibrate the restraining component more precisely. This requires combining the technical with the normative, both in our investigation of the causes of the crisis and in our evaluation of policy responses. It suggests that behavioural economics must play a critical role in identifying and adjudicating how incentives and preferences are arrived at.[8] Other disciplines too have significant roles to play: law, through its primary but not exclusive focus on rules; political science and public policy, for its emphasis on the dynamics of power and institutional design; ethnography, for its detailed examination of cultural rituals; philosophy, for its emphasis on ethics; management, for the attention placed on organisational frameworks; and the accounting

---

[5] See L Stout, 'Social Norms and Other-regarding Preferences' in J Drobak (ed), *Norms and the Law* (New York, Cambridge University Press, 2006) 13 (reviewing results from social dilemma, ultimatum games and dictator games and postulating 'taken as a whole, the evidence strongly supports the following proposition: *whether or not people behave in an other-regarding fashion is determined largely by social context tempered—but only tempered—by considerations of personal cost*', 22; original emphasis).

[6] D North, *Structure and Change in Economic History* (Cambridge, Cambridge University Press, 1981) 47 (suggesting that they are the 'cement of social stability').

[7] For original formulation, see A Greenspan, 'The Challenge of Central Banking in a Democratic Society', speech delivered at the American Enterprise Institute Dinner, Washington DC, 5 December 1996. Greenspan asked rhetorically 'How do we know when irrational exuberance has unduly escalated asset values, which then become subject to unexpected and prolonged contractions as they have in Japan over the past decade?' The remarks provided the title for a seminal analysis of the dynamics of speculative bubbles: see R Shiller, *Irrational Exuberance* (Princeton, NJ, Princeton University Press, 2000). Shiller, along with a Nobel prize winning economist at University of California at Berkeley, has applied similar reasoning to the global financial crisis: see R Shiller and G Akerloff, *Animal Spirits* (Princeton, NJ, Princeton University Press, 2009) 4 ('The crisis was caused precisely by our changing confidence, temptations, envy, resentment, and illusions—and especially by changing stories about the nature of the economy').

[8] Psychological factors such as confidence, perception of fairness, toleration of or condemnation of corrupt and antisocial behaviour, money, illusion tempered by narratives, influence market actors in a profound, if imperfectly understood, manner: see Shiller and Akerloff, ibid, 5–6.

discipline, for its work on the value of disclosure. This list is far from exhaustive; however, it does serve to suggest that the search for more effective and more accountable governance necessitates an understanding of the dynamic interaction between all these variables and disciplinary foci, as Charles Sampford points out in the opening essay. Suspicious of a new regulatory contract or the restraining power of fiduciary duty without explicit reference to renegotiated adherence to values, for Sampford, effective reform requires the combination of three distinct but overlapping modes of intervention: legal regulation, explicit ethical standard setting and institutional reform. Practically, this involves asking

> vital questions that must be asked of any institution or organisation: what is it for? Why should it exist? What justifies the organisation to the community in which it operates, given that the community generally provides privileges? Why is the community within which it operates better for the existence of the government/corporation etc? Asking those questions involves an institutional and collective effort under its own formal and informal constitutional processes (including getting acceptance from relevant outsiders, such as shareholders and/or relevant regulators).

This analysis helps frame and inform the substantive chapters examining the causes and consequences of the crisis that follow.

The first sign of stress occurred in the US sub-prime market, the subject of exegesis by Robin Malloy. For Malloy, the problems were not caused by securitisation per se but the inappropriate uses to which it was placed. As will be explored in later sections, this distinction also has important implications for regulatory reform. First, however, it is necessary to trace the wide macro-level impacts of the initial shock. In their examination of how the securitisation crisis crossed the Atlantic with such ferocity, Barrell, Hurst and Kirby place the blame on the combination of 'light-touch regulation' for failing to prevent the crisis and excessive fear of counter-party risk in its immediate aftermath for exacerbating it. The result has been the most severe financial crisis in a century, with severe credit rationing and a very sharp contraction in output. Barrell and his co-authors argue that, while financial crises happen with depressing regularity, the severity of this one is likely to leave permanent scarring, not least because of the external costs of a collective misjudgement in the financial sector now borne by wider society. They maintain that, as a direct consequence, there is now a pressing need for deeper more intrusive regulation.

As noted above, despite the media focus on investment bankers and conflicted rating agencies whose flawed valuation of risk helped legitimate the entire enterprise, it is important to emphasise the critical role played by the legal community. For Doreen McBarnet,

> a crucial component of the new banking products was legal creativity. The legal work behind such practices as securitisation was not confined to drafting the contracts to sell on risk. It was also about creatively removing the 'obstacles' of prudential regulation, accounting requirements and other legal and regulatory constraints intended to control or disclose risk. Indeed, circumventing capital adequacy regulation was a crucial driver behind much structured finance.

Building on earlier work on creative compliance in the audit profession, McBarnet argues that part of the problem rests on the fact that legal representatives took a very narrow compartmentalised view of their work. What is particularly striking is the degree to which the securitisation contracts were themselves standardised, a point highlighted by Jeffrey Golden, one of the leading London-based securitisation and derivative lawyers. Golden argues that while 'we do not have a world parliament to legislate such matters . . . the markets have created a kind of global law by contract'. This raises profound risks, not only for the legal practitioners who designed the mechanisms but also in determining the outcome of (inevitable) future litigation. As Golden points out, widespread usage of the same terms can 'amplify any mistakes that a court makes in deciding the proper meaning of such terms'. He warns that consolidation of the global legal services market magnifies the problems. 'If, as a result, the experts in the field become unavailable when litigation arises because of traditional notions of "conflict", practice designed to protect clients and promote justice could have the opposite effect.' It would appear, therefore, that what eventually mushroomed into a multi-trillion dollar market was designed and executed with little or no reference to longer-term operational or reputational risk. The unresolved question is why? The answer, in large part, takes us back to the underpinning ideational agenda that denigrated attempts to impose formal restraint. As Paddy Ireland argues in a penetrating critique, meaningful reform requires us to resolve, definitively, the existential conflict between public and private law imperatives in the regulation of the corporation and the markets in which it is nested. Unless this question is resolved, it is likely that reform will not only be ad hoc and piecemeal, it will also fail to address the underlying problems.

B.   Regulatory Techniques and Practice

The financial crisis has inevitably raised serious questions about the capacity of regulatory systems to anticipate or prevent such developments or to act when warning signs become apparent. These questions focus, in particular, on the role of risk-based regulation; the formulation and application of capital adequacy rules; the reliance on disclosure and transparency as a primary regulatory technique; and the role of enforcement in ensuring compliance with regulatory rules. The reliance on risk-based regulation has been the subject of particularly strong criticism. It is not that it is wrong in principle to adopt a risk-based approach to financial products and services, since it is a well-established policy framework in other regulatory domains. Moreover, it provides a means of prioritising the use of scarce regulatory resources. The problem centres on an over-reliance on this approach, particularly its quantitative dimension.

In his overview of the UK regulatory framework, Roman Tomasic argues that, whilst risk is an inherent feature of modern times, the question that arises here is

> the degree to which banking regulation should depend upon the use of risk models and the extent to which these need to be supplemented by the application of legal rules as well as other regulatory techniques that have emerged from the study of corporations and professionals.

He concludes that

> the much touted claims of the superiority of the UK's light touch and principles based system of market regulation has been shown to be hollow as, at the end of the day, this has merely amounted to a lack of regulation.

The reputational costs to the FSA, in particular, have been enormous and have not been helped by poor media management. As Joanna Gray points out, the problem is that

> It is much harder for regulators, especially when engaged in post-crisis reform, to emphasise the persistence and possibility of unknowable uncertainty than it is for politicians.

For Gray, the very future of the risk-based approach is under question unless market participants, including, crucially, the FSA itself are,

> more open and explicit about the persistence of uncertainty and the fact that no amount of regulation, whatever its model or approach, can guard against the truly catastrophic 'killer event'.

Such change, notes Gray, requires 'political and social leadership and honesty' and 'is one that policymakers are only just beginning to wake up to'.

MacNeil concurs that, despite its failures, risk-based regulation is likely to remain embedded within the system. He questions, however, not only its foundational assumptions but also its capacity to prohibit, limit or remedy potential or actual risks to systemic stability. For MacNeil,

> Capacity is a function of the institutional and normative structure of a system of regulation and of the underlying legal system on which it is superimposed. It is also a function of the mix of risk control strategies that are adopted within the system, since each strategy offers a distinctive approach to the process of regulation.

For MacNeil, the foundational assumptions of risk-based regulation have been falsified and, more fundamentally, policymakers in the UK have, to date, been unable to demonstrate how the regime can or should be recalibrated. As he puts it, echoing Tomasic, there is something 'deeply unsatisfactory about a regulatory system that is designed to avert risk and yet when the risk materialises is unable to hold the primary decision-makers to account in any meaningful way'. Although the FSA has been subject to withering criticism, other regulatory authorities failed within the banking matrix, not only in the UK but also in Ireland, Germany, the US and, most, catastrophically, Iceland.

The common feature was a reliance on internal risk models to determine regulatory capital. It is also demonstrated by the integration of third-party, partially conflicted measurements of risk (such as credit ratings) into the regulatory system. When considered alongside the limited historical basis on which most models were constructed, the outcome was a system that relied to a dangerous degree on a hubristic capacity to identify and measure risk.[9] These observations can be applied equally to capital adequacy rules. They form the core of risk-based rules that focus on the quantitative matching of risk and regulatory capital. The basic concept of creating a capital buffer to protect a financial institution's creditors is long established. The operation of the principle has, however, been frustrated in recent years by a number of developments which have led to a much more rapid growth in risk assets than in the associated regulatory capital.[10] These include the use of conduits (such as special purpose vehicles) to transfer risk 'off balance sheet' for regulatory purposes (without a corresponding transfer of economic risk); the sanctioning by Basel II of the use of banks' own risk models to determine regulatory capital; the proliferation of complex products which are difficult to value and to allocate regulatory capital against; and crucially the willingness of regulators to permit higher leverage ratios in the knowledge that all these developments were occurring (even if the finer details may in some cases have remained obscure). Thus, it eventually transpired that regulatory capital was woefully inadequate. As Persaud explains in a later chapter, at best the crisis derives

---

[9] See N Taleb, *The Black Swan: The Impact of the Highly Improbable* (New York, Penguin, 2008).

[10] For a graphical representation of the increasing divergence between global risk-adjusted assets and regulatory capital prior to the crisis see the Turner Review: Financial Services Authority, *The Turner Review: A Regulatory Response to the Global Banking Crisis* (London, FSA, 2009) 19.

from a reliance on microprudential oversight: improving the condition of the individual bank. He argues that it is a fallacy of composition to believe that, if each individual institution behaves 'prudently', the system as a whole will be safe. Even here, however, there is significant evidence that the regulators did not ask sufficient questions, as the painful experience with Northern Rock so tellingly reveals. It is therefore not surprising that attention is now focusing, both in regulatory agencies and the markets, on the need for much higher levels of capital.

Moving forward, however, the extent of policy intervention required to temporarily stabilise the financial sector raises its own discrete set of policy conundrums. Campbell and Lastra argue that there is pressing need to revisit conventional wisdom about the extent and effectiveness of bank crisis management instruments and to reassess the degree of government intervention needed to safeguard confidence. Many of the interventions, although undoubtedly ingenious, pose significant questions for the theory and practice of central banking. For Campbell and Lastra,

> The financial crisis has meant that the role of the Bank of England, the Federal Reserve System and other central banks in providing lender of last resort assistance or emergency liquidity assistance is never likely to be the same again.

George Walker, by contrast, cautions that despite failures, the existing market and regulatory rulebooks do not require fundamental overhaul. For Walker, great care must be taken not to overreact to the severity of the recent crisis and subsequent downturn. This could have the effect of unnecessarily limiting future innovation and benefit while possibly overextending the duration and depth of the crisis with unnecessary measures that would only restrict liquidity and credit creation and supply.

He advances instead an incremental approach to 'create a new more balanced and effectively managed market system'. Whether such an incremental approach will be adopted depends, in large measure, on the capacity of lobby groups to keep the discussion focused on technical or on broader normative issues. Here it is both inevitable but dispiriting that the policy response seems fixated on the silver bullet of greater transparency and disclosure.

The causal role of disclosure and transparency in the crisis is complex. On the one hand, the crisis can be viewed as the result of a lack of transparency in certain markets, with the 'over-the-counter' market in which much derivatives trading occurs being an obvious example. From this perspective, we have experienced not so much a failure in markets but a failure in the proper structuring and operation of markets which require adequate disclosure and transparency to price risk and allocate capital efficiently. The alternative approach is to argue that too much reliance has been placed on disclosure and transparency as regulatory techniques because of an unfounded belief in the market's capacity to self-correct when provided with the information required to make rational decisions. As noted above, there are many influences that result in investors making irrational decisions even when they are fully informed; such influences include psychological factors, herding behaviour, reliance on heuristics as a substitute for analysis and 'irrational exuberance'. In the light of recent experience, it is hardly surprising that regulators across the world are signalling a much more interventionist stance. As Emilios Avgouleas points out,

> Most of the risks that led to the creation of the 2008 catastrophe were often fully disclosed but the markets failed to understand what was disclosed and appreciate the implications . . . Accord-

ingly, there is a clear need to devise strategies that make disclosure work under actual (not hypothetical) market conditions.

He argues that, given the evidence of failure in prudential regulation, disclosure will only work if it is supplemented by protective measures and imaginative regulatory techniques, such as the use of experiments to complement empirical studies in the measurement of the actual contribution of disclosure to effective investor protection. It is possible, he concludes, that such studies will show that, in the case of unsophisticated investors (who have been shown to include many deemed sophisticated), the establishment of an independent financial products committee is a better investor protection strategy than enhanced disclosure.

Here it is important to emphasise that the problem is not the product but how irresponsible usage is legitimated. Joseph Tanega revisits securitisation—the trigger, if not the cause, of the global collapse of confidence. Tanega argues that the current regulatory framework has encouraged the production of ever increasingly complex financial instruments and that,

> With the unfolding phenomenon of the credit crisis, these complex financial transactions show an asymmetry at a social level which threatens to undermine social cohesion by discrediting the financial system.

Tanega argues that, unless the asymmetry at a social level is dealt with, there is a profound risk that the financial system will be further discredited, leading, in turn, to an undermining of social cohesion.

The crisis also raises issues about the role of enforcement in financial regulation and the capacity of regulators to use discretionary powers at the appropriate point in time to ensure financial stability both within individual firms and across the system. It now seems clear that there were many instances in which discretionary powers were not used, in particular as regards the potential to require higher levels of regulatory capital to reflect increasing levels of leverage. Attention must now turn to developing regulatory structures and systems that place the relevant regulatory authorities in a position to act even when that goes against the grain of current political and market perceptions of their role. Enforcement is linked with that agenda, especially in the UK, where, as MacNeil has pointed out, the 'light-touch' approach has resulted in relatively few cases of formal enforcement and a perception that the regulator lacked teeth. Viewed from the interaction of both perspectives, a failure to prevent and a failure to enforce known weaknesses, what we are witnessing is a massive systemic failure of regulation. Ultimately, however, enforcement is only one weapon in the regulatory arsenal. Securing improvements in ex ante regulatory techniques and practice require us to transcend an increasingly sterile debate over whether it is preferable to privilege rules over principles. Moreover, as has long been recognised in regulatory studies, rules need to work hand in glove with principles within an interlocking system of incentives and disincentives. In some areas, compliance with rules might be more important than alignment with principles. On the other hand, for some problems in other areas, for example potential conflicts of interest, the emphasis might need to be on principles in the context of verifiable procedural requirements, such as an internal but independent mechanism for determination of any conflict of interest. In still other areas, such as disclosure requirements, principles and rules might both need to be met. More generally, principles may require ongoing testing to ensure consistency and coherence in terms of application. How to ensure that rules and principles mutually reinforce one another—rather than competing with one another—is central to regulatory effectiveness.

C.   Controlling the Corporation:
Towards Ethical Governance

In the search for responsibility and for solutions, it is essential that self-reflection extend to the academy, which failed to internalise (or, more accurately, ignored) insights from classical economics on how markets can be (and often are) corrupted by a lack of restraint.[11] Adam Smith's disdain of the joint-stock corporation is (almost but not quite) as well known as his fleeting and largely flippant reference to the invisible hand metaphor. Indeed, the need for governmental intervention to engineer aspiration over mere duty informs his more philosophical writing, particularly the *Theory of Moral Sentiments* (1759).[12] The rise of the corporation magnified the need for impartial adjudication. As Edward Mason noted as early as 1958, corporate power had a profound impact on the 'carefully reasoned' laissez-faire defence that 'the economic behaviour promoted and constrained by the institutions of a free market system is, in the main, in the public interest'.[13] For Mason, as for Smith before him, this rested on foundations that depended largely on the general acceptance of a reasoned justification of the system on moral as well as on political and economic grounds.[14] The emergence of major corporations, immune from meaningful controls, along with its 'apologetics' within the management literature, 'appears devastatingly to undermine the intellectual presuppositions of this system' without offering 'an equally satisfying ideology for twentieth century consumption'.[15] As such, 'the entrepreneur of classical economics has given way to something quite different, and along with him disappears a substantial element in the traditional capitalist apologetic'.[16] Despite Mason's misgivings, the economic conception of the corporation as a 'nexus of contracts' extended well beyond the boundaries of the economics tradition. In a highly influential essay,[17] Easterbrook and Fischel, for example, maintain that wider social issues are and should remain outside the purview of the market, citing approvingly Adam Smith in defence of the proposition that 'the extended conflict among selfish people produces prices that allocate resources to their most valuable uses'.[18] In this context, the role of corporate law is solely 'to establish rights among participants in the venture'.[19] For Easterbrook and Fischel, the key normative advantage is that it

[11] See K Polanyi, *The Great Transformation: The Political and Economic Origins of Our Time* (Boston, MA, Beacon Press, 1944).

[12] See also L Fuller, *The Morality of Law* (New Haven CT, Yale University Press, 1964) 5–9.

[13] E Mason, 'The Apologetics of Managerialism' (1958) 31 *Journal of Business* 1, 5.

[14] Ibid, 5.

[15] Ibid, 6, 9.

[16] Ibid, 10.

[17] F Easterbrook and D Fischel, 'The Corporate Contract' (1989) 89 *Columbia Law Review* 1416.

[18] Ibid, 1422.

[19] Ibid, 1428. The authors note, however, circumstances where the corporate contract can be trumped. As they state, 'the argument that contracts are optimal applies only if the contracting parties bear the full costs of their decisions and reap all of the gains. It applies only if contracts are enforced after they have been reached. The argument also depends on the availability of the full set of possible contracts. If some types of agreements are foreclosed, the ones actually reached may not be optimal', 1436.

removes from the field of interesting questions one that has plagued many writers: what is the goal of the corporation. Is it profit (and for whom)? Social welfare more broadly defined? Is there anything wrong with corporate charity? Should corporations try to maximise profit over the long run or the short run. Our response to such questions is: 'Who cares?'[20]

In many ways, this construct reached its apogee with the publication in 2001 of Hannsmann and Kraakman's landmark essay, 'The End of History for Corporate Law'.[21] The normative claim of 'the end of history' thesis was always exceptionally vulnerable to contestation, not least because of its circular reasoning.[22] Furthermore, the foundational assumption of maximising individual utility, while informing the transformation from democratic capitalism to financial capitalism,[23] cuts against the plurality approach to governance that is embedded in stakeholder and stewardship conceptions of corporate purpose. The credit crisis has now fundamentally falsified its normative assumptions.

Alan Greenspan's admission that he was 'partially' wrong in his deference to the capacity of the market to exercise necessary restraint marks an important but insufficient step forward. The remaining challenge for a now weakened financial sector and for society as a whole is to build corporate governance and capital market regulation in ways that emphasize duties and responsibilities as well as corporate rights. As noted earlier, it requires a settled accommodation 'between a public law, regulatory conception of corporate law on the one hand, and a private law, internal perspective on the other'; between 'a body of law concerned solely with the techniques of shareholder wealth maximization [and] a body of law that embraces and seeks to promote a richer array of social and political values'.[24] President Obama has neatly encapsulated this dilemma.

> There's always been a tension between those who place their faith in the invisible hand of the marketplace and those who place more trust in the guiding hand of the government—and that tension isn't a bad thing. It gives rise to healthy debates and creates a dynamism that makes it possible for us to adapt and grow. For we know that markets are not an unalloyed force for either good or for ill. In many ways, our financial system reflects us. In the aggregate of countless independent decisions, we see the potential for creativity—and the potential for abuse. We see the capacity for innovations that make our economy stronger—and for innovations that exploit our economy's weaknesses. We are called upon to put in place those reforms that allow our best qualities to flourish—while keeping those worst traits in check. We're called upon to recognize that the free market is the most powerful generative force for our prosperity—but it is not a free license to ignore the consequences of our actions.[25]

This admonition forces us to address the intractable failure of the traditional mechanisms used to assert control over corporate governance which failed so spectacularly, most notably the reliance on independent directors. For Blanaid Clarke, observing the crisis from Dublin, which has seen its economy devastated by an interlinked regulatory, political and commercial failure, the problem has both cultural and structural dimensions. Both

---

[20] Ibid, 1446.

[21] H Hansmann and R Kraakman, 'The End of History for Corporate Law' (2001) 89 *Georgetown Law Review* 439.

[22] See K Greenfield, 'September 11th and the End of History for Corporate Law' (2001) 76 *Tulane Law Review* 1409, 1426.

[23] See R Reich, *Supercapitalism, The Transformation of Business, Democracy and Everyday Life* (New York, Vintage, 2007).

[24] D Millon, 'Theories of the Corporation' (1990) *Duke Law Journal* 201, 201–2.

[25] Remarks on Financial Regulatory Reform (White House, Washington DC, 17 June 2009).

have been made manifest in the failure of Anglo Irish Bank, a high-profile casualty of the banking crisis. As Clarke makes clear,

> Although substantially exposed to the Irish property market, Anglo did not engage in sub-prime lending or possess significant 'toxic assets'. It was regulated by the Irish Financial Regulator pursuant to a principles-led supervisory system. In addition, it appeared to comply with the Combined Code and in some instances seemed to go further than the Combined Code in terms of internal controls.

It is therefore hard to see how reliance on strengthened codes alone could be sufficient. Sally Wheeler argues that the problem comes from interlocking boards of directors that lack the will, training or accountability to challenge executive decision-making. Taking as a starting point the observation in the Higgs Report on Corporate Governance that 'the key to non-executive director effectiveness lies as much in behaviours and relationships as in structures and processes', she addresses the impact of gender imbalance, in terms not of sexuality but of feminised practices.

If the board of directors is an insufficient bulwark, what then about institutional investors? As Charlotte Villiers points out,

> the growth in the proportion of shares held by institutional shareholders gives to them considerable voting power to encourage directors and managers to run the company properly . . . Yet the current crisis suggests that, at least in the context of innovative financial products, institutional shareholders failed to act as effective corporate governance monitors.

Villiers traces this failure in part to the difficulty of integrating 'the long-term interests of their beneficiaries into their fiduciary responsibilities and the fund managers are easily put at risk of breaching their fiduciary duty to their beneficiaries'. Curtiss, Levine and Browning, themselves professional fund managers, note the lack of incentive to monitor investments actively and concur with Avgouleas that increased disclosure will be in itself insufficient. This suggests that there is a pressing need for the kind of early warning system approach now contemplated in Brussels and Washington to redress the problem caused by destructive creation, the literal subversion of Schumpeter's famous claim about the inherent instability of capitalism. Howard Adelman addresses this deficit directly by noting that 'we constantly rely on regulatory mechanisms that are designed for what has happened in the past'. What is needed, according to Adelman, 'is an institutional mechanism specifically tailored to do that job and no other'. For Adelman, the critical question is

> How do we create new rules and new regulatory mechanisms on the heels of creative enterprise? The issue is anticipation as a precondition of regulation and accountability. We have to be able to ascertain when and how the creativity is getting onto dangerous ground just as we have to anticipate when weather systems threaten storms and when low level conflicts can become violent.

Pamela Hanrahan, a former academic at the University of Melbourne and now a practising regulator, sees the problem as a conflict of values; in other words, a conflict over what constitutes integrity in practice.

Given the enormous externalities involved, such confusion is no longer politically or socially acceptable. All of this, however, begs the question: what kind of institutional reform can deliver the kind of change we can believe in? For Werner Jeanrond, a leading theologian, the critical issue is the consequences of the attempt to decouple the economy and specifically the market from society. As he puts it, what we have been urged to do, and what we also did, was all the time to increase our trust in the market's own absolute mechanisms, to free the market's own dynamics, to grow in faith in the coming blessings of the market (first for us and eventually even for poorer societies) and to hand over our future to the competent hands of our financial agents. The market thus assumed control of and power over our destiny.[26]

The resulting crisis of confidence (and of faith) necessitates realignment with fundamental values not only within the industrialised north but also between it and the south. The turmoil created by the financial crisis has exacerbated the underlying inequality between the relatively affluent developed world and the developing world for which the financial crisis has more fundamental effects on the basic requirements for a life with dignity. Barry and Peterson approach this issue from the perspective of responsibility for 'severe deprivations' caused by the financial crisis and argue that

> When the livelihoods of the world's poorest people are at stake, as they are here, we ought to construct standards that err in their favour. We suggest that any plausible specification of those standards would hold the world's financial giants, especially the US and UK, morally liable for contributing to harm in the developing world.

The rapid growth of China, its increased muscularity in recent months, including its call for a new reserve currency, and the emergence of the G-20 as the key legitimating international body in the global regulatory conversation are testament to a shift in the balance of international power. The zeitgeist has moved decisively from governing to governance, from governance to accountability and from accountability to integrity. Policymakers and practitioners across the world have acknowledged that there is a pressing need for the development of a regulatory and corporate architecture based on principles of integrity.[27] If the concept is to have meaning beyond rhetoric, it is essential to parse its multifaceted dimensions from an applied ethics perspective.

Integrity is an exceptionally nebulous concept. What it means in practice and how to rank competing, potentially incommensurable interpretations of what constitutes appropriate behaviour are contestable issues. Can one say, for example, that acting within the confines of the law evidences integrity? This cannot be a satisfactory answer, given the ethical void experienced in both fascist and totalitarian societies, each governed by legal (if morally repugnant) frameworks.[28] The scale of ethical failure witnessed in the global financial crisis demonstrates the inherent limitations of black-letter law as a sufficient bulwark even within the liberal democratic state. It is equally unsatisfactory to claim that one evidences integrity if one acts consistently. Consistently engaging in deceptive misleading practice may demonstrate 'wholeness' or 'completeness', but it cannot be a constituent of integrity. Integrity therefore requires of us not only duty (that is,

---

[26] In large measure this argument reflects those first advanced by Polanyi, above n 11.

[27] Integrity has also long been recognised as an important intangible asset or liability in strategic management studies: see M Kaptein and J Wempe, *The Balanced Company: A Theory of Corporate Integrity* (Oxford, Oxford University Press, 2002) 145–52 (noting that organisational structure and culture generate the execution of specific corporate practices in a reflexive manner).

[28] This is the classic focus of a legendary debate in contemporary legal philosophy as to what constitutes law. The positivist approach suggest law is merely what is in the statute book, a historical record made by properly constituted legislatures: see, eg HLA Hart, *The Concept of Law* (Oxford, Clarendon Press, 1961). Others have argued that properly constituted law cannot be vouchsafed unless underpinned by an explicit moral component: see Fuller, above n 12. A third approach suggests that propositions of law are true if they figure in or follow from principles of justice, fairness and procedural due process, which provide the best constructive interpretation of agreed legal practice: see R Dworkin, *Law's Empire* (Cambridge, MA, Belknap Press, 1986).

compliance with the law; consistent and coherent actions), but also principles that contribute to (and do not erode) social welfare (treating people, suppliers and stakeholders with fairness and respect). Seen in this context, enhancing integrity through higher standards of business ethics is a question of organisational design.

Business ethics research tends to calcify around one of four main theoretical approaches: deontological, consequential or utilitarian, virtue ethics and contextual ethics. The deontological approach derives from Immanuel Kant's categorical imperative, namely 'act only according to that maxim whereby you can at the same time will that it should become a universal law'.[29] Reliance on short-term profiteering, if universalised (and condoned by regulatory and political authorities), would destroy the credibility of the market and would be ultimately self-defeating. In deontological terms, the crisis displays systemic unethical tendencies. Moreover, deceptive or misleading conduct debases moral capacities (indeed, it may well also be illegal if the action can be demonstrated to contravene relevant legal rules). The third categorical imperative is to ensure that corporate actions have societal beneficence. In Kantian terms, this can only be vouchsafed if the organisation acts and is seen to act within defined ethical parameters. Even if one views the global financial crisis from the less demanding utilitarian perspective, the consequential impact—unintended, to be sure—makes both the activity itself and the underpinning regulatory framework equally ethically suspect.

Here it is essential to differentiate between the product and the inappropriate uses to which it was put to work. There is nothing unethical about securitisation per se. However, from an ethical perspective it is a deficient defence for chief executive officers to claim ignorance either of how these products were structured or how unstable the expansion of alchemistic engineering had made individual banks or the system as a whole.[30] It is now recognised, for example, that the originate–distribute–relocate model of financial engineering significantly emaciated corporate responsibility precisely because it distanced institutional actors at every stage of the process from the consequences of their actions. Likewise, given the huge social and economic cost, it is deficient for policymakers to profess shock at the irresponsibility of banks, insurance companies and the rating agencies. The failure to calculate the risks and design or recalibrate restraining mechanisms at the corporate, regulatory and political levels grossly exacerbated the externalities now borne by wider society.

The third major approach to evaluate the ethical dimension of corporate activity is perhaps more demanding. It is also more fruitful in terms of refashioning corporate and regulatory action. The focus of virtue-based analysis is not on formal rules (which can often be transacted around) or principles (which lack the definitional clarity to be enforceable). Rather, it focuses on how these rules and principles are interpreted in specific corporate, professional or regulatory practice. This, ultimately, is a question of individual and collective character, or integrity. In a narrowly defined context, it could be argued that the corporate form itself is inimical to virtue. There is prescience to Alasdair MacIntyre's argument that the 'elevation of the values of the market to a central social place' risks creating the circumstances in which 'the concept of the virtues might suffer at first

---

[29] I Kant, *Grounding for the Metaphysics of Morals* (1785) 30.

[30] Indeed, in the US it is illegal under s 404 of the Sarbanes-Oxley Act. In other jurisdictions, such as Australia, it amounts to misleading, deceptive and unconscionable conduct, and can be prosecuted under the Trade Practices Act 1974 and the Corporations Act 2001.

attrition and then perhaps something near total effacement'.[31] This builds on an earlier insight that suggested that 'effectiveness in organisations is often both the product and the producer of an intense focus on a narrow range of specialized tasks which has as its counterpart blindness to other aspects of one's activity'.[32] Compartmentalisation occurs when a

> distinct sphere of social activity comes to have its own role structure governed by its own specific norms in relative independence of other such spheres. Within each sphere those norms dictate which kinds of consideration are to be treated as relevant to decision-making and which are to be excluded.[33]

For MacIntyre, the combination of compartmentalisation and focus on external goods, such as profit maximisation, corrode capacity for the development of internal goods, which should be developed irrespective of the consequences. While the policy response to scandal has traditionally been to emphasise personal character, much less attention has been placed on how corporate, professional, regulatory and political cultures inform, enhance or restrain particular character traits.[34] As Doreen McBarnet has observed, it is incumbent upon regulatory authorities (formal and informal) to identify and break down the compartmentalisation imperatives at corporate and professional levels and to integrate the form and purpose of business ethics into a wider social contract.

It is in this context that the fourth key dimension of business ethics theory comes into play: the contextual framework. What is required, therefore, is a synthesis between an appreciation of context, the need for virtuous behaviour, and the importance of deontological rules and consequential principles of best practice within an overarching framework that is not subverted by compartmentalised responsibilities.[35] The problem, therefore, is not the relative importance of virtue but whether it can be rendered operational in a systematic, dynamic and responsive way, with specific benefits to business.[36]

---

[31] A MacIntyre, *After Virtue: A Study in Moral Theory* (Notre Dame, IN, Notre Dame University Press, 1984) 196, 254; see also J Schumpeter, *Capitalism, Socialism and Democracy* (London, Allen & Unwin, 1943) 137 (arguing that the stock market is a poor substitute for the Holy Grail).

[32] A MacIntyre, 'Why Are the Problems of Business Ethics Insoluble' in B Baumrin and B Friedman (eds), *Moral Responsibility and the Professions* (Notre Dame, IN, Notre Dame University Press, 1982) 358.

[33] A MacIntyre, 'Social Structures and their Threats to Moral Agency' (1999) 74 *Philosophy* 311, 322; see also, however, J Dobson, 'Alasdair MacIntyre's Aristotelian Business Ethics: A Critique' (2009) 89 *Journal of Business Ethics* 43. For application of the need to avoid compartmentalisation from a practising law perspective, see S Day O'Connor, 'Commencement Address', Georgetown Law Center, May 1986 ('lawyers must do more than know the law and the art of practicing it. They need as well to develop a consciousness of their moral and social responsibilities . . . Merely learning and studying the Code of Professional Responsibility is insufficient to satisfy ethical duties as a lawyer'). See also A Kronman, *The Lost Lawyer: Failing Ideals of the Legal Profession* (Cambridge, MA, Belknap Press, 1995) 16 (lamenting the demise of an ideal in which reputation was defined by who the person was as much as by technical mastery).

[34] For exceptions, see R Sennett, *The Culture of the New Capitalism* (New Haven, CT, Yale University Press, 2006) and R Sennett, *The Corrosion of Character: The Personal Consequences of Work in the New Capitalism* (London, Norton, 1998).

[35] One suggested approach derives from an integrative social contracts theory approach, which sets out corporate and reciprocal arrangements and expectations. Microsocial contract norms must be compatible with hypernorms (ie norms sufficiently fundamental that they can serve as a guide for evaluating authentic but less fundamental norms): see T Donaldson and T Dunfee, *Ties that Bind: a Social Contracts Approach to Business Ethics* (Boston, MA, Harvard Business School Press, 1999).

[36] For application to business as an intangible asset, see J Petrick and J Quinn, 'The Challenge of Leadership: Accountability for Integrity, Capacity as a Strategic Asset' (2001) 34 *Journal of Business Ethics* 331; for original formulation of the model, see J Petrick and J Quinn, 'The Integrity Capacity Construct and Moral Progress in Business' (2000) 23 *Journal of Business Ethics* 3.

Accountability is, therefore, as noted above, a design question at both the corporate and regulatory levels. To be effective it needs to be mutually reinforcing and address dynamically the calculative, social and normative reasons for behaving in a more (or less) ethically responsible manner.[37] Here five alternative propositions are put forward, ranging from the normative to the practical. McPhail argues that while 'There is undoubtedly some truth in the observation that the crisis represents further evidence that the individualising nature of developed global capital systems undermine the possibility of society' a response based on 'a reversion to state intervention in the form of aggressive deterrents would seem rather simplistic'. McPhail proposes instead that 'more analysis is required into the failings of professional associations and how the notions of professional competence, integrity and professional education could be reformulated'. Building on the responsive regulatory framework pioneered by the Australian sociologist John Braithwaite, McPhail argues that this is best achieved by engaging in an agonistic dialogue within the epistemic community itself. McPhail, like his University of Glasgow colleague George Walker, cautions the need for an incremental approach built on further embedding associational groupings. Others, however, go further.

For Seumas Miller, resolution of the integrity deficit requires a much broader engagement, which has both preventive and reactive responsive dimensions. This necessitates the design of institutional mechanisms for promoting an environment in which integrity is specified and rewarded, and unethical behaviour is specified and discouraged. This requires an ongoing process of engagement across three interlocking dimensions: a reactive–preventive axis; an internal–external axis; and the self-interest–ethical attitude axis. Any conceptual redesign must, as Sampford has also argued, assess the adequacy of each of the elements of the above systems. For Miller, however, the key criterion on which to build support within the organisation or professional group for a holistic integrity system approach pertains to motivational attitudes: specifically, self-interest and ethical attitudes. On the one hand, and most obviously, there must be some shared moral values in relation to the moral unacceptability of specific forms of behaviour, and in relation to the moral desirability of other specific forms of behaviour: for example, market actors must actually believe that bribery is wrong. That is, there needs to be a framework of accepted social norms, and a means for inculcating these norms. On the other hand, there also needs to be a shared ethical conception in relation to what institutional and other measures ought to be taken to minimise corruption, criminality and unethical behaviour more generally; very harsh penalties and other draconian measures, for example, may simply alienate reasonable, ethical people.

For Dubnick, the problem is not too much or too little reform, but, rather, a lack of focus. What is required is to 'shift and raise our sights from the arena of institutions and regulatory mechanisms to the domain of governance regimes'. While the regulatory regime is in many ways understood and understandable, the problem with sustainable reform centres on a lack of clarity about the dimensions of accountability. As Dubnick frames it,

---

[37] S Winter and P May, 'Motivation for Compliance with Environmental Regulations' (2001) 20 *Journal of Policy Analysis and Management* 675; see more generally I Ayres and J Braithwaite, *Responsive Regulation: Transcending the Deregulation Debate* (New York, Oxford University Press, 1992); for a study suggesting the power of outsiders to frame the emphasis on effective internal controls only if there is a perception within the company that performance is being monitored, see C Parker and V Nielsen, 'To What Extent Do Third Parties Influence Business Behaviour' (2008) 35 *Journal of Law and Society* 309 (reporting survey evidence from 999 large Australian companies).

'[t]he difficulty with designing reforms for the accountability regimes of governance can be traced to our inability to understand and appreciate what this important area of governance entails'. The role of accountability as both problem and solution—cause and cure—begs for clarification if we are to make some sense of the accountability regime's place and role in governance. What does accountability mean to those engaged in these searches for causes and cures, and in what way(s) do various views of accountability impact on our understanding of the financial crisis and/or our responses to it? Accountability regimes are primarily about the management of expectations, thus making variations of expectations extremely important in the description, assessment and design (and reform) of domain governance.

D.   The Trajectory of Reform

As this book goes to press, in regulatory jurisdictions across the world innovation, renewal and stagnation conflict and conflate. This is most apparent in the piecemeal attempts in the US to deal with the thorny issue of how to wean the banking sector off its addiction to irresponsible and unsustainable lending and trading practices. Treatment options were clarified with the release on 7 May 2009 of stress tests, conducted by the Federal Reserve in conjunction with the Department of Treasury, into 19 of the most important banks. Not surprisingly, given the extensive media management that preceded publication, prognosis was favourable. As widely reported, the Charlotte-based Bank of America remains the most exposed. The bank is required to enhance capital reserves by $34 billion. Citigroup, by contrast, one of the weakest major banks, requires only $5.5 billion. The former investment banks Morgan Stanley and Goldman Sachs have fared much better. Morgan Stanley has been cautioned to raise just $1.5 billion. Goldman Sachs is regarded as adequately capitalised, as is JP Morgan Chase, which has managed the integration of Bear Stearns much more successfully than the hapless management at Bank of America, where empire building led to the disastrous acquisition of Merrill Lynch and Countrywide at the peak of the crisis. Remarkably, this exercise in regulatory oversight did not identify the need to change senior management. Indeed, the overall picture presented was of relative strength not weakness. In total, only $75 billion was deemed necessary to insulate the banking sector. For Timothy Geithner, the US Treasury Secretary, investors should now be reassured that all losses were accounted for and that entrenched management was credible. The suggestion overstates the case.

The content and conduct of the tests and the way in which the results were disseminated leave huge questions about the ultimate purpose and who will stand to gain most of all from this exercise in managing expectations. As O'Brien observes, there are a number of profound methodological flaws. The tests used worst-case scenario baselines that have already been proved optimistic. More problematically, the banks were able to negotiate privately with the government over how the latter interpreted the results. None of this gives confidence in the veracity of claims that the banking sector as a whole is adequately capitalised or would remain so if explicit and implicit guarantees were removed. What is clear, however, is that a process of differentiation has begun that is likely to intensify in coming months. The banks perceived to be stronger will seek to extricate themselves from congressionally imposed remuneration caps and trading restrictions. JP Morgan Chase and Goldman Sachs have already sought to repay mandatory loans advanced under the Troubled Asset Relief Program. For the moment, economic policymakers appear to favour creative ambiguity. As O'Brien argues, creative ambiguity may well be an effective short-term strategy. Unless, however, a more calibrated practical, ethical framework underpins the agenda, the opportunity for fundamental transformation will be lost. Suggesting that the marketplace is somehow cleansed and chastened by the experience is naive. There is simply no evidence of the Pauline conversion that policymakers in the Obama administration and elsewhere suggest has occurred. Moreover, the focus on executive remuneration, while laudable, derives from imperatives imposed by Congress rather than the White House, which had initially argued that such policies were too invasive. What makes matters even more problematic is the laxity of the conditions to allow banks to exit Congressional oversight. Securing partial Wall Street approval for industrial policy, which may yet be deemed unacceptable by the bankruptcy courts, could allow the banks to get away with what, in financial and moral terms, amounts to the crime of the century. The stage is now set for one of the largest transfers of wealth in US banking history. Those with the highest rating, including Goldman Sachs, Morgan Stanley and JP Morgan Chase, are best placed to take advantage. This occurs precisely because differentiation flatters disproportionately. Far from controlling Wall Street, O'Brien argues, it is likely to increase its capacity at precisely the same time as the economic crisis hits Main Street with increasing force.

In the UK, legislative change also threatens to promise more than it can deliver. The most immediate regulatory response to the emerging crisis in the autumn of 2007 was to address the deficiencies in the system of deposit protection and the insolvency regime for banks, both of which had contributed to the collapse of Northern Rock. The Banking Act 2009 introduced a 'special resolution regime' for failing banks, with the Bank of England designated as the principal actor within that regime, reflecting both the leading role played by the Bank in crisis management and a perception that, in the past, the regulatory structure had not properly balanced the roles of the FSA as prudential regulator and the Bank as a supplier of liquidity and ultimately a lender of last resort. The Act also formalised the Bank's role in ensuring financial stability, although a lack of powers associated with that role has led the Governor to complain that the Bank can do no more than 'issue sermons or organise burials'.[38] From there the focus shifted to the process of recapitalisation of the major banks and the emergence of the government as the major or majority shareholder in the banking groups Lloyds, HBOS (later to be combined into a single entity known as Lloyds/HBOS, in which the government has a 43% shareholding) and Royal Bank of Scotland (in which the government now has an 84% shareholding).[39] This process shifted the focus to the potential role of the government as a major or majority shareholder[40] in restraining past excesses in dividend payments to shareholders and remuneration to executives, as well as to reinvigorating bank lending. While it remains to be seen just how active the government will be in its new role as major or majority shareholder, the initial indications are that the government will be less interventionist than

---

[38] Mervyn King, Governor of the Bank of England, Mansion House speech of 17 June 2009, available at www.bankofengland.co.uk/publications/speeches/2009/speech394.pdf (accessed on 19 June 2009).

[39] This is in addition to the 100% shareholdings in Northern Rock and Bradford and Bingley, two former building societies that were nationalised following financial difficulties.

[40] The government's shareholdings are managed by a Treasury-owned company, UK Financial Investments Ltd.

many had expected.[41] There has been little evidence to date of the British government using its power as major or majority shareholder to require (as opposed to encouraging) changes in the lending practices or governance structures of the banks; and much of the potential effect of restrictions on dividends that were part of the initial recapitalisation package has been removed by subsequent changes to the structure of the government shareholding. Meanwhile, the issue of remuneration has been left to the FSA, which plans to introduce a code that focuses on procedures rather than substantive controls.[42]

This all fits into a broader perspective in which government ownership is a temporary measure and in which the regulatory and governance reform is pursued better across the entire market rather than being confined to those entities in which the government happens to have a substantial shareholding at any particular point in time. That regulatory reform agenda was addressed by the Turner Report published in March 2009.[43] Turner focuses in particular on the need for a 'macroprudential' approach that combines macro-economic analysis with the more traditional focus in prudential supervision on individual firms. This is envisaged as making the system 'more intrusive and more systemic', with a stronger focus on liquidity and a stricter regime for regulatory capital. The FSA's 'principles-based' approach will survive, but its association in the past with 'light-touch' regulation will not. Broadening the regulatory regime so as to counter the possibility of regulatory arbitrage through the 'shadow' banking system is another priority. Reflecting the very broad nature of regulatory discretion in the UK system (both in design and implementation), it is envisaged that this change in regulatory style can be achieved within the existing legislative framework, albeit that important elements of the overall reform package will be linked with action at the international level. That in itself represents something of an indictment of the FSA's role in the emergence of the crisis, since it is clear that it was not legal powers that were lacking but rather the authority and determination to use them. It is interesting in this regard that FSA rhetoric is moving in tandem with regulatory reform, with market participants being warned that in future they should 'be afraid' of the FSA.[44] Whether that is a credible threat remains very much an open question. As Kern Alexander points out, moves towards macroprudential regulation are likely to have a profound impact on the theory and practice of regulatory policy in the UK as 'macroprudential regulation will require that principles-based regulation become more rules-based because tighter *ex ante* constraints will need to be applied to the risk exposures of individual firms'. As a consequence, FSA regulation will gradually become more rules-based in order to achieve macroprudential regulatory objectives. This, undoubtedly, will cause jurisdictional dilemmas not only within the UK, but also on the regional and global levels.

At a supranational level, the G8 meeting in Italy in July 2009 advanced calls for systemic early warning systems, but the proposals lack the detail required to ascertain the capability of advancing substantive behavioural change. While the EU is the source of much of the

---

[41] See the 'Framework Agreement' between UK Financial Investments Ltd and the Treasury (17 June 2009), available at www.ukfi.gov.uk/releases/UKFI%20Introduction.pdf, making clear that 'The Company will manage the Investments on a commercial basis and will not intervene in day-to-day management decisions of the Investee Companies (including with respect to individual lending or remuneration decisions)'.

[42] See FSA, 'Reforming Remuneration Practices in Financial Services', Consultation Paper 09/10 (March 2009), available at www.fsa.gov.uk.

[43] Above n 10.

[44] See BBC News, 18 June 2009, available at news.bbc.co.uk/1/hi/business/7939619.stm, reporting comments made by FSA Chief Executive Hector Sants at a London Conference in March 2009.

regulatory rules that are in place in the Member States, there is no European financial regulator. Although there are arrangements in place to promote a common approach, it remains the case that supervision and enforcement are the responsibility of the individual Member States. The European Central Bank has demonstrated during the crisis that it has an important role to play in supplying liquidity to the markets, but it is ultimately limited in its role by the fact that it is not a regulator; by the fact that the internationally-significant financial markets in London are not in the eurozone; and by the fact that only Member States can provide the financing that is required for crisis management. The UK government in particular has expressed reservations about moving towards a more centralised European system. Two other reform proposals are viewed with much less enthusiasm in the UK than in continental Europe. One is the European Commission proposal for greater regulation of hedge funds;[45] the other is the European Parliament proposal to mandate that some segments of the 'over-the-counter' (OTC) market in derivatives and other complex financial instruments be traded on regulated markets.[46] Since the growth of both hedge funds and OTC trading in derivatives and other complex instruments is particularly associated with London, there is some perception in the UK of an 'anti-London' agenda. To the extent that the 'light-touch' regulatory regime favoured by the UK has been viewed in some parts of the EU as one of the main causes of the crisis, that perception is probably correct; however, it remains to be seen how the dynamics of EU politics as well as the trajectory of economic recovery will affect the outcome of these proposals.

As Avinish Persaud points out, it is important to emphasise that the regulatory gaps plugged as a consequence of this crisis will be insufficient to deal with the next one. Moreover, while the crisis has pointed to problems within the shadow banking system, the miscreants at the heart of this scandal in both the EU and the US were highly, if inappropriately, regulated. Indeed, the instruments that the banks used were disclosed to the market and the risks quantified—if, again, inappropriately. Persaud argues instead for smarter regulation, the admixture of rules, principles and norms within a more responsive, dynamic macroprudential framework. This is not, he maintains, a question of simply raising the capital adequacy requirements. This represents a much more holistic approach to regulatory purpose, which concentrates on systemic problems exposed and at times exacerbated by herding behavioural instincts, which, while rational for individual institutions, may and indeed have posed grave economic, social and political risks. The difficulty, however, is that booms have their own political economy, which, as Persaud acknowledges, severely inhibits the capacity of regulators to take the pre-emptive action required.

This task is addressed directly by Jeremy Cooper, the Deputy Chairman of the Australian Securities and Investments Commission. In relative terms, the Australian economy and regulatory system have fared much better than many of its OECD counterparts. Cooper notes the strengths of oversight in the regulatory system but acknowledges too the risk of regulatory overreach, in particular in the immediate aftermath of scandal. He advocates instead a pre-emptive model of oversight that negates the capacity of irrational investor behaviour to shape economic policy, either during the boom, when it

---

[45] See ec.europa.eu/internal_market/investment/docs/alternative_investments/fund_managers_proposal_en.pdf (19 June 2009).
[46] See 'Parliament to Take Lead on Derivatives Regulation', available at www.euractiv.com/en/financial-services/parliament-take-lead-derivatives-regulation/article-179170 (19 June 2009).

precludes or inhibits counter-cyclical measures, or in its aftermath, when the search for scapegoats may result in regulatory measures which in themselves may have counter-productive unintended consequences. Cooper cautions that disclosure is an insufficient bulwark, even for allegedly sophisticated investors. Financial literacy measures and greater enforcement are also applauded, but are recognised as insufficient. Instead, Cooper urges the implementation of what he terms 'architectural solutions'. As he puts it,

> More attention needs to be paid to how things work. It is a fair point that more time and effort seems to be expended on ensuring a toaster is safe from catching fire than is the case with many financial products. Many systems have tolerated relatively dangerous financial toasters, so long as the risks of incineration are disclosed.

This concern also lies at the centre of debates in the US on the remit of the proposed financial products safety commission and whether the remit should extend to allegedly sophisticated investors. How this debate resolves will provide a telling indication of the relative power of financial actors in the regulatory matrix. Much more work is required if we are to transcend the desultory failure of the trajectory of financial regulation reform and embed higher standards of professional responsibility, integrity and corporate excellence. What is clear, however, is that current models are outdated and attempts to build a credible framework on those falsified assumptions represent not only poor policy but also poor social science. This book explains the reasons why.

1

Adam Smith's Dinner

CHARLES SAMPFORD*

A. Introduction: The Walls Came Tumbling Down

In 1961, the East German government erected what they claimed was an anti-capitalist barricade. In 1989, this barricade was dismantled by those whom it was supposed to keep apart: the forces it was intended to contain had overwhelmed it. In the aftermath, the victims of Stalinist oppression and the planned economy opted for radical change. Some might have hoped that they would intellectually march resolutely westwards towards the forms of social democracy that had proven so successful in their nearest neighbours—Scandinavia, Germany and Austria—and stop when they had reached a point on the political spectrum with which they felt comfortable, and which worked for them. Unfortunately, they went to the opposite end of political economy. That choice was celebrated by those theorists who wanted other nations to move in the same direction. Eastern Europe suffered a decline of 50% in its GDP.

Much earlier, in 1653, Peter Stuyvesant had erected a wall of earth and wood to protect the westernmost settlement of a great commercial nation (the US) from those they imagined to be barbarians. In 1699 Stuyvesant's barrier was dismantled by the British, who replaced it with a street named after the wall. So it came to be that one of the most inconsequential walls in history became one of history's most famous streets. I am not sure if the Dutch left some tulip bulbs on either side of the wall of New Amsterdam, perhaps as a reminder of capitalism's first bubble and an inspiration to later bubbles. However, many of the victims of the latest burst bubble are pretty keen to tear down that wall.[1] As in 1989, they want to take action against the guardians of the system that failed them. And the more they suffer, the more likely it is that they will demand radical change, and the more likely that the resulting change will go too far—as seems to have been the case in Eastern Europe after the terminal crisis of communism, and in the majority of democracies that fell in the dozen years following the Great Crash.[2] The current reaction is so strong that some are even wondering what role there will be for markets. I was invited to address a conference in the EU Parliament last November on the topic 'Capitalism: Quo Vadis?'. I

---

* Professor of Law, Griffith University and Director of Institute of Ethics Governance and Law.

[1] Eric Hobsbawm, for example, discusses the comparison between the nonsense of the former USSR that you could plan everything and the equally nonsensical western notion that you could leave it all unregulated. See E Hobsbawm, *The Age of Extremes: A History of the World, 1914–1991* (New York, Pantheon Books, 1994).

[2] Of all the 1929 democracies, only the US, UK, Canada, Australia, New Zealand, Ireland, Switzerland, Sweden, Chile and Venezuela survived to 1941.

apologised to the international audience that the topic was posed in a dead European language because the answer to this question is not going to be determined by the west alone. The problems of capitalism emerged in the west and have affected the rest. However, the answers will not come solely from the west, and may even come primarily from the south and the east.

B.   W[h]ither Capitalism?

At the November conference I suggested that the best literal translation was 'Whither capitalism?', but a freer and more appropriate definition would be 'Wither capitalism?' In answer to the question, 'Capitalism—quo vadis?', three broad answers have been propounded. Some have said 'nowhere', some have said 'everywhere' and others have suggested that capitalism has a vital but defined role within a larger ethical order. During the 1930s, statists of the right and anarchists of the left said that capitalism had nowhere to go. It was left to the American social democrats, in the end, to save capitalism from itself. In the 1970s, the statists of the left said that capitalism had nowhere to go. However, the anarchists of the right saw it as going everywhere; in fact, some of them started to say how superior markets were to democracy. The social democrats were the ones who saw capitalism playing a vital role in a larger order—with clear spaces for both the democracy of the dollar and the democracy of the vote. Some also recognised the need to police the boundary lest those with dollars buy votes or government action (a common form of 'public–private partnership' that some call 'corruption'). From 1980 to 2008, the 'everywhere' option seemed to be very popular, and it is interesting how a number of extremists from the left became extremists on the right. A couple of the quite famous ones have decided to start moving backwards: it could well be that they are third time lucky. Yet I suggest we seek counsel elsewhere, and look to the role of values to save capitalism from itself a second time, and also to let us all glean a better understanding of the proper place of capitalism. I was profoundly unimpressed in 1989 that Francis Fukuyama should without irony herald the failure of the last ideology that proclaimed the end of history only to make a similar claim for his own. At the time, some of us had noticed a few problems with capitalism, and it is a pity that the decision by Gorbachev to end the cold war and to attempt gradual change towards more liberal democratic models led us to ignore those clear problems. I maintained then that there would be a role for markets, and that the extremism of statists or anarchists of the left or right had been a large part of the political and economic upheavals of the twentieth century, offering no prospects for solving problems in the twenty-first century. We should recognise the dynamic power of markets, which allow us to trade what we have for what we would prefer, but also recognise that this is one element in an effective order that serves the interests of the community.

C.   Adam Smith's Dinner and the Missing Variable

Adam Smith famously said: 'It is not from the benevolence of the butcher, the brewer, or the baker, that we expect our dinner, but from their regard to their own self-interest'.[3] We might equally say that it is not the malevolence of the mortgage broker who writes the NINJA loan,[4] or the ratings agency that anoints it AAA. It is not the malevolence of the arms manufacturer that invents the cluster bomb or the polluter who destroys the planet; rather, it is their regard to their own self-interest. Self-interest is an important motivation, but there are other critical variables or preconditions, determining, for instance, whether self-interest puts food on our plantation timber table, or cluster bombs in an overheated and flood-prone backyard that has been repossessed by a zombie bank. The key question is: what are those other variables, and why and how has their variation dealt so much damage so quickly? As we all know, this is the 250th anniversary of *The Theory of Moral Sentiments*,[5] the work Adam Smith regarded as his most important, and which provided the essential grounding for his *Wealth of Nations*. The former is now seen primarily to concern moral philosophy and the latter economics, so that some might say moral philosophy or ethics is prior to and more important than economics, and constitutes the relevant variable. But Smith would not have said that. He and other contemporaries lived before the separation of disciplines and, like Bentham, Smith would have seen little point in separating the modern disciplines of law, ethics, politics and economics, whose separate formation post-dates their work and their insights. Two and a half centuries later, with the modern separation of disciplines now so broad, what might we say about Smith's missing variable?

Smith's eighteenth-century petit bourgeoisie did business with regard to their own self-interest (rather than, say, their customers' interest or the greater good), but precisely what self-interest signified to them—and to him—can only be understood from an overarching view of the specific institutional landscape in which they found themselves. This kind of overarching understanding—or the attempt at it—seems by and large to have been missing from contemporary academic debate. The study of institutions, their problems and solutions, what they are and what they mean, is divided into strongly theorised but limited discipline-specific fields, which can easily aggravate any nascent contemporary misunderstanding of the thrust of Smith's observation. Each discipline provides vital yet severely limited insights into the institutional settings in which putatively self-interested agents go about their everyday business. Our missing variable concerns the institutional settings in which people live and in which they interact with one another—sometimes, as in Smith's example, through the medium of markets. Yet how do we best conceive of and govern these intermediary institutions, given the current interdisciplinary (and intra-disciplinary) proliferation of theoretical approaches to institutional governance? The question is especially pressing if our aims include ameliorating and preventing the kinds of system-wide failures—the current world economic crisis furnishes a vivid example—that have occasionally spilled over and devastated butchers, brewers, bakers and their customers alike.

---

[3] A Smith, *An Inquiry into the Nature and Causes of the Wealth of Nations* (Oxford, Oxford University Press, 1976 [1776]) 26.

[4] 'No Income, No Job, No Assets'.

[5] A Smith, *Theory of Moral Sentiments* (Oxford, Oxford University Press, 1976 [1759]).

D.   Institutional Governance and Disciplinary Compartmentalisation

Despite the western emphasis on rational individual agency, we live our lives with other human beings, largely in and through the institutions into which we were born and educated, and in which we work, think, feel, play, procreate and age. Even when we try to act like the idealised rational individuals we are sometimes assumed to be, our lives are played out in an environment characterised by powerful institutions capable of shaping and influencing our deepest motives and most important deliberative decisions. Indeed, institutions and their governance play a significant part in many, if not most or all, of our most pressing collective problems. Institutions are also almost invariably a key part of solutions to these problems, whether the institutions be non-government organisations (NGOs), corporations, industry groups, regulators, government agencies, regional bodies or international agencies. The importance of good institutional governance is recognised by many disciplines which might make a contribution to institutional governance and reform. The problem is not that it is ignored: the problem is that each discipline has a strongly theorised but limited conception of institutions, which colours and structures their view of the nature of institutional problems and the best means for addressing them. For example, lawyers look at institutions and see sets of formal norms, ethicists see informal norms and the values the institution claims to further, economists see incentives and disincentives, political scientists see power relations, social psychologists see complex webs of interpersonal and group relationships, and management theorists see structures and systems. Accordingly, the problems are seen in the deficiency of laws, ethical standards, incentives, power relations, systems and so on, and the solutions are seen as lying in remedying those specific deficiencies.

All these partial insights into institutions and their problems are important and any solution that ignores them is likely to fail. However, as proffered solutions tend to be developed from only one disciplinary perspective, they are necessarily limited, perhaps overemphasising legislative solutions or the impact of economic incentives. As indicated above, this was not a problem when Smith and Bentham were writing. However, the explosion of literature within each of the relevant disciplines means that we need strong interdisciplinary teams with mutual understanding and respect for what their disciplines can contribute. Those who study governance generally engage in a further specialisation in the kinds of institution whose governance they research. Many concentrate on government institutions, but others focus on corporations, professions, NGOs or international organisations, among others. However, many of the most intractable governance problems occur when inadequacies at one level of governance are reinforced and exacerbated by inadequacies at other levels. This has always been the case, for instance, in issues of peace and security, where the inadequacies of global governance are exposed by governance failures within states. This is paradigmatically the case in the response to climate change, where governance issues at the global, national and corporate levels contribute to the problem and make finding solutions difficult. It is also most certainly the case with the 2008 global financial crisis (GFC), where problems of global, regional, national, corporate and professional governance have produced the greatest set of interlocking governance failures since the 1930s.

E.   Multiple Governance Failures and Globalisation

One thing that is very clear from the essays in this book is that the crisis has been the result of multiple and reinforcing governance failures. Globalisation has certainly been a factor in the genesis and spread of the GFC. If globalisation involves the flow of people, ideas, goods and money, the last mentioned has grown most rapidly—indeed, well in excess of the flow of goods and investment that it is supposed to support. Employees in developed countries have entrusted the comfort of their post-retirement lives to financial intermediaries. Developing countries have entrusted their enormous and growing surpluses to western banks and other financial intermediaries. Some have been pressed by western-run multilaterals to entrust the proceeds of extractive industries in Wall Street and other financial centres on the basis that it was less likely to be eroded by corruption. The amounts entrusted to such intermediaries in the US and elsewhere on the basis that funds would be invested on a secure and conservative basis were unprecedented. It now appears that entrusted powers were abused.

Many within financial intermediaries pursued strategies that focused on the maximisation of fees and short-term profits. The ratings practices were scandalous and incredibly insulting to well-run businesses and governments whose default risk was, in reality, far less than 100%-plus non-recourse mortgages provided to NINJA borrowers ('No Income, No Job, No Assets'). The fact that risk models were based on the probabilities of individual defaults and ignored the possibility of an overall decline in property markets is less of an excuse than an indictment. Once such ratings could be secured, the signing up of mortgagees, the packaging of those loans, their rating and their sale to local citizens and foreigners resembles a well-oiled 'corruption system'. Even though these intermediaries did not see themselves as corrupt, several parties were maximising their fees while squandering profits at the expense of those who entrusted them with their funds. The unedifying subsequent sharp shift from greed to blind panic adds to the contempt seen in talk radio and readers' letters across the world. The damage that was subsequently inflicted on those engaged in the production and distribution of goods and services has caused shock and anger, and has raised profound questions not just about the future of financial regulation but about many elements of global and national financial systems.

The pathways for transferring funds to where they can most usefully and profitably be deployed have become the pathways through which the financial contagion has spread. It is like a financial influenza pandemic which has jumped from another species to humans and has spread toxic products through the pathways of our interconnected world. And just like an influenza pandemic, it is capable of infecting perfectly healthy institutions. Alternatively, one might draw the analogy that some terrorists are so completely committed to an extreme version of a widely shared religion that they are not constrained by normal rules, and are contemptuous of the more moderate faith held by a majority of their co-religionists. Substitute extreme fundamentalist market theory for extreme fundamentalist religion and the metaphor of financial terrorism may stick. The financial terrorists may not believe in an afterlife with 60 virgins, but $218m can buy a lot of whatever you fancy in this life. I am not suggesting that Guantanamo be kept open for a new batch of the 'worst of the worst', but I do not rule out the possibility that a condition of continuing to lend money is that we will demand an explanation of how so much of the money lent was squandered, who squandered it, what we have done to ensure it does not happen again and what we have done to punish those responsible.

The inability of any one discipline to find adequate answers and the multiple reinforcing governance failures such as those that gestated the current global economic malaise might tempt us to argue for a radical change of the kind we had in the 1930s, in which many rejected markets, democracies or both; or the kind of extreme and rapid reversal that cut the Russian and several other economies by half. I do not think that we should discard markets or democracy, but we should recognise and address the institutional problems in each, and the ways they interact. I would argue that we should question every assumption on which our theories are based and on which they are separated. If not, a fresh round of enormous policy mistakes may be made. Failure could produce desperation, extremism and, in more countries than one might imagine, disorder and even revolutionary rejection of markets or democracy. The stakes are especially high because of huge mistakes made over the last 10 years; yet a global institutional consensus for the greater part of the decade leading up to the current crisis had hailed the then status quo (the 'great moderation'), thought to have been achieved through well-crafted and effective global governance and the skilful deployment of appropriate institutional power.

F.   The Missing Variable: Regulatory Contracts?

Having already accentuated the limitations of disciplinarily limited analyses of institutional governance, I must also express reservations about whether contract-based notions provide the missing variable or can provide a useful way of examining the problems that have occurred, or the solutions that are needed. Is the metaphor of a regulatory contract a useful way of looking at the relationship between corporations (in this case financial corporations, but more usually utilities) and governments? Or is the contractual metaphor one that obfuscates more than it illuminates? Even before expressing my reservations, I do not wish to endorse what might be seen as the opposite view: that states should or even do have the power to vary regulatory arrangements at will, without regard to the legitimate interests and expectations of those who are being regulated. Briefly, I want to fully endorse the following ideas about good regulation that supporters of regulatory contracts might prefer to see furthered:

1.   maximum clarity in advance about the rules of engagement;
2.   caution about change;
3.   consultation with all stakeholders;
4.   giving a very clear indication of the sorts of things that might be changed;
5.   harnessing the commercial interests of corporations to publicly stated goals;
6.   developing regulatory mechanisms that are self-enforcing.

However, I would argue that any contractarian approach to the relationship between states and citizens is fundamentally flawed, for (at least) the following reasons:

1.   A contract assumes a bilateral relationship. In reality, governance issues involve many parties: states, corporations, consumers. As privity is central to contracts, relaxing privity is not the answer and other models should be explored.

2.   It also assumes an equal relationship. States and citizens do not have equal relationships. Prior to the enlightenment, it was a one-way relationship in which subjects had to prove their loyalty to their sovereign. After the enlightenment, a Feurbachian moment reversed the relationship, so that henceforth states had to justify themselves to citizens. However, as the duty of states is to citizens (and, possibly, residents) and not corporations, it is the job of states to ensure that corporations operate for the benefit of citizens and not against them.

3.   It generally assumes, falsely, that the parties to a contract already have property and bargain on the basis of the advantages that gives them.

4.   It assumes that both parties are equally free to contract or not and are entitled to play 'hold-out'. In fact, states are expected to deliver services to citizens. The purpose of establishing private utilities, banks and so on is to deliver better and more efficient services. That has to be built into the DNA of the relevant corporations—part of their 'justification', as I have traditionally put it. The argument that a profit motivated company can do this better and more efficiently is not a priori true or false. If privatised utilities and service providers are to live up to that claim, it becomes a central duty of the corporation to ensure that it is true; quoting Smith will not do. Smith did not assume that the unseen hand ensured that monopolies (often granted by mercantilist sovereigns in return for money or favours) served the public interest.

5.   Contracts are one way of governing relationships within society. However, you need another mechanism for determining when contracting will be used and when it will not. To use a contract to determine when contracts will be used is circular and hence is tantamount to a category mistake, if not an attempt to rig the books or an unwitting expression of ideological preference.

6.   While I consider the idea of a 'relational contract' very fruitful, especially in explaining long-term business relationships, and some very interesting contributions to the 'new institutional economics' of the 1980s, I tend to see this as a useful single disciplinary insight that needs to be integrated with those from other disciplines.

In the case of the regulatory contract, I have six specific reservations:

1.   This appears to be a relatively recent conceptual development constructed during the recent neo-liberal 'capitalism spreading everywhere' period. Regulatory contracts may not sit so well in the period that follows as they seek to avoid the excesses and assumptions of that era.

2.   It has become particularly popular in an era of deregulation and privatisation. One of the myths of privatisation was that this would be much simpler because managers would no longer have to manage for multiple values. The companies that ran public facilities would be motivated by profit, and any public interest elements could be determined by regulation. I wrote at the time that this showed a remarkable faith in regulation from a group who generally decried the difficulties of effective legislation. While not as chary about the possibility of effective regulation, I thought I had a pretty good idea of the difficul-

ties as principal advisor to the Queensland Scrutiny of Legislation Committee. I also thought that separating the relevant decision-making into the utility company, the regulator and the government would be a recipe for complexity. Rather than questioning the original assumptions and the commercial ownership of 'natural' monopolies,[6] the relational contract was seen as an even more complex answer.

3.   One of the biggest problems is dealing with future eventualities. Two kinds of futures are unknown:

    a.   Future policy flexibility to deal with changing circumstances. If the government builds a toll road or toll bridge and later decides that it should upgrade alternative routes, it will take into account the effect on the tolls it receives. However, if the toll road is privately owned, then the government has to make promises as to what it will do that would have an effect on the toll.

    b.   The policies that the opposition may take to the electorate and win. Regulatory contracts need to recognise this or be fundamentally undemocratic. In one example, the Victorian government reversed an election promise that a proposed highway would have no toll. It changed its mind and signed a contract not long before the next election. The value of the company with the contract increased by $2,000,000,000. When the leader of the opposition said he would make the reinstatement of the government's earlier promise the cornerstone of the upcoming election, the company with the contract threatened to sue for the loss of the $2,000,000,000 it had just gained without turning a sod.

4.   This illustrates the problems with what might be called 'one-way compensation'. Sidak and Spulber[7] argued that changing the regulations to the detriment of the corporation should lead to compensation because this amounts to a 'taking' of property. There is no suggestion that the corporation would automatically pay the government for windfalls if its decisions enriched it. However, if governments have to pay the downside while not sharing the upside, then this reflects a systemic risk to such arrangements.

5.   The confidentiality of much contracting with privatised utilities provides a real danger of corruption. The flexibility of regulatory contracts provides another opportunity.

6.   Much of the rhetoric of regulatory contracts and PPPs is based on assumptions that seem particularly shaky:

    a.   Private capital is needed for infrastructure when most of the money is borrowed at rates that are more expensive than government infrastructure.

    b.   Risk can be identified, priced and allocated.

---

[6] I am aware of the debate about what are natural monopolies, but they apply to the margins rather than the core of networks which cannot be economically or ecologically duplicated.

[7] JG Sidak and DF Spulber, *Deregulatory Takings and the Regulatory Contract* (Cambridge, Cambridge University Press, 1998).

c. In fact, one of the greatest risks is the differential knowledge, skills and experience of the government and privatisers in dealing with the complex contracts involved.

d. Other risks include the bankruptcy risk of the private utility. As in so many other contexts, the corporations got the upside while governments were effectively forced to come in and pick up the downside if it materialised (something that happened, for instance, in the Asian Financial Crisis).

Finally, for what it is worth, it seems to me that Smith's original work is incompatible with the idea of a social contract, notwithstanding John McCain's reference to Wall Street breaching Adam Smith's 'social contract'.

G. The Missing Variable: Equity, Trust and Fiduciary Duty?

Another popular way of conceiving the missing variable is to use the terminology of trust, which is significantly more flexible than contract (indeed, equity was developed expressly to relieve the rigidities of common law). A trust involves a fiduciary relationship between one or more beneficiaries and a trustee who holds property on their behalf, and who has a fiduciary duty to exercise his or her powers over that property in the interests of the beneficiaries. The trustees and beneficiaries may never have met, and the latter may not even know of the relationship. The relationship may be set up by agreement between the former owner of the property, or may be implied because of the position or conduct of the trustee. There can be multiple beneficiaries, whether named or in classes. There can also be multiple trustees, or the trustee may be a corporation or an institution. This approach became very influential in political theory as the enlightenment reversed the polarities of the relationship of sovereign and subject to make states responsible to citizens, and required them to justify the exercise of state power to the citizens who were the beneficiaries of the new implied trust. A breach of that implied trust would give the subjects or citizens a right to rebel. With the coming of elections, changeovers could be achieved with less disruption, but it was—and still is—common to see the elected representatives holding power on trust for those who have conferred it. The terminology of trust also influences the way that administrative law imposes various constraints on the exercise of governmental discretion. This approach has been even more central in understanding the relationship between directors and shareholders in corporate law. For example, in the aftermath of the corporate and political scandals in Western Australia that tarnished and then came to define the 'WA Inc' of the 1980s, Professor (now Justice) Paul Finn re-emphasised equity and saw it as a way of understanding the relationship between state and citizen as well as director and shareholder. Trust-based thinking also influences Transparency International's definition of corruption as the abuse of entrusted power for private gain. The trust approach is thus very fruitful and may be perfectly satisfactory for many. It is particularly useful in looking at the ethical duties of government and corporate officials. However, it remains rooted in the model of an interpersonal relationship, and in this regard may fail to capture the institutional character of governments and corporations.

H.   The Missing Variable: An Institutionalist Approach

For the last 19 years, I have taken an institutionalist approach[8] in which I have argued that government and corporate institutions need to justify themselves to the communities in which they operate for a number of reasons, including:

1.   The various privileges they are accorded—most notably, limited liability of joint stock companies (banks also have the ability to create credit and access to central bank 'lender of last resort' facilities).

2.   The various benefits that are provided—in particular, bank guarantees and, as we have seen, the bailing out of corporations that are 'too big to fail', as well as a general expectation (for some, an obligation) of governmental powers being used to prevent some of the worst problems afflicting economies.

3.   The legal protection of property rights that are backed up by state power.

The reasons why these privileges, benefits and protections are provided is not for the benefit of the government agencies and corporations, but for the community as a whole. In general terms, we allow the creation of joint stock companies because they are seen as increasing the likelihood that we will be able to put dinner on our table (as well as have the many other things that people have wanted in the past and want now). However, there is another, and in my opinion decisive, reason why governments, corporations and, indeed, all institutions need to justify themselves to the communities in which they operate. All institutions concentrate power, people and resources to achieve certain publicly stated goals that are, or are seen to be, of benefit to the relevant community. However, that concentration of power, people and resources could be used for other purposes that might harm that same community. Police forces and the armed services are supposed to protect citizens, but could use their coercive force to secure bribes, to terrorise inhabitants or even to seize state power. Banks and other financial institutions concentrate the resources of their shareholders, depositors and others who entrust them with their money. These resources are supposed to ensure liquidity for those who engage in the provisions of goods and services to others. Yet those resources can be used in transactions that generate very high fees for the financial intermediaries at the same time as they create great risk for those who have entrusted their money to them.

For anarchists, the dangers are just too great, but most of us are prepared to take a risk. The American revolutionaries considered this very carefully. Governments are instituted to support the 'inalienable rights to life, liberty and the pursuit of happiness', but they could turn against the people they were supposed to benefit, justifying revolution and the establishment of governments that could perform the relevant function (or in my terms, justify themselves). The revolutionaries did not decide to abandon the idea of government because government power had been abused. However, they wanted to reduce the risk of future abuse by creating a system of 'checks and balances' that provided a form of 'risk management'.

While Adam Smith saw virtue in competition, he certainly recognised the dangers of the abuse of economic power in his warnings about combinations of merchants and large

---

[8] See, in particular, the Keynote Speech at the 1990 ALTA Conference, C Sampford, 'Law, Institutions and the Public Private Divide' (1992) 20 *Federal Law Review* 185; see also C Sampford and N Preston, *Encouraging Ethics and Challenging Corruption: Public Sector Ethics in Theory and Practice* (Sydney, Federation Press, 2002).

mercantilist corporations. Over the intervening two and a half centuries we have seen many cases where governmental and corporate power have been abused and our 'risk management systems' have been improved. The three responses typically tried are legal regulation, explicit ethical standard setting and institutional reform. I have long argued that the three are relatively ineffective if tried on their own, but can be highly effective if used in combination and directed towards making it more likely that institutions will live up to the public justifications for the powers and privileges they exercise. I have argued that ethical standard setting provides the most effective means of integrating the three by encapsulating the core of explicit ethical standard setting, the principled basis of laws and the ultimate criteria for judging whether institutional reforms have been effective.

This 'institutional' approach that brings together ethical standard setting, legal regulation and institutional design will need to be implemented at a number of levels—at the corporate level (with individual financial institutions, regulators and other players); and, in co-ordinating regulators and oversight bodies into 'financial integrity systems', at the national, global and, in some cases, regional[9] levels. I will comment briefly on the first level and then discuss the application of the idea of national integrity systems to finance at the global level.

I.   Integrity Systems for Individual Firms

I have long argued[10] for a values-based approach to the governance of institutions—be they corporations,[11] government agencies[12] or professional groups.[13] Such an approach uses a form of 'institutional ethics' to integrate ethical standard setting, legal regulation and institutional design, and to utilise the insights of the four main governance disciplines in looking for potential norms. This approach starts with Peter Singer's basic ethical question—how are we to live?[14] Answering that question involves asking yourself hard questions about your values, giving honest and public answers, and trying to live by those answers. If you do, you have integrity in the sense that you are true to your values and true to yourself. In fact, if you do not live up to the answers you give, the first person you cheat is yourself.

Institutional ethics applies the same approach to institutions. It involves an institution asking hard questions about its value and values, giving honest and public answers, and living by them. Doing so for an institution is more complex than for an individual, but it is both possible and necessary. The first vital questions that must be asked of any institution

---

[9] Regional level financial integrity systems are important in Europe and their further development may be the key to solving the diverse problems of countries with financial systems in difficulties, such as Ireland, Latvia and Iceland, and countries with recessional problems, such as Germany.

[10] See above n 5.

[11] C Sampford and DAR Wood, 'The Future of Business Ethics: Legal Regulation, Ethical Standard Setting and Institutional Design' (1992) 1 *Griffith Law Review* 56.

[12] C Sampford, 'Institutionalising Public Sector Ethics' in N Preston (ed), *Ethics for the Public Sector: Education and Training* (Sydney, Federation Press, 1994).

[13] C Sampford and C Parker, 'Legal Ethics: Legal Regulation, Ethical Standard Setting and Institutional Design' in C Parker and C Sampford (eds), *Legal Ethics and Legal Practice: Contemporary Issues* (Oxford, Oxford University Press, 1995).

[14] P Singer, *How Are We to Live? Ethics in an Age of Self-interest* (Melbourne, Text Publishing, 1993).

or organisation are: what is it for? Why should it exist? What justifies the organisation to the community in which it operates, given that the community generally provides privileges? Why is the community within which it operates better for the existence of the government/corporation etc? Asking those questions involves an institutional and collective effort under an organisation's own formal and informal constitutional processes (including getting acceptance from relevant outsiders, such as shareholders and/or relevant regulators).

An organisation has integrity if it lives by its answers. However, it does so in a different way to an individual. It cannot merely be a personal commitment but must be an institutional commitment that involves creating mechanisms which make it more likely that the organisation keeps to the values it has publicly declared and to which it is publicly committed. These mechanisms are collectively called an 'integrity system'. Leaders of financial institutions would do well to commence this process and consider the justification for their existence, for the concentration of resources within them and the special privileges accorded them. Is the community better off for their existence? If so, why? These are questions that should always be asked—the difference is that there is now a demand for answers from outside as well as a need to provide them internally.

I will not rehearse this complex process but I will reprise a thought that a common-room conversation generated 20 years ago, when we were going through a property boom as investors burnt by the stock market crash went searching for what they thought was safety in real estate. I had a post-doctoral fellowship at Monash University and a new colleague introduced himself as the first person appointed to teach Banking Law in the Faculty. I enunciated a view of banking and banking law:

> The first principle of banking is to ensure that as much money passes through your hands as many times as possible ensuring that a little bit sticks each time. The first principle of banking law is that what sticks is yours.

A decade later, I added: 'The first principle of banking ethics is that the transaction and the stickiness are justified as a service to the community to which banking claims to be a service industry.' Paul Krugman has pointed out that financial services now account for 8% of the US economy—up from 4% half a century ago.[15] Does this mean that it is doing twice as much or does it mean that they are half as efficient—or just that a lot more clients' money is sticking to their hands—and in ways that do not serve the interests of the economy and the community?

J.   National Integrity Systems and Financial Integrity

At the national level, various ways of integrating legal regulation, ethical standard setting and/or institutional reform have been tried. Twenty years ago, the Hong Kong model (a strong law and a powerful agency) was the general model for fighting corruption. However, when Queensland sought to address the endemic corruption problems that had plagued it, they did not opt for that model. Since then, preference has shifted to 'national integrity systems' in which several institutions, agencies, laws and codes simultaneously

---

[15] P Krugman, 'The Market Mystique', *New York Times*, 26 March 2009, 29.

seek to promote 'integrity' and limit corruption—to increase the probability that entrusted powers will be used for its publicly justified and democratically endorsed ends and reduce the likelihood that those powers will be abused. The choice of the term 'integrity system' rather than 'anti-corruption' system was inspired. Corruption (the abuse of entrusted power for personal gain) is a derivative concept and a derivative goal. One cannot know what an abuse is without knowing what the legitimate uses of those powers are. Integrity (the use of entrusted power for publicly justified ends) is primary. We want effective institutions that deliver a sufficient proportion of their promises. If all we wanted was to avoid institutional corruption, that goal could be achieved in theory by not having institutions of the offending type at all, and in practice from anti-corruption practices that prevented such institutions from wielding any power. But the potential for corruption is built into all institutions because of the dynamics of collective action and agency. The reason why we create and support governments, joint stock companies and international NGOs is because often more can be achieved collectively than individually with the pooling of people power and resources for shared goals.

However, this pooling of power opens the possibility that institutional leaders may turn that entrusted power to their own benefit or use it against their citizens, stockholders, bondholders and employees. While it is not true that all power corrupts, it has to be recognised that it will not only attract those who wish to exercise it for its publicly justified purpose but also those who wish to use it for their own purposes. Hence anti-corruption agencies still have a place, but it is a place within a system that is primarily directed to channelling institutions into using their powers in the ways that they claim and by which they justify their existence. I would argue that this approach is very apt for application and we should see ourselves creating and refining national and international financial integrity systems. There are already multiple agencies from government, corporate and NGO sectors with mutually complementary and supportive institutional goals. In any case, most public officials and company directors are more than happy to engage in such justification. They genuinely believe that their activities do make society better off. Very few see themselves as social parasites benefiting at the expense of the community.

While there is a need for immediate action to limit the fallout to a 'mere' global recession, serious global research is required to understand these interlocking and mutually reinforcing problems and then totally to rethink the responses needed. This will involve rethinking the nature and function of corporations and financial intermediaries, and the capital markets in which they are nested, including what is now called "smart regulation"—designing and integrating rules, principles and norms to enhance security while simultaneously ensuring that sustainable innovation will not be compromised. This task requires, in turn, an integrated approach that transcends the limited solutions suggested by particular disciplines, and which looks to the 'integrity system' approach that was so successful in post-Fitzgerald Queensland. Such integrity systems involve ethical standard setting, economic incentives, organisational structures and the professionalism of those involved. The provision of oversight by lawyers, accountants and journalists is also vital. Moreover, the reality of global capital flows and the nature of the problems involved mean that the search for an equitable and sustainable solution cannot be undertaken by one nation, or solved by using the conceptual frameworks privileged by one disciplinary perspective. What is required is never just a new law but a reformed and effective 'global financial integrity system'. Not for the first time, capitalism needs to be saved from itself, so that it can live up to its claims of advancing human wellbeing rather than live down to the deficits which its critics have long claimed lie at its heart.

The best and most complete contemporary solution to Smith's missing variable thus lies in establishing a new global financial integrity system. What will this look like? A proper answer to that question would be better following rather than in advance of a 'global financial integrity systems assessment' based on the methodology we pioneered with Transparency International.[16] Luther nailed 95 theses to the door of a German church. I will not be so ambitious, but here are a dozen to begin with:

1. The explicit recognition of power in the market economy, including:
    a. Concentration of political and social power, people and resources within organisations.
    b. The inevitabilities of asymmetries in knowledge and the fact that the exploitation of these is a feature of all market and political systems and the basis of much profit-making.
    c. The inevitability of agency problems that mean that markets cannot operate unregulated—and that those who have power and asymmetric knowledge may well propose unregulated markets to make it easier to exercise their power and asymmetric knowledge.
2. Recognition of ideology and recognition of self-interest in public debates, including:
    a. Recognition of the self-interest of financiers arguing that privatisation and public private partnerships are necessary and desirable.
    b. The existence of ideology—political, economic, social, moral—within debates about governance of financial markets and the tendency to make self-serving comparisons between ideologies in which the ideal version of one's preferred ideology is compared with actualised versions of others.
    c. Questioning how efficient markets theory ever got going and the ideological controls on appointments in so many economics faculties, including the role of think tanks in pressing the interests of their donors. Economists especially must recognise that their insights are partial and limited and can only be useful in conjunction with other disciplinary perspectives.
3. Organisations should publicly justify themselves to the communities in which they operate, including:
    a. Asking deep questions about their values, giving honest and public answers and demonstrably exemplifying them.
    b. Being transparent.
    c. Taking public responsibility for failures as well as celebrating successes.
4. Repudiating the externalisation of costs and risks onto others.
5. Recognising the dangers of executives enjoying a large share of upside and limited downside risk—an agency problem that has materialised in many financial institutions.

---

[16] The most recent statement of this is found in my conference discussion paper: C Sampford, 'From National Integrity Systems to Global Integrity Systems: Conference Discussion Paper', presented at the 13th International Anti-Corruption Conference, Global Transparency Fighting Corruption for a Sustainable Future, Athens, 30 October to 2 November 2008, available at www.13iacc.org/files/IACC_discussion_paper.doc (accessed on 18 August 2008).

6.   Ratings are not done by New York firms and must be dissociated from ideology.

7.   The international financial system will not be a means for supporting domestic illegality, meaning specifically:

    a.   Corporations not paying their taxes.[17]

        i.   This is a quid pro quo for bailouts that save the system. We cannot expect ordinary citizens to bail out financial corporations and not expect those companies that remain profitable to avoid their responsibilities.

        ii.   Those who are still profitable should be glad that they are and willing to take on their responsibilities.[18]

        iii.   But we should implement simpler taxes—basic income and flat taxes.

    b.   Hiding of dictators' money.

    c.   Lending to dictators other than secured on assets that are built with the loans.

    d.   Odious debt and toxic debt.

8.   The international financial system will have to take into account climate change.

9.   The immediate response has to be national, or rather internationally coordinated but nationally based. However, the new system will have to be truly international, because it is going to depend on some countries continuing to lend to others.

10.   The response will have to include the creditor nations. They are going to be the ones who do the bailing out. If debtor nations like the US have a place at the table, so do other debtor nations. The US would not want its creditors to give the same weighting to creditor nations over debtor nations as in International Monetary Fund (IMF) deliberations. In recognising the reasonableness of that position, they should be promoters of a change in the IMF.

11.   We must recognise that American power is going to wane more quickly than had been thought. American hyper-power never existed and attempts to preserve it were consequently doomed to failure.

    a.   Ten years ago, the US possessed huge reserves of both soft power and hard power.

    b.   It squandered the former and overestimated the latter, leading to a weakening of its military and financial power and an exposure of those weaknesses.

12.   We may need the global equivalent of a truth and reconciliation commission. The US and other liberal democracies may need to give up some of those who appear to be corporate criminals to that process as a way of indicating that their priority is fixing the problems rather than protecting the perpetrators. This may be an essential condition for restoring confidence among those whose continued and possibly increasing loans will be necessary.[19] The alternative might be handing them over for prosecution.

---

[17] Tax avoidance is important for a number of reasons. It detracts from the revenue available to states to look after their people and bail out the system. It is also quite likely that the attitudes to tax avoidance within law firms helped establish the culture in which regulatory avoidance came to be legitimated in large law firms.

[18] I have never had much sympathy with those who complained of having 'taxation problems'. The real problems are income problems!

[19] At other times, the sacrifice of a few heads to the tumbrils might be seen as a good way of assuaging the anger of developing country creditors whose entrusted funds were squandered. The insistence of a fair trial is a reasonable modern caveat—made more difficult because of the treatment of those at Guantanamo.

K.   Financial and Human Security Issues: From Climate Change to Capital Flows

In the current global crisis, activities to combat climate change may or may not be part of the stimulus packages introduced by some countries. Just as important may be the warning signals it sends for carbon trading schemes. For most of this decade there has been general agreement that we need to send price signals to those engaging in unsustainable activity, and most have favoured carbon trading over a carbon tax. I have been quite sceptical of carbon trading ever since I was invited to speak on this matter for a World Council of Churches colloquium in 2000. As soon as I started to see merchant banks salivating over the money to be made on the carbon market I was sure that it was a bad idea. Who would now suggest that those who destroyed more than five trillion dollars of value (and counting) should be given the role of building the carbon market that is supposed to save the planet? Beyond climate change, human security goes to a range of domestic governance issues, but it also goes to the issue of the distribution of capital flows.

When I was on a World Bank Governance mission to East Timor, I was surprised that most of the foreign aid bodies thought that the spike in proceeds of East Timorese oil government should be invested in New York. There were some short-term reasons for this—the capacity of the economy to absorb large-scale infrastructure investment, the uncertainty of what the best infrastructure would be, the lack of a developed integrity system to ensure that the funds were used for the purposes intended rather than corruptly appropriated, or spent on pet projects that had not been properly examined and pork barrelling. However, once those impediments had been addressed, East Timor should have been an entirely appropriate place for East Timor to invest in. Traditionally the wealthiest economies have generated a lot of capital and exported it. This is because the greatest growth and the greatest opportunities have occurred in developing countries.[20] In the meantime, putting all their money into one country, especially one with the known global debt problems at the time, should have seemed narrow. Investments might well have been made in developing countries that were clean and that were ahead of East Timor in the above desiderata.[21] I was glad to discover, however, that most of East Timor's sovereign wealth fund was invested in fixed interest securities, so no harm was done to that particular sovereign wealth fund of a poor country.

If globalisation involves the flow of people, ideas, goods and money, the last has grown most rapidly—indeed, well in excess of the flow of goods and investment that it is supposed to support. Developing countries have entrusted their enormous and growing surpluses in western banks and other financial intermediaries. Some—such as East Timor—were pressed by western-run multilaterals to entrust the proceeds of extractive industries in Wall Street on the basis that it was less likely to be eroded by corruption. The amounts entrusted to such intermediaries in the US and elsewhere on the basis that they would be invested on a secure and conservative basis were unprecedented. As I have already observed, it now appears that entrusted powers over vast sums of money were abused for personal gain.

---

[20] This has since been pointed out by the President of the Chinese Central Bank.
[21] This would have had the advantage of focusing on businesses whose work might be applicable in East Timor.

This does not mean that banks should not be rescued. The fact that they were poorly run is not the point. If they had been well run, they would not need to be rescued. Rescues are instigated to protect the wider economy, confidence and depositors who were not accepting suspiciously high rates—while seeking to ensure that the owners and managers of such banks remain as exposed as possible to the consequences of their mistakes. Nor does this mean that all participants acted unethically or illegally. However, if confidence in the international financial system is to be restored in the long term, and if the proceeds of developing country surpluses and western superannuation are to continue to be entrusted with intermediaries for investment in the globalised economy—thereby supporting sustainable globalisation rather than undermining it—then this can only happen if there is a full investigation of what went wrong and options for the establishment of adequate financial integrity systems are debated, selected and implemented as part of the global integrity system. Such an investigation will have to include members of developing as well as developed countries, and must be supported by the work of international researchers, NGOs and international organisations. In this process, the Equator Principles, the UN Global Compact and the UN Principles of Responsible Investment will need to be reconsidered and implemented.

In reforming the international financial system, we should set the goal of ensuring that those who are entrusted with investing funds for others do not abuse that entrusted power to increase their own wealth at the expense of those for whom they invest. At the same time, we should set the international banking system the goal of establishing a regime that is sufficiently transparent so that no rational corrupt official or tax avoider would put his money in an offshore bank. I have long argued that this is the single most important contribution that developed nations can make to the reduction of corruption in developing nations. While some developed nations had resisted such a goal, 9/11 has stimulated the development of relevant tools.

L.   Conclusion

I have argued that we do not need a new 'regulatory contract'—a concept that is potentially useful but more misleading than it is helpful. The concept of trust and fiduciary duty is more helpful, but I suggest an institutionalist approach in which institutions are required to justify themselves to the community of which they are a part. That justification is in part because of the special privileges granted to financial institutions in limited liability. The reality of global capital flows and the nature of the problems involved mean that the search for an equitable and sustainable solution cannot be undertaken by one nation or solved by using the conceptual frameworks privileged by one disciplinary perspective. What is required is not just a new law but a reformed and effective 'global financial integrity system'. Not for the first time, capitalism needs to be saved from itself so that it can live up to its claims to advance human well-being rather than live down to the defects which its critics have long claimed lie at its heart. If confidence in the international financial system is to be restored in the long term, and if the proceeds of developing country surpluses and western superannuation are to continue to be entrusted to intermediaries for investment in the globalised economy (thereby supporting sustainable globalisation rather than undermining it), there must be a full investigation of what went wrong. Subsequently, options for the establishment of adequate financial integrity systems must be debated, selected and implemented as part of the global integrity system. Such an investigation will have to include members of developing as well as developed countries, and must be supported by the work of international researchers, NGOs and international organisations. In this process, the Equator Principles, the UN Global Compact, the UN Principles of Responsible Investment will need to be reconsidered and implemented. In reforming the international financial system, we should set the goal of ensuring that those who are entrusted with investing funds for others do not abuse that entrusted power to increase their own wealth at the expense of those for whom they invest. If so, we can, like Adam Smith, enjoy our dinner—and get a good night's sleep.

2

US Mortgage Markets:
A Tale of Self-correcting Markets, Parallel Lives
and Other People's Money

ROBIN PAUL MALLOY*

A. Introduction

The collapse of global financial markets and in particular US mortgage markets has had a dramatic impact on business, government and people everywhere. The magnitude of the consequences of this market shakeout draws attention to the need for reform in mortgage and financial market operations. Examining the causes of the crisis and suggesting reforms does not mean that we can or should eliminate these markets. In fact, we need these markets to facilitate economic growth, spreading of risk, enhancement of liquidity and promotion of development. At the same time, it is clear that reform is needed.

In approaching reform we must first recognise that markets are the product of volitional arrangements that incentivise particular networks and patterns of exchange. The current crisis in the US housing and mortgage markets reflects poorly incentivised exchange relationships. We cannot simply blame the current financial crisis on 'the market' or fall back on meaningless metaphors related to being caught in 'the perfect storm'. The crisis in the US, which also underlies the crisis globally, stems from an overly optimistic view of self-regulating markets and of the belief in an unregulated invisible hand. The current crisis demonstrates the need for strong and purposeful regulation of housing and of mortgage market activity.

In this paper I examine the meltdown of the mortgage market in the US from the perspective of the underlying real estate transaction and the related activities of the primary mortgage market. My goal is to explain that the future of financial regulation must include the focusing of substantial attention on reforming the underlying real estate transaction upon which mortgaged-backed securities are dependent. In doing this, my focus is primarily structural. By this I mean that I intend, in this short chapter, only to address a couple of key structural ideas that need to be adjusted as we think about creating new arrangements for the future. To accomplish this goal, I proceed in several steps. First, I provide a brief overview of the relationship among the underlying real estate transaction,

* EI White Chair and Distinguished Professor of Law, Director, Center on Property, Citizenship, and Social Entrepreneurism, College of Law, Syracuse University.

the primary market and the secondary market in mortgages.[1] In this setting I explain the fallacy of self-correcting markets. Next, I examine Hernado DeSoto's idea of creating parallel lives for property and the transactions based on the representation of property.[2] I argue that this is an inappropriate metaphor that leads to bad regulation. And thirdly, I touch on the problem of having integrated financial markets where most of the players are playing with other people's money.

B.   Self-correcting Mortgage Markets

Markets are not objects that can be observed as something real. Markets involve a dynamic process of human interaction and exchange. This process is complex, multi-valued and ever changing. When economists speak of the financial market, the mortgage market or any other market they are speaking in metaphorical terms in which the underlying networks and patterns of human exchange are expressed in terms of economic models.[3] While these models are useful, they are not the markets to which they refer.[4] The difference is important, particularly when we consider the idea of self-correcting markets.

When one speaks of self-correcting markets one provides iteration on Adam Smith's invisible hand metaphor[5]—one suggests that markets are naturally occurring objects or real physical places that automatically adjust to changing circumstances, as if market activity were being directed by an invisible hand. Markets, however, are the institutional product of human action and not naturally occurring environments in which people happen to be placed. There are, in fact, probably few better examples of the volitional creation of a market institution than that of the secondary mortgage market. The secondary mortgage market in the US is purely a creation of the federal government. The government has long subsidised and supported the growth of primary markets and the management of primary market funding via money supply operations and initial programmes of buying and holding originated loans.[6]

In the 1980s the government created the secondary mortgage market to achieve greater liquidity and reduce risk for financial intermediaries operating at the primary market

---

[1] See generally RP Malloy and JC Smith, *Real Estate Transactions*, 3rd edn (New York, Aspen Publishers, 2007) 379–84 (2007); RP Malloy and JC Smith, *Real Estate Transactions*, 2nd edn (New York, Aspen Publishers, 2002) 617–26; RP Malloy, 'The Secondary Mortgage Market—A Catalyst for Change in Real Estate Transactions' (1986) 39 *Southwestern Law Journal* 991; CA Stone and A Zissu, *The Securitization Market Handbook: Structures and Dynamics of Mortgage- and Asset-backed Securities* (Princeton, NJ, Bloomberg Press, 2005).

[2] H DeSoto, *The Mystery of Capital: Why Capitalism Triumphs in the West and Fails Everywhere Else* (New York, Basic Books, 2000).

[3] RP Malloy, *Law and Market Economy: Reinterpreting the Values of Law and Economics* (Cambridge, Cambridge University Press, 2000); DN McCloskey, *The Rhetoric of Economics* (Madison, Wisconsin Press, 1985); DN McCloskey, *If You're So Smart: The Narrative of Economic Expertise* (Chicago, IL, Chicago University Press, 1990).

[4] Malloy, ibid; RP Malloy, *Law in a Market Context: An Introduction to Market Concepts in Legal Reasoning* (Cambridge, Cambridge University Press, 2004).

[5] A Smith (E Cannon, ed), *An Inquiry into the Nature and Causes of the Wealth of Nations* (Chicago, IL, Chicago University Press, 1976) Book I, 477–78; A Smith (EG West, ed), *The Theory of Moral Sentiments* (Indianapolis, IN, Liberty Press, 1969) 304.

[6] Malloy, 'The Secondary Mortgage Market' above n 1; D Reiss, 'The Federal Government's Implied Guarantee of Fannie Mae and Freddie Mac's Obligations: Uncle Sam Will Pick Up the Tab' (2008) 42 *Georgia Law Review* 1019.

level. They also hoped to expand the investment appeal of instruments and securities that would attract additional funds to the real estate markets. The demand for housing and real estate development in the US was mismatched in terms of spending and savings rates in different regions of the country, and the country in general needed to tap into foreign capital in an effort to fuel the American demand for property development.[7] Thus, as is the case with most institutional markets of any considerable size, public intervention created structures to define and incentivise particular networks and patterns of exchange, and these actions were taken in pursuit of beliefs concerning the cost effectiveness of achieving particular value-based outcomes.

When we think of markets, therefore, we should think in terms of purposeful institutional frameworks designed to incentivise and privilege certain networks and patterns of exchange over others.[8] These institutional frameworks provide the constraints and terms of trade. Within the constraints of the institutional arrangements prices may be self-correcting because price is an interpretation of value, and prices simply respond to changing value relationships within a give framework. The idea of self-correcting or relative changes in prices, however, is not the same as the idea of a self-correcting market. People change markets (the institutional structures of exchange) even if prices within a given structure adjust in response to new patterns of exchange within the system.

This distinction is particularly important when one considers the political commitment to minimal regulation in the US. The iconic representation of invisible hands and self-correcting markets are useful political constructs used to reject and constrain government oversight and regulation. They play into a deeply held self-image of the free spirited and independent American pioneer, cowboy and entrepreneur. They are also offered as a foil of reassurance of American superiority with respect to the arrangements pursued in the capitals of Europe and elsewhere, where paternalism and social connectedness allegedly receive more legitimisation than in the US. Of course, the American love affair with the invisible hand is conveniently dismissive of any regard for Adam Smith's notion of the impartial spectator, and of the roles of morality and ethics in the marketplace.

More importantly, the assumption of self-correcting markets reinforces the American commitment to a highly protective form of constitutional property. As Gregory Alexander pointed out in *The Global Debate over Constitutional Property*, a strong commitment to private property raises tensions within liberal democracies.[9] This is because it makes efforts at redistribution very difficult and counters the efforts of political majorities to respond to questions of equity and fairness. Given the American commitment to a very strong constitutional property right, efforts at redistribution are often done by indirect means, such as in subsidising credit. This is the case with the mortgage markets. The sub-prime market was a tool for expanding ownership to lower-income people and to assist in opening ownership opportunities to a more diversified population.[10] As a substitute for building more public housing that is often times politically frowned upon, the indirect subsidies to mortgage markets appeared to be a purely private market

---

[7] Ibid.

[8] D Bromley, *Sufficient Reason: Volitional Pragmatism and the Meaning of Economic Institutions* (Princeton, NJ, Princeton University Press, 2006).

[9] G Alexander, *The Global Debate Over Constitutional Property* (Chicago, IL, Chicago University Press, 2006).

[10] See, eg Malloy and Smith 3rd edn, above n 1, 313–14 (charts on ownership rates between 1994 and 2004 showing rapid gains by minority groups); S Schmidt and M Tamman, 'Housing Push for Hispanics Spawns Wave of Foreclosures', *Wall Street Journal*, 5 January 2009, A1.

operation capable of appealing to the American dream of home ownership without the 'stigma' of wealth redistribution. The problem, of course, is that mortgages that make little or no economic sense (as is the case with many of the so-called toxic mortgage loans) are unsustainable in the private marketplace.

The commitment to self-correcting markets allowed for too little regulation, and led to a slow response to perverse market incentives in US housing and mortgage markets. When government officials should have been rethinking their beliefs about the appropriateness of the institutional structures that were in place for these markets they simply relinquished responsibility and waited for the markets to correct themselves. Not until catastrophic results became obvious to everyone did anyone actually take volitional action to seek a restructuring of the market arrangement.

When we think about financial innovation and mortgage markets we must, therefore, think beyond financial product development and include consideration of innovation in exchange relationships. The current structure of the mortgage market connects homebuyers with loan originators in the primary market and primary lenders with secondary mortgage market intermediaries and investors in mortgage related securities. In the underlying purchase and sale of a home, the buyer and seller enter a contract wherein the seller agrees to convey the property to the buyer for monies paid. The buyer generally obtains a mortgage to assist in the finance of the purchase and this mortgage is obtained from the primary mortgage market. The basic set of relationships today is depicted in Figure 1.[11]

In these markets, borrowers approach primary lenders in order to obtain funding to facilitate the purchase of real estate. Lenders provide funding and secure a promise to pay back the loan with a mortgage lien placed against the property. In the old days, a lender would hold the mortgage in its portfolio until it was repaid (a loan and hold strategy). This gave them an ownership stake and a continuing risk related to the quality of

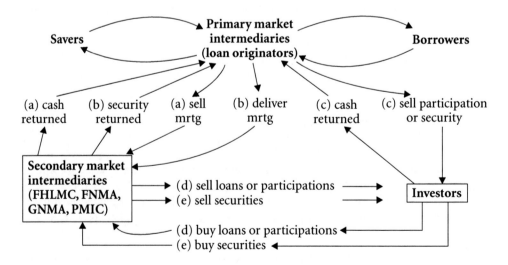

Figure 1. The relationship between primary and secondary mortgage markets.

---

[11] Malloy and Smith 3rd edn, above n 1, 382.

the loans that they originated. Now, most lending takes a different form. The loan originator makes the loan and then sells it to a secondary market intermediary, earning fees for originating and servicing of the loan, not from holding it long term (a loan-and-sell strategy). Likewise, the secondary intermediaries spread the risk by packaging the loans, issuing securities based on the cash flow represented by the underlying promises to pay on the mortgages and selling these securities in the financial markets. In all of these inter-market exchanges, actors are rewarded for originating and selling mortgages, and financial instruments related to such mortgages. There is very little responsibility for the quality of what is originated, and very big rewards for how much is originated.

Under pressure from Congress, the government-related intermediaries in the secondary market experimented with lower and lower underwriting standards for the mortgages they purchased. In addition, the incentive arrangement for top executives at Fannie Mae and Freddie Mac were structured to reward the quantity of originations and purchases in the respective institutional portfolios, not the quality.[12]

A significant point for global understanding of this approach is one of appreciating that in the US many public policy issues have a race as well as a social class dimension. In general, income continues to have a correlation with race, and this raises a number of concerns with respect to equity and fairness. For a number of years the complaint had been that housing ownership unfairly discriminated against certain identifiable racial groups and worked in favour of whites. One reason for promoting the sub-prime market, therefore, was its ability to open home ownership to a larger and more diverse population; and it actually had this effect.[13] At the same time, the effort was abused by lenders willing to make too many loan originations on terms that made little or no economic sense.

The end result of these inter-market relationships and incentive structures was that everyone in the underlying real estate transactions received fees, commissions and benefits from papering a loan origination, working on an incentive structure that rewarded lots of originations at lower and lower standards of quality. They did this because the secondary intermediaries created a profitable market for off-loading these loans. The secondary intermediaries kept buying 'substandard'-quality loans because they could package them and sell them to investors for a high profit. The fall-back position in all of this was a political and regulatory ideology based on the idea that markets were self-correcting— even when the current market in mortgages was itself the product of purposeful government regulation and intervention. Basically, the logic goes something like this: since investors kept buying these securities backed by mortgages, the products must have been fine; otherwise the market would have corrected itself. Even Federal Reserve Chairman Alan Greenspan is famously quoted as saying he was shocked to find that this did not happen.[14]

Innovation in the structure of home financing dramatically changed the underlying real estate transaction. In simple terms, a couple of significant changes occurred.[15] Prior to the new secondary mortgage market environment, the local depositors and homebuyers

---

[12] See JR Hagerty, JR Wilke, JD McKinnon and JS Lublin, 'After Fannie Shake-up, Regulators Focus on Pay', *Wall Street Journal*, 23 December 2004, A1; JR Hagerty, 'Fannie Will Use New Benchmarks In Setting Incentive Pay for 2005', *Wall Street Journal*, 14 March 2005, A2.

[13] See the sources above n 10.

[14] K Scannell and S Reddy, 'Greenspan Admits Errors to Hostile Home Panel', *Wall Street Journal*, 24 October 2008, A1.

were considered to be critically important customers earning the bank's attention.[16] After the innovative integration of primary and secondary markets, banks quickly changed focus and understood that the key customer base was not the depositor/borrower but the secondary market intermediaries, and ultimately investors in mortgage-related securities.[17] The development of the secondary market redefined the customer service focus of lending and incentivised lenders to set terms and make loans according to the preferences of the secondary intermediaries and their investors.

A second significant change resulting from the innovation of the mortgage market was the way in which it reshaped the business plan for loan originators. Prior to the integrated market, lenders were operating under a business model of loan and hold. After the development of the integrated market, the business model switched to one of working to efficiently generate high volumes of loan files that could quickly be sold so that new funds would be funnelled back to the originator to be used for yet more lending. Thus, loan origination became a fee-based operation for the production of standardised input items for the securities market.[18] This is a very different business model from that of the old loan-and-hold operation.

Consequently, innovation in the structure of mortgage market operations generated new opportunities for problems. Prior to the development of secondary mortgage market, transactions were done on a much more local scale, a scale on which economic models of two-party transactions, with individuals bargaining for a wealth-enhancing outcome, could come closer to Adam Smith's ideal of having private exchanges advance the public interest even though it forms no part of the intention of the underlying parties.[19] This maxim diminishes in relevance as the scale changes to global, integrated, multi-party exchanges with numerous externality issues. Secondary mortgage market incentive structures changed all of the relational dynamics in the underlying transaction, and the obsession with following an invisible hand of efficiency resulted in a misunderstanding of the continuing importance of the underlying real-estate transaction. Not only is the amoral and self-interested quest for efficiency unsustainable, as I have argued extensively elsewhere,[20] the obsession with the securities end of the market incentivised paper generation with a sense that the quality of the underlying property transaction no longer mattered.

The wake-up call on the collapse of US mortgage markets is one that reminds us of the fundamental importance of the underlying real estate transaction to the asset value of innovative securities backed by pools of mortgages. Just as all property lawyers know that a mortgage is meaningless without a promise to pay standing behind it, all investors should know that a mortgage-backed security is only as valuable as the quality of the underlying mortgage. The incentive structure of mortgage markets prior to the collapse, however, provided incentives for quantity of production with little or no attention to quality of production. Consequently, the innovation in the market structure was critically flawed,

---

[15] Malloy, above n 3, 50–6 (a market analysis of structural changes in mortgage market relationships brought about by development of the secondary mortgage market).

[16] Ibid.

[17] Ibid.

[18] Ibid; Malloy and Smith 3rd edn, above n 1, 367–406.

[19] Malloy, *Law in a Market Context*, above n 4, 27–30 (discussing this point with reference to Adam Smith).

[20] Malloy, above n 3.

independent of the complex innovation in the development of new financial instruments backed by home mortgages.

C. Parallel Lives

The seeming lack of focus on the underlying real estate transaction, as discussed above, is highlighted by the acceptance of an erroneous understanding of a metaphor offered by Hernado DeSoto. As DeSoto explains in *The Mystery of Capital*

> In the west, . . . every parcel of land, every building, every piece of equipment, or store of inventories is represented in a property document that is the visible sign of a vast hidden process that connects all of these assets to the rest of the economy. Thanks to this representational process, assets can lead an invisible, *parallel life* alongside their material existence. They can be used as collateral for credit. The single most important source of funds for new business in the United States is a mortgage on the entrepreneur's house. These assets can also provide a link to the owner's credit history, an accountable address for collection of debts and taxes, the basis for the creation of reliable and universal public utilities, and a foundation for the creation of securities (like mortgage-backed bonds) that can then be rediscounted and sold in secondary markets. By this process the West injects life into assets and makes them generate capital.[21]

Seemingly building on DeSoto's metaphor of creating parallel lives of economic activity between real property and the documentary representation of such property, government regulators have failed to fully appreciate the connection between the underlying real estate transaction and the activity in the secondary mortgage market. Contrary to DeSoto's imaginative metaphor, the transactions in the documentary representations of property do not live a life parallel to the property itself. These documents represent the property in some respects and can generate additional economic activity, creating leverage and extending the reach of markets, but they occupy a derivative place in the market. These documentary transactions, like the mortgage-backed securities in the financial markets, have little or no value when the underlying real estate transaction is degraded and non-performing.

A key problem associated with issuing mortgage-backed securities is one of transactional authentication. The secondary market deals in abstractions and representations of underlying real estate transactions. Thus, a critical valuation issue in the secondary market is one of assurance that the investment in the abstract and representative instruments reflects the reality of an actual underlying real estate transaction. In other words, there is a need for greatly improved protocols to ensure that the representations of a deal are authentic. We know that this was not the case with respect to many underlying transactions where appraisals had no relationship to the actual value of a property, and information on properties, borrowers and sellers was untrue, misrepresented, unavailable or poorly authenticated.

Consequently, there is a need to recognise that these transactions do not take place in a parallel universe because they are always linked to the underlying property. It is easy to misunderstand this and to begin to think that the mortgage-backed securities have a life of their own, but they do not. Setting aside what to do with currently non-performing loans,

---

[21] DeSoto, above n 2, 6 (emphasis added).

the basic structure of the simple residential home transaction has to be examined. The future of financial regulation must avoid the mistake of spending too much time on the securities end of these transactions and too little time on restructuring the regulation of the underlying real estate transaction. Effort must be expended to develop appropriate transactional structures and protocols for ensuring the authenticity and quality of the underlying transactions on which mortgage-backed securities are issued.

D.   Other People's Money

A third critical factor to address is the fact that the mortgage market game is played with other people's money. From top to bottom, the housing and the primary and secondary mortgage markets operate on using other people's money; likewise, the trillion dollar bailout undertaken by the US government is yet another gamble taken with other people's money. Consequently, no one has any 'skin' in the game, as they say. Everyone who plays gets benefits, but the downside risk falls heavily on non-players—the people who did not borrow recklessly, who did not commit to loans that they cannot repay, who did not use fraudulent appraisals, who did not make commissions from speculative flips and who did not engage in other activities that substantially degraded the quality of the underlying real estate transactions. The people who saved and played by the rules are now asked to cover the risks and bail out the losers.

Such a bailout clearly creates a moral hazard, but more importantly it shines a light on the perverse incentive structure of a primary mortgage market in which homebuyers borrow with little or no money down;[22] loan originators collect fees and commissions for packaging paper files for which they have little or no responsibility once they sell them; and secondary intermediaries shift much of their risk to investors. Everyone works on leveraged funds while pocketing all the profits in real dollars. There is no incentive for caution but great reward for speculation.

In addition, when one considers the alignment of interest among real estate salespeople and loan originators earning commissions for pushing loans, and lenders for packaging loans in the secondary market, one can appreciate the presence of what might be called an 'inverse prisoner's dilemma'.[23] In the exchange patterns of the mortgage markets every participant gained from promoting and processing more loans, without regard to quality. Cooperation among parties facilitated the kind of transactional misbehavior that degraded the overall loan process and the mortgage market. Whereas the prisoner's dilemma typically concerns itself with the problem of getting people to cooperate, it is the inverse problem that plagued the US mortgage market: cooperation was too easy. The exchange pattern needs to be corrected to introduce more safeguards and authentication protocols. This may increase transaction costs from increased policing, added documentation and a more adversarial bargaining process, but it will enhance the quality of the loans in the underlying real estate transaction. The end result of imposing such costs is that we may need to accept increased transaction costs at the micro-level in exchange for

[22] Malloy, *Law in a Market Context*, above n 4, 115.
[23] Ibid, 130–32; RH McAdams, 'Beyond the Prisoner's Dilemma: Coordination, Game Theory, and Law' (2009) 82 *Southern California Law Review* 209.

the benefits of positive externalities at the macro-level. In other words, individuals may need to spend more to verify and authenticate an economically sound real estate transaction but in so doing the public will gain much more than the individuals will lose.[24]

Consequently, future financial regulation must find ways of policing the quality of loan originations, requiring significant down payments (like required capitalisation rates), and ways of having participants in the underlying transaction retain liability for the loans they originate.

E.   Implications and Conclusion

The current crisis in the US mortgage market reflects a complex set of factors. Thus, there are many factors to consider in addressing the future of financial regulations with respect to securities backed by real estate mortgages. One key implication is that we need to focus on fixing the underlying real estate transaction because the mortgage-related securities are only as sound as the underlying mortgages on which they are based. Thus, reform of financial markets must include a re-evaluation of the underlying property and mortgage market fundamentals. Secondly, since these mortgage-related securities trade in global markets, there should be a global role in establishing sound underwriting standards for transactional operations and disclosure rules. Thirdly, we must move away from the ideology of self-correcting markets and of imagining that an amoral approach to a calculus of wealth maximisation is sustainable. Markets are not an end in themselves, they are a means; and ethical and normative beliefs direct our attention to praiseworthy goals to which particular market incentive structures might properly be addressed.

Markets are a means for achieving certain desirable outcomes, and we can incentivise transactions in a variety of ways to achieve particular goals. One way to reduce the incentive for originating high-risk loans is to eliminate speculation for quick gains in housing values. Many low-quality loans were originated on assumptions that housing prices would continue to rise at a rapid pace, making it possible to justify such loans by assuming that rapidly rising equity would make up for the unsustainable economic realities of the original loan. Eliminating the incentive to speculate on short-term gains in housing values would be beneficial to housing and mortgage market stability. After all, housing policy is about subsidising affordability and the virtues of ownership, citizenship and connection to a community, not about get-rich-quick schemes and speculation. Thus, government can justify limiting short-term equity appreciation gains in the first few years of home ownership. This would undercut the perverse incentives to engage in flipping properties and borrowing beyond one's current means. It would also be a good first step in returning stability and reality to the underlying real estate transaction.

The future of financial market regulation must be based on active and volitional measures, not on the fiction of self-correcting markets directed by an invisible hand. Similarly, the regulation must be holistic in addressing the full range of activities from the underlying real estate transaction to the ultimate investment in a mortgage-related

---

[24] The idea is that transaction costs are not always a bad thing. Sometimes transaction costs at one level of the market are more than offset by gains elsewhere. See, eg DM Driesen and S Ghosh, 'The Functions of Transaction Costs: Rethinking Transaction Cost Minimization in a World of Friction' (2005) 47 *Arizona Law Review* 61.

security. Regulatory policy cannot be based on a metaphor of parallel lives because there is a direct and continuing relationship between real estate transactions and the derivative activities of the secondary market. Reform efforts must include restructuring the supervision and confirmable authenticity of the underlying real estate transactions. New protocols must be developed to assure transactional authenticity so that investors can be confident that the documents representing the transaction actually reflect a real and substantive exchange consistent with those documents.

Finally, regulatory reform needs to affirm accountability by making market participants responsible for the quality as well as the quantity of the exchanges that they undertake. Loan originators, packagers and everyone else in the mortgage market business needs to have a stake in the market, they cannot be allowed to simply play with other people's money. This includes looking at the potential for degraded transactions resulting from what I have identified in the last section of this chapter as a reverse prisoner's dilemma problem. Assuring quality real estate transactions may impose some additional transaction costs at the micro-level to discourage the reverse prisoner's dilemma problem but will generate large positive externalities at the macro-level. Therefore, we should not be reluctant to impose additional transaction costs on the parties to the underlying transactions in the primary markets. Nor should we be hesitant to return to the practice of reviewing mortgage quality in loan originations as part of the process of rating mortgage-related securities. The added costs will be offset by positive and public externalities.[25]

---

[25] In this chapter I have focused on a few key structural matters relevant to a global market perspective. For information on specific reform recommendations that I have for the underlying real estate transaction under US law, see a related piece by me entitled, 'Mortgage Reform and the Fallacy of Self-correcting Markets' to be published in a symposium on Real Property, Mortgages and the Economy: A Call for Ethics and Reform, to appear in the fall issue of 30 *Pace Law Review* (2009).

3

The Current Financial Crisis and the Economic Impact of Future Regulatory Reform

RAY BARRELL, IAN HURST AND SIMON KIRBY[*]

A. Introduction

This paper evaluates the roots of the current financial crisis and provides insight into the costs and benefits from the tightening of financial regulation. These are linked, and an evaluation of how the crisis has been dealt with depends upon the costs and benefits of action and inaction in the run up to a crisis, the process of dealing with it and in the aftermath. We begin by briefly summarising previous financial crises in advanced economies. Section B summarises the precursors to the current financial crisis. Section C discusses how the current crisis can be modelled using NiGEM, the global econometric model of the National Institute of Economic and Social Research (NIESR). The next section takes a first look at the costs and benefits of regulatory changes, and we then conclude.

B. Financial Crises

Contrary to popular wisdom, recent research indicates financial crises occur with depressing regularity. Demirgüc-Kunt and Detragiache[1] used a sample of 77 systemic crises over the period 1980–2002 in their research. Caprio et al[2] found 117 episodes of systemic banking crises (with much or all of bank capital being exhausted) in 93 countries from 1970 to 2002. Davis and Karim[3] found seven systemic crises took place between 1980

[*] National Institute of Economic and Social Research, London. Previous versions of this paper have been presented at the IMF in Washington, at the IfW in Kiel and at Brunel University. Funding has been provided by the FSA and by the NiGEM model user group, which includes the IMF, the ECB, the Bank of England and most European central banks. Opinions and errors remain ours.

[1] A Demirgüc-Kunt and E Detragiache, 'Empirical Analysis of the Causes and Consequences of Banking Crises' (2005) 192 *National Institute Economic Review* 68.

[2] G Caprio, D Klingebiel, L Laeven and G Noguera, 'Banking Crisis Database' in P Honohan and L Laeven (eds), *Systemic Financial Crises: Containment and Resolution* (Cambridge, Cambridge University Press, 2005).

[3] EP Davis and D Karim, 'Could Early Warning Systems Have Helped to Predict the Sub-prime Crisis?' (2008) 206 *National Institute Economic Review* 35.

and 2000 in advanced OECD countries, with minor crises in the US, Portugal and Italy, and large-scale systemic crises in Japan, Norway Sweden and Finland. With the probability of a serious banking crisis in any OECD country approximating 2.5 standard deviations away from the mean (around 2%), instituting preventative measures should be a priority. Barrel, Davis, Karim and Liadze[4] undertook a logit analysis of the determinants of OECD crises since 1980, and suggested that levels of liquidity and capital reserves as measured by leverage in the run up to the crisis are significant determinants of the risks of a crisis. They also showed that the pre-existence of a bubble in real property prices also raises the risk of a crisis. Other factors that are common in studies dominated by emerging markets are shown to be not significant in OECD crises.

The Nordic crises were associated with rapid and poorly designed financial deregulation that led to excessive consumer and commercial real-estate borrowing and housing market and commercial property bubbles that had a significant effect on output. The collapse of consumption spending and commercial real-estate companies that came with the pricking of the asset bubbles was a factor behind the large-scale losses in the banking sectors, as were exposed positions in foreign exchange dealings. Real house prices fell 30% in Finland between 1991 and 1993, whilst they fell by 25% in Sweden over the same period. Output losses, commonly calculated as the cumulated drop below trend growth, were large, but there seems to have been little effect on longer-term growth prospects.

The Japanese crisis also followed from ill-judged deregulation and an expansion of borrowing, but involved fewer failures. The crisis lasted for a significantly longer period and the cumulated output loss appears to have been large. The economy was also trapped in a period with zero interest rates, making monetary policy essentially ineffective. The Japanese crisis was driven as much by falling commercial property prices after an extreme bubble and by corporate sector over-indebtedness as by personal sector problems. This led to a re-evaluation of risk premia in Japan, which, in turn, raised the user cost of capital and reduced trend output growth for some time. The Japanese crisis has probably had a permanent effect on the sustainable level of output in that economy. A fast resolution may have been a wiser option. In this paper we look at the build-up to the current global crisis, the events of the past 15 months and some implications of theory for policy.

Table 1. The Effects of Selected Banking Crises

	Norway	Sweden	Finland	Japan
Date	1989–92	1991–94	1991–94	1991–2001
Direct cost to taxpayers	3.4	2.1	10.0	14.0
Output loss (% of GDP)[a]	27.1	3.8	44.9	71.7

Source: Hoggarth and Sapporta (2001).
[a]Per cent of annual GDP at end of episode.

---

[4] R Barrell, EP Davis, D Karim and I Liadze, 'Bank Regulation, Property Prices and Financial Crises in OECD Countries', NIESR Discussion Paper No 330 (London, National Institute of Economic and Social Research, 2009).

C.   Precursors of the Crisis

The period 2000–07 was one of low global interest rates and high levels of global liquidity. Countries such as China built up current account surpluses and foreign exchange reserves, maintaining artificially low exchange rates and a positive saving investment balance. As a result of such pressure, global real interest rates fell after 2001 and long-term real rates were probably 100 or more basis points below their level of the previous decade. This, in turn, contributed to the rapid credit expansion and rising asset prices that preceded the crisis.

The monetary stance in the US and UK contributed to the asset bubbles, with low short-term real interest rates prompting a hunt for yield on the part of banks and institutional investors. Financial innovations sought to provide higher returns to serve this desire, but the consequence was higher risk and/or increased opacity—for example, via higher credit risk in structured products and sub-prime loans.

Lending to households grew at unprecedented rates, particularly in Spain, the US and the UK, where house prices also rose rapidly. The lending was often to types of borrower (notably sub-prime and buy-to-let borrowers) who had been previously excluded or quantity rationed, especially in the US, and to a lesser extent in the UK. Real house prices in the UK and the US rose far above their longer-term trend. This of course could have been due to structural factors, as Cameron et al[5] suggest. However, simpler analyses, such

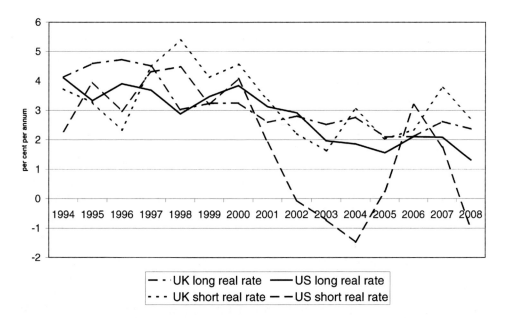

Figure 1. Real interest rates in the US and UK.

---

[5] G Cameron, J Muellbauer and S Murphy, 'Was there a British House Price Bubble? Evidence from a Regional Panel', CEPR Discussion Paper No 5619 (Center for Economic Policy Research, 2006).

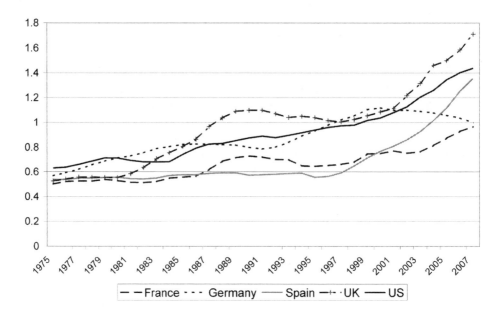

Figure 2. Personal sector borrowing as a proportion of disposable incomes.

as that of Barrell, Kirby and Riley,[6] which included the impacts of the real interest rate decline, have led us to think that house prices were 30% or more above fundamentals in the past few years in the UK, for example. Figure 3 suggests that house prices are similarly overvalued in Spain and France, and perhaps a little less so in the US. In all these countries borrowing had expanded rapidly.

At a deeper level, it can be argued that the pattern of asset price bubbles also reflected policy errors. One aspect is the monetary policies, notably that of the US, which were a partial cause of low nominal and real interest rates. The monetary stance was initially eased as a response to the equity bear market of 2000–03, whose feared deflationary impact they were introduced to counteract. However, it can be argued that the equity price fall was soon more than offset by a debt-financed housing boom in many OECD countries, which gathered strength as equity prices recovered in 2003–04. This was not counteracted by monetary policy, which stayed 'too loose for too long', especially in the US. Even from an inflation targeting point of view, as in the UK and the Euro Area, it can be argued that wealth effects of the housing bubble were inadequately taken into account.

Moreover, there were failures of regulation. As noted in Davis and Karim,[7] many central banks have developed 'macroprudential surveillance' in recent years, with teams of analysts producing financial stability reviews. These, in turn, have often highlighted the risks of high leverage by home owners, accompanied by house prices above sustainable levels. They also, albeit to a lesser extent, saw the risks of opaque financial innovations and the risk of a liquidity crisis in the financial markets as in 1998 (the Russia–LTCM episode).

---

[6] R Barrell, S Kirby and R Riley, 'The Current Position of UK House Prices' (2004) 189 *National Institute Economic Review* 57.
[7] Davis and Karim, above n 4.

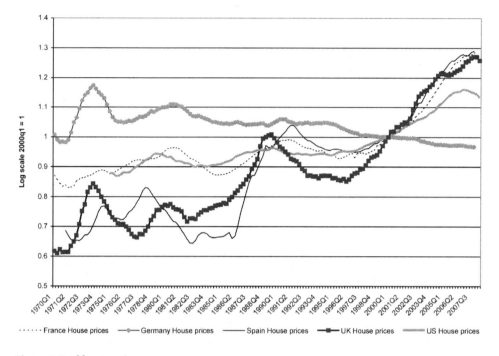

Figure 3. Real house prices.

The problem was that, beyond speeches by Central Bank Governors (moral suasion), there were no effective policy instruments for macroprudential action in the hands of these central banks beyond the interest rate, which was devoted to price stability. They could, as in the case of Sweden, have 'leaned against the wind' in the context of inflation targeting, as Wadhwani suggests,[8] but that was not considered appropriate in the UK or the US. It appears that the UK central bank seemed relaxed about the house price bubble, believing that it was not a major support for demand or a problem if it burst. The US authorities were convinced they could mop up the bubble once it burst. They can, but at a much greater cost to the US and the global economy than they had anticipated.

The situation was arguably aggravated by the fragmentation of microprudential regulation in the US, its separation from the Central Bank in the UK in 1997 and the lack of a unified regulator in the EU.[9] All of these arguably contributed to a division of microprudential and macroprudential regulation. In this context, although capital adequacy regulation continued to be focused on avoiding systemic risk as well as individual institution failure (and hence a difference between 'regulatory' and 'economic' capital), there seems to have been a tendency to greater focus in recent years on microefficiency at the cost of macrostability. The sharp potential reductions in capital needs when banks adopted the advanced internal ratings-based approach under Basel II

[8] S Wadhwani, 'Should Monetary Policy Respond to Asset Price Bubbles? Revisiting the Debate' (2008) 206 *National Institute Economic Review* 25.

[9] R Barrell and EP Davis, 'Policy Design and Macroeconomic Stability in Europe' (2005) 191 *National Institute Economic Review* 94.

are a symptom of this. Another is the lack of response of regulators to the concerns expressed in financial stability reports by central banks, given that they had the scope to warn institutions against the background of a threat of tighter capital standards. A third is the tendency of the financial system to become increasingly procyclical, as pointed out repeatedly by the Bank for International Settlements.[10] The Spanish approach of requiring higher provisions from institutions with rapidly growing balance sheets shows the scope for better integration of micro- and macroprudential policies in that, although it did not prevent a major debt and real-estate boom, it has left Spanish banks in a reasonable state of robustness. However, the Spanish banking system became more reliant on wholesale funding than others in Europe, and has been the major user of the ECB's short-term facilities. Hence its business model, which was similar to that of Northern Rock, was not robust to a crisis where interbank interest rates rose.

Looking more closely at European issues, over the past decade or so the European Commission has created a single market in financial services, and has recognised the need for a single, or at least coordinated, regulatory framework. Little was done in response to this felt need, and solvency concerns were left in the hands of country regulators, whilst host regulators could only concern themselves with the liquidity of foreign banks (in the case of branching). This took place as EU banks grew highly dependent on wholesale, often cross-border, funding, which eventually proved unreliable. The inadequacy of this approach is best illustrated by the problems of the Icelandic banking system. Icelandic banks took retail deposits in many countries and invested in equity assets (directly or via lending) as if they were holding companies or hedge funds. There was little that regulators in the UK or elsewhere could have done about this, and Icelandic banks built up asset bases that summed to more than 10 times Iceland's GDP. Accordingly, bank failures following liquidity crises, which on standard definitions of crises often involve losses of 10% or more of assets, could not easily be covered.

The year 2007 saw growing realisation of potential losses on sub-prime mortgages as US house prices fell and defaults increased. Whereas initial estimates in July 2007 quoted by Federal Reserve Chairman Bernanke were for $50–100 billion in losses, by February 2008 Greenlaw et al[11] were forecasting $500 billion, and by October 2008 the IMF[12] was reasonably sure that losses could be as high as $1.4 trillion, around $450 billion more than the figure they had suggested as a possibility in April 2008. The capital reserve assets of the US banking system in 2007 were not much larger than this number, and if all defaults had been contained within the system, it would have failed. As Honohan notes,[13] over half of the assets backed by sub-prime loans had been offloaded, mainly on European banks. There had also been a significant amount of recapitalisation from sovereign wealth funds

[10] C Borio, 'Monetary and Financial Stability, So Close and Yet So Far' (2005) 192 *National Institute Economic Review*, 84; C Borio, C Furfine and P Lowe, 'Procyclicality of the Financial System and Financial Stability: Issues and Policy Options' (2001) 1 *BIS Papers* 1.

[11] D Greenlaw, J Hatzius, A Kashyap and HS Shin, 'Leveraged Losses: Lessons from the Mortgage Market Meltdown', available at http://faculty.chicagobooth.edu/anil.kashyap/research/MPFReport-final.pdf

[12] International Monetary Fund, 'Global Financial Stability Report: World Economic and Financial Surveys' (Washington, DC, October 2008).

[13] P Honohan, 'Risk Management and the Costs of the Banking Crisis' (2008) 206 *National Institute Economic Review* 15.

in the early months of the crisis,[14] with up to $400 billion raised, much of which was subsequently lost by the investors as bank equity prices fell in 2008.

The paper investigates the impacts of widespread credit rationing and a significant rise in the spread between lending and borrowing rates for both producers and consumers in a rational expectations dynamic general equilibrium version of the widely used NiGEM model. Credit rationing is a ubiquitous result of financial crises, and it reduces consumption and investment.[15] Quantity rationing of this form may reflect increased asymmetry in information and increased risk aversion on the part of banks. A rise in spreads increases price rationing and can also help banks wishing to rebuild their capital after a crisis. In either case they represent the immediate impacts of a crisis in the banking sector. The paper also investigates the impact on output of a permanent regulation-induced rise in margins in the financial sector, taking into account the impacts of regulation on equity market valuations.

When leveraged institutions such as banks lose part (or all) of the value of their capital base they have to find ways to rebuild it and reduce their loan portfolio. If the losses are concentrated in just a few banks, then they are insolvent, and either have to be allowed to go bankrupt or be taken into public ownership and wound down in an orderly way. Bank bankruptcies can be disastrous for an economy, and should not have been contemplated.[16] Once they begin on the scale seen recently with Lehman Brothers in the US, there is a faultline shift between debtors and creditors and a serious recession is almost inevitable. Widespread credit rationing would normally develop after a large-scale bank bankruptcy as lenders have to reduce their risks rapidly and cannot evaluate appropriate risk premia for borrowers.

If most banks in a market have lost some of their capital asset base and choose to reduce their loan books, then the supply curve for loans will shift up the demand curve for loans. The price of loans increases with a greater spread between loans and deposits. Leverage will improve as their capital asset base will rise with higher earnings and their loan book will shrink. Another way to rebuild their base is to make rights issues, but these are unlikely to succeed unless banks are clear that they are taking better account of risk in future and that losses have been fully identified. This information failure during a financial crisis of the scale we are seeing can be seen as the major aspect of capital market failure, and bank recapitalisation has to come about some other way—almost certainly through state acquisition of some or all of the banking system.

D. Modelling the Crisis

The potential impacts of credit rationing and increases in spreads and margins are modelled using NiGEM configured in its dynamic stochastic general equilibrium version,

---

[14] Greenlaw et al, above n 12.

[15] R Barrell, EP Davis and O Pomerantz, 'Costs of Financial Instability, Household-sector Balance Sheets and Consumption' (2006) 2 *Journal of Financial Stability* 194.

[16] They are dangerous because of the destruction of the information in the credit relationship and the decline in liquidity that comes with freezing assets in insolvency. This decline in liquidity can lead to further insolvencies as agents have to sell assets in 'fire sales'.

which is equivalent to the model described by Harrison et al.[17] The long-run structure is based on the same theoretical framework, and the dynamics of adjustment to that equilibrium are estimated or the result of rational expectations jumps.[18]

If investment spreads rise and externally financed capital rationing for firms develops, then the user cost of capital will increase and investment will fall. Capital rationing means that the shadow price of borrowing rises significantly, but the scale of the increase is not directly observable. The standard Hall–Jorgenson definition of the user cost of capital (user) in formula (1) below depends on the weighted average of equity and bond finance.[19] The rate of return on equity capital can be gauged by the earnings–price ratio in the stock market (cec). The cost of bank and bond finance can be gauged by the rate of return on corporate bonds, which is made up of the real return on risk-free government bonds (lr) plus a corporate spread (spread).

$$\text{User} = ((\text{eqs} \times \text{cec} + (1 - \text{eqs}) \times (\text{lr} + \text{spread}) \times (1 - \text{ct}) + \text{dep} + \text{pt})/(1 - \text{ct})) \qquad (1)$$

where ct is the corporate tax rate, dep is the depreciation rate, pt is the rate of change in capital goods prices, and interest payments are tax deductible. The more dependent firms are on equity markets, the less vulnerable they are to increases in borrowing costs as long as real equity prices remain constant. Corporate sector vulnerability to increases in borrowing costs is likely to be highest in Germany, Italy and Ireland since they have the lowest stock market to capital stock ratios, and hence probably the highest levels of corporate sector borrowing from banks and other lenders.[20] However, in a generalised financial crisis, equity prices change. Forward-looking equity prices (eqp) are determined by the discounted present value of profits net of corporate taxes (prof). The discount factor includes the equity risk premium (prem):

$$\text{eqp}_t = \text{prof}_t + \text{eqp}_{t+1}/[(1 + \text{rh}_t)(1 + \text{prem}_t)] \qquad (2)$$

In a crisis the risk premium on equity investment rises, inducing falls in equity prices. This, in turn, raises the user cost of capital, and hence gives a further impulse to reductions in investment. Countries that are more dependent on equity markets, such as the UK, the US and Canada, will be more affected through this channel.

Output (Q) is determined in the long run by supply factors and technology, and we assume all economies are open and have perfect capital mobility. This implies that they follow changes in the world real rate of interest. The production function is CES, where output depends on capital (K) and on labour services (L), which is a combination of the number of persons in work and the average hours of those persons. Output also depends on the scaling (α), distribution (δ) and substitution (ρ) parameters. Technical progress (λtech) is assumed to be labour augmenting and independent of the policy innovations considered here:

---

[17] R Harrison, K Nikolov, M Quinn, G Ramsay, A Scott and R Thomas, *The Bank of England Quarterly Model* (London, Bank of England, 2005).

[18] The adjustment speeds may be slightly slower and more realistic as Barrell and Kirby suggest: R Barrell and S Kirby, 'Interest Rates and the UK Economy' (2007) 202 *National Institute Economic Review* 61. The effects of a financial crisis are less in this style of model because equilibrium effects are brought forward. It is to be hoped that we are using the correct model, and that a more old-fashioned 'backward-looking' Keynesian model is not a better description of the world we live in. Barrell, Hurst and Kirby expand on this point: R Barrell, I Hurst and S Kirby, 'Financial Crises, Regulation and Growth', NIESR Discussion Paper No 313 (London, National Institute of Social and Economic Research, 2008).

[19] R Brealey and S Myers, *Principles of Corporate Finance* (New York, McGraw Hill, 2000).

[20] The tax treatment of corporate bonds may be one of the reasons for excess issuance of complex securities.

$$Q = \alpha[(\delta(K)^{-\rho} + (1 - \delta)(L(e^{\lambda tech}))^{-\rho}]^{-1/\rho} \qquad (3)$$

We assume forward-looking behaviour in production and because of 'time to build' issues investment depends on expected trend output four years ahead and the forward looking user cost of capital. However, the capital stock does not adjust instantly, as there are costs involved in doing so.[21] The elasticity of substitution is estimated from the labour demand equation; in general, it is around 0.5. This estimate is used in the calibration of the other parameters of the production function, and an estimate of technical progress is calculated. Prices are determined as a constant mark-up over marginal costs in the long term, are consistent with factor demands and are influenced by capacity utilisation.

Increases in perceived lending risks can lead to higher borrowing margins. Personal income would be affected by the margin as it includes gross income receipts on deposits and other assets held with the financial sector (PA) at an average rate of r_d minus interest payments (at r_d + margin) on liabilities to the financial sector (PL), where margin is the difference between borrowing and lending rates for the personal sector. When assets exceed liabilities it is possible that an increase in interest rates will raise other personal income, although it would reduce incomes when debts are larger. An increase in the spread between borrowing and lending rates for consumers always reduces incomes, and hence consumption. We may write net interest receipts as

$$NIR = r_d \times PA - (r_d + margin) \times PL \qquad (4)$$

It is assumed that consumers react to the present discounted value of their future income streams, which we may call total wealth (TW), although they may face liquidity constraints from their personal disposable income in the short run:

$$TW_t = Y_t - T_t + TW_{t+1}/((1 + rr_t)(1 + my_t)) \qquad (5)$$

where Y is real income, T are real taxes. The variable with suffix t+1 is an expected variable, and it is discounted by the real interest rate rr and by the risk and myopia premium used by consumers, my. The equation represents an infinite forward recursion, and permanent income is the sustainable flow from this stock. The dynamics of adjustment may depend on financial- and housing asset-based wealth, but in the long run housing assets are not considered as real wealth, much as Buiter suggests.[22] The dynamics of adjustment to the long run are important in policy analysis and are largely data based, and differ between countries to take account of differences in the relative importance of types of wealth and of liquidity constraints. Barrell and Davis[23] discuss the impact of financial liberalisation on the dynamics of adjustment in a group of countries where housing wealth can be utilised for borrowing.

Financial wealth depends on foreign and domestic equity and bond prices, and on the accumulation of assets. Each country on the model has a stock of foreign assets and a

[21] The approach to the estimation of the production function is set out in R Barrell and N Pain, 'Foreign Direct Investment, Technological Change, and Economic Growth within Europe' (1997) 107 *Economic Journal* 1770.

[22] WH Buiter, 'Housing Wealth isn't Wealth', NBER Working Paper No W14204 (National Bureau of Economic Research, 2008). House prices on the model depend in the long term on the user cost of housing capital, and this is affected by the mark-up over risk free rates, much as the user cost of business capital depends on the investment premium.

[23] R Barrell and EP Davis, 'Financial Liberalisation, Consumption and Wealth Effects in 7 OECD Countries' (2007) 54 *Scottish Journal of Political Economy* 254.

stock of liabilities linked to the stock of domestic financial assets and the stock of domestic private sector and public sector liabilities. A proportion of government debt is owned abroad, as are proportions of the national stock of equities and the stock of banking assets. Some national financial wealth is held in foreign equities and bonds, as well as by banks. Income flows from asset stocks are allocated in relation to ownership, and hence net property income from abroad depends on income receipts and payments on bonds, equity holdings and banks. The wealth and accumulation system allows for flows of saving onto wealth and for revaluations of existing stocks of assets in line with their prices determined as above. When foreign equity and bond prices change, domestically held assets change in value. The fully forward-looking model used here is stock flow consistent as all flows come from or go onto stocks.

Exchange rates are forward looking in the uncovered interest parity condition. The current exchange rate depends on the expected future path of interest rates and risk premia. Interest rates are determined by policy rules adopted by monetary authorities. The exchange rate equation is written as:

$$RX_t = RX_{t+1}[(1+rh_t)/(1+ra_t)](1+rprx_t) \tag{6}$$

where RX is the exchange rate, rh is the home interest rate, ra is the interest rate abroad and rprx is the risk premium. Relationships of this form are investigated empirically by Al-Eyd, Barrell and Holland,[24] and the implications for risk premia for the evolution of current accounts are discussed by Barrell, Holland and Hurst.[25] The monetary rules on the model determine rh and are discussed by Barrell, Hall and Hurst.[26] The rules contain forward-looking expectations of the rate of inflation. All countries have fiscal closure rules.[27] Budget deficits are kept within bounds in the longer term through a targeted adjustment of income tax rates.

Table 2. Modelling the financial crisis

Crisis component	NiGEM shock
1. Credit rationing and increases in spreads for firms	Raise the spread in (1) by 800 basis points for two years
2. Equity markets	Rise of 800 basis points for two years in the equity premium in (2)
3. Attempts by banks to rebuild margins and cover risk.	The margin in (4) is raised by 800 basis points for two years
4. Credit rationing when evaluating the net present value of future incomes	Discount factor in (5) is raised by 800 basis points for two years

[24] A Al-Eyd, R Barrell and D Holland, 'A Portfolio Balance Explanation of the Euro Dollar Rate' in D Cobham, D (ed), *The Travails of the Eurozone* (London, Palgrave, 2006).

[25] R Barrell, D Holland and AI Hurst, 'Sustainable Adjustment of Global Imbalances' in A Aslund and M Dabrowski (eds), *Challenges of Globalization* (Washington DC, Peterson Institute of International Economics, 2008).

[26] R Barrell, S Hall and I Hurst, 'Monetary Policy Rules' (2006) 93 *Economics Letters* 1.

[27] R Barrell and J Sefton, 'Fiscal Policy and the Maastricht Solvency Criteria' (1997) 65 *Manchester School* 259.

We assume firms, consumers, labour markets and financial markets are all fully forward looking and have rational, outcome consistent expectations. Additionally, we have assumed no active fiscal response to the crisis.

We introduce this sharp crisis in the fourth quarter of 2008, which would give negative growth in the fourth quarter in each of the UK, the US and the Euro Area. Figure 4 plots the quarterly growth paths that we would have projected using information available to the end of September 2008 and also the crisis scenario paths that deviate from this. This would exacerbate a worsening situation in the Euro Area and the UK, and bring a sharp halt to growth in the US. The slowdown would be largest in the US, but that economy might also recover more strongly, as it is more flexible than either the UK or the Euro Area. The Euro Area would see negative quarterly growth from the second quarter of 2008 to early 2010, whilst negative growth would last until mid-2010 in the UK.[28]

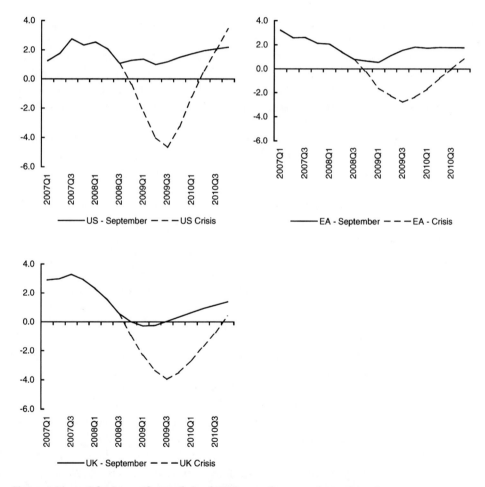

Figure 4. Financial crises and growth (real GDP growth, per cent per annum).

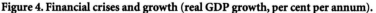

[28] Much else happened around the end of the third quarter of 2008, with major changes in exchange rates taking place. Further details of the crisis are discussed in the *National Institute Economic Review* No 206 (2008).

Table 3. Impacts of the financial crisis on GDP growth (percentage points)

	2008	2009	2010	2011	2012
Canada	−0.27	−3.41	−1.35	2.75	2.05
Euro Area	−0.23	−3.51	−2.18	2.37	2.70
France	−0.25	−3.87	−2.52	2.58	2.59
Germany	−0.26	−3.15	−1.06	2.45	1.69
Italy	−0.16	−3.26	−3.10	1.24	3.11
Spain	−0.18	−4.06	−3.48	2.58	4.45
UK	−0.24	−3.23	−2.21	1.89	2.72
US	−0.41	−4.83	−0.80	4.42	2.78

Table 3 gives details of the impacts of such a crisis on growth in the major economies. Output growth would be reduced by 3–4% in the major economies, with the effects being largest in the US, as we might expect. Our scenario does not include any permanent scarring from the crisis, but this is a clear possibility. Barrell and Kirby[29] suggest that the premium applied to investment will be permanently higher after the events of the past year. If this is the case, then it is necessary to reassess longer-term growth prospects and we turn to this below.

These outcomes look poor, but are predicated on a relatively rapid resolution to the crisis. In a forward-looking world, if a crisis is expected to lengthen, then its impacts will strengthen now. Forward-looking consumers re-evaluate their wealth when an increase in the discount premium is expected to last longer. As a result, they consume less now as well as in the future. Equity prices would fall more, and the user cost of capital would rise as a result. However, a more extended crisis would lead to a greater and more extended monetary response, and long-term interest rates would be lower, partly offsetting the effects of the longer equity premium increase. Figure 5 plots the worsening of the prospects in response to an expected lengthening of the period to full resolution. We assume that all the changes in rationing and risk premia are the same as discussed above, but that they are sustained for four years rather than two. Although nothing changes in the crisis in the quarters plotted, in a forward-looking world the impact of extending the crisis is brought forward to the start of the crisis.

Financial innovation can reduce borrowing costs and this will reduce the user cost of capital, hence, for a period at least, it can be important for raising growth.[30] However, it is difficult to distinguish between sustainable innovation and excessive risk taking. Regulators have to ensure that they encourage the former and discourage the latter. New financial instruments are difficult to stress test against downturns, and it is often impossible to gauge how they will behave. Financial sector regulation is extremely difficult and financial innovation often finds ways around regulation. However, good regulation revised to keep up with developments is essential if financial markets are to be constrained from

---

[29] R Barrell and S Kirby, 'The Budgetary Implications of Global Shocks to Cycles and Trends in Output' [2008] *ESRI Budget Outlook* October.

[30] There is an extensive literature both on financial innovation and on banking crises. The literatures on these two topics are discussed in R Kroszner, L Laeven and D Klinggebiel, 'Banking groups, Financial Dependence, and Growth' (2007) 84 *Journal of Financial Economics* 187.

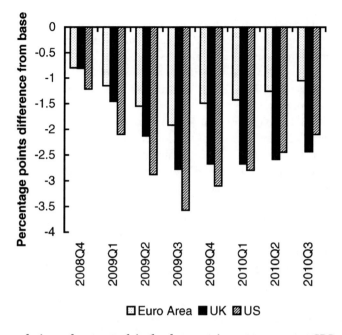

Figure 5. Slow resolution reduces growth in the short run: impacts on current GDP growth of lengthening the time before the crisis is resolved

generating a depression on the scale seen between 1929 and 1933. Given that we have generated a crisis, a quick resolution is essential to reduce the current costs.

E. Cost and Benefits of Bank Regulation in the UK

One response to the current crisis is to contemplate building better defences against a recurrence by improving, or at least changing, regulation. Barrell and Davis[31] argue that the single financial market in Europe necessitates a single regulatory approach that would cover all members of the European Economic Area, including Iceland and Norway. Unfortunately no such framework has been put in place. A set of directives on prudential regulation was in place, but they were interpreted differently in different countries. No single framework for crisis management exists, as is reflected in the disparate approaches to bank guarantees in Europe in late September and early October 2008.

It is clear that there is a need to improve the regulatory structure in the UK and elsewhere, and that those changes will involve tighter regulation. Changes in bank regulation change the structure of bank costs, and the implications can be analysed using dynamic stochastic general equilibrium models. If banking markets are competitive, these changes in costs will be passed on to the users of bank services in either increased costs for using services or increased charges on loans. These, in turn, will affect

[31] Barrell and Davis, above n 9.

behaviour, and change consumption and investment. The best way to model these implications is to presume that the change in costs comes through as an increase in the margin between borrowing and lending rates. The change in costs and the increase in margins, or spreads, will affect both individual consumers, who deposit money and borrow from banks, and firms, who finance part of their investment from bank or market-related borrowing.

The impact of a change in bank margins on firms depends upon its impact on the user cost of capital and hence on the level of the desired capital stock. It is possible to calculate the user cost with the standard finance formula, which takes the average cost of equity finance and bank (or other sources of) finance and adjusts this for depreciation and corporate taxes. In the UK the value of the stock market is about half the value of the private sector capital stock, which suggests that on average British firms finance about half of their investment from the stock market and half from either internal funds or from external borrowing. The user cost of capital in the UK is around 13–14%, well above risk-free untaxed rates. If banks were to raise their margins permanently by 0.50% (50 basis points), then, before second-round effects were taken into account, the user cost of capital facing firms would rise by about half this number and the desired capital stock (and the sustainable level of output) would be smaller, with the impact depending upon the elasticity of substitution between capital and labour. It is very unlikely that banks would only raise costs to firms, as they have no profit-related incentive to do this. Hence, we would expect the margin between borrowing and lending rates facing consumers to increase by a similar amount to that faced by firms.

Overall, an increase in bank costs as a result of increased prudential regulation will lead to a fall in consumption and national saving will rise. Domestic investment will also fall and real interest rates will be marginally lower, but the main effect will be small, as the UK is a small open economy without capital controls. The major consequence of the increased national saving with lower domestic investment will be an improvement in the current account of the balance of payments and a gradual accumulation of foreign assets.

Table 4 details the impacts on consumption and investment, as well as on GDP. A rise of 50 basis points in the spread between borrowing and lending rates would reduce output in the long run by around 0.2%, all else being equal. As long as all consumers and investors

Table 4. The effects of a permanent 50 basis point rise in spreads in the UK

	Private sector investment	Consumption	Output
Year 1	−0.17	−0.23	−0.02
Year 2	−0.54	−0.51	−0.08
Year 3	−0.79	−0.67	−0.14
Year 4	−0.93	−0.75	−0.18
Year 5	−0.99	−0.78	−0.20
Average 10–14	−0.70	−0.68	−0.17
Average 15–20	−0.62	−0.60	−0.17
Average 21–25	−0.63	−0.54	−0.18

Note: Levels are per cent difference from base.

fully understand the policy, output growth would be lower by about one-third of this for three years and would then stabilise on its new trajectory, with the trend growth rate then being unchanged as it is driven by population and technology. Private sector investment would be about 0.67% lower, whilst public sector investment is assumed to move in line with trend output in the long run. Consumption would also fall by around 0.5–0.75% as compared to baseline, which would be rather more than the fall in income. The increase in saving, along with the lower level of private sector investment, would result in an improvement in the balance of payments. Assets would accumulate abroad, and the income flow on them would mean that consumption would start to grow relative to domestic output.

Our analysis is undertaken with a standard interest rate reaction function for the central bank. The slower growth over a number of years would leave room for a small cut in interest rates and, given our assumption that financial markets are forward looking and fully understand the implications of the changes, sterling would immediately decline by around 2%, boosting net exports and reducing the impacts of the increase in spreads on the economy.

Good bank regulation is difficult and, as it reduces output, at least at first glance, is unpopular. Liquidity ratio regulation may be easily avoided by moving items off balance sheet, even at a small cost, but it may be of use. Changing the asset quality rules for judging capital adequacy is also possibly useful. Perhaps the most effective change in regulations would come from requiring that secured loans (by anybody) could not have more than (say) 90% recourse to the security in case of a default on the loan. Lenders would then be unwilling to lend at low rates above this ceiling. Asset bubbles would be less common, and securitised assets less vulnerable to default.

Our assumption that all else would be equal means that in this analysis there are no second-round implications for either bank equity prices or for the risk premium associated with investing in assets in the UK as compared to elsewhere. Both may change as a result of the change in bank regulation that increases the spread, and the effects of these changes would help offset the impacts of the change and might even be larger, giving an overall positive outcome. The equity premium should fall, boosting the stock market and investment, and the general volatility of the economy should be lower, which should lead to a lower country specific risk premium and hence to overall lower real interest rates.

F.   Conclusions

The recent financial crisis that has emanated from the US mortgage market has been driven by excessively risky lending disguised by complex financial products. Default rates have risen as high as 20%. Losses have worn away at the capital base of the banking system in the US, the Euro Area, Switzerland and the UK. We appear to be in the middle of the largest financial crisis since the Second World War. Complex products were sold to people inside and outside the US who did not understand the risks they were taking, and they have lost money. There are calls for improvement in regulatory structures and for coordinated actions. Coordination of European regulators should also be discussed, as countries do not have full oversight of their banking systems in the current dispersed responsibility structure.[32]

There are ways to give incentives for banks to follow regulations, and hence reduce debts. Regulators will always need to innovate in response to the market, but they should not give up the task just because it is hard. Financial markets improve the efficiency of the economy and the welfare of citizens. Regulation can make them operate more effectively, but it can also induce costs. Although the direct effects of regulation might be to reduce output and consumption marginally, the general reduction in risk in the economy could have beneficial effects that could more than offset the costs. A quantification of the impacts on margins and default risk is needed before a cost–benefit analysis can be undertaken fully.

---

[32] Country regulators look at liquidity needs of foreign banks but do not supervise their capital adequacy, and hence must remain ignorant of many risks that banks on their soil take.

4

Financial Engineering or Legal Engineering? Legal Work, Legal Integrity and the Banking Crisis

DOREEN McBARNET*

A. Introduction

One strand of analysis in the banking crisis has been the issue of financial engineering gone wrong. Problems are attributed to innovative financial products that were too readily believed to disperse risk,[1] backed by mathematical models[2] that senior banking executives took at face value, without, it is said, questioning or even comprehending them.[3] The financial structures set in place were so complex that risk[4] and even ownership became untrackable.[5] People were blinded by 'disaster myopia'[6] and, indeed, market ideology.[7] There was a dominant belief in the rationality of the market and a collective failure to recognise the limits of market, maths and risk management. Regulators are portrayed as carried along on this tide of false confidence, regulating through only a light touch with the focus on internal and market controls, and encouraged, or instructed,[8] by politicians to do so. People questioning the reality of the emperor's new clothes were dismissed as the ones who did not understand, lacking the sophistication to handle the magic of financial

* Professor of Socio-Legal Studies, University of Oxford and Visiting Professor, University of Edinburgh. Thanks are due to the ESRC for funding this research (Professorial Fellowship RES-051-0031).

[1] A Turner, 'The Financial Crisis and the Future of Financial Regulation', *The Economist*'s Inaugural City Lecture, 21 January 2009.

[2] J Teanor, 'Toxic Shock: How the Banking Industry Created a Global Crisis', *The Guardian*, 8 April 2008.

[3] B Hutter and N Dodd, 'Social Systems Failure? Trust and the Credit Crunch' [December 2008] *Risk and Regulation* 4; R Tomasic, 'Beyond "Light Touch" Regulation of British Banks', paper presented at the Conference on the Future of Financial Regulation, Glasgow University, 29–30 March 2009 (chapter 7 of this volume).

[4] 'Product complexity has introduced increased opacity into our financial system, making it almost impossible to determine where risk lies and making it much more difficult to achieve financial stability', John McFall, chairman of the House of Commons Treasury Committee, quoted by A McDermid, 'Banks "Refused to Believe the Good Times Were about to End"', *The Herald*, 3 March 2008.

[5] S Schwarcz, 'Protecting Financial Markets: Lessons from the Sub-prime Mortgage Meltdown', Duke Law School Legal Studies Research Paper No 175 (2008). Failure was exacerbated because ownership could not be tracked in order to restructure.

[6] See, eg J Plender, 'Analysis: Error Laden Machine', *Financial Times*, 3 March 2009.

[7] R Peston, *Today* (Radio 4, 18 March 2009).

[8] A Turner, chairman of the FSA, was reported as saying that the FSA was put under pressure by Prime Minister Gordon Brown not to be 'heavy and intrusive', to make regulation 'more light touch', *Daily Telegraph*, 26 February 2009.

engineering. The subsequent crisis has revealed that the emperor was indeed unclothed, and the demand is for tougher regulation to stop this situation recurring, though with concerns, even in the throes of crisis, that regulation should not be so heavy handed as to stifle the lifeblood of financial innovation.[9]

Characterising the financial products and transactions that led to the crisis primarily as financial engineering, however, tends to gloss over the other innovative skills and creative participants involved in their construction. A crucial component of the new banking products was legal creativity. The legal work behind such practices as securitisation was not confined to drafting the contracts to sell on risk. It was also about creatively removing the 'obstacles' of prudential regulation, accounting requirements and other legal and regulatory constraints intended to control or disclose risk. Indeed, circumventing capital adequacy regulation was a crucial driver behind much structured finance.

This chapter seeks to reconceptualise the significant practices behind the banking crisis as not just a matter of financial engineering but a matter of legal engineering—legal engineering that is common practice in all sophisticated business. It seeks to set the financial crisis in the context of the wider practice of creative transaction structuring in which the driving characteristic is deliberately and systematically to thwart regulation and bypass regulatory control. The analysis is based on documentary analysis and on interviews over a period of many years at major companies, banks, accountancy and law firms, in the context of a wide range of regulatory, tax and accounting issues, although the interviews quoted from here relate specifically to banking.[10] These were conducted before the banking crisis and give some insight into the legal practice and culture that I would argue contributed to it. The focus is sociological rather than legal. It explores the practice of legal engineering, and the attitude to law and compliance at its core. It is therefore concerned less with banking regulations than with how banks and their lawyers have reacted to them, and it is less about the financial instruments created than about the motivations behind them, depicting them as part of a pervasive strategic response to regulation, which itself needs to be critically reviewed.

Reconceptualising the issue as one of creative legal circumvention rather than simply financial innovation suggests a different set of issues that need to be addressed in the wake of the financial crisis. This chapter first analyses the role of legal engineering in the banking crisis, showing it to be a conscious strategy in which regulatory circumvention, complexity and opacity were integral parts. It then sets out some specific implications for future practice in business, government, regulation and the professions, and argues the

---

[9] International Monetary Fund, 'Global Financial Stability Report' (Washington, DC, 2007) 126. See E Engelen, I Erturk, J Froud, A Leaver, K Williams, 'Reconceptualising Financial Innovation: Frame, Conjecture and Bricolage', paper presented at the Conference on the Future of Financial Regulation, Glasgow University, 29–30 March 2009.

[10] This research was carried out over a period of some 25 years, in a series of projects on business regulation, in particular in the areas of corporate finance, creative accounting (especially off-balance-sheet financing in both corporate and banking sectors) and tax avoidance, and covering issues in the UK, the EU and the US. The projects all involved in-depth interviews with a wide range of big firm lawyers and accountants, bankers, corporate executives, in-house counsel and regulators. For examples of the work, see D McBarnet, *Crime, Compliance and Control* (Aldershot, Ashgate, 2004). One key issue to emerge from that research was the routine practice of 'creative compliance', and it was the role of creative legal work in accomplishing that which became one of the key issues researched under the ESRC professorial fellowship (RES-051-0031). The broad analysis in this chapter is therefore based on a whole range of research projects over many years, while the interviews quoted took place as part of research conducted in 2004 and 2006–07.

need not just for new law and regulation, but more fundamentally for a new respect for the rule of law, for a new legal integrity.

B.   Legal Engineering, Intent and Complexity

A prime excuse for the financial crisis has been that those involved simply did not understand the complex financial instruments in use or realise the risk, organisational and systemic, they were creating. It is hard not to see this incomprehension as, in the kindest interpretation, a willing suspension of disbelief. Like the courtiers in the tale of the emperor's new clothes, a lot of people were doing rather nicely out of this apparently misunderstood scenario. Indeed, it might be fairly argued that if senior banking executives, taking vast rewards for the stewardship of their businesses, did not understand the products at their core, they ought to have, and a failure to probe was itself, to the layman if not the lawyer, a failure of duty.

What is clear, however, is that the image of financial disaster as the result of ignorance or of unintended consequences simply does not wash when we view the innovative financial instruments through the lens of legal rather than just financial creativity. The legal creativity involved was knowingly and deliberately aimed at avoiding laws and regulations put in place to control risk and to ensure its disclosure. Of course regulators may have been lax and regulations insufficiently demanding, too permissive, perhaps naïve. But the fact of the matter is that however the regulations had been formulated they would have met with the same response: here is a constraint; how do we gain a competitive advantage by getting round it?

Finding arguably legal ways round legal and regulatory obstacles is a key function of the lawyer's role for sophisticated clients such as banks, and sophisticated legal circumvention has been integral to the construction of innovative financial products in banking. As one banking lawyer put it in interview:

> The traders talk to people in the marketplace. 'What problems do you have at the moment, what would you really need if you could have something devised for you?' Then they look at pricing models, and mathematical models, and then the next stage is the law. This could be very good, very lucrative, what legal hurdles are there?[11]

Or again:

> The credit group at [X] Bank is a specialist structured group in the capital markets which focuses on credit instruments to securitise and it's a wonderfully lucrative business, but there are lots of laws, regulations and concepts and natural justice principles which, you know, inconveniently get in the way and they have to be reformed or modified or creatively dealt with.[12]

These quotations articulate particularly clearly a culture and approach to law which is not always so baldly verbalised but which is clearly and consistently demonstrated in the practice of legal work described to me over many years in corporate and professional interviews. Regulation is an obstacle to be overcome. In the particular context of banking, laws and regulations that obstruct financial engineering have to be removed by legal

---

[11] Research interviews, 2004.
[12] Ibid.

engineering: 'If law is inconvenient to the economic features of the proposal the lawyer must get round it.'[13]

1.   The Banking Crisis in Context

Legal engineering lies at the heart of the banking crisis, and there is nothing new or unique about the practice. In that sense, the banking crisis needs to be seen in a wider context. It is just part of an approach to law that has been pervasive in business over a long period of time and in a range of contexts, and there have been warnings enough of the dangers inherent in it, notably via Enron.[14]

Problems created by securitisation of sub-prime assets have constituted one of the key triggers of the banking crisis. Securitisation is a form of off-balance-sheet financing (OBSF), and both OBSF in general and securitisation in particular can be seen as prime examples of a long-standing practice of legal engineering to deal with 'obstructive' laws. Though both securitisation and OBSF in general have been defended as, properly used, of real value to business and society, they have also been systematically and pervasively exploited over a period of many years as a deliberate means of undermining attempts at regulatory control.

OBSF, particularly through the use of the 'special purpose entities' (SPEs) or 'vehicles' (SPVs) that feature so centrally in securitisation—separate companies or other legal forms that have been carefully constructed to be, technically, legally distinct from the originating company—has a long history. It has been widely used in corporate creative accounting as a technique for consciously circumventing company law obligations to disclose a 'true and fair view' of corporate finances to shareholders. It has been used to keep debts or liabilities out of the accounts, enhancing apparent performance and misleading the market. Since accounts are used as the basis of all sorts of further specific corporate governance controls, OBSF has also been used to circumvent them. Bank loan covenants might stipulate tolerance of only a certain level of debt to equity before a loan can be called in. Keeping debt off the books—even if it might ultimately come back to haunt the company in the future—removes this control. It has also meant the negation of shareholders' rights, often written into the company's memorandum and articles of association, to call an EGM if a particular debt/equity ratio is exceeded. Performance-related pay and bonuses have also been magnified by profits and growth reported in the books, even if they had no funda-mental economic substance.[15]

Banks have played a key role not only in engineering their own OBS practices but in creating and very actively marketing schemes to corporate clients to relieve the clients' books of liabilities and losses, with all the advantages just noted. Many corporate inter-viewees in my research emphasised the active role of investment banks in corporate OBSF schemes, sometimes indeed, in hindsight in more recent interviews, with some vituper-ation. One major bank's head of compliance complained about 'the snake oil salesmen

---

[13] Ibid.

[14] D McBarnet, 'After Enron: Will Whiter than White Collar Crime Still Wash?' (2006) 46 *British Journal of Criminology* 46; B McLean, 'Enron Was the Pit Canary but its Death Went Unheeded', *The Guardian*, 4 October 2008.

[15] D McBarnet and C Whelan, *Creative Accounting and the Cross-eyed Javelin Thrower* (Chichester, John Wiley, 1999).

from the investment banks coming in and saying "Everyone's doing this, why aren't you?" putting enormous pressure on young directors'.[16]

Banks were also active participants both in corporate-initiated schemes and in the schemes they were purveying themselves. They would, for example, play the crucial role of independent third party in the structuring of an SPV, this being a key element in meeting the criteria that would let the SPV be treated as a legal entity separate from the originating company. Or they might temporarily buy liabilities to get them off the client's balance sheet at a legally significant moment.

Banks could indeed be in the interesting situation where one department of the bank was actively marketing a device to take debts off a client's balance sheet, so undermining the covenants of the bank loans lent by another department of the same bank. It might be worth noting here the wider implications of the banks' role in general corporate off-balance-sheet financing. It was not just bank risk that was disguised, but general corporate indebtedness and therefore corporate vulnerability in the face of the kind of credit crunch the banking crisis has produced. Banks' OBSF activities have played a part in the economic and not just the financial crisis.

Banks were also heavily implicated in Enron's OBSF practices, a fact that led to some interesting developments in the deferred prosecutions that followed, of which more later. Enron famously, or infamously, used a host of SPEs, derivatives and other creative legal devices to hide liabilities and boost apparent profits, while at the same time constructing a vast range of tax avoidance devices to the point where it received tax rebates.[17] Enron executives, of course, also resorted to, and were prosecuted for, fraud, but the reality is that the corporation was doing a pretty good job of misleading the market even without resort to fraud. Indeed, comments at Congressional investigations repeatedly drove this point home.[18] Many of the devices used by Enron were standard business practice. Indeed, at the 2002 annual meeting of the US Bond Market Association one member is reported as asking: 'How do we help the market distinguish between what we do and what Enron did?' The question was put to speaker Harvey Pitt, then chair of the SEC, and the report notes 'he had no ready answer'.[19] Enron's use of legal engineering to circumvent regulatory control was far from unique.

A single device of legal engineering can often circumvent multiple regulatory obstacles. SPEs have been used to circumvent all manner of other laws and regulations, such as tax, disclosure rules in takeovers and trade embargoes. Synthetic securitisation, described in interview as 'the transfer of economic or credit risk associated with assets without transferring the assets', was credited by the interviewee as being:

> helpful in the face of anti-assignment clauses, transfer restrictions under the laws or jurisdictions where the assets are located, securities law registration issues regarding transfers of assets or securities, legal investment restrictions, withholding tax and stamp duty . . .[20]

[16] Research interviews, 2007.

[17] McBarnet, above n 14.

[18] 'The real scandal here may be from not what is illegal, but what is totally permissible. If the GAAP allow the bookkeeping shenanigans that have been reported in the press then we should all go into the derivative business. It seems that all too often the name of the corporate game is to conceal the true financial situation of the company while doing the minimum amount of disclosure to avoid legal exposure' (US Senate 2002, Senator Thompson).

[19] A Osterland, 'Commercial Paper Chase', *CFO Magazine*, 1 June 2002.

[20] Research interviews, 2004.

A useful tool indeed.

And, of course, both synthetic securitisation and securitisation in general, along with derivatives and other innovative legal structuring, gave banks an escape route from the constraints of capital adequacy regulation, an escape route that was precisely the purpose of the innovation.

2.   Creative Legal Responses to Regulation

Regulation and regulators have been criticised strongly in the wake of the banking crisis, and with justification, but it is also important to remember that, whatever regulation is put in place, business—in this case banks—will routinely respond by seeking out ways to circumvent it. Reviewing the history of off-balance-sheet practices in banking, a 2003 report by one international bank noted that '[t]he motivation [for OBSF] was heightened in the late 1980s by the introduction of risk-based capital guidelines for banks and thrifts'.[21]

In this the banks were behaving no differently from any other big business. Introduce a new regulatory strategy and the business response will be a new circumvention strategy. Require companies to consolidate subsidiaries and the response is creative structures to constitute 'non-subsidiary subsidiaries' or SPVs that fall beyond the definition of subsidiaries. Capture in the tax net the practice of 'bed and breakfasting' shares to artificially crystallise tax losses and the response is share-'weekending' to tweak the technique using parallel but technically different criteria. Count the loans on the books as part of a regulatory risk assessment and the response is to come up with some creative legal engineering to get those loans off the books.

The first Basel concordat on banking regulation in 1988 prompted a flurry of creativity to circumvent its constraints and, indeed, to use it as an opportunity to secure competitive advantage through that circumvention. Legal engineering involves close scrutiny of the wording of laws and regulations in order to work out how to package a transaction in such a way that it can claim to meet the technical demands of the regulation even if the result is not what the creators of that regulation had in mind. Definitions and criteria involving clear rules or thresholds make particularly valuable material for legal engineers to work on. The criteria set out in Basel I were scrutinised in just this way and the distinction between tier 1 and tier 2 capital provided, according to the *Financial Times*, 'a rich vein of material with which financial engineers have worked'[22]—with, it should be noted, legal engineering integral to the process.

Tier 1 capital was the safest capital with higher weighting, equity being the prime example since it did not have to be repaid in the event of crisis. The challenge therefore became how to invent an instrument which could claim to meet the tier I criteria while still attracting investors by offering them the kind of investor security that, for example, a bond would give. It had, in short, to do the magic trick of apparently involving no risk to either bank or investor.

One early response (1989) was the construction of preference shares with dividends which could be interrupted if the bank got into trouble. They were also, in legal form, 'permanent', meaning that in theory they need never be repaid, all of this enabling them to

---

[21] Nomura Fixed Income Research, 'Off-balance Sheet Update', 11 March 2003, 2.
[22] *Financial Times*, 6 December 1990.

be claimed as tier 1 capital, although in practice they were structured such that they could be redeemed after five years. The attraction of this instrument was that it raised money that, it was claimed, had the same tier 1 status as equity, while avoiding the rights issue that equity raising would involve and, since it was done through an SPV, also avoiding the need to seek the approval of shareholders.[23] Reports on this instrument noted that the banking supervisors intended to keep a close eye on innovative instruments to prevent the Basel agreement being subverted. There were similar concerns with RBS's early innovative floating rate notes (also 1989). The Bank of England prevaricated on whether to accept the bank's claim that they qualified as upper tier 2 capital, allowing the first issue, only to disallow further issues when the Basel Committee made it clear it saw the instrument as a threat to the regime: it 'would open the door to a variety of innovations that might ultimately undermine the Basel Agreement'.[24] From the beginning, in short, there were creative challenges for the regulators which only became more sophisticated over time in response to both competition and changing regulations.

In legal engineering, any new regulation is seen simply as a new challenge to be overcome. OBSF regulation was significant for the banking industry both in relation to banks' own securitisation practices and, as we have seen, in relation to the lucrative services they were marketing to clients. So, when the US Financial Accounting Standards Board (FASB) introduced new rulings on off-balance-sheet financing after Enron,[25] the banks' response was not to capitulate and accept more activities would now go on the balance sheet, but, as one international bank noted in an analysis of current trends, to search for 'practical solutions to avoid consolidation'.[26]

In the same 2003 document the bank analysed the new regulations to explore possible ways to avoid the consolidation they required. It suggested restructuring collateralised debt obligations and asset-backed commercial paper programmes to fall within an exclusion in the rules, which did 'not apply to a "qualifying special purpose entity" or QSPE under FAS 140(14c)'. This approach was predictable, exploitation of exclusions and exemptions being a standard technique of legal engineering. Concern was expressed, however, that this would constrain the ability to actively market the asset portfolios backing the deals. Another route, the bank's researchers suggested, looking closely at the wording of the regulation, would be 'to disperse a VIE's [Variable Interest Entity's] economic risks and benefits among many parties, so that none holds a majority of variable interests requiring consolidation', though there would be problems with this 'if third party holders of variable interests insist on having a measure of control proportionate to their economic stake'. The ideal way would be another route, finding an 'aggressive (but not manifestly unreasonable) basis for measuring variable interests in a way which does not closely correspond to their economic risks and benefits . . . [then] . . . dispersing variable interests without dispersing the economic risks and benefits'.[27]

Such a device, the document noted, would be the 'holy grail' to search for. This is just one example of how every new regulation becomes a challenge to be creatively overcome, and to be scrutinised for escape routes, usually with some success. Certainly *Accountancy*

[23] Barclays, reported in the *Financial Times*, 9 May 1989.
[24] *The Independent*, 1 June 1989.
[25] Financial Accounting Standards Board, 'Consolidation of Variable Interest Entities, an Interpretation of ARB No 51', FASB Interpretation No 46 (17 January 2003).
[26] Nomura Fixed Income Research, above n 21, 1.
[27] Ibid.

Age in 2008 reported a general loss of confidence within the FASB on how to tackle off-balance-sheet financing: though new rules were introduced in the US after Enron, 'the banks found a way round these'.[28]

Over time, regulatory initiatives to control or ensure the disclosure of risk have spawned a range of new and ever more complex securitisations which let banks expand their lending without having to increase their risk capital. This has, of course, been argued to have real value: 'Structured finance allows people to raise money they might not otherwise be able to raise, and that access to capital contributes to productivity.'[29]

And where risk really has moved from the banks, the argument goes, then it is right to treat innovative forms as substantively and not just technically compliant. One question that arises from the current crisis, however, is how far were the risks truly removed? There is also the issue of how adequately they were disclosed. In addition, the apparently infinite capacity to lend off balance sheet without the need for balancing capital encouraged much riskier lending than could otherwise have been undertaken. Indeed, the legal capacity to securitise itself stimulated a hunger for opportunities to create loans or other assets that could be securitised.[30] Rather than securitisation being built on pre-existing assets with their own economic logic, the possibility of securitisation prompted the creation of assets—such as sub-prime loans—to securitise, regardless of their intrinsic economic logic. Small wonder that there was concomitant expansion of systemic risk.

Economic risk issues are beyond the scope of this chapter, as is the adequacy of the regulations themselves. The focus of this chapter is the strategic approach taken to law and regulation by the regulated, and the point there is that regulatory attempts to control bank risk were—as is routine and pervasive practice in any big business context—consciously and deliberately met by attempts to innovate out of them, and that innovation involved not just mathematical or financial creativity but legal creativity. For banks, capital adequacy regulations, designed to control risk, were 'obstructions' to be 'dealt with' through creative legal engineering.

3.   The Role of Tax in Structured Finance

This legal engineering was right at the core of structured finance. Legal engineering is what translated the financial whizz-kid's idea into a legally and therefore economically viable product: 'the potential of the product depends on the ratio of cost it would incur to get round legal, regulatory, tax or accounting difficulties'.[31]

The reference to tax is pertinent. Creative tax avoidance was a frequent driver of securitisation as well as a key element in profit and, indeed, in marketability. There was always a basic issue in any legal engineering of ensuring that devices intended to circumvent one set of regulations, such as capital adequacy rules, did not end up with adverse tax repercussions, and an equally basic practice of working to retain both tax and regulatory

---

[28] P Sukhraj, 'FASB Probes Off-balance Sheet Rules', *Accountancy Age*, 29 February 2008, available at www.accountancyage.com/accountancyage/news/2210839/fasb-investigates-balance-sheet.

[29] Lynn Turner, former chief accountant at the SEC and professor of accounting at Colorado State University, quoted in T Reason, 'Reporting: See-through Finance', *CFO magazine*, 1 October 2002, available at www. cfo.com/magazine/index.cfm/3046581?f=bc.

[30] An example of insurance products being created in order to securitise them is given in the next section.

[31] Research interviews, 2004.

advantages even where logically the securing of one advantage should have been at the expense of the other.

Legal engineering is about having your cake and eating it too. Hybrid capital, for example, was designed to achieve both the capital adequacy advantages of equity and the tax advantages of debt. In normal usage equity would be best for the capital adequacy count but equity does not generate the tax-allowable costs of debt which boost the return on equity. 'Hybrid capital' was conjured up to claim qualification as tier 1 capital under the Basel framework while still being tax deductible. As noted by one UK regulator, it is

> capital that acts like debt as far as the taxman is concerned, and capital that acts like equity as far as the depositor is concerned . . . Market participants have been quite imaginative in devising structures that meet diverse requirements in different jurisdictions to qualify as debt for tax purposes and equity for accounting purposes.[32]

This is parallel to the convertible bonds created in the corporate sector in the 1980s to simultaneously meet the apparently contradictory criteria of both debt and equity for different regulatory purposes.

Tax avoidance can itself be a primary driver of structured finance, and the source of the profit generated. In its 2009 'Tax Gap' series, *The Guardian* reported structured finance deals, such as those where '"investments" of £6 billion at a time . . . moved in circles between RBS and other banks . . . [as] . . . an important factor in driving the 'securitisation' boom which led to worldwide financial calamity'.[33]

Creatively structuring in tax avoidance can also be key to the marketability of the underlying assets for securitisation—and it is important to remember here that assets have sometimes been created in order to securitise them rather than the securitisation following from the pre-existence of the assets. A securitisable insurance product, for example, might be dreamed up in the abstract, and successfully legally engineered. But then the insurance policies had to be sold—to give the product 'an insurance wrap'[34] and to constitute the underlying asset. In marketing the policies, the lure of tax avoidance for the purchasers proved key: 'The objective is the securitisation but we use the legal benefits to get the policies sold. It's sold as a cheap way for high net worth individuals to leave money to heirs, avoiding IHT [inheritance tax].'[35]

In a number of ways, then, the legal engineering of tax avoidance has also been a key driver of, and integral to the profit in, banks' securitisation and other structured finance transactions, and this has added further layers of complexity to transaction structures.

4.   Legal Engineering and the Production of Complexity

In highly structured transactions of any kind—and these instruments were, as one lawyer put it, 'hellishly structured'[36]—there is typically complexity and opacity. It is hardly surprising, therefore, if the securitisation transactions behind the banking crisis were

---

[32] Thomas Huertas, Director, Banking Sector, FSA 'Hybrid Capital', speech at the City and Financial Bank Capital Seminar, 26 June 2008.

[33] F Lawrence and D Leigh, 'RBS Avoided £500m of Tax in Global Deals: State-supported Bank Admits Billions Were Put into Schemes to Cut Tax Bill', *The Guardian*, 13 March 2009, 1.

[34] Research interviews, 2004.

[35] Ibid.

[36] Ibid.

retrospectively deemed too complex and opaque for their risk to be comprehended.[37] But a key factor in why highly structured finance became highly structured was the desire to circumvent regulation.

Dealing with regulatory obstacles involves complex and sophisticated legal work in long chains of transaction structures. This is neither accidental nor incidental, but inherent in the task of regulatory circumvention. A solution to one regulatory problem will inevitably throw up new legal, regulatory, accounting and tax problems, which in turn need to be dealt with. Solving them will involve the addition to the transaction structure of further complex steps, partners, legal entities or jurisdictions, and the final product may indeed be a 'labyrinthine' structure that is hard to comprehend. If financial instruments are too complex to understand, it is important to recognise that one of the reasons for that complexity is the legal engineering that lies behind them and the multiplicity of laws, regulations, taxes and jurisdictions that are being circumvented in order to avoid regulatory control.

The complexity, incomprehensibility and opacity of risk attributed to innovative financial instruments can then be characterised not simply as an unfortunate by-product of financial engineering but as an integral part of legal engineering. And whether or not there was awareness of the financial risk being created, there was most certainly a very clear awareness that the regulations intended to control and disclose financial risk were being systematically circumvented by legal engineering. That indeed was its purpose. In fact, my research over the years has underlined to me that the risks that primarily concerned legal engineers, whether in the corporate or the banking sectors, were not financial risks at all but 'structural risks'[38]—the risk that the regulatory and tax circumvention integral to the transactions might be challenged by the authorities.

C.   Redefining the Problem, Redefining the Solution

Reconceptualising financial innovation as legal innovation gives a different take on some of the problems underlying the banking crisis and raises different issues that need to be addressed. I will consider the implications of this analysis for four issues:

— changing the regulations;
— principles-based regulation;
— the allocation of responsibility; and
— the relevance of current events, movements and mood.

1.   Changing the Regulations

Regulations and regulators have themselves come under fire as a result of the current financial crisis. Capital adequacy regulations have been described as inadequate and promises have been made that they will become more demanding.[39] However, as we have

---

[37] See n 4 and the quote there from John McFall.
[38] Research interviews, 2004.
[39] Eg Callum McCarthy, chairman of the FSA, 'Lessons from the Financial Crisis', speech at the Manchester Business School (13 May 2008) 3; and Mansion House Speech (18 September 2008).

seen in the course of this paper, any new regulation tends to be met with the same energetic drive to circumvent it, and there should be no expectation of a quick fix from increasing the capital adequacy ratios required or prohibiting specific instruments currently in use.

Legal engineering is all about getting round the rules, whatever shape they currently take. We saw instances of that earlier in this chapter in our discussion of the banks' response to the introduction of new regulations on off-balance-sheet financing. New regulations can simply stimulate new devices to escape them. Financial innovation has been discussed as 'bricolage',[40] with 'bricoleurs' using 'whatever is at hand' to construct new products from the current finite materials around them. One of those materials is law. Legal engineers use whatever law is available at any given moment, sometimes drawing from areas of law and regulation not hitherto seen as relevant to the context in hand, in order to construct new ways out of control. Law is both the obstacle to be overcome and the 'raw material to be worked on'[41] in order to achieve that. However regulations are changed, they will be complied with 'creatively', and there needs to be awareness that the same could happen in the current context with new regulations unless the whole approach to compliance is addressed.

That is not to say that regulations should not be enhanced, that creative compliance cannot be made a little more difficult, that legal engineers should not be challenged by presenting them with tougher obstacles to surmount. And the pleas of ignorance at the top could be addressed. On this, lessons might be learned from the post-Enron deferred prosecutions in the US.

Several of the banks that had been involved in Enron's schemes, along with KPMG, were not immediately prosecuted for their roles, but were monitored under deferred prosecution agreements. Prosecution was deferred so long as the firms undertook a range of obligations, with the threat of prosecution dropped after a specified time. These agreements included a number of obligations of direct relevance to the kind of legal engineering discussed in this paper.[42] Firms were, for example, required to set up committees of senior executives ('Head of Group or experienced designee') from all the 'disciplines' in the firm, to review and approve transactions, with the need for agreement of all the Heads before a transaction structure was approved. This review obligation extended, to cite the Merrill Lynch agreement, to 'all complex structured finance transactions effected by a third party with Merrill Lynch'.[43] This requirement for the direct involvement of top management is in line with the call from the Financial Services Authority (FSA) for responsibility at the top of organisations, it is best practice in some organisations[44] and it might be a mechanism that should be given greater emphasis, especially in the wake of senior bankers' protests that they simply did not realise what was going on or the risk it involved.

Under the deferred prosecution agreements, these committees were required not just to

---

[40] Engelen et al above n 9; D MacKenzie, 'An Equation and its Worlds: Bricolage, Exemplars, Disunity and Performativity in Financial Economics' (2003) 33 *Social Studies of Science* 831.

[41] D McBarnet, 'Law and Capital: The Role of Legal Form and Legal Actors' in D McBarnet (ed), *Law and Capital, Special Issue of International Journal of the Sociology of Law* (London, Academic Press, 1984), reprinted in McBarnet, above n 11.

[42] For a detailed analysis, see McBarnet, above n 14.

[43] US Department of Justice, 'Enron Task Force Agreement with Merrill Lynch on Deferred Prosecution' (2003).

[44] Research interviews, 2007.

ensure that the transactions did not technically break the law; they also had to consider their wider effects. The agreements prohibited firms from engaging in any transaction intended to 'achieve a misleading earnings, revenue or balance sheet effect'[45] for the corporation involved. Note the reference to 'misleading' rather than just 'fraudulent' effects. There was also a demand that, in assessing these structures, there should be a shift of focus from technical compliance to a concern with the 'objectives' of the structuring, with a purely accounting or tax objective deemed inappropriate.

Given the impact of Enron at the time, it is not surprising that the focus in these agreements was on the bank's role in facilitating OBSF deals for other corporations. Hence the concern with third-party transactions and with the effects on the third party's accounts. But there is no reason why the same standards could not be set for monitoring a bank's own transactions and the effect on its own balance sheet. The underlying concept was that it was not enough for a transaction to be, under a strict or literal reading of the law or regulation, technically not illegal: there needed to be some responsibility taken, too, for its wider purpose and effects. This reflected public concern at the time not just over Enron's fraud but over the whole idea of legally engineered structures that could claim to be 'perfectly legal', or 'not illegal', but nonetheless defeated regulatory policy. The same public concern is clear now in relation to banking practice itself.

2.   Principles-based Regulation

As a result of the banking crisis, principles-based regulation—the flagship approach of the FSA—has come in for severe criticism. Julia Black has described the approach as having suffered 'a potentially fatal blow'.[46] Indeed, FSA officials themselves have declared principles-based regulation a failure in that 'a principles-based approach does not work with individuals who have no principles'.[47] However, critics seem to be equating principles with soft touch regulation and the two do not necessarily have to coincide.

There are different philosophies and strategies behind principles-based regulation. Sometimes the approach is to provide a broad goal in order to allow for variations in detail or implementation. This approach characterises regimes bent on harmonisation of different bodies of regulation, and is often a way of achieving broad harmonisation—or the appearance of harmonisation—without every party having to agree on every detail. It can be a product of political expediency or of an approach which finds it more appropriate to delegate detail to a lower regulatory rung. The FSA's approach—and it was also bringing into one regime a range of different organisations with different regulations—was to set very broad behavioural standards but allow for variation in the methods used to achieve those standards, allowing a broad sweep of laissez-faire so long as the 'outcomes' met the goals. This exhibited a great deal of trust in the regulated and their ability to self-regulate, and it tied closely with the dominance of market ideology.

There can be another philosophy behind principles-based regulation, however, where it is driven not so much by trust in the regulated and their capacity for restraint, but by

---

[45] US Dept of Justice, above n 43.

[46] J Black, 'The Death of Credit, Trust—and Principles-based Regulation?' [December 2008] *Risk and Regulation* 8.

[47] Hector Sants, chief executive FSA, speech at Thomson Reuters, 12 March 2009, reported in *The Guardian*, 13 March 2009.

distrust, based on experience, and by the need for constraint. Driving this approach is an explicit recognition that any specific rule will be met by legal engineering to circumvent it, and principles-based regulation is seen as the only realistic response, the only way to try to capture the spirit of the law in the face of constant creativity and technical challenge. This approach featured to some extent in the FSA's adoption of principles-based regulation, but it was the overwhelming driving force behind the adoption of principles-based regulation in the 1990s by the Accounting Standards Board (ASB), which saw it as an essential bastion against opportunistic legal engineering.

It would be unwise in the extreme for the FSA to abandon the idea of principles-based regulation because of the current debacle. A reversion to rules will simply result in legal engineers developing ways out of them with bright line rules to point to in their defence. Creative compliance thrives on rule-based regulation, for tight specific rules provide particularly solid material for legal engineers to work with.

Importantly, though, principles will certainly not stop legal engineering if they are not strongly enforced. The ASB emphasised the need for principles to control creative compliance with law and regulation through legal and accounting engineering. However, the body responsible for enforcing accounting standards, the Financial Reporting Review Panel (FRRP), was not noted for its use of principles in its enforcement practices, tending instead to monitor for and enforce compliance with specific rules. ASB chairman David Tweedie frequently stated that the requirement in company law to give a true and fair view in accounts should override even compliance with specific rules if such compliance did not result in a true and fair view of the financial situation. However, research[48] on the FRRP's enforcement practice showed that it did not use the 'true and fair' requirement in this way. The Panel quite frequently refused to accept situations where a company had invoked the true and fair override as a reason for not following specific rules. However, there were no instances of the Panel doing the opposite, that is, itself using the override to reject a company's technical compliance if it was not deemed to result in a true and fair view of the accounts, even though it was for this situation that Tweedie had particularly advocated its use.

The FSA has used principles as a means of enforcement in cases where there were deemed to be unacceptable effects even though there was arguably no breach of a specific rule. In one case, there was no specific rule to deal with the situation; in the other, the infringement took place outside FSA jurisdiction.[49] Using principles in this way helps tackle the kind of legal engineering which takes advantage of an absence of rules and innovates into a vacuum. However, it would take more to challenge legal engineering based on a claim to technical compliance with extant rules, despite the fact that the net result is not what was intended. For that approach to be challenged, principles need to be brought in not just to fill a vacuum in the book of specific rules but also to override the rulebook if the principles have not been met. That is the only way to ensure that technical compliance with the letter of the law is subjugated to a requirement to comply with its spirit. For this to be meaningful, it would have to be the basis not just of regulatory rhetoric but also of regulatory enforcement.

However, too much can be expected of principles-based regulation. It is difficult to

---

[48] McBarnet and Whelan, above n 15.

[49] Citigroup and Deutsche Bank, 2006. In the case of Citigroup there is no suggestion that a specific rule was infringed. In the case of Deutsche Bank, the infringements occurred in foreign markets not regulated by the FSA, so that the FSA's specific rules did not apply. Enforcement took place by invoking FSA principles.

enforce principles. There is not always consent on whether a practice constitutes compliance with the spirit of the law.[50] Some financial products seem to have left regulators stumped as to whether or not they are legitimate. Thomas Huertas, Director of the Banking Sector of the FSA, discussing hybrid capital, pondered on whether it was 'admirable alchemy or invidious innovation'.[51] There is a real reluctance to use principles in enforcement because of the criticisms of subjectivity, retrospectivity and too much power being usurped by regulators, and even principles and broad abstract concepts take the form of words which can still provide material for legal engineers to work on.[52]

Principles should not be abandoned, but neither are they the panacea. Indeed, underlying the issue of principles or rules is a more fundamental problem: the culture that fosters legal engineering and its presumption of legitimacy.

3.   Legal Engineering and Responsibility

The rule of law may be seen as a fundamental of democratic society, but that is not how it is approached in the practice of legal engineering. In the mindset of the legal engineer, law or regulation is not a legitimate and authoritative command to be taken at face value, respected and obeyed; rather, it is simply a nuisance, an obstacle to be overcome, a material to be worked with and reshaped to one's advantage, a challenge in a regulatory game of cat and mouse.

Legal engineers know they are not following the intentions or spirit of the law. Bankers and banking lawyers talk in interview about their legal practices as 'bullish' or 'sailing close to the wind'. Indeed, they are sometimes surprised when they succeed, when regulators fail to see through what a lawyer described as the 'fog' of complexity and opacity, a fog which indeed can be developed for just that purpose. In the mindset that underlies and fosters legal engineering, all the responsibility for control is being placed on the regulators. If they cannot make regulations legal engineering proof or spot the failings in the schemes, it is fair game to exploit that situation. Ideas such as responsibility, the public good, morality, ethics or integrity do not enter into the equation. All, it seems, is fair in love and law.

But should all the responsibility for securing compliance rest with writers and enforcers of regulation? Or should the regulated also be seen as having a responsibility to comply with the spirit of the law? Black describes the regulations on capital adequacy as too easy to get round,[53] but that takes the culture of circumvention as given. The present crisis may indicate that it is time to question that culture and its legitimacy, and to place more responsibility for the efficacy of regulation on the regulated.

What this chapter has also reminded us of is the behind-the-scenes but active and crucial role of the legal profession in creative compliance. At the core of financial engineering is legal engineering, which depends heavily on lawyers and legal work. Professional responsibility therefore also needs to be questioned, and the meaning of professional ethics in relation to the rule of law needs to be addressed.

---

[50] Though it is sometimes forgotten that this can be equally true of specific rules.
[51] Huertas, above n 32.
[52] 'When Compliance is not the Solution but the Problem: From Changes in Law to Changes in Attitude' in V Braithwaite (ed), *Taxing Democracy* (Aldershot, Ashgate, 2003), reprinted in McBarnet, above n 10.
[53] Black, above n 46.

If the legitimacy of legal engineering and creative compliance is to be reassessed, politicians also need to put their own house in order, since they have been as guilty of legal engineering, creative compliance and disrespect for the law as banks and corporations have. Politicians and governments have themselves thoroughly exploited this 'bullish', technical and literal approach to law, not just in such practices as the careful technical packaging of party donations as loans in the 'peerages for loans' scandal, but also in core financial policy. UK Prime Minister Gordon Brown has said he wants 'all companies to bring out their bad assets and put them back on their balance sheet so the financial system can move forward'.[54] Yet for years, the government itself used off-balance-sheet financing techniques in the form of the Private Finance Initiative to enhance public accounts. There is more than a whiff of hypocrisy in politicians denouncing such activities as tax avoidance and off-balance-sheet financing while themselves using the letter of the law to defeat its spirit. If a more responsible approach to the rule of law is to be encouraged, there must be more of what corporate responsibility consultants and regulators have referred to as 'tone at the top'.[55]

4.   Carpe Diem

There has been a growing regulatory rhetoric, especially since Enron, for a more ethical stance in relation to law and compliance and for greater emphasis on compliance with the spirit of the law.[56] The financial crisis may provide an opportunity—if, and it is a very big 'if', the political and professional will is there—to shift from rhetoric to practice. The banking crisis has added force to a public discontent with business that began with Enron, a discontent that demonstrates growing awareness of, and strong objections to, the practice of technical compliance with the letter but not the spirit of the law, and the lack of basic ethics in business and public life. Recent UK experience over politicians' approach to expenses has strengthened this public mood to a level of public disgust that could be harnessed to change. Taxpayer funding of banks could also provide an opportunity for setting new standards of social and legal responsibility in the banking sector itself.

There are also other trends and forces at work that might be harnessed. The corporate social responsibility movement has been expanding its agenda beyond pressures for environmental responsibility and human rights to concerns with a more ethical approach in business to finance and to legal compliance. This has been expressed particularly in the context of tax avoidance, but has the potential to be harnessed to a wider critique of cavalier approaches to law—by business, professions or politicians—and to a call for compliance with the spirit of the law.[57] The banking crisis has demonstrated that clever manipulation of law and circumvention of regulation may not be quite so clever after all, and that its social costs can be devastating. There is a growing awareness of the unfairness

[54] Institute of Financial Accountants, 'Gordon Brown Has Vowed to Force Banks and other Businesses to Put their Off-balance Sheet Liabilities into their Books' (25 September 2008), available at www.ifa.org.uk/news.

[55] 'Tone at the Top: Getting It Right', speech delivered at the Second Annual General Counsel Roundtable, Washington DC, 3 December 2004.

[56] D McBarnet, 'Compliance, Ethics and Responsibility: Emergent Governance Strategies in the US and UK' in J O'Brien (ed), *Private Equity, Corporate Governance and the Dynamics of Capital Market Governance* (London, Imperial College Press, 2007).

[57] For a detailed analysis see D McBarnet, 'Corporate Social Responsibility beyond law, through law, for law: the new corporate accountability' in D McBarnet, A Voiculescu and T Campbell (eds), *The New Corporate Accountability: Corporate Social Responsibility and the Law* (Cambridge, Cambridge University Press, 2007).

by which those with the resources to do so can buy their way out of legal control at the expense of those who cannot.

The time may be appropriate for a new aspiration towards a greater respect for the rule of law, a greater respect for democracy in law and a new legal integrity. Certainly it will require a shift as fundamental as that, and not just some tinkering with the rules, for there ever to be any hope of effectively regulating banking or, indeed, business in general.

5

The Future of Financial Regulation: The Role of the Courts

JEFFREY B GOLDEN[*]

A. Introduction

What role would we wish to see our courts play in dealing with complex financial instruments, matters arising from the financial crisis and, in due course, the new regulatory regime that we have been discussing and expect will emerge from this crisis? Do we think that the courts, as currently constituted, are prepared to play that role? Is there more, in any event, that the markets, the profession and academia can do to ready them? The other papers in this collection and the conference that inspired them have focused on financial regulation as a kind of 'preventive medicine' and the importance we attach to getting it right. It would be foolish to challenge the utility of our doing so. Preventive medicine in matters of both personal and financial health is important. Moreover, the malaise afflicting the financial markets is already of epidemic proportions and arguably the contagion is spreading. In addition, once cured of it, we do not want to experience a relapse.

It is a little surprising that, with all the debate around us about the future of financial regulation, and the statements being made or reported by regulators and politicians, by lawyers and economists, by academics and in the media, so little attention (in fact, almost zero column inches) has been paid to the judges around the world who can be expected to interpret that regulation, fill in gaps or resolve ambiguities in it, and peacefully settle any number of disputes—some of them highly complex and technical—that are likely to follow from the considerable losses, and in some cases the demise, of major financial institutions and their counterparties.

To take the medical analogy a little further, preventive medicine is all well and good; however, we know that we have 'patients' who are seriously, if not terminally, ill, and we

[*] General Editor, *Capital Markets Law Journal*; Founder Partner, US Law Group and Senior Partner, Global Derivatives Group at Allen & Overy LLP. This article is based on a paper delivered at the Future of Financial Regulation Conference, 30–31 March 2009, University of Glasgow, and the portions of it which first appeared with the title 'The courts, the financial crisis and systemic risk' in (2009) *Capital Markets Law Journal*, Special Issue 1 are reprinted here by permission of Oxford University Press. The author gratefully acknowledges the assistance of Sarah Newton and Suyash Paliwal, students at Columbia University School of Law, and Dr Peter M Werner, Policy Director at International Swaps and Derivatives Association, Inc (ISDA), in preparing this expanded version for this publication.

can expect more accidents and victims in the future, so perhaps we should worry a bit more about the conditions of our 'hospitals', that is, our courts, and whether we have enough qualified staff to run them.

B.   The Stakes Are High

We did not need a financial crisis to make us aware of the enormous scale of the global financial markets. What can be observed in conjunction with the collapse of the financial markets, however, is that complex products sold globally will be tested in litigation for the first time. The amounts potentially at risk here are staggering. For example, when the Bank for International Settlements last reported its semi-annual statistics on positions in the global over-the-counter (OTC) derivatives markets, notional amounts outstanding of all types of OTC derivatives stood at $605 trillion at the end of June 2009.[1] This represents a six-month increase of 10% (and follows the only reported decline since collection of data began in 1988). At growth rates prior to the crisis it was predicted that, just for OTC derivatives, we would see volumes in excess of $1 quadrillion by 2010.[2] We may still see the crossing of that threshold in the not too distant future.

At the time of writing, lawyers are also predicting a 'tsunami' of financial market litigation from the crisis.[3] So the stakes are high, and, with the amounts involved, it is important that decisions in major financial market cases, and any precedents they produce, are correct, are in context and foster legal certainty.

C.   The Results So Far Are Less Than Satisfactory

While the jury is still out, so to speak, as to how the courts will perform in this next wave of cases, there have already been worrying signs. In several past cases, some dealing with contractual issues that global markets thought important (for example, the close-out mechanics of industry standard contracts like the ISDA Master), there were concerns (either because of where the case was brought or who the parties were) that the court would not have been adequately briefed on the subtleties of complex documentation or as

---

[1] Bank for International Settlements, 'OTC Derivatives Market Activity in the first half of 2009', Monetary and Economic Department Report (12 November 2009), available at www.bis.org/publ/otc_hy0911.pdf. The notional amounts reported are a measure of derivatives market activity and reflect both new and existing transactions. These amounts, however, are not a measure of risk. The marked-to-market values of outstanding trades and the estimated credit exposure after netting would be significantly less, although still measured in trillions of dollars.

[2] The $1 quadrillion figure was cited by more than one senior derivatives market participant in conversation with the author in early 2008.

[3] See E Weinburger, 'Financial Crises Litigation Wave Forming its Crest', *Law 360*, 17 March 2009, available at http://securities.law360.com/articles/90495: 'Massive financial calamity is often accompanied by great, crashing waves of litigation. Although the raw number of lawsuits filed following the generalized meltdown of the financial markets are up at historic levels, those expecting an even bigger wave shouldn't put away their surfboards yet.'

to wider market practice and interest—and, indeed, the extent of that interest.[4] In other cases, stretching back over a longer period of time, including the local authorities cases in the UK arising in the early 1990s, market reaction has been critical of decisions, in whole or in part, because it was thought that one or more judges lacked a fuller appreciation of the products or markets involved.[5]

The fact is that the nature of the claims in complex product litigation has evolved. Early cases concentrated on whether the activity contemplated by the contract was authorised or ultra vires, whether the parties' conduct gave rise to formation of a contract and on what terms, on counterparty relationships and the duty of care[6]—subjects that judges not versed in new financial products nevertheless both understood and felt comfortable with. However, in more recent disputes, parties have challenged, and increasingly can be expected to further challenge, results produced by complex financial models and formulaic calculations and their suitability in assessing complicated contractual remedies—remedies which were created by the markets in part to insolvency-proof the parties' contract in a wide range of jurisdictions, some of them very pro-debtor, around the world. These remedies are very different from the remedies of the loan and bond markets, even though the contemplated cash flows may be similar.[7] Global market facts and practices are highly relevant, and need to be understood and accounted

---

[4] Concern was expressed, for example, by the ISDA over a series of recent rulings in the Seoul Central District Court in relation to Knock-in Knock-out (KIKO) currency option litigation cases, citing 'fundamental misconception' on the part of the court and the risk of 'upsetting financial stability' if the decisions were upheld. ISDA news release, 'ISDA Expresses Concern Over KIKO Case Ruling' (1 April 2009). As of 10 March 2009, there were more than 330 such cases pending before the Korean courts, including preliminary injunctions. Presentation by Keith Noyes, ISDA Regional Director, Asia Pacific at the ISDA Annual General Meeting, April 2009. See also ISDA webcast at secure.webex.com/g2.asp?id=H8MY4GH2; WY Bay and J Gu, 'Ringfencing and Contract Enforceability Challenges' [April 2009] *Asia Risk* 23–24; 'KIKO Case May Hinge on Judges' (6 April 2009) 18 *Derivatives Week* 13. *Peregrine Fixed Income Limited (In Liquidation) v Robinson Department Store Public Company Limited* [2000] All ER (D) 1177 was an earlier decision provoking a similar reaction from practitioners: see eg Allen & Overy's Client Bulletin on Peregrine v Robinson (May 2000): 'The Judge's decisions on the issues before him, and his reasoning for those decisions, raise potentially serious issues in relation to the valuation and close-out mechanics of the 1992 ISDA Master Agreement . . . It should be noted that ISDA itself was not a party to the case, was never invited to express its views or to make representations to the Court on these issues and did not do so.'

[5] Such claims were levied by many market participants following the House of Lords decision in *Hazell v Hammersmith & Fulham London Borough Council* [1992] 2 AC 1. As a result, the Bank of England established the Legal Risk Review Committee to consider how best to tackle legal uncertainties in a way that would promote market confidence in English jurisprudence. This objective, together with the aim of fostering a better understanding by the English judiciary of matters relating to the wholesale financial markets, led first to the creation of the Financial Law Panel in 1993 and subsequently to the establishment of its successor, the Financial Markets Law Committee, in 2002. See generally Joanna Perkins, 'Legal Certainty and the Role of the Financial Markets Law Committee' (2007) 2 *Capital Markets Law Journal* 155. See also Roger McCormick, 'How the Financial Markets Law Committee works and why we need it: an interview with Lord Woolf' [January 2007] *Law and Financial Markets Review* 3.

[6] See, eg *Powercor Australia Ltd v Pacific Power* [1999] VSC 110; *Hazell v Hammersmith & Fulham London Borough Council* [1992] 2 AC 1; *Westdeutsche Landesbank Girozentrale v Islington London Borough Council* [1994] AC 669; *Kleinwort Benson Ltd v Lincoln City Council and Ors* [1998] 3 WLR 1095; *Intershoe Inc v Bankers Trust Co* 77 NY2d 517, 569 NYS 2d 333 (1991); *Bankers Trust International PLC v PT Dharmala Sakti Sejahtera, PT Dharmala Sakti Sejahtera v Bankers Trust International PLC and Another* [1996] CLC 518; *Gibson Greetings v Bankers Trust Co* (CV No C-1-94-620, SD Ohio); *Proctor & Gamble v Bankers Trust Co* 925 F Supp 1270 (SD Ohio 1996), 78 F 3d 219 (6th Cir 1996).

[7] There is, of course, a risk that, when a non-expert court lacks familiarity or experience with derivatives and other complex financial products, the judge may be tempted to recharacterise such 'new' products and treat them as something more familiar (like loans or even traditional insurance contracts) but rather different from what the parties have bargained for.

for.[8] There is little to demonstrate a propensity for this across the courts that are likely to field cases from the crisis.[9]

D.   The Phenomenon of Standardisation

Of particular importance is the phenomenon of standardisation of legal terms across geographical, cultural and even linguistic divides. Widespread usage of master agreements and standard terms can facilitate legal certainty and huge cost efficiencies.

We do not have a world parliament to legislate such matters, but the markets have created a kind of global law by contract. The risk, however, is that widespread usage of the same terms can amplify any mistakes that a court makes in deciding the proper meaning of such terms. It becomes difficult to attribute a result to the actual intent of the parties when their contract emerged from a room in which perhaps they never were present or even represented and at a place and time far removed from their transaction. In such a case, the courts should perhaps instead 'look to the overall history of a term, the process by which the term became a standard (or one of the standards) in the industry, and its context within the greater commercial environment'.[10] For a host of reasons, in the current scheme of things, there is a high risk that this will not happen.

For example, the parties to a dispute may not spot an issue of importance to the markets. Or, having spotted it, they may have difficulty finding the requisite experts to give evidence in court. They may just not wish to, or may be unable to, spend what it takes to get a right answer. There may be other strategic reasons why a party may not frame or develop an issue that others in the market view as extremely important.

It also has to be recognised that conflict of interest rules and procedures, presumably designed to protect clients, may give rise to unintended consequences in future when applied to complex financial market cases. Practice in this area and the subject matter of many cases we are likely to see are highly specialised. Very few lawyers and even fewer law firms as such are expert. Given the consolidation that has arisen in global legal services,

---

[8] SJ Choi and CM Gulati, 'Contract as Statute' (2006) 104 *Michigan Law Review* 1130.

[9] Concerns about systemic pressures and the effectiveness and cost-efficiency of court settlement of disputes arising from derivatives trading may have inspired recent market initiatives to provide arbitration-like contractual remedies. In March 2009, ISDA formed so-called 'Determinations Committees' to make binding determinations in credit derivatives market disputes, such as whether a triggering credit event has occurred, whether an auction will be held and what obligations are deliverable for purposes of the auction. A separate committee for each of five geographical regions has been formed, each comprising ten dealer and five non-dealer ('buyside') ISDA members: ISDA news release, 'ISDA Forms Credit Derivatives Determinations Committees' (31 March 2009). The Determinations Committees have been busy since their formation. More recently it has been reported that ISDA is also developing dispute resolution procedures to deal privately with a material increase in the number of collateral calls in the OTC derivatives market that have been disputed. 'ISDA Preps Margin Call Dispute Protocols' (18 May 2009) 18 *Derivatives Week* 19. See also R Davidson, 'Derivatives Industry Focuses Attention on Collateral Disputes' (2009) 22 *Risk Magazine* 6. Of course, both the Determinations Committees and any protocol that emerges for the resolution of disputed collateral calls derive their authority from the parties' contract. Further challenges in domestic courts to any prescribed outcome cannot be ruled out entirely. For a recent US court case involving a disputed margin call made under a credit default swap, which raised issues of market practice relating to the interpretation of contractually defined terms, see *VCG v Citibank, NA*, 08-CV-01563 (BSJ) 2008 WL 4809078 (SDNY Nov 5, 2008); see also AH Scheiner, 'The Next Wave: Developments in Credit Default Swap Litigation' *Business Law Today* (May/June 2009) 53.

[10] Choi and Gulati, above n 8, 1131.

most of these lawyers can be found at large, international firms that represent a multitude of financial institutions in their transactional work. If, as a result, the experts in the field become unavailable when litigation arises because of traditional notions of 'conflict', practice designed to protect clients and promote justice could have the opposite effect. The search for a law firm without the taint of commercial conflict, as some banks currently see it, could engender a 'race to the bottom'.[11] It could take a very long time to get litigators unfamiliar with relevant market practice and the complexity of the products up to speed—assuming you ever could. It would certainly be a lot more expensive than engaging experienced lawyers who understand the subject.

Moreover, traditional aids that assisted courts to get it right in the past have been problematic in this context. Not only has their scarcity and perceptions of conflict made it difficult to ensure that experienced and expert counsel argue key cases, but for similar reasons it has also been a challenge to find suitable expert witnesses in complex product cases. One key reason is that some of the relevant markets are so new and emerging, and the practitioners so young, that retired practitioners are—at least for now—rare (although, for reasons discussed below,[12] the pool of such retirees could deepen). Still another challenge arises from the fact that the markets in question are dynamic and practice moves on rapidly, so that retired practitioners who have moved out of the market quickly lose their expertise. As a result, as things stand at the moment, those in a position to serve best as experts have been unavailable, while there is a risk that those who may now become available could quickly lose their effectiveness.[13]

[11] Interestingly, client perceptions of conflict, or potential conflict, in a litigation context can vary considerably from the approaches often adopted when clients choose legal counsel for their transactional work. The handful of international law firms that specialise in complex derivatives and structured finance transactions tend to represent a multiplicity of market competitors when advising on and documenting their clients' trading activities. It is not unusual to see such firms 'switch sides', appearing for Bank X in one transaction and for a counterparty of Bank X in a transaction with Bank X (and with Bank X's permission) on another occasion. Permission is usually readily granted and justified on the basis that it is more comforting than threatening to see a knowledgeable firm across the table, provided that confidential and proprietary information is protected and, where appropriate, walls or screens are employed. That attitude seems to change dramatically when the sides are drawn up for litigation. Law firms with leading finance practices have been reluctant for some time to act in a lawsuit that targets a major financial institution, even in the absence of actual conflict, and, as a result of agreements reached with bank clients, may be prevented from doing so. See, eg H Power and J O'Connor, 'Wanted: Law Firm to Sue the UK's Big Five Banks', *The Lawyer*, 27 September 2004, available at www.thelawyer.com/wanted-law-firm-to-sue-the-uk's-big-five-banks/112203.article. For the reasons set out in this article, it may be time for the markets and the profession to rethink their traditional views on conflicts of interest in such a highly specialised and technical market. In any such future consideration regarding financial market litigation, it may be particularly useful to distinguish between actual and commercial conflicts, on the one hand, and between unfair advantage and protecting confidentiality, on the other. Relevant experience and competence must be key factors.
[12] See discussion below, E–G.
[13] *Bank One Corporation v Commissioner* (2003) 120 TC 174 is a case in which the court can be seen to be struggling with the challenge of obtaining suitable expert testimony in relation to complex financial products. At trial, each party called expert witnesses in support of that party's position. In addition, and emphasising that it did so for the first time, the court decided to appoint its own experts to testify to relevant subject matter: ibid 276. The court noted that the parties were engaged in complex litigation with novel issues of first impression and significant importance relating to taxation of financial derivatives: ibid 276–77. It also noted that the taxpayers affected by the issues before the court were 'plentiful' and the tax dollars affected by the reporting requirement at issue in the case 'reach into the billions, if not trillions': ibid 175. In a postscript to the case, the court discusses the weight it gave to the expert testimony it heard, while also describing the proper role that the court thought experts should play and its impression of the experts before it: ibid 332–34. It can be reasonably inferred from its decision that the court's unprecedented decision to appoint its own experts reflected a sense of insecurity about the evidence otherwise being offered.

In appropriate cases, provision of an amicus-type brief could help bridge the gap.[14] Such a filing could ensure that the judge is made aware of relevant issues and the potential market impact of the decision and, in so doing, could lend credibility to controversial decisions which do affect the market. I have argued elsewhere that this is a topic probably worthy of further consideration.[15] However, for the moment, utilisation of 'friend of court' briefs varies widely from jurisdiction to jurisdiction. Embracing a global perspective on their helpfulness in financial market litigation may be desirable. At present, though, in some courts, including the English courts, there is no precedent or procedure for a court to resort to a third-party brief in such cases or request such a brief if it is not offered. Indeed, there is no practice to suggest that such input would be accepted or considered even if offered. There is also a bit of a 'chicken and egg' issue to sort out before we can expect reliance on advice of this sort to make a positive difference. It is a question of what has to come first: absent greater familiarity with relevant markets, judges will not necessarily know where to look for a helpful brief, even if the court in question has the option to seek one, and, given the decentralised nature of dispute settlement for these markets, it is currently near impossible for the markets to stand ready to interject relevant background in all the fora where the need to do so might arise.

E.   We Need a Settled Body of Law

So what could make a positive difference? Right now, it is widely accepted that we have the potential for very complicated cases. The best guess is that there will be a growing number of such cases (remember the tsunami).[16] However, getting correct answers from our courts is fraught with challenge. The potential for getting a wrong decision is particularly great in the absence of specialised courts,[17] judges with directly relevant experience, expert counsel

---

[14] See eg *In re National Gas Distributors, LLC* 556 F 3d 247 (4th Cir 2009), a case which involved the first major interpretation of the Financial Netting Improvements Act of 2006 and Bankruptcy Abuse Prevention and Consumer Protection Act of 2005. ISDA played an amicus role at all stages through the appeal of the case to the US Court of Appeals. See more generally ISDA's website www.isda.org, which reports amicus brief filings by the trade association in numerous US and Canada court proceedings during the period commencing in 2000 to the present.

[15] J Golden, 'Do We Need a World Court for the Financial Markets?' in RD Vriesendorp, FA Nelisson and M Wladimiroff (eds), *The Hague Legal Capital?* (The Hague, Hague Academic Press, 2008).

[16] See above, text to n 3.

[17] Specialised courts covering particular subject matters or areas of law have often been created alongside courts of general jurisdiction. The judges for these specialised courts typically bring relevant experience and background to provide more competent and possibly more cost-efficient adjudication, and their decisions create an informed and responsive *lex specialis* pertaining to that field. In the US, for instance, a variety of specialised courts have been created by Congress to address specific areas of law. The Court of Federal Claims has competence to hear cases by individuals against the US allowed by statutes or the Constitution. Every district court has a specialised unit, the bankruptcy court, empowered to conduct core bankruptcy proceedings. The Court of International Trade hears only civil claims arising under import transactions. The Court of Customs and Patent Appeals, merged in 1982 into the Court of Appeals for the Federal Circuit, has appellate jurisdiction over both the Court of International Trade and administrative decisions relating to patents. The US Tax Court was established to hear claims against the Internal Revenue Service. The specialised courts often have subject-matter jurisdiction concurrently with courts of general jurisdiction. This affords claimants the right to choose which court provides the best balance of ease and expertise. Regarding tax matters, for instance, US taxpayers have the right to raise tax claims both in the Tax Court and in courts of general jurisdiction. An aggrieved taxpayer may pay the tax and sue for a refund in district court. The taxpayer may also pay and sue for a refund in the US Court of Federal Claims. Concurrently, the aggrieved taxpayer has the right to file a petition for

conflicted out, difficulties in identifying and retaining suitable experts, and, in many juris-dictions, the difficulty of bringing in the briefs of third parties. Moreover, the intent of the parties may be less important than that of working groups, often far removed from the parties, who developed the terms for trading. The standardisation of these terms creates the risk of serious knock-on effects from wrong decisions.

All this is complicated by the current decentralised nature of the dispute settlement system for the financial markets. The cases can be and are brought anywhere. There are now not just more cases arising but also many more participants in the game. They, too, can be from anywhere, and they are increasingly more geographically spread out.[18] This gives rise to another anomaly which complicates things: the widespread usage of common-law-governed standard-form contracts by multi-jurisdictional system partici-pants. Ad hoc arbitration does not fix the problem,[19] though it does offer the theoretical potential of selecting people with the requisite expertise and background to decide the matter.[20]

---

review of the Commissioner of Internal Revenue's decision before paying the tax. The Tax Court hears only tax-related cases. Jury trials are not allowed and the judges bring the advantage of coming from tax backgrounds. Juries are available in district court, but the judges are not always as knowledgeable in the economics and policy underlying tax. Relative costs may be another factor that weighs in the balance. See generally CA Wright and MK Kane, *Federal Practice Deskbook 5. Federal Practice & Procedure* (St Paul MN, West Group, 2002) 20–28. See also KM Clermont, *Principles of Civil Procedure* (St Paul MN, Thompson/West Publishing, 2005) 174. Until now, the financial markets have been slow to inspire separate, special subject matter courts. However, interestingly we are seeing new financial courts appearing in developing countries which aim to establish regional financial centres. Qatar, for example, recently created a new civil and commercial court along with an associated regulatory tribunal to deal with commercial and regulatory disputes. The Court has recruited several senior judges from outside the country in an attempt to enhance its international nature and standing, including the former Chief Justice of England and Wales, the former Chief Justice of India and a judge of the Federal Court of Australia: F Gibbs, 'New Qatar Court will Blend Legal Cultures of West and East' *TimesOnline* (London 4 June 2009). Nigeria, which has undertaken a long-term project to develop a financial system strategy, has also recently announced that its National Assembly is in the process of establishing a special court to handle financial crimes. The new court, which will be known as the Enhanced Financial Crimes Court, will hear cases where actions are alleged that could have the effect of sabotaging the economy and recognises the particular difficulty of dealing with the specialised nature of financial crimes and disputes: 'Nigeria: Special Court for Financial Crimes' *Legal Brief Africa* (25 May 2009) 332.

[18] As evidence of the breadth of market participation, see the list of more than 2,000 parties who signed up earlier this year to ISDA's so-called 'Big Bang' CDS Protocol, available at www.isda.org/whatsnew/. The protocol incorporates certain auction settlement terms into the adhering parties' documentation for credit derivatives. The geographically diverse list of adherents includes banks and insurers, funds, universities and even governments.

[19] ISDA recently co-chaired a meeting with academics as well as legal and banking practitioners in Europe at which the potential for arbitration in financial market disputes was discussed. See ISDA, *ISDA News* III (2009). It was reported that a number of participants shared a current preference for administered arbitration rather than ad hoc arbitration, citing difficulties stemming from delays due to lack of agreement on submission to arbitration clauses and a lack of meaningful dialogue at present between the arbitral community and the wholesale financial markets. See also 'Flaws Emerge in Arbitration Clauses' (18 May 2009) 18 *Derivatives Week*, 9, available at www.iiderivatives.com/pdf/DW051809.pdf. Arbitration clauses were looked at recently in some detail by the US Supreme Court in *Vaden v Discover Bank*, 129 S Ct 1262 (2009). While there has been a precedent favouring the enforceability of agreements to arbitrate, the *Vaden* case may limit this long-standing tradition.

[20] In fact, however, in a report of the settlement of the first derivatives related dispute in Brazil to be referred to arbitration by the national courts, a leading Brazilian lawyer acknowledged that, had the matter reached an arbitration hearing, 'the selection of arbitrators with specific knowledge in derivatives transactions' would have been a major challenge: 'First Derivatives Arbitration in Brazil Settles' *Global Arbitration Review* (29 May 2009), available at www.globalarbitrationreview.com/news/article/5313/first-derivatives-arbitration-brazil-settles/. One could almost hear a collective sigh of relief from the Brazilian market when the case settled, and it was unnecessary to cross that bridge.

However, there is another issue: we need a settled body of law.[21] We need the benefit of collective wisdom to build upon and to learn from our mistakes.[22] The results thus far from national courts and ad hoc arbitration do not get us there.

Arguably we need a new jurisprudence as well. Two US law professors contend that, where standard terms are employed in these markets, we may wish to rethink traditional views on contract interpretation.[23] In their view, contracts like the ISDA Master function more like statutes, and courts should look to the intent of the original drafters—rather like looking to legislative intent in interpreting statutes or preparatory work in interpreting treaties—instead of the actual intent of a specific pair of contracting parties.[24]

These same professors also argue that '[d]eference to the intentions of the specific parties is especially inappropriate where there are third party effects', and of course there will be such effects when the 'interpretation of the contract language in one case will impact the contracts for a multitude of other parties who all have essentially the same boilerplate language in their contracts'.[25] In such cases, how do we protect the broader interests of the markets and others in those markets who have no say in the proceedings before the court?

Now here is a radical thought: can we see a blurring of lines—lines that historically have divided civil from criminal proceedings—as a result of a new appreciation of a serious public, or at least market, interest in the outcome of certain financial market cases? Consider: A shoots B and stands trial for the shooting. B forgives A. The state says,

> All well and good. However, we have an issue with people using guns to settle their disputes and a public interest to protect. It's not for you alone to decide to settle this case. That is for the state to decide, and it is also for the state to decide how to progress the matter.

Now that we have seen considerable systemic consequence from market defaults, not just for counterparties but also for a wide range of stakeholders and even pensioners and taxpayers, [26] should we devise better ways to ensure that court decisions take cognisance of

---

[21] The success of the State of Delaware in becoming the 'go to' choice for companies as a place to incorporate in the US turns in no small measure on the fact that its laws are watched over by a sophisticated bench and, through judicial precedents, are particularly well understood.

[22] The contribution of the courts in the build-out of US securities regulation has been widely acknowledged. See eg GM Brown, *Soderquist on the Securities Laws*, 5th edn (New York, Practising Law Institute, 2006) 1–11; TL Hazen, *The Law of Securities Regulation*, 6th edn (St Paul MN, West Publishing Co, 2009) 8: 'In some areas of federal securities law, notably in the registration provisions of the 1933 Act, most of the "law" is found in the rules, forms and policy statements of the Commission, and very little in the form of decided "cases". In other areas, however, notably under general anti-fraud provisions of the 1934 Act, there is very little in the way of formal rules, and the law has developed in the traditional "common law" manner, with courts and other tribunals deciding each case on the basis of precedents.' See also K Pistor and C Xu, 'Incomplete Law' (2003) 35 *New York University Journal of International Law and Policy* 931, 947, pointing to the role of courts to fill in the gaps: 'Interpretation, even if narrowly construed, involves an element of residual lawmaking.'

[23] See Choi and Gulati above n 8.

[24] Ibid, 1131–32.

[25] Ibid, 1132.

[26] Much has been written about the cost to taxpayers of the financial bailout programmes recently announced by a number of governments in response to the financial crisis. However, recognition of taxpayer interest in the outcomes of financial market disputes certainly pre-dates these more recent developments. In earlier financial market cases previously mentioned, courts have recognised the interest of non-party taxpayers and ratepayers in the outcome of the decision. See eg *Hazell v Hammersmith & Fulham London Borough Council* [1992] 2 AC 1; *Bank One Corporation v Commissioner* 120 TC 174 (2003). See also K Matussek, 'Deutsche Bank Wins Swaps Case With German Utilities' *Bloomberg* (11 May 2009), available at www.bloomberg.com/apps/news?pid= 20601100&sid=ay6mLRYjZ.Mo, noting possible adverse consequences for taxpayers of recent German court dismissals of claims following losses on derivatives entered into by state-owned companies and local authorities in Germany and Italy.

a wider market or public interest in appropriate civil cases? Should it be easier for third parties, in order to protect that interest, to have a right to intervene? Should more be invested in getting to right answers, even if that entails approaching aspects of the proceedings in a more prosecutorial way?

F.   Do We Need a World Court?[27]

How do we ensure that (i) national courts stay up-to-date with developments in financial market products and practices, (ii) judges have the requisite competence to unravel facts and apply laws that often predate and did not anticipate these markets (or that were too hastily drafted in response to political pressure resulting from the crisis) and (iii) the risk of a wrong decision contributing to systemic risk in a global and highly interconnected marketplace is mitigated? Do we need an international tribunal for private party financial market disputes or which could perform an advisory role? Let us call it TIME—a Tribunal of International Market Experts (or PRIME—a Panel of Respected International Market Experts . . . but not SUBPRIME!!). That could give us the flexibility to get the right judges (as, in theory, arbitration should, but there are reasons why it has not), which may be a mix of judges with legal training and experience, on the one hand, and lay experts, on the other. It may be not only judges with common law training, but also judges with knowledge of civil code and Islamic finance concepts who collectively represent broad linguistic capability as well. 'The whole that is greater than the sum of its parts.' Indeed, it should be hoped that we can create a college of relevant thinking, with a tribunal or panel at the centre but with feeds from and dialogue with academia, trade bodies, regulators and, in particular, a specialised bar (with relevant experience trumping commercial conflict to a greater extent).

There is a big question mark as to whether our national courts currently have judges competent in these matters. Ad hoc arbitration has been just that—too ad hoc. It has not given us a settled body of law. It also has not attracted the right people. Are there the right people out there? Well, ironically, there are, but we could easily lose them. By the same token, we have a unique opportunity to capture their talent for a greater good.

In the sociology of the financial markets, the phenomenon of a global industry legislating by contract, benefiting from but also building in systemic risk by standardising legal terms for trading and generating these in working groups with sophisticated lawyers from around the world contributing, is not the only phenomenon. Another phenomenon—our opportunity but also our challenge—is that we are about to 'graduate' by retirement a generation of market participants and their advisors, the real experts in this field. They built the legal theory and infrastructure of the derivatives and structured finance industry through the formative years of the business. They understand it.

Until now, they have not been involved to any extent in the litigation from these markets. They have not been available as experts because they have been too actively involved in the markets and, frankly, being an expert has not been remunerative enough to

[27] See also Golden, above n 15. For further developments, see R Davies, 'Courting Attention' (2009) 22 *Risk Magazine* 5. See also J Watson, 'Lawyers Pick Up the Pieces as States Go Bust', *International Bar News*, June 2009, which floats the idea of a world bankruptcy court.

compensate for the lost opportunity cost of involvement (or because they have been conflicted out). This group of sixty-somethings might otherwise disperse, and along with them their collective wisdom—they do not need the money—but a number of them have shown signs of wanting to 'give back' and could perhaps be recruited, in much the same way as world court judges, to play a senior gate-keeping role—and to preserve their legacy.

G.   Conclusion

World financial market law litigation is probably increasing. It is certainly potentially complicated and, partly because of standard contracts and terms and the volume of trading covered by these, wrong decisions threaten systemic risk. In this sense at least, the interest of the markets in the outcome of a case may be far greater than the interest of the parties to that case.

The current reliance on national tribunals of general jurisdiction and ad hoc arbitration is unsatisfactory. It is too decentralised, too inefficient and expensive, and, perhaps most importantly, it is failing to produce a settled and authoritative body of law or the predictability that the markets crave and on which financial stability may depend.

Can we imagine circumstances such as would give rise to a public, or at least a market, interest in certain financial market cases that, because of the potential systemic implications of the facts underlying the case, or any decision on those facts, would justify the proceedings or some aspect of it being taken out of the control of the parties and being pursued in a more prosecutorial way? If we can, how do we cater for that interest in civil litigation?

We need to think creatively about solutions that might move things to a better place. After all, the financial markets have not been shy about being creative, and the issue is, in no small way, the pace of change, the complexity and the multi-cultural influences which must be accommodated—all of which are of the highest order.

We also have another challenge, which is at the same time an opportunity: to capture the collective experience of the financial and legal architects who best understand the complexity and key issues (but who otherwise might exit the business).

Think about it. World trade benefits from the existence of the WTO tribunal and the dedicated bar that it has nurtured. Can it be that international financial market law is any less global than, say, international trade law? Would anyone today say that it is less important or less systemically relevant? Can it be that we should be any less inspired than WTO lawyers in seeking a specialised international tribunal and a specialised bar to appear before it?

I don't think so. What do you think?

6

The Financial Crisis: Regulatory Failure or Systems Failure?

PADDY IRELAND*

A. Introduction

Many people are blaming the current economic crisis on the lack, or laxity, of financial regulation. It is easy to see why they are doing this, for it is not difficult to identify a series of 'regulatory failures' in the field of finance. The views espoused only a few years ago by Howard Davies, the first Chief Executive and Chair of the Financial Services Authority (FSA)—'Consenting Adults in Private? That's Their Problem Really'[1]—now seem rather misguided. As the recent Turner Report observed, the philosophy of the FSA, shared with regulators across the developed world, assumed that 'wholesale market customers are by definition sophisticated and do not need protection' and that 'financial markets innovation delivers benefits to customers and the economy'.[2] It was a philosophy, the Report adds, rooted in 'an overt and authoritatively stated theory that financial innovation had resulted in a significant reduction in financial stability risks'. Unsurprisingly, since the crisis, the whole tenor and tone of the debates surrounding financial and economic regulation has changed. No one doubts that we are going to see a series of regulatory reforms, but how radical will they be? Will they entail paradigmatic change? What vision of the world will animate them?

It has become increasingly clear that many leading politicians and policymakers, including Barack Obama and Gordon Brown, are wedded to the idea that while there is indeed a need for significant regulatory reform, there is nothing fundamentally wrong with the financial system or, indeed, with the economic system as a whole. In the UK, for example, few deny the need to deal with 'specific regulatory failings' and 'excessive and irresponsible behaviour', but both Brown and Alastair Darling have been anxious to stress the inherent value and benefits of free and open markets, and of free financial markets in particular, repeatedly seeking to emphasise that, at a time when their efficacy is being challenged, the benefits of such markets need more than ever to be highlighted and explained. The UK government has been extraordinarily passive in its role as a substantial

---

* Professor, University of Kent Law School.
[1] R Wade, 'Financial Regime Change?' (Sept/Oct 2008) 53 *New Left Review.*
[2] Financial Services Authority, 'The Turner Review: A Regulatory Response to the Global Banking Crisis' (2009) 108–09.

shareholder of bailed out banks, stressing, rather perversely, given the billions spent lifting them off the commercial rocks, its unwillingness to interfere in their commercial decision-making and emphasising its desire to reprivatise them as quickly as possible. In the US, one only has to look at the composition of Obama's top appointees to suspect that the process of regulatory reform is likely to be relatively modest in scope and ambition, and slanted in a very particular direction. Many of them are recycled senior Democrats from the Clinton administration—Summers, Geithner, Gensler, Schapiro—who oversaw the dot.com mania, deregulation binge and stock market bubble and crash of the late 1990s.[3] It is not insignificant that in terms of campaign contributions, Wall Street switched allegiances in 2007–08, offering significantly more to Obama than McCain. In Europe, the approach taken to the problems arising out of derivatives tells a similar story. Initially, the Commission sought a voluntary agreement. Only when this failed to materialise did it propose the establishment of a central clearing house to monitor credit derivatives, and credit default swaps in particular. While this policy marks the abandonment of market self-regulation, it is hardly radical and certainly does not mark a decisive shift away from neoliberal financialisation. In short, then, it has become increasingly clear that the goal of regulatory reform is not likely to be fundamental change but a resurrection of as much of the old system as is reasonably practicable. As many have observed, the reform agenda seems to being driven more by the needs of finance than by the wider needs of society as a whole. This has been vividly reflected in the grave warnings issued by prominent and influential politicians about the dangers of 'politically driven', 'excessive or ill-thought regulation', of 'stifling innovation' and 'swinging the pendulum too far and falling prey to populist tendencies'.[4]

B.   The End of Neoliberalism?

There are, however, good reasons for thinking that the problems are more serious than suggested by the modest reform agenda which is emerging; that what we are seeing is not a mere failure of regulation, but a more fundamental, more systemic failure—a failure, if not of capitalism as a whole, at least of the free market, neoliberal, stock-market-based, financialised, Anglo-American model of capitalism which has been so vigorously promoted in recent years by a host of international institutions and agencies. There are good reasons for thinking, in other words, that what we are facing is a problem with the system rather than a problem within it. From this perspective, what is required is not merely financial reform but what Robert Wade has called 'financial regime change'. But is this likely to be forthcoming? Or are we going to see little more than a reformulation of neoliberalism?

    There is no doubt that, at the ideological level, neoliberalism has suffered a major blow. Notwithstanding the attempts of some of the more zealous market theologians to portray

---

the crisis as a natural disaster[5] and the contorted efforts of others to suggest that it is primarily the fault of 'big government', of insufficient rather than too much market freedom,[6] it will be much harder in the future not only to defend claims about the beneficence of market 'deregulation' but to sustain the idea that there is or can be such a thing as a 'deregulated' or 'free' market. Neoliberalism, with its radical separation of the economic (the market) from the political (and legal), has always been based on misconceptions about the 'naturalness' of markets and these have been cruelly exposed in recent months by the measures now being taken to try to get markets functioning again and the economy back on its feet. The image of some of the most market-oriented institutions rushing headlong, cap-in-hand, to the government for help will not be easy to erase, not least because we are going to be paying for the bail-outs for many years to come.[7] It is not, therefore, only specific theories—such as the 'efficient capital markets' hypothesis—that have lost plausibility, it is the whole intellectual edifice of neoliberalism. The claim that, if 'depoliticised' and allowed to function without political interference, 'the market' and its purely economic rationality will operate to maximise efficiency, wealth and welfare for the benefit of all is hard to sustain as governments frantically intervene to bail out banks, get markets functioning and prevent a complete system-wide financial collapse. So too is the claim that markets are, in essence, purely 'economic' phenomena which somehow exist independently of, and prior to, law and regulation—an idea which finds commonplace expression in the notion that states (political entities) 'intervene' (or 'interfere') in and 'regulate' markets (economic processes). The current debates about regulatory reform are likely to highlight further that markets (and their many different rationalities) and, indeed, private property and private property rights are regulatory products: the creations, not merely the objects, of regulation.[8]

The undermining of neoliberalism at the ideological level does not, however, mean that neoliberalism is going to disappear. The crisis is unlikely to mark the end of neoliberal policies and practices, or the demise of the financialisation and 'new finance capitalism' which lie at the root of today's problems. Joseph Stiglitz was overstating when he claimed that the 'fall of Wall Street is to market fundamentalism what the fall of the Berlin Wall was to communism'.[9] In this context, we should not forget that many thought that the East Asia crisis of 1997–98 would mark the demise of neoliberalism and the end of the Washington consensus, and herald the emergence of a 'new international financial architecture'. In the event, however, the crisis was contained in the periphery and blamed on faults in the affected countries, in particular their 'crony' capitalisms. Indeed, if anything, the reforms which were implemented—the construction and imposition of global standards of so-called 'good governance', exemplified by such things as the OECD's

[5] Alan Greenspan likened it to 'a once-in-a-century credit tsunami' in his testimony to the Committee of Government Oversight and Reform, 23 October 2008.

[6] See, eg M O'Grady 'The Weekend Interview with Gary Becker: Now is no Time to Give up on Markets', *Wall Street Journal*, 21 March 2009, A9. After recovering their poise following the initial shock, many neoliberals, like Becker, have pointed the finger of blame at irresponsible government policies, especially monetary policies, and thus at Greenspan himself.

[7] Leading the undignified rush in the UK, of course, was Northern Rock, whose non-executive chairman in the period preceding the bank's near collapse (2004–07) was Matt Ridley, who in 2006, in response to the question 'What's your dangerous idea?', answered that it was that 'government is the problem not the solution': *The Edge*, 1 January 2006.

[8] See P Ireland, 'Property, Private Government and the Myth of Deregulation' in S Worthington (ed), *Commercial Law and Commercial Practice* (Oxford, Hart Publishing, 2003)

[9] J Stiglitz, *Huffington Post*, 16 September 2008, available at www.huffingtonpost.com/.

Principles of Corporate Governance[10] and the IMF's Reports on the Observance of Standards and Codes—created a platform for the further growth of financial capital, not least by promising outside investors greater protection. The mere fact that we are likely to see a raft of regulatory reforms does not, therefore, in itself mark a shift away from neoliberalism. All markets are, in important senses, regulatory products, and neoliberalism is characterised not so much by 'deregulation' as by regulation of a certain tenor and type: it is quite possible to have regulation which is neoliberal in orientation. As David Harvey has observed, there is a yawning gap between the anti-state, anti-regulatory rhetoric of neoliberalism and actual neoliberal practices and policies, which often entail extensive state regulation.[11]

Nor should we forget how far neoliberal ideas and policies have become institutionally embedded around the world, and how far our culture and social practices have been financialised. Despite the calls for a new Bretton Woods, the sorts of regulatory reforms currently being proposed seem unlikely to effect major changes in this regard. In the corporate governance context, for example, the idea of 'shareholder value'—one of the principal expressions of neoliberal financialisation—has in recent years become the guiding light of corporate governance in Anglo-American jurisdictions. Vigorously promoted by the OECD and the World Bank, a highly financialised, Anglo-American, shareholder value model of governance has also made progress in places such as Japan and Germany.[12] Will the crisis see this model challenged? While the recent comments of the former CEO of General Electric, Jack Welch, to the effect that shareholder value was a 'dumb idea'[13] suggest this is a possibility, the seemingly rapid restoration of the 'bonus culture' among executives suggests otherwise. So too does the initial OECD response to the implications of the crisis for corporate governance. In a recent report, the OECD concedes that the crisis can 'to an important extent' be attributed to 'failures and weaknesses' in corporate governance arrangements. What is recommended, however, is not a fundamental re-examination of the shareholder-oriented, shareholder-value model, but more safeguards against excessive risk taking, better board oversight and more carefully designed remuneration systems.[14] In short, neoliberal ideas are not going to disappear simply because reality seems to be disproving them. In this context, it is worth noting that the Geithner plan for dealing with the 'toxic' (or 'legacy') assets held by US banks is ultimately based on the belief that the underlying problem is the absence of a market for them (the result of nobody knowing what they are worth). The proposed solution thus entails using state subsidies to create such a market. As the state/taxpayer bears most of the risk, the solution amounts to an invitation to private investors to have a flutter on the value of these assets: if they are worth something, investors could make pots of money; if they are not, the taxpayer will pick up (most of) the bill. It is hardly surprising that this has been described as socialism for the rich, in which profits are privatised and losses socialised.

Finally, we should not forget just how powerful and influential financial interests are. One only has to look at the furious reaction of UK hedge funds and private equity firms to

---

[10] Organisation for Economic Cooperation and Development, *Principles of Corporate Governance* (Paris, OECD, 2004); International Monetary Fund, Reports on the Observance of Standards and Codes, available at www.imf.org/external/np/rosc/rosc.asp.

[11] D Harvey, *A Brief History of Neoliberalism* (Oxford, Oxford University Press, 2005).

[12] See, eg R Dore, 'Japan's Conversion to Investor Capitalism' in DH Whittaker and S Deakin (eds), *Corporate Governance and Managerial Reform in Japan* (Oxford, Oxford University Press, 2009).

[13] F Guerrera, 'Welch Condemns Share Price Focus', *Financial Times*, 12 March 2009, 1.

[14] G Kirkpatrick, 'The Corporate Governance Lessons from the Financial Crisis' (Paris, OECD, 2009).

the draft EU Directive on Alternative Investment Fund Managers and the response their threats elicited from the UK government to see the political power they wield. Stepping up their campaign against the draft Directive, they warned the Treasury that they might have to leave the UK and relocate unless significant changes were agreed. The government response was swift. Lord Myners chastised the Commission for producing 'naive' proposals and, at a meeting organised by the FSA, a Treasury representative reassured 'almost a dozen of London's top managers' that 'they would fight for changes' on their behalf.[15] This serves to remind us that the hegemony of neoliberal ideology was always based more on the powerful interests supporting and promoting it than on its real-world plausibility or achievements.

C.   The Neoliberal Vision

If the regulatory reforms are primarily aimed, as they were following earlier crises, at getting as much of the old system—with all its economic, social, environmental and ethical flaws—up and running again, will they work? Unlike the reforms implemented following the 1997–98 crisis, it seems inevitable that some constraints will be placed on finance. Things such as new rules on capital adequacy and on the licensing or quasi-licensing of acceptable financial products are virtually inevitable following a crisis which has dwarfed previous crises and centred not on the periphery but the very heart of modern global capitalism, the US. It remains to be seen, however, how great these constraints will be. As events unfold, it is likely to become ever clearer that for the majority of people what we have is a much deeper-rooted, systemic failure which is unlikely to be remedied by a few modest regulatory reforms. At the moment, policymakers seem to have managed successfully to stabilise the financial system. They might also—though this is far from certain—be able to get the economy moving again in the coming months and years. But even if they succeed, the neoliberal vision of the path to individual and collective health, wealth and happiness, which has been so vigorously and ruthlessly promoted around the world by policymakers, is, for most people, unravelling.

Neoliberalism suggests that by using market mechanisms, and in particular by developing and expanding financial markets, economic efficiency, growth and welfare can be maximised. At the general economic level, the vision it promotes is one of shareholder-oriented enterprises, operating in a world of open capital and product markets which compel managers to maximise 'shareholder value' and economic efficiency. At the individual level, the vision is one of a world of autonomous, self-reliant, 'responsible', 'financially literate' owners of intangible financial property (property which confers on its holders rights to receive revenues in the future) who achieve personal security not through social insurance but through the ownership of assets (houses) and financial property (private pensions). Thus, recent decades have seen social welfare and security around the world increasingly 'privatised'. The key to personal security, especially in old age, we have

---

[15] See J Macintosh, G Parker and N Tait 'Hedge Funds Threaten to Quit UK over Draft EU Investment Laws', *Financial Times*, 3 June 2009, 1. The Directive would regulate a range of funds from hedge funds and private equity funds to real estate funds and commodity funds. It is hardly very radical and has been described by Poul Nyrop Rasmussen, President of PES (Party of European Socialists), as having 'more holes than a Swiss cheese' (29 April 2009) available at www.pes.org.

been told, is no longer to be found in collective action by the state but in the expansion of individual financial property ownership through pension funds and the development of capital markets. It is to be found, in other words, in the 'financialisation of the masses'.[16] The neoliberal world is thus what Jose Pinera, the architect of pension privatisation in Chile and now one of its most vigorous global advocates, has called a world of 'worker-capitalists'. It is a world of 'shareholder democracies' and 'ownership societies'. Indeed, the link between these two different dimensions of the neoliberal vision was made explicit in the 1994 World Bank report which marked the beginning of its campaign to privatise pensions. In *Averting the Old Age Crisis: Policies to Protect the Old and Promote Growth*, the 'and' was deliberately underlined.[17] Both parts of the vision are now unravelling.

D.   The Neoliberal Vision Unravels

Quite apart from the growing number of commentators—particularly in the relatively affluent, developed world—who are questioning whether the search for endless economic growth is indeed the route to social welfare and 'happiness',[18] the neoliberal vision of the road to growth and increased material prosperity and welfare for all is beginning to look increasingly threadbare.

Despite the claims made for the benefits which flow from free markets, free finance and neoliberalism, overall growth rates in the period 1980–2000—the era of finance-dominated growth—were lower than in the earlier, post-Second World War, Bretton Woods era of financial repression. 'The presumption, widely held before 1997,' wrote John Eatwell and Lance Taylor in 2000, 'that financial liberalization is invariably beneficial has now been abandoned by almost [all?] serious commentators.'[19] Post-crisis, of course, the prospects for sustained growth in the coming years are pretty bleak. If the short-to-medium term economic consequences of the crisis for many in the developed world are likely to be damaging, for many in the developing world they are likely to be catastrophic. Indeed, it now seems clear that such growth as was achieved in recent years was based in significant part on the reckless expansion of credit and a string of bubbles in the values of assets (such as houses) and intangible financial property forms (from collateralised debt obligations to corporate shares). In similar vein, in the corporate context, there is growing evidence that the obsession with 'shareholder value' and with maximising the short-term financial performance of corporations has impeded 'real' productive performance; that the techniques deployed to enhance shareholder value and financial performance have served to diminish rather than increase 'real' investment and improvements in productive performance. Although there is recognition that the corporate incentive structures that were created have operated somewhat perversely, there are few signs that they are going to be

---

[16] See I Erturk et al (eds), *Financialization at Work* (London, Routledge, 2008).

[17] World Bank, *Averting the Old Age Crisis: Policies to Protect the Old and Promote Growth* (Washington, DC, World Bank, 1994).

[18] See, eg R Layard, *Happiness: Lessons from a New Science* (London, Penguin, 2006); O James, *Affluenza* (Sydney, Random House, 2007).

[19] J Eatwell and L Taylor, *Global Finance at Risk: The Case for International Regulation* (New York, New Press, 2000) ix.

radically overhauled. The focus on finding ways, using share options and other perfor-mance-related remuneration packages, and the constant threat of hostile takeover or leveraged buy-out, to align the financial interests of managers with those of shareholders seems likely to continue, as does the drive to maximise shareholder value. At the moment, the changes which look likely to be implemented seem to entail adjusting corporate incentive structures to try to ensure that managers take a slightly more 'enlightened', longer-term view of shareholder value. The paradoxical result is that, while regulatory reform in this context might temper the highly financialised forms of corporate governance which have emerged in recent years, it might also entrench and reinforce them.

E.   An Alternative Account of Neoliberalism and Financialisation

It is not only the neoliberal vision of the road to growth and development that is unrav-elling, however. The rapid decline in house prices and, even more importantly perhaps, the collapse of private pensions has left the vision of a world of neoliberal individuals—auton-omous, self-reliant, financial property owners—and of shareholding 'ownership societies' in tatters.[20] It is possible that this will prove politically quite significant.

An alternative account of the neoliberal project and of the forces underlying financialisation has been sketched by commentators such as David Harvey and Robert Brenner.[21] This alternative account suggests that neoliberalism is best and most accurately seen as a class project aimed at restoring profitability and increasing the share of the social product accruing to capital and financial property.[22] Thus Brenner argues that the vitality of advanced economies everywhere has been declining since the 1970s, and especially since 2000, with economic performance in the US, western Europe and Japan steadily deterio-rating in terms of standard economic indicators such as GDP, investment and real wages. The business cycle that began in 2001 and ended in 2007 was, he suggests, 'by far' the weakest of the post-war period, despite 'the greatest government sponsored economic stimulus in US peacetime history'. Brenner attributes these problems to a deep and lasting decline in the rate of profit dating from the end of the 1960s, a decline which has not been reversed despite increasingly stagnant real wages. These profitability problems, he argues, are ultimately attributable to a chronic, systemic tendency towards overcapacity. Ironically, therefore, the attempt to restore profitability by holding down wages failed to solve the problem in large part because it simultaneously served to depress aggregate demand. In the 1970s and 1980s, and again from the mid-1990s,[23] an alternative strategy was adopted,

---

[20] Though this has not prevented the recent emergence of so-called 'Red Toryism', led by Philip Blond and based on strikingly similar notions of expanding 'financial citizenship'.

[21] See Harvey, above n 10; R Brenner, *The Economics of Global Turbulence: the Advanced Capitalist Economies from Long Boom to Long Downturn, 1945–2005* (London, Verso, 2005); R Brenner, 'Interview' (March–April 2009) *Against the Current*.

[22] See Harvey, above n 10; G Duménil and D Lévy (trans D Jeffers), *Capital Resurgent: Roots of the Neoliberal Revolution* (Cambridge, MA, Harvard University Press, 2005).

[23] Led by the Clinton administration, in the early 1990s an alternative strategy of balanced budgets was tried out. However, the moves to reduce deficits hit demand, bringing about the recession and slow growth of the early 1990s and prompting (from around 1995) the policy of low interest rates, which precipitated the growth of private borrowing and debt.

that of boosting demand by increasing public and private debt: hence the encouragement given by both governments and regulators to the spiralling debt, bubbles and speculation which have sustained the economy in the last decade or so. It is this strategy which has imploded.

For a while, however, it appeared to be working. Growing home ownership, rising house prices and increased financial property ownership helped to compensate for increasingly stagnant real wages. Amidst the rise of the credit card culture, household debt increased massively, often on the strength of rising equity in homes. Together these developments helped not only to create a false sense of prosperity but also to build political support for the ruling, neoliberal ideas of the age. It was, for example, the spread of financial property ownership through utility privatisations and the growth in private pensions that underlay the claim that 'we are all (more or less) shareholders now' and the claim that shareholder-oriented corporations seeking to maximise shareholder value operate for the benefit of us all. In reality, however, despite its undoubted spread in recent years, financial property ownership has remained very heavily concentrated in the wealthiest elites of the population. In the US, for example, the wealthiest 10% own over 80% of total financial property and the wealthiest 1% alone own over 40% of company shares.[24] From this perspective, it is hardly surprising that one the most striking effects of neoliberalism in the last three or so decades has been the stagnation of 'real' wages for most people and the rise in income and wealth inequalities. Moreover, it is now clear that the money that was being poured into mortgages and into financial markets by people seeking to provide for themselves, particularly in old age, was, compounded by the global savings glut, simply fuelling the asset price bubbles.

With the bursting of those bubbles, the last 18 or so months have seen the gradual but inexorable disintegration of the key elements of the neoliberal 'ownership society'. House prices have now plummeted and private pension schemes are in a catastrophic state, as are public finances; unemployment has risen and is still rising. It is becoming ever clearer that for most people social security simply cannot be achieved through financial property ownership. The US sub-prime mortgage crisis was prompted in significant part by the desire to incorporate—through financialisation—the American working class—starting with the relatively well-off working class before moving on to the less-well-off, predominantly African-American and Latino, working class. In what amounted to an alternative social welfare plan, people with no income were debt-financed. The authorities, still engaged in fire-fighting, have yet to confront the longer term implications of the collapse of this vision fully.

F.   Towards a More Radical Reform Agenda

Despite the undoubted damage done to neoliberal ideology, we can expect huge efforts to be made to try to secure the pre-eminent economic position of finance and to re-establish the integrity and value of financial property—whatever the cost for the majority of the population in terms of reduced public services and wages, higher taxes and personal (and

[24] G Draffan, 'Facts on the Concentration of Wealth', available at http://www.endgame.org/primer-wealth.html (accessed on 21 August 2009).

old age) insecurity. If, from this perspective, the bank bail-out represented a kind of coup by finance and wealthy financial property owners, the regulatory reforms which are now being implemented might well turn out to be the process whereby those groups regain their equilibrium and power and secure their interests for the future. It seems likely that we are about to enter a new era of 'prudent', but nevertheless fundamentally neoliberal, financial regulation.

This is not to say, however, that the present conjuncture does not provide an opportunity—a policy window—for more radical reform. The financial architecture is going to be redesigned, at least to some extent, and it is clear that the authorities themselves do not know exactly what the new architecture will or should look like: the term 'bricolage' may well turn out to be apposite here too. Politically, radical reform does not, at present, seem likely. However, things could change, particularly if, as seems inevitable, the measures that have to be taken to protect financial institutions and financial property interests require the adoption of very particular social and economic policies entailing long-term mandated austerity for the masses. If profitability is to be restored and state debt reduced, public expenditure will have to be severely reduced and taxes raised. We are already seeing calls for pay restraint, and these calls are likely to become even louder in the future. Crucially, this mandated austerity is likely to highlight further both the disparities in the treatment of different groups—exemplified for many by the forgiveness being shown towards the debts of the rich but not towards the victims of foreclosure—and the collapse of the neoliberal vision of an 'ownership society'. Will this prompt a populist backlash? And, even it did, would the backlash be directed against executive remuneration, corporate bonuses and the power of financial interests, rather than immigrants and crooked MPs? And would it lead to a deeper and more focused struggle?

There are good reasons for thinking that the structural problems are as serious as Brenner suggests and that there will much hardship in the coming years, so this is not out of the question. There are, therefore, very good reasons for trying to begin to develop a more radical reform agenda. Here, briefly, are a few starting points. First, at the most general level, there is an urgent need to reduce finance to the role of servant, not master. This would entail, inter alia, banning, rather than merely regulating, certain speculative financial instruments. Banks need to be turned into genuine public utilities—nationalised in quite a different way from that at present. This would pave the way for what Keynes called the 'somewhat comprehensive socialization of investment'.[25] We also need to re-conceptualise the large public corporation as a social or quasi-social institution, something which in many cases would entail the demotion of shareholders to the status of something like preferred creditors. Finally, as part of the process of making finance, financial markets and financial property socially and economically less important and of making proper provision for most people in old age, we need to restore the state pension.

---

[25] JM Keynes, *The General Theory of Employment, Interest and Money* (London, Macmillan, 1936).

7

Beyond 'Light Touch' Regulation of British Banks after the Financial Crisis

ROMAN TOMASIC[*]

A. Introduction

We have reached a turning point in our efforts to regulate banks and financial institutions by resorting to current risk-based models and regulatory structures. As is evident from failures during the global financial crisis that burst upon the scene in late 2007, the use of these risk-based and self-regulatory models has been seen by many to be seriously flawed. This failure may be attributed to many causes, such as flawed assumptions of rating agencies, the limits of model building as an exercise, and the ease with which such efforts have been compromised by behavioural and political factors that influence markets. These behavioural factors include the power of market euphoria and the influence of perverse incentives, which have driven excessive risk taking.[1] Political factors have included the uncritical commitment to self-regulation and the capacity of markets to regulate themselves.[2]

Whilst risk is an inherent feature of modern times, the questions that arise here are the degree to which banking regulation should depend exclusively upon the use of narrow (and inevitably imperfect) mathematical risk models[3] and the extent to which these need to be supplemented by the application of legal rules, as well as other regulatory techniques that have emerged from the study of corporations and professionals.[4] However, the limits of law as a mechanism for social ordering should also not be

---

[*] Professor, Durham Law School.

[1] See further RJ Shiller, *Irrational Exuberance*, 2nd edn (New York, Currency Doubleday, 2007); and H Shefrin, *Beyond Greed and Fear—Understanding Behavioral Finance and the Psychology of Investing* (Oxford, Oxford University Press, 2007).

[2] JC Coffee, 'What went wrong? An initial inquiry into the causes of the 2008 Financial Crisis' (2009) 9 *Journal of Corporate Law Studies* 1; Also see generally: RA Posner, *A Failure of Capitalism—The Crisis of '08 and the Descent into Depression* (Cambridge, MA, Harvard University Press, 2009). In regard to the effect of other human factors, see generally P Augur, *Chasing Alpha—How Reckless Growth and Unchecked Ambition Ruined the City's Golden Decade* (London, The Bodley Head, 2009); and G Tett, *Fool's Gold—How Unrestrained Greed Corrupted a Dream, Shattered Global markets and Unleashed a Catastrophe* (London, Little Brown 2009).

[3] An excellent overview of efforts to understand risk is provided by PL Bernstein, *Against the Gods—The Remarkable Story of Risk* (New York, John Wiley & Sons, 1998).

[4] Some useful scholarly studies of this area include those by: DW Arner, *Economic Stability, Economic Growth and the Role of Law* (Cambridge, Cambridge University Press, 2007); A Campbell and P Cartwright, *Banks in Crisis—The Legal Response* (Aldershot, Ashgate Publishing Limited, 2002); and BE Gup

overestimated.[5] Other factors, such as the existence of mutual trust and an appreciation of wider stakeholder interests, are also important ingredients of any effective regulatory system. This has led to calls for more responsive forms of regulation, although little of this work has focused upon the banking and finance sectors.[6]

It is interesting to note that the economic historian Eric Hobsbawn recently expressed the view that the current economic crisis is 'the end of the era in the development of the global capitalist system'.[7] He added that, just as centrally planned communist economies were doomed to failure, so too was the organisation of the global economy on an 'effectively unregulated basis'.

The Deputy Governor of the Bank of England, Charles Bean, also pointed recently to the magnitude of the credit crisis by observing that '[t]his is a once in a lifetime crisis, and possibly the largest financial crisis of its kind in human history'.[8] Other key former US finance officials, such as Hank Paulson, the former Secretary of the Treasury, and Alan Greenspan, the former Chairman of the Federal Reserve, have also frequently referred to the magnitude of the current crisis.

The lack of rigorous regulation of financial markets in the UK may be attributed to the retention of features of the older gentlemanly system of self-regulation that had prevailed in the City of London prior to the internationalisation of the financial sector after London's 'big bang'.[9] The establishment of the Financial Services Authority (FSA) and the enactment of the Financial Services and Markets Act 2000 were intended to resolve this weakness by creating a single stronger regulator.[10] However, the regulatory objectives of this new scheme were soon seen as being very weak or 'woolly', as AE Goodhart had noted in 2000.[11]

Goodhart's assessment proved to be accurate if we reflect upon what has occurred during the current financial crisis, and it also suggests that we should now be looking for more sophisticated models of regulation to deal with the new environment that we now find ourselves in. For example, the strong adherence in the UK to a large number of regulatory rules and private codes in regard to financial services when compared to other

(ed), *Corporate Governance in Banking: A Global Perspective* (Cheltenham, Edward Elgar, 2007). Also, see generally E Ferran and AE Goodhart, *Regulating Financial Services and Markets in the 21st Century* (Oxford, Hart Publishing, 2002).

[5] See generally D McBarnet, 'Corporate Social Responsibility beyond Law, through Law, for Law: The New Corporate Accountability' in D McBarnet, A Voiculescu and T Campbell (eds) *The New Corporate Accountability—Corporate Social Responsibility and the Law* (Cambridge, Cambridge University Press, 2007).

[6] See generally R Baldwin and J Black, 'Really Responsive Regulation' (2008) 71 *Modern Law Review* 59. See also J Gray and J Hamilton, *Implementing Financial Regulation* (Chichester, John Wiley & Sons, 2006).

[7] See further 'Will the Bail-out Work?', *vox pop*, 9 October 2008, available at www.guardian.co.uk/commentisfree/2008/oct/09/economy.creditcrunch (all URLs accessed on 27 December 2009); also see A Bruce interview with E Hobsbawm, 3 November 2008, money.uk.msn.com/investing/articles/morecommentary/article.aspx?cp-documentid=10465208.

[8] Reuters, 'Bank's Bean Says Crisis May be Worst in History' (24 October 2008), available at www.iht.com/articles/reuters/2008/10/24/business/OUKBS-UK-BRITAIN-BANK-BEAN.php.

[9] See further P Augar, *The Death of Gentlemanly Capitalism* (London, Penguin Books, 2000).

[10] E Ferran, 'The Liberalisation of Financial Markets: The Regulatory Response in the United Kingdom' in R Grote and T Marauhn (eds), *The Regulation of International Financial Markets—Perspectives for Reform* (Cambridge, Cambridge University Press, 2006) 59–62.

[11] Referred to by Ferran, ibid, 65. Professor Ferran also noted (75) that the FSA faced enormous challenges after it was established as it was given heavy responsibilities, but had been provided with a small number of staff and an inadequate funding base. See further AE Goodhart, 'Regulating the Regulator: An Economist's Perspective on Accountability and Control' in E Ferran and AE Goodhart (eds), *Regulating Financial Services and Markets in the Twenty-First Century* (Oxford, Hart Publishing, 2001).

countries, such as Australia and the US, might need to be reassessed.[12] Also, as has been officially recognised, current government regulatory structures in this area are in need of a major overhaul or replacement. The passage of the Banking Act in 2009 was but the first of many efforts that will be required to be made to refashion existing regulatory arrangements.[13]

B.   In Search of Risk Models for Banks

Acknowledgement of this comprehensive systemic failure has come from some of those who tried most vocally to support efforts to develop reliable risk models.[14] One of those who have acknowledged the limits of modelling was Alan Greenspan. Greenspan had for some time been pointing to the fact that markets were driven by what he described as 'irrational exuberance' and that 'we will never have a perfect model of risk' as the market models that had been used to describe market forces did not fully capture irrational 'innate human responses'. These arguments served merely to avoid directly confronting more fundamental problems.[15]

Interestingly, others, such as the Bank of England's Director for Financial Stability, have also pointed out that the cause of the current crisis can be found in unrealistic risk models that were based on very short-term views of the past, usually only based on economic events from the previous decade.[16] As is now widely acknowledged, risk models need to draw upon a much longer data set to be reliable.

Writing in April 2008, Greenspan remained largely confident that government regulation of financial markets was as effective as it was capable of being and that 'free competitive markets are the unrivalled way to organise economies'.[17] Implicit here was a reluctance to accept suggestions that there was a place for government in the market; adherence to this view was, however, to fail several months later.[18] Confidence in the

---

[12] See generally J Black, 'Law and Regulation: The Case of Finance' in C Parker et al (eds), *Regulating Law* (Oxford, Oxford University Press, 2005) 45.

[13] See further R Tomasic, 'Creating a Template for Banking Insolvency Reform After the Collapse of Northern Rock' (2009) 22 *Insolvency Intelligence* 65 (Part 1) and (2009) 22 *Insolvency Intelligence* 81 (Part 2).

[14] The Chief Executive of Goldman Sacks, Lloyd Blankfein, has, for example, provided a reasoned defence of the need to preserve opportunities for risk taking; Blankfein calls for a separation of risk control and business functions in banks and the need to take into account the full implications of off-balance sheet exposures: L Blankfein, 'Do Not Destroy the Essential Catalyst of Risk', *Financial Times*, 9 February 2009, 13.

[15] A Greenspan, 'We Will Never Have a Perfect Model of Risk', *Financial Times*, 16 March 2008). Similar arguments had been made by behavioural economists such as RJ Shiller, *The New Financial Risk in the 21st Century Order* (Princeton, Princeton University Press, 2003); RJ Shiller, *Irrational Exuberance*, 2nd edn (New York, Currency Doubleday, 2005); RJ Shiller, *The Subprime Solution—How Today's Global Financial Crisis Happened, and What to Do About It* (Princeton, Princeton University Press, 2008); and GA Akerlof and RJ Shiller, *Animal Spirits—How Human Psychology Drives the Economy and Why it Matters for Global Capitalism* (Princeton, Princeton University Press, 2009).

[16] N Cohen, 'Financial Meltdown Blamed on Risk Models', *Financial Times*, 14–15 February 2009. More extensive statements of similar arguments have been made by others: see, eg NN Taleb, *The Black Swan—The Impact of the Highly Improbable* (London, Penguin, 2007); BB Mandlebrot and RL Hudson, *The (Mis)Behaviour of Markets—A Fractal View of Risk, Ruin and Reward* (London, Profile Books, 2008).

[17] A Greenspan, 'The Fed is Blameless on the Property Bubble', *Financial Times*, 7 April 2009.

[18] A Greenspan, 'The World must Repel Calls to Contain Competitive Markets', *Financial Times*, 5 August 2008, 11. This approach has not gone without criticism; see, eg J Kay, 'Greenspan could have found a cure at the pharmacy', *Financial Times*, 25 February 2009, 13.

self-regulatory capacities of markets was to suffer considerably after the collapse of Lehman Brothers with its filing for bankruptcy in September 2008. In late October 2008 Greenspan appeared before the Congressional Committee on Oversight and Government Reform in Washington DC and, during questioning, he noted that the credit crisis had been precipitated by 'the failure to properly price . . . risky assets'. Greenspan added that he had been 'partially' wrong in his opposition to stronger government regulation of markets.[19]

The selfish conduct of banks in failing to support each other during the current financial crisis came as a shock to Greenspan, as was evident when he admitted before a US Congressional Committee in October 2008 that he had been wrong in placing complete faith in the self-regulatory powers of financial markets. Greenspan pointed to the extraordinary nature of current events and told the Congress that we were experiencing a 'once in a century credit tsunami'. In discussing the failure of banks to provide credit to each other, Greenspan admitted: '[t]hose of us who have looked to the self-interest of lending institutions to protect shareholders' equity, myself included, are in a state of shocked disbelief'. Committee Chairman Henry A Waxman asked Mr Greenspan: 'Do you feel that your ideology pushed you to make decisions that you wish you had not made?' In reply, Greenspan conceded, 'Yes, I've found a flaw. I don't know how significant or permanent it is. But I've been very distressed by that fact.'[20]

The notion that government should not intervene in markets has led to an almost blind faith in the power of the 'invisible hand' to ensure that markets are self-correcting. It also traumatised governments and regulatory agencies, and prevented them from assuming greater responsibilities in the face of excessive risk taking behaviour in the market. The failure of banks to support each other by providing credit seemed to imply a more fundamental instability in financial markets than Greenspan had been prepared to acknowledge. In this regard, it is interesting to note that economists such as Joseph Schumpeter had long pointed to the self-destructive features of capitalism (which he famously saw as a process of creative destruction).[21] Later Hyman Minsky was to elaborate upon this theme when he pointed out that '[f]inancial instability is a deep-seated characteristic of a capitalist economy with a sophisticated financial system'. He then argued that an institutional framework needed to be created to seek to 'attenuate if not eliminate the economy's thrust towards instability'.[22]

For Minsky, big government was both a blessing and a curse. This was in contrast to those, such as Milton Friedman, whose confidence in the power of markets was such as to lead them to argue that market processes will create a full-employment equilibrium.[23] Friedman's trust in the capacity of markets to achieve equilibrium parallels Greenspan's faith in the self-correcting power of financial markets, something that has been shown to have collapsed in the current crisis. The ideological adherence to Friedmanite ideas in the UK has done much to undermine the role of government as a stabilising and supportive institution in relation to markets. A system that has also stressed shareholder value at the

---

[19] T Bawden, 'Alan Greenspan Admits some Mistakes', *Times Online*, 23 October 2008, available at http://business.timesonline.co.uk/tol/business/economics/article5003610.ece?print=ye.

[20] Quoted by EL Andrews, 'Greenspan Concedes Error on Regulation', *New York Times*, 23 October 2008, available at www.nytimes.com/2008/10/24/business/economy/24panel.html?_r=1&hp.

[21] See further JA Schumpeter, *Capitalism, Socialism and Democracy* (New York, Harper & Row, 1976).

[22] HP Minsky, *Stabilizing an Unstable Economy* (New York, McGraw Hill, 2008) 315.

[23] Referred to by Minsky, ibid, 196.

expense of other considerations[24] has been vulnerable to short-sighted and narrow conceptions of corporate objectives; this 'short-termism' is as applicable to banks as it is to other companies in a society in which financialisation has become the dominant feature of the economy.[25] It was therefore interesting to note that the former CEO of General Electric, Jack Welch, once regarded as the champion of the shareholder-value orthodoxy, pointed out that this short-term approach was 'the dumbest idea in the world' as 'shareholder value' should be seen as a result and not as a strategy: 'Your main constituencies are your employees, your customers and your products.'[26]

Before the crisis, the Bank of England had adopted an approach to banking regulation that seemed to have been heavily influenced by Greenspan's market-based approach. An illustration of the enthusiasm for these ideas is reflected in the fact that the UK awarded Alan Greenspan an honorary knighthood in 2002 'in recognition of his outstanding contribution to global economic stability and the benefit that the UK has received from the wisdom and skill with which he has led the US Federal Reserve board'.[27] According to Sir John Gieve, the former Deputy Governor of the Bank of England, this approach meant that markets should be allowed to have their effect and that government should only get involved to 'mop-up' after a bubble has burst.[28] This restraint is in part attributable to economists' obsession with the moral hazard that may be caused by government intervention. That idea seems to have suffered a major blow after repeated government efforts to bail out heavily indebted banks. Gieve went on to point out that 'one lesson we have learnt from the crisis is that we cannot leave risk management to the banks'.[29]

However, as Satyajit Das pointed out in his very readable book on derivatives trading, risk management has a clear purpose for banks as they 'must take risks in order to make money. Increasingly, banks have to take more and more risks as client business just doesn't pay'.[30] Of the four types of risk that Das identified (market risk, credit risk, liquidity risk and operational risk), banks often do not focus upon those that affect them most. As Das explained,

> In banks, the biggest risk by a significant margin is credit risk, and liquidity and operational risk are probably next. Market risk is the smallest. Perversely, banks have, until recently, spent much of their efforts in quantifying and managing market risk, which may be because it lends itself to quantification. The precision is mostly false.[31]

Das also pointed to the 'illusion of precision' in risk management and noted that risk

---

[24] Not surprisingly, neo-liberal ideas of this kind are also found in the ideas of FA Hayek, who had argued that in a system that assumes the primacy of shareholder value, wider considerations are difficult to justify; see generally FA Hayek, *Law, Legislation and Liberty*, vol 3 (Chicago, IL, University of Chicago Press, 1979) ch 15, especially 82; also see D Harvey, *A Brief History of Neoliberalism* (Oxford, Oxford University Press, 2007). These kinds of ideas dominated Thatcherist policies and continued to have influence until recent times in regard to financial markets, despite efforts to adopt a broader stakeholder approach to corporate governance in reforms now found in the Companies Act 2006.

[25] See generally J Froud, C Haslam, S Johal and K Williams, *Financialization and Strategy* (London, Routledge, 2006).

[26] Quoted by F Guerrera, 'Future of Capitalism: A Need to Reconnect', *Financial Times* supplement: The Future of Capitalism: The Big Debate, 12 March 2009, 33, available at www.ft.com.capitalism.

[27] *Daily Telegraph*, 7 August 2002.

[28] C Giles, 'Gieve Challenges many Bank Orthodoxies', *Financial Times*, 20 February 2009, 2.

[29] Quoted by N Pratley, 'Viewpoint—Past Failings Catch Up with FSA', *The Guardian*, 26 February 2009, 27.

[30] S Das, *Traders, Guns & Money—Known and Unknowns in the Dazzling World of Derivatives* (Harlow, Prentice Hall, 2006) 178. See also generally E Avgouleas, 'The Global Financial Crisis, Behavioural Finance and Financial Regulation: In Search of a New Orthodoxy' (2009) 9 *Journal of Corporate Law Studies* 23.

[31] Das, ibid, 158.

models are usually only well understood by those with advanced mathematical skills, adding that '[m]ost bank managers, directors and regulators didn't have the requisite skills' and that '[m]ost of the inputs required were either unavailable or difficult to verify'.[32] This makes adequate risk management by senior executives and directors in banks problematic.

Within financial institutions, those professional risk managers who speak out about perceived risks are also in danger of being silenced during market bubbles (as was seen with the dismissal of Paul Moore at HBOS).[33] Moreover, as risk managers usually enjoy much less prestige than frontline traders in banks, risk concerns are not easily articulated in an organisation that is overwhelmed by market euphoria.[34] As a result, as Taleb and Triana[35] pointed out, it was commonplace for risk managers to simply act as silent bystanders, even though they knew the limits of risk models that continued to be in use, and even though similar models were known to have clearly failed, such as in the collapse of Long-Term Capital Management a decade earlier.[36] On the other hand, excessive risk taking has been tolerated as it has been linked to bankers' compensation packages, which, as Henry Kaufman has argued, 'often favour aggressive risk-taking'.[37] This unbalanced incentives structure tended to foster 'short-termism' and perverse motivations and rewards within banks. A recent OECD report pointed to the need to match risk management and the incentives structure of a company, and noted that in the current crisis '[t]here appears to have been in many cases a severe mismatch between the incentive system, risk management and internal control systems'.[38]

C.   Beyond Exclusive Reliance upon Self-regulation in Financial Markets

Until the bursting of the credit bubble in late August and early September 2007 at the time of the collapse of Northern Rock, there was almost universal agreement that markets could be allowed to regulate themselves and that industry actors would see it as being in their self-interest to ensure that markets continued to operate effectively. In the US these hopes were not completely dashed until the collapse of Lehman Brothers a year later. These market assumptions have now been shown to be false, and we have seen an unprecedented surge of public money being poured into failed banks and financial institutions in an effort to prop them up so as to preserve systemic stability.

---

[32] Das, ibid, 159–60.

[33] See further the P Moore memo at ftalphaville.ft.com. Also see: A Cox, '"Confident" Moore Stands by his Claims', *Financial Times*, 12 February 2009, 2; J Croft, 'Evidence Triggered Crosby's Departure', *Financial Times*, 12 February 2009, 3; J Eagleman and J Hughes, 'Opposition Queries PM's Judgment', *Financial Times*, 12 February 2009, 2.

[34] See further OECD Steering Group on Corporate Governance, *Corporate Governance Lessons from the Financial Crisis* (Paris, OECD, 2009) 11.

[35] NN Taleb and P Triana, 'Bystanders to this Financial Crime Were Many', *Financial Times*, 8 December 2008.

[36] R Lowenstein, *When Genius Failed—The Rise and Fall of Long-Term Capital Management* (London, Fourth Estate 2002).

[37] H Kaufman, 'Finance's Upper Tier Needs Closer Scrutiny', *Financial Times*, 21 April 2008, 15.

[38] OECD, above n 34, 6.

The fashioning of new dimensions of a regulatory order to deal with banks, and other financial institutions that have been seen as comprising a 'shadow banking' system, has now become a broadly based endeavour.[39] Even Prime Minister Gordon Brown, one of the architects of London's growth as a financial centre, has begun to see the need to 'bring the shadow banking system and tax havens into the regulatory net'.[40] In contrast to views espoused by other influential economists like Greenspan, others such as Professor Willem Buiter have pointed to the overexpansion of the banking sector that occurred in both the UK and the US, and, in looking for an explanation, argued that:

> Financial stability was undermined by thoughtless financial liberalisation, especially in the US and the UK. Light-touch (really soft-touch) regulation permitted an explosion of opaque instruments often held by non-transparent 'shadow banking' institutions. The UK was revealed to have no functioning deposit insurance scheme, no functioning lender of last resort arrangements and no special resolution regime for insolvent or badly impaired banks. In the balkanised regulation and supervision regime of the US, no one was in charge; few were even aware of the dysfunctional developments that were taking place.[41]

Nevertheless, many former bankers continue to be in a state of denial in regard to their responsibility for events and continue to resist efforts to build a new regulatory structure which moved beyond the current system which has largely lacked effective external and internal regulation.[42] This applies especially to hedge funds, which have lacked transparency.[43] This state of denial also extends to a reluctance to change internal governance practices[44] and uncritical attitudes to the desirability of rewarding bank employees with extravagant bonuses and retirement packages. The publicity regarding these matters surrounding the Royal Bank of Scotland (RBS) and other failed banks has highlighted this problem well.[45] Nevertheless, there has been criticism in the US from conservative think-tanks, such as the American Enterprise Institute, of efforts to impose regulatory rules over products that have been found to create systemic risks, such as credit default swaps.[46]

---

[39] See generally N Roubini, 'The Shadow Banking System is Unravelling', *Financial Times*, 21 September 2008.

[40] Reuters, 'Brown Urges Crackdown on Bonus Culture at G20' (6 March 2009), available at http://reuters.com/article/idUSTRE52558G20090306.

[41] W Buiter, 'Welcome to a World of Diminished Expectations', *Financial Times*, 6 August 2008, 11.

[42] See generally C Giles, R Atkins and J Wilson, 'Bankers Act to Head Off Tighter Regulation', *Financial Times*, 10 April 2008; Leader, 'The Regulators are Coming', *The Economist*, 29 March 2008, 17. See also PT Larsen and G Tett, 'Political Interference "is Biggest Risk" for Banks', *Financial Times*, 31 January–1 February 2009, 7.

[43] See further: P Davis, 'Hedge Funds Prepare for Legal Crackdown', *Financial Times*, 26 January 2009, 7; J Mackintosh, 'Hedge Funds Move to Limit Rules Burden', *Financial Times*, 19 January 2009, 19.

[44] One much publicised example of such denial was the statement by Vikram Pandit, the Citigroup CEO, that, despite a virtual nationalisation of the bank, there would not be any changes made to the 'strategy, operations or governance' of the bank; see further F Guerrera and A Beatte, 'US Government to Take Biggest Stake in Citigroup', *Financial Times*, 28 February–1 March 2009, 1; F Guerrera, 'Rivals are Poised to Take Advantage of Ownership Limbo', *Financial Times*, 28 February–1 March 2009, 16; J Kay, 'How Competent Bankers can be Assisted', *Financial Times*, 4 March 2009, 25.

[45] PT Larsen, 'Goodwin's Undoing—RBS and the Crisis', *Financial Times*, 25 February 2009, 11; P Wintour, 'Bank Executive Bonuses may be Clawed Back, Warns Brown', *The Guardian*, 13 February 2009, 6; J Treanor, 'RBS Chief "Empathises" with Public Anger on Bonuses', *The Guardian*, 12 February 2009, 7; J Eaglesham, 'Goodwin Action could Start "in Weeks"', *Financial Times*, 4 March 2009, 2; J Oliver et al, 'Payback Time for Culture of Greed', *Sunday Times*, 1 March 2009, 14.

[46] J Grant and N Tait, 'Plea for Caution on Re-regulating Financial Sector', *Financial Times*, 4 February 2009, 6.

D.   Improving the Quality of Banking and Financial Regulation

Parliamentary inquiries in both the UK and the US have sought to ask searching questions of bankers about some of the major risks that they have taken in recent years.[47] Apart from gaps in the current regulatory structure, a key issue here must concern the quality of regulation itself. This has been found to be very poor and recently led to bodies such as the FSA announcing that they would enhance their supervisory activity[48] and the US Securities and Exchange Commission (SEC) beginning to follow up on serious market abuses, such as the Madoff[49] and Stanford[50] ponzi schemes. In the US, the SEC seemed to have been caught on the back foot by the credit crisis (such as the collapse of Bear Stearns[51]), which meant that the leading roles were taken instead by the US Treasury and the Federal Reserve. There was also much room for improvement in the UK, given the FSA's acknowledged lack of a deep understanding of some of the banks it was supposed to regulate, such as Northern Rock and the RBS.[52]

Not surprisingly, shortly after commencing in his new position, the current Chairman of the FSA, Lord Turner, sought to 'wipe the slate clean' as he foresaw that the regulator would be seeking to develop more effective strategies for dealing with banking failures, because, as Lord Adair Turner added, 'we have been doing supervision on the cheap'.[53]

The history of recent failures upon the part of UK corporate regulation, which has included the FSA's acknowledged poor handling of the collapse of Northern Rock and the FSA's and Department of Trade and Industry's (DTI) much criticised handling of the Equitable Life saga,[54] suggests that, despite the positive intentions of Lord Turner, there

---

[47] For the UK see J Treanor and P Wintour, 'Bankers Admit They Got it Wrong as RBS Announces 2,300 Job Cuts', *The Guardian*, 11 February 2009, 6–7; PT Larsen, 'Cuts and Bruises but no Fatal Blow', *Financial Times*, 11 February 2009, 3; For the US, see A Clark, 'Do or Die for Banks as Knives are Sharpened on Capitol Hill', *The Guardian*, 13 February 2009, 28.

[48] J Hughes, 'FSA to Step Up its Supervisory Role', *Financial Times*, 1 December 2008, 3.

[49] See further J Chung, P Hollinger and S Pignal, 'SEC "Illiteracy" to Blame for Madoff Failings', *Financial Times*, 5 February 2009, 21; A Rappeport, and J Chung, 'Madoff Records Put More Pressure on SEC', *Financial Times*, 21–22 February 2009, 16; J Treanor and A Clark, '"It Was All One Big Lie": $50bn Black Hole Engulfs Global Funds', *The Guardian Weekly*, 19 December 2008, 3; *The Economist*, 'The Madoff Affair, Con of the Century', *The Economist*, 20 December 2008, 119; M Goldstein, 'The Humbling of Hedge Funds', *BusinessWeek*, 29 December 2008–5 January 2009, 26; B Masters, 'Off the Fairway—Behind the Madoff Scandal', *Financial Times*, 27 January 2009, 11.

[50] See further SM Ishmael and J Chung, 'Stanford Charged with Fraud by SEC', *Financial Times*, 18 February 2009) 1; SM Ishmael, 'Twenty20 Hindsight: The Stanford Scandal', *Financial Times*, 21–22 February 2009) 9; A Clark, 'Stanford Scandal—Alarm Bells Sounded in 1995—but Regulators Did Not Listen', *The Guardian*, 20 February 2009) 6; J Chung, T Alloway and J Lemer, 'The Stanford Scandal—Why Were Red Flags Ignored?', *Financial Times*, 19 February 2009, 22; M Peel, 'The Stanford Scandal—An Empire Long on Claims and Short on Data', *Financial Times*, 20 February 2009, 20.

[51] 'The Wreck and Rescue of America's Fifth-biggest Wall Street Bank', *The Economist*, 22 March 2008, 94.

[52] See further R Tomasic, 'Corporate Rescue, Governance and Risk-taking in Northern Rock' Part 1 and Part 2 (2008) 29 *The Company Lawyer* 297 and (2008) 29 *The Company Lawyer* 330.

[53] See further PT Larsen 'Banking Regulator Calls for Clean Slate', *Financial Times*, 17 October 2008, 1.

[54] The UK government has been severely criticised by the Parliamentary Ombudsman for the failure of government regulators to intervene in the long-established insurance company Equitable Life, even though evidence of this failure was plain to see. The Ombudsman pointed to 'passive, reactive and complacent' regulators in the form of the Department of Trade and Industry (DTI), the Government Actuary's Department and the FSA, which the Ombudsman accused of being guilty of 'comprehensive failure': see Y Essen, 'Equitable Sank as Regulators Stood By', *Daily Telegraph*, 31 October 2008, B1.

was a case for more fundamental reform. This could even include replacing the FSA entirely and refashioning the system of tripartite regulation into a different shape.

Some have even suggested that this might, for example, involve a dual structure, with one body concerned only with prudential regulation and another concerned only with consumer issues, with protocols for cooperation between them. Such a dual regulatory model is found in other parts of the world, such as in Australia, Canada and the Netherlands, having been developed out of an earlier banking crisis in the 1990s. Interestingly, the former Secretary to the US Treasury, Hank Paulson, is said to have favoured this dual model, and the value of this approach has also been recognised recently in the UK in a report written for the Conservatives by former Treasury official James Sassoon.[55] The failure of the FSA to deal adequately with corporate fraud may also need to be dealt with structurally, although corporate prosecutions are a notoriously difficult area to deal with and need adequate funding and specialised enforcement staff with a commitment to the enforcement of legal rules and not mere light-touch regulation.[56]

Concurrently with Lord Turner's announcement of a clean slate, the FSA set aside years of modelling of financial risks by forcing banks to recapitalise. In his first major interview as the FSA's new chairman, Lord Turner observed that:

> We are going to have to return to a rule driven approach and ideally that should be an international set of rules. And we are just going to have to see how rapidly the world can get back to an agreed set of rules.[57]

Up until recently, the FSA also seemed unable to move beyond the use of failed regulatory models, despite criticism of its approach in the US; as one analyst of the FSA's commodities regulation practices has noted, for example, the FSA 'is frank about not being enforcement-driven. It prefers a system of "credible deterrence", which requires senior management at firms to show they have "good systems and control" to prevent misconduct—or face sanction.'[58]

Contemporaneously, the UK government has been severely criticised by the Parliamentary Ombudsman for the failure of government regulators to intervene in the affairs of the long-established insurance company Equitable Life, even though evidence of its failure was plain to see. The Ombudsman pointed to 'passive, reactive and complacent' regulators in the form of the DTI, the Government Actuary's Department and the FSA, which the Ombudsman accused of being guilty of 'comprehensive failure'.[59] If this is yet another illustration of the UK's much vaunted light-handed regulation, it has had extraordinary consequences. As with Northern Rock, it also suggests some bureaucratic conflict between the relevant regulatory bodies that enabled the avoidance of regulatory responsibilities.

The collapse of Northern Rock was also followed by a staggering internal audit of the FSA that highlighted the failure of risk-based light-handed regulation.[60] This kind of

---

[55] J Sassoon, 'Britain Deserves a Better System of Financial Regulation', *Financial Times*, 9 March 2009, 15; and J Eaglesham, 'Overhaul of FSA Needed, Says Review', *Financial Times*, 9 March 2009, 3.

[56] On the problems of using criminal sanctions in areas that are dominated by a civil law culture, see further R Tomasic, 'Corporate Crime in a Civil Law Culture' (1994) 5 *Current Issues in Criminal Justice* 244.

[57] PT Larsen, 'Turner Rises to the Challenge of Calming Financial Markets', *Financial Times*, 17 October 2008, 17.

[58] J Grant, '"London Loophole" Leaves US at Odds with FSA', *Financial Times*, 7 July 2008, 21.

[59] See Essen, above n 54.

[60] See further www.fsa.gov.uk/pages/Library/Other_publications/Miscellaneous/2008/nr.shtml.

attitude prevailed up until the collapse of Northern Rock. In some ways, the financial crisis facing the UK has been more severe than elsewhere because of the 'success' that the UK has had in building up its financial services industry as a proportion of the overall business sector; arguably, this meant that when this sector failed the damage would be much greater than would otherwise have been the case.[61]

The FSA's Chief Executive, Hector Sants, also acknowledged that the FSA failed to adequately understand the companies that it was charged with regulating and that it would need to develop better mechanisms for overseeing them. In announcing a move to appoint more qualified personnel to the agency, he observed that '[w]e do want to have a somewhat more intrusive approach to regulation'. In an unusually strident tone, Sants added, '[w]hat we absolutely should be doing is delivering an effective supervisory regime' and admitted that '[w]e are acknowledging that we could have challenged those business models more before they went into the downturn'.[62] However, the forces of resistance to such re-regulation are not going to be easy to deal with, having been so much a part of the boom years of the credit bubble.

Writing in July 2008, Lawrence Summers, now chairman of the US President's National Economic Council, outlined some of the key features of a new regulatory order. These key features of any new system include the avoidance of competition between regulatory agencies;[63] assuming that institutions and regulators will be unable to predict market conditions with much more confidence; and ensuring that the risks that arise from the 'parallel' or shadow banking system are monitored properly. Like many others, Summers also noted that: 'it should be recognised that to a substantial extent self-regulation is deregulation. Allowing institutions to determine capital levels based on risk models of their own design is tantamount to letting them set their own capital levels.'[64]

The much touted claims of the superiority of the UK's light-touch- and principles-based system of market regulation has been shown to be hollow as, ultimately, this has merely amounted to a lack of regulation. Successive UK governments sought to attract foreign companies to set up operations in London on the grounds of its superior light-handed regulatory approach. This created what has been described by Martin Wolf[65] as the problem of 'regulatory arbitrage', or what might also be described as a kind of 'race to the bottom'.

The problems created by the lack of (or minimal) regulation have been accentuated by the massive growth of the financial centre in London and the tendency that London's low levels of regulation have had to attract even more risky financial products, such the credit default swaps offered, for example, by AIG's London office.[66] On one estimate, the collapse

---

[61] See further A Shipman, 'UK Financial Sector Size, and Vulnerability, Questioned from Within', *Finance Week*, 5 November 2007, available at www.financeweek.co.uk/item/5683.

[62] Quoted by Hughes, above n 48.

[63] This is something that has undercut the effectiveness of the UK's tripartite authorities in dealing with the crisis, as the Treasury Committee of the House of Commons found in its inquiry into the collapse of Northern Rock. Similar criticisms have been made in the US by Timothy Geithner about the need to streamline the regulatory infrastructure: T Geithner, 'We Can Reduce Risk in the Financial System', *Financial Times*, 9 June 2008, 11; see also G Tett and K Guha, 'Multi-layered Patchwork Will Be Tough to Unpick', *Financial Times*, 24 April 2008, 13.

[64] L Summers, 'Six Principles for a New Regulatory Order', *Financial Times*, 2 June 2008, 12.

[65] M Wolf, 'Seven Habits that Finance Regulators must Acquire', *Financial Times*, 7 May 2008, 15. See further M Wolf, *Fixing Global Finance—How to Curb Financial Crises in the 21st Century* (New Haven, CT, Yale University Press, 2009).

[66] A Clark, 'Mayfair's $600bn House of Horrors', *The Guardian*, 7 March 2009, 37.

of AIG is likely to cost US taxpayers up to $250bn.[67] In any event, the existence of regulatory arbitrage undermines efforts to build a global regulatory approach to what is probably one of the most globalised industries.

Shortly after being appointed as FSA Chairman, Lord Turner promised a revolution in the FSA's regulatory practices with more bank like rules for hedge funds and further probing of whether senior bankers are 'fit and proper' for their jobs.[68] This was to be more fully articulated with the publication in March 2009 of The Turner Review, which signalled a new regulatory approach. This review of the regulatory response to the global banking crisis examined the causes of the crisis and went on to make a call for a systemic approach to regulation rather than an approach that merely focused upon the risk profile of individual banks.[69]

The release of the Turner Review was also accompanied by an extraordinary refocusing of the FSA's new regulatory stance by its CEO, Hector Sants. Up until that time, the dominant ethos of light-handed regulation had been accompanied by the idea of principles-based regulation, which sought to avoid an overly legalistic approach to regulation of the kind often associated with the US Sarbanes-Oxley Act. It should be emphasised that these were two different approaches to regulation. The principles-based approach had often been seen as reflecting a major difference between the regulatory approaches found in the US and the UK. On 12 March 2009 Sants told an audience that the 'principles-based' approach had been flawed to the extent that it provided the sole basis for regulation. As he explained:

> Historically, the FSA characterised its approach as evidence-based, risk based and principles-based. We remain, and must remain, evidence- and risk-based but the phrase 'principles-based' has, I think, been misunderstood. To suggest that we can operate on principles alone is illusory particularly because the policy making framework does not allow it . . .

Sants went on to call for the use of more intensive supervision of markets as 'the limitations of a pure principles-based regime have to be recognised. I continue to believe the majority of market participants are decent people; however, a principles-based approach does not work with individuals who have no principles.'[70]

Sants was concerned that the FSA's credibility was not being taken seriously enough and warned that people 'should be very frightened of the FSA'.[71] This suggested the adoption of a more proactive regulatory stance, especially in regard to those persons who might be seen as acting in an unprincipled manner. This conceptualisation focused attention upon the impact or effectiveness of legal regulation in regard to market actors.

It is interesting to contrast this approach with the conceptualisation of law developed by the American lawyer and judge Oliver Wendell Holmes, who had used a similar metaphor for persons 'who have no principles', calling such a person the 'bad man'. In an influential argument, Holmes defined law as a reflection of legal outcomes and not legal principles when he said:

---

[67] Clark, ibid, quoting D Vickery, founder of the US research firm Gradient Analytics.

[68] J Hughes, 'FSA Head Promised Regulation Revolution', *Financial Times*, 26 February 2009, 1.

[69] Financial Services Authority, *The Turner Review—A Regulatory Response to the Global Banking Crisis* (London, Financial Services Authority, 2009) ch 2.

[70] H Sants, 'Delivering Intensive Supervision and Credible Deterrence', speech at Reuters Newsmakers Event, 12 March 2009, available at www.fsa.gov.uk/pages/Library/Communication/Speeches/2009/0312_hs.shtml.

[71] Ibid.

If we take the view of . . . the bad man we shall find that he does not care two straws for the axioms of deductions, but that he does want to know what Massachusetts or English courts are likely to do in fact.[72]

In other words, the real meaning of the law or of legal regulation is to be found in the law in action or in what courts and regulatory bodies do. To make the regulation of financial markets effective, Sants has generated a new sense of market credibility for the FSA by adopting a more outcomes-based approach. It is too soon to know how effective this more assertive approach will be.[73]

E.   Improving the Quality of Regulation through Enhanced Corporate Governance[74]

Another approach to enhancing the performance of financial institutions is to focus more effectively upon internal regulation within these firms; this might be called improved corporate governance. Corporate rescue and insolvency often arise where there are poor corporate governance standards, although this is not always so, as excellently governed companies may also fail for other reasons. Indeed, it could be argued that corporate insolvency and good corporate governance are often the opposite sides of the same coin. Government responses to the current financial crisis have once again placed a focus upon corporate governance issues, especially where government has become a major stakeholder in high street banks and other entities that have been seeking and have received taxpayer support.

Many have argued that, as a significant stakeholder in these companies, government should place pressure on boards to make them act in a more socially responsible way. This has seen mixed responses from banks: some, like the government-supported RBS, have in recent times been more receptive to these pressures, whilst others, such as Barclays, have sought to avoid receipt of public funds due to a fear of unwanted external pressures being placed upon them.

Early recognition of the central place of corporate governance in ensuring financial stability of banks is to be found in an insightful 2001 study that emerged out of an earlier Nordic financial crisis of the early 1990s.[75] Taking a broader stakeholder approach to corporate governance, Mayes, Halme and Liuksila argued that '[g]ood corporate governance is a key element in a satisfactory framework for financial supervision' and saw 'good corporate governance as being a precondition for the successful operation of financial

---

[72] OW Holmes, 'The Path of the LAW' (1897) 10 *Harvard Law Review* 457. See further the discussion of this concept by W Twining, *Globalisation & Legal Theory* (London, Butterworths, 2000) 108–27.

[73] See further the FSA consultation paper on enforcement, 'A Regulatory Response to the Global Banking Crisis', Discussion Paper 09/2 (2009).

[74] Some of the material in this and the next section of this paper is drawn from R Tomasic, 'Raising Corporate Governance Standards in Response to Corporate Rescue and Insolvency' (2009) 2 *Corporate Rescue and Insolvency* 5.

[75] This crisis followed a deregulation of financial markets, an economic boom and a subsequent asset market bubble. The effect of the shock when this bubble collapsed was especially severe in Finland because of the collapse of the Soviet Union; see further J-C Rochet, *Why Are There so many Banking Crises? The Politics and Policy of Bank Regulation* (Princeton, NJ, Princeton University Press, 2008); J Tirole, *Financial Crises, Liquidity and the International Monetary System* (Princeton, NJ, Princeton University Press, 2002).

supervision'.[76] Mayes et al sought to map the features of good corporate governance that are likely to facilitate financial stability. In a somewhat prescient observation that is applicable to the current crisis, they noted that:

> The banking crises of recent decades have highlighted the importance of a well functioning legal, regulatory and supervisory framework in ex ante prevention of massive banking crises and the reduction of the resulting pain. The crises have clearly demonstrated that there can be serious negative outcomes in situations where the incentives influencing the behaviour of legislators, regulators, supervisors or banks (management, board, shareholders) are inappropriate.[77]

These Finnish authors also noted that focusing merely upon shareholder value causes biased decision-making so that management needs to 'internalise the welfare of all stakeholders, not just shareholders.'[78] They argued persuasively that a system of incentives-based rules and regulations is likely to create the most effective corporate governance arrangements.[79] These insights have been echoed in subsequent reports and studies. A recent report by the International Corporate Governance Network has, for example, found that poor corporate governance was a significant cause of the current financial crisis as company boards 'failed to understand and manage risk and tolerated perverse incentives'.[80]

A 2009 report prepared by the OECD Steering Group on Corporate Governance also pointed to the close relationship between risk management and corporate governance. This report noted that recent research had found that 'risk governance was a key responsibility of bank boards' but that only one-third of banks that had been involved in the study 'were confident that their strategy and planning functions had a detailed understanding of their companies' risk management methodology'.[81] The OECD Group concluded that the failure to embed risk management more deeply into the organisation was 'a clear corporate governance weakness'.[82] On top of this there is a need to have adequate numbers of board members with some substantial financial competence; but, as the OECD Group noted, prior banking experience alone is not enough.[83] As the OECD Group concluded:

> the financial crisis can be to an extent attributed to failures and weaknesses in corporate governance arrangements. When they were put to a test, corporate governance routines did not serve their purpose to safeguard against excessive risk taking in a number of financial services companies [banks]. A number of weaknesses have been apparent. The risk management systems have failed in many cases due to corporate governance procedures rather than the inadequacy of computer models alone: information about exposures in a number of cases did not reach the board and even senior levels of management, while risk management was often activity rather than enterprise-based.[84]

It is clear that regulatory and legal efforts need to be directed to ensuring that more effective systems of checks and balances are embedded within financial institutions to ensure that corporate governance is more meaningful than it has been in companies such

---

[76] DG Mayes, L Halme and A Liuksila, *Improving Banking Supervision* (Houndmills, Palgrave, 2001) 91.
[77] Ibid, 93.
[78] Ibid.
[79] Ibid, 95.
[80] Quoted by P Skypala, 'Time to Reward Good Corporate Governance', *Financial Times*, 17 November 2008, 6.
[81] OECD, above n 34, 17, referring to a 2008 study by Nestor Advisers.
[82] Ibid, 17.
[83] Ibid, 19–20.
[84] OECD, above n 34, 3.

as Northern Rock, HBOS and RBS. This calls for more effective checks and balances within financial institutions so as to deal with overbearing bank chief executives, ineffective non-executive directors, complacent shareholders, and weak internal compliance and risk-assessment mechanisms. This is important as external regulatory processes by bodies such as the FSA will inevitably only provide a partial solution to the problems encountered by financial institutions during the current financial crisis.

F.   Improving Corporate Governance in UK Banks

In the UK, many of the above failures were evident in the collapse of Northern Rock, and have caused controversy in other banks such as HBOS and RBS.[85] In this context, it is interesting to note that the UK City Minister, Lord Myners, has long championed better corporate governance on bank boards, although this has not had enormous success. Myners recently pointed to the complexity of introducing better corporate governance when he said:

> I think regulation is one aspect of enhancing confidence in financial institutions. Others include self-healing through improved governance, more effective boards, more considered analysis of incentive plans and the behaviours they will produce, and stronger capital. There isn't a single silver bullet here, regulation in itself without support of those other features will lead to a potential frustration of innovation and probably higher cost of funding.[86]

Regrettably, progress has been slow in adopting some of the recommendations made by Myners, such as those found in his 2001 HM Treasury-initiated report into the corporate governance roles of institutional investors; for example, efforts to urge institutional investors to be more proactive in regard to corporate governance matters have not been very successful.

We are currently witnessing a conflict between the prevailing ideology that promotes the superiority of unregulated markets (where 'principles-based' and 'light-touch' forms of regulation have been favoured) and a more rigorous approach to handling issues of corporate governance within the banking sector and other financial institutions. How this conflict will be resolved will be vital for the future health of financial markets and of the corporate sector as a whole.

During the credit boom little regard seems to have been given to corporate governance issues encountered by banks and other leading financial institutions, despite the potential significance of better corporate governance to moderate reckless risk-taking. Thus, regardless of whether one adopts a director primacy model of the modern corporation or whether one leaves more room for stakeholder arguments to operate, duly elected boards should be free to manage the company as they alone see as being in the best interests of the company.

However, this does not preclude shareholders, whether they are individuals, institutional investors or government agencies, from making inputs through the normal institutional structures of the corporation and being listened to seriously. For example, if a

---

[85] See further House of Commons Treasury Committee, 'The Run on the Rock: Fifth Report of Session 2007–08', vol 1 (London, The Stationery Office, 2008); R Tomasic, above n 52.

[86] Interview with A Davidson, 'Paul Myners, the City's Middle Man', *Sunday Times*, 12 October 2008.

shareholder has a sufficient number of shares in a company, she should be able to use these rights to appoint directors to the board to work with the board in settling policies and making major policy decisions for the company. These two ideas can and do coexist, even though they conflict with assumptions built into a director primacy model that has dominated corporate governance in many companies.[87]

Regrettably, for a number of reasons, most institutions have been somewhat timid as investors in British companies (whether they be banks or other types of companies), and as a result company boards in the UK have felt free to manage companies without much concern for shareholder opinions. For example, we have seen this in regard to decisions of the board in Marks & Spencer to persist in retaining a chairman who is also its CEO, despite prevailing corporate governance principles which suggest that these key roles should be held by different persons; also, the actions of the board of Barclays Bank in seeking over £7 billion in equity capital directly from a sovereign wealth fund and a wealthy member of the Abu Dhabi royal family, rather than acknowledging the pre-emptive rights of its existing shareholders, might be seen as another illustration of boards being prepared to act without regard for the views (and the rights) of their shareholders. The Association of British Insurers was so concerned about this action that it issued a rare 'red top' alert to its members.[88]

This reflects a broader failure of corporate governance ideas to be properly embedded within the financial and corporate sectors in the UK. Despite the enactment of new statutory duties of directors which emphasise the importance of looking more broadly at stakeholder interests in the corporation, this pattern of conduct calls for a more thorough-going re-evaluation of judicial and regulatory attitudes to corporate governance. Whilst 'conditionality' was a key feature of efforts by the International Monetary Fund to rescue banks and other key institutions during the Asian Financial Crisis, and saw efforts to impose often quite onerous western market ideas, such as deregulation and modern business laws, upon Asian countries, the 'new conditionality' is focused more upon issues of corporate social responsibility.[89]

However, it should also be noted that this is not a good time to be a shareholder of a bank, insurance company or financial institution, especially in the context of nationalisations, which effectively destroy shareholder equity.[90] One commentator has emphasised this point in the context of recent US government bank actions:

> By deciding essentially to wipe out shareholders in Fannie Mae and Freddie Mac and acting even more harshly to the shareholders of Lehman Brothers this weekend, Mr. Paulson has sent the clearest possible message to investors around the world: do not buy shares in any bank or insurance company that could, under any conceivable circumstances, run short of capital and need to ask for government help; if this happens, the shareholders will be obliterated and will not be allowed to participate in any potential gains should the bank later recover.[91]

[87] See further SM Bainbridge, *The New Corporate Governance in Theory and Practice* (Oxford, Oxford University Press, 2008).

[88] See further K Burgess and PT Larsen, 'Barclays Practises Appeasement', *Financial Times*, 19 November 2008, 21.

[89] See J Eaglesham and J Croft, 'Darling to Set Out Bank Rescue Terms', *Financial Times*, 18 November 2008, 2; and A Barker, 'Brown Rethinks Legislation Priorities', *Financial Times*, 1 December 2008, 2.

[90] See further the High Court decision in regard to former shareholders in Northern Rock: *R (on the application of SRM Global Master Fund LP) v Commissioners of HM Treasury* [2009] EWHC 227, [2009] BCC 251. See also the National Audit Office report into the nationalisation of Northern Rock: National Audit Office, *HM Treasury The Nationalisation of Northern Rock* (London, The Stationery Office, 2009).

[91] A Kaletsky, 'Hank Paulson Has Turned a Drama into a Crisis', *The Times*, 16 September 2008.

Of course, we need look no further than the nationalisation of Northern Rock for expressions of similar concern. This makes corporate governance problematic and suggests that the only shareholder that counts is government itself.

A succession of industry-sponsored efforts to legitimise and improve prevailing corporate governance practices in the UK has seen the development of the Combined Code on Corporate Governance. This was based on recommendations drawn from industry-initiated inquiries, including the Cadbury Committee (1992), the Greenbury Committee (1995), the Hampel Committee (1998) and the Turnbull Committee (1999). To a large degree, these industry-inspired efforts seem to have been taken because of the fear that government would intervene and introduce more stringent requirements if industry did not seek to set down some self-regulatory rules.

During the 1990s the UK government was committed to the idea of industry self-regulation and minimal government interference. The promise of corporate governance, as echoed in these privately sponsored committee reports, as a means of achieving greater corporate accountability has so far failed to eventuate.[92] Inquiries such as those undertaken by Cadbury were often stimulated by the occurrence of some significant market scandal; for example, the appointment of the Cadbury Committee followed the BCCI and Maxwell scandals. Scandals have long been the engines of corporate law reform. Sometimes, governments themselves are prompted to take the leading role as a result of such scandals, as we saw in the US with the passage of the Sarbanes-Oxley Act following the collapse of Enron. In the UK, however, governments have been slow to act unilaterally.

The establishment of the FSA in 1997 (taking the place of the old Securities and Investments Board) was aimed at bringing together previously disparate regulatory bodies in the light of regulatory failures such as the collapse of Barings and BCCI in 1995 and the pension mis-selling scandal. The collapse of Northern Rock produced an equally severe legislative response in the form of the Banking (Special Provisions) Act 2008. These rapid reactions have not developed well-articulated and broadly based corporate governance rules. Overall, there has been timidity in the UK upon the part of government, regulators and the courts in fashioning more intrusive and more effective governance rules for the finance sector, even if industry might be prepared to readily accommodate such higher standards.

The regulatory response to crises that have precipitated these modest legal changes has been tempered for a variety of reasons. One of these was the desire to protect and preserve London's position as a financial centre. For example, after BCCI collapsed, the former head of banking supervision at the Bank of England allegedly argued that '"overzealous" regulation of the fraud-ridden bank BCCI and other banks would have damaged London's standing as a major financial centre'.[93] This concern has continued to be a prevailing factor in government policy responses, with massive negative consequences for the British taxpayer.

---

[92] For one explanation of this see further Froud et al, above n 25, 49–64.
[93] J Kollowe, 'Supervisory Chief Defends Bank over BCCI Collapse', *The Independent*, 27 September 2005.

G.   The Modest Role of UK Courts in Enhancing Corporate Governance

It is interesting to reflect briefly upon the haphazard manner in which corporate governance rules have been developed by British courts since the mid-nineteenth century. If the collapse of Northern Rock plc stands out as a landmark in the current crisis, the collapse of another bank, Overend, Gurney & Co in 1866, also stands as a landmark of sorts. Like the collapse of Northern Rock, it too led to a bank run, but, unlike Northern Rock, the (then private) Bank of England decided not to organise a rescue of this once proud bank.[94] The failure of subsequent litigation against the directors of Overend, Gurney & Co was to cast a shadow over the way in which courts were to deal with issues of corporate governance and define the duties of directors.

In his famous 1925 decision in *Re City Equitable*,[95] Romer J traced principles regarding the duties of directors through earlier cases back to *Overend & Gurney Co v Gibb*.[96] Although the basis of those principles was already being questioned at that time, Romer J followed Lord McNaughten's approach in *Dovey v Cory*,[97] namely, that it was not for the courts, but for Parliament, to lay down more precise rules for directors in the conduct of their business affairs. This judicial self-restraint is curious, especially when leading business commentators in the 1870s had urged that higher standards would actually be appropriate. It was clearly not seen as acceptable for the courts to take judicial notice of changing commercial attitudes in this area. This timidity effectively froze the development of this area of law; in other countries (eg the US and Australia) the courts have been more active in developing the law to align it with community standards.

As is well known, Romer J reviewed the earlier cases and noted that the authorities did not provide clear answers as to the degree of care and skill expected of a director: 'It has been laid down that so long as a director acts honestly he cannot be made responsible for damages unless guilty of gross or culpable negligence in a business sense'.[98] His Honour went on to state some well-known 'general propositions' derived from the reported cases:

> (1) A director need not exhibit in the performance of his duties a greater degree of skill than may reasonably be expected from a person of his knowledge and experience . . . [and] (2) A director is not bound to give continuous attention to the affairs of the company. His duties are of an intermittent nature . . .

Romer J added:

> Whether or not the directors exceeded the powers entrusted to them, or whether they did not so exceed their powers they were cognisant of circumstances of such a character, so plain, so manifest, and so simple of appreciation, that *no man with an ordinary degree of prudence acting on their own behalf* would have entered into such a transaction as they entered into.[99]

This decision set a fairly low standard of care for directors and clearly raised some interesting questions of proof. But should directors of banks be treated like this or should we

---

[94] See generally G Elliott, *The Mystery of Overend & Gurney* (London, Methuen, 2006).
[95] [1925] Ch 407.
[96] [1872] LR 5 HL 480, 486.
[97] [1901] AC 477.
[98] [1925] Ch 407, 425.
[99] [1925] Ch 407, 426 (emphasis added).

expect a higher standard from them? The case law has not developed greatly in the UK since this old decision, although there have been some suggestions that this older standard is wanting. However, by way of contrast, it is interesting to refer to the higher standard that has been adopted in the US where the business judgement rule is dominant. In the 1981 New Jersey case of *Francis v United Jersey Bank* it was said of directors by Pollock J that:

> The sentinel asleep at his post contributes nothing to the enterprise he is charged to protect . . . Directorial management does not require a detailed inspection of day-to-day activities, but rather a general monitoring of corporate affairs and policies . . . A director is not an ornament, but an essential component of corporate governance . . .[100]

This approach was adopted by the New South Wales Court of Appeal in *Daniels v Anderson*[101] and, in the course of adopting a higher and more objective standard, the court departed from the subjective standard set by Romer J in *Re City Equitable*. Some British commentators have suggested that UK law is currently moving in the direction of adopting this higher standard.[102]

The slowness of UK chancery courts in developing this area of law is surprising, especially if one notes that, as early as 1873, Walter Bagehot, a leading authority on British banking and financial markets, had urged a higher standard than the courts in cases such as *re City Equitable* have adopted. In some way, Bagehot can be compared with Sir Adrian Cadbury in more recent times.

In his classic work on banking, *Lombard Street—A Description of the Money Market*, first published in 1873, Walter Bagehot reflected upon what had happened in the management of Overend, Gurney & Co and observed that 'the business of a great bank requires a great deal of ability, and an even rarer degree of trained and sober judgment'. This suggests that much greater skills were required to manage larger banking institutions than smaller ones. Bagehot went on to argue that:

> Till now private banks have been small; small as we now reckon banks. For their exigencies a moderate degree of ability and an anxious caution will suffice. *But if the size of the banks is augmented and greater ability is required*, the constant difficulty of an hereditary government will begin to be felt.[103]

The difficulty Bagehot was referring to arose at the time that Overend, Gurney & Co was under the control of the family elders who had built the company; subsequently, younger members of the family had risked the company by engaging in questionable ventures. In some ways this is reminiscent of UK banks that were once building societies. In the case of Northern Rock, for example, the board's skills base changed little from the time when it was a building society to when it became a FTSE 100 company. Bagehot had warned against this over 130 years earlier, but this seems to have had little effect on corporate governance practices, although Bagehot is still often cited for his advice on best practice in bank risk management.

As Professor Paul Davies has also argued, the best practice guidelines that can be found in the UK Combined Code on Corporate Governance and in industry reports, such as the Higgs review, could also serve as a similar expression of appropriate business standards for

---

[100] 432 A 2d 814 (1981), 822.
[101] (1995) 16 ACSR 607.
[102] See discussion in P Davies, *Principles of Modern Company Law*, 8th edn (London, Thomson, 2008) 490–94.
[103] W Bagehot, *Lombard Street—A Description of the Money Market* (New York, John Wiley & Sons, 1873, 1999) 274 (emphasis added).

directors, and that courts could take judicial notice of these standards in developing the duties of directors. Indeed, as Davies also notes, courts seem to have begun to do this in some areas, such as in regard to the disqualification of directors, as is evident in the 2000 decision in *Re Barings Plc (No 5)*.[104] Whether judges will do this in duty of care cases under the Companies Act remains unclear.

Romer J was probably not referred by counsel to the relevant statements by Walter Bagehot when he decided *Re City Equitable*. He was obviously resistant to straying too far from previous cases and, as we have seen, in any event saw innovation as a matter for Parliament. Subsequent cases have begun to suggest that a more objective standard of care should be applied to directors, as we saw in the 1989 decision of Hoffman J in *Dorchester Finance Co v Stebbing*.[105]

In his judgment, Hoffman J drew upon the more objective standards applicable to directors of companies facing insolvency found in section 214(4) of the Insolvency Act 1984. In his 1991 decision in *Norman v Theodore Goddard*,[106] Hoffman J found that the objective standard in section 214 correctly reflected the common law duty of directors. A similar view was expressed by him in *Re D'Jan of London*.[107] Professor Andrew Keay has noted that Hoffman's decisions in reality 'did not depart significantly from that put forward by Romer J in *re City Equitable*'.[108] Keay went on to observe that UK judicial decisions in this area during the 1980s and 1990s 'saw a change in the approach of the courts rather than an essential change in the law'.[109] Chancery courts in the UK have been reluctant to interfere in decisions made by directors, tending to see them as akin to trustees.[110] In this context, Keay has also recently observed that UK judges 'have consistently refrained from reviewing business judgments made by directors'.[111]

This standard has now been repeated in section 174 of the Companies Act 2006, although section 170(4) may present a difficulty in developing a more objective standard as it states that the 'general duties shall be interpreted and applied in the same way as common law or equitable principles, and regard shall be had to the corresponding common law rules and equitable principles in interpreting and applying the general rules'. Some, such as Davies, have suggested that courts should be cautious about using the older common law authorities, given legal developments that have occurred in other parts of the Commonwealth.[112]

However, the government-appointed management of Northern Rock plc recently announced that, after some inquiry, they would not take legal action again the bank's former directors. Thus, the company announced that:

> A review of the conduct of the previous board in respect of funding and liquidity has been undertaken with the assistance of external advisers, (lawyers) Freshfields and (accountants) KPMG Forensic. The board has concluded that there are insufficient grounds to proceed with

---

[104] [2000] 1 BCLC 523; see also Davies, above n 102, 492–94.
[105] [1989] BCLC 498.
[106] [1991] BCLC 1028.
[107] [1994] 1 BCLC 561.
[108] A Keay, *Directors' Duties* (Bristol, Jordans Publishing Limited, 2009) 184.
[109] Ibid, 184–88.
[110] See generally D Arsalidou, *The Impact of Modern Influences on the Traditional Duties of Care, Skill and Diligence of Company Directors* (Leiden, Kluwer Law International, 2001).
[111] Keay above n 108, 213.
[112] Davies above n 102, 491.

any legal action for negligence against the former directors, and has no intention of bringing any such action. The board has also completed a similar review in respect of the company's auditors and has determined that no action is warranted.[113]

This was presumably based upon legal advice from their lawyers as to the limited state of UK law in this regard. Essentially, insofar as the decided cases are concerned, the common law has not moved much beyond the standard set out in *Re City Equitable*. It is too early to say whether the new, more objective language of the Companies Act 2006, which came into effect after the events that led to the collapse of Northern Rock, would produce a different outcome. Uncertainty remains on the question of whether the courts will seek to modernise corporate law doctrine applying to directors' duties in the light of developments in other jurisdictions and the passage of new companies legislation in the UK.

H.   Some Conclusions

This chapter has sought to sketch the strands of the debate that has emerged from the financial crisis with a view to seeing the range of alternative approaches that will need to be pursued as we look beyond 'light-touch' regulation of banks and financial institutions in the UK. This is not the place to rehearse the detailed features of more appropriate corporate governance arrangements, based on what we know of the key determinants of good corporate governance, but the chapter has instead sought to identify some of the major issues which will need to be addressed as this debate develops.

Unfortunately, we are still too close to the pain and suffering that the financial crisis has delivered to be able to develop comprehensive solutions. However, the groundwork needs to be laid for building new regulatory structures and governance strategies over the coming years. These will inevitably have to be international ones. There is, of course, a danger of 'knee-jerk' reactions, but on the other hand, there is no better time to seek to fashion new regulatory arrangements than in the aftermath of a crisis as minds remain open to consideration of reform issues.

What is clear is that governments will need to be more comprehensively involved and that bank boards will need to consult their various stakeholders in a more effective way. Whilst irrational exuberance and ideology may have stood in the way of reform efforts during the bubble that preceded the current crisis, there is clearly more room for assessment of how the diverse range of disciplines and ideas that bear upon understanding our current predicant are utilised in fashioning new solutions. These need to be able to move more quickly and effectively in dealing with the unwanted results of greed, hubris and plain dishonesty. It is clear that our current systems have not delivered satisfactory outcomes in this regard.

---

[113] As quoted in 'No Legal Action against Northern Rock Bosses', *The Independent*, 14 October 2008, available at www.independent.co.uk/news/business/news/no-legal-action-against-northern-rock-bosses-960607.html.

8

What Next for Risk-based Financial Regulation?

JOANNA GRAY*

A. Envisioning the Future(s) of Financial Regulation

This conference challenges us all to think about very many specific aspects of financial regulation at global, regional, national and indeed firm specific level. The global, multi-causal nature of this crisis has been widely acknowledged,[1] and proposals for reform of financial regulation have emerged with some degree of international consensus and coordination.[2] Others address these aspects in detail and assess some of the more concrete international and national reform proposals. This chapter does something more abstract, but is sited in a UK context. It seeks to draw out from the enormous quantity of official sector comment and analysis that has emerged in the UK alone since the depositor run on Northern Rock in September 2007 what may have been lacking in UK financial sector regulation and governance systems leading up to the current global banking crisis.

The emergence of global financial markets has been accompanied by careful design, redesign and refinement of financial regulation over the past 20 years, and throughout that time the UK has thought of itself as having been in the vanguard of this process.[3] Indeed, it does not seem long since the UK model of financial regulation and its championing of a pioneering 'principles-based' and light-touch framework of rules coupled with supervisory and enforcement practices that were driven by one unified organising principle—that of the minimisation of 'risk' to the four core objectives of the Financial Services Authority (FSA)[4]—was the envy of the world.[5] Such risk-based approaches to

---

* Professor of Law, Newcastle University.

[1] See Communique from Leaders of the G20 Countries at Washington Summit Agreeing Common Principles for Reform of Financial Markets (15 November 2009), published in *The Independent*, 16 November 2008, available at www.independent.co.uk/news/business/analysis-and-features/g20-summit-communiques-in-full-1020692.html.

[2] G20 Leaders, 'The Global Plan for Recovery and Reform: Statement Issued by the G20 Leaders' (London, 2 April 2009).

[3] From the Chancellor's Commons Statement, May 1997, which heralded the setting up of the Financial Services Authority as a new unitary financial sector regulator for the UK right through to the setting up on 13 January 2009 of the new International Centre for Financial Regulation, available at www.icffr.org/getdoc/81a17260-b506-4951-bc7a-efb1980c9092/Press-Releases.aspx.

[4] Financial Services and Markets Act 2000, s 2.

[5] US Treasury, 'Blueprint for a Modernised Financial Regulatory Structure' (2008) 115. In 2006 the US Committee on Capital Markets Regulation canvassed options for stemming the post-Sarbanes-Oxley haemorrhaging of foreign IPOs from New York to London, and amongst its recommendations were that 'Regulations and the oversight of such regulations by the regulatory authority should be risk-based and

regulation are far from being unique to UK financial regulation. They are found in many different regulatory regimes at both the national and international levels, and a vast literature exists on risk and regulation across many disciplines.[6] Using the examples of banking, actuarial and accounting regulation, Franklin makes a positive case for such risk-based and principles-based legal regimes which he claims result in law based on sound abstract principles pursuant to which financial institutions correctly evaluate their risk, overseen by regulators within legal regimes 'free of the idiosyncrasies endemic to individual legal systems'.[7] He argues that more lawyers and political theorists should be trained in the statistics of risk to understand the power and global reach of technical risk expertise.

In the context of the UK financial sector, however, we must surely ask now whether 'risk-based' financial regulation as it has developed since 1997 could ever have delivered the outcomes it purported to promote and, if not, how it could be improved so as to do.[8] This is exactly what the FSA has done for us in the recent Turner Review. The relationship between 'risk' and regulation is under review the world over now. Mapping where and how the consequences of the tidal wave of systemic risk that has beset global financial markets have been felt in countries, regulatory systems, financial institutions, investors, employees and real economies will occupy social scientists for years to come and is itself a fascinating exercise,[9] but this chapter sites the examination of regulators and risk closer to the author's home in the depositor run on Northern Rock and in the consequences of its nationalisation, for the questions being asked now by and of financial regulators and governments around the world first began to be most publicly asked in the UK after September 2007. It is argued here that in its design, techniques and consequences financial regulation has failed to acknowledge the essential humanity of its subject matter and its subjects. In order to illustrate this missing link in financial regulation, the paper uses two examples: first, the losses incurred in the wake of the Northern Rock run and nationalisation; and secondly, our awakening to the limits of mathematical risk modelling as a tool to reliably foretell the future of how markets and the people who comprise them will behave, and hence how regulators should seek to respond to risk and uncertainty.

---

principles-based'. This call was echoed by the 2007 McKinsey Report into sustaining NYC and US global financial services leadership commissioned by NYC Mayor Michael Bloomberg.

[6] M Power, *Organised Uncertainty* (Oxford, Oxford University Press, 2007); J Black, 'The Emergence of Risk-based Regulation and the New Public Risk Management in the UK' (2005) *Public Law* 512; J Black, 'Tensions in the Regulatory State' (2007) *Public Law* 58; J Franklin, 'Risk-driven Global Compliance Regimes in Banking and Accounting: the New Law Merchant' (2005) 4 *Law, Probability and Risk* 237.

[7] Franklin, ibid, 250.

[8] B McDonnell, 'Financial Regulation after the Storm: Heavy Hand after Light Touch' (2008) 10 *Journal of International Banking and Financial Law* 519.

[9] G Dymski, 'The Political Economy of the Subprime Meltdown: Crisis at Different Spatial Scales', Centre for Urban and Regional Development Studies Annual Distinguished Lecture (February 2009); M Lewis, 'Wall Street on the Tundra', *Vanity Fair*, 4 March 2009.

B. Accounts of FSA's Risk-based Supervision of Northern Rock

Confidence in financial capitalism itself, and in the ability of political, legislative and regulatory authorities to maintain its stability, have suffered most markedly of all in the wake of the UK run on Northern Rock and subsequently in bank runs, collapses and rescues the world over. Over this same period there has been the most intense Parliamentary scrutiny of the structure and operation of the institutions, laws, rules and processes responsible for refereeing modern financial capitalism in the UK since the passage of the Bank of England Act 1998 and the Financial Services and Markets Act 2000. The changes made to the institutional structure of UK financial regulation as a result of the former created the tripartite structure whereby the Bank of England, HM Treasury and the FSA shared responsibility for the maintenance of financial stability, acting as watchdogs against systemic risk and shoring up confidence in capitalism.[10] Despite losing responsibility for prudential banking regulation in 1998, the Bank of England retained its lender of last resort function and hence shared responsibility for guarding against risk to the financial system with the FSA (which is formally charged with the objective of maintenance of confidence in the financial system as one of its four statutory tasks) and with HM Treasury. It is HM Treasury that must always enjoy ultimate political responsibility for a safe and stable financial system—even if the ability of national governments to exert influence now within a globalised financial system is more apparent than real.[11] However, this tripartite shared responsibility has been found wanting. Some of the conclusions drawn by two Treasury Select Committee reports that have examined (inter alia) the performance of the regulatory bodies and of government in the events leading up to the run on Northern Rock are sharply critical of the way in which FSA's risk-based financial regulatory model was applied both to its supervision of Northern Rock itself,[12] and to the failure to follow through the implications for the stability of UK financial institutions of the growing threat to the supply of wholesale liquidity posed by the very mispricing of risk about which FSA had long been warning in the credit markets, triggered by the emerging problems in the US housing market.[13] These criticisms have been echoed more recently by the National Audit Office[14] and acknowledged by the FSA itself, both in the specific context of its lessons learned from the supervision of Northern Rock review,[15] which has led to a programme of supervisory process enhancement,[16] and more fundamentally in the recent Turner Review.[17]

[10] Responsibility for the various tasks seen as necessary to the maintenance of systemic stability and confidence was allocated between the three authorities according to the following principles: clear accountability; transparency; avoidance of duplication; and regular information exchange.

[11] The UK Prime Minister has now acknowledged the shortcomings of the unitary system of financial regulation he announced in 1997 that led to the settlement of respective responsibilities between the Bank of England and the FSA (interview, *The Guardian* 17 March 2009).

[12] House of Commons Treasury Committee, 'Fifth Report of Session 2007–08', vol 1, HC 56-1, ch 3.

[13] House of Commons Treasury Committee, 'Sixth Report of Session 2007–08', HC 371, ch 9.

[14] Great Britain, Comptroller and Auditor General, 'HM Treasury: The Nationalisation of Northern Rock' (National Audit Office, 2009).

[15] Financial Services Authority, 'The Supervision of Northern Rock: A Lessons Learned Review' (March 2008).

[16] See Financial Services Authority, 'Stress and Scenario Testing', FSA Consultation Paper 08/24 (2008).

[17] Financial Services Authority, 'The Turner Review: A Regulatory Response to the Global Banking Crisis' (2009).

A recurrent theme throughout the various post-mortems on the run on Northern Rock that have taken place is the muddy and unclear boundary between 'risk' and 'uncertainty'. The board of Northern Rock, in evidence to the Treasury Committee, stated that the decline in interbank liquidity in August 2007 fell into the latter category. Rather than being a measurable and foreseeable 'risk', they argued that it was an unforeseeable 'unknown' that materialised.[18] It was less easy for the FSA to mount this kind of defence of its application of its risk-based supervisory framework (widely known as the ARROW model of supervision[19]) to Northern Rock, but nevertheless there were echoes of it, while at the same time the FSA acknowledged the shortcomings in assumptions underlying its stress testing of Northern Rock's business model.[20]

The comments from board members about the unexpected and unforeseeable way in which 'normal' wholesale bank funding seized up and the FSA's comments about its failure to stress test in such a way as to predict the consequences of such a seizure in liquidity raise serious questions about a supervisory framework that is calibrated in terms of discrete and finite 'risks'. Were the systemic effects of the congruence of different factors and influences from different parts of the banking system so as to cut off Northern Rock's wholesale funding flows an ascertainable and foreseeable 'risk' or an unknowable, blind-siding 'uncertainty'? The board appears to argue that it was indeed the latter, whereas the FSA has acknowledged that its conceptualisation and modelling of risk in its ARROW supervisory process failed to spot the true level of liquidity risk to which Northern Rock was exposed, and hence it failed to react appropriately to it. However, the FSA did not seek to argue that it could never have done so, or that it was any kind of an 'unknowable unknown'.[21] The distinction between risk and uncertainty has now been acknowledged by the FSA in the Turner Review. Indeed, it may well surface in a courtroom in the course of litigation against bank boards and intermediaries, and could well be determinative of its outcome. However, the fact that some events and consequences could not be and were not captured by ARROW-type models (whether or not it is correct to call them truly Knightian uncertainties[22]) signals dangers of a mismatch of expectations between the various stakeholders in financial regulation as to what it can and cannot achieve. Although, until recently, the FSA never really emphasised the risk/uncertainty boundary, it had already attempted to dampen down unrealistic and unachievable expectations of financial regulation in its discussion of the persistence of failure in regulated markets.[23] It tried to sketch the limits of financial regulation's capacities and has pointed to the existence of the principles accompanying the four core objectives as statutory exhortations to look for market-based solutions to threats to those objectives. In explaining that regulated firms can and should still fail, the FSA has argued that every such instance should not automatically be seen as evidence of regulatory failure. The regulator's

---

[18] Evidence given by the former Chairman and Chief Executive of Northern Rock to Treasury Select Committee, 16 October 2007.

[19] Advanced, Risk-responsive Operating Framework; the framework had last been revised in 2005/2006 and is set out in detail in *The FSA's Risk-Assessment Framework* (FSA, August 2006). See further Black, above n 6; J Black, 'The Development of Risk Based Regulation in Financial Services: Just "Modelling Through"' in J Black, M Lodge and M Thatcher (eds), *Regulatory Innovation: A Comparative Analysis* (Cheltenham, Edward Elgar, 2005).

[20] Evidence given by Hector Sants, CEO of FSA, to Treasury Select Committee, 9 October 2007.

[21] Financial Services Authority, above n 15.

[22] F Knight, *Risk, Uncertainty and Profit* (1921), available at www.econlib.org/library/Knight/knRUP.html.

[23] Financial Services Authority, 'Regulation in a Non-zero Failure World' (2005).

role in seeking to reduce or minimise risks posed by regulated firms should not be confused with the ability to isolate those firms from the risks posed by the wider economic context.[24] However, the FSA has revisited this analysis and has been more explicit about the implications of the risk/uncertainty boundary.[25]

C. What Can Litigation Arising from Northern Rock Run and Nationalisation Tell Us about Risk and Financial Regulation?

Many different areas of law and financial regulation have played a key role in mediating events leading up to, during and after the depositor run on Northern Rock plc.[26] The nationalised bank has now announced that it will not pursue litigation to recoup the losses to shareholder value in the bank against any of the executive or non-executive members of the board of Northern Rock plc.[27] Such litigation could have raised some quite fundamental questions concerning the extent of company directors' duties in company law, especially those owed by the non-executive directors, in companies doing business in highly regulated sectors. In a preliminary hearing of the ultimately abandoned litigation against members of the Equitable Life board in *Equitable Life Assurance Society v Bowley & Others*,[28] the High Court hinted that there might have been some room for argument that non-executive directors should bear a special responsibility of independent assessment of the executive board.[29]

Arguably, in the Northern Rock case, non-executive directors' responsibilities could have extended to stress-testing a banking business model more than usually reliant on wholesale short-term funding than most and to insuring such a business model against liquidity shortage. However, those directors' duties questions will not now be rehearsed in court following the decision by the company not to proceed with any claims against the board members.

Although, now, direct government equity investment in and involvement in the banking sector are all around us, an important milestone was still reached in UK financial markets on 22 February 2008 with Northern Rock's nationalisation.[30] The liabilities of the

---

[24] Ibid, para 3.5.

[25] Turner Review, above n 17, ch 1, para 1.4(iii).

[26] R Tomasic, 'Corporate Rescue, Governance and Risk-taking in Northern Rock' (2008) 29 *Company Lawyer* 297 and (2008) 29 *Company Lawyer* 330; Robert Falkner, 'How to React to Northern Rock' (2007) 26 *International Financial Law Review* 479; D Greene, 'Northern Rock: Potential False Market Shareholder Claims' (2008) 23 *Butterworths Journal of International Banking and Financial Law* 67; C Bamford, 'Northern Rock and the Single Market' (2008) 29 *Company Lawyer* 65; G Walker, 'Sub-prime Loans, Inter-bank Markets, Financial Support' (2008) 29 *Company Lawyer* 22; W Lindsay-Poulsen, 'Regional Autonomy, Geographic Selectivity and Fiscal Aid: Between "The Rock" and a Hard Place' (2008) 29 *European Competition Law Review* 43; B McDonnell, 'Northern Rock: Was Mervyn King Right?' (2007) 22 *Butterworths Journal of International Banking and Financial Law* 623; H Weenink, 'State Aid in the Financial Services Sector' (2008) 23 *Journal of International Banking Law and Regulation* 2008 514.

[27] Northern Rock Q3 Trading Statement, issued on 8 October 2008.

[28] [2003] BCC 829.

[29] Ibid para 41, per Langley J.

[30] *The Northern Rock plc Transfer Order 2008* (SI 2008/432); a good chronology of events is provided in Part One of the National Audit Office's Report, above n 14.

bank were transferred to the government's account in return for compensation to be paid to its shareholders. That compensation was to be based on certain valuation assumptions, namely that the value of the securities transferred on nationalisation be assessed on the basis that all financial assistance made to Northern Rock by either the Bank of England or HM Treasury has been withdrawn and no more is forthcoming, that it is unable to continue as a going concern and that it is in administration.[31]

1.   Shareholder Claims

Various Northern Rock shareholders have challenged the compatibility of this legislation with Article 1 Protocol 1 (A1P1) of the European Convention on Human Rights.[32] They have argued that the valuation assumptions it contains will inevitably fail to result in compensation that meets the requirements of A1P1. That application was unsuccessful both at first instance and on appeal.[33] The High Court found the essential facts giving rise to the proceedings easy to state:

(a)   Northern Rock had a good-quality loan book.

(b)   At all relevant times the assets of Northern Rock exceeded its liabilities. It was solvent on a balance sheet basis.

(c)   However, in August or September 2007 it became insolvent in the sense that it could not pay its debts as they fell due.

(d)   Government support for Northern Rock was provided because there was 'a genuine threat to the stability of the financial system and in order to avoid a serious disturbance in the wider economy'. It may also have been provided in order to protect depositors.

(e)   The loans and guarantees provided for Northern Rock were not gratuitous. A premium rate of interest was payable on the loans, and a fee 'set at a higher rate than the interest premium' was charged for the guarantee arrangements provided on 9 October 2007 and later.

(f)   The loans to Northern Rock provided by the Bank of England were repayable on demand. If repayment had been demanded at any time before nationalisation, the company would have been insolvent in that it would have been unable to pay its debts as they fell due.

(g)   The financial support required by Northern Rock was not available from any source other than the government.

(h)   The government may make a profit from the nationalisation of Northern Rock in addition to the price paid for the financial support.[34]

---

[31] Banking (Special Provisions) Act 2008, s 5(4); Northern Rock Compensation Scheme Order 2008 (SI 2008/718) para 6.

[32] A1P1 provides: 'Every natural or legal person is entitled to the peaceful enjoyment of his possessions. No one shall be deprived of his possessions except in the public interest and subject to the conditions provided for by law and by the general principles of international law.

The preceding provisions shall not, however, in any way impair the right of a State to enforce such laws as it deems necessary to control the use of property in accordance with the general interest or to secure the payment of taxes or other contributions or penalties.'

[33] *R v HM Treasury ex parte (1) SRM Global Master Fund LP (2) RAB Special Situations (Master) Fund Ltd (3) Dennis Grainger & Ors* [2009] EWHC 227; and on appeal [2009] EWCA Civ 788.

[34] Ibid, para 82.

The Court provided useful analysis of the principles governing the Bank of England's role as lender of last resort, emphasising how such support is provided solely as a means for pursuing wider objectives of systemic stability and should never be seen as any kind of special protection for depositors or employees, and that in fact owners and managers should expect to be penalised.[35] In further support of their allegations, the claimants had argued that it was wrong that HM Treasury was to profit from the nationalisation since it was its failings, along with those of the Bank of England and the FSA in their tripartite management of both Northern Rock and of the financial sector during the credit crisis more generally, that led to the nationalisation of Northern Rock. Therefore, the shareholders argued, to allow the government to profit in the sense of permitting a basis for shareholder compensation which rewards them at the expense of the shareholders is incompatible with A1P1. HM Treasury countered by arguing that such an argument would put difficult and sensitive questions of macro-economic policy management before the Court for which judicial review proceedings were wholly inappropriate. The Court did not accept the shareholders' argument about unfair government potential profit from the nationalisation upon the successful turnaround and sale of Northern Rock back into private hands, pointing out that the government would in the meantime bear considerable trading risk and was thus not precluded from benefiting from its own management of the bank should it be successful.

2.   Allegations of Regulatory Failure

The most interesting aspect of this case from the point of view of thinking about the future of financial regulation is the way in which the Court dealt with the allegations of regulatory failure on the part of the tripartite authorities. These were essentially that the Bank of England was insufficiently proactive in response to the drying up of inter-bank liquidity and failed to use its lender of last resort powers consistently and in a timely fashion, and that the FSA had failed in the exercise of its regulatory functions vis-à-vis its supervisory responsibilities for Northern Rock.

The Court made it clear that it was not deciding whether or not there had been any regulatory failure that constituted negligence, these being judicial review proceedings. It cautioned that FSA statements made in the aftermath of the run on Northern Rock which appeared to be admissions of supervisory failure were informed by hindsight and it emphasised what the FSA had to say about the extreme unforeseeability of complete wholesale funding closure and just what a long tail risk it was.[36] However, even if it were possible for the claimants to establish regulatory failure, the Court stated it did not advance their claim for two principal reasons. First, it was the management of Northern Rock who were first and foremost responsible for its insolvency due to their business model's extreme reliance on short-term wholesale funding as opposed to retail deposits. It had been open to shareholders to monitor and assess this business model, and to influence

---

[35] Ibid, para 21.

[36] The Court cited the evidence given to the Treasury Select Committee by the CEO of the FSA on 9 October 2007, referred to above on the text to n 20. That there was clear regulatory failure in the case of the supervision of Northern Rock has now been acknowledged by the FSA in the Northern Rock 'Lessons Learned' Internal Audit Report (March 2008) and by Lord Turner, Chairman of FSA, both in evidence to Treasury Select Committee (25 February 2009, Q 2143) and in the Turner Review, above n 17, para 2.7(i).

(and, if need be, replace) the directors responsible for stewardship of the bank. As owners of the bank, they had the option of using voice and/or exit in accordance with the classical model of corporate governance, which visits any losses of shareholder value on those who fail to protect it. Secondly, the Court made it clear that the shareholders in Northern Rock were owed no duty by either the Bank of England or the FSA, and that their interests fell outside the range of interests to be considered by the regulators in exercise of their public law duties.

In any event, said the Court, these arguments as to regulatory failure did not avail the first and second claimant shareholders, both hedge funds which had acquired their shareholdings after the events that were said to constitute regulatory failure had taken place. But what of the third group of claimants? The law assumes that a shareholder is a shareholder and that their different characteristics, backgrounds and profiles matter not one jot for equality literally is equity, and only the rights and terms on which their shares were allotted govern their ultimate status and entitlements.[37] However, if we ask the question who are these shareholders who are challenging the government's handling of the Northern Rock crisis and nationalisation, then we see, de jure orthodoxy aside, that equality is very far from being equity. For, if we focus for a moment or two on the identity of the third group of small shareholder claimants, a very different type of investor/owner is revealed:

> Some acquired their shares on demutualisation; others are or were employees who acquired their shares under an approved profit share scheme or share incentive plan, or other incentive schemes, or by contributions to the company pension fund. Others were small investors who purchased their shares on the stock exchange. Three of the small group of representative shareholders had purchased shares after the Bank had issued the statement on 14 September 2007 that it had provided financial support to Northern Rock. At the date of nationalisation there were some 150,000 small shareholders.[38]

While the Court repeatedly expressed sympathy for these small shareholders (especially those for whom Northern Rock shares had formed a substantial part of their pension funding), it reverted to the narrow lens of company law orthodoxy through which to see their position at law, saying:

> All shareholders, large or small, professional or private, are investors in the fortunes of the company the shares of which they hold, and the small shareholders had the misfortune to hold investments in a company that by 13 September 2007 was cash flow insolvent.[39]

The third group of claimants did not seek in argument to distinguish their position in any way from that of the hedge fund claimants. It was not argued for them that A1P1 would extend its protections to them as individual, (largely) long-term owners of the company in any way differently or with more subtlety and sensitivity than it would to offshore-based institutional investors who epitomised short-termism. It is to be regretted that they did not seek to advance arguments based on such a distinction, for it too readily enabled the Court to conclude:

> [W]e can see no basis for holding that A1P1 required the Government to treat small shareholders differently from professional investors such as the First and the Second Claimants . . . The shares

---

[37] *Birch v Cropper* (1889) 14 App Cas 525.
[38] Above n 33, para 9.
[39] Ibid, para 103.

acquired from the small investors were identical to and had the same value as the shares acquired from professional investors.[40]

In a context where we as scholars of financial regulation are discussing questions of the nature of financial citizenship, asking what financial regulation is actually for and how it can be made more responsive and democratic, as well as narrower questions about its efficacy and effectiveness, the position of the small shareholders in Northern Rock should not be seen in such simple terms. If human rights law protects anything in the context of property, surely it must have something to say about financial citizenship?[41] Ought human rights law not have some role to play in identifying, drawing out and safeguarding the essentially human aspects of that concept? The Court heard no evidence as to the circumstances in which the small shareholders acquired their Northern Rock shares, their motives for such acquisition or retention, their understanding of the risks and incidents of liability of equity investment, their awareness of the extent to which the financial regulatory system extended its surveillance and protection, or their understanding of and practical ability to participate meaningfully in the governance of Northern Rock. Although we are constantly being told that the credit crisis is a truly global one, it has to be pointed out that its most painful effects are being felt unevenly, both geographically and demographically. An interesting piece of research would be to obtain the shareholder register of Northern Rock as at February 2008 and to map the geographic locations, identities, longevity of shareholding and household wealth of its shareholders. It is highly likely that a much higher proportion of shareholders would be found in the North East of England region, and of these many would have held parcels of original demutualisation shares which, over time, would have come to represent significant proportions of household wealth. Further research would as likely as not reveal specific individual and personal shareholder stories which could create quite a powerful narrative of how the effects of the run and nationalisation have been felt especially sharply in one region by individuals who do not fit the usual mould of shareholder/equity investor, despite the presumptions applied by the law that a shareholder is a shareholder whoever they are and is not owed any duty of care by financial regulators. It may be argued, too, that the vast majority of the individual North Eastern shareholders (26,000 or so) rather became shareholders not 'as a windfall' but by agreeing to a demutualisation process whereby they swapped one solid and more democratic form of financial citizenship (regional building society membership) for another model of financial citizenship (shareholding in a publicly listed company).[42] As corporate governance scholarship has revealed to us, there is far more of a democratic deficit inherent in the latter form of financial citizenship. The same government now cancelling that form of citizenship (ie nationalising shares) set up the context which allowed building societies to convert into proprietary institutions and encouraged employee share ownership, greater private pension saving and wider retail participation in equity markets—all things which led many regional shareholders to build up further stakes in an institution they knew and trusted. Perhaps it is the case that hard legal argument based on human rights law principles would not acknowledge the relevance of such a narrative or be assisted by them, but they deserve rehearsing.

---

[40] Ibid, para 169.

[41] Just as Reich once argued in the context of citizenship constructed by welfare entitlements and its place in US public law: CA Reich, 'The New Property' (1964) 73 *Yale Law Journal* 733.

[42] The way was paved for such demutualisation by the Building Societies Act 1986.

The legal process as it stands has failed to see financial regulation as relevant to the form of financial citizenship engaged in by those who chose to keep their Northern Rock demutualisation shares as opposed to those who sold and reinvested the proceeds in a deposit account with the same bank. What, if anything, does this tell us about the FSA's twin statutory objectives of consumer protection and public awareness of the financial system when viewed from the bottom up by those who feel the effects of fault lines in the financial system as opposed to being viewed by those who design policy? Indeed, the Turner report has acknowledged for the future that there will be instances when extreme 'uncertainty' strikes and losses occur such that the only sensible policy response to system failure is the socialisation of risk.[43] It seems that the small Northern Rock shareholders are to bear that risk alone, though. It is interesting that the Court made no comment at all on the fact that Northern Rock had been advised against legal action against the board—in its (and the government's) view the principal authors of the shareholder losses.

D.   The Future for Risk-based Regulation?

What has been remarkable about the official sector and political rhetoric surrounding the crisis in confidence in UK financial regulation has been the shift from a position where the model of high-level 'principles-based' and 'risk-related' regulation was at first defended as a regulatory approach[44] to a position where it has been acknowledged that it enabled regulation to take place that was simply too 'light touch'[45] and needed to be seen in a broader political context that constrained the ability of regulators to operate a more restrictive and intrusive model of regulation.[46] Foreshadowing the Turner Report's emphasis on a less pro-cyclical, more macro-prudential[47] and systemic approach to

---

[43] Turner Review, above n 17, para 1.4(iii).

[44] For example, Hector Sants (chief executive, FSA), 'The UK Approach to Regulation', speech to the FSA Financial Services Seminar, British Embassy, Tokyo (7 November 2007); Verena Ross (director, Strategy & Risk, FSA), 'London's Financial Markets and the FSA's Approach to Financial Regulation', speech to *The Economist* Conference, 4 December 2007; BBC Radio 4 *Today Programme*, interviews with Alistair Darling, 23 September 2008, and Gordon Brown, 24 September 2008.

[45] A phrase that both politicians and regulators refused to apply to UK financial regulation but was eventually used as a descriptor of the UK model by both the Chairman of the Bank of England and the Governor of the Bank of England on successive days while giving evidence to the Treasury Select Committee on the Banking Crisis (25 and 26 February 2009).

[46] 'I think . . . that [a system of regulation which focused on organisation structures, processes, systems and whether the reporting lines were correct rather than casting questions over the overall business strategy of the institution] existed within a political philosophy where all the pressure on the FSA was not to say : "Are you looking more closely at these business models?" but to say: "Why are you being so heavy and intrusive? Can you make your regulation a bit more light touch?"' (Lord Turner, evidence in response to Q 2145, HC Treasury Select Committee, 25 February 2009). See also Mervyn King in response to Q 2354, HC Treasury Select Committee, 26 February 2009, making the point that regulators would have been both put to proof and faced vocal lobbying had it asserted that the risks being taken by what appeared to be highly successful and profitable institutions were excessive and should be curtailed.

[47] For a good discussion of the differences in objective and approach between 'micro' and 'macro' prudential perspectives on financial regulation and supervision see C Borio, 'Towards a Macroprudential Framework for Financial Supervision and Regulation?', BIS Working Papers No 128 (Bank for International Settlements, February 2003); these points had been made by other commentators earlier in the unfolding of the current financial crisis: see C Goodhart, 'The Regulatory Response to the Financial Crisis', CESIFO Working Papers No 2257 (March 2008); C Borio, 'Change and Constancy in the Financial System: Implications for Financial Distress and Policy', BIS Working Papers No 237 (Bank for International Settlements, October 2007).

regulation in the future, Mervyn King and other Bank of England witnesses made some very interesting comments to the Treasury Select Committee about the need for regulators and those entrusted with governance in financial institutions to go out on a limb, to be a voice (lone, if need be) against received wisdom and orthodoxy, to think and act counterfactually and to 'think big, [sticking] to first principles'.[48]

Mervyn King set out the task for the Turner Review perfectly in his statement to the Committee that:

> The real challenge is to build into the institutions something which bequeaths to our successors our institutional memory of the dangers of relaxing regulation too much and of not having a framework which builds in some sand in the wheels to a rapid rate of expansion.[49]

Before turning to how the Turner Report seeks to achieve that, it is worth noting that the literature on risk measurement, management and modelling has been growing more critical and less accepting of the claims of predictive power of financial risk modelling.[50] Statistical and quantitative finance scholars have long struggled to deal with extreme, outlier or 'fat tail' risks which lie outside standard distribution patterns and are less easily modelled,[51] but shy away from questions of whether such risks are knowable unknowns or unknowable unknowns, a distinction that, it is argued here, has significance in terms of designing regulation. The behavioural finance literature provides a developing intellectual framework for a more fundamental critique of the predictive power of risk models.[52] Gerding has recently used insights from both behavioural finance and the domain of cyber-law to critique what he argues has been effectively an outsourcing of what is properly the responsibility of financial regulation to proprietary risk models developed by and operating within financial institutions themselves, a process that finds its most extreme and ultimate expression in Basel II.[53] Using Gilson and Whitehead's recent analysis of the role of securitisation and derivatives finance in risk transfer and diffusion leading to a retreat from public equity, Gerding charts the use of different proprietary computer-based risk models at every point along the tortuous and long 'originate and distribute' chain. It starts with the use of data mining and credit scoring software at the customer facing point of risk origination. This might be when the sub-prime, teaser rate, self-certified mortgage is transacted in a previously red-lined zip code in South Central Los Angeles.[54] The consumer finance risk to be securitised will then be run through the financial institution's own pricing model, and subsequently rated by a credit rating agency employing its own models for the computation of ratings. Insofar as the risks of these asset-backed securities are hedged, then the derivatives used will be priced by computational models, and the financial institutions that ultimately end up holding these

---

[48] Answering Q 2362 HC Treasury Select Committee, 26 February 2009.

[49] Ibid, answering Q 2363.

[50] K Dowd, *Beyond Value at Risk: The New Science of Risk Management* (New York, Wiley, 1998); J Danielsson, 'VaR: A Castle Built on Sand' (2001) 5 *Financial Regulator* 46; M Nwogugu, 'Further Critique of GARCH/ARMA/VAR/Stochastic-Volatility Models', ssrn.com/abstract=859985; M Power, *Organised Uncertainty: Designing a World of Risk Management* (Oxford, Oxford University Press, 2007); NN Taleb, *The Black Swan: The Impact of the Highly Improbable* (London, Penguin, 2008).

[51] P Embrechts (ed), *Extremes and Integrated Risk Management* (London, Risk Waters Group, 2000).

[52] R Shiller, *Irrational Exuberance* (Princeton NJ, Princeton University Press, 2000); A Shleifer, *Inefficient Markets: An Introduction to Behavioural Finance* (New York, Oxford University Press, 2000).

[53] E Gerding, 'The Outsourcing of Risk Models and the Global Financial Crisis: Code, Crash and Open Source' *Washington Law Review* (forthcoming) ssrn.com/abstract=1273467.

[54] Dymski, above n 9.

asset-backed securities will employ their own investment management models in the running of their portfolios with their risk management policies being set and driven by technical models too. Gerding terms all these proprietary models and software 'the new financial code' and likens it to the early generation of proprietary software that built the worldwide web but has now been opened up and made more transparent and democratic by the advent of open source code. However, in finance he argues that financial regulators have been complicit in the dominance and dominion of these closed and private models. Regulators have, through mechanisms such as linking 'investment grade' debt to credit rating agency decisions or by endorsement of relating regulatory capital to banks' own risk management techniques in Basel II, enrolled the models as proxies for their own judgements and decision-making about some extremely complex and opaque risks to such an extent that regulators have almost retreated to the sidelines, leaving risk and uncertainty to the reductive magic of models. Gerding uses language intelligible to those who are not expert in quantitative finance to show that even those who are conversant with it also struggle with risk models' ability to quantify Knightian 'uncertainty', due to the models' reliance on historical data patterns, the limits of these data patterns and even more sophisticated assumptions about their interaction with each other when randomly sampled (the so-called 'Monte Carlo' variant of the value at risk model). He concludes that even these cannot pin down uncertainty and change it into risk about which we can say anything meaningful ex ante.

In considering why and how this new financial code crashed so spectacularly in failing to mediate efficient risk transfer and regulation, evidenced by widespread foreclosures and failure of financial institutions, as well as how it can be improved, Gerding struggles with the same problems that faced Turner. He identifies a need to come up with practical and workable policy recommendations that at the same time acknowledge the inherent limitations of man-made risk models in ever knowing the unknowable unknowns that constitute true 'uncertainty'. He finds Taleb's radical critique of risk modelling 'philosophically provocative' yet somewhat ethereal in terms of charting ways forward from here.[55] Risk management models are not going to go away. Delphic omniscience will not suddenly suffuse regulators, bank boards and investors worldwide. Instead, those charged with charting a way forward, in their prescriptions to fix risk models and reorient regulators' and financial institutions' use of models, must also be more open and explicit about the persistence of uncertainty and the fact that no amount of regulation, whatever its model or approach, can guard against the truly catastrophic 'killer event'.[56]

1.   Turner and Flaws in Risk Modelling

Turner makes this non-zero failure point in his questioning of some fundamental assumptions underlying what many of us had always believed about market efficiency. He refers to the need to distinguish between 'risk' and true 'Knightian uncertainty' in any efforts to fix the mathematics of models and counter their limitations. Our inability to model uncertainty, he argues, lends weight to the need for a more macro-prudential approach but also 'suggests that no system *could* ever guard against all risks/uncertainties and that there may

---

[55] Gerding, above n 53, 53, accompanying text to n 198.
[56] Taleb, above n 50.

be extreme circumstances in which the back up of risk socialisation . . . is the optimal and the only defence against system failure'.[57]

Having sounded this caveat about the inherent limits within ex ante regulation, Turner finds plenty within the UK financial regulatory system to fix and improve. These include his recommendations as to how to engineer more macro-prudential and systemic capital regulation for banks that can form a buffer against the economic cycle, a greater focus on and improved liquidity regulation, correction of skewed incentive structures (whether they be in the influence of credit rating agencies or the operation of remuneration practices) and improvement of cross-border and particularly European-level bank regulation and supervision, along with his recommendations as to deposit insurance and bank resolution. Of most relevance to the future of risk-based financial regulation are his recommendations relating to changes needed to the FSA's supervisory approach and to firms' capacity for and engagement with risk management and governance. Although he expresses the by now familiar disclaimer that the FSA's supervisory approach was never 'light touch', he does signal a very clear break with the past, having reviewed and found wanting the assumptions that underpinned FSA's risk-based and principles-based approach to supervision and regulation, namely a belief that markets are self-correcting,[58] that primary responsibility for risk management lies properly with senior management of regulated actors and that consumer protection is best pursued by retail conduct of business regulation and minimal wholesale market regulation. This approach, Turner admits, led to the FSA focusing too much on the micro and the individual at the cost of macro and systemic oversight; to focus too much on systems and processes rather than on the substance of the way in which business was being done and planned; to place too great a focus on integrity rather than on technical competence of the key people driving the financial industry forward and responsible for its governance; and to a skewing of regulatory effort, attention and focus towards conduct of business regulation over prudential regulation so that system-wide, macro-prudential fault lines and pressure points within the latter were missed.[59] The terms 'risk-based' and 'principles-based' do not appear anywhere in the Turner Report applied to any overarching philosophy or model of regulation. Terms such as 'intrusive', 'aggressive' and 'systemic' are used by Turner to describe the regulatory philosophy that will characterise the FSA's approach to supervision in future. Indeed, Turner points out that the various initiatives that comprise the FSA's Supervisory Enhancement Programme settled in the wake of its Northern Rock lessons-learned review have already begun this shift towards more intensive and intrusive supervision.[60] However, echoing Mervyn King's arguments before the Treasury Committee

---

[57] Turner Review, above n 17, para 1.4(iii) (emphasis added).

[58] He echoes Alan Greenspan's admission that he had placed too much faith in the inherent ability of markets to manage risk (evidence on the Financial Crisis and the Role of Federal Regulators, to Congressional House of Representative Committee on Oversight and Government Reform (October 2008); see transcript of Committee hearing, oversight.house.gov/documents/20081024163819.pdf).

[59] Turner Review, above n 17, para 2.7.

[60] Turner highlights examples of the kind of more intensive supervision being put in place since April 2008, such as more frequent and comprehensive ARROW risk reviews for high impact firms; increased FSA resources devoted to sectoral and firm comparator analysis; closer examination of the technical competence of those with and applying for Approved Person status under Part V FSMA 2000; more expertise within the FSA on specialist areas such as liquidity risk analysis and greater attention to liquidity risks; more willingness to vary capital and liquidity prudential requirements when the FSA judges this is required; and greater likelihood of intervention when specific business strategies are perceived to pose undue individual prudential or wider systemic risk: see Turner Review, above n 17, para 2.7(ii).

for more robust and counterfactual thinking and judgement in financial regulation, Turner adds the need for greater capability within the FSA to operate truly counter-cyclical and macro-prudential supervision. He also adds to the list of changes needed for more intrusive and intensive supervision the need for a greater critical engagement with and understanding of banks' accounting processes and judgements. The extent of the recent bank recapitalisations and their ongoing nature resulting in the need for the Asset Protection Scheme (and similar elsewhere) to clean out the Augean stables of bankers worldwide has revealed mark-to-market accounting techniques that have been all but meaningless in producing credible value narratives. In order to prevent the kind of unprecedented capital write-downs and revaluations that UK banks have engaged in over the past year or so, the FSA will involve itself more closely and intensely with banks' auditors and management and why and how the accounting judgements that are made are made at the point when values are first ascribed to bank books and from thereon as they are kept under review. The Audit Committee of any UK bank in the future may find that it has a de facto, ex officio member in the form of a more sceptical and enquiring FSA.

Despite Turner's conclusion that there are limits to how much can be achieved at the individual firm level, he nonetheless recommends improvements in risk management, oversight and governance at that level, although detailed recommendations will await the outcome of the Walker Review into bank governance. He does, however, single out the need for shorter and more direct links between a more professional and independent firm risk management function and board level risk committees, and for remuneration policy not to distort the independence and integrity of risk management. He makes the by now familiar call for more technically skilled, competent, committed and independent bank non-executive directors, and for greater shareholder monitoring and involvement of strategic issues within banks.[61] These points echo a spate of recent corporate governance and company law reviews as well as the analysis of poor governance as the root cause of the near collapse and takeover at one of our major clearing banks in the evidence given to the Treasury Select Committee by the former Head of Group Regulatory Risk at HBOS plc.[62]

2.   Did Turner Miss a Valuable Opportunity to Help Develop a New 'Politics of Uncertainty'?

Finally, it is worth asking whether or not Turner, in a highly reflective report characterised by a welcome degree of intellectual honesty and openness, nevertheless missed an opportunity to future-proof redesign of financial regulation against accusations of failure and the opprobrium that will inevitably ensue once the next 'killer event' hits and widespread financial losses occur, whatever that event turns out to be. This brings us back to the risk/uncertainty distinction again. Prior to the Turner Review, the FSA understandably sought through its Supervisory Enhancement Programme to improve the effectiveness of the implementation of regulatory standards and objectives through the medium of

---

[61] Turner Review, ibid, para 2.8.

[62] See evidence of Paul Moore in the Part Three Memorandum of Evidence to Treasury Select Committee, Hearings on Banking Crisis (February 2009) paras 4.2–4.7; Further Memorandum of Written Evidence from Paul Moore to Treasury Select Committee, 26 February 2009.

improved, more effective supervision, and Turner has taken that process further. The FSA and the Bank of England have now both gone on record as arguing that the way in which the implosion of wholesale bank funding markets transpired as a result of loss of confidence between counterparties in that market as a result of a widespread loss of trust in the quality of bank assets represented the fruition of a 'macro-prudential' risk. They appear to see it as a systemic fault line that shifted in a manner that was, though wholly unexpected in many quarters, not exactly unimaginable, and could have been picked up by a better designed, more counterfactual and systemically sensitive regulatory Richter scale. It was not therefore an 'unknowable uncertainty' and, although difficult to measure, predict and foresee, and obviously beyond the bounds of many individual bank risk models, it could have been stress tested by regulators worldwide and was thus not true Knightian uncertainty. However, that admission should not occlude or obscure the FSA's earlier message in its warning about the impossibility of a non-zero failure world[63] and, given the degree of opprobrium being heaped on regulators worldwide now, they would do well to sound that warning again even as they redesign and seek to increase the risk detection capacity of regulatory supervisory models for the future. What results may (indeed, it is to be hoped, will) enhance the ability for 'unknown uncertainties' to be factored into how financial capitalism is controlled and regulated. More improved systemic, macro-prudential risk management and more independent, holistic and sceptical thinking and actions may indeed come from regulators in the future. One means by which some jurisdictions choose to pursue that may be a brake on financial innovation through the application of a precautionary principle that prohibits financial products, services and institutions beyond a simple and narrower range, in the hope of benefiting from a 'race to the top' effect in financial regulation. However, there will still remain with us the 'unknowable uncertainties' that Taleb has so effectively brought to the popular imagination,[64] yet economists and practical risk managers have been puzzling over for some time now. Although he uses the term 'significant risk' when he is talking of these kinds of unknowable uncertainties, one professional risk manager, Jablonowski, has written that '[a] realistic view of risk demands some belief in the idea of immediate powerlessness in the face of significant risk'.[65] The same point was made by Turner as he cautioned against the inherent limits of regulation in the face of true Knightian uncertainty. It is the same point made by the FSA in its analysis of a non-zero failure world,[66] and was made by Power in his call for a new 'politics of uncertainty' to accompany the proliferation in risk based regulatory regimes.[67] As Power points out, although regulators in the very act of using and developing risk-based regulatory standards and techniques appear to be implicitly acknowledging that there will be events and circumstances where unknowable uncertainty reigns supreme and their standards and techniques cannot and will not operate, this is a very difficult point for regulators to make politically, especially at times of crisis, collapse and disaster (as now). For, as Power has put it:

---

[63] FSA, above n 23.
[64] Taleb, above n 50.
[65] M Jablonowski, 'Facing Risk in the 21st Century' (2004) 51 *Risk Management* 26; see also M Jablonowski, *Precautionary Risk Management* (London, Macmillan, 2006).
[66] FSA, above n 23.
[67] M Power, *The Risk Management of Everything* (London, Demos, 2004).

> Risk has become reflexively applied to regulatory bodies themselves; risk-based approaches become central to an active blame management process via the ability to demonstrate a rational process trail. Existing public discourses sit uneasily with a 'risk-based' ethos and tend to have a more zero tolerance character.[68]

It is much harder for regulators, especially when engaged in post-crisis reform, to emphasise the persistence and possibility of unknowable uncertainty than it is for politicians. Jablonowski has argued that the two simple and appropriate responses to truly unknowable uncertainties are precaution and rational fatalism.[69] It is for regulators to turn to the former (emphasising that there is no guarantee that even that will work) and for political and social leaders to turn to the latter through education, leadership and, as Turner put it, presenting real politically honest choices about socialising the consequences of uncertainty. Of course, this raises a further difficult question of what is an ex ante 'unknowable uncertainty/risk' and what is simply an 'unknown uncertainty/risk' for, to be the victim of the former may result in some lifeline through compensation or other form of loss socialisation, whereas, with the regulatory immunities as they are currently structured, to be the victim of the latter is to be left high and dry. The Northern Rock small shareholders illustrate this point perfectly. Insights from decision theory appear to indicate that it may be easier to develop a politics of uncertainty and a public reconciliation to the truly unknowable than we might at first think. When faced with choices as between the three types of uncertainty—known, unknown and unknowable—individuals are reported to prefer and to express less dissatisfaction with the outcomes of known, unknowable and unknown uncertainties in that order.[70] This suggests that it may be easier to procure some public acceptance and reconciliation to the inevitable existence and persistence of true Knightian uncertainty than uncertainty that was not wholly latent and could have been modelled for, stress tested for, or imagined and identified ex ante, prior to its transpiring. Viewed like this, the Northern Rock small, long-term shareholders' feelings of being wholly let down by government and regulators are understandable, for it is government and regulators who exhorted and encouraged the kind of financial citizenship in which those small shareholders had engaged, and who have admitted that the gaps in the supervision of Northern Rock were of the unknown kind rather than the unknowable. Hence, when those shareholders are directed by the Courts to look to the board and not the regulators for redress, that same board claiming that as far as they were concerned the seizure in inter-bank liquidity was an unknowable when viewed from their individual (non macro-prudential) perspective, the shareholders can be forgiven for feeling exactly the kind of dissonance that decision theorists would predict.

If the same 'uncertainty' can be unknowable by one set of actors (individual boards never imagining that inter-bank trust would evaporate and block up financial capitalism) and yet merely unknown by others (regulators missing vital macro-prudential and systemic indicators), this does not really help us in practical terms and shows how politically loaded is the decision whether to characterise something as a truly unknowable uncertainty.[71] If a real politics of uncertainty can be developed, then these questions ought

---

[68] M Power, *Organised Uncertainty: Designing a World of Risk Management* (Oxford, Oxford University Press, 2007).

[69] Jablonowski (2006), above n 65.

[70] CC Chow and RK Sarin, 'Known, Unknown and Unknowable Uncertainties' (2002) 52 *Theory and Decision* 127.

[71] P O'Malley, *Risk, Uncertainty and Government* (London, Glasshouse Press, 2004).

to be brought out into the open and be settled in as transparent, democratic and participative a way as possible, for if financial capitalism does get back on its feet, then it will surely stumble again in spectacular and painful fashion in the future, albeit over something else next time. Whether regulators (and all of us) do not or cannot know what that stumbling block may be is beside the point for those who will feel the effects of the stumble. However, from a regulators' point of view, whether what causes losses next time is more widely perceived as an unknowable may affect the degree to which blame is attributed to it and so, for that reason alone, this opportunity for regulatory redesign ought to make clear that there will be much to come in the future that will be genuinely unknowable by it as opposed to merely unknown.

E.   Some Very General Conclusions

This paper has raised the question whether all aspects of financial regulation that have failed to deliver desired outcomes and objectives and have resulted in such public disaffection and dissatisfaction are amenable to being fixed by legal, regulatory and institutional changes in financial regulation. It suggests that when it comes to responding appropriately to the effects of uncertainty, whether they be properly characterised as unknowable or unknown unknowns of the future, then legal and regulatory redesign are at best a sideshow and at worst a false signal to unrealistic expectations on the part of the 'financial citizenry' for whose benefit regulation purports to exist.[72] It has argued that the changes for which Power calls in a new 'politics of uncertainty' need to be made closer to home within the psyche of those who regulate, those who are regulated and those for whose benefit regulation exists.

This can be illustrated with the following example from the current financial crisis. When asked by the Treasury Select Committee what was the one key 'macro-prudential' risk signal in the various business models and strategies that was missed in recent years by regulators and bank boards to whom much control of risk had been outsourced, the Governor of the Bank of England singled out leverage.[73] Or, as Lewis puts it in his essay on the impact of the financial crisis on the life and soul of one small nation (Iceland):

> When you borrow a lot of money to create a false prosperity, you import the future into the present. It isn't the actual future so much as some grotesque silicon version of it. Leverage buys you a glimpse of a prosperity you haven't really earned.[74]

That gives us a glimpse of how great counterfactualism in regulatory policy may need to be in order to challenge the psyche of market and individual. It will require much more of its proponents than econometric skills, legal and regulatory tools and technical expertise. It is a challenge that calls for a subtle and honest understanding of the link between people and money, possibly informed as well by insights of behavioural finance and by the new

---

[72] CAE Goodhart et al, *Financial Regulation, Why, How and Where Now* (London, Routledge, 1998); see ch 1 for the moral hazard effects of regulation.
[73] M King, evidence to HC Treasury Select Committee, answering Q 2364, 26 February 2009.
[74] M Lewis, above n 9.

economics of happiness[75] and psychological resilience.[76] The problem of disappointed expectations of regulation in a non-zero failure world will not go away, and will surely be triggered by future events. Whether one sees such events as counterable 'macro-prudential' factors (unknown unknowns) or, to use Taleb's descriptor, true 'black swans' (unknowable unknowns), some of the negative externalities of future financial failures can be contained and reduced by the socialisation of certain politically unacceptable consequences of failure,[77] and also by a reordered relationship between individuals, risk and financial wealth. It certainly calls for the reconstruction of the notion of financial citizenship that has developed over the past 20 years or so. If more responsive and effective financial regulatory policy is to be achieved, then fundamental change is needed in individuals' thinking about money, wealth, status, entitlements and senses of security and fulfilment, for it is people, not institutions, processes, models and technical elites, that matter most as the ultimate stakeholders in financial regulation. Change here requires political and social leadership and honesty. It is one that policymakers are only just beginning to wake up to, but must be central to financial regulatory reform.

---

[75] R Layard, *Happiness: Lessons from a New Science* (New York, Penguin Press, 2005).

[76] RS Lazarus and S Folkman, *Stress, Appraisal, and Coping* (New York, Springer, 1984). Systemic economic change and widespread financial losses are identified as macro-stressors by psychiatry: see, eg DR Williams and H Neighbors, 'Social Perspectives on Mood Disorders' in D Stein, D Kupfer and A Schatzberg (eds), *Textbook of Mood Disorders* (Washington, American Pychiatric Publishing, 2005).

[77] Gerding, above n 53.

9

Risk Control Strategies: An Assessment in the Context of the Credit Crisis

A. Introduction

The concept of risk-based regulation is now well established in the UK regulatory framework for financial services. It is perhaps surprising that it has risen to such prominence in the absence of formal recognition by the legislative framework contained in the Financial Services and Markets Act 2000 (FSMA 2000). Its roots nevertheless do lie in the legislative framework, or at least in its interpretation by the UK regulator, the Financial Services Authority (FSA).[1] The statutory objectives[2] of financial regulation in the UK have been interpreted by the FSA as requiring that the regulator adopt a 'non-zero failure' approach, meaning that there are practical limitations on the extent to which regulation can eliminate risks to the statutory objectives.[3] Viewed in that light, risk-based regulation is 'based on a clear statement of the realistic aims and limits of regulation'.[4]

Underlying the model of risk-based regulation adopted by the FSA are two assumptions. The first is that risk can be identified and, at least in some contexts, measured. In the FSA's own words, risk is taken to be 'the combination of impact (potential harm that could be caused) and probability (the likelihood of the particular issue or event occurring)'. The main focus of risk identification and measurement is the individual firm, and this has two consequences. First, there is less attention paid to aggregation of risk across firms. This is reflected both in the limited significance that has been attached to systemic risk within the

---

[*] Alexander Stone Professor of Commercial Law, University of Glasgow.

[1] The FSA was created in 1997 as the successor to the Securities and Investments Board, which had been created by the Financial Services Act 1986. It is an integrated regulator with responsibility for prudential supervision and conduct of business regulation. Under the terms of a memorandum of understanding between the Treasury, the Bank of England and the FSA (the 'tripartite authority'), the Treasury is responsible for the overall intuitional structure of regulation and the legislative framework, while the Bank of England has responsibility for overall financial stability. The recently purchased government shareholdings in the financial sector are held by UK Financial Investments Ltd, a company in which the Treasury is the sole shareholder, and will be managed on an arms-length basis.

[2] The statutory objectives are: market confidence; public awareness; protection of consumers; and reduction of financial crime (FSMA 2000, ss 3–6).

[3] See FSA, 'Reasonable Expectations: Regulation in a Non-zero Failure World' (September 2003).

[4] See FSA, 'The FSA's Risk-assessment Framework' (August 2006), 7.

regulatory system[5] and also in the determination of the intensity of supervision at the firm level.[6] Secondly, the focus on measurable risk means that the regulatory system pays little attention to uncertainty, at least in its 'Knightian' form.[7] That omission has been particularly exposed by the recent credit crisis, which has focused attention on the threat posed by uncertain future events for risk models (both regulatory and proprietary) that are limited to measurable risk.[8]

The second assumption is that risk can be controlled inter alia by varying the intensity of regulatory supervision by reference to risk. From the perspective of an authorised firm, this means that the initial pattern of supervision and any subsequent change should be determined by the risk profile of the firm. From the perspective of the regulator, it implies that there is capacity to detect and measure changes in risk and to respond accordingly. Both facets of the second assumption have been tested in the recent credit crisis and in several instances have been shown to be weak.[9]

The process of risk-based regulation can be characterised as control over activity that is prima facie desirable but nevertheless poses risks associated with individual firms (insolvency), individual transactions (information asymmetry and conflicts of interest) and in aggregate across the market (systemic risk and market integrity). The challenge for risk-based regulation is to find a balance between facilitating regulated activity and ensuring that there is adequate control over risk. It will never be possible to satisfy everybody in this regard, so there will inevitably be an ongoing struggle in any system of risk-based regulation between proponents of the 'light-touch' approach and those favouring a more 'belt-and-braces' approach to the control of risk. It seems clear both that 'light-touch' regulation has been in the ascendancy in the years preceding the credit crisis and that a correction will follow, even if the precise direction and pace of change remains at this point uncertain.

An assessment of the causal role of risk-based regulation in the emergence of the crisis must consider two issues. One is the relative position of risk-based regulation in the range of causal influences that contributed to the crisis.[10] The second, which is the main focus of this chapter, is the extent to which the crisis provides evidence of limitations in risk-based regulation that may require its role to be recast. One line of argument has been that there are fundamental flaws in the very concept of risk-based regulation that call into question

---

[5] See M Brunnermeier, A Crocket, C Goodhart, A Persuad and H Shin, 'The Fundamental Principles of Financial Regulation' (January 2009), available at www.voxeu.org/index.php?q=node/2796.

[6] See further Part B below.

[7] This refers to the distinction drawn by Frank Knight between measurable risk and non-measurable uncertainty: see FH Knight, *Risk Uncertainty and Profit* (New York, Sentry Press, 1921) 233, commenting that 'The practical difference between the two categories, risk and uncertainty, is that in the former the distribution of the outcome in a group of instances is known (either through calculation a priori or from statistics of past experience) while in the case of uncertainty this is not true, the reason being in general that it is impossible to form a group of instances, because the situation dealt with is in a high degree unique'.

[8] For example, the distinction is evident in the treatment of regulatory capital, where the risk of probable default is taken into consideration in calculating risk-adjusted assets but not the uncertainty relating to possible downgrades in credit ratings that will carry consequences for regulatory capital.

[9] Examples are the failure to respond adequately to a rapid expansion in lending at Northern Rock and failure to appreciate and respond to the broader implications of the 'originate and distribute' model in the mortgage market.

[10] See FSA, 'Financial Risk Outlook 2009' (February 2009), citing the following as causal influences: a property price boom; increasing leverage in the banking and shadow banking system; rapid expansion of credit and falling credit standards; increasing complexity of the securitised credit model; and underestimation of bank and market liquidity risk.

its dominant position within the UK regulatory approach.[11] An alternative (the FSA approach[12]) has been that the concept itself is sound but that there have been some errors and misjudgements in implementation that, in conjunction with a range of other causal factors, have been instrumental in the genesis of the credit crisis.

Whatever the merits of each of those critiques, it seems clear that risk-based regulation is now so embedded in the regulatory system that it will survive in some form and therefore the regulatory reform debate should focus on what that form should be. I propose to do this by investigating the capacity of the regulatory system to control risk through three generic strategies. Capacity is a function of the institutional and normative structure of a system of regulation and of the underlying legal system on which it is super-imposed. It is also a function of the mix of risk control strategies that are adopted within the system, since each strategy offers a distinctive approach to the process of regulation. The paper is structured as follows. Part B discusses three generic risk control strategies and how they can be mixed so as to create a system of regulation with a distinct character. Part C sets out the system of risk control that has been developed in the UK under the FSMA 2000. Part D compares that system of risk control with corporate regulatory regimes that operate in parallel with FSMA 2000. Part E discusses the manner in which responsibility for regulatory compliance can be and is in fact distributed between individuals and firms under FSMA 2000 and parallel regulatory regimes. Part F attempts to link these insights into the capacity of the regulatory system to control risk with some of the key failings that have been brought to light by the crisis. The purpose is to identify what regulatory reform may be able to achieve.

B.   Risk Control Strategies

1.   Generic Risk Control Strategies

While the descriptor 'risk-based regulation' is of relatively recent origin, the technique itself is not. The concept of controlling excessive or abuse instances of activity that is prima facie socially beneficial has a long history both within discrete regulatory regimes and in the general law. Regulatory regimes generally adopt three high-level strategies for controlling risk-taking:[13] prohibition, limitation and remedy (see Table 1). Whilst in principle each represents a different approach, there is some overlap, and regulatory regimes typically combine the three approaches. The three generic approaches remain the same irrespective of the institutional arrangements for regulation within any system, although there may well be issues as to how well each strategy can operate when responsibility is split across different regulatory authorities.

---

[11] See J Gray, 'Is it Time to Highlight the Limits of Risk-based Regulation?' (2009) 4 *Capital Markets Law Journal* 50.

[12] See FSA, above n 10.

[13] Risk-taking behaviour is a subset of the entire set of risks that a regulatory system confronts (see the introduction above). It is most obviously linked with credit risk, market risk and systemic risk, all of which lie at the root of the current crisis.

Table 1. Generic Risk Control Strategies

	Prevent	Limit	Remedy
Substance	Prohibition	Risk threshold	Liability standard
Process			
Ex ante	Licensing	Supervision	Deterrence
Ex post	Enforcement: exclusion/containment/ penalty	Negotiated correction/penalty	Enforcement: restitution/compensation/ penalty

The prohibition strategy is used for three main purposes: (i) to control entry[14] into regulated activity; (ii) to constrain the activities of authorised firms; and (iii) to prohibit conduct within the system that directly threatens the objectives of the regulatory system. Examples of the first within the UK regulatory system are the criminal offence of engaging in regulated activity without authorisation and the prohibition on 'controlled activities' being performed by anyone other than an 'approved person'.[15] An example of the second is the constraint imposed on authorised firms by the concept of 'permitted activities', which represent the sub-set of regulated activity in which an authorised firm is permitted to engage. An example of the third is the 'market abuse' regime.[16] The attraction of the prohibition strategy is that it draws a clear dividing line between what is and what is not permitted. It does, however, have several disadvantages. First, at least in it simplest form, it is a crude mechanism that lacks flexibility. Moreover, in its more sophisticated forms (eg the market abuse regime) it risks losing legal certainty since the prohibition becomes so nuanced that it can be difficult to understand and to apply. Secondly, the prohibition strategy limits the potential role of the regulator as a supervisor as opposed to an enforcer of regulatory rules. The extent to which that occurs will depend on how the prohibition is framed. Thus, for example, a 'fit and proper' test for entry into regulated activity by firms and individuals can in itself open up a broad role for a regulator even within a system that emphasises prohibition. Thirdly, the prohibition strategy is open in some cases to avoidance through regulatory arbitrage. That will be the case particularly when activities can be transferred to jurisdictions in which the activity is not prohibited or can be functionally replicated through alternative techniques (eg 'off-balance-sheet' financing or derivatives).

The limitation strategy is more sophisticated in the sense that it permits activity subject to the observance of risk thresholds that cannot be exceeded. Such risk thresholds can be either quantitative (eg regulatory capital requirements by reference to tiers of capital) or qualitative (eg the requirement to have 'adequate financial resources'). From the perspective of process, the limitation strategy focuses on supervision, undertaken through provision of information and direct contact between regulators and the firm. As the experience of the credit crisis has shown, breach of risk thresholds tends to be dealt with as a matter of negotiated correction rather than formal enforcement. This reflects both the

---

[14] And in some cases exit: see the rules on de-listing of SEC-registered companies, which constrain the ability of companies to de-list.

[15] FSMA 2000, ss 19 and 59, respectively.

[16] FSMA, pt XVIII, implementing the EC Directive on Market Abuse (Dir 2003/6, OJ L96/16).

priority given to supervision over enforcement within the limitation model and the practical constraints imposed on the possibility of formal enforcement where regulators have failed to use their full range of powers prior to the emergence of a crisis. In such a situation, regulators cannot credibly claim that there has been non-compliance when the exercise of discretionary powers would have averted (or at least mitigated) the crisis.[17] The limitation strategy is particularly appropriate in situations where alignment of the interests of regulated firms and their customers creates an incentive to observe the regulatory thresholds without resort to enforcement.[18] It also offers the potential to respond more quickly through supervision than through formal enforcement. The drawback of the limitation strategy is that it depends heavily on the capacity of the regulator to engage in effective supervision and, as recent events demonstrate, that may not always be a realistic expectation.

The remedial strategy attracts less attention as a regulatory technique probably for two reasons. One is that regulation is often equated with a model in which the regulator has an active supervisory role, whereas the remedial strategy does not envisage such an active role for the regulator but relies instead on the deterrent effect of the liability standard. The limitation strategy typically gives a significant role to the courts in enforcing the liability standard, although it is also possible for this process to take place within the regulatory system.[19] By setting a standard that may trigger liability (to investors, customers), a liability standard has the capacity to control risk-taking ex ante, at least to the extent that risk-taking can be causally linked with harm.[20] A second reason for its lower profile is that the remedial strategy bridges the divide between the general law and discrete regulatory systems (in the pure sense as something distinct from law), and can therefore be characterised as much as a general legal strategy as a regulatory strategy associated with risk-based regulation. However, it remains the case that the remedial strategy plays an important role in many systems of financial regulation. Prime examples in the UK are the liability associated with false or misleading statements in prospectuses and disclosures to the market and actions in damages or for restitution for regulatory contraventions. In the US, securities class actions stand out as the most distinctive example of the remedial approach. The strategy in principle encompasses both public and private enforcement, albeit that the relative role of each will depend on a range of factors.[21] The objective of enforcement under the remedial model is to secure compensation (or restitution) in respect of loss caused by breach of the liability standard. That objective also represents a limitation on the potential use of the strategy since there are instances in which the

---

[17] This is the position in respect of regulatory capital since the FSA is already empowered to require levels of capital above the minimum requirement.

[18] That has been the case with regard to the recent strengthening of the regulatory capital of banks but only as a result of the onset of the financial crisis. It seems clear that banks (and their counterparties in the wholesale markets as well as regulators) were prepared to tolerate much lower levels of regulatory capital during the boom years.

[19] For example, FSMA 2000 authorises the FSA on its own initiative to make restitution and compensation orders in connection with regulatory contraventions (see s384). While there is little formal use of this power, it does provide a 'stick' to back up negotiated settlement in individual or industry-wide cases (eg pensions mis-selling).

[20] It is for this reason that a liability standard is of little use in controlling systemic risk, whereas it has a major role to play in regulating individual transactions.

[21] They include the powers of the regulator and the incentives for private lawsuits in the legal system generally and in the system of financial regulation.

avoidance of the materialisation or risk is such a priority within the system that it is inappropriate to deploy a regulatory strategy that focuses on resolution ex post.[22]

2.   The Mix of Regulatory Strategies

Regulatory systems can and do adopt different combinations of the three generic strategies outlined above. It is the mix that largely defines the individual character of any regulatory system, and it is likely to be driven by a range of different factors. The legislative framework has a direct effect on the mix to the extent that it adopts clear choices between the three strategies. As far as the UK system is concerned, the legislative framework adopts the prohibition and remedial strategies to a significant extent, but does not emphasise the limitation strategy. That does not mean, however, that the limitation strategy is excluded. On the contrary, the wide discretion enjoyed by the regulator in the UK in defining its approach to regulation opens up the possibility of adopting the limitation technique across the board. That is precisely what has occurred through the adoption of risk-based regulation. Linked with this is the fact that the UK legislative framework does not deal with the issue of the risk preference that should be favoured by the regulatory system[23] and it has therefore fallen to the FSA to delimit tolerable risk. In so doing, the FSA has implicitly prioritised the limitation strategy, albeit that there are important elements of the prohibition and remedial strategy within the system. The limitation strategy offers a more active role and greater flexibility to a regulator than do the other two options, and in that sense is hardly a surprising choice within a system that leaves the determination of basic regulatory policy to the regulator.

   Another factor that should influence the mix but does not always clearly do so is how the system of financial regulation meshes with the general legal system and in particular the extent to which corporate and fiduciary law as well as governance codes provide a normative substratum on which the system of financial regulation is built. That issue is relevant not only for the determination of whether regulatory intervention should occur but also for the manner in which it should occur. In this context, attention should be paid to the regulatory strategies adopted in regimes that operate in parallel with FSMA 2000. They are significant since, to the extent that they pursue similar objectives to the FSMA, different regulatory strategies are liable to lead to confusion and lack of coherence. The principles/rules debate is also relevant here since principles-based regulation maps very directly onto the limitation strategy with its focus on flexibility and supervisory engagement. Risk-based regulation and principles-based regulation together reinforce the limitation strategy and may even cause a degree of 'path-dependence' that will make it difficult to move away from the limitation strategy so long as they remain at the heart of the FSA's approach.[24]

---

[22] That argument applies both to the risk of insolvency of individual firms and systemic risk, although it is possible for ex post mechanisms such as deposit protection to prevent the materialisation of (insolvency and liquidity) risk.

[23] Despite calls for it to do so. See, eg a letter published in the *Financial Times* of 2 September 2008 from Ronald Bowie, President of the Faculty of Actuaries, arguing that 'The decision about which end of the [risk] spectrum banks should be at is one for elected politicians. Only when this has been made clear should regulators be asked to implement the political will. If politicians leave regulators to make these decisions then they will be in dereliction of their duty.'

[24] In this respect, the recent move away from principles-based regulation by the FSA in response to the credit crisis is significant—see further below.

C.   Risk Control under FSMA 2000

1.   Risk as a Determinant of Regulatory Response

Risk identification and assessment, driven by statutory objectives, lies at the heart of the regulatory system in the UK because it is what determines the regulatory response. In principle, the regulatory response encompasses the entire range of powers that are made available to the FSA by the legislative framework. The appropriate regulatory response will depend on a range of factors. If there are no regulatory rules in place, the risk must justify regulatory intervention. and the FSA follows economic orthodoxy in maintaining that intervention is only justified when there is market failure. Moreover, even when there is some evidence of market failure, regulatory intervention will only be justified when other mechanisms (eg contractual[25]) cannot mitigate the risk effectively. If there are already regulatory rules in place, risk identification and assessment across the market may result in changes to the rules or a decision that the matter can be adequately dealt with through supervisory engagement. In that sense, the determination of the regulatory response at the market level is linked with the model of supervision for individual firms since the latter can be adjusted by the FSA for different levels of risk tolerance. As risk tolerance levels rise for individual firms, it can be expected that the capacity of the system to generate rules or rule changes will decline and vice versa. There may also be a form of reflexive relationship here since it can also be expected that a greater tolerance of risk across the system will feed back into greater tolerance of risk at the firm level.

2.   Risk as a Determinant of Supervisory Intensity at the Firm Level

The 'ARROW' risk model used by the FSA to model the risk of individual firms focuses on the impact of the occurrence of a risk event and the probability of that event.[26] The risk profile of a firm is a combination of these two characteristics and results in a firm being categorised as falling into one of four risk categories: low, medium low, medium high and high. In the case of low impact firms, the FSA undertakes supervision primarily through remote monitoring of the firm and thematic assessment. For other firms, the FSA undertakes individual assessments that vary in their intensity according to the risk profile of the firm and result in a risk mitigation programme (RMP) being agreed with the FSA. It is envisaged that the FSA will monitor the RMP and follow up the actions within it to ensure that its objectives are achieved. In the periods between these formal assessments the FSA undertakes 'baseline monitoring' for all firms and 'close and continuous monitoring' for firms that are designated 'high-impact'. These two processes are intended to identify emerging risks promptly, verify the reliance placed on senior management and the control systems of a firm, and keep up to date with organisational and personnel changes in complex firms. Crucially, the ARROW risk model can be adjusted to reflect changes in the risk tolerance of the FSA. In the FSA's own words, 'We have constructed the ARROW II risk model to be very flexible. The model contains parameters that can be set by our senior

---

[25] Contracting can only operate in this way when there is access to adequate information and regulation will often be framed (in the form of disclosure obligations) to allow it to occur.

[26] For more detail, see 'The FSA's Risk-assessment Framework' (August 2006) ch 3.

management to reflect their risk appetite.'[27] This approach provides a mechanism through which changes in the FSA's risk tolerance has a direct effect on the RMP of individual authorised firms and on the process of supervisory engagement.

It seems clear that the model may not always work as it should, and the FSA itself has admitted as much in the context of its supervision of Northern Rock.[28] However, just as important, from the perspective of regulatory reform, as the reasons why the system failed in particular cases is the more fundamental issue of whether it is appropriate to rely as much as we have on the capacity of the regulator to vary the intensity of supervision (and, by implication, require changes in regulatory capital and liquidity) in response to changes in risk profile. That question should be linked with the broader issue of the extent to which regulatory discretion is built into the system (discussed below) since variation in the intensity of supervision is just one example of the very broad discretionary powers that are available to the regulator in the UK system.

3.   Risk Control through Capital Adequacy and Liquidity Rules

The principle of controlling risk-taking in banks by reference to the capital of the bank has a long history, at least in its most basic form. Risk-weighting of assets was introduced by the first Basel Accord, while the second Basel Accord refined the system and emphasised the role of supervisory engagement and market discipline in ensuring capital adequacy for individual institutions. In the EC, the Basel Accords have been implemented by a series of directives that have overlaid a market integration framework objective on the substantive regulatory rules and applied them to investment firms which face market risk as a result of trading in financial instruments. Both the Basel and EC systems have focused on the solvency of individual institutions, with much less attention being paid to systemic risk or liquidity, both of which have featured prominently in the credit crisis.

In the UK context, the minimum levels of regulatory capital set by the Basel accords and the EC Directives are of limited practical relevance for two reasons. First, market counterparties may demand higher levels of capital as a condition for access to certain forms of money-market finance and higher levels of capital will, *ceteris paribus*, generate a higher credit rating for a bank's own debt, thereby lowering its funding cost. Secondly, the FSA is empowered to set individual capital adequacy standards for banks in the form of individual capital guidance (ICG), which then represents 'a regulatory intervention point' for the purposes of supervision.[29] However, following the principles-based approach that prevails in the UK (see Table 2), responsibility for ensuring adequate regulatory capital and liquidity rests with the management of an authorised firm. This is made clear by the FSA Handbook:[30]

> A firm must at all times maintain overall financial resources, including capital resources and liquidity resources, which are adequate, both as to amount and quality, to ensure that there is no significant risk that its liabilities cannot be met as they fall due.

---

[27] FSA, ibid, 15.
[28] See FSA, 'The Supervision of Northern Rock: A Lessons Learned Review' (March 2008).
[29] See FSA, above n 26 39.
[30] FSA Handbook, GENPRU 1.2.26R.

Table 2. Risk Control under FSMA 2000

Risk	Strategy	Substance
Failure to meet regulatory capital requirements (solvency & liquidity)	Risk threshold	FSA Principle 4 FSA GENPRU
Internal systems and control (firms)	Risk threshold	FSA Handbook SYSC
Competence and integrity (individuals)	Prohibition Risk threshold	FSA Handbook APER

Moreover, the FSA makes clear in its risk assessment of individual firms that '[t]he FSA's issuance of the ICG should not be seen as an alternative to the responsibility of a firm's management to monitor and assess the level of capital appropriate to its needs'.[31]

Thus, in theory, the regulator is in a powerful position as regards capital adequacy in that it can both adjust the required level of regulatory capital and, even if that goes wrong, can ultimately hold the senior management to account for getting it wrong. That seems too good to be true and in reality it is. The problem for the regulator is twofold. First, if it fails to set the ICG at a sufficient level, it is difficult to hold the senior management to account (even if possible in a technical legal sense) when the regulator has failed to identify and/or act on the problem. A pure principles-based system would have no difficulty in acting against the senior management in those circumstances because they are responsible for outcomes, so it might also be observed at this point that recent events point to the UK version of principles-based regulation being a compromise version. Secondly, even if the regulator acts against the senior management, there may be little to gain since some form of systemic risk may already have been activated. Of course, to the extent that action against the senior management in those circumstances would promote deterrence and individual responsibility, there would be some benefit for the system a whole.

4. Risk Control through the 'Senior Management, Systems and Controls' (SYSC) and 'Approved Persons' (APER) Components of the FSA Handbook

In tandem with the regulatory capital regime, the UK regulatory system attempts to control risk taking through two distinct but related components of the rulebook (see Table 2). One (SYSC) focuses on organisational structure, governance and risk management, while the other (APER) is more clearly focused on the competence and integrity of individuals who carry out a range of functions referred to as 'controlled functions'.[32] The scope of APER is much wider than SYSC since APER operates without reference to the seniority of the relevant individual.

[31] FSA, above n 26, 38.

[32] One of the innovations of FSMA 2000 was to introduce an 'approved person' regime ('APER' in the FSA Handbook) under which persons performing 'controlled functions' require the approval of the FSA. Approval is subject to the FSA being satisfied that the relevant person is 'fit and proper' to perform the relevant controlled function.

At the level of principle, the objective of the SYSC component of the FSA Handbook of Rules and Guidance is expressed by Principle 3 of the Principles for Business: 'A firm must take reasonable care to organise and control its affairs responsibly and effectively, with adequate risk management systems.'[33] In more detailed terms, the FSA Handbook describes the purposes of SYSC as being:

1.   to encourage firms' directors and senior managers to take appropriate practical responsibility for their firms' arrangements on matters likely to be of interest to the FSA because they impinge on the FSA's functions under the Act;
2.   to increase certainty by amplifying Principle 3, under which a firm must take reasonable care to organise and control its affairs responsibly and effectively, with adequate risk management systems;
3.   to encourage firms to vest responsibility for effective and responsible organisation in specific directors and senior managers;
4.   to create a common platform of organisational and systems and controls requirements for firms subject to the CRD[34] and/or MiFID[35]; and
5.   to set out high-level organisational and systems and controls requirements for insurers.

The third of these purposes represents the first step in a move towards individual responsibility because it requires the implementation of management systems that provide a basis for identification of individual responsibility. The second step is the link between SYSC and the mechanisms that are available for taking enforcement action against individuals.

Persons to whom SYSC functions are allocated are automatically included within the APER regime because such functions are designated as 'controlled'. This has the effect that the sanctions[36] available for breach of APER are available in respect of persons performing or failing to perform SYSC functions. Moreover, it has been noted that close linkage in rule formulation between the SYSC and APER ensures that failings in relation to SYSC can be positively identified as contraventions of the approved person's regime, thereby opening up the possibility of action against an individual.[37] Furthermore, accessory liability, in circumstances in which an approved person is 'knowingly concerned' in a contravention for which a firm bears primary responsibility, represents another route for enforcement action against individuals.[38]

5.   The Role of Regulatory Discretion in Risk Control

Regulatory discretion is a key feature of risk-based regulation in the UK. It is evident both at the level of design of the regulatory system and at the level of the regulator's relationship with authorised firms. At the level of design, the legislative framework leaves

---

[33] These are high-level principles that bind authorised firms.

[34] The EC Capital Requirements Directive: Dir 2006/49, OJ L177/201.

[35] The EC Markets in Financial Instruments Directive: Dir 2004/39, OJ L145/1.

[36] The relevant sanctions include: withdrawal of 'approved person' status (s 63); a financial penalty (s 66); or a public statement of misconduct (s 66). A prohibition order (under s 56) preventing an individual from engaging in specified regulated activities is a broader sanction that is not limited to the approved persons regime and is regarded by the FSA as a more serious penalty than withdrawal of approval.

[37] J Gray and J Hamilton, *Implementing Financial Regulation: Theory and Practice* (Chichester, Wiley, 2006) 75.

[38] See FSMA 2000, s 66; see also the enforcement action against Deutsche Bank/David Maslen discussed in MacNeil, below n 53.

considerable freedom to the FSA to select the appropriate regulatory technique (eg disclosure, conduct of business regulation), to determine the structure of its rulebook (eg as between principles and rules) and to allocate responsibility for regulatory compliance (as between authorised firms and individuals). This remains true even when account is taken of the substantial extent to which the UK regulatory system is based on standards and regulatory rules emanating from international sources (such as the Basel Committee) and the European Union. At the level of the regulator's relationship with individual firms, discretion is evident in: the manner in which the regulator can issue individual capital and liquidity guidance to a firm that exceeds the levels set by the FSA Handbook; the ability to review and update a firm's RMP as a result of specific events that affect a firm; and the ability to adjust the permitted activities of an authorised firm in order to protect the interests of consumers or potential consumers.[39]

Recent events raise doubts over the capacity of a regulator to exercise discretion at the point in time when, from the perspective of the financial position of individual firms and systemic stability, it is necessary. That point will be before a crisis has emerged, and the problem faced by a regulator in these circumstances is that intervention will most likely be resisted and resented by firms on the basis that increasing regulatory capital inevitably increases costs. It may also be characterised as heavy handed, stifling innovation and limiting wider access to credit. Cast in that light, the question becomes one of whether it is appropriate from a public policy perspective to rely on the exercise of regulatory discretion or, alternatively, to design a system in which the regulator plays a less active role as a supervisor and a greater role as an enforcer of rules. The choice reflects a trade-off between a flexible and dynamic system (which requires some discretion) and a more static system which limits discretion but sets regulatory requirements in a way that stability is prioritised over flexibility.

D.   Risk Control under Parallel Regulatory Regimes

Several corporate regulatory regimes operate in parallel with FSMA 2000 and share the objective of controlling risk-taking. Each is linked with the role of directors and, viewed as a whole, they both underpin and overlap with the provisions of the FSMA 2000 regulatory system that apply to directors and senior managers. They underpin the regulatory system because it is structured on the assumption that there are already basic corporate law rules that govern the function and liability of directors in all companies and not just FSMA-regulated entities. They overlap with the regulatory system in that there are sets of circumstances in which both FSMA 2000 and one or more of the parallel regimes 'bite'.

What lessons can be learnt from the operation of risk control in these parallel regulatory regimes? To answer that question, a brief survey is necessary to set out the basic elements of those regimes (see Table 3).

The legal provisions relating to the abuse of limited liability constrain risk-taking on the part of both directors and shareholders. The legal regime is focused on creditor protection because limited liability has the capacity to transfer risk from shareholders to

---

[39] FSMA 2000, s 45. 'Consumers' in this context means any customer of an authorised firm, not just private individuals.

Table 3 Risk Control Strategies in Parallel (Corporate) Regimes

Risk	Strategy	Substance
Abuse of limited liability (creditor protection)	Liability standard	'Veil-lifting' when 'façade' established
	Liability standard	Directors: CA 2006 (various)
Breach of directors' duties (investor/creditor protection)	Risk threshold	Ratification: CA 2006 s239
	Liability standard	CA 2006: s178
	Prohibition	CDDA 1986
Fraudulent/wrongful trading (creditor protection)	Liability standard	Contribution to creditors' pool of assets in insolvency
Failure of internal control systems (investor/creditor protection)	Risk threshold	Combined Code

creditors since creditors stand to lose all debts owed by a company while shareholders stand to lose only their capital contribution. The legal technique is to define a liability standard that results in either (i) the corporate legal entity being ignored or (ii) liability being imposed on shareholders or directors for debts of the company. In the first case, the common law has developed the concept of 'lifting the veil of incorporation' when the company is a 'mere façade'.[40] As a liability standard, 'mere façade' is inherently uncertain, even if judicial policy provides a clear message that the courts will not lightly ignore the legal personality of companies, even those within corporate groups. In the second case, the liability standards are varied, but they have in common the culpability of directors in the manner in which a company is run, to the detriment of creditors.

The legal regime governing directors' duties seeks inter alia to constrain excessive risk-taking.[41] It contains elements of the three generic approaches to risk control: prohibition, risk threshold and liability standard. Prohibition operates ex post in this context since it only arises following insolvency, when a director can be disqualified for 'unfitness' in the running of a company prior to insolvency.[42] Risk threshold operates in this context in the form of authorisation ex ante of potential breaches of duty and ratification ex post of actual breaches of duty. Viewed in this light, the board and general meeting engage in supervision of directors' duties and in negotiated correction through authorisation and ratification. The liability standard operates only in the zone beyond authorisation and ratification, and is subject to the proviso that the courts will not review the 'business judgements' of directors as long as they are in good faith.[43] While the liability standard may be said to have some 'teeth' in respect to its application to integrity (via fiduciary

[40] The leading authority is *Adams v Cape Industries* [1990] Ch 433.
[41] The legal regime is now contained in ss170–81 of the Companies Act 2006, but the pre-existing common law remains relevant for the interpretation and application of the statutory provisions.
[42] Under the Company Directors Disqualification Act 1986. For an example linked with the collapse of a bank, see *Re Barings plc (No 5)* [2000] 1 BCLC 523, in which a director was disqualified for failing properly to supervise functions delegated to an employee.
[43] While the law in the UK is not framed around the concept of a 'business judgement' rule (as it is in the US), it is functionally similar in the manner in which it defers to directors' business judgement.

duty), that outcome is much less clear in relation to competence, since there are very few instances in which directors have been or can be found to be in breach of the duty of care and skill. This issue is to the fore in the credit crisis, with shareholders in Northern Rock receiving legal advice that there was no credible case against the directors of the company and Royal Bank of Scotland receiving advice that there were no grounds on which to dismiss its CEO for incompetence.[44]

The 'fraudulent/wrongful trading' regime contained in the Insolvency Act 1986 seeks to protect creditors from the risk that, as insolvency approaches, directors may be tempted to take risks that expose creditors to losses that would be greater than if the company were to be wound up and its assets distributed. Creditors are particularly exposed in those circumstances since it can be assumed that shareholders' equity has little or no value and thus shareholders may have little or no incentive to constrain risk-taking on the part of directors in the way that they might when a company is trading profitably. The regime is directly linked with the company law provisions relating to directors' duties since the wrongful trading provision[45] (the remedy most commonly pursued by liquidators of an insolvent company) is formulated in the same manner as the duty of care and skill,[46] by reference to both an objective and a subjective element. In this case, however, it is a liability standard that is the dominant feature of the regime since a director[47] becomes liable to contribute to the pool of assets available to the creditors if either fraudulent or wrongful trading is established. There is no possibility within this regime for the operation of the authorisation or ratification procedures that operate in relation to directors' duties outside the zone of insolvency (above) since it would be inappropriate to permit shareholders to sanction risk-taking by directors that jeopardises the position of creditors, especially since it is only creditors who are left with any real financial interest in the company's assets. The prohibition strategy features only indirectly in this regime in the form of the possibility that the court making a contribution order against a director may simultaneously make a disqualification order against the director.[48]

The provisions of the Combined Code relating to internal control systems encompass financial, operational and compliance controls, as well as risk management systems. In the words of the Code itself, they are intended to 'safeguard shareholders' investment and the company's assets'. Viewed from that perspective, they protect the interests of both shareholders and creditors. The 'comply or explain' approach adopted by the Combined Code means that, in terms of generic risk-control strategies, it is the limitation strategy that is to the fore. The 'comply or explain' model envisages that 'supervision' and 'negotiated correction' will occur through market discipline as the market (institutional investors) either accepts explanations for non-compliance or requires changes either explicitly (through negotiation) or implicitly (through selling based on protest against a company's governance arrangements). However, the operation of this model has been the subject of considerable adverse comment. It has been noted that many firms do not explain

---

[44] There does not appear to be any instance of a director being dismissed (at least expressly) for incompetence related to the credit crisis.

[45] Insolvency Act 1986, s 214.

[46] See s 172 of the Companies Act 2006.

[47] The fraudulent trading provision (IA 1986, s 213) applies to 'any person' while the wrongful trading provision applies only to directors. In practice, most cases under both provisions relate to the actions of directors.

[48] Under s 10 of the Company Directors Disqualification Act 1986.

non-compliance or, when they do, the explanations typically fail to justify a deviation from the Code.[49] Moreover, it appears that in the case of companies whose share price is performing well shareholders are unlikely to be concerned about non-compliance or inadequate explanations, preferring to allow discretion to the incumbent board.[50] Thus, the internal control provisions of the Combined Code (in common with its other provisions) do not represent a credible risk control technique since the risk threshold is not effectively controlled by the process of supervision and negotiated correction.

This brief survey of parallel regulatory regimes provides some insights that are relevant in assessing the capacity of risk-based regulation to deliver on its objectives. First, there is a strong focus on individual responsibility (other than in the case of the Combined Code, which in any event is the worst example of risk control in operation in the parallel regimes). Secondly, as might be expected in 'legal' as opposed to 'regulatory' regimes, none give as much significance to the limitation strategy as the FSMA regulatory regime. Thirdly, there are real problems in defining liability standards, especially in relation to the conduct of directors, in a manner that represents meaningful control of risk-taking behaviour, but these problems may be no greater or less than in other areas of the law (uncertainty is an endemic problem).[51] Fourthly, the potential harm that can result from the materialisation of risk within these regimes is less than in the case of the FSMA system, where systemic risk poses a much larger scale threat. To that extent, the FSMA system should arguably be more risk averse as a system of regulation. That is a matter of regulatory system design and a separate issue from the degree of risk tolerance within the system. Regulatory system design should pay attention both to linkage with the underlying legal system and to the risks associated with the risk control strategies that are adopted. The emergence of the credit crisis provides evidence that reliance on the limitation strategy, at least in the form of risk-based regulation as practiced in the UK, carries with it the risk that regulators may lack either the capacity or the willingness to meet the expectations associated with it. While other deficiencies (such as too little focus on systemic risk and liquidity regulation) are common to many regulatory systems and are likely to generate a response at the international level, the UK should not ignore the unique features and limitations of its own system, especially since it is an outlier in international terms by reference to its reliance on a combination of an integrated regulatory authority, risk-based regulation and principles-based regulation. Thus, attention should focus on the potential benefits that might be gained from readjustment of the regulatory system towards the other two generic risk-control strategies. Although not the focus of this paper, there is also increasing support for adjusting the institutional structure of regulation to focus more clearly on financial stability and systemic risk.[52]

---

[49] SR Arcot and VG Bruno, 'In Letter but not in Spirit: An Analysis of Corporate Governance in the UK' (May 2006) ssrn.com/abstract=819784.

[50] I MacNeil and X Li, '"Comply or Explain": Market Discipline and Non-compliance with the Combined Code' (2006) 14 *Corporate Governance: An International Review* 486.

[51] See, eg I MacNeil, 'Uncertainty in Commercial Law' (2009) 13 *Edinburgh Law Review* 68.

[52] Changes have already been made in the Banking Act 2009 to give the Bank of England a formal role in financial stability: see s 238 of the Act and ch 10 of this volume.

E.   Attribution of Responsibility for Compliance between Firms and Individuals

Linked with the issue of whether risk-based regulation represents an appropriate combination of regulatory strategies by reference to the capacity of a regulatory system to control risk-taking is the issue of who bears responsible for regulatory compliance. There are in principle three models (see Table 4): the corporate entity; the board of directors (or more broadly senior management) as a collective entity; and the directors and senior managers as individuals.[53] In principle, locating responsibility in any one of the three potential options, whether in isolation or cumulatively, carries implications for risk-taking incentives within a regulated entity as a whole and also for the levels within the organisation at which risk-taking will occur and the techniques that will be adopted. Thus, for example, the corporate entity model of responsibility will effectively punish the shareholders for regulatory contraventions and will place considerable reliance on governance techniques to protect shareholders from directors' excessive risk-taking. Similarly, the individual responsibility model may result in directors and senior managers becoming risk averse to the extent that the interests of the company may be harmed.[54] Moreover, the possibility of the distribution of responsibility being altered through Coasean 'risk-shifting'[55] does not arise, since regulatory obligations cannot be contracted around,[56] nor can companies indemnify directors in respect of criminal or regulatory fines.[57]

While the FSMA regulatory system has moved a considerable way towards recognition of senior management and individual responsibility by reference to rule formulation,[58] enforcement action against senior management as a group or individuals is a relatively rare occurrence. The legislative framework itself adopts a cautious approach, requiring the FSA to consider whether it is appropriate to take action against an individual in respect of a regulatory contravention.[59]

In that sense, the FSMA regulatory system does not operate in symmetry with the parallel corporate regimes (above), which do focus on individual responsibility, even if they have difficulty in formulating the relevant liability standards. The question therefore is whether the FSMA regulatory regime should move in that direction. While it may be tempting to conclude that none of the regulatory regimes have demonstrably constrained risk-taking in the run up to the financial crisis, there are grounds for considering further movement within the FSMA regulatory regime towards individual responsibility. One is

---

[53] See generally I MacNeil, 'The Evolution of Regulatory Enforcement Action in the UK Capital Markets: A Case of "Less Is More"' (2007) 2 *Capital Markets Law Journal* 345.

[54] Such arguments were made following the introduction of the 'Sarbanes-Oxley' corporate governance rules in the US in 2002 but have since receded.

[55] This refers to the proposition made by Ronald Coase that, absent transaction costs, it does not matter how the law sets liability standards since parties will contract round the law to reach efficient outcomes: see R Coase, 'The Problem of Social Cost' (1960) 3 *Journal of Law and Economics* 1.

[56] See s 234 of the Companies Act 2006.

[57] Although it is possible for companies to purchase 'directors' and officers' insurance' to cover negligence and that represents an indirect form of risk-shifting.

[58] See MacNeil, above n 53, discussing the development of individual responsibility within the APER and SYSC regimes. See also Gray and Hamilton, above n 37, ch 4.

[59] FSMA 2000, s 66(2)(b). The FSA maintains that personal culpability is an essential element of a decision to take enforcement action against an individual—see FSA, 'The Regulation of Approved Persons', Consultation Paper No 26 (1999) 115.

Table 4. Distribution of Responsibility for Regulatory Compliance between Firms and Individuals

Regulatory regime	Responsibility	Risk control strategy
Directors' duties	Individual	Liability standard
Combined Code	Board/Collective	Market discipline (FRC/FSA Enforcement)
APER	Individual	Liability standard
SYSC	Firm	Liability standard

that it has the potential to counterbalance over-reliance on supervision as a regulatory technique and to compensate for weaknesses in supervision. That is so because rebalancing the system more towards individual responsibility will generally represent a movement away from the limitation strategy since supervisory engagement is a process primarily between the regulator and authorised firms whereas individual responsibility is more clearly linked with the prohibition and liability strategies. Greater individual responsibility would also readjust the incentives for risk-taking. Under the prevailing model, taking both directors' duties and the FSMA regulatory system together, an unduly protective stance is adopted towards directors and senior managers, thereby encouraging excessive risk-taking.[60] A less protective model, particularly within the FSMA system, would place greater emphasis on stability by comparison with risk-taking.

F.   Assessment: Capacity for Risk-control and the Appropriate Techniques

The emergence of the credit crisis and the severity of the disruption associated with it raise fundamental questions regarding the capacity of risk-based regulation to deliver on its objectives. This is not an issue of whether risk-based regulation worked as it should in the pre-crisis period, but an issue of whether it would be possible even in an idealised world for risk-based regulation to meet the expectations that have in the past been associated with it.

The main criticism that can be levelled against risk-based regulation is that the credit crisis provides clear evidence that the two assumptions on which it relies are false. The first is that risk can be accurately measured. This has been shown to be false in multiple dimensions. First, the regulators did not properly take account of the extent to which leverage and risk were being increased within individual firms and across the system. Had they done so, we would have seen at a much earlier stage the moves currently being made to strengthen regulatory capital. Secondly, rating agencies were unable to measure (default)

---

[60] Remuneration practices often exacerbate the problem since it is widely recognised that, particularly in the financial sector, remuneration has not been properly aligned with risk-taking or performance. In response to the financial crisis, the FSA proposed changes to remuneration within authorised firms: see 'Reforming Remuneration Practices in Financial Services', FSA Consultation Paper 09/10 (March 2009). A new Remuneration Code will take effect from 1 January 2010: see FSA, 'Reforming Remuneration Practices in Financial Services, Feedback on CP09/10 and Final Rules', Policy Statement 09/15 (August 2009).

risk accurately, and their mistakes were compounded by reliance on ratings in measures of regulatory capital and proprietary risk models. Thirdly, banks and other financial agents operating in the market were unable to measure risk accurately for the purposes of pricing transactions. This multiple failure in the measurement of risk is one of the salutary lessons of the credit crisis and surely acts as a warning against over-reliance on risk measurement in the future. That is not to say that the regulatory system should not be sensitive to risk, simply that we must adjust the confidence levels that are attached to such measurement.

The second criticism is that the capacity of regulators to exercise discretion when it is most required is quite limited. In the UK context, the emergence of the credit crisis is not (despite the popularity of this version of events) a story of the triumph of self-regulation over formal regulation. The UK moved decisively away from self-regulation in its system of financial regulation with the introduction of FSMA 2000, despite leaving remnants of the old self-regulatory approach in place in adjacent regulatory domains.[61] The regulators in the UK have very broad powers, and the emergence of the credit crisis is therefore much more directly linked with a failure to use powers rather than a lack of powers. That observation must, however, be understood by reference to two (implicit) complications that arise from the practice of risk-based regulation. The first is that the risk tolerance of the regulator is variable, and this can be expected to complicate the exercise of discretion. The second is that the regulator's reliance on firms' risk models in the process of supervision makes the risk tolerance of the regulator difficult to disaggregate from that of the firm.[62] Thus, it would seem correct in principle to focus reform on changing the role of the regulator to focus less on discretionary supervision and more on the enforcement of rules.

Another notable aspect of the credit crisis has been the failure to hold individuals to account for their role in excessive risk-taking. In contrast with the position in the US, where a significant number of regulatory and private enforcement actions against individuals are underway, there has been very little action in the UK (or, at least, very little that has reached the public sphere). Part of the reason for this relates to the different incentives to litigate in each system (eg the presence of contingency fees and class actions in the US but not in the UK), but the protective stance of the UK legal and regulatory system towards directors and senior managers also plays a part. There is something deeply unsatisfactory about a regulatory system that is designed to avert risk and yet when the risk materialises is unable to hold the primary decision-makers to account in any meaningful way. It is true that there have been high-profile dismissals, but the power to dismiss is a core component of corporate law to which the system of financial regulation seems to have added little by way of additional accountability standards or mechanisms. Thus, there are clear incentives for individuals to engage in conduct that 'sails close to the wind' on the basis that, even if a regulatory contravention is established, it is more likely to be the authorised firm than the individual who bears responsibility.

It is more difficult to assess the extent to which risk-based regulation and principles-based regulation are linked as causes of the crisis. At a theoretical level, the two are distinct, even if they are often conflated: risk-based regulation is a policy choice that carries implications for the entire system, whereas principles-based regulation is concerned primarily with the structure and formulation of regulatory rules. It is possible

---

[61] Primarily corporate governance and takeover regulation, the latter having been subsumed into the statutory framework following implementation of the EC Takeovers Directive (Directive 2004/25, [2004] OJ L142/12).

[62] It is in that (limited) sense that the self-regulatory account of the emergence of the crisis is true.

for the regulatory system to incorporate neither, one or both approaches, and, irrespective of which option is selected, the system can gravitate towards 'light-touch' or 'belt-and-braces' regulation. None of these outcomes is inevitable and they depend on policy choices that are made either at the level of the legislative framework or in the exercise of regulatory discretion. That remains true even in the UK, where risk-based regulation, principles-based regulation and light-touch regulation have been combined to create a regulatory mix with a very distinct character. While a case can be made for principles-based regulation being the component of the mix that is least implicated in the crisis, it seems that its days are already numbered, with the FSA chief executive recently commenting that: 'The limitations of a pure principles-based regime have to be recognised . . . A principles-based approach does not work with individuals who have no principles.'[63]

That comment should, however, be understood by reference to the link between principles-based regulation and light-touch regulation. Subsequent clarification from the FSA makes it clear that principles-based regulation will continue in the sense of a continued focus on outcomes and 'judging the results of the actions of the firms and individuals the FSA supervises'.[64] Nevertheless, as an indicator of capacity for regulatory reform, the move is encouraging since it shows a willingness on the part of the FSA to restrict or even abandon techniques that have not worked, even when, as in the case of principles-based regulation, they formed a central part of the UK regulatory mix.

G.   Conclusion

The credit crisis has exposed inherent limitations in the system of risk-based regulation that operates in the UK. In particular, it has drawn attention to the fact that reliance on risk measurement and variation in the intensity of supervision are likely to be prone to failure at times when they are needed most. Those times are particularly when innovation causes risk to change in ways that are not always clear and when regulators become over-reliant on authorised firms setting and controlling their own risk appetite. At least in those circumstances, and arguably in others, the capacity of risk-based regulation to deliver on its objectives is constrained. These limitations are exacerbated by an unduly protective stance towards directors and senior management in the FSMA regulatory system and more generally in corporate law. In tandem with inappropriate remuneration structures, the effect is to shift risk and cost from the drivers of risk-taking (directors and senior managers) to shareholders and (to a lesser extent) bondholders.

Thus, some movement away from the limitation strategy (as represented by risk-based regulation) towards the other two generic risk-control strategies (prohibition and remedy) seems sensible. That change could occur regardless of how the institutional framework is reshaped, although there would be a certain degree of symmetry in combining it with a 'twin peaks' approach in which prudential regulation is separated from conduct of

---

[63] H Sants, 'Delivering Intensive Supervision and Credible Deterrence', speech at Reuters Newsmakers Event, 12 March 2009, available at www.fsa.gov.uk/pages/Library/Communication/Speeches/2009/0312_hs.shtml.
[64] FSA, 'A Regulatory Response to the Global Banking Crisis', FSA Discussion Paper 09/2 (March 2009) para 11.6.

business regulation.[65] Since the former is focused essentially on the prohibition and limitation strategies and the latter is focused on the remedial strategy (albeit with components of the prohibition and limitation strategies), there is arguably a clearer approach to the practice of regulation in the 'twin peaks' model.

In terms of regulatory process, a movement away from the current model of risk-based regulation would mean a greater role for prohibition and the criminal law. The FSMA regulatory system has largely marginalised the criminal law as a regulatory technique, focusing instead on a more informal approach to enforcement even when criminal prosecution may be possible. There are now signs that this approach is changing, with the FSA adopting a more robust line on the prosecution of insider trading. More could be done, for example by bringing into play the 'misleading statements and practices' provisions of s397 FSMA 2000 in the context of the credit crisis. There would also be a greater role for the courts if the system were to move more towards the remedial approach, though many would no doubt oppose such a move without further consideration since there is a traditional reluctance to involve the courts in matters relating to the financial markets in the UK. However, it is certainly arguable that standards of integrity in financial markets have now become too remote from those prevailing elsewhere and that it is only greater involvement on the part of the courts that will resolve that problem.

From the perspective of regulatory practice, these changes would have far-reaching effects for rule formulation, supervisory engagement and enforcement. It is virtually inconceivable that such fundamental changes would occur absent a crisis, but now that the wind of change is in the air, it is possible to envisage that they may become reality. It is important to bear in mind, however, that even a reformed system of financial regulation will not eliminate asset bubbles or financial crises. History proves that they will recur. The best we can hope for is to mitigate their severity.

---

[65] This option is canvassed in the Turner Review: FSA, 'The Turner Review: A Regulatory Response to the Global Banking Crisis' (2009) 19.

10

Revisiting the Lender of Last Resort—
The Role of the Bank of England

ANDREW CAMPBELL AND ROSA LASTRA[*]

A.   Introduction

Banking crises are a regular occurrence in international finance and during the last 30 years have taken place in over 100 countries.[1] As a result of this, most countries have put in place a financial sector safety net which comprises a mix of the following: a supervisory and regulatory framework, a deposit protection system, bank insolvency laws[2] and a lender of last resort role by the central bank. There are also government measures of implicit protection of depositors, the payment system and the financial system at large. This article concentrates on the lender of last resort role and the emergency liquidity assistance (ELA) operations available to the Bank of England (the Bank). The term 'lender of last resort' (LOLR) evokes collateralised lines of lending, while emergency liquidity assistance encompasses a broader array of operations, as we discuss further below. LOLR/ELA operations have acquired a new significance in the light of the turmoil in financial markets over the last months, leading to remarkable changes in the UK and elsewhere. Two UK banks, Northern Rock and Bradford & Bingley, have been nationalised, Alliance & Leicester has been taken over by Santander (via Abbey, its UK subsidiary) and a significant recapitalisation programme has been introduced which has led to the government having substantial ownership stakes in Royal Bank of Scotland (RBS), Lloyds TSB and Halifax Bank of Scotland (HBOS).

The inter-bank liquidity crisis, which arrived seemingly unexpectedly in August 2007 and with a rapidity that took the financial sector by surprise, provides the starting point of

[*] Andrew Campbell is Reader in Law, University of Leeds; and Rosa Lastra is Professor of International Financial and Monetary Law, Centre for Commercial Law Studies, Queen Mary University of London. This is a shorter version of an article published in the *Banking & Finance Law Review* in 2009 entitled 'Revisiting the Lender of Last Resort'. The authors thank Thomson Reuters for giving permission to publish this amended version. The authors are also grateful to Gillian Garcia, Francois Gianviti, Charles Goodhart, René Smits and Geoffrey Wood for helpful comments on the original article.

[1] IMF Statistics. See S Heffernan, *Modern Banking* (London, Wiley, 2005) generally and at ch 8 in particular. See also A Campbell and P Cartwright, *Banks in Crisis: the Legal Response* (Aldershot, Ashgate, 2002).

[2] These can consist of either a special insolvency law for banks or the general corporate insolvency laws with some additional provisions relating to banks.

our discussion.[3] From a legal perspective, LOLR/ELA policies raise a number of interesting issues, which we consider in our analysis.

A lot of soul searching is happening in the EU, the UK and the US (and many other countries) as regards the institutional design of supervision and crisis management. LOLR sits squarely in that debate. This article focuses solely on London.

The Banking Act 2009 gives a statutory mandate with regard to financial stability to the Bank and introduces a bank resolution and insolvency framework. However, the legal framework for the provision of emergency liquidity assistance and the role of the Bank as lender of last resort are only partially considered[4] in the Act. The important notion of 'financial stability' is not defined in the new Banking Act (nor was it defined in any of the consultation documents), even though it is the key objective, a fundamental concept in the reform process that is at the core of the LOLR/ELA policies of the central bank.

The serious financial difficulties experienced by Northern Rock bank brought the issue of the safety of banks and the protection of depositors to the attention of the public in the UK. Despite having in place a financial sector safety net which included the provision of emergency liquidity assistance and a depositor compensation scheme, Northern Rock suffered a humiliating old-fashioned bank run, much to the embarrassment of the UK government, the Financial Services Authority (FSA) and the Bank.[5]

B.   Market Liquidity, Individual Assistance and other Definitional Issues

Our initial consideration is that central banks provide liquidity, not capital. Though the crisis moved beyond the liquidity squeeze phase some time ago, and concerns about liquidity have mutated into concerns about solvency, the provision of central bank liquidity remains a key instrument to confront the crisis.

There are two main types of crisis situation where the provision of emergency liquidity assistance could be critical. The first is the case, in many if not all financial markets, of a general liquidity dry up (of which we have ample examples from the last 18 months), leading to a widespread and generalised questioning of the liquidity of different sorts of financial institutions. Open market operations is the classic instrument in this type of crisis. The second, the classic case of LOLR assistance (elaborated by Thornton and Bagehot, as explained further below), refers to collateralised loans to an illiquid banking sector. A particular crisis situation can arise, for example, when one or more financial institutions gets into trouble due to problems which originate in the payment system and which can lead to a payment system gridlock.

---

[3] Both authors have written extensively on this subject in the past but, in view of the ways in which the provision of liquidity financing by central banks has come into focus as a result of the crisis, it seems timely to revisit the subject at this time. See, eg R Lastra, 'Lender of Last Resort, an International Perspective' (1999) 48 *International and Comparative Law Quarterly* 340; R Delston and A Campbell, 'Emergency Liquidity Financing by Central Banks: Systemic Protection or Bank Bailout?' in *Current Developments in Monetary and Financial Law*, vol 3 (Washington, DC, International Monetary Fund, 2005).

[4] Aspects have been addressed, but some of the arguably most important ones have not. This is discussed later in the article.

[5] At the time of writing, Northern Rock bank is operating in the marketplace as a mortgage bank that is in public ownership.

The confines of our subject have appeared like a moving target as events have unfolded, and other crisis management mechanisms have often overlapped with liquidity assistance operations. Various forms of government intervention have triggered a debate on whether banking in future should be treated as a utility, that is, as an essential public service. The wisdom of having the government as insurer of last resort is also being questioned.

Another definitional issue where the contours are becoming less clear concerns the distinction in times of crisis between regular discount policies (a classic instrument of monetary policy) and extraordinary or emergency lending. LOLR is an instrument that affects monetary and financial stability.

The distinction between ordinary monetary policy and extraordinary liquidity assistance gets further complicated when we consider the 'non-standard monetary policy operations' undertaken by central banks in recent months; for example, the 'quantitative easing' announced by the Bank to expand the money supply sharply, now that interest rates cannot go much lower; the announcement by the Bank of a programme of asset purchases of £75 billion, financed by the issuance of central bank reserves, mean that monetary policy has taken a turn into the unknown.[6] From a legal point of view, if a central bank is both in charge of monetary policy and the LOLR, as the Bank is, this is not a problematic issue.

Bearing in mind these difficult definitional issues and the fact that we are dealing with a moving target, we try in this chapter to confine our analysis to the liquidity assistance that the Bank provides in extraordinary circumstances, such as those that the financial markets, and the economy at large, have lived through over the last 18 months.

C.   Background to the Liquidity Crisis

During the summer of 2007, liquidity started to dry up significantly in many markets, including New York and London, the two major inter-bank markets. The speed with which liquidity disappeared was quite unexpected, and the extent and severity of the difficulties were unforeseen, although a number of institutions and commentators had previously demonstrated concerns about a number of practices in the financial markets.[7]

The recent crisis has exposed a number of problem areas and deficiencies in the UK financial sector safety net. This crisis has provided the first test of the safety net that was introduced in 1997. In a number of respects it has been found wanting. As noted above, the crisis has led to the nationalisation of banks, a series of consultations and proposed new legislation. A new landscape for financial sector regulation is being developed and the role to be played by the Bank as LOLR needs to be addressed.

---

[6] See Bank of England, 'Quantitative Easing Explained: Putting More Money into Our Economy to Boost Spending' (2009), available at www.bankofengland.co.uk/monetarypolicy/assetpurchases.htm.

[7] According to Charles Goodhart, 'virtually all of the major central banks and international financial institutions had been warning about the underpricing of risk and excessive leveraging by 2006–07' [July 2008] *FMG Review* 3.

D.   Liquidity and the Bank

Liquidity support is normally only available to banks and not other types of business.[8] It is necessary to have a source of liquidity available to try to ensure the stability of the financial system as the structure of banks and the ways in which they operate make them particularly vulnerable. Banks have traditionally raised most of their funds from depositors and used this money to lend to borrowers. This creates some potential liquidity problems in that the funds deposited will normally be available on demand or with a relatively short notice period, whereas loans[9] are generally made for a fixed period. This is usually referred to as 'borrow short—lend long'. As a result of this, should there be unusually high demand by depositors to withdraw savings, the bank will face a squeeze on liquidity. In such a situation, provided the bank's balance sheet is in good shape, it will normally turn to the inter-bank market for assistance or, if that is not available, to the central bank.

In the past few years the position has changed somewhat, with many banks, rather than relying on deposits to fund lending, turning to the money markets to borrow large sums for fixed periods and also using securitisation of loan portfolios. This, as has been demonstrated in the last 18 months, significantly increased liquidity risks. As a result of such developments, there is a need to discuss, from the legal perspective, the scope and parameters of what has traditionally been referred to as 'lender of last resort', a function undertaken by central banks.[10]

E.   Two Important Features of LOLR Financing

Before considering the history and theory of the LOLR function, there are two particularly important features of emergency liquidity assistance which make it such a valuable tool in the prevention and control of banking crises, and which need to be considered. The first is the immediacy of the availability of central bank assistance (the central bank being the ultimate supplier of high-powered money) that makes the LOLR particularly suitable to confront emergency situations. This is a key feature that distinguishes lender of last resort from other support operations and crisis management procedures. This 'immediacy' contrasts with the 'time framework' of other crisis management instruments. The second important feature is the unlimited capacity of the central bank to provide liquidity, either to the market in general or to individual banks as needed.

By being able to act quickly and to provide adequate liquidity it should be possible in a well-regulated financial environment to prevent liquidity problems from developing into serious financial crises. Neither deposit insurance nor bank insolvency proceedings can

---

[8] See, eg Delston and Campbell, above n 3, on why this is.

[9] Apart from overdrafts, which under English common law are repayable on demand unless there is agreement to the contrary. See *Rouse v Bradford Banking Company* [1894] AC 586; *Crips v Wickenden* [1973] 1 WLR 944.

[10] This change of approach has also led to significant developments in relation to other relevant matters, including the adequacy and effectiveness of the regulation and supervision of banks, capital and liquidity adequacy and others. These are not being considered in this article.

achieve this. By their very nature they are lengthy and complicated processes, which take into account the interests of many stakeholders and are subject to legal constraints. They are both necessary and valuable, but cannot provide immediate assistance to prevent a crisis worsening. In most countries the central bank will undertake the role of providing lender of last resort assistance, but this can be more complicated in certain situations.

F. Lender of Last Resort—History and Theory[11]

The historical and theoretical basis of LOLR assistance was originally developed by Henry Thornton[12] in the early part of the nineteenth century, then by Walter Bagehot some 70 years later.[13] Both of these authors used the term 'lender of last resort' in their writings, and this is still widely used at the present time. Other terms, such as 'emergency liquidity assistance' and 'emergency liquidity financing', are also used. Since it is becoming increasingly difficult to ascertain what constitutes LOLR,[14] it is useful to go back to the origins of the doctrine first and to then establish how much we have departed from that traditional doctrine (or from 'good practice').

The essence of the theoretical basis is that there are four 'pillars', or conditions, that are to be applied when providing LOLR assistance. These are not legal principles, but rather principles attributed to LOLR since the doctrinal elaboration by Thornton and Bagehot. First, financial assistance should be made available to banks which are illiquid but solvent[15] to stem a crisis which could lead to the failure of a bank or banks. Secondly, the central bank should lend 'freely', that is, it should lend as much as is needed, but the rate of interest charged should be high. This is frequently referred to as a penalty rate in the literature, but there is some disagreement about this.[16] So what did Bagehot actually say? He said that these loans should only be made at 'a very high rate of interest' and went on to say that 'this will operate as a heavy fine on unreasonable timidity and will prevent the greatest number of applications by persons who do not require it'.[17] It was clearly the

---

[11] The term lender of last resort is reputed to have originated as far back as 1797 with Sir Francis Barings, who referred to the Bank of England as the *dernier resort* from which all banks could obtain liquidity in times of crisis. See TM Humphrey and RE Keleher, 'The Lender of Last Resort: A Historical Perspective' (1984) 4 *Cato Journal* 275. For further reading on this topic see A Campbell, 'Emergency Liquidity Financing for Banks and Distress: a Legal Framework for Developing Countries' [2006] *Lloyds Maritime and Commercial Law Quarterly*, Part 1, 96; X Freixas, C Giannini, G Hoggarth and F Soussa, 'Lender of Last Resort—a Review of the Literature' in C Goodhart and Gerhard Illing (eds) *Financial Crises, Contagion, and the Lender of Last Resort* (Oxford, Oxford University Press, 2002); R Lastra, 'Crisis Management and Lender of Last Resort' in R Lastra and H Schiffman (eds), *Bank Failures and Bank Insolvency Law in Economies in Transition* (Kluwer,1999); see also GE Wood, 'The Lender of Last Resort Reconsidered' (2000) 18 *Journal of Financial Services Research* 203.

[12] H Thornton, 'An Enquiry into the Nature and Effects of the Paper Credit of Great Britain' (London, F & C Rivington, 1802).

[13] W Bagehot, *Lombard Street: a Description of the Money Market* (London, C Kegan Paul & Co, 1873).

[14] According to A Milne and G Wood, 'Shattered on the Rock: British Financial Stability from 1866 to 2007' (2009) 10 *Journal of Banking Regulation* 108, 'The decision to provide support to Northern Rock has been described as a "lender of last resort" operation but it was *not* what we would term a classic lender of last resort operation'.

[15] In his comments to our paper, Geoffrey Wood wrote: 'There need at this point in the operation be no discussion of solvency, as the lending is on collateral expressly so that solvency need not be evaluated at a moment when time is of the essence.'

[16] See C Goodhart, 'Myths about the Lender of Last Resort' (1999) 2 *International Finance* 339.

[17] Bagehot, above n 13, 197.

intention of Bagehot that the availability of this sort of financing was to be at a price significantly greater than that being charged by other lenders to ensure that recourse to such assistance would only be made after all other avenues had been tried. The third pillar is that the central bank should accommodate anyone who can provide 'good' collateral, which is valued at lower than pre-panic prices but higher than it would have been valued had the central bank not entered the market. The issue of what amounts to appropriate collateral is discussed further below. Fourthly, while the central bank should let it be known in advance that it will be ready to lend, it will also exercise discretion in whether or not to provide assistance.[18] This is sometimes referred to as 'constructive ambiguity', although, as will become apparent, neither author agrees that this is a constructive feature and indeed we believe that more often than not 'destructive' would be a more appropriate term to use, hence our preference for the word 'discretion': the central bank's LOLR role is discretionary, not mandatory. The assumed benefits of 'constructive ambiguity' do not actually exist. Ambiguity and uncertainty as to the procedures and loci of power are not constructive. In the event of a crisis, the procedures to follow should be crystal clear ex ante for the institution affected, the other market participants and the public at large. The only 'ambiguity' that can be constructive in LOLR is the discretionary component in the provision of such assistance, in the sense that there is no obligation for the central bank to provide LOLR loans. It is this discretionary nature that reduces the moral hazard incentives inherent in any support operation, together with the fact that once an institution's collateral has run out it gets no further assistance. Bagehot and Thornton contended that the LOLR's responsibility is to the market—to the entire financial system—and not to specific institutions.

Freixas et al[19] provide the following description of the use of LOLR in modern times:

> the discretionary provision of liquidity to a financial institution (or the market as a whole) by the central bank in reaction to an adverse shock which causes an abnormal increase in demand for liquidity which cannot be met from an alternative source.

Prior to the international financial crisis, modern-day practice in most countries was still largely based on these four pillars. Bagehot, it should be noted, was clearly of the opinion that an insolvent bank which could not provide good security should not receive assistance and should be allowed to fail.[20] A widespread reluctance to allow banks to fail, even when clearly insolvent, has been demonstrated in many countries in the recent past.

It would appear that the discretionary nature of the LOLR is perhaps the most important and controversial aspect. The central bank will assess whether what it faces is a situation of illiquidity or insolvency and will also consider whether the failure of the institution involved would be likely to trigger contagion within the marketplace, bringing with it the danger of the failure of other institutions.[21] The discretionary aspect is intended to assist in preventing the increase in moral hazard which would exist should the central bank be obliged to lend in all cases. We would argue, however, that the risk to contagion posed by a refusal to assist an insolvent bank must be weighed against the effect on moral

---

[18] Neither Thornton nor Bagehot ever made this suggestion.
[19] Freixas et al, above n 11, 151.
[20] Bagehot, above n 13, ch VII.
[21] For a fuller discussion of contagion see, eg R Lastra, *Legal Foundations of International Monetary Stability* (Oxford, Oxford University Press, 2006) 138–50.

hazard that a bailout would create. The central bank, before exercising its discretion to act or not to act as LOLR, should conduct a cost–benefit analysis of the results of its intervention (this is, of course, a difficult exercise, since it is done under pressure and with the need to reach a decision as promptly as possible). The costs are typically the risk of loss to the central bank and the creation of moral hazard incentives. The benefits accrue from the speed, flexibility and decisiveness with which the central bank can cope with an emergency crisis. In this cost–benefit analysis due consideration should be given to the interests of depositors, other creditors, shareholders and taxpayers. A generalised banking crisis is different from an individual banking crisis in a healthy economy, an important element that the Bank will also consider. The central bank should be held accountable for the use of its discretionary LOLR powers. Such accountability needs to be articulated carefully, particularly in cases where the central bank has no direct role in bank supervision; due consideration should also be given to the degree of central bank independence from the Treasury with regard to the exercise of the LOLR function.

G.   Revisiting LOLR: A Moving Target

Lending to insolvent institutions is a departure from the classical LOLR principles. The risk of loss to the central bank is ultimately a risk of loss to the public (taxpayers). However, in practice, and this is particularly acute in times of crises, it is often hard to distinguish between illiquidity and insolvency. A situation of bank illiquidity (that is, with lack of liquid funds) can be an indication of technical insolvency (that is, where value of liabilities exceeds market value of assets) or can quickly turn into insolvency if assets are sold at a loss value or 'fire-sale' price. And an insolvent institution, if allowed to continue operations, will almost certainly run into liquidity problems. The immediacy of the need for assistance often makes it difficult to assess whether an institution is illiquid or insolvent. If central banks provide inadequately collateralised support to insolvent rather than illiquid institutions, the traditional short-term nature of the LOLR assistance is likely to be insufficient to solve the troubles of such institutions. Therefore, in practice, the LOLR will be the first step in a chain or process that is likely to include a bank insolvency proceeding. Another spin-off regarding the differentiation between illiquidity and insolvency refers to the multiple problems and difficulties experienced in the valuation of various assets (a feature of the financial crisis 2007–09), which present a very serious information problem. Concerns about liquidity can be uncertainty about insolvency.

Lending over an extended period of time (which is often an indication that the problems are not of mere illiquidity) increases the risk of loss to the central bank and the risk of loss to the public. Any extended lending—committing taxpayers' money—should ideally be done by the fiscal authority. To minimise the risk of moral hazard, it is important to demarcate clearly what the central bank can and cannot do—or should not do—through its LOLR. The central bank can provide emergency liquidity—quick cash upfront—over a short period of time when no other sources of funding are readily available. What the central bank should not do is to lend over an extended period of time, committing taxpayers' money, without the explicit approval of the fiscal authority. The central bank can provide liquidity, not capital. Any extended lending becomes the responsibility of the fiscal authority. Neither should the central bank use its LOLR to bail out bank owners; the LOLR's ultimate responsibility remains to the market—to the entire financial sector—and not to any particular institution.

A punitive rate or a high rate of interest has typically been considered a tenet of classic LOLR operations. However, several authors have suggested a rate lower than the market rate.[22] Goodhart argues that the cost of the initial [borrowing] tranche should be kept very low to avoid the stigma problem associated with borrowing from the central bank.[23] The expansion of central bank liquidity operations has turned what ought to be extraordinary into 'ordinary'—ordinary in the sense that with the crisis the central bank has often been the lender of primary or only resort. The central bank's commitment to fight the crisis has signified a departure from this otherwise typically applied principle. Rather than discourage its use, the central bank has been keen to encourage various types of lending operations, whatever qualification one wishes to attribute to them: ordinary or extraordinary. With the drying up of the inter-bank market, the central bank has often been the only provider of liquidity to the money markets. It is worth noting that it is possible for the interest rate to be high, while lower than it would have been without central bank lending.

One of the four pillars of traditional LOLR practice is that the institution receiving assistance should provide 'good' collateral.[24] How exactly this has been applied has varied from country to country and crisis to crisis. In some instances collateral has not been provided at all, while in others only the best quality collateral has been considered to be acceptable, for example treasury bonds. As speed is invariably of the essence when a request for emergency liquidity assistance is received, it will often be difficult to accurately assess the value of any collateral that is being offered or the suitability of the type of asset. For example, the various types of collateralised debt obligations which have been developed in the recent past range from those which are backed by top-quality loans to others which may relate to the sub-prime mortgage market.[25]

The recent financial crisis has exposed a significant weakness in the securitisation process. Individual banks started to refuse to accept securitised loan obligations for a number of reasons. In some instances there has been doubt about the quality of the underlying assets, thus suggesting that the bonds may be worth significantly less than face value. On the other hand, in many cases good-quality assets have been securitised and such bonds should, in normal market conditions, be easily tradable on the financial markets. However, as the liquidity crisis developed it became clear that even those securitised obligations of supposedly high quality had become virtually impossible to use, as trust between banks evaporated.

---

[22] See C Goodhart, *The Regulatory Response to the Financial Crisis* (Cheltenham UK, Edward Elgar, 2009) 71; JC Rochet, *Why There are So Many Banking Crises?* (Princeton, NJ, Princeton University Press, 2008) 89; R Repullo, 'Who should Act as a Lender of Last Resort? An Incomplete Contract Model' (2000) 32 *Journal of Money, Credit and Banking* 580, available at ftp://ftp.cemfi.es/pdf/papers/repullo/Liquidity%202005.pdf.
[23] Ibid.
[24] According to W Bagehot, 'these advances should be made on all good banking securities': Bagehot, above n 13, 197.
[25] W Buiter has argued that central banks as 'markets maker of last resort' should accept a wider range of assets as collateral (including non-investment grade and impaired assets) as long as they can establish a price for them and apply an appropriate 'haircut'. See maverecon.blogspot.com/2007/08/central-bank-as-market-maker-of-last.html.

The Special Liquidity Scheme (SLS) developed by the Bank of England recognised the need for banks holding such assets to be able to raise liquidity against them. The SLS is not a replacement for the Bank of England's lender of last resort policy. However, it does raise the issue of what sort of collateral should be acceptable to the Bank when undertaking its role as lender of last resort. If it is acceptable under the SLS to use collateral of good quality, but which is not in the form of government-issued securities, it is arguable that this should be allowed to continue. The question of what, if any, collateral should be taken by the Bank of England when exercising its lender of last resort function is not currently set out anywhere in law and traditionally it has been left to the Governor and Court of the Bank to decide policy on this. It is suggested that it would be better practice to have legislative provisions which set out clearly what types of collateral will be acceptable and on what terms (for example, what 'haircut' should apply? This means that banks receive Treasury bills with a lower nominal value than the assets they have provided in the swap).

The policy on collateral needs to be addressed and an approach formulated to ensure that all banks operating in a particular market are fully aware of what will be acceptable to the central bank and, equally important, what will not. In most jurisdictions the position appears to be unclear, and this is a situation which can only assist in exacerbating a difficult situation. Weak collateral runs against the essence of the credibility that central bank LOLR/ELA operations are meant to achieve.

It is worth returning to the words of Walter Bagehot, who wrote

> The object is to stay alarm, and nothing therefore should be done to cause alarm. But the way to cause alarm is to refuse some one who has good security to offer. The news of this will spread in an instant through all the money market at a moment of terror . . .[26]

He went on to say

> principle requires that such advances, if made at all for the purpose of curing panic, should be made in the manner most likely to cure that panic. And for this purpose, they should be made on everything which in common times is good 'banking security'.[27]

H.   Financial Sector Safety Net and the Financial Crisis from Northern Rock Onwards

The structure of the regulation of financial services in the UK underwent a significant reform in 1997, which led to the passing of the Financial Services and Markets Act 2000, the creation of the Financial Services Authority and a Memorandum of Understanding between HM Treasury, the Bank and the Financial Services Authority. This new financial landscape brought about many reforms which at the time were generally considered to be very positive, with particular praise for the move to give independence to the Bank. Although the Bank was no longer to be the banking regulator (this role was to be undertaken by the FSA), it retained its traditional role of LOLR.

---

[26] Bagehot, above n 13.
[27] Ibid, 205.

Although the reforms were significant and led to a substantial piece of legislation, which in turn has led to the FSA designing and implementing an extremely detailed rule book, no statutory or other guidance is given as to how the Bank is to undertake its lender of last resort role. From 1997 until the late summer of 2007 this issue had received much attention, but the drying up of liquidity on the inter-bank market in London created a number of problems. However, in the late summer of 2007 the focus in the UK turned to one bank, Northern Rock, a former building society that had become a fast-growing mortgage bank. The Northern Rock story has been described in detail elsewhere and will not be discussed further here.[28]

I. The Special Liquidity Scheme

On 21 April 2008, approximately 8 months after the problems at Northern Rock became public and the panic ensued, the Bank announced the launch of a scheme, the SLS,[29] to deal with the failure of the inter-bank markets to return to some state of normality. It was recognised by then that the normal conditions in this market were showing no signs of returning and, as a result, it had become necessary to find a way of injecting liquidity into the banks in the UK, on a temporary basis, while at the same time avoiding the dangers of an increase in moral hazard. It was envisaged that this scheme would satisfy the requirements of ensuring that both the risks and financial costs would remain with the banks receiving financial assistance and not with the Bank or the Treasury. Subsequent developments resulting from the global financial crisis have meant that the SLS, which, when introduced, was not intended to be a permanent scheme but one aimed at providing a temporary solution to the continuing problems associated with the lack of liquidity in the financial markets, had to be extended and expanded. Eligibility to use the SLS for draw-downs ended on 30 January 2009, but the scheme will remain in place for another three years which, according to the Bank of England, provides 'participating institutions with continuing liquidity support and certainty'.[30]

The SLS is essentially a vehicle through which good-quality but illiquid assets held by banks in the UK could be 'swapped' for liquid government securities. It provides, in effect, a repo transaction. By the end of January 2009, Treasury Bills with a total face value of £185 billion had been lent to banks and building societies under the scheme,[31] with a total of 32 banks and building societies accessing the scheme. At the time of the introduction of the SLS it was intended that it would close to new applications at the end of October 2008, but, due to the conditions in the financial markets at that time it, became necessary for it to be developed and expanded. The original idea was for a return to normality to be achieved by providing a temporary swap of 'high quality mortgage-backed and other

[28] For a detailed account of all aspects of the Northern Rock story see House of Commons Treasury Committee, 'The Run on the Rock' (24 January 2008); R Lastra, 'Northern Rock, UK Bank Insolvency and Cross-Border Insolvency' (2008) 9 *Journal of Banking Regulation* 165; and A Milne and G Wood, 'Shattered on the Rock: British Financial Stability from 1866 to 2007' (2009) 10 *Journal of Banking Regulation* 89.
[29] Bank of England news release, 21 April 2008.
[30] Bank of England news release, 3 February 2009.
[31] Bank of England, 'Special Liquidity Scheme: Market Notice' (3 February 2009), available at www.bankofengland.co.uk/markets/marketnotice090203c.pdf.

securities' for UK Treasury Bills.[32] It was recognised that, at least for the short term, there would be no market for trading some of these assets held by UK banks.

The SLS actually allows assets to be swapped for a relatively long period of time, and this indicates that the Bank and the Treasury feel that the inter-bank market is not likely to return to normal for a significant period. It works in the following way.[33] Initially a swap of assets was made for a fixed period of one year, but it is possible that this may be renewed up to three years in total. An important feature of the original scheme was that only assets which were in existence at the end of 2007 were eligible for swapping. That was to ensure that banks did not use the SLS to finance new lending. An important feature of the SLS is that the risk of losses remains with the individual banks. The Bank does not intend taking on any of the risk, and the design of the SLS, while not totally eliminating any risk to public funds, has certainly reduced it to an acceptable level.

If this process proves to be successful, it will result in increased liquidity for individual banks and the banking system. The governor of the Bank, Mervyn King, has stated that

> the Bank of England's Special Liquidity Scheme is designed to improve the liquidity position of the banking system and raise confidence in financial markets while ensuring that the risk of losses on loans they have made remains with the banks.[34]

The period for which initial swaps could be made ran for six months from 21 April 2008. During this time, each bank had to decide how much of its assets, in existence at the end of 2007, should be swapped. Thus, by 20 October 2008 the Bank and the Treasury were in a position to know the extent to which the SLS has been used. However, by that time events had moved on, and, as noted above, it was necessary to extend the life of the SLS and also to greatly increase the funds to be made available. Of course, what is not yet known is whether or not the banks receiving assistance will wish to continue beyond the initial period of 12 months, but it appears increasingly likely that this will be the case. It is a significant feature of the SLS that, although each swap will be for a period of one year, the banks will be able to request a renewal for a further one-year period and then at the end of that period make a further request for another one-year period. Renewals will not be automatic, however, but will be subject to the discretion of the Bank. So far no detailed guidance has been given as to what factors the Bank will take into account in exercising that discretion, and that is something which needs to be clarified. Presumably, factors such as the overall liquidity position of the general marketplace will be taken into account, but the liquidity position of individual banks requesting the renewal will also be a relevant factor.

The SLS, despite its design, does not come without risks. This has been recognised in that the Bank has been indemnified by HM Treasury, but, to ensure that any risks are minimised, banks will need to take a 'haircut'. It has already been seen that the Bank requires that the illiquid assets that are being swapped be of 'sufficiently high quality',[35] and a list of the classes of eligible securities was set out in a Market Notice.[36] Importantly,

---

[32] Bank of England, 'Special Liquidity Scheme: Information' (21 April 2008), available at www.bankofengland.co.uk/markets/sls/sls-information.pdf.

[33] Ibid.

[34] Bank of England, 'Special Liquidity Scheme: Money Markets News Release' (21 April 2008), available at www.bankofengland.co.uk/publications/news/2008/029.htm.

[35] Ibid.

[36] Bank of England, 'Special Liquidity Scheme: Market Notice' (21 April 2008), available at www.bankofengland.co.uk/markets/money/marketnotice040821.pdf.

UK- and EEA-covered bonds (including own-name bonds) secured by mortgages (residential and commercial) are included. Most of the other classes are public-sector-issued securities from the UK, EEA and US, including debt securities issued by Fannie Mae and Freddie Mac, although there is some argument about the quality of these. An additional requirement is that an eligible security must be triple-A rated by at least two of the major credit-rating agencies.[37]

The SLS was due to close to new applications in October 2008 but the deepening international financial crisis led to an increased need for liquidity assistance. In fact by late September and early October the position of many UK banks, both in relation to capital and liquidity, was so bad that a major operation was required in an attempt to save several major banks from insolvency. So, instead of announcing the termination of the temporary SLS after its initial six-month period ended in October 2008, on 8 October 2008 the government announced a rescue plan which has had the effect, inter alia, of expanding and extending it.[38]

This stabilisation plan, announced by the Chancellor, has three parts, one of which is concerned with liquidity. Although this chapter is concerned with lender of last resort issues, it is important, for an understanding of the way in which the continuing SLS is to operate, to consider all aspects of the stabilisation plan.

The Chancellor announced that the government had established a Bank Recapitalisation Fund (BRF) to enable UK banks[39] to increase their capital positions. Eight major UK banks immediately announced that they planned to join the scheme and increase their capital. Some of the new capital was to be raised in the open market, with the remainder being raised through the BRF. Where recapitalisation is to be made through the BRF, this will be by way of an issue of preference shares by the relevant bank to the government, which are to rank in priority over ordinary shares of the bank. Attached to these preference shares will be a fixed rate of interest, which is set at the significantly, and punitively, high level of 12%. This is aimed at protecting public funds, thereby ensuring that the source of capital, while necessary in the short term, is sufficiently unattractive because of cost to ensure that those banks which have raised capital in this way will make every attempt to repay the government as soon as they are in a position to do so. It is interesting to note that no other country which has introduced a similar scheme has set the interest rate at such a high level and there are legitimate concerns about whether this could actually make it more difficult for UK banks which are using the BRF to operate effectively.

Since the introduction of the scheme, three major UK banks have applied for capital through the BRF (HBOS, Lloyds TSB and RBS). Barclays announced its intention to increase capital by £10 billion from private sources; Santander is transferring £1 billion to its UK operations; HSBC has already injected £750 million of new capital; Standard Chartered is adequately capitalised and does not need any injection; and Nationwide Building Society, which is mutually owned, will increase its capital by £500 million. HBOS, Lloyds TSB and RBS[40] have also attempted, without success, to raise some capital from

---

[37] Standard & Poors, Moody's and Fitch.

[38] HM Treasury, 'Financial Support to the Banking Industry', Press Notice 100/08 (8 October 2008), available at www.hm-treasury.gov.uk/statement_chx_081008.

[39] And building societies.

[40] The attempt by RBS to raise capital by way of a rights issue to existing shareholders proved to be an absolute flop, with less than 2% of the shares on offer being taken up.

existing shareholders, but all needed the government to take substantial shareholdings. In the case of RBS, the government has a majority stake in the bank.[41] The government has continually asserted that it has no intention of running UK banks, but it does want to rebuild them. The Chancellor has announced that it is the government's intention to sell the public share in the participating banks as soon as this can be done.

In addition to the recapitalisation, the Chancellor significantly increased the amounts available to the Bank to lend through the SLS. He announced in the House of Commons that he had agreed further immediate liquidity measures with the Governor of the Bank[42] and stated that 'until markets stabilise, the Bank will extend and widen its injections of funds into the system'.[43] The amount available to the Bank to lend through the SLS was increased 'to a total of at least £200 billion',[44] thereby indicating that it was thought at that time that the final amount needed may have been considerably more. As has been seen above, the final figure came close at £185 billion. It was also announced that the Bank would lend in both sterling and US dollars against a wider range of collateral[45] than had been the case under the original SLS. The Chancellor emphasised once again that this was designed to ensure that the risks of losses would be with the banks receiving assistance, not with the UK taxpayer.

On 13 October 2008, the Chancellor made a further statement on financial stability in the House of Commons[46] in which he announced that, with immediate effect, the provision of liquidity would include an unlimited amount of dollar funds available to banks to be swapped for sterling funds and continued loan operations through the SLS.[47]

The third part of the stabilisation programme is the temporary underwriting of eligible new debt issued by banks. The aim of this is to encourage banks to start lending to each other again and this, if successful, would also assist in increasing the amount of liquidity in the banking system. This would work in tandem with the SLS. The Chancellor has recognised that many banks have simply lost confidence in each other and that medium-term lending between them has frozen up. He noted that if banks do not lend to each other they are also unlikely to lend in the normal marketplace to businesses and individuals. To remove what is perceived to be a key barrier, the government is offering to temporarily underwrite any new eligible debt issued by banks which participate in the BRF. This is to be priced on commercial terms and the expected amount available is to be in the region of £250 billion, but the Chancellor indicated that this sum is to be kept under review. The guarantee under the scheme will be provided directly by the Treasury and will cover new lending issued during a six-month period. This period is to be renewable. The actual cost

---

[41] The government will have appropriate representation on the board of directors of each of these institutions. It also announced that these shareholdings will be managed on a fully commercial basis by a company, at arm's length, which will have a precisely defined remit to ensure that it is acting in the interests of taxpayers. Individual agreements have been reached in relation to each of these banks, and these contain conditions with respect to such matters as executive pay, bonuses, continued lending to small businesses, homebuyers and other relevant matters.

[42] HM Treasury, 'Statement by the Chancellor on Financial Stability' (8 October 2008) para 13. available at www.hm-treasury.gov.uk/statement_chx_081008.htm.

[43] Ibid, para 14.

[44] Ibid, para 16.

[45] Ibid, para 15.

[46] HM Treasury, 'Statement by the Chancellor on Financial Markets' (13 October 2008), available at www.hm-treasury.gov.uk/statement_chx_131008.htm.

[47] Ibid, para 15.

can be varied at the discretion of the Treasury, but has initially been set at a premium of 50 basis points above the recent average cost of default insurance for each of the participating banks and accordingly is risk-based. It is worth reiterating that it is only those banks (and building societies) that participate in the BRF that are eligible for this assistance.

On 16 October 2008 the Bank published details of a permanent regime to underpin liquidity in the banking system.[48] This permanent regime is designed 'to improve the functioning of the existing framework and introduce two new permanent liquidity insurance facilities for banks to access in stressed financial circumstances'.[49] The Bank's existing Standing Facilities were to be replaced with what are to be known as Operational Standing Facilities. The existing standing facilities were introduced in 2006 and allowed banks to borrow unlimited amounts from the Bank at any time and also to deposit any surplus cash, but the Bank believes that the existing facility 'became stigmatised after August 2007 when operational use was misinterpreted as a sign of financial difficulty'.[50] It was to get rid of this stigma that the Bank announced the replacement of the then existing Standing Facilities with Operational Standing Facilities and a Discount Window Facility. Importantly, the Bank has amended its approach to the disclosure of the use of these facilities. From 20 October 2008 average use of the Operational Standing Facilities will only be disclosed after the end of the relevant maintenance period.[51] This, the Bank believes, should cause the cessation of any potential stigma.

The Discount Window Facility is to be a permanent feature that will allow banks to swap securities for either government securities or, in some cases, cash. According to the Bank, 'the facility is explicitly designed to help contain system stress by providing financing against assets that may become illiquid in stressed conditions'.[52]

The original SLS provided important liquidity assistance for many of the banks which are currently experiencing liquidity problems, but what is as yet unclear is the position of banks which are denied assistance on the basis that the assets being offered are not considered by the Bank to be of sufficiently high quality. Were this to happen, the bank being denied assistance would clearly have significant problems. Both the application by the bank and the refusal by the Bank would not be in the public domain, but it would quickly become clear to the market that the bank in question had been unable to obtain additional liquidity on the basis of a swap under the SLS.

To coincide with the ending of the drawdown period of the SLS, the Chancellor announced the creation of an Asset Purchase Facility (APF). The Bank is to operate the scheme, the objective of which 'is to increase the availability of corporate credit, in order to support the Bank's responsibilities and financial stability and monetary stability in the UK'.[53] The Chancellor authorised the Bank to purchase up to £50 billion of what he describes as 'high quality private sector assets'.[54] The Bank is to be indemnified by the government to ensure that it is protected in connection with any losses. The APF will allow banks to sell a wide range of assets to the Bank, which should assist in allowing banks to

---

[48] Bank of England news release (16 October 2008); and 'The Development of the Bank of England's Market Operations: Market Notice' (16 October 2008).
[49] Ibid.
[50] Bank of England, 'The Development of The Bank of England's Market Operations' (16 October 2008) 2.
[51] Ibid.
[52] Ibid, 3.
[53] Letter from the Chancellor to the Governor of the Bank of England, 29 January 2009.
[54] Ibid.

operate with greater liquidity.[55] The Governor of the Bank immediately announced that it would establish a new company to undertake these transactions and that it will provide a clear, transparent mechanism for monitoring the operations conducted under the facility.[56] It will also publish a quarterly report on the transactions undertaken in the APF.[57]

J.   Liquidity, LOLR and Constructive Ambiguity— Where Are We Now?

In the consultation paper "Financial Stability and Depositor Protection: Further Consultation", published in July 2008,[58] it is recognised that 'through the provision of liquidity to the financial system the Bank of England plays a key role in contributing to maintaining financial stability and implementing monetary policy'.[59] In addition, it states that the government intends to introduce legislation to support this (and has since introduced the Banking Act 2009), but what is contained in the document is minimalist in relation to policy on providing emergency liquidity assistance, with little detail being provided and, importantly, it does not deal at all with the question of constructive ambiguity.[60] Also, despite legislative reforms in the Banking Act, there is no sign as yet of any legislative developments in relation to the provision of liquidity. It is recognised that, while at present the Bank's responsibility for monetary policy is clearly set out in legislation,[61] this is not the case in relation to financial stability. This is to change, and the Bank will be given 'statutory responsibility for contributing to the maintenance of financial stability within the UK'.[62] This is to be a high-level objective which will ensure that the central bank is given the flexibility it needs to attain its objective. No further details of how this will operate are provided.

The proposals relating to liquidity support arrangements deal with certain specific issues. The first of these is a proposal to provide the Bank with 'statutory immunity from liabilities and damages arising from acts or omissions in carrying out its responsibilities in relation to financial stability and other central bank functions'.[63] The second proposal is to clarify the Bank's position as a creditor.[64] The third proposal is to extend

---

[55] According to the Chancellor, the following sterling assets are eligible for purchase by APF: paper issued under the Credit Guarantee Scheme, corporate bonds, commercial paper, syndicated loans and asset-backed securities created in viable securitisation structures. The Bank must also be satisfied that there will be a viable private market demand for the types of assets it purchases.

[56] Letter from the Governor of the Bank of England to the Chancellor, 29 January 2009.

[57] The quantitative easing (QE) policy adopted by the Bank of England announced on 5 March 2009; see above n 6.

[58] Chancellor of the Exchequer, 'Financial Stability and Depositor Protection: Further Consultation', Cm 7436 (London, HM Treasury, 2008).

[59] Ibid, 52, para 3.15.

[60] Ibid, 52, para 3.16.

[61] Bank of England Act 1998.

[62] Chancellor of the Exchequer, above n 58, 88, para 6.3.

[63] Ibid, 52, para 3.17.

[64] This relates to the Settlement Finality Regulations 1999. It aims to make it easier for the Bank of England to realise collateral more effectively and, in particular, to insulate it from the effects of insolvency collateral which has been pledged to it.

financial assistance to building societies, and this has already been done.[65] To strengthen the position of the Bank further, the government is to allow building societies to grant floating charges in relation to emergency liquidity financing.[66]

The question of liquidity disclosure was clearly an important issue in the Northern Rock case and the apparent 'stigma' of LOLR assistance surfaced. This subject is considered within the consultation and it is recognised that there are circumstances in which disclosure can have a damaging effect on the provision of liquidity assistance. This is certainly not a new viewpoint. In 1994 Sir Edward George, former Governor of the Bank, wrote

> we usually try to keep the fact that we are providing systemic support secret at the time . . . If people know that we are so concerned about systemic fragility that we have judged necessary to provide support, [it] could lead to a wider loss of confidence. They would wonder how far that support would be extended, and we could rapidly find ourselves in the position where we were in practice underwriting all the liabilities of the banking system.[67]

The former Governor was merely advocating that it is better to keep assistance confidential at the time when it is actually being provided. He was not arguing for secrecy and emphasised that it should be made public as soon as possible thereafter. This is generally recognised as a sensible approach. Under the system where the Bank lent to the discount houses, no one knew which bank or banks needed the funds.

Market transparency is undoubtedly of utmost importance and this is recognised by the UK authorities, who also recognise that it is very difficult to strike the right balance between the transparency which is afforded by disclosure and the protection which is afforded by secrecy.[68] To achieve a balanced response, the consultation paper contains two specific proposals. First is the publication of the Bank's weekly return.[69] It appears that most respondents to the January consultation supported this proposal. While any decision has yet to be taken, it seems likely that this will be done. Also of significance are the other statutory reporting requirements of the Bank which require disclosure of liquidity assistance operations. For example, the Annual Report and Accounts do not contain details of specific liquidity assistance operations until there is no longer a need for confidentiality.[70] The need for banks to be able to access liquidity without stigma is recognised as being particularly important[71] and the proposals on disclosure should assist in this respect.

In October 2008 the Bank published a consultative paper on the development of the Bank's market operations.[72] However, this is concerned with normal market operations, not about lender of last resort, and, while it is helpful to see such developments, no guidance about the operation of the lender of last resort role is given.

---

[65] The Building Societies (Financial Assistance) Order 2008 was approved by Parliament in June 2008.
[66] Chancellor of the Exchequer, above n 58, 53, para 3.21.
[67] 'The Pursuit of Financial Stability' [February 1994] *Bank of England Quarterly Bulletin* 60.
[68] Chancellor of the Exchequer, above n 58, 53, para 3.22.
[69] The Bank Return is a weekly statement of the financial position of the Bank, available at www.bankofengland.co.uk.
[70] Chancellor of the Exchequer, above n 58, 53, para 3.24.
[71] Ibid, 88, para 6.4.
[72] Bank of England, above n 50.

K.   Concluding Observations

Lender of last resort as a central bank function has substantially changed over the last 18 months in response to the financial crisis. The concept of constructive ambiguity has been altered. In times of extreme uncertainty and volatility, market participants want little ambiguity from their central bank. In the UK, the SLS has not yet become a permanent feature, but it is possible at some time in the future that it may have to. If that were to happen there would be no place for ambiguity, constructive or otherwise, and, providing the collateral requirements are satisfied, the role of the Bank would not be to decide whether or not to assist but simply to evaluate the quality of the security being offered and then to provide assistance. The bank being assisted would be hit by a 'haircut' and would have to pay for the privilege.

LOLR as a crisis management instrument has always been related to other crisis management procedures, notably deposit insurance and insolvency proceedings. A major issue that must be considered following recent events is the role that insolvency should play, in view of the introduction of the Special Resolution Regime (SRR). Under classic LOLR, as has already been seen, the central bank would only lend to banks which were illiquid but still solvent. In practice, of course, the speed with which an assessment of a bank's financial position had to be made meant that assistance was no doubt sometimes provided to banks which had crossed the threshold of insolvency. In November 2007 the traditional position was reiterated by the Bank, but that, of course, was before the introduction of the SLS, the SRR and the other measures that have taken place since then. Banks which had become insolvent have certainly been assisted in the UK since the troubles at Northern Rock, though on the basis of having a capital injection as well as liquidity through the SLS. The UK government has shown a real reluctance to allow any high-profile bank to fail.[73]

Does this imply that where a bank is of sufficiently low profile and therefore systemically unimportant no attempt is likely to made by the authorities to keep it afloat? What is certainly clear following the events over the last 18 months is that ensuring that depositors are fully protected remains sacrosanct. The financial crisis has meant that the role of the Bank in providing lender of last resort assistance or emergency liquidity assistance is never likely to be the same again. While many countries have introduced clear legal frameworks for the provision of liquidity, it does not appear that the UK is going to adopt this approach, in particular since the recently adopted Banking Act 2009 does not go into details in this regard.

The effect of the introduction of the SRR probably means that a bank approaching the Bank for LOLR assistance will risk the possibility of finding itself subject to this procedure. Is this likely to be a factor in reality? If so, what effect might it have on the behaviour of the bank's management? The Treasury is to publish a Code of Practice in relation to the use of the SRR and that might assist in clarifying the position. Some guidance from the Bank of England on how it sees its lender of last resort role would be very welcome.

Reputation and confidence are and were at the core of what LOLR/ELA operations aim to achieve. In this sense, the revision of the traditional principles ought to mitigate the

---

[73] Although London Scottish Bank plc, in contrast to Northern Rock, was allowed to go into administration at the end of November 2008.

issues of 'stigma' (resulting from a perception that only the desperate go to the LOLR/ELA) that were evident in the Northern Rock case. Disclosure is generally a good thing, but, given the psychological component in the rapid spread of a crisis, the provision of covert as opposed to overt assistance should remain in the arsenal of the Bank. The importance of a clear mandate and a set of enabling rules for the Bank with regard to financial stability, in particular with regard to its LOLR/ELA operations, contributes positively to safeguard confidence and has a positive reputational effect.

Central banks and public authorities can claim that if they are to assist an institution on 'a rainy day' they should regulate that institution on 'a sunny day'. Hence, regulation and protection tend to be mutually reinforcing. The downside of 'protection' is moral hazard. In the absence of protection, individuals and institutions tend to be more conservative and less prone to risk. Public opinion is usually sympathetic towards regulation in the aftermath of crises. And the longer a crisis lasts and the more severe its effects are, the greater the public sympathy for regulation.

11

The Global Credit Crisis and Regulatory Reform

GEORGE A WALKER[*]

A. Introduction[1]

The recent crises in financial markets have caused significant damage and hardship, especially with the onslaught of the global recession beginning in October and November 2008. This never developed into a full depression, with the downturn levelling during the second quarter of 2009 as financial markets began to recover in advance of the rest of the economy. A number of significant lessons must now be considered with regard to supervisory and regulatory revision, as well as in terms of the more general monetary and economic policy management of modern complex economies.

The global financial crisis unfolded with a brutal and remorseless continuity and predictability. We have now moved through three clear phases of turmoil, from an initial credit contraction in August 2007 to successive bank and financial failures and bailouts in the summer of 2008, and then to a full stock-market crisis and consequent global recession in autumn 2008. We are now in the third stage of the most tumultuous period in financial history since the stock market crash in 1929 and consequent Great Depression. If the five days between Monday 15 September and Friday 19 September 2008 were not unsettling enough, the global financial system teetered on the edge of collapse three weeks later, between Monday 6 and Friday 10 October 2008. US markets had stabilised little following the protracted and untidy agreement on 3 October on the US$700bn bailout plan, while European leaders singularly failed to agree any common collective response. The British government was then forced into undertaking an inspired but uncharacteristically dramatic lead (especially following Northern Rock) in adopting the first informed and comprehensive package of response measures to the crisis on 8 October.

Many nevertheless anticipated that these measures would only be given bland or formal recognition at the G7 Finance Ministers and central bankers' meeting on the weekend of 11–12 October 2008. These discussions then shifted to the G-20 'Bretton Woods 2' meetings held in Washington on 14–15 November, which were followed by further events in Paris and then London. Whether the necessary domestic and coordinated international

[*] Professor of International Financial Law, Centre for Commercial Law Studies, Queen Mary, University of London and Professor of Financial Regulation and Policy, University of Glasgow.
[1] This paper is based on GA Walker, 'Credit Markets, Bretton Woods II and Global Response' (2009) Butterworths *Journal of International Banking and Financial Law* 75; and G Walker, 'Credit Contraction, Financial Collapse and Global Recession' (2009) *Journal of International Banking and Financial Law* 5.

action will be taken to limit the damage from the current crisis and to prevent future crises recurring remains to be seen.

B.   From Credit Contraction to Crisis in the US and Beyond

The turmoil originated with the credit tightening on inter-bank markets beginning on 9 August 2007. Inter-bank credits froze after BNP Paribas suspended payments on three investment funds. The German Sachsen Landesbank was sold to the Landesbank Baden-Wuerttenberg on 28 August 2007 and IKB reported a loss of US$1bn in US sub-prime debt. Shares in Northern Rock fell on 14 and 15 September 2007 following the announcement of its request for liquidity assistance from the Bank of England, with Northern Rock eventually being brought into public ownership (nationalised) on 17 February 2008 after the Treasury's rejection of the remaining private sector bids.

Société Général suffered a €4.9bn (£3.7bn) loss through its trader Jerome Kerviel, while Evan Dooley misplaced US$41.5m at MF Global. The instability spread to the US Monoline insurance market, worth US$2.3tn, with the Federal Reserve having to announce a special US$30bn facility to allow JP Morgan to purchase Bear Stearns initially for US$2 per share on 17 March 2008. This was the first occasion in recent times that the Federal Reserve has acted to bail out a non-bank financial institution. The most dramatic episodes of the crisis then appeared to be over following the managed acquisition of Bear Stearns by JP Morgan. The subsequent escalation six months later took everyone completely by surprise.

The credit crisis spread to other financial sectors at the end of summer 2008, with a number of major non-bank financial institutions announcing further losses. The original pressure in the credit markets then infected other parts of the financial system, with the most infamous casualties being the giant US mortgage lenders Fannie Mae and Freddie Mac and the remaining major independent Wall Street investment firms, Lehman Brothers, Merrill Lynch, Morgan Stanley and Goldman Sachs, the largest global insurance company, American Insurance International (AIG), and other US commercial banks, including Wachovia and Washington Mutual (WaMu).

The US government announced that it would take control of Fannie Mae and Freddie Mac on Sunday 7 September 2008. This amounted to a de facto nationalisation, with confirmation that the government would provide up to US$100bn (£56.3bn) as required. This would allow both agencies to remain solvent and continue to cover their debts, with the government acquiring US$5tn (£2,825bn) of mortgage-backed securities. By way of comparison, the UK Treasury only acquired £100bn of mortgage debt on the nationalisation of Northern Rock. The effect was to stabilise the US$12tn US mortgage market, though at the expense of shareholders and investors in both entities. This would act as a significant disincentive for future capital injection by private investors.

The market capitalisation of Lehman Brothers halved during the week to Friday 12 September 2008 after it recorded US$3.9bn in losses. Chairman and Chief Executive, Dick Fuld, had attempted to placate the markets with a survival plan involving the sale of 55% of its asset management unit, worth US$30bn, the US$30bn commercial real estate portfolio and a further US$4bn in UK property assets, with dividends being cut. Lehman was then forced to contact other banks to find a possible 'white knight', although any rescue plan would have been unattractive without Treasury support. Treasury Secretary Hank Paulson had taken the decision that the US authorities could not bail out another investment bank and that a private sector solution would have to be found. Lehman was then forced into Chapter 11 bankruptcy on 15 September 2008 after Barclays walked away from negotiations. Barclays would later acquire Lehman's North American investment banking business for less than US$2bn. This terminated Lehman's 158-year history as an independent investment bank and became the largest bankruptcy in US corporate history. While the US authorities had calculated that the closure of Lehman would not have any major systemic consequences, this would later be identified as the main causal event that led to the subsequent and much more severe second stage of the financial crisis.

With the crisis at Lehman, Merrill Lynch was forced to accept a $50bn offer from Bank of America after a week of negotiations, with the deal being announced on the same day as the Lehman bankruptcy. Shares in the remaining two largest US independent investment banks, Goldman Sachs and Morgan Stanley, continued to fall on Thursday 18 September. Morgan Stanley approached the Wachovia Bank in the US and the China Investment Corporation (CIC) for capital support, though concerns arose with regard to the political sensitivity of allowing the CIC to acquire a major stake in a Wall Street firm. Wachovia was later acquired by JP Morgan. Goldman Sachs and Morgan Stanley would subsequently be forced to reregister as bank holding companies, thereby ending the inglorious days of large-scale aggressive independent investment banking on Wall Street.

The Treasury then had to provide a separate support package for AIG, which was the world's largest insurer, with a market value of US$239bn. An US$85bn credit facility was made available on 16 September 2008 to run for a two-year period in return for a 79.9% stake in the group. This was subsequently increased to $153bn in the middle of November. An attempt had again been made to arrive at a private sector solution worth US$70bn, although this was not possible following a further collapse in the share price. AIG's problems had arisen with its development of a niche practice in the area of credit default swaps (CDSs) in combination with its less risky life insurance and retirement services. This included writing CDSs on many of the largest financial institutions in the world as well as other financial contracts, including collateralised debt obligations (CDOs). AIG had to report in May 2008 that its total losses would be over US$10bn. Treasury support was considered necessary in light of its central position in the US and international insurance and reinsurance markets, including through its extended and complex subsidiary group structure. AIG support was subsequently increased to $150 billion, with the Treasury Department to purchase $40 billion in preferred shares as part of its Capital Repurchase Plan and the Federal Reserve buying $52.5 billion in mortgage-backed securities to allow AIG to retire many outstanding credit default swaps and lend more.

Considerable market pressure had also been placed on WaMu, although it was decided to allow WaMu to close at the end of September 2008. This was the largest individual US bank failure. WaMu had assets of US$307bn and deposits of US$188bn at the end of June 2008, with US$46.6bn in equity and bonds outstanding. WaMu was closed down by the Federal Deposit Insurance Corporation on the evening of Thursday 25 September 2008, with JP Morgan acquiring its deposit and retail branch business and mortgage portfolio but without any unsecured debt or liabilities of the holding company. JP Morgan became the largest banking group in the US. The effect of the closure was again to wipe out the shareholders and bondholders in WaMu, with another bank being allowed to come and purchase the assets following the closure at a substantial discount rather than support the failing entity. Thirteen other lenders were allowed to close during 2008, although WaMu was by far the largest.

C.   The US Regulatory Response

A number of initiatives were taken forward in the US, UK and other countries, as well at the EU and international levels, in response to the crisis. Many of these were initially only reactionary or isolated and fundamentally protectionist in effect, if not in immediate intent. National governments had to face the reality of the global financial contagion that had erupted and the inevitable inadequacy of any solely national-based solution. The need for coordinated action nevertheless only became apparent slowly, which itself revealed the continuing inadequacies of the post-war international financial architecture. The need for a more carefully coordinated and structured collective response was recognised but immediately postponed to a series of more general 'new Bretton Woods' conference meetings to begin in Washington in October 2008 and London in April 2009.

The US authorities were forced into undertaking a series of increasingly desperate attempts to contain the crisis. These were essentially based on massive continued liquidity injections into the markets and a distressed asset purchase programme, which was subsequently abandoned in favour of bank recapitalisation and direct intervention in the corporate commercial paper market.

1.   Liquidity Support

Following the rescue plan announced for Fannie Mae and Freddie Mac and the AIG support programme, the Federal Reserve injected US$180bn in global liquidity. The funds were made available through the Federal and other national central banks, including the Bank of England, the Bank of Japan and the European Central Bank, as well as in Switzerland and Canada. Dollar funds were provided through central bank currency exchange and swap arrangements. This represents possibly the most significant extension of global lender of last resort funding in history intended to maintain dollar liquidity within the markets.

A number of new initiatives have since been introduced by the Federal Reserve. In addition to regular Open Market Operations and the Discount Window, facilities set up in 2007 include the Term Discount Window Programme, the Term Auction Facility and Reciprocal Currency Arrangements entered into with other selected investment banks. Other primary dealer facilities were launched in 2008 with the Primary Dealer Credit Facility, the Term Securities Lending Facility, the Term Securities Lending Facility Options Programme and other Securities Lending. Additional facilities are now also available with Transitional Credit Extensions for US and London broker-dealer subsidiaries of Goldman Sachs, Morgan Stanley and Merrill Lynch, as well as the asset-backed commercial paper (ABCP) Money Market Funding Liquidity Facility, the Commercial Paper Funding Facility, the Money Market Investing Funding Facility and the Term Asset-Backed

Securities Loan Facility. A range of significant new credit and other official support options have accordingly been introduced in the US which must be considered as part of any larger new response programme to the financial crisis.

2.   The Troubled Asset Recovery Programme

The most significant US initiative was Hank Paulson's plan to establish a US$700bn mortgage rescue plan to purchase distressed debt from leading US financial institutions. The possibility of such a scheme had been raised at the end of the week of Friday 19 September 2008 and then confirmed by Paulson on the following Sunday 21 September. Under the Troubled Asset Recovery Programme (TARP), a new corporation would be established to purchase distressed residential and commercial mortgage-backed securities from any major institution operating in the US, including foreign banks. The range of securities to be covered could be extended at Treasury and Federal Reserve discretion, with the assets acquired being managed by privately appointed fund managers acting on behalf of the Treasury. Securities would be purchased over the first two years and then held and disposed of over a further period to be determined. This was similar to the scheme set up during the Great Depression in the 1930s and the savings and loan crises in the 1980s and in Sweden in the 1990s. A private sector 'superSIV' had also been attempted in the US more recently, but was abandoned.

It was later announced that US$250bn of the funds made available would be used to recapitalise the banking system based on the UK model, although it was then decided in November that the scheme would focus on supporting the direct ABCP market facility already in place. The removal of the asset purchase component within the TARP halted the improvement in inter-bank lending rates that had taken place. It was later confirmed that up to $1,800bn would be provided by the Federal Reserve directly to corporate issuers in the US commercial paper market (above).

3.   Stimulus Package

Incoming President Obama's response to the crisis was taken forward with the announcement by Tim Geithner, the new Treasury Secretary, of the proposed bailout proposals on 10 February 2009 and Congressional agreement on the US$789bn (later US$838bn) stimulus package on 11 February 2009. The new Administration's Fiscal Stimulus Bill was passed by the Senate on the same day, although with the support of only three Republicans. The stimulus package was ceded 'to the fractious Congressional Democrats', and degenerated into a 'divisive partisan battle'.[2] This was a lost opportunity. President Obama would nevertheless later confirm that he would proceed with the introduction of new restrictions on offshore tax avoidance by US companies.

---

[2] 'The Trouble with Obama's Rescue', *The Economist*, 12 February 2009, http://www.economist.com/opinion/displaystory.cfm?story_id=13108724.

4.   US Bailout II

Geithner subsequently clarified the US$2tn (£1.38tn) package of measures to support the US banking system. Geithner referred to this as being 'comprehensive and forceful', and would 'clean up and strengthen the nation's banks, bring in private capital to restart lending' and 'go around the banking system directly to the markets that consumers and businesses depend on'. Shares nevertheless fell because of the absence of detail provided, especially with regard to the distressed asset component, and the absence of any insurance guarantee support for other portfolio assets affected by the recession. The plan consisted of an unspecified capital injection, credit market support of up to US$200bn–US$1tn, asset purchases of up to US$1tn and US$50bn in foreclosure relief. Specific conditions were imposed with regard to dividend payments (other than a nominal US$0.01 per share) until the government assistance had been repaid in full. The most important element of the new bailout plan was the stress testing to confirm which banks were solvent and which were not.

The results of the US stress testing of the 19 largest banks in the country were released on 7 May 2009. The carrying out of the tests had been announced in February with a series of assumptions being made with regard to the possible extent of the economic downturn. Tangible common equity is being used in preference to the Basel Committee's risk weight system to avoid possible further dilution. Separate initiatives have been announced by Geithner to stimulate other credit markets with only one-third of funding being provided by banks in the US. The release of the stress test results was important in terms of market and public interest and consumption, even though the figures were predictable, and it has to be expected that the US authorities would not have proceeded with the exercise if they were not confident about the outcome.

It was confirmed that Bank of America would require an additional US$34bn (£26.6bn) in capital and Citigroup US$6bn. Bank of America's tier 1 ratio had been 10.7% and Citigroup's 11.9% at the end of the first quarter of 2009. Commentators have questioned the ability of the 10-year-old Basel Standards, which established the 8% minimum capital requirement and 12.5% obverse leverage (capital to assets) ratio. This nevertheless fails to take into account the size of the non-backed trading losses suffered that was dealt with under the separate market risk rules.

D.   The UK Regulatory Response

The first major casualty from the global credit tightening in the UK was Northern Rock, which was forced to ask for liquidity support from the Bank of England on 14 September 2007. The Banking (Special Provisions) Act 2008 was specifically enacted on a short parliamentary procedure to allow Northern Rock to be brought into temporary public ownership in February 2008. This also assisted with the reconstruction of Bradford & Bingley (B&B) in September 2008. A decision was eventually taken to nationalise the mortgage and loan business, worth £43.3bn, under the 2008 Act but to sell the £22bn of retail deposits and 200 branch business to Spanish Banco Santander.

As markets continued to fall and with the leak of a possible UK rescue plan during the week beginning 6 October, the government was placed under increasing pressure to bring forward more substantial response package. The final Treasury refinancing plan involved the making available of up to £50bn to the eight largest UK banks in exchange for preference shares. The Bank of England's Special Liquidity Scheme (SLS) was doubled from £100bn to £200bn—with Treasury bills being exchangeable for lower-quality liquid collateral assets (although with strict discounts being maintained). The Treasury also provided commercial guarantees worth up to £250bn on new wholesale funding for up to three years. The objective of the guarantees was to allow banks to raise further medium-term funds on the money markets as existing facilities matured. In effect, the UK government had created the first coherent reform package to the crisis—although this was still on strict commercial terms. This was not the 'giveaway' portrayed in parts of the press, with the strict terms imposed not allowing any immediate improvement in money market lending.

The government confirmed on the morning of Monday 13 October 2008 that £37bn would be invested in RBS (£19bn), HBOS (£12bn) and Lloyds TSB (£5bn), with Barclays attempting to raise £7bn directly from the capital markets. As many of the banks had also already issued large amounts of preference shares (with higher dividends but no voting rights), it was confirmed that the government would purchase a larger amount of ordinary shares in each institution. The effect of this was that the government would acquire a controlling interest in at least RBS and HBOS, while the holdings of existing institutional investors would be further diluted—which would act as a further disincentive to any private uptake. The government separately confirmed that it would prohibit cash bonuses and that dividend payments would be frozen for five years, although these conditions had to be relaxed subsequently. The Chief Executives and Chairmen of RBS and HBOS confirmed their resignations. RBS would be forced to enter into a further, more comprehensive, bailout arrangement on 26 February 2009 with the UK Treasury. RBS announced losses of £24.1bn for 2008, with a £2.5bn restructuring plan and 20,000 job losses to follow. The government agreed to inject £25.5bn in new capital, with £325bn in distressed assets being supported by the Treasury guarantee in return for a fee £6.5bn. RBS would accept a first loss of £19.5bn. Stephen Hester, the new RBS chief executive, announced plans to divide its operations into two entities, with three-quarters of the successful parts of the business being retained and the other quarter prepared for disposal.

The UK bailout plan was supported by the G7 at their meeting on the weekend of 11–12 October. Commentators had been nervous about the degree of commitment that would be displayed and then acted on. The G7 leaders nevertheless confirmed that they would use all available tools to support systemically important financial institutions and prevent their failure, which was interpreted as meaning that there would be no more Lehman-style collapses. The G7 further confirmed that they would take all necessary steps to unfreeze credit and money markets, and ensure that banks and other financial institutions had broad access to liquidity and funding. They would also ensure that banks and other major financial intermediaries could raise capital from public as well as private sources in sufficient amounts to re-establish confidence. The UK refinancing plan was subsequently approved and implemented with various national revisions at EU level during the week beginning Monday 13 October 2008. Germany established a €100bn fund to support banks, with a total package of €300–400bn, including inter-bank guarantees and direct loans. Portugal confirmed that it would provide a credit line of up to €20bn to guarantee bank liquidity.

1.   The Tripartite Response

The tripartite authorities have issued a number of papers in response to the UK and global crises.[3] The tripartite authorities are made up of the Bank of England, the Financial Services Authority (FSA) and HM Treasury under the Memorandum of Understanding entered into between them in 1998 and updated in 2006. An initial discussion was issued in October 2007 reviewing the current systems in place for dealing with banks in distress, including the deposit protection scheme managed by the Financial Services Compensation Scheme (FSCS). A series of objectives were stated to support the government's key purpose of maintaining financial stability. Consumers had to be confident that an appropriate, credible and reliable guarantee scheme operated in a timely fashion. There had to be full transparency (including funding) in the event of a disruption in banking services. Critical banking functions must be maintained for retail, business and wholesale customers, allowing, where necessary, an orderly transition to an alternative banking provider. Any reform must maintain the UK's reputation as a pre-eminent location for financial services, must protect the taxpayers' interest and must ensure an appropriate sharing of costs between all parties concerned.

The tripartite authorities issued a separate statement on a revised financing structure for Northern Rock on 21 January 2008,[4] with three further consultation documents on Financial Stability and Depositor Protection being issued by HM Treasury, the FSA and the Bank of England on 1 July 2008.[5]

In the July 2008 paper on financial stability and depositor protection, the authorities reconfirmed their adherence to the five key policy objectives set out in the earlier January consultation document. A number of specific recommendations were developed with regard to stability and resilience in the financial system, individual bank difficulty, impact failure (including the new Special Resolution Regime, or SRR), compensation and the role and function of the Bank of England, including inter-agency coordination. The paper confirmed that the UK would implement all of the recommendations in the Financial Stability Forum (FSF) report on enhancing market and institutional resilience (April 2008).

The FSA had separately strengthened individual bank oversight through its supervisory enhancement programme (SEP) and has consulted on changes to the Disclosure and Transparency Rules to clarify circumstances in which a corporate issuer in receipt of liquidity support from a central bank can have a legitimate interest to delay disclosure. The

---

[3] The Treasury, the Bank of England and the FSA, 'Banking Reform—Protecting Depositors: a Discussion Paper' (October 2007); the Treasury, the Bank of England and the FSA, 'Financial Stability and Depositor Protection: Strengthening the Framework', Cm 7308 (January 2008); Tripartite Authorities, 'Financial Stability and Depositor Protection' (July 2008); and Tripartite Authorities, 'Financial Stability and Depositor Protection: Special Resolution Regime' (July 2008) CM 7459. See also HM Treasury, 'Financial Stability and Depositor Protection: Cross-Border Challenges and Responses' (September 2008).

[4] HM Treasury press release, 'Northern Rock', 21 January 2008.

[5] Tripartite Authorities, 'Financial Stability and Depositor Protection' (July 2008); Tripartite Authorities, 'Financial Stability and Depositor Protection: Special Resolution Regime' (July 2008) CM 7459; and HM Treasury, 'Financial Stability and Depositor Protection: Cross-Border Challenges and Responses' (September 2008).

FSA has consulted on deposit guarantee limits that apply across all sectors, with bank deposit limits being increased to £50,000 on Friday 3 October 2008.

The Bank of England was to be given express statutory responsibility for contributing to the maintenance of financial stability, and a new Financial Stability Committee has been created to report to the Governor and Court. The number of Court members would be restricted to 12, and all new appointments will be made on an advertised and open competitive basis. The Bank's role in connection with financial stability has unfortunately only been expressed in loose and non-specific terms in the Banking Bill introduced to the House of Commons in October 2008. This is an unfortunate omission and lost opportunity.

2.   Special Resolution Regime

The new SRR was referred to in the July paper and separate consultation document released at the same time. The stated purpose was to assist the resolution of banks in difficulty. It was accepted that a range of powers were already available, including voluntary firm and regulatory action, although the SRR may be required in specific cases. The SRR was described in terms of a set of existing and new tools to permit the authorities to take control of a bank that is judged to be failing—and with all other options having been deemed to be insufficient. Relevant tools included transferring part or all of the failing bank to a private sector third party or a publicly controlled 'bridge bank', a new special bank insolvency procedure (BIP) and updated bank administration procedure (BAP), temporary public ownership and financial support, as currently provided by the Bank of England. The most controversial element was possibly the decision to make the Bank of England responsible for determining which SRR option will be used, with the FSA deciding when the regime will be triggered following a bank's failure to comply with its threshold conditions. The FSA should clearly remain responsible for day-to-day management of any restructuring, although the Bank of England may have insisted that it was involved in the original option selection. This is nevertheless an unfortunately untidy compromise. The specific issues that arise with regard to maintaining financial stability on a cross-border and global basis were considered in a further Treasury paper in September 2008.[6]

The Banking (Special Provisions) Bill was introduced to the House of Commons within two days of the acquisition announcement of Northern Rock on 19 February 2008 and had received Royal Assent by 21 February 2008. The purpose was to create an interim regime to allow the Treasury to make a transfer order of the securities issued by an authorised deposit-taking institution or a building society or the property, rights and liabilities of such an institution. These provisions were then replaced by the permanent measures set out in the Banking Act 2009 following the Bills introduced to the House of Commons on 6 October 2008 (Bill 147).

The SRR consists of three stabilisation options (transfer to a private sector purchaser (section 11), a bridge bank (section 12) and temporary public ownership (section 13)), as well as a BIP (part 2) and a revised BAP (part 3). The stabilisation options are exercised through the stabilisation powers, including share transfer powers (sections 15, 16, 26–31

---

[6] HM Treasury, Financial Stability and Depositor Protection: Cross-Border Challenges and Responses, ibid.

and 85) and property transfer powers (sections 33 and 42–46). The Act contains five new special resolution objectives (section 4), with the issuance of a code of practice provided for (under section 5). Specific duties and powers are conferred on the Bank of England, the FSA and the Treasury under the Act. The Act also contains measures intended to improve the operation of the FSCS, consumer protection and a strengthening of the Bank of England, including the establishment of a new Financial Committee within its Court.

The Act came into effect with a number of supporting statutory instruments, including a Commencement Order, a Parts 2 and 3 Consequential Amendments Order and a Restriction of Partial Property Transfers Order. Separate regulations were issued in connection with the application of the bank administration procedure to temporary public ownership banks and multiple transfers, as well as sharing information and third-party compensation arrangements for partial property transfers. The Treasury has also issued the SRR Code of Practice. The government had been assisted by an expert liaison group in bringing the legislation forward, with a special Banking Liaison Panel being vreated to assist the Treasury in connection with the operation of the SRR under the Code. The Treasury has consulted separately on the insolvency arrangements to apply with regard to investment firms.

3.   Turner Review

The FSA published a review of the global banking crisis by its new Chairman, Lord Adair Turner, along with a supporting discussion paper.[7] The review considers the causes of the crisis ('What Went Wrong?' in chapter 1) and proposed reforms ('What to Do?' in chapter 2), with certain further additional issues ('Open Questions' in chapter 3) and implementation and transition (chapter 4). The principal causes of the crisis are identified in terms of macroeconomic imbalance, financial innovation without supporting social value and deficiency in key capital and liquidity controls, which factors were aggravated by an excessive reliance on rational and self-correcting markets. The principal recommendation is that a more general systemic (macro-prudential) approach should be adopted with regard to financial regulation in place of an earlier policy of firm-specific supervision and control. The Review generally rehearses and restates other regulatory initiatives already identified or commenced either within the UK or elsewhere. It nevertheless provides a substantive discussion of the key issues involved either in the report directly or in the supporting discussion paper. This, then, provides the intellectual basis for a new post-crisis 'regulatory debate', with the announcement of several further important new initiatives.

The FSA has issued a separate draft code of practice on remuneration policies.[8] While boards and shareholders were to set remuneration levels, the code was concerned with ensuring that policies were consistent with sound risk management and did not create excessive risk. The code applies to all firms regulated by the FSA and is based on general

---

[7] Financial Services Authority, 'The Turner Review: A Regulatory Response to the Global Banking Crisis' (2009); and Financial Services Authority, 'A Regulatory Response to the Global Banking Crisis', Discussion Paper 09/2 (March 2009).

[8] The draft Code was issued on 18 March 2009. FSA, 'Reforming Remuneration Practices in Financial Services', Discussion Paper CP 09/10 (March 2009).

principles that firms must ensure that their remuneration policies are consistent with effective risk management. Ten more specific principles are then developed in connection to governance, performance measurement for bonuses and long-term incentive plans and composition.

The FSA had issued further papers on the strengthening of liquidity standards.[9] The December 2008 consultation paper explains the need for strong liquidity regulation and summarises the key features of the new regime.[10] The new regime is based on five components of adequate liquidity and self-sufficiency, systems and controls, individual liquidity adequacy standards, group and cross-border management, and qualitative and quantitative supervisory reporting. In its April 2009 paper, the FSA estimates that the potential incremental costs for UK banks to implement the new liquidity reporting regime could be over £2.4 billion. This could cost from £49,000 each for the 58 building societies surveyed and £3.3 million for 157 UK banks, with up to £7.4 million for 244 full-scope investment firms. Banks may have to spend between £517,000 and £775 million on an ongoing basis, depending on how much crisis reporting is required. These are substantial amounts and, while liquidity security is of significant importance in terms of regulatory revision, the authorities have to be careful not to isolate UK markets with potentially little overall benefit in terms of financial stability if crises may again simply be imported from elsewhere.

4.   Treasury Committee

A number of the issues that have arisen as a result of the financial crisis have been considered by the House of Commons Treasury Committee. The Treasury Committee examines the expenditure, administration and policy of the Treasury, as well as of HM Revenue & Customs and other associated public bodies. It is one of the departmental select committees of the House, with its powers set out in House of Commons Standing Orders. The Chairman of the Committee during the crisis was the Rt Hon John McFall MP and the Principal Clerk was Colin Lee. The Treasury Committee had been examining financial stability since early 2007, including, in particular, the Memorandum of Understanding between the Treasury, the Bank of England and the FSA, which was revised and reissued on 22 March 2006.[11]

The Treasury Committee had undertaken an examination of Transparency in Financial Markets and the Structure of UK Plc[12] and decided to examine the issue from a financial stability perspective specifically following the crisis that had occurred with the withdrawal of funds and run on the Northern Rock Plc between 14 and 17 September 2007. A formal

---

[9] FSA, 'Strengthening Liquidity Requirements', Discussion Paper CP08/22 (December 2008); and FSA, 'Strengthening Liquidity Standards 2: Liquidity Reporting", Discussion Paper CP 09/13 (April 2009). See also FSA, 'Review of the Liquidity Requirements for Banks and Building Societies', Discussion Paper 07/7 (December 2007).

[10] Design and Scope (ch 2); Systems and Controls (ch 3); Individual Liquidity Adequacy Standards (ILAS) (ch 4); Quantitative Standards for Simpler Firms (ch 5); Liquid Assets Buffer (ch 6); Group-wide Management (ch 7); and Liquidity Reporting (ch 8). A cost–benefit analysis (CBA) is also provided (ch 9), with a compatibility statement having regard to the FSA's objectives and principles of good regulation (ch 10).

[11] Treasury Committee, 'Financial Stability', HC (2006–07) 292-i.

[12] Treasury Committee Press Notice No 36, 'Session 2006–07'. See also Treasury Committee, 'Tenth Report of Session 2006–07, Private Equity', HC 567-I.

report was then issued on 26 January 2008.[13] This considered the nature and operation of the business model adopted by Northern Rock and its regulation by the FSA, the circumstances surrounding its forced support in August and September, the special position of banks and the need for official support, including lender of last resort and deposit protection provision. Principal conclusions and recommendations were made with regard to the regulation of Northern Rock, support operations, bank resolution regimes, deposit protection and supervisory oversight.

The Treasury Committee published a further report on Financial Stability and Transparency on 3 March 2008.[14] The government issued its Response to the Committee's Sixth Report on Financial Stability and Transparency in July 2008.[15] The report examines the nature of the changes that have taken place in financial markets since the early 1990s with the 'great moderation' or 'great stability' and the new financial instruments, including specifically structured finance products, and alternative capital pools that developed in search for higher returns or yield.

The Treasury Committee issued a report on the extent to which reform was required of the statutory system for the regulation of banks in the UK in September 2008[16] in response to the tripartite consultation document on financial stability in July 2008, with a further Treasury Committee paper in May 2009.[17] The Committee has issued a separate report on the Icelandic banks and a further report on executive remuneration in the banking area and the extent to which this contributed to the crisis.[18] In its report on the Icelandic banks, the Committee did not accept that there was a need to provide assistance to local authorities, although it did recommend that, on this occasion only, all charities should be compensated for losses incurred as a consequence of the failures of the Icelandic banks.

5.   National Audit Office Review

The National Audit Office published its report on the nationalisation of Northern Rock in March 2009.[19] This first considered the background to the immediate crisis at Northern Rock and then the circumstances surrounding the search for a longer-term solution. The report accepted that the Treasury was entitled to conclude that the nationalisation of

[13] Treasury Committee, 'The Run on the Rock', HC 56-I (26 January 2008). The House of Commons held a debate on the Committee's report on The Run on the Rock (January 2008) on 10 March 2008. HC Deb, 10 March 2008, cols 21–84.

[14] Treasury Committee, 'Financial Stability and Transparency', HC 371 (3 March 2008). This followed the earlier Fifth Report on The Run on the Rock (HC 56-I) and a separate Inter-Parliamentary Conference on Crisis Management and Financial Markets with the Economic and Monetary Affairs Committee of the European Parliament in Brussels on 22–23 January 2008.

[15] Treasury Committee, 'Financial Stability and Transparency: Government Response to the Committee's Sixth Report of Session 2007/08', HC 919 (10 July 2008).

[16] Treasury Committee, 'Banking Reform', HC 1008 (11 September 2008). The specific purposes of the report were: (i) to examine what can be achieved under existing legislation and the extent to which new legislation was required; (ii) to consider existing proposals for and make further proposals concerning the content of the forthcoming legislation; and (iii) to examine how the new legislation and wider framework would work in practice and, in particular, with regard to future crises. September 2008 Report, para 4.

[17] Treasury Committee, 'Banking Crisis: Dealing with the Failure of the UK Banks', HC 416 (1 May 2009).

[18] See also Treasury Committee, 'The Impact of the Failure of the Icelandic Banks', HC 402 (4 April 2009); and Treasury Committee, 'Banking Crisis: Reforming Corporate Governance and Pay in the City', HC 519 (15 May 2009).

[19] The National Audit Office, 'HM Treasury: the Nationalisation of Northern Rock' HC 298 2008–09 (20 March 2009).

Northern Rock offered the best prospect of protecting the taxpayers' interest and was based on a sufficiently sound analysis of all the options available. The Treasury had met its objective in protecting depositors and halted the run on the bank. It correctly concluded that the private sector bids gave insufficient prospect for safeguarding the taxpayers' interest. The capacity of the Treasury to deal with the crisis was nevertheless stretched, while it could have conducted a more systematic assessment of the risk that it was taking on and more carefully tested the initial business plan after nationalisation.

E. The International Response

A number of parallel economic and regulatory initiatives were taken forward at the international level by various bodies. The politically strengthened G-20 held two major summits, with an initial meeting in Washington in November 2008 under the departing Bush Administration and a follow-up meeting in London in April 2009 hosted by UK Prime Minister Gordon Brown. The FSF has issued a number of papers, including its key document on enhancing market and institutional resilience in April 2008, and has subsequently acted as a central coordinating organisation in terms of cross-sector technical and regulatory reform. Capital adequacy and other bank-related corrections have been taken forward by the Basel Committee. The Group of 30 (G-30) issued a report entitled 'Financial Reform and Financial Stability' in January 2009, and a separate European paper entitled 'Financial Supervision in the EU' was produced by a High-Level European Group chaired by Jacques de Larosière that was later adopted by the European Commission in May 2009 as the basis for its institutional reform programme.

1. G-20 and Bretton Woods II

The call for a revision of the international financial architecture by French and EU President Nicolas Sarkozy and UK Prime Minister Gordon Brown led to the G-20[20] 'Leaders Summit on Financial Markets and the World Economy' held in Washington on 14–15 November 2008. The November 2008 meeting was referred to as 'Bretton Woods II' as the structure and operation of the international monetary and financial system was to be discussed, although it was not expected that the results would be as ambitious as the original Bretton Woods conference held in July 1944, which led, in particular, to the establishment of an international currency system based on the US dollar and to the creation of the International Monetary Fund (IMF), the creation of the World Bank and the adoption of the General Agreement on Tariffs and Trade, which was eventually superseded by the World Trade Organisation in 1996.

The root causes of the crisis were explained in the communiqué in terms of market participants seeking higher yields without adequate appreciation of the risks involved and

---

[20] The G-20 consists of the finance ministers and central bank governors of the G7 (Australia, Canada, France, Germany, Japan, UK and US) and Argentina, Brazil, China, India, Indonesia, Italy, Mexico, Russia, Saudi Arabia, South Africa, South Korea, Turkey and the EU (the 20th member), with representatives also attending from the European Central Bank, the IMF, the World Bank, the International Monetary and Financial Committee and the Development Committee.

the failure to exercise proper due diligence, with vulnerabilities being created through weak underwriting standards, unsound risk management practices, increasingly complex and opaque financial products and excessive leverage. Policymakers, regulators and supervisors 'in some advanced countries' had not adequately appreciated the risks building up in financial markets, kept pace with financial innovation or taken into account the systemic effects of domestic regulatory action. The crisis was then explained somewhat over-simply in terms of yield pursuit and risk management aggravated by product complexity and high leverage. Major underlying factors also included inconsistent and insufficiently coordinated macroeconomic policies and inadequate structural reforms, which led to unsustainable global macroeconomic conditions.

Existing action was summarised in terms of economic stimulus, liquidity, recapitalisation, deposit protection, regulatory correction, credit market release and the support of international financial institutions. Further action was still necessary to stabilise the markets and to support economic growth as economic momentum slowed substantially. It was accordingly agreed that a broader policy response was needed based on closer macroeconomic cooperation to restore growth, avoid negative spillovers and support emerging market economies. Relevant action would include recognising the importance of monetary policy support having regard to domestic conditions and using fiscal measures to stimulate domestic demand at the same time as maintaining 'a policy framework conducive to fiscal sustainability'. Action would be taken to stabilise the financial system where necessary and to provide funding to support the IMF, World Bank and other multilateral development banks to allow them to carry out their crisis roles.

The declaration contained a separate commitment to an 'open global economy' based on free market principles, including the rule of law, respect for private property, open trade and investment, competitive markets, and efficient and effectively regulated financial systems. Five common principles for financial market reform were identified, based on strengthening transparency and accountability; enhancing sound regulation; promoting integrity in financial markets; reinforcing international cooperation; and reforming the international financial institutions. This work would be taken forward by finance ministers, with priority actions being completed by end March 2009 in advance of the April 2009 follow-up meeting in London.

The summit was possibly of more value than many had expected, although it was always unclear to what extent the overall objective was political rather than economic stability. The reform principles listed are a mixture of objectives, aspirations and mechanisms. Some useful and necessary recommendations are included, such as with regard to securities valuation and rating agencies, although many are simply repetitive or too general and simplistic, such as with regard to mitigating pro-cyclicality. The general approach adopted is one of delegation, with the reform menu simply being passed back to accounting bodies, national regulators, the Basel and other technical committees, the FSF, the IMF and the World Bank. Other, separately existing agendas are also incorporated, such as with regard to uncooperative and non-transparent jurisdictions, money laundering and tax information exchange, although these have little direct relevance to financial stability. No technical details are included and no attempt is made to deal with more general structural issues, such as the massive US current account deficit, undervalued exchange rates, unbalanced export led growth, capital flight, existing trade restrictions, economic cycles, price bubbles and development finance.

The subsequent April G-20 meeting represented one of the most important meetings of world leaders in modern history. The agenda was correspondingly expansive and expectations high but qualified. The leaders of 90% of the world's trading economy had to determine the action to take following the onslaught of the most devastating global recession for 80 years. The dominant ideal was fiscal stimulus in almost all countries and quantitative easing where appropriate. The particular circumstances, needs and financial condition of each country had nevertheless to be taken into account on an individual basis and an appropriate mix of stimulus, easing and fiscal contraction produced. The leaders had also to convince the markets that necessary reforms would be undertaken in the financial regulatory area in each country and globally while any trade protectionism was avoided. International institutions would also be strengthened to assist countries in difficulty.

2.   The Financial Stability Forum

The most comprehensive set of technical recommendations at the international level were issued by the FSF. The G7 Finance Ministers and Central Bank Governors asked the FSF in October 2007 to undertake an examination of the causes and weaknesses that had produced the turmoil in financial markets and to issue recommendations for increasing resilience of markets and institutions by April 2008. The FSF worked with other international bodies and committees as well as national authorities in the main financial centres to produce its report on enhancing market and institutional resilience.[21] This draws together the work of many of the other agencies involved.[22] The report was presented to the G7 on 11 April 2008 following final discussions at the FSF's Rome meeting on 28–29 March 2008 on the challenges in financial markets and the action necessary to correct them.[23] A further report was issued on implementation in June 2008 and in October 2008.[24]

3.   Basel Committee on Banking Supervision

The Basel Committee on Banking Supervision announced its strategy to address fundamental weaknesses following the financial crisis in global markets in November 2008. This was based on eight objectives concerning the strengthening of the risk capture of the Basel II framework (especially for trading book and off-balance-sheet exposures), enhancing the quality of tier 1 capital, building additional shock absorbers into the capital framework

---

[21] FSF, 'Report of the Financial Stability Forum on Enhancing Market and Institutional Resilience' (April 2008). Preliminary and interim reports were issued in October 2007 and February 2008. These are available on the FSF website, www.financial stabilityforum.org/publications.

[22] This includes the Basel Committee on Banking Supervision, the International Organisation of Securities Commissions, the International Association of Insurance Supervisors, the Joint Forum on Financial Conglomerates, the International Accounting Standards Board, the Committee on Payment and Settlement Systems, the Committee on the Global Financial System, the IMF and the BIS.

[23] Statement by Mario Draghi, Chairman of the FSF, before the International Monetary and Financial Committee Meeting, Washington DC, 12 April 2008.

[24] FSF, 'Update on the Implementation of FSF's Recommendations' (11 June 2008); and FSF, 'Report of the Financial Stability Forum on Enhancing Market and Institutional Resilience—Follow-up on Implementation' (10 October 2008).

during stress and to limit pro-cyclicality, leverage review through possible supplementing risk with gross measures in prudential and risk management frameworks, strengthening cross-border liquidity supervision, strengthening risk management and governance practices under Basel II, strengthening counter-party credit risk capital, risk management and disclosure at banks. and promoting globally coordinated supervisory follow-up exercises to ensure implementation of supervisory and industry sound principles.

The Committee issued a subsequent package of documents to strengthen the Basel II capital framework as part of its review of action necessary to strengthen the regulation and supervision of internationally active banks following the recent crises. The changes specifically relate to trading book exposures (including complex and illiquid credit products), complex securitisations in the banking book (including CDOs of asset-backed securities) and off-balance-sheet vehicle exposures (including ABCP conduits). The supervisory review process was also to be strengthened to ensure more effective supervision and risk management of risk concentrations, off-balance-sheet exposures, securitisations and related reputation risks, with other improvements to valuations, the management of funding liquidity risks and firm-wide stress testing practices. There would be enhanced disclosure of securitisations and the sponsorship of off-balance-sheet vehicles. Trading book changes would come into effect by December 2010, the other revisions by the end of 2009.

The Basel Committee separately confirmed in March 2009 that its membership would be extended to include representatives from Australia, Brazil, China, India, Korea, Mexico and Russia, thus taking the total number of members to 20. This was considered necessary to enhance the Committee's ability to carry out its core mission in strengthening regulatory practices and standards worldwide, and followed the G-20 call by major standard-setting bodies to review their current memberships.

4.   G-30 Financial Reform Report

The Group of 30 (G-30) issued the report 'Financial Reform—A Framework for Financial Stability' in January 2009. A steering committee had been set up in July 2008 under Paul Volker, with Tommaso Padoa-Schioppa and Arminio Fraga Meto as vice chairmen. The report considers the policy issues relating to redefining the scope and boundaries of prudential regulation, reforming the structure of regulation (including the role of central banks and market support arrangements), improving governance, risk management, regulatory policy and accounting practices and standards, as well as securing improvements in transparency and financial infrastructure arrangements. The report provides an overview programme for reform and contains 18 specific recommendations on the scope of prudential regulation, structure of regulation and international coordination, governance standards and transparency and incentives.

5.   EU Financial Supervision Group

An EU group chaired by Jacques de Larosière published its report, entitled 'The High-Level Group on Financial Supervision', in the EU in February 2009.[25] The purpose of

---

[25] See http://ec.europa.eu/internal_market/finances/docs/de_larosiere_report_en.pdf (accessed on 20 August 2009).

the report was to establish a framework for the construction of a new EU regulatory agenda, stronger coordinated supervision and effective crisis management procedures. The report examines the cause of the financial crisis and develops recommendations for policy and regulatory repair, EU supervisory repair and global repair. The Group explains the crisis in terms of substantial balance sheet expansion and leverage following high levels of macroeconomic liquidity and low interest rate and yields, inadequate risk management, defective credit ratings, corporate governance failures and regulatory, supervisory and crisis management failure (paragraphs 6–13). The dynamics of the crisis are also reviewed (paragraphs 32–37). Regulation and supervision are distinguished in terms of control and oversight (paragraph 38), with reference being made to the parallel G-30 report on financial reform (paragraph 30).

The report contains 31 recommendations on regulatory and policy correction, including with regard to Basel II and the EU Capital Requirements Directive, credit rating agencies, mark-to-market accounting principles, the EU Solvency II Directive and ensuring effective national supervision. Supervision had to be strengthened through the establishment of a new European Systemic Risk Council (ESRC), chaired by the President of the European Central Bank, with an effective risk warning system under the ESRC and the Economic and Financial Committee, with a separate formalised system of European System of Financial Supervisors (ESFS) being set up. The ESFS would include a European Banking Authority, a European Insurance Authority and a European Securities Authority, which would replace the existing Committee of European Banking Supervisors, Committee of European Insurance and Occupational Pensions Supervisors and Committee of European Securities Regulators, with the specific role of coordinating the application of supervisory standards and guaranteeing strong cooperation between national supervisors.

F. Post-crisis Reform

A number of areas of reform have to be considered in terms of national economic and regulatory practice as well as regional and cross-border relations in the new post-crisis era. Some of this was referred to in the original G-20 declaration, although it did not create any clear, complete or coherent framework, with decisions on almost all issues being delegated to technical committees or deferred until further meetings. It must nevertheless be stressed that existing market and regulatory rulebooks do not require fundamental overhaul and great care must be taken not to overreact to the severity of the recent crisis and subsequent downturn. This could have the effect of unnecessarily limiting future innovation and benefit while possibly overextending the duration and depth of the crisis with unnecessary measures that would only restrict liquidity and credit creation and supply. A balanced and proportionate response is required. A more complete reform model can then be constructed on the basis of financial system revision, regulatory revision, supervisory revision, crisis management revision and institutional revision. The following key elements of any new reform framework can be identified.

1.   Financial System Revision

Monetary authorities must monitor money and credit growth to contain inflation but also to avoid cyclic disruption. Growth in money supply must be linked to an increase in domestic GDP. Credit levels must be managed to avoid destabilising excesses through such instruments as interest rates, bank reserve requirements and other money market operations. Regulatory penalties may also be imposed on specific activities or products where necessary, including on predatory and abusive sales techniques. Authorities must monitor asset price inflation and attempt to limit asset price bubbles. Relevant interest rate, exchange rate, economic and fiscal policies must all be coordinated. Cheap credit may not be a problem in itself, although excessive credit effects must be monitored carefully.

2.   Financial Regulation

A number of more specific regulatory revisions should be considered in developing any meaningful emerging post-crisis reform. The immediate need is to identify any continuing areas of lack of proper supervisory oversight and regulatory gap. This would apply specifically to the federal regulation of mortgage sales and specifically sub-prime mortgage commissions in the US. The operation of the increasingly extended 'shadow banking system' must be reviewed to ensure that all credit suppliers and non-bank financial intermediaries are brought within effective supervisory oversight and control.

This 'perimeter' review must include the use and operation of all forms of off-balance-sheet financing, such as structured investment vehicles and bank conduits, as well as other specialist asset managers, such as hedge funds, private equity firms and sovereign wealth funds. There must be maximum transparency and disclosure in all cases. Much of this work is already continuing, although this has to be updated and extended to include all necessary post-crisis lessons.

Regulatory attention must then focus on ensuring that all financial institutions maintain effective risk management systems covering all on- and off-balance-sheet exposures. As banks have extended the range of their activities and operations, including through the use of securities and dealing in increasingly complex financial products, internal control processes must be correspondingly improved. This was one of the key elements of the new UK system of integrated regulation set up under the Financial Services and Markets Act 2000, although these arrangements must be further reviewed in light of the more recent changes that have taken place within the industry.

3.   Capital Reforms

It is inevitable that capital adequacy standards will be further revised following the crises. This was nevertheless a liquidity rather than capital crisis, with capital only becoming relevant with the subsequent collapse of share prices on stock markets. This was again, then, principally concerned with business models and leverage rather than underlying capital, with massive capital injections being required to prevent further falls far in excess of that prescribed under the regulatory rules. The Basel sub-committees are already working on a series of 'Basel III' revisions, the general effect of which will be to allow banks to rely increasingly on internal measurement systems and to align regulatory and economic capital more closely. This will now include strengthening various aspects of the Basel II regime, including securitisation and credit risk mitigation allowances such as CDSs. These more technical reforms will now be reassessed in light of recent events, though they will be of limited effect in themselves.

(a)   Counter-cyclical Charging

A number of commentators have pressed in particular for the adoption of counter-cyclical capital charging. This would require banks to raise additional capital during economic growth periods that could be used to contain losses in a downturn. This was supported by the Turner Review. Difficulties nevertheless arise with regard to the complexity of such a proposal and with the number of distinct models and metrics that can be used. These may also operate on either a formulaic or a discretionary basis, with discretionary systems inevitably leading to abuse and formulaic systems to inconsistency. In either case, the new charges may be expensive to administer and may impose additional unnecessary costs on banks.

It may also prove to be impossible to reach any clear agreement on the most desirable relevant standard at the European and global levels. Countries would then be at a significant competitive disadvantage if they attempted to introduce counter-cyclical charging on their own at the national level. More generally, this is counter-intuitive and an anti-normal market process, which may only delay recovery and subsequently interfere with normal market operations. Equivalent effects could be secured through simply strengthening tier 1 and, in particular, common equity capital positions, as many of the largest banks have already achieved. There is also to be resolved the more difficult policy issue of whether regulatory charges should be used to secure separate, more general, monetary objectives. Opinion differs and debate continues on this point.

It is clearly necessary to strengthen core tier 1 capital, especially in equity. Regulatory authorities already have the necessary discretion under the Basel II provisions and national regulation. The earlier 8% minimum under Basel I was only set as an absolute floor figure, with many countries, including the UK, maintaining average ratios of between 12 and 14% or above in higher risk situations. This can most easily be strengthened by setting new core tier 1 limits at either 4 or 6%, which, in turn, would take the average total capital to up to 15 or 16%. National regulators would have to set and give effect to the relevant limits in each case. Once markets recover, it is possible that a 4% core tier 1 (common equity) requirement would be more than sufficient and would avoid the need for additional and over-complex counter-cyclical charging.

It must also be stressed that the size of the losses suffered on structured finance products (distressed assets) was so severe in the case of the recent financial crisis that no amount of adjusted minimum capital would have been sufficient. Authorities must further ensure that they have effective extended support arrangements in place, including appropriate capital support facilities where necessary (see below). The authorities will always have to support the banking markets in light of the importance of the functions that they carry out and their inherent instability. This cannot be ignored or forgotten in determining any new capital minima.

(b)   Leverage Ratio Ceilings

One major deficiency revealed by the crisis was the high level of leverage operated by many investment firms and banks. Regulators should consider the reintroduction of more basic financial ratios, including debt/capital (leverage) limits, to act as supplementary guidelines in assessing risk management and capital adequacy. It may be considered inappropriate to impose specific numeric values due to the inflexible and arbitrary effects these may have. Basic ratios may nevertheless be used to reassess the value of the revised capital rules to be brought into effect under Basel II and Basel III, and the effectiveness of underlying risk management systems.

(c)   'Systemic or Crisis' Reserves

There have been separate calls for counter-cyclic capital charges to be imposed, with banks putting aside higher levels of capital during growth periods. This may be too complicated to work effectively in practice and would not have prevented the collapse in bank share prices in September and October 2008. It would also operate as a counter-intuitive penalty for economic success that only penalised borrowers. It could be more easily achieved through adjusting existing margins in excess of the minimum 8% required under Basel I to include a possible 'systemic or crisis reserve'. Most banks in the UK and elsewhere already operate at between 12 and 14% in any case, and this could be reallocated to a systemic or crisis reserve.

4.   Bank Liquidity

National and international regulators are currently examining liquidity requirements, with the FSA having continued its earlier Liquidity Mismatch and Sterling Stock measures on an interim basis until an agreement is achieved. The revised rules will specifically have to take into account the danger of sources of wholesale liquidity and parent bank support drying-up. Specific guidance should also be issued to ensure that banks hold predominantly safer government debt instruments for liquidity reserve purposes as opposed to the high yielding structured finance products used more recently. This was a major source of shortfall in the recent crisis.

5.   Financial Innovation and Complex Product Design

Important policy decisions have to be taken with regard to the development of securities based 'originate-to-distribute' models (including securitisation) as opposed to more traditional bank-based 'originate-to-hold' models. While the apparent separation of risk management is not a problem as such (to the extent that the administration, processing and management of the debt are delegated back to the originating intermediary), more significant difficulties arise with banks holding considerably higher levels of securities on their balance sheets. Separate securities-based capital requirements are imposed (as introduced under the 1996 Basel Market Risk Amendment and then incorporated into Basel II, as well as the EU Capital Adequacy Directive and later the Capital Requirements Directive). Where banks suffer losses on these security positions and require central bank lender of last resort (LLR or LOLR) support, these arrangements have to be extended to cover such activities. Central Banks then have to determine whether they are prepared to support such losses on whether more specific limits should be imposed on bank securities exposures. Key policy decisions have to be taken in this area.

Further guidelines could be issued in connection with the development of more complex financial products. These would essentially ensure that appropriate development and design principles are applied and that no excessive risk is created. Maximum disclosure and transparency would again apply in all cases.

6.   Financial Supervision

Supervisory returns and assessments must be extended to allow authorities to monitor all of the activities of banks and other financial institutions, including off-balance-sheet positions. Extended measures should be adopted in connection with high-risk institutions such as those the UK FSA's SEP adopted following its internal review of the supervision of Northern Rock. Consideration should also be given to creating a new form of 'systemic reporting' using returns designed to identify changes in financial condition that would indicate possible future systemic threats, including financial ratios. Authorities could then either undertake 'systemic inspections' or impose specific 'systemic conditions or directions' with regard to the activities of such institutions. The effectiveness of cross-border supervisory arrangements must be strengthened especially in connection with large, globally active complex groups. Informal sets of contacts and relations already exist, although these should be formalised under dedicated cross-border committee arrangements (referred to as 'colleges' under the G-20 declaration).

7.   Crisis Management

The principal area in which further official work is required is in connection with crisis management at the international, regional and global levels.

(a)   Clarified Lending of Last Resort

The rules in which support is provided by central banks must be reclarified following the recent crises. The more traditional 'Walter Bagehot' rules have had to be reassessed in light of changing conditions. The nature of a more traditional 'bank run' and deposit withdrawal has to be extended to include the drying-up of wholesale funds on inter-bank markets, withdrawal of credit on other money markets and possibly speculative attacks on bank share prices or other share price collapses. The most recent difficulties faced by individual banks have not been based on deposit withdrawal (as with Northern Rock) but were driven by wholesale credit and then share prices.

(b)   Extended Lending of Last Resort

Extended LLR facilities have to be made available in light of the higher levels of inter-connection and dependence created by the disintegration of the distinctions between traditional financial sectors and the emergence of complex groups. The specific difficulty that arises is with regard to 'cross-sector loss transfer',[26] with exposures in more volatile securities, derivatives, currency, commodities or other asset markets undermining the stability of the banking or insurance sectors. Modern market support and LLR systems have to be managed on a more extensive and comprehensive basis, although funds can still be channelled through the banking sector.

(c)   Deposit Protection

Existing deposit protection arrangements have to be revised to increase limits to appropriate levels (such as with the new £50,000 award in the UK), provide for timely payment and ensure that scheme operators have sufficient funds either on a full or partial pre-funded basis or with the assistance of central banks or other government lending facilities. All of these amendments are to be introduced in the UK following the earlier tripartite documentation produced following Northern Rock and the Banking Bill introduced to the House of Commons on 7 October 2008 (Bill 147). Cross-border payment arrangements also have to be strengthened, especially following the difficulties experienced with UK depositors at Icelandic banks.

(d)   Inter-bank Liquidity

In addition to individual bank liquidity, authorities must try to ensure that adequate liquidity levels are maintained in all of the principal inter-bank markets. The Bank of England has already announced a review of its Red Book and possible replacements of such temporary facilities as its Special Lending Scheme (SLS). The SLS was increased from £100bn to £200bn under the financing package announced by the government on 8 October 2008. Difficult policy issues nevertheless arise in this area. Once external sources of funding dry up (such as those placed by money market funds, institutional investors or corporate treasuries), it is difficult to reactivate inter-bank lending, especially with banks having to use existing deposit funds to cover their own direct and contingent liabilities. It is not sufficient for authorities to claim that they have made funds available where these are only on strict commercial terms with high interest or dividend charges (12% under the UK recapitalisation) or additional risk premium (as with the UK three year guarantee scheme), or have to be fully collateralised (under the Bank of England's extended SLS). The authorities either have to assist banks in providing funds at competitive rates or provide direct funds for on lending.

(e)   Crisis Management Tools

A full range of support tools must be available in the event of a major crisis arising with as much flexibility as possible being provided. This should include being able to conduct 'systemic inspections' and issue 'systemic directions' based on the earlier 'systemic returns' referred to. A full range of bank transfer options must be available, including private transfers, regulatory ('bridge bank') transfers and public transfers (nationalisation). A special BAP, a BIP and an enhanced deposit protection procedure must all be in place. Many of these facilities were already available in the UK, although the government has

---

[26] GA Walker, *International Banking Regulation—Law, Policy and Practice* (The Hague, Kluwer Law, 2001) ch 3.

assisted by clarifying them under the provisions contained in the Banking Bill, which includes the new bank SRR.

A range of special support facilities (SSFs) should also be set up for use in extreme cases. These could include a Liquidity Support Facility, a Capital Support Facility, a Guarantee Support Facility, an Asset Purchase Facility and a Direct Credit Facility. These would be used to inject liquidity into the inter-bank markets, recapitalise banks, support wholesale lending, purchase distressed (toxic) assets and provide direct credit facilities to banks for passing on to corporate or individual customers where no other sources of funding are available. Appropriate institutional arrangements will also have to be set up to hold government interests for a temporary period, as with UK Financial Investments Limited. The effect of these arrangements should be to allow banks to operate effectively even in extreme conditions, although the extent to which they will be able to continue to make new funds available will depend on the terms set and amount of credit made available by the government.

A number of other special corrective mechanisms should also be considered. These include confirming that central bank support can be provided on a non-disclosed basis (following the difficulties at Northern Rock), as well as possibly suspending mark-to-market valuation rules where these provide no useful purpose and only aggravate individual bank crisis. Further corrective devices could include bans on 'naked' short selling of financial stock or full bans on short selling in times of stress, as well as share trading suspensions in particular cases for temporary periods.

8.   International and Institutional Revision

A series of further international and institutional amendments should be considered as part of the new 'international financial architecture' announced at the Bretton Woods II summit, even though these may take longer to put into place. This would include coordinating cross-border crisis management and deposit protection arrangements. A Global Financial Rulebook should be created based on the FSF's existing 'Compendium of Standards', which currently operates on a 'virtual' basis by collecting the main papers from each of the principal international financial institutions, standards bodies and technical committees. This must also include a new Global Crisis Management rulebook or section to clarify cross-border support arrangements.

A global Financial Stability Facility has to be set up managed by the IMF to provide support to countries in need of assistance for domestic crisis management purposes, with funds principally made available through special lending facilities agreed with countries with substantial foreign exchange reserves, such as in the Middle East and China. Appropriate institutional or other diplomatic concessions would have to be made in return, including amending the composition and voting rights on the IMF, World Bank and other international financial institution boards.

A new Financial Stability Committee should be set up to coordinate crisis management activity at the international level, with a permanent International Financial Committee being considered to coordinate other related areas of international importance, including monetary policy, currency valuation, revaluation and convergence and market support. Rather than attempt to reform the role and function of existing entities (such as the IMF) or extend the operations of others (such as the BIS), a new core directing body should be set up with a clear and specific mandate. This is necessary to deal with the problems of 'mandate lock' and 'legacy practice' that would arise to prevent any meaningful reform.

F.   Conclusion

We are now at the beginning of a new financial world. This does not mean the rejection or demolition of the old one but only that a new, more streamlined and rebalanced financial marketplace has been created. Cheaper credit conditions will return although not in the same volumes as before and with a substantial deleveraging of positions having to take place. Considerably higher degrees of transparency and disclosure will be introduced, including of off-balance-sheet assets. The role and function of credit rating agencies and the accuracy and validity of their grading processes will be reassessed. The economic and regulatory value of credit protection, including through the use of CDSs, will be recalibrated.

The global economy is essentially market and financial market based. This has allowed significant welfare benefits and gains in individual and social wealth. Significant difficulties can nevertheless arise where core banking services are mixed with more volatile securities markets and stock market trading. Originate-to-distribute models have not been wholly discredited, nor has the larger process of securitisation of debt been undermined. Bank and security-based credit will continue to be offered together with banking and capital markets working in parallel. The authorities must nevertheless reassess the effects of this relationship to ensure that an effective balance is maintained at all times. A similar dilemma arose in the 1930s that has now to be reconsidered and re-resolved having regard to modern markets and credit conditions. The ultimate objective remains one of protecting confidence in the safe and stable operation of the financial system. This should be possible provided that the new post-crisis global marketplace operates on a clear and transparent basis, with excess credit being removed and with more complex innovative forms of financing being kept within reasonable limits having regard to their potential systemic effects. Revised and extended market support operations must also be installed and made available at all times.

The crisis has resulted in substantial loss and damage across national economies and across the globe. Any arguments with regard to predictability or natural cycles are of no assistance to those suffering consequent hardship. The correction was nevertheless necessary to restore many asset and commodity prices to more proportionate levels. The crisis has also provided the opportunity of redesigning a new national and international infrastructure for market supervision and regulation. A number of the initiatives announced in the G-20 communiqués are of value and should be taken forward. National authorities must also adopt all necessary reforms to prevent such extreme crises and damage in future. In so doing, authorities must remember that this was a full financial and financial system crisis and not simply one limited to the banking sector. All necessary lessons on a cross-sector, cross-border and cross-disciplinary nature must be learned.

The financial world almost collapsed but was salvaged at the last instance. It should still be possible to realise the benefits of modern finance and credit supply at the same time as manage and limit the underlying risks and exposures created. The challenge of the post-crisis world is to create a new, more balanced and effective managed market system. Blind unregulated financial capitalism driven by individual greed and profit without corresponding responsibility and accountability is hopefully over. Innovative and dynamic financial markets and services must nevertheless be preserved and extended to support national and global trade and relations and longer term economic growth and social development. It only remains to be seen whether all of the necessary actions will be taken this time.

12

What Future for Disclosure as a Regulatory Technique? Lessons from Behavioural Decision Theory and the Global Financial Crisis

EMILIOS AVGOULEAS[*]

A. Introduction

Inadequate disclosure has been at the heart of most policy analysis of the global financial crisis. According to the inadequate disclosure critique, investors had insufficient information regarding the risks involved in structured securities, the flaws of credit ratings and the impact of excessive executive compensation, all among the main causes of the financial market collapse. However, the global financial crisis has also exposed the many limits of disclosure as an effective regulatory tool. Most of the risks that led to the creation of the 2008 catastrophe were often fully disclosed but the markets failed to understand what was disclosed and appreciate the implications. The reasons for this failure were product complexity and the impact of socio-psychological factors such as bounded rationality, strategic trade behaviour (herding) and cognitive biases. These findings pose a great challenge to the prevailing rational choice view of disclosure as a regulatory remedy for most market failures. At the same time, the issue of transparent financial markets dominates the global regulatory reform agenda. Accordingly, there is a clear need to devise strategies that make disclosure work under actual (not hypothetical) market conditions. This chapter argues that in specific contexts, such as the field of prudential regulation of banks, disclosure will only work if it is supplemented by protective regulation, for example, licensing barriers between 'utility' and 'casino' banking. It also argues that only through the use of experiments, as a complement to empirical studies, will policymakers and regulators be able to measure the actual contribution of disclosure to investor protection. It is possible that such studies will show that, in the case of unsophisticated investors, the establishment of an independent financial products committee is a better investor protection strategy than enhanced disclosure.

Contemporary financial regulation has made disclosure the centrepiece of the regulatory armoury. Although disclosure has traditionally been viewed by English case law as an effective way to protect investors in the context of public offerings, even in the laissez faire

[*] Reader in International Financial Law, School of Law, University of Manchester. This paper is based on research funded by the UK's Arts and Humanities Research Council (AHRC) and was completed while spending time as the Global Capital Markets Center Fellow at the School of Law, Duke University.

arm's length securities markets of the nineteenth century,[1] it really became an indispensable weapon of the regulatory arsenal in the early 1930s. In an attempt to clean up US markets from abuse in the post-1929 crash era, the Roosevelt administration created widespread disclosure regimes for securities issuers and traders by means of the so-called New Deal Statutes: mainly the Securities Act 1933[2] and the Securities and Exchange Act 1934.[3] However, disclosure completed its ascent to the 'regulatory Olympus' in the past 25 years for reasons that had little to do with the battle against fraud and market abuse.

With the advent of financial liberalisation and with the aid of modern finance theory, but not with its full endorsement, policymakers and regulators came to view financial markets as an agglomeration of rational investors who make optimal resource allocation and wealth maximisation decisions when provided with sufficient information and appropriately structured economic incentives. So all regulators had to do to safeguard efficient markets and help investors was to ensure that a vast volume of pertinent information entered the public domain in any given area of financial market activity. Then, on the basis of all available information, market actors would adjust their investment decisions, positions and strategies to the information's content and the market would essentially regulate itself. Thus, no further consideration was usually given to other very important issues, such as the question whether market actors used all of the disclosed information and, if so, what kind of decisions they took on the basis of abundant supplies of information.

As a result, based on the rational investor model, modern financial regulation stretched the disclosure paradigm and reliance on self-regulation way beyond its original realm of issuer disclosure and prevention of market abuse to financial services consumer (retail investor) protection and even prudential regulation with mixed results. For example, disclosure was utilised, in lieu of protective regulation (for example, position limits), as a principal supervisory tool in banking regulation. The third pillar of Basel II[4] (market discipline) mandates extensive disclosure obligations for banks operating under this framework, on the assumption that timely informed rational actors are capable of acting as 'supervisors' and 'enforcers' of prudential regulation rules. Essentially, Basel II gave to market self-regulation a crucial and strategic role in preventing institutional collapses and systemic crises. For the reasons explained below in section C, this view was seriously flawed, and the way banking markets have behaved in the course of global financial markets has also proved that it was dangerous.

Given the predominance of the disclosure-based rational investor model in policymakers', analysts' and regulators' thinking, it is not surprising that inadequate disclosure has been widely cited as almost the sole cause of the global financial crisis.[5]A s this argument goes, investors had insufficient information regarding the risks involved in structured securities, such as asset-backed securities (ABSs),[6] collateralised

---

[1] Eg *Central Railway of Venezuela v Kisch* (1867) LR 2 HL 99 and *New Brunswick and Canada Railway Company v Muggeridge* (1860) 1Dr & Sm 381.

[2] Securities Act of 1933, 15 USC §§77a–77mm (1994).

[3] Securities Exchange Act of 1934, 15 USC §§78a–78mm (1994).

[4] Basel Committee on Banking Supervision, 'International Convergence of Capital Measurement and Capital Standards, A Revised Framework (Updated November 2005)' (Basel II Accord).

[5] The President's Working Group on Financial Markets, 'Policy Statement on Financial Market Developments' (March 2008).

debt obligations (CDOs)[7] and credit default swaps (CDSs),[8] the flaws and limitations of credit ratings, and the impact of excessive executive compensation. Had rational investors been given higher quality information they would have approached structured credit securities with caution and would not have been overexposed to these markets. Moreover, well-informed capital markets would have punished companies with executive and trader compensation schemes that fostered short-termism, in spite of bringing to them mega-profits.

The inadequate disclosure critique has not, however, been fully endorsed by all analysts of the global financial crisis. A minority of commentators have argued that closer examination shows that in many cases investors had sufficient information about the risks of their investment strategies and of the financial products used to implement them.[9] Yet market actors could not process available information properly in those cases and adjust their positions to the riskiness of structured credit securities for a variety of reasons. First, due to product complexity, boundedly rational investors failed to understand the mechanics and risks of shadow banking and structured credit securities.[10] Secondly, because of market players' tendency to herd, responding strategically to other market actors' behaviour, they did not have the capacity or the desire to use the disclosed information in a rational way and take contrarian positions. Thirdly, the influence of other behavioural factors, such as the use of heuristics,[11] and investor overconfidence in times of market euphoria, because of abundance of easy credit and rising market prices, meant that investors chose to ignore the warning signals in the disclosed data in favour of over-reliance on credit ratings.[12] Arguably, the view taken by this second group of commentators makes the inadequate disclosure argument a much less powerful explanation for the global financial crisis, and the initial focus on increased disclosure as the lynchpin of global regulatory reform puzzling!

---

[6] ABS is normally a security whose value and income payments are derived from a specified pool of underlying assets, which may be credit card or auto loans, mortgages, claims from leasing contracts etc. The assets in the pool usually cannot be sold individually and, by gathering them in a pool of assets and selling them to a special purpose vehicle, the asset seller transforms illiquid assets to a liquid source of income.

[7] CDOs are typically set up by investment banks or fund managers and comprise securitised interests in pools of generally non-mortgage assets. Assets in the pool, called collateral, usually comprise loans or debt instruments and are called collateralised loan obligations or collateralised bond obligations, depending on whether the collateral is only loans or bonds respectively.

[8] CDS is a swap in which two parties enter into an agreement whereby one party pays the other a fixed periodic coupon for the specified life of the agreement. The other party makes no payments unless a specified 'credit event' occurs. CDSs are normally concluded under the International Swaps and Derivatives Association architecture and 'credit events' are typically defined to include a material default, bankruptcy or debt restructuring for a specified reference asset. If a 'credit event' occurs, the party makes a payment to the first party and the swap then terminates. The size of the payment is usually linked to the decline in the reference asset's market value following the occurrence of such a 'credit event'.

[9] S Schwarcz, 'Disclosure's Failure in the Subprime Mortgage Crisis' [2008] *Utah Law Review* 1109. Schwarcz notes accurately: 'In the subprime mortgage crisis, there is to date relatively little dispute that the disclosure documents describing MBS, CDO, and ABS CDO securities and their risks generally complied with the federal securities laws' (1113).

[10] S Schwarcz, 'Protecting Financial Markets: Lessons from the Subprime Mortgage Meltdown' (2008) 93 *Minnesota Law Review* 373.

[11] The best analysis of the limitations that financial product complexity posed for investors' understanding of them and the catastrophic consequences of this limited understanding is S Schwarcz, 'Regulating Complexity in Financial Markets', Duke Public Law & Legal Theory Research Paper Series No 217 (revised 26 February 2009).

[12] E Avgouleas, 'The Global Financial Crisis, Behavioural Finance and Financial Regulation: In Search of a New Orthodoxy' (2009) 9 *Journal of Corporate Law Studies* 121.

It is not, therefore, surprising that more recently sceptical voices have been raised, at the highest level, about the view that holds increased disclosure as the remedy for all market illnesses; the recent Turner Review is the leading example of such scepticism.[13] The above findings are not totally lost on global policymakers either. Thus, while the Washington Summit of the G-20 in November 2008 fully endorsed the inadequate disclosure critique and declared the willingness of its members to redress disclosure failures and enhance the transparency of global financial markets, the G-20 summit in April 2009 in London took a much more balanced view, placing significant emphasis also on protective regulation and the imposition of restrictions on market activities that were highly implicated in the building up of the crisis, chiefly shadow banking.[14]

This chapter sets out to investigate the standing of disclosure as a protective technique in the new regulatory era that will dawn soon on global financial markets. In this context, it opens two lines of enquiry. First, it investigates whether the prominent role of disclosure in banking regulation as a facilitator of market discipline is justified. Secondly, it considers the value of extensive disclosure in financial markets under conditions of complexity, discussing also the impact of socio-psychological factors on investor decision-making. Consequent to these analyses, the chapter argues that policymakers should try to understand disclosure's limitations and, until this happens, disclosure will remain a puzzling regulatory technique of a mythical standing and limited effectiveness.

The chapter is divided into five sections. The first section is the present introduction. The second section provides a concise overview of the main welfare benefits of disclosure rules. It also examines the limitations of disclosure regulation under the lens of behavioural decision theory. The third section explains how inadequate disclosure, as well as investors' flawed use of information, due to socio-psychological factors, built many of the conditions that led to the global financial crisis. The fourth section provides a number of proposals that can help to place disclosure techniques on a more effective and realistic footing in the context of financial regulation. It is proposed that, with respect to prudential regulation, disclosure should only be seen as a supplement to strict protective rules, such as institutional segregation of commercial and investment banking and position limits. In the field of investor protection regulation, it is suggested that disclosure's effectiveness may increase if relevant rules adapt to actual market conditions. Arguably, this may only be achieved through the extensive use of empirical studies complemented by properly calibrated economic experiments.[15] The fifth section brings the strands of the present discussion to a comprehensive conclusion.

---

[13] Financial Services Authority, 'The Turner Review, A Regulatory Response to the Global Banking Crisis' (2009).

[14] 'The Global Plan for Recovery and Reform', statement issued by the G-20 leaders, 2 April 2009, available at www.number10.gov.uk/Page18914.

[15] For an overview of experimental methods to test legal rules see C Camerer and E Talley, 'Experimental Study of Law' in AM Polinsky and S Shavell (eds), *Handbook of Law and Economics* (Amsterdam, North-Holland, 2007) 1619.

B.   The Benefits and Limitations of Disclosure Regulation

1.   Disclosure as a Tool to Promote Efficient Markets and Protect Investors

Disclosure has been regarded as one of the most potent tools of corporate and financial market regulation for six reasons:[16] (i) by increasing publicly available information, it enables market actors to make informed investment decisions; (ii) it improves market efficiency: increased availability of information leads to better pricing of securities and other financial instruments enhancing allocative efficiency; (iii) it reduces the cost of information searches, which, when excessive, is pure social waste in zero sum securities markets; (iv) it fosters fair, ethical and competitive markets, as it obliterates (along with prohibitions of insider dealing) the information advantage that insiders enjoy over outsiders in financial markets; (v) it may help market stability by containing market volatility that is usually caused by limited information regarding the merits or risks of financial products; and (vi) it deters fraud—as the much celebrated US Supreme Court Justice Louis Brandeis observed almost nine decades ago, ample provision of information is the best 'disinfectant' for the markets to drive out abuse, which may be easily identified under conditions of transparency.

Arguably, some of the aforementioned benefits of disclosure regulation are not only indisputable but have also served multiple causes. For instance, mandatory (securities issuer) disclosure has not only helped to improve the integrity of securities markets, it has also advanced the cause of democratic capitalism by eradicating the information advantages of the established economic elites, where corporate insiders normally belong. However, the above benefits are not the only reasons why disclosure has become the cornerstone of modern financial regulation. Nor is it because it is an inexpensive or non-intrusive regulatory technique—it is both very costly and intrusive for the subject of relevant disclosure requirements, whether a securities issuer or a financial firm. Regardless of context, for example, periodic issuer disclosure or offer prospectus, an army of auditors, lawyers and compliance officers are assigned the task of processing and verifying disclosable information. As mentioned in the first section, disclosure's ascent is rather due to the pre-eminence of rational choice theory in modern financial regulation.

In one way or another rational choice theory proposes that human agents strive to maximise their utility from a stable set of well-defined preferences, accumulating, in the process, an optimal amount of information and other inputs in a variety of contexts.[17] Thus, in the face of uncertain outcomes, individuals will choose a decision or a course of action that maximises expected utility, the so-called Expected Utility Hypothesis, first

---

[16] For an overview of the many studies that provide an economic analysis of the merits and demerits of disclosure regulation see E Avgouleas, *The Mechanics and Regulation of Market Abuse, A Legal and Economic Analysis* (Oxford, Oxford University Press, 2005) 173. The two most convincing academic analyses in favour of disclosure regulation are J Coffee, 'Market Failure and the Economic Case for a Mandatory Disclosure System' (1984) 70 *Virginia Law Review* 717; and J Cox, 'Insider Trading and Contracting: A Critical Response to the "Chicago School"' [1986] *Duke Law Journal* 628. Other authors have dismissed the benefits of mandatory disclosure mostly because of the high costs of compliance it entails, but also because of a quasi-metaphysical belief in self-correcting efficient markets that make the mandatory disclosure of information unnecessary, eg FH Easterbrook and DR Fischel, 'Mandatory Disclosure and the Protection of Investors' (1984) 70 *Virginia Law Review* 669.

[17] See GS Becker, *The Economic Approach to Human Behavior* (Chicago, IL, University of Chicago Press, 1976), 14; and R Posner, *Economic Analysis of Law*, 6th edn (New York, Aspen Law and Business, 2003) chs 1–3.

clearly expressed by Daniel Bernoulli in 1738[18] and further refined by the two leading game theorists, Von Neumann and Morgenstern.[19] That is, the 'homo economicus' is supposed to act to maximise expected utility because his/her preferences are given consistently and representably in the form of a utility function.

Provision of information becomes very important in this model of decision-making because, where individuals operate in conditions of uncertainty about the results of their actions, they are assumed to be able to assess the probability distribution in accordance with their level of knowledge. If new information can be collected from the environment and individuals know the information's possible content, they assess it, in accordance with Bayes's law, by calculating the probability distribution based on the interplay between the new information's content and their prior knowledge.

2.   Limitations of Disclosure Regulation

(a)   Prospect Theory, Experimental Economics, and Disclosure Regulation

As mentioned above, under the rational investor model of regulation, disclosure leads to informed investment decisions in accordance with investor risk and return preferences. Thus, rational and self-disciplined wealth-maximising investors need large volumes of information in order to calculate the risk and return possibilities of an investment, in order to maximise their expected utility (expected profit) in accordance with their risk and return preferences.

This is also the first statement that would fall foul of a Prospect Theory analysis of disclosure. Kahneman and Tversky's Prospect Theory[20] constitutes the core of the so-called psychology of choice and judgement, one of the two pillars of Behavioural Decision Theory (BDT).[21] Prospect Theory assumes that preferences are not constant and choice may be manipulated through the framing of information. If the assumptions of Prospect Theory are correct, namely that by changing a reference point human actors' evaluation of gains and losses will change and that in any case individuals' ability to make actuarial calculations is limited, then the utility of the provision of vast amounts of information to both retail and institutional investors looks much diminished. These limitations make disclosure even less effective as a regulatory technique that helps investor decision-making if the effects of problem description or framing[22] are also taken into account. Barberis and Thaler note that there are numerous demonstrations of a 30–40% shift in preferences depending on the wording of a problem.[23] This means that individuals'

---

[18] D Bernoulli, 'Exposition of a New Theory on the Measurement of Risk' (1738), reproduced in (1954) 22 *Econometrica* 23.

[19] J Von Neumann and O Morgenstern, *Theory of Games and Economic Behavior* (Princeton, NJ, Princeton University Press, 1944).

[20] See D Kahneman and A Tversky, 'Prospect Theory: An Analysis of Decision under Risk' (1979) 47 *Econometrica* 263.

[21] The other pillar is, of course, experimental economics. Experimental economics reflects equally the rational and behavioural intellectual traditions. Its main findings do not discard rational choice theory; they merely challenge the idealistic foundations of neoclassical economics that people exhibit unbounded rationality, pure self-interest and complete self-control when making economic decisions.

[22] A Tversky and D Kahneman, 'Rational Choice and the Framing of Decisions' (1986) 59 *Journal of Business* 251.

[23] N Barberis and R Thaler, 'A Survey of Behavioral Finance', National Bureau of Economic Research Working Paper No 9222 (2002) 20.

choices can be manipulated depending on the way relevant information is presented. The effect of framing is stronger among the less sophisticated members of any group.[24] However, even thoughtfulness is not sufficient to counter the effect of framing; thoughtful individuals are still in need of a relevant cue in order to untangle the impact of framing.[25]

The assumption that preferences are not affected by variations in irrelevant features of options or outcomes, namely, that choices are independent of the problem description or representation, called extensionality[26] or invariance,[27] is an essential aspect of rational choice theory. As explained in the next section, the impact of the aforementioned behavioural factors was very evident in exposing the limitations of disclosure in the context of the global financial crisis.

Nonetheless, the above is not the full story. The critical importance of disclosure in promoting clean markets and protecting investors should not be easily dismissed, nor should rational choice theory be proclaimed dead. In fact, there is plenty of empirical and experimental evidence that validates and refutes the assumptions of both BDT and rational choice theory. For example, experimental economics shows that in reality human activity is diffused and dominated by unconscious, autonomic, neuropsychological systems.[28] These enable people to function effectively without always calling upon the brain's scarcest resource: attentional circuitry. However, through trial-and-error learning, individuals may eventually make decisions that are compatible with expected utility theory.

This conflicting evidence leads to the plausible assumption that 'human decision-making is simply a more nuanced phenomenon than unitary-process theories permit'.[29] According to Arlen and Talley, this means that human actors:[30]

[M]ay employ multiple decision-making programs concurrently, and the actuation of each program may depend on the underlying context in systematic ways. In some contexts, conscious decision-making may share many features of Rational Choice Theory. In other moments, unconscious or intuitive processes may intervene, affecting the information that reaches our deliberative processes, the weight we give to various pieces of information, the time and attention devoted to choosing through deliberation, and our willingness to choose based on the outcome of deliberation instead of an 'intuition' about what is right.

The above observation essentially means that, instead of focusing on the unitary theories of decision-making like rational choice and prospect theory, it is better to understand human decision-making as the product of multiple processes.[31] As a result, individual cognitive processes may become dominant in different context-specific situations and

[24] RA LeBoeuf and E Shafir, 'Deep Thoughts and Shallow Frames: On the Susceptibility to Framing Effects' (2003) 16 *Journal of Behavioral Decision Making* 77.

[25] Ibid.

[26] KJ Arrow, 'Risk Perception in Psychology and Economics' (1982) 20 *Economic Inquiry* 1.

[27] Kahneman and Tversky, above n 20.

[28] See VL Smith, *Papers in Experimental Economics* (Cambridge, Cambridge University Press, 1991) and JH Kagel and AE Roth (eds), *The Handbook of Experimental Economics* (Princeton, NJ, Princeton University Press, 1995).

[29] JH Arlen and EL Talley, 'Introduction' in JH Arlen and EL Talley (eds), *Experimental Law and Economics* (Cheltenham, Edward Elgar, 2008) xix. This work has also appeared as JH Arlen and EL Talley, 'Experimental Law and Economics, New York University Law and Economics Working Paper No 149 (2008).

[30] Ibid.

[31] Ibid, xviii–xx.

cross-context comparisons may potentially lead to observed inconsistencies in behaviour.[32]

In my view, the phenomenally inconsistent way that market actors use disclosed information constitutes evidence of employing multiple decision-making programmes concurrently. This view is further reinforced by the emerging discipline of neuro-economics,[33] which, relying on the findings of neurosciences, increasingly views human actors as (often simultaneous) users of multiple decision-making programmes. In fact, neuroeconomics has raised doubts as to whether the two identified systems of decision-making even exist or operate separately. Three well-known neuroscientists noted in a recent paper that '[t]here is, for example, no evidence that there is an emotional system, per se, and a rational system, per se, for decision making at the neurobiological level'.[34] They added that viewing the human brain as a collection of two distinct decision-making processes/systems, one emotional/irrational and the other deliberative/rational, may serve economists well in trying to make sense of human behaviour, but it has no grounds in neurobiology.[35]

Taking into consideration the above observations, it is assumed that it would be difficult, probably impossible, to untangle conscious and deliberative processing of disclosed information by market actors in order to evaluate its impact on their decision-making. Relevant research would possibly show that sometimes the disclosed information is used in a deliberative way, leading to outcomes that are consistent with rational choice theory. At other times, non-conscious (intuitive), automatic decision-making processes will be found to account for market phenomena that do not fit with the outcomes prescribed by rational choice. Behavioural finance scholars called these 'market puzzles' or 'anomalies'.[36] Because these automatic processes intervene, short-circuit or overrule deliberative processes they may develop into a cognitive bias, which induces behaviour inconsistent with rational choice/expected utility theory.[37] As explained below (section D), this finding also means that only through the use of both empirical and experimental studies will the actual value of disclosure as a protective regulatory technique be properly ascertained, leading to the formulation of disclosure policies, techniques and formats that really aid individual investor and market welfare.

---

[32] Ibid, xviii.

[33] CF Camerer, G Loewenstein and D Prelec, '"Neuroeconomics": How Neuroscience Can Inform Economics' (2005) 43 *Journal of Economic Literature* 9. See also PW Glimcher, C Camerer, E Fehr and RA Poldrack (eds), *Neuroeconomics: Decision Making and the Brain* (New York, Academic Press, 2008) esp chs 4 (A Rustichini, 'Neuroeconomics: Formal Models of Decision Making and Cognitive Neuroscience') and 15 (E Fehr, 'Social Preferences and the Brain'). A concise journalistic analysis of the origins development and main findings of neuroeconomics may be found in J Cassidy, 'MIND GAMES—What Neuroeconomics Tells us about Money and the Brain', *The New Yorker*, 18 September 2006.

[34] PW Glimcher, MC Dorris and HM Bayer, 'Physiological Utility Theory and the Neuroeconomics of Choice' (2005) 52 *Games Economics Behavior* 213.

[35] 'Recently, a number of economists have begun to suggest, at a psychological level, that human decision making can be broken down into two categories; typically rational and irrational . . . What we cannot stress strongly enough is that the vast majority of evolutionary biologists and neurobiologists reject this view. There are probably two principal reasons that biologists reject this dualist view of the nervous system; one neurobiological and one behavioral. First there is no neurobiological evidence that emotional and non-emotional systems are fully distinct in the architecture of the primate brain. Secondly, there is no evidence that rational and irrational behavior are the product of two distinct brain systems, one of which is uniquely rational and one of which is uniquely irrational.' Ibid.

[36] See Barberis and Thaler, above n 23.

[37] Arlen and Talley, above n 29, xix, xx, xxviii.

(b)   Bounded Rationality and Herding as Barriers to Rational Reaction to Disclosed Information

There are two additional factors that seem to limit the effectiveness of disclosure. First, bounded rationality[38] may account for market actors' limited understanding of disclosed information regarding highly complex financial instruments.[39] Secondly, herding (strategic trade behaviour), either due to peer pressure or in response to career/reputational concerns, also means that disclosed information is ignored in favour of the safer 'follow the herd' strategy.[40] Thus, herding places a very powerful limitation on rational reaction to all kinds of disclosed information.

Because individuals are boundedly rational, as securitisation markets grew and products became more complex, expert investors showed limited capacity for understanding the disclosed mechanics and calculating the attendant risks of structured credit products, and for developing tools to value them. Instead, as explained below, investors replaced rigorous credit controls and valuation models with over-reliance on credit ratings.

Furthermore, institutions' herding has been recognised as one of the main builders and amplifiers of the crisis in the recent review by Lord Turner of the causes of the global financial crisis.[41] Herding is often due to irrational exuberance, yet it is even more often caused by the 'beauty contests', first described by Keynes,[42] in their post-modern form, which intrinsically links them to the agency problem.

Today, bank shareholders' or institutional investors' money is managed by expert individuals who, as agents, allocate the money of their principals. Their interests, as in most principal–agent relationships, are not perfectly aligned and sometimes diverge considerably. While shareholders or fund investors are concerned, under the rational choice model, with an optimal mixture of risk and return that ensures sustained profitability, bankers' and fund managers' concerns are markedly different. They have to show that their performance is equal to or better than the rest of the market.[43] Performance affects bonus payments and the bankers' and fund managers' tenure in the job.[44] Individuals who work for institutional investors are in the market in order to make money

---

[38] This concept was introduced as a potential determining factor in the making of economic decisions by Herbert Simon. See HA Simon, 'A Behavioral Model of Rational Choice' (1955) 69 *Quarterly Journal of Economics* 99; HA Simon, 'Rationality as Process and Product of Thought' (1978) 68 *American Economic Review: Papers and Proceedings* 1. Essentially it means that individuals have limited ability to process information because of their limited computational ability and flawed memory.

[39] See Schwarcz, above nn 9–11.

[40] See Schwarcz, above n 10; Avgouleas, above n 12.

[41] Turner Review, above n 13.

[42] '[P]rofessional investment may be likened to those newspaper competitions in which the competitors have to pick out the six prettiest faces from a hundred photographs, the prize being awarded to the competitor whose choice most nearly corresponds to the average preferences of the competitors as a whole; so that each competitor has to pick, not those faces which he himself finds prettiest, but those which he thinks likeliest to catch the fancy of the other competitors, all of whom are looking at the problem from the same point of view. It is not a case of choosing those which, to the best of one's judgment, are really the prettiest, nor even those which average opinion genuinely thinks the prettiest. We have reached the third degree where we devote our intelligences to anticipating what average opinion expects the average opinion to be.' JM Keynes, *General Theory of Employment, Interest and Money* (New York, Harcourt Brace, 1936) ch 12 (emphasis added).

[43] For an analysis of the impact of the principal–agent relationship (within financial institutions) on the failure of disclosure in the market for structured credit securities see Schwarcz, above n 9.

[44] See J Chevalier and G Ellison, 'Career Concerns of Mutual Fund Managers' (1999) 114 *Quarterly Journal of Economics* 389.

and save their jobs, not in order to 'correct' prices through arbitrage trading, as the Efficient Market Hypothesis (a direct brainchild of rational choice theory) assumes. Thus, they are very likely to follow the herd,[45] conveniently forgetting the value of painstaking risk-management controls and the costs of possible long-term market reversals.

This might seem like a reasonable response to noise trader activity. Professional investors follow the herd and its trading choices, playing the 'momentum game'[46] in the hope that they will be able to sell and materialise their gains before the noise traders decide to sell. That is, bankers, traders and fund managers concentrate on trades and trading techniques that enable them, if not to beat the market, at least not to post returns inferior to the market average, saving their jobs and securing large compensation packages.[47] However, as their reaction prolongs and deepens an eventual asset bubble,[48] the short-term and non-contrarian nature of their behaviour goes counter to the game theory (strong) view of rationality.[49] The next section explains both the role of inadequate disclosure in building up the conditions that led to the global financial crisis and the way the crisis has exposed disclosure's limitations.

C.   The Global Financial Crisis and the Impact of (In)adequate Disclosure

1.   The Rational Choice Critique

Inadequate disclosure is blamed for building up the conditions that created the global financial crisis in five contexts: (i) inadequate disclosure of risks to sub-prime borrowers; (ii) opacity of highly structured financial products, which also incorporate very complex pricing formulas, and sometimes possible obfuscation by financial institutions of the risks associated with such products, in spite of relevant legal and regulatory requirements; (ii) inadequate disclosure by financial institutions of their on- and off-balance-sheet exposures; (iv) inadequate disclosure by credit rating agencies of the limitations of credit ratings and their conflicts of interest; and (v) inadequate disclosure of the short-termist nature of executive and trader compensation.

It is an indisputable fact that, as regards structured credit products, lack of standard-isation—and, in the case of CDSs, inherently limited, if not non-existent, disclosure—meant that the market had considerable difficulty in filling the gaps and properly evalu-ating the risks of those securities. Thus, it could not price them with any degree of

---

[45] P Gompers and A Metrick, 'Institutional Investors and Equity Prices' (2001) 116 *Quarterly Journal of Economics* 229; R Wermers, 'Mutual Fund Herding and the Impact on Stock Prices' (1999) 54 *Journal of Finance* 58; see also DS Scharfstein and J Stein, 'Herd Behavior and Investment' (1990) 80 *American Economic Review* 465.

[46] DC Langevoort, 'Taming the Animal Spirits of the Stock Markets: A Behavioral Approach to Securities Regulation' (2002) 97 *Northwestern University Law Review* 135, 158–59.

[47] PM Healy and K Palepu, 'Governance and Intermediation Problems in Capital Markets: Evidence from the Fall of Enron' (2003) 17 *Journal of Economic Perspectives* 3–26.

[48] JR Nofsinger and RW Sias, 'Herding and Feedback Trading by Institutional and Individual Investors (1999) 54 *Journal of Finance* 2263.

[49] J Nash, 'Equilibrium Points in n-person Games' (1950) 36 *Proceedings of the National Academy of the USA* 48; J Nash, 'Non-Cooperative Games' (1951) 54 *Annals of Mathematics* 286.

accuracy. This built uncertainty, which eventually gripped the markets following the trigger of the credit crisis. The same uncertainty also prevented new entrants to the structured products market. Furthermore, banks, either deliberately or because of their own ignorance, gave the market incomplete information regarding their on- and off-balance-sheet exposures to structured credit products. As a result, fears about the true size of their exposures led to considerable reluctance by counterparties to trade and the subsequent amplification of the market turmoil.

Moreover, in the highly complex and fast-moving environment of global financial markets it is easy for regulators to make the wrong choice regarding the kind of data that has to be disclosed. Thus, either because of the nature of the Basel Capital Adequacy standards[50] or of the inherently flawed supervisory focus on institutional capital adequacy,[51] financial intermediaries were not requested to make any kind of assessment of the systemic implications of their market activities and did note have to disclose such assessment.

However, in other areas there was considerable disclosure of information regarding the risk of investment products and techniques that have been highly implicated in the building up and amplification of the global financial crisis. In those cases, market actors either simply did not read the warning signals properly or did not understand or act on the disclosed information. An unbiased observer would particularly focus on three areas of protective regulation where disclosure as regulatory technique did not work as expected: (i) risk assessment/management; (ii) prudential regulation/systemic stability; and (iii) consumer protection. These disclosure failures are discussed analytically in the next few paragraphs.

2. The BDT Critique

(a) Risk Assessment

A recurring theme in every regulatory report on the causes of the global credit crisis is the role of lax risk management controls within financial institutions. The failures of internal risk management controls were concentrated in five areas: (i) failing credit control and borrower vetting standards; (ii) inability to value positions in structured credit securities properly; (ii) excessive reliance on credit ratings in spite of their widely known short-comings; (iv) inadequate use of information when this was provided; and (v) ignorance by senior bank management of the true function of special investment vehicles (SIVs) and thus of the institution's actual exposure to them.[52] The cause of some of these failures, however, was not lack of information but inappropriate use of what was disclosed, due, no less, to behavioural factors.

For example, in the case of credit ratings, institutional buyers and sellers of structured

---

[50] See in general M Brunnermeier, A Crockett, C Goodhart, AD Persaud and H Shin, 'The Fundamental Principles of Financial Regulation', Geneva Reports on the World Economy No 11 (London, Centre for Economic Policy Research, 2009) ch 4, also called the Goodhart Report.

[51] M Hellwig, 'Systemic Risk in the Financial Sector: An Analysis of the Subprime-Mortgage Financial Crisis', Preprints of the Max Planck Institute for Research on Collective Goods No 2008/43 (2008) 56.

[52] According to the President's Working Group, above n 5, 15, these weaknesses 'were particularly evident with respect to the management of certain business lines: (a) CDO warehouses; (b) syndication of leveraged loans; and (c) conduit businesses (sponsorship or liquidity support for SIVs and other conduits that issued ABCP)'.

credit securities used credit ratings in order to price them, when reliable price quotations were unavailable,[53] which in the case of structured credit products was not unusual. As a result, credit ratings came to play a key role in the 'valuation of customized or illiquid structured credit products'.[54] However, these highly sophisticated market participants knew all too well that the ratings produced by the major credit rating agencies (CRAs) suffered several shortcomings. First, they were built to measure. Namely, the issuers of the products were using CRA know-how and software in order to build baskets of securities that would ensure an AAA rating. Secondly, the insatiable appetite of global markets for credit ratings and the fact that the relevant market was highly oligopolistic (three major agencies—Standard & Poors, Fitch and Moody's—have traditionally dominated the market) meant that the industry suffered from a serious lack of incentives to seriously stress test credit ratings, a fact that was well known to most market professionals. Thirdly, CRAs were often subject to considerable conflicts of interest, as the buyers of their ratings were the issuers whose products they rated.[55] Fourthly, in the case of structured credit securities, which normally bundle together underlying debt obligations emanating from a multitude of obligors, CRAs did not make public the estimated correlation of obligors in the asset pool; disclosure of the cross-correlations would have greatly assisted investors in assessing whether the rating was based on expectations which were in line with their own. Finally, asset value in the case of securities is often intrinsically linked to the market-ability/liquidity of a financial product, but this parameter was not measured by credit ratings.

Of course, modellers and risk managers in most institutions understood very well the implications of the absence of such information, yet chose to continue relying on credit ratings. It is thus mystifying why so much importance was placed on ratings and why big, well resourced and highly sophisticated banks and other institutional investors chose to ignore all of the aforementioned faults and perform little or no in-house credit analysis of their investments.

Arguably, there are two ways to explain why big institutions chose to substitute proper analysis and due diligence for 'a subscription to a ratings publication'.[56] The rational choice explanation is that, in order to economise on substantial research costs and thus facilitate transactions, investors chose to ignore the known flaws of credit ratings. However, given how pronounced, serious and well known those flaws were, this explanation does not sound convincing. Therefore, the second explanation, which highlights the behavioural aspects of investor reliance on credit ratings, is also worth considering.

It is possible that investor 'irrational' reliance on credit ratings was the result of the operation of the availability and representativeness heuristics.[57] Namely, market participants relying much more heavily on heuristics rather than on any rational computations

---

[53] International Monetary Fund, 'Global Financial Stability Report, Containing Systemic Risks and Restoring Financial Soundness' (2008) 55.

[54] Ibid.

[55] For an excellent analysis of the Credit Rating Agencies' paradox see SL Schwarcz, **'Private Ordering of Public Markets: The Rating Agency Paradox'** [2002] *University of Illinois Law Review* 1.

[56] M Carney, 'Addressing Financial Market Turbulence', remarks of the Governor of the Bank of Canada to the Toronto Board of Trade, 13 March 2008, 3–4.

[57] The availability heuristic controls estimates of the frequency or probability of events, which are judged by the ease with which instances of such events come to mind. In other words, the availability heuristic is an assessment of accessibility. The representativeness heuristic is used by individuals to evaluate probability. Much of the time, representativeness is a helpful heuristic, but it can generate some severe biases.

came to the conclusion that painstaking and accurate calculations of market value were not necessary for structured credit products. There was no memory of serious failures of the ratings process, since structured credit securities were predominantly new products without long trading histories. On the contrary, given also the prevailing conditions of market euphoria, credit ratings, in spite of their shortcomings, could serve as a usable, though inaccurate, benchmark of value so that trading and profiteering could go on. Specifically, rational actors' cognitive limitations and focus on short-term profit forced sophisticated investors to ignore the warning signals. This explains both the incredible amount of trust placed on the ratings of CRAs and why these 'had grown more powerful than anyone intended'.[58]

Additional credibility to the above argument is lent by the fact that, while investors and regulators were placing nearly blind trust on credit ratings, CRAs frequently warned the market about the true function of their ratings. Naturally, their warnings were neither very prominent nor widely publicised,[59] yet a rational investor, given also the vast technical sophistication and expertise available to institutional investors, would easily have identified and properly incorporated them into their decision-making model, discounting instead of exaggerating the importance of credit ratings.

(b)   Consumer Protection

There is a rational choice explanation of the sub-prime crisis that focuses on inadequate disclosure of risks (especially once so-called 'teaser' rates had ceased and interest payments had been adjusted to higher rates) and of the mortgage brokers' conflicts of interest.[60] According to this approach, US sub-prime borrowers did not obtain loans that they could not afford on the basis of their income, their job prospects and the value of their asset, they simply did not have enough information to make a rational risk analysis of their investment. This approach is, of course, not inaccurate when it comes to the unscrupulous practices of US mortgage brokers, but it also greatly discounts an indisputable fact. US sub-prime borrowers were buying into a 'dream': the infinite rise of the US housing market. Even if the risks of the mortgage were not properly disclosed, it was not difficult to figure out that US housing price markets were at historical highs and that this growth could not last forever. Nor was it a secret to both borrowers and lenders that they borrowed/lent money in excess of the already overpriced asset's value. Therefore, it seems unlikely that inadequate disclosure and sharp practice were the sole culprits of the explosion of US sub-prime loans.

Collective speculative fever—usually called irrational exuberance—and perhaps the inherent inability of a segment of the population, due to low levels of education and financial expertise, to fully understand the risks involved were possibly more important factors. A rising US housing market, which was also followed by rising housing markets in most western countries, led to credit consumer overconfidence. That is, mortgage

---

[58] International Monetary Fund, above n 53, 56.

[59] Ibid, 55: 'Although credit rating agencies insist that ratings measure only default risk, and not the likelihood or intensity of downgrades or mark-to-market losses, many investors were seemingly unaware of these warnings and disclaimers.'

[60] The Becker-Posner blog, 'The Subprime Mortgage Mess—Posner's Comment', 23 December 2007, available at www.becker-posner-blog.com/archives/2007/12/the_subprime_mo.html.

borrowers in the US and the rest of Western world, anchored[61] to the prevailing environment of low interest rates and overconfident that rising house prices would last forever, rushed to jump on the property bandwagon, playing the 'momentum game'. In doing so they were rather reluctant to engage in careful calculations regarding the sustainability of their borrowings. Of course, if overconfidence and inability to make an informed financial decision were at the heart of consumers' credit decisions in the context of sub-prime loans, it is unlikely that consumers would have acted very differently if they had been given accurate information about the risks of sub-prime lending and the conflicts of interest of the intermediating brokers.

'[U]nderwriting standards for US adjustable-rate sub-prime mortgages weakened dramatically between late 2004 and early 2007' and mortgages were extended to borrowers with weaker credit histories.[62] Irrational exuberance and bounded rationality may account for the relaxed attitude of credit providers as much as the perverse incentives created by the originate-to-distribute model, which focused on commission earned from loan generation and not credit controls. Arguably, lenders were themselves gripped by overconfidence, because of the easy availability of credit, due to excessive levels of liquidity in global financial markets, and rising asset prices. Also they misunderstood the mechanics of innovative financial instruments, due to their complexity, and believed that the credit risk they were transferring to SIVs through securitisations or to counterparties through CDSs was, in fact, disappearing from the system and from their balance sheets. This belief was totally flawed and highlighted their limited understanding of financial innovation.[63]

(c) Banking Regulation

The chief objective of banking regulation is the prevention of financial collapses, because they are highly contagious, due to the nature of the banking industry, and can evolve, aided by market panic, to full-scale financial cascades threatening the stability of the financial system. Probably the most important regulatory tool used to buttress banking institutions' financial health and soundness is the regulatory standards of so-called capital adequacy. The standards currently applicable to the majority of international banks are those fashioned by the Basel Committee on Banking Supervision. The third pillar of the Basel II Accord provides an increased number of regulatory and market disclosures by regulated banks in order to enhance market discipline.[64] This is based on the assumption that, if the regulatory capital positions and risk exposures of international banks are

---

[61] Anchoring refers to the process by which an individual decision maker gravitates to a reference point that she or he subsequently uses as an initial condition for arriving at a final decision. Experimental evidence shows that people anchor too much on the initial value, eg on prevailing current interest rates or stock prices, and subsequent adjustment is often insufficient.

[62] President's Working Group on Financial Markets, above n 5, 8.

[63] In fact, banks kept an exposure to the securitised loans with the lowest quality in order to make the issue desirable to investors. At the same time, credit risk was piling up in hidden parts of the system because of shadow banking and credit default swaps, but did not at all disappear.

[64] Banks are required under the Basel II Accord to regularly disclose, inter alia, (i) the composition of their tier 1 and tier 2 capital, the total amount of capital, and the accounting policies they use for the valuation of their assets and liabilities; (ii) an exposure assessment comprising information about the asset side of balance sheet, the different types of risk to which the bank is exposed and the amounts exposed, the method used for calculating those risks, the external credit agency used for the risk-weighting purposes, in the case of banks using the standardised approach; and (iii) general information on the risk assessment methodology used, in the case of banks using the internal ratings-based approach, the capital requirements for each different type of risk and the total capital requirements.

regularly disclosed, banks facing difficulties, because, for instance, they pursue risky business policies, will be restrained/disciplined, as the rest of the market will become increasingly unwilling to lend them money. Thus, disclosure has become one of the most important tools of monitoring and enforcement of capital adequacy regulation.

However, this view was either naive or just exhibited a metaphysical belief in self-regulation. In the absence of properly calibrated objectives, because of the possibility of public bank rescues and deposit insurance, the role of market discipline is rather marginal.[65] The fact that all big banks enjoy an implicit public guarantee means, in practice, that even badly run banks will probably not be allowed to fail, and, if they do, the taxpayer and the deposit insurance scheme will cover most of the creditors' losses. This means that, first, the ailing bank's management can afford to continue behaving irresponsibly and, secondly, its creditors may continue lending it funds without any substantial fear of losses that an institution's bankruptcy would entail, significantly weakening market discipline.

This obstacle to market discipline is magnified by the fact that by the very nature of its business the banking industry creates interconnectedness. Given the operation of the government guarantee, banking institutions have a strong incentive to grow their asset book (loans), since the larger and more interconnected the institution becomes the more likely it is that its failure will also drag down other interconnected institutions. The Goodhart Report calls this risk the 'interconnectedness spillover'.[66] Obviously, the bigger and more interconnected the institution the more likely it is that the government will rescue it in the event of failure.[67] This, in turn, creates powerful perverse incentives to expand a banking institution's balance sheet, obliterating the restraining power of market discipline.

However, even if it was possible to eliminate moral hazard and fashion appropriate incentives so that bank creditors became effective monitors of banks—in which case extensive market disclosure would have been very useful—still market monitoring would mean little in terms of preventing institutional failures and/or safeguarding systemic stability for two reasons. First, as Hellwig observes:[68]

> Because of systemic interdependence, the individual bank's risk exposure cannot be ascertained by just looking at the bank's assets and liabilities, on balance sheet and off balance sheet. If the bank's asset position involves a certain risk and the bank has hedged this risk by contracting with a third party, the effectiveness of the hedge depends on the third party's ability to fulfil its obligations when needed. If the risk in question is of macroeconomic dimension, an interest rate risk, exchange rate risk, or a housing-price risk, the counterparty's ability to fulfil its obligation depends on how many similar contracts it has concluded with other market participants. If risk

---

[65] A view that was tentatively based on CW Calomiris and CM Kahn, 'The Role of Demandable Debt in Structuring Optimal Banking Arrangements' (1991) 81 *American Economic Review* 497. This analysis focused on the role of demandable bank debt in disciplining bankers. However, the strength of the countervailing power possessed by the 'too big to fail' doctrine and, of course, deposit insurance was not accounted for. To account for these limitations, Calomiris argued in a subsequent article for banks to maintain a minimal proportion of subordinated debt finance, while at the same time restricting the means by which government recapitalization of insolvent banks occurred. See CW Calomiris, 'Building an Incentive-compatible Safety Net' (1999) 23 *Journal of Banking and Finance* 1499.

[66] Goodhart Report, above n 50, 20–21.

[67] Ibid.

[68] Hellwig, above n 51, 59–60. Hellwig accurately notes that: 'The difficulties that the monoline insurers of credit risk in mortgage-backed securities have had over the past year—or the more recent crisis of AIG—provide a telling example of the problem.'

correlations across contracts are such that the counterparty to the hedge must deliver on many of them at the same time, this in itself may destroy the counterparty's viability.

In today's globalised markets, there is no private institution that possibly has the ability, resources and access to information to be able to conduct a credit analysis of all other financial institutions, regulated or unregulated. Furthermore, even if such an institution existed, the colossal costs of universal monitoring would far exceed the expected benefits.

Secondly, even if a financial institution behaves individually in a prudent way, or even if all financial institutions behave in a prudent, but uncoordinated way, a systemic crisis may not be averted. Especially in the event of a liquidity crunch even the prudent behaviour of one financial institution can create spillovers that may undermine the stability of other institutions leading to systemic instability. This problem is due to another (risk-spillover) externality: fire sales.[69] According to the Goodhart Report:

> [T]he fire-sale externality arises since each individual financial institution does not take into account the price impact its own fire-sales will have on asset prices in a possible future liquidity crunch. Hence, fire-sales by some institutions spillover, and adversely affect the balance sheet of others, causing a negative externality.

D.   What Future for Disclosure Regulation?

1.   Prudential Regulation

As mentioned in the introduction to this chapter, none of the limitations of disclosure as a regulatory technique diminish its importance: they just call for a radical rethinking of the disclosure paradigm in financial regulation. Clearly, in the context of capital markets the pre-eminence given to disclosure as a regulatory technique is unwarranted, given also the costs it entails for the producer of the disclosed information if information so disclosed is not properly processed by investors and does not target specific areas of market activity, where it is most effective. In other areas, such as banking regulation, disclosure is not suffi-cient to enforce, by means of market discipline, the prudent operation of individual institutions and the protection of the system from the risk of contagion.

In the field of banking regulation, disclosure will remain a strong supervisory tool only if it is used to supplement the impact of protective rules. It is not accidental that both of the influential reviews of banking regulation issued in recent months, the Goodhart Report and the Turner Review, place much more emphasis on revamped capital adequacy regulation and straitjacket protective rules and less, if any at all, on disclosure.

Proposals for the introduction of restrictive regulation in banking markets include calls for the imposition of dynamic pre-provisioning obligations, so that banks set aside more capital in good times in order to restrain the credit flows to the economy that may feed asset bubbles;[70] and of an upper level (maximum gross) leverage ratio for

---

[69] This externality was first explained in a model in J Geanakoplos and H Polemarchakis, 'Existence, Regularity, and Constrained Suboptimality of Competitive Allocation when the Asset Market is Incomplete' in WP Heller, RM Starr, and DA Starrett (eds), *Uncertainty, Information and Communication, Essays in Honor of Kenneth J Arrow*, vol 3 (Cambridge, Cambridge University Press, 1986).

[70] Goodhart Report, above n 50, 35, 38–39, 59–60.

banks.[71] Furthermore, academic commentators have suggested that inherent moral hazard in the banking industry, the cognitive limitations of human actors, the impact of the agency problem and the inability of disclosure to solve any of these problems call for the imposition of restrictions on the kind of business activities savings and loans banks should undertake. The same commentators have called for the imposition of limits on the use of securitisation by commercial banks and of their exposure to the capital markets.[72] Such restrictions would of course herald a radical transformation of regulatory thinking in this field at a global level, as reforms with a domestic focus are bound to prove ineffective due to regulatory arbitrage. They would also mean the separation of commercial banking from 'casino banking', as the Turner Review calls the capital market activities of banks.[73]

2.   Can Economic Experiments Help?

To the untrained eye the future of disclosure as a regulatory technique in the context of capital markets could look rather bleak. However, there are good reasons why this is not so. These include the indisputable benefits disclosure brings in battling market abuse and democratising capital markets, and thus encouraging access to them, fostering liquid markets. What is really required is the adaptation of disclosure techniques, volume, format and content to actual market conditions. Arguably, this means that disclosure regulation reform should be guided by empirical and experimental studies[74] that measure the actual impact of disclosed information, and thus the effectiveness of disclosure rules.

As mentioned in section B, experimental studies may be particularly useful in this context. The focus of experimental economics on an ecological concept of rationality, which asks questions as to why a specific social practice or specific game has been chosen instead of another, may be exactly what is needed to measure the true impact of disclosure rules on investor decisions and market efficiency. For instance, experimental economics holds that, in competitive markets—and financial markets are normally highly contested markets—institutions (the rules of the game) matter, because they determine information and private incentives.[75] However, the incentives to which people respond are sometimes not those one would expect based on the canons of economic theory. Thus, it is very doubtful whether financial incentives could act as generalised substitutes to prescriptive regulation.[76]

Testing how expert and lay investors process and utilise and strategically use disclosed information in the context of financial markets in order to measure the impact of disclosure rules will require highly complex and sophisticated experiments conducted by a broad alliance of lawyers, economists, psychologists and regulators. Thus, relevant teams

---

[71] Turner Review, above n 13, 7, 53, 95, 118.

[72] For a first approach and the description of this new licensing/supervisory model for the banking industry see Avgouleas, above n 12, 149–50.

[73] Turner Review, above n 13, 43, 94.

[74] The value of experimental studies in testing financial regulation has also been stressed elsewhere, especially in evaluating the effectiveness of laws designed to limit market imperfections such as asset price bubbles in the context of complex adaptive markets. See EF Gerding, 'Laws Against Bubbles: An Experimental-asset-market Approach to Financial Regulation' (2007) *Wisconsin Law Review* 977.

[75] VL Smith, 'An Experimental Study of Competitive Market Behavior' (1962) 70 *Journal of Political Economy* 111.

[76] For a summary of relevant studies see G Mitchell, 'Why Law and Economics' Perfect Rationality Should Not Be Traded for Behavioral Law and Economics' Equal Incompetence' (2002) 91 *Georgetown Law Journal* 67.

will probably present serious coordination issues. Furthermore, in order to have credibility, relevant experiments must engage real-life investors, traders and other human participants, and try to observe how these react to different pieces of information and what the result of their reaction in terms of market outcomes is. Naturally, conducting experiments with real-life actors will require expending considerable public resources. Overall the number of experiments attempting to explain market actors' behaviour, including the way they react to differential volumes of disclosed information, is on the rise.[77] Furthermore, a recent experiment on herding behaviour in financial markets, conducted by IMF economists using market professionals, has shown that the use of experiments in this context is both feasible and very useful to test theoretical assumptions.[78]

However, the use of experiments to test the impact of disclosure rules will not prove unproblematic. Given strong evidence that individuals do not use exclusively unitary processes of decision-making, as rational choice and prospect theory hold, but rely instead on multiple processes, what should be tested here is this new 'meta-theory', as Arlen and Talley call it.[79] Nonetheless, 'the recognition that people may employ multiple processes seriously complicates efforts to derive broad normative policy prescriptions from isolated experimental results'.[80] Also, in terms of methodology, experimenters should observe the six criteria set by Arlen and Talley, for successful experimental testing of legal rules: control, internal validity, falsifiability of theory, replicability, external validity and contextual attentiveness.[81]

A plausible and serious objection that may be raised here is regarding the need for experiments. Is it not enough to just conduct empirical studies? The answer to this objection is rather straightforward. First, experimental evidence should be used to complement, verify or nullify empirical research and not as a self-standing body of evidence. Secondly, since what is really required to be identified here is why, rather than how, market actors behave in particular ways while in possession of full information, such evidence is difficult to derive from empirical studies. Thirdly, assessing how market actors process information is a rather complex issue and will also require the conduct of qualitative studies (interviews, questionnaires) to accompany/interpret empirical data observations. However, qualitative studies in this context are open to manipulation by the subjects of the study, who will probably lie in many contexts in order to present themselves as much more clever, alert or rational, and much less prone to peer pressure than their actual market behaviour would indicate. On the other hand, in the controlled environment of an experiment using real-life subjects, many of these problems may be overcome. This makes experiments a very useful and reliable method to gauge the actual impact of disclosed information on market actors' behaviour, though their results would only be a useful basis for law reform if they did not conflict with the results of quantitative empirical studies.

---

[77] Eg J Beshears, JJ Choi et al, 'How Does Simplified Disclosure Affect Individuals' Mutual Fund Choices?' (11 September 2008), available at www.som.yale.edu/faculty/jjc83/summaryprospectus.pdf.

[78] See M Cipriani and A Guarino 'Herd Behavior in Financial Markets: An Experiment with Financial Market Professionals', IMF Working Paper 141/08 (June 2008). Their research comes to validate to some degree older experimental evidence on the impact of herding. LR Anderson and CA Holt, 'Information Cascades in the Laboratory' (1997) 87 *American Economic Review* 847.

[79] Arlen and Talley, above n 29, xxviii.

[80] Ibid, xviii.

[81] Ibid, xxxii.

It is hoped that, following the conduct of the suggested extensive empirical and experimental studies, a new framework for the use of disclosure as a regulatory technique in capital markets will emerge. One of the issues that will have to be addressed is financial product complexity. Important steps have already been taken in this area with respect to increased product standardisation and enhancement of clearing and settlement infrastructure. These initiatives are bound to improve the transparency of the market for structured credit securities, and complexity may well stop being the problem that it proved to be during the global financial crisis. However, experiments may also prove helpful in this area, if what is tested is whether complex financial contracts should at any rate be marketed and sold to certain investor classes.

3. A Financial Products Safety Committee?

The above observation leads us to one of the thorniest questions that experiments on the effectiveness of disclosure regulation must address. Is disclosure enough with respect to the investment decisions taken by certain classes of retail investors, who present limited financial sophistication and are also at the lower ranks of the earnings and education ladder? On the basis of present evidence, there is room for a prediction that experiments may lead to the conclusion that disclosure of information under whatever format or technique might have to be complemented with soft paternalism mechanisms,[82] such as a default investment/savings option.[83] These, in turn, may be inserted by a public or other non-profit consumer body in relevant financial contracts.

The assumption that simply modifying the volume of disclosed information may have an imperceptible impact on investor behaviour is reinforced by a recent experiment conducted by Laibson et al on the way individuals may use the 'summary prospectus' proposed by the US Securities and Exchange Commission (SEC) to be issued by mutual funds. The main objective of this proposal was to improve retail investors' processing and digestion of product information, something that is not usually possible with the bulky and very detailed full prospectus that mutual funds are obliged to issue. The experiment, where subjects were Harvard staff, showed that 'the Summary Prospectus [did] not meaningfully alter subjects' investment choices. Average portfolio fees and past returns [were] similar whether or not subjects receive[d] the Summary Prospectus.' The welfare gains the authors identified were in relation to spending less time to read the prospectus and wasting less paper—not exactly the gains intended by the SEC when it proposed the Summary Prospectus.[84]

---

[82] C Camerer, S Issacharoff, G Loewenstein, T O'Donoghue and M Rabin, 'Regulation for Conservatives: Behavioral Economics and the Case for "Asymmetric Paternalism"' (2003) 151 *University of Pennsylvania Law Review* 1211. For an analysis of possible uses of soft paternalism mechanisms to protect investors see E Avgouleas, 'Reforming Investor Protection Regulation: The Impact of Cognitive Biases' in M Faure and F Stephen (eds), *Essays in the Law and Economics of Regulation in Honour of Anthony Ogus* (The Hague, Intersentia, 2008) 143.

[83] From the ever expanding literature on the effect of defaults on savings planning see JJ Choi, D Laibson, BC Madrian and A Metrick, 'Optimal Defaults' (2003) 93 *American Economic Review* 180; and idem, 'For Better or For Worse: Default Effects and 401(k) Savings Behavior' in DA Wise (ed), *Perspectives in the Economics of Aging* (Chicago, IL, University of Chicago Press, 2004). For the active choice of defaults by the financially literate see GD Carroll, JJ Choi, D Laibson, B Madrian and A Metrick, 'Optimal Defaults and Active Decisions' 124 *Quarterly Journal of Economics* 1639.

[84] See Beshears et al, above n 77.

Accordingly, in the absence of a default option, disclosure of information alone, in whatever format or volume, may not be enough to counter individuals' tendency to prefer instant gratification over long-term rewards, which, of course, fosters speculation, and their general exhibition of limited self-control. Of course, this finding raises a more general question as to who should have the duty of scrutinising financial products targeting the unsophisticated retail investor market and be responsible for the identification of the right default option.

Harvard Professor Elizabeth Warren suggested in an article in 2007 that the US mortgage catastrophe would have been averted if there had been an independent financial products watchdog guarding against hazardous financial products, such as adjustable rate sub-prime mortgages.[85] This is an idea that has been embraced by US Congress,[86] where Warren now heads the Congressional Oversight Panel for the Troubled Asset Relief Program adopted by the Obama administration. Thus, there is an expectation that legislation will soon be introduced establishing an independent financial products safety commission in the US.

The EU and many other geographical regions did not experience a sub-prime mortgage scandal, suggesting such a strongly paternalistic solution to the problems retail financial services consumers face may be found unacceptable in many countries. On the other hand, just expecting brokers and other financial advisors to act as champions of consumer protection for their clients on the basis of relevant suitability and general conduct of business rules is an inadequate and sometimes unrealistic protection mechanism. Relevant rules oblige providers and sellers (financial advisors and brokers) of financial products to disclose as much information as possible about the products' nature and risk, and to ascertain whether it is suitable for the customer's risk profile. Sometimes, however, these rules do not work properly. First, brokers/financial advisors try as much as legally possible to avoid complying with them, no less due to the complexity of relevant rules. Secondly, the rules' effect is limited because of the limited ability of consumers to understand what is disclosed and to regularly act on such information in a rational way (as explained above). Therefore, on the basis of the preceding discussion, an independent experts/consumers watchdog that would advise, scrutinise and recommend options for financial products, rather than regulate them or prohibit them from entering the market, as the US proposals seems to suggest, would be a very positive development.

---

[85] See E Warren, 'Unsafe at Any Rate' (2007) *Democracy a Journal of Ideas*, available at www.democracyjournal.org/article.php?ID=6528. Warren has famously quipped: 'It is impossible to buy a toaster that has a one-in-five chance of bursting into flames and burning down your house. But it is possible to refinance an existing home with a mortgage that has the same one-in-five chance of putting the family out on the street—and the mortgage won't even carry a disclosure of that fact to the homeowner. Similarly, it's impossible to change the price on a toaster once it has been purchased. But long after the papers have been signed, it is possible to triple the price of the credit used to finance the purchase of that appliance, even if the customer meets all the credit terms, in full and on time. Why are consumers safe when they purchase tangible consumer products with cash, but when they sign up for routine financial products like mortgages and credit cards they are left at the mercy of their creditors? The difference between the two markets is regulation.'

[86] Senator Charles E Schumer press release, 'Durbin, Schumer, Kennedy ask Treasury to Support Creation of a Financial Product Safety Commission', 24 April 2009, schumer.senate.gov/new_website/record.cfm?id=311958.

E. Conclusion

The old disclose and self-regulate paradigm in financial markets is dead, no less because of its role in bringing about a global financial catastrophe. However, this does not diminish the value of disclosure as a regulatory technique; it simply calls for a substantial overhaul of its processes, volume, timing and format in order to make it more effective. This chapter undertook the bold task of considering disclosure's future in the aftermath of the global financial crisis in order to incorporate into the new disclosure paradigm the lessons learnt by the crisis. After highlighting the disclosure rationale in contemporary financial regulation, it opened two new lines of enquiry intending to measure the welfare benefits of disclosure. First, it investigated whether the prominent role which international banking regulation accords to market discipline aided by extensive disclosure, in order to prevent behaviour that endangers systemic stability, is justified. Secondly, it considered how useful extensive disclosure of information is to retail/unsophisticated investors, especially for those lower down in the income and educational pyramid.

The chapter's findings show that premising banking regulation on disclosure and market discipline was a flawed approach that endangered the stability of the global financial system. Disclosure can have a constructive role in banking regulation only as a supplement to strict protective rules that limit the kind of activities an institution may undertake and restrain its risk-taking appetite. Furthermore, it has been argued that the disclosure conundrum in capital markets will only be resolved if disclosure rules are subjected to extensive and rigorous empirical and experimental studies. It is possible that such studies will show that, in spite of the existence of extensive disclosure regimes, certain classes of individual investors also need to be aided by the introduction of default choices. This is a role that should be assigned to an independent public body that is not susceptible to regulatory capture.

13

Credit Crisis Solutions: Risk Symmetric Criteria for the Reconstruction of Socially Fair Asset-backed Securities

JOSEPH TANEGA[*]

A. Introduction

In this essay, I compare investors' rights to ever-increasing complex financial instruments under US and EU securities law, and explore the various differences through the lens of a risk symmetries theory.[1] This is part of a larger project examining the logic of securities regulations from philosophical and anthropological perspectives. The scope of my enquiry is to identify a set of high-level principles relating to investors' disclosure rights to ever increasingly complex financial instruments and to focus on the features of disclosure requirements of a particular complex financial instrument in its generic form, namely, the asset-backed security and the legal-financial technique, more generally called securitisation. My focus on asset-backed securities and securitisation is not entirely arbitrary since these instruments and their implied originate-to-distribute business model are generally considered to be the catastrophic epicentre of the global credit crisis.[2] In many minds, asset-backed securities, especially residential mortgage-backed securities (RMBS) linked to sub-prime mortgages and securitisation, need to be understood before we can comprehend the aetiology[3] and continuing illiquidity[4] of the credit crisis. My purpose, however, is not to provide a detailed history of the credit crisis but rather to examine the logic of investors' rights to disclosure as found in US and EU securities regulations in terms of a risk symmetries analysis, which are now being asserted in the form of a giant

---

[*] Reader in International Financial Law, University of Westminster School of Law.

[1] See generally J Tanega, 'Securitization Disclosures under Basel II: Part II-Applications of the Risk Symmetry Principle to Economic Substance over Legal Form' (2006) 21 *Journal of International Banking Law and Regulation* 1.

[2] M Crouhy and S Turnbull, 'The Subprime Credit Crisis of 07' (5 March 2008) ssrn.com/abstract=1112467, 3.

[3] Ibid, 4–8. See also Y Demyanyk and O van Hermert, 'Understanding the Subprime Mortgage Crisis' (5 March 2008) ssrn.com/abstract=1020396, 1–2, claiming that the 2007 credit crisis was detectable in 2003; AB Ashcraft and T Schuermann 'Understanding the Securitization of Subprime Mortgage Credit', Wharton Financial Institutions Center Working Paper No 07-43 (2008) i–iii, for analysis of economic frictions of the credit crisis.

[4] See M Wolf, 'Why Britain's Economy Will Change', *Financial Times*, 2 May 2008, 13, for illiquidity in RMBS market in the UK. See J Mackintosh 'Government Bond Traders pulled into Deleveraging Vortex', *Financial Times*, 2 May 2008, 39, on extreme volatility and illiquidity.

wave of litigation[5] and politicised calls for increased government aid to the foreclosures and delinquency problems in the housing market.[6] From the perspective of market participants, the problem in the short term is how to kickstart the asset-backed securities market, which has now been on strike for almost two years,[7] and in the long term how to fashion financial regulations with aim to eradicate or at least reduce future bubbles and ameliorate systemic risk.[8] I ask:

1. What are the genuine rights of investors to asset-backed securities in the worlds pre-default and post-default of the credit crisis?
2. How might we wish to design investor rights that are fair given the complex nature of the financial instruments?

I hypothesise that, if complex financial instruments were designed with the specific objective of social fairness, they would have the catalytic power of kickstarting the asset-backed securities market, and it would require only a little more regulation to clarify or enhance the disclosure requirements of already existing disclosure regimes.

This paper comes in three parts. In part I, I define asset-backed securities operationally and in terms of the disclosures regimes of the US and EU. In part II, I re-examine the theory of disclosures à la Akerloff's classic Nobel Prize-winning 1970 paper on lemons and find an ironic twist to the theoretical tale. In part III, I present investor rights to disclosure in the context of before and after states of the world corresponding to the pre-default and post-default states of asset-backed securities, and ask if we can innovate better. In part III, I also show how the image of the pre- and post-credit crisis asymmetry requires the reassessment of the basal theory of infinitely complex financial instruments wrought by Arrow (1964) and Debreu (1959) as promoted by Sharpe (1995). Instead of following this normal financial-economic path, which I believe is intractable, I reduce the infinite complexity of the states of the world into a risk symmetric approach making use of translational and bilateral symmetries. This simple general framework generously points to solutions to the credit crisis. As a necessary preliminary, I provide operational and regulatory definitions of asset-backed securities and the rights of investors to disclosure therein.

---

[5] R Evans 'It Will Be Hard to Prove Issuer Fraud', *International Financial Law Review*, 22 April 2008, available at www.iflr.com/default.asp?Page=9&PUBID=263&ISS=24675&SID=705703&LS=EMS176061, stating 'more than 280 class actions were filed with federal courts in 2007 that relate to sub-prime'. See also JE Bethel, A Ferrell and G Hu, 'Legal and Economic Issues in Subprime Litigation', Harvard Law and Economics Discussion Paper No 612 (2008), for the types of claims made.

[6] See B Frank, 'FHA Housing Stabilization & Homeownership Retention Act' (13 March 2008), available at http://www.house.gov/frank/fha0308.html.

[7] For an explanation of the continuing illiquidity of triple-A CDO bonds despite their historical cheapness, see G Tett 'Why Triple A Prices Are Out of Sync with Fundamentals', *Financial Times*, 2 May 2008, 38.

[8] J Eatwell 'The Challenges Facing International Financial Regulation' in AK Dutt and J Ros (eds), *Development Economics and Structuralist Macroeconomics, Essays in Honour of Lance Taylor* (Cheltenham, Edward Elgar, 2003) 354.

B.   Definitions of Asset-backed Securities

1.   Operational and Regulatory Definitions of Asset-backed Securities

(a)   Operational Definition

In general, asset-backed securities finance or securitisation may be defined as the set of legal and financial techniques that transforms illiquid assets into tradable financial instruments. The practice of securitisation throughout the world, whether or not there are securities regulations governing their special purpose nature, is a multi-step procedure which requires:

1.   the recognition of the legal rights to assets that are, in effect, obligations of payment to an originator;
2.   the transfer of these legal rights to a clean, unencumbered legal vehicle in the form of either a trust or special-purpose corporate vehicle (SPV), the transfer of which achieves the legal effect of 'bankruptcy remoteness' from the credit risk of the originator; and
3.   the sale of the rights to the cash flows of the assets in the SPV to investors.

Securitisation is the process of transferring the title or the assignment of the rights to receivables to an SPV, which, in turn, sells notes to investors. The underlying assets which provide the basis for the cash flow to the asset-backed securities can be anything that can have legal title or be legitimately owned, but are usually of a homogeneous character formed by standard contracts, such as mortgages, credit card receivables, car loans and student loans.[9]

In its simplest diagrammatic form (see Figure 1), securitisation is normally portrayed in terms of the obligors forming the underlying assets to an originator, which in turn transfers the title or assigns the rights to the cash flows of the underlying assets to an SPV. The SPV, being bankruptcy remote from the originator, then issues tranches of securities that are bought by investors. The proceeds from the securities sales are then used to purchase the title or rights to the cash flows of the underlying assets.

Under US Regulation AB,[10] which governs all asset-backed securities disclosures in the US from 1 January 2006, all underlying assets to an asset-backed securities transaction must have a 'self-liquidating' character,[11] meaning that the underlying receivables convert into cash within a finite period of time,[12] and the definition does not include synthetic securitisations.[13] In sharp contrast, under EU law, asset-backed securities are not limited to self-liquidating assets but may even include open-investment-type funds, with

---

[9] See 'Debt Innovations' in JD Finnerty and DR Emery, *Debt Management: A Practitioner's Guide* (Boston MA, Harvard Business School Press, 2001); A Davidson, A Sanders, L-L Wolff and A Ching, *Securitization: Structuring and Investment Analysis* (Hoboken NJ, Wiley, 2003) (various types of asset-backed securities); 'Asset-Backed Securities: Final Rule', *Rules and Regulations*, 17 CFR parts 210, 228 ff (2005) 70(5) *Federal Register* 1506 (7 January 2005) (herein the Final Rule).

[10] 17 CFR §229.1100–23.

[11] US Regulation AB, §1101(c)(1).

[12] Ibid.

[13] Final Rule, 1514.

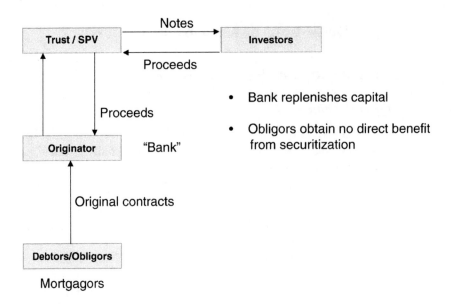

Figure 1. Simplified asset-backed securities transaction.

managers having discretion to select any type of asset,[14] and, by regulatory definition, include derivative and synthetic types of transactions.[15] Since the underlying assets are bundled together and their payment streams are assessed in a statistical manner, almost all securitisation transactions rely on the relative certainty of payment of a large group of obligors. Although there are large differences in disclosure between EU and US law, the common principle underlying both is that parties who have a significant interest in the transaction should be made to disclose their identity and their interests in the transaction in order to avoid any conflict of interest. This disclosure principle is also consistent with the principle of overcoming the information asymmetry that favours the seller.

(b)   Parties Responsible to Disclose or be Disclosed under EU Prospectus Regulation (PR)

Under EU law, the investor's rights to disclosure not only obligate the issuer-SPV[16] to provide disclosures, but also requires disclosures of all parties that have contributed to the prospectus, including any persons responsible for any information contained therein,[17] statutory auditors,[18] persons having direct or indirect ownership or control between the parties to the securitisation programme,[19] persons working within the issuer who have

---

[14] European Commission Regulation (EC) No 809/2004, Annex VIII, item 2.3; US Regulation AB, §1101(c)(2)(i) prohibits the 'depositor or the issuing entity' to become an 'investment company under the Investment Company Act of 1940 (15 USC 80a-1ff)' as a result of the asset-backed securities transaction.

[15] See EU Prospectus Regulation (PR), Art 2(5)(a) and (b); J Tanega 'Some Principles of Disclosure for Asset Backed Securities under the EU Prospectus Regulation' (2008) 23(6) *Journal of International Banking Law and Regulation* 294.

[16] See EU PR, Annex VII, items 4ff and US Regulation AB, §1101(f).

[17] EU PR, Annex VII, items 1.1 and 1.2.

[18] Ibid, 2.1.

[19] Ibid, 5.2.

duties outside of the issuer in administrative, management and supervisory bodies,[20] partners with unlimited liability,[21] major shareholders of the issuer,[22] names of governmental, legal or arbitration proceedings which may have a significant effect on the issuer,[23] third-party experts identified in the registration document,[24] and providers of undertakings or obligors.[25] This list may appear rather innocuous since it merely requires the identification of potential parties to the transaction, but from a risk symmetric analysis it tells us what the regulators think are the parties that pose an expected risk to the investor and, therefore, should be disclosed. Pre-credit crisis, this list is unexceptionable. However, post-credit crisis, we see that a major party underpinning the transaction, namely the obligor, is excluded from any benefits in the transaction. This fact forces us to re-evaluate the risk symmetric fairness of securitisation transactions.

(c) Parties Responsible to Disclose or be Disclosed under US Regulation AB

Under US law, specifically section 11(a) of the Securities Act of 1933, the person having the direct and primary liability to the investor for false disclosure or omission for a false registration statement is the issuer who signs the registration statement.[26] This general rule is further limited and specified by Regulation AB to include primarily the depositor[27] deemed as the 'issuer' and, therefore, primarily liable for any material misstatements or omissions.[28] Similar to the PR, Regulation AB requires that a number of 'transaction parties' be identified in the prospectus who may have indirect liability if the information which they provide is inaccurate or misleading. These parties include: the sponsor,[29] issuing entity,[30] trustee,[31] servicers and back-up servicers,[32] originator,[33] significant obligor,[34] providers of credit enhancement,[35] counter-parties to derivative instruments,[36] parties in legal proceedings against the sponsor, depositor, trustee, issuing entity or servicers,[37] parties representing other asset pools,[38] parties who prepared or provided reports,[39] affiliates or parties to related transactions,[40] and nationally recognised statistical rating organisations (credit rating agencies).[41] It is important to note that, whilst the number of transaction parties required to be disclosed under Regulation AB is explicitly larger than those required under the EU PR, the general language of the PR which refers to

---

[20] Ibid, 6.1(a).
[21] Ibid, 6.1(b).
[22] Ibid, 7.1.
[23] Ibid, 8.3.
[24] Ibid, 1 and 9.2.
[25] EU PR, Annex VIII, items 1.2, 2.2 and 2.2.11.
[26] See Securities Act of 1933, s 11(a) for persons liable for a false registration statement.
[27] US Regulation AB, §1106.
[28] See Final Rule, VI. Offerings of Asset-backed Securities, C signatures, 1618.
[29] US Regulation AB, §1104.
[30] Ibid, §1107.
[31] Ibid, §1109.
[32] Ibid, §1108(a)(1) and (2).
[33] Ibid, §1110.
[34] Ibid, §1112(a).
[35] Ibid, §1114(b)(1).
[36] Ibid, §1115.
[37] Ibid, §1117.
[38] Ibid, §1100(d)(1).
[39] Ibid, §1118.
[40] Ibid, §1119.
[41] Ibid, §1101(h).

parties who should be disclosed means that the issuer has a discretion to disclose trans-action parties that is wider than that found under Regulation AB. In the language of the PR, the issuer is 'entitled' to provide the appropriate set of disclosures.[42]

After the final prospectus is filed under US law, there are other disclosure reports, such as the Form 10-D for regular monthly reporting, Form 8-K for exceptional reporting, Form 10-K for annual reports and certification under section 302 of Sarbanes-Oxley, all of which must be signed by either the depositor or the servicer.[43] The rules regarding viola-tions of these particular securities regulations (except for section 302 of Sarbanes-Oxley, which is a matter of US Securities and Exchange Commission enforcement) may be actionable under section 12(a)(2) for private investors. And, if there are false communica-tions to the public that are actionable as fraud, then Rules 10b and 10b-5 under the Securities Exchange Act of 1934 are possible bases for liability. Given this panoply of remedies under the US securities law which could potentially 'open the floodgates' to litigation, it is not surprising that the US Supreme Court has recently interpreted the legal basis for class actions relating to securities fraud claims rather restrictively.[44]

(d)   Other Meaningful Differences in Disclosure Requirements

Although the EU entitles the issuer to use his discretion to ferret out disclosures which are relevant to the investor's ability to make an informed assessment,[45] there are simply too many categories of disclosure which are not defined well enough in comparison to US Regulation AB. For example, under the PR, the disclosure requirements for the structure of the asset-backed securities transaction is stated in just 13 words,[46] while under Regulation AB the disclosure requirements for the transaction structure[47] is stated in 1,551 words! This difference is so staggering for such an essential disclosure that one can only wonder whether the entire system of disclosures is being called into question. This difference cannot be explained plausibly in terms of a difference between principles-based versus rules-based approaches because both disclosure systems require disclosures to factual levels of specificity for the sake of investor protection. Ironically, Regulation AB is essentially disclosure by self-declaration[48] and, by its own internal logic, is much more principles-based than the PR, since it has a tightly defined legal concept of asset-backed securities with all the other requirements logically connected to the principled definition, while the PR has an extraordinarily broad definition of asset-backed securities for which there are lacunae of required expected risks.

One giant gap which can only be interpreted as a win for the powerful pro-issuers' lobby composed of European financial institutions to the detriment of the investors is the lack of any mandatory disclosures by the servicer. Although the definition of asset-backed securities includes the bare mention of the word 'servicing',[49] there is no explicit

---

[42] See EU PR, recital (5).

[43] Final Rule, 1526.

[44] *Tellabs Inc v Makor Issues & Rights Ltd* (United States Supreme Court, No 06-484, 21 June 2007), available at www.law.cornell.edu/supcrt/html/06-484.ZS.html; *Stoneridge Inv Partners LLC v Scientific-Atlanta Inc* (United States Supreme Court, No 06-43, 15 January 2008), available at www.law.cornell.edu/supcrt/html/06-43.ZS.html.

[45] Council Directive (EC) 2003/71, Art 5(1).

[46] EU PR, Annex VIII, item 3.1.

[47] Regulation AB, §1113.

[48] Final Rule, 1508, stating: 'We are adopting a principles-based definition of asset-backed security . . .'

[49] See EU PR, Art 2(5)(a) and (b) for the definition of asset-backed security.

requirement of disclosures relating to the servicer, leaving the matter to the discretion and morals, one supposes, of the enlightened issuer.

C.   Criteria for Judging Successful Solutions to the Credit Crisis

1.   Information Asymmetry Leads to Degrees of Emptiness

Akerloff's 1970 information asymmetry theory[50] sets out a rather rational and plausible argument for the justification of disclosures based on a world where individuals are Machiavellian, and can be used as a means for explaining why disclosures are required for securities transactions. I will, however, use it to explore the limits of investor rights to complex financial instruments and show how, by a cruel extension, it gives rise to both ever increasing complexity of financial instruments and ultimately market failure. Akerloff's argument about lemons comes in two parts. The first part has been woven into the fabric of information asymmetry analysis like a magical origination myth, while the second part is much ignored. Both parts sound too simple to be true, but, as we shall see, together they form what might be called 'logically complete and symmetric arguments' which are disturbingly persuasive if the premises are accepted.[51]

Since disclosures are at the heart of securities regulations[52] and are set to influence behaviour,[53] the purpose of disclosures in securities regulations, at least at the level of the initial public offering, is to mitigate the information advantage which issuer-sellers have over investor-buyers. As Akerloff[54] famously argued, markets in which the sellers have an information advantage have a temptation to sell and represent lower quality items as higher quality items to less informed buyers. Let us call this form of information asymmetry 'dysfunctional asymmetry'. As a consequence of this dysfunctional asymmetry, the lower quality goods will tend to drive out higher quality goods from the market. This, if iterated over time, will lead to an equilibrium where there is no trading at all or market failure where it becomes impossible for the participants to calculate the market value of the goods in question. Ironically, there is less chance of market collapse where the information advantage favours the buyer. Let us call this form of information asymmetry 'functional asymmetry'. Since the buyer will be able to assess the quality of the goods more accurately, the forces of supply and demand will prevail, and poor quality items will be seen for what they are and more accurate pricing will occur. That is, transactions will occur at prices distinguishing between lower level and higher quality goods.[55] Although

---

[50] G Akerloff, 'The Market for Lemons: Quality Uncertainty and The Market Mechanism' (1970) 84 *Quarterly Journal of Economics* 488.

[51] J Tanega, R Turkmenov and T Koroleva, 'Codeword STRIDE: Standard Risk Disclosure Environment' (IFC World Bank Group, November 2007) forthcoming, available from Andrey Milyutin, IFC, amilyutin@ifc.org.

[52] TL Hazen, *Treatise on the Law of Securities Regulations*, 4th edn (St Paul MN, West Group, 2002), 740, where the author states that 'federal securities law's exclusive focus is on full disclosure'.

[53] JR Brown Jr, 'Corporate Governance, the Securities Exchange Commission and the Limits of Disclosure', University of Denver Legal Studies Research Paper No 07-27 (2009), 48ff.

[54] Akerloff, above n 50.

[55] J Tanega, 'Securitization Disclosures and Compliance under Basel II: A Risk Based Approach to Economic Substance over Legal Form' (2005) 20 *Journal of International Banking Law and Regulation* 617.

scholars have called this latter situation information asymmetry in favour of the buyer, it would be more precise to say that the situation in which buyers and sellers transact is when they are in a state of risk symmetry.[56] That is, when their subjective perceptions of the risk for a given level of information are equivalent. Schwarz, in summarising the Akerlof solution to the 'lemons problem', states that it is 'it is up to the seller to achieve a solution to this problem of quality uncertainty' and 'one obvious solution is guaranties, such as warranties on the sale of goods, in order to shift the risk from the buyer to the seller'.[57] However, the lesson to be learned for the asset-backed securities markets is that mandatory disclosures by the seller help overcome dysfunctional asymmetry so long as such information is pertinent to the investor understanding the quality of the investment. A well-structured disclosure regime that aims at functional asymmetry therefore should reduce the risk of market failure since more accurately informed investors will be able to distinguish between lower and higher quality issues, encouraging market expansion.

It is important to note that Akerloff's information asymmetry idea was developed further by Stiglitz and Weiss in their pivotal paper focusing on the credit rationing behaviour of financial institutions in relation to risk-seeking and risk-averse borrowers.[58] Other researchers, such as Zywicki and Adamson, have used Stiglitz and Weiss to argue that financial innovations 'have ameliorated and in many cases even reversed the traditional information asymmetry to the point where today lenders have more information than borrowers about the borrower's ability to repay loans or the suitability of certain terms for certain borrowers.'[59]

We might think of the Akerloffian idea as three different states. In state 1 the information asymmetry favours the seller, so, if the buyer and seller iterate the trade, the market price falls to zero and the market collapses. In state 2 the information asymmetry favours the seller but there is a guarantee which the buyer accepts and pays for that completely covers any risk to the buyer. In state 3 the information asymmetry favours the buyer, which is the situation alluded to by Zywicki and Adamson (above), where the trade, if iterated, establishes a sustainable market price, never falling to zero. State 1 would appear to be the normal state of affairs and, if nothing more, predicts an inevitably gloomy market collapse. State 2 draws a picture of the world where the market continues so long as the guarantees are credible to the buyer. State 3 is relatively rare, where the expertise, experience and competence and inside knowledge of the buyer are superior to that of the seller. State 2 of Akerloff's argument may help explain the 'market expansion' of the ever increasing complexity of financial instruments towards market collapse, if not extinction. This is not an empirical argument so much as a logical one.

Consider dysfunctional asymmetry in relation to asset-backed securities. The underlying policies of securities regulations in both the US and the EU emphasise both

---

[56] Ibid.

[57] SL Schwarz, 'Rethinking the Disclosure paradigm in a World of Complexity' (2004) *University of Illinois Law Review* 25.

[58] JE Stiglitz and A Weiss, 'Credit Rationing in Markets with Imperfect Information' (1981) 71 *American Economics Review* 393.

[59] TJ Zywicki and JD Adamson, 'The Law & Economics of Subprime Lending', George Mason Law & Economics Research Paper No 08-17 (March 2008) 73, set out the arguments made by Engel and McCoy in KC Engel and PD McCoy, 'A Tale of Three Markets: The Law and Economics of Remedies for Predatory Lending' (2002) 80 *Texas Law Review* 1255 (separating mortgage markets into prime, legitimate sub-prime and predatory segments).

'investor protection'[60] and 'market confidence',[61] as well as 'financial innovation'.[62] There is no inherent limit to financial innovation. If we allow financial innovation to continue because of dysfunctional asymmetry, we are merely transferring the uncertainty from one party to another and asking for a guarantee. But then what is the nature of a financial instrument? Essentially, a financial instrument is an unfulfilled promise—and here is the fault of the Akerloffian analysis. Whilst we may swap real goods for money, if we swap what should be a payment for a financial instrument, all we are doing is emphasising the character of the unfulfilled promise. In somewhat metaphysical-sounding terms, we are merely swapping the empty promise for another empty promise. If we allow further guarantees, credit enhancements and liquidity support, as they are so elegantly allowed under US Regulation AB and the EU PR, we are actually allowing further and further degrees of emptiness.

Under the Akerloffian analysis of dysfunctional asymmetry, the credit substitution function is sufficient to stave off market collapse. However, this is simply not true. The substitution function allows greater and greater pressure of performance risks to build up since the reputational risk of each party can only be substituted for by the performance risk of another. As more transaction parties are required to fulfil the essential epistemo-logical gap—'guaranteeing the future', so to speak—the performance risk of the legally dependent financial instruments increases. If any of the parties in the credit substitution game have even a whiff of discredit, then the house of promises will fall precipitously, because, after all, they are all just paper, not goods. At the same time, the very complex financial instruments are hit the hardest because it was through the credit substitution mechanism that the financial instruments grew ever increasingly complex. The ever increasing complexity justified in the name of financial innovation was also justified under the pretext of meeting market demand. The just-so story told by the investment banking tribe is this: 'Ever increasingly complex financial instruments were necessary because there was huge market demand for them, otherwise they would not have grown.' Yes, market demand for instruments that linked and depended on the worth of other instruments so that their 'inherent risks' could be sliced, diced and distributed to others who believed that they would act like primary level stable financial instruments (triple A) used to purchase goods. In the period from September 2007 to April 2008 triple-A simply descended into untradable paper.[63] Pre-credit crisis, this type of ontological essentialist argument against the nominative nature of money and the essential emptiness of financial instruments would have been laughed out of court. But the world is different now. Faith in the signs, symbols, rites and rituals of the investment banking tribe have been shaken and stirred.

---

[60] See, EU PR, recital (41) and US Final Rule on Asset-backed Securities, 1515.
[61] EU PR, recital (41) and US Final Rule Asset-backed Securities, 1590–91.
[62] EU PR, recital (41); US Final Rule on 'capital formation', 1557 and 1591.
[63] M Mackenzie, '"Super-senior" CDO Investors Begin to Flex their Muscles', *Financial Times*, 15 April 2008, 15.

D.   Proposals to Change the Social Reality of the Credit Crisis

1.   A Social Reality of Disclosures Increases Noisy Complexity

Given the wide array of disclosures for asset-backed securities under EU and US securities regulations, it is important to keep in mind the reality amongst practitioners. The widely practised disclosure game is that, so long as the issuer does so in a manner that is not misleading or inaccurate, he is most likely absolved of any harm to the investor caused by the item so disclosed. Thus, the rule among the lawyers who intend to reduce their client's risk of liability rule for false disclosure is 'disclose if in doubt'. This means that in the US the issuing entity of any security has a strong incentive to disclose any material fact that verges on being relevant to the decision making of the investor. In the EU, the rule is similarly broad ranging, requiring the issuer to disclose any fact or any risk that has an impact on the investor's ability to make an informed assessment of the investment.[64] Although the US Final Rule on Asset-backed Securities repeatedly cautions against the urge to repeat the legal babble of boiler-plate provisions,[65] lawyers have no incentive but to do otherwise in order to protect their client-issuers from potential claims by investors that the disclosures were legally indefensible, that is, that the client-issuer had the chance to disclose, but did not do so.

Although the disclosure regime for asset-backed securities is very complex, there is a large body of literature defining and tracing the history of asset-backed securities as part of US legal practice, mostly on the 'cheerleading' side as Professor Kettering says,[66] but surprisingly little academic scrutiny of what the assumptions of securitisation mean to society. In order to partially redress the balance, consider Figure 2.

In Figure 2 are presented two states of the world, with pre-default on the left-hand side and post-default on the right-hand side, and a population pyramid, with the taxpayers representing the base of the population and homeowners who have mortgages as obligors representing a smaller part of the taxpaying population. At the top of the triangle are CEOs, investment banks and commercial banks, which comprise a tiny fraction of the population, representing the community who thrive on the trading of complex financial instruments. The tribe represents not only investment bankers per se, but also all those whose businesses depend on the primary production of complex financial instruments, generally known as the primary markets, and the trading of these instruments, known as the secondary market. The list of transaction parties under Regulation AB outlined above corresponds roughly to the main functional parties involved in the primary production of asset-backed securities. Identifying all the characters is not important for our purposes. The important point of the figure is that it shows how the money pumped from the homeowners up to the banks allowed banks to have an accelerated replenishable supply of cash to lend, with fees earned by all the various parties involved in the transaction.

---

[64] EU PR, Art 5(1).
[65] Final Rule, 1509.
[66] KC Kettering, 'Securitization and Its Discontents, The Dynamics of Financial Product Development' (draft, 12 September 2007) 5, ssrn.com/abstract=1012937.

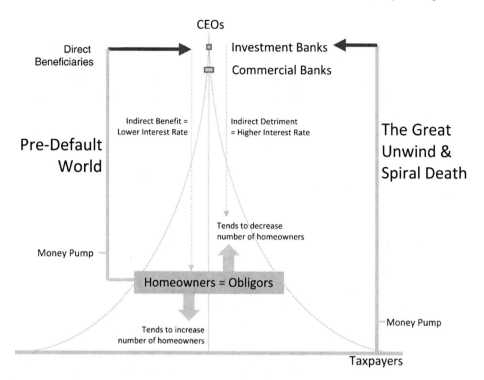

Figure 2. The logic of the pre-default versus post-default world.

In brief, from the early 1980s, with a surge in growth in the late 1990s and again from 2002 to 2007, many trillions of dollars worth of asset-backed securities were manufactured with many thousands of bankers or financiers making many tens of billions in fees. Kettering quotes a figure of $3.6 trillion as the aggregate outstanding value of securitisation in the US for 2006.[67] So much cash being made available provided an indirect benefit to homeowners by increasing the amount of funds available for lending and thus contributing to the lowering of interest rates to the homeowners. In this virtuous pre-default world, securitisation allowed more money to circulate, significantly increasing the prospect of homeownership via mortgages to millions of people in the US and other jurisdictions where RMBS took hold.

When securitisation fails, this virtuous circulation comes to an almost dead stop. Where, before, hundreds of billions of dollars worth of asset-backed securities per year were being pumped out, as of late August 2008, there were hardly any issues in private label residential mortgage-backed securities while government-chartered mortgage finance in the US accounted for about 90% of the market by the end of 2007.[68] Structured finance products, especially collateralised debt obligations (CDOs), which were created with mortgage-backed securities as their underlyings, have seen massive losses with Standard & Poor announcing more than 4,000 downgrades in 2008, or '90 per cent of all

---

[67] Ibid 4–5, citing Board of Governors of the Federal Reserve System, 'Federal Reserve Statistical Release Z.1: Flow of Funds Accounts of the United States, Flows and Outstandings, Fourth Quarter 2006' (8 March 2007) 79 (table L.126), available at www.federalreserve.gov/releases/z1/.

[68] S Scholtes, 'Fannie and Freddie Drive Home Loans' *Financial Times*, 2 April 2008.

downgrades issued to CDOs', with recovery rates for single-A or lower likely to be zero, and for double-A 5% at best.[69] Although many of the top banks have reported billions or tens of billions of dollars worth of loss,[70] the reported figures themselves are susceptible to vast miscomprehension, confusion and incredulity because the standard accounting principles for the determination of fair value of complex financial instruments appear to be unable to provide a reasonable rule for the determination of their value.[71] The headline numbers generated by the 'authorities' include the OECD estimate that the sub-prime debacle will cost approximately $420 billion,[72] the IMF estimate of the fallout from the sub-prime mortgage crisis at $945 billion,[73] and one of the gloomiest predictions from Professor Roubini, not to be outdone by anyone, estimating the loss at about $3 trillion, roughly 20% of the US's GDP.[74]

From one perspective, mainly the investors who believed that they had bought 'cash-like' tradable financial instruments, this is a terrible loss. From another, this is a terribly good opportunity to make a fortune.[75] The anecdotal evidence is that, at the start of the Great Unwind in August 2007, members of the investment banking tribe were in denial and said that the market would come back in a few months or a few years. As of March 2009, with the announcements of thousands of redundancies, there is no more talk about the market for asset-backed securities returning so soon, and much more grimness about selling asset-backed securities portfolios at a fraction of their original price.[76]

Returning to Figure 2, the arrow marked as 'The Great Unwind and Spiral Death' shows that taxpayers' money is being through government intervention used to help stem the losses. There are a number of policy mechanisms which the central banks, and especially the US Fed, has used to try to kickstart the asset-backed securities market, especially the RMBS market, such as allowing investment banks to put up AAA-rated mortgage-backed securities as collateral for 3-month US treasury paper to the Fed. A similar operation was begun in the UK as per a 24 April 2008 announcement by the government, whereby £50 billion worth of UK gilts is borrowable with AAA-rated mortgage-backed securities as collateral. Howard Davies, former Chairman of the Financial Services Authority, likens this game to that of putting 'dead mice' at the central bank's counter and getting 'hard cash'.[77] The US experience so far has been for the government to technically 'lend' support rather than purchasing out-and-out the ownership of the asset-backed securities notes in question. As the taxpayers' money is put at risk to support the market and give it confidence that the major financial institutions will not fall, other areas of the financial system are put at risk. For example, with the continued stagnation of the money market, institutions are wary of counter-party credit risk, the risk of insolvency and the reputational risk of banks or funds being trapped without sufficient liquidity to meet their obligations

[69] PJ Davies, 'S&P Delivers Blow to CDOs', *Financial Times*, 29 April 2008, 39.

[70] K Guha, 'IMF Points to High Cost of Global Credit Crisis' *Financial Times*, 8 April 2008.

[71] International Accounting Standards Board, 'Reducing Complexity in Financial Reporting', Discussion Paper (March 2008), available at www.iasb.org/NR/rdonlyres/A2534626-8D62-4B42-BE12-E3D14C15AD29/0/DPReducingComplexity_ReportingFinancialInstruments.pdf; D Tweedie, 'Solutions now Sought to Add Transparency' *Financial Times*, 20 March 2008.

[72] D Strauss, 'OECD Predicts Sub-prime Loss of £450bn', *Financial Times*, 16 April 2008.

[73] Guha, above n 70.

[74] M Wolf, 'A Rising Auction of Scary Scenarios', *Financial Times*, 11 March 2008.

[75] A Gangahar and H Sender, 'John Paulson Sub-prime Bet Pays $3.7bn', *Financial Times*, 16 April 2008.

[76] F Guerrera, B White and H Sender, 'Banks under Pressure to Follow $30 bn Merrill Cut Price Debt', *Financial Times*, 30 July 2008.

[77] H Davies, 'Sharks Circle Paulson's Aussie Plan', *Financial Times*, 1 April 2008, available at www.ft.com.

when due. Given that UBS's loss relating to sub-prime residential mortgages for the year 2007was $18.7 billion, as reported in an extremely revealing 'Shareholder Report on UBS's Write-Downs'[78] dated 18 April 2008, one can only wonder how exposed investors in investment banks and investors in asset-backed securities must feel when only £50 billion (approximately $100 billion) of UK taxpayers' money is offered to stem the tide. In this rumbling mess, a few traders and funds speculating on the failure of financial institutions and the market have made fortunes in short-selling.[79] The appreciable asymmetry between the pre-default world and the Great Unwind is that homeowners, as the long-suffering obligors, have lost because of higher lending rates and higher foreclosure rates. And, most importantly, beyond the homeowners the entire society is at risk, with the genuine worry of government actions which take options on moral hazard and stoke inflation by allowing the good money of the taxpayer to be traded for the bad money of the asset-backed securities.

To put the matter in risk symmetries terms, the pattern of trades and the flow of risks from one segment of society to another is asymmetric between the pre-default and post-default world states. For purposes of simplification, the essential pattern in risk symmetric terms for Figure 1 is symbolised in Figure 3.

This childish picture serves to remind us that the flow of funds, the actual trades, concerning a complex financial instrument, such as an asset back security, are limited to transaction parties and the expected risks of the transaction are not captured symmetrically in the post-default state since the taxpayers' funds are implicated in the post-default state of the world. In the post-default state, where the transactions are 'unwinding' and where there are insufficient cash flows to make good the promises made on the contracts, more actors and agents are involved than those explicitly stated in the prospectus or transaction documents. This is symbolised by the larger square on the right. In a strong sense, financial instruments which pose this sort of risk asymmetry are unfair to societies in which they are unfair to the investors since (i) the parties to the original transaction,

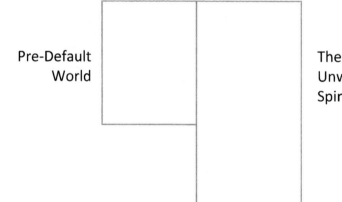

Figure 3. Asymmetry between pre-default and post-default world states.

[78] UBS, 'Shareholder Report on UBS's Write-Downs' (18 April 2008), available at www.ubs.com/1/ShowMedia/investors/topics?contentId=140333&name=080418ShareholderReport.pdf.

[79] Gangahar and Sender, above n 75.

especially the investors, are not apprised of the specific extreme tail-end risks[80] and (ii) the external or social parties, ie the taxpayers, are not beneficiaries to the risk taking generated by the original transaction. Kettering, after reviewing the major scholarship critiquing securitisation in the pre-default era, has argued persuasively that the 'prototypical securitisation structure has no purpose, and no significant effect, other than to circumvent the burdens that the Bankruptcy Code places on the lender of a simple secured loan to an Originator who has gone bankrupt'.[81]

Kettering's argument is about how the securitisation structure is against the fundamental rights to reapportion debt that is regulated by the Federal government, and therefore by society in general. This is a normative legal argument pre-credit crisis. However, post-credit crisis, Kettering's argument does not go far enough, because securitisation does not merely deny 'bankruptcy tax' but, in crisis, when the conditions of the securitisation are required to be read and used to distribute allocations of cash flow, the parties required ultimately to foot the bill are the taxpayers. The asset-backed securities are sufficiently complex so as to require the entire society in the jurisdiction where the issuer has failed to provide sufficient cash flow to fill the shortfall, which is arguably 100% of the transaction value. The contention that asset-backed securities are just too big to fail is simply another expression for the asymmetry between the pre-default and post-default worlds.

The question arises, is it possible to design complex financial instruments which are more socially fair and more risk symmetric? Before answering this question, let us dip once again into the deep theory of financial innovation.

2.   A Digression into the Nuclear Financial Economics of Financial Alchemy

Sharpe, in a pivotal article entitled 'Nuclear Financial Economics',[82] describes the nuclear foundations of financial economics alluding to Arrow[83] and Debreu.[84] It is important to note that standard finance theory and much of financial engineering is based implicitly on Arrow and Debreu's fundamental idea of an infinitely divisible contingent world, with the financial economic definition of a financial instrument, as being the set of all conditions of the world at time 1 being the same at time 2 except for the one condition of payment or the fulfilment of a particular determinable condition, meaning that any and all financial instruments can describe any and all states of the world. The fascinating theoretical assertion is that, between time 1 and time 2, the only other condition of this model is that the world be absolutely unchanged. Thus, simply because we can describe a particular state of the world at time 1 as having a particular set of rights over the world embedded

---

[80] It is arguable that they are 'apprised' in the sense that the documentation defines various types of default. However, prior to the credit crisis it would have been very difficult to comprehend, let alone believe, that triple-A asset-backed securities would become illiquid. Anecdotal evidence suggests that fund managers who called the market correctly during the credit crisis failed to make the appropriate hedges by buying triple-A paper.

[81] Kettering, above n 66, 8.

[82] WF Sharpe, 'Nuclear Financial Economics' in WH Beaver and G Parker (eds), *Risk Management Problems & Solutions* (New York, McGraw-Hill, 1995) 17.

[83] KJ Arrow, 'The Role of Securities in the Optimal Allocation of Risk-bearing' (1964) 31 *The Review of Economic Studies* 91.

[84] G Debreu, *The Cowles Foundation Monograph 17. Theory of Value: an Axiomatic Analysis of Economic Equilibrium* (New Haven, Yale University Press, 1959).

within a particular financial contract means that, so long as there are no 'discontinuities', financial contracts can define well the state of the world from time 1 to time 2. The consequence of these deep ideas is that financial innovation (ie the construction of new financial instruments) moves irrevocably towards an ever more complete coverage of the infinite contingent states of the world—the movement of which is called market completion.[85]

Against this theoretical background of an infinitely dynamic growth towards market completion with ever increasing complexity of financial instruments to meet particularly unique conditions of the contingent world we have the counterfact of the failure of complex financial instruments in the time of the Great Unwind.[86] We can think of the premises of the Arrow and Debreu model as being either true or false in relation to the post-credit crisis world. If the Arrow and Debreu model were incorrect, then we would not have a movement towards complete markets. However, this is contradicted by the facts in the Great Unwind because there were short-sellers in the derivative markets that allowed individuals to take positions on credit collapse. Assuming that the Arrow and Debreu model is fundamentally correct, how was it possible for the Great Unwind to occur? And is there a way for us to remove the bind of Akerloff's dysfunctional asymmetry that results in the accumulation of worthless paper? Put another way, is there a way of formulating complex financial instruments that can avoid the asymmetry of the pre-default and post-default worlds?

Clearly, one of the major shortcomings of a purely financial theory relating to financial contracts is that it tends to ignore totally the risk transmission of 'failed bargains', that is, of the translation of financial risk into the realm of law, remedies and litigation. Perhaps one other assumption should be added to the Arrow and Debreu model, and that is that any and all financial contracts, while they may fully describe any particular state of the contingent world in time 1, at time 2 when the explicitly defined contractual pay-off should occur but does not, then a time 3 occurs which requires the contract to be interpreted in an entirely different world called the law where contingencies are not infinite, but rather reducible to explicitly stated rights with their attendant judicial remedies. In the legal world, the financial contracts are no longer bilaterally symmetric and determinable, but rather are trilaterally symmetric in relation to judicial interpretation. The decision of value which the market cannot take in the credit crisis is taken for them in the court of law. The before and after picture of the world of securitisation in Figure 3 tells us that there is a major asymmetry between the distribution of benefits and the accumulation of risks amongst the population. One of the fundamental questions relating to investor rights within this framework is: 'Were investors properly informed of the asymmetric risks of securitisation?' Again, pointing to the paradox of the Arrow and Debreu model, while the financial contract at time 1 may have defined, or rather willed, the world to be within a particular contingent frame, by time 2 the world had changed in a completely unanticipated manner. Should investors be able to claim any rights for failure to disclose exactly that which was not anticipated?

---

[85] Sharpe, above n 82, 18–19.

[86] John Plender, 'The Return of the State: How Government is Back at the Heart of Economic Life', *Financial Times*, 22 August 2008, quoting Paul Volcker: 'Simply stated, the bright new financial system—for all its talented participants, for all its rich rewards—has failed the test of the market place.'

3.   Constructing Socially Just Complex Financial Instruments

Taking account of the above, that is, the disclosure requirements for asset-backed securities, the investor rights to these disclosures, the dangers of the information asymmetry of Akerloff, and the potential to capture any particular condition of the world through complex financial instruments based on the nuclear financial economics of Sharpe, Arrow and Debreu, is it possible to design a socially fair complex financial instrument? For our purposes, a socially fair transaction is one in which two conditions are fulfilled: (i) that the parties to the original transaction anticipate the expected risks to the transaction and agree to share the risks and rewards of such a transaction; and (ii) that exogenous parties, such as the taxpayers through government agents, are not required to rejig the risks allocated by the parties. Although this sounds like an extraordinarily complex problem, according to a risk symmetries approach, the range of solutions to this problem would simply be something requiring the shape in Figure 4, as per the symbolism of Figure 3.

Again, as before in explaining Figure 3, Figure 4 looks like a childish and inane picture of possibly exceedingly complex financial instruments and their markets across two periods of time, pre-default and post-default. In Figure 4, the two boxes are indicative of the circulation of cash flows and the risks, coming to and going from the same parties as set out in the original transaction. Nirvana would be to not have the taxpayer burdened with any residual risk in the post-default period. There is a strange message from this picture about the securitisation states of the world, because the right-hand box should represent the post-default world as not asymmetric to the pre-default world.[87] How is this possible?

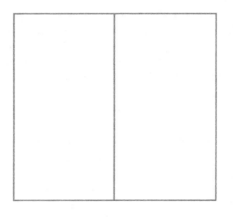

Fair Transactions Over Time

=

The Bilaterally and Translationally Risk Symmetric Worlds

Figure 4. Risk symmetric transaction.

---

[87] Technically, under a risk symmetries theory, the partition between the 'past' and 'future' states of the original set of contracts is equivalent in the sense that any and all conditions relating to their full performance are reflected continuously throughout the lifetime of the entire transaction. This is a definition of the existence of the legal relations embedded within the set of contracts and not about the value of the contracts which can flux over time.

It is possible because the cash flows (rewards) and the entirety of the risks are shared by all the parties to the transaction. Recall, one of the odd asymmetries of the prototypical mortgage-backed securitisation structure is that the obligors are long suffering and continue to pay for their mortgages until a long-dated maturity of 20 or 25 years. They receive only an indirect benefit in the pre-default world of generally lower market interest rates, but no explicit direct benefits from the securitisation transaction. This is despite the fact that all the other parties to the transaction are expected to make profits from the collective payments of the obligors through time.

A fairer and therefore risk symmetric securitisation programme would be for the obligors to be given a tranche in their favour. I together with a few colleagues who prefer to remain anonymous[88] but may be said to be highly experienced professionals in structuring mortgage-backed securities, have generated a simple model of a four-tranche mortgage-backed security. Tranches are the notes that are normally structured for the purpose of satisfying the particular interests of particular institutional investors' demands. If this model were applied to, say, the Northern Rock situation, where the UK government has, say, a mortgage book of £100 billion, our model would require that the government merely be at risk for half the amount of the coupon for the life of the notes. The additional major benefits of this structure include: (i) the obligors would benefit from pre-payment risk; (ii) the obligors would have an incentive to remain good payors and be given an incentive to pay down their principal balance; and (iii) investors would have objectively less risk of obligors defaulting. Since this model has not been road-tested, we can only say that it exists as a theoretical possibility that is close to achieving the risk symmetry symbolised in Figure 4. Figure 4 and its risk symmetric implications should be taken rather seriously since there are now a number of proposals by well-intentioned regulators and fervent politicians who believe that some kind of new regulations in the area of mortgage origination and government-sponsored programmes are required. According to the risk symmetric analysis, these new proposals should be measured against risk symmetric principles and outcomes.

4.   Credit Reconstruction: Risk Symmetric Solutions to the Credit Crisis

Since 2008 there have been a number of government interventions (for example, in the US, the Emergency Economic Stabilization Act of 2008, including 'Title I: Troubled Assets Relief Program' (TARP), signed by President Obama on 3 October 2008, and the Term Asset-Backed Securities Loan Facility (TALF), [89] which is a $1 trillion funding facility for newly initiated asset-backed securities;[90] in the UK, the government purchase of majority

---

[88] See my blog on 'New Plain Vanilla'; for access, contact me at joetanega@gmail.com.

[89] Board of Governors of the New York Federal Reserve press release, 25 November 2008, available at www.federalreserve.gov/newsevents/press/monetary/20081125a.htm. The original terms and conditions of the TALF programme are available at www.federalreserve.gov/newsevents/press/monetary/monetary 20081125a1.pdf.

[90] V Bajaj, 'US Tries a Trillion-dollar Key for Locked Lending', *New York Times*, 19 February 2009, available at www.nytimes.com/2009/02/20/business/20lend.html?_r=1, where it was reported that the US Treasury will provide $20 billion and the US Federal Reserve will provide $180 billion. The Treasury Secretary Timothy F Geithner is reported to have said that the Treasury could increase its commitment to $100 billion to allow the US Federal Reserve to lend up to $1 trillion.

stake in RBS[91] and in Lloyds Banking Group[92]) and precipitous exits of financial institutions (the biggest of which was Lehman Brothers[93]) which have aimed at recapitalising the banking sector and parts of the insurance sector. Illiquidity has turned into fears of insolvency, which in turn has resulted in a form of dictatorial finance. The Great Unwind of financial contracts has become nearly synonymous with the image of Spiral Death, where the original manifestation of risk in the asset-backed securities markets has raised doubts about the credit quality of financial institutions, which in turn have caused them to attempt to raise cash to meet their tier 1 capital requirements and where small community banks (defined as having assets of less than $1 billion) have seen drops in their investment portfolios breaching their regulatory capital requirements and forcing them into bankruptcy. This danger is an accelerating cycle of payment failure running rampant throughout the global economy, ie a full-blown depression, 1930s style. From the bursting of the complex financial instruments bubble to the manifestation of liquidity risk to credit risk and, finally, to bankruptcy and liquidation, these actualised risks have deeply affected all sectors of the US[94] and UK[95] economies. In response, the US and UK governments have propounded 'quantitative easing'[96] with an unease that reflects dreaded associations with the Weimar Republic, Zimbagwe and Argentina, which in effect means printing money rather than selling bonds. At the same time, because so much paper is expected to be issued in the form of corporate and government-backed bonds (over $2,000 billion estimated alone in government bonds for 2009[97]), there is a genuine risk of massive failure to raise sufficient capital for both the corporate and government sectors. It is not difficult to see a direct parallel to the freezing of credit leading to the Great Depression driven by the failure of equity speculation in 1929. This time, instead of equities being overleveraged

[91] J Werdigier, 'UK Takes Over Royal Bank of Scotland', *New York Times*, 28 November 2008, available at www.nytimes.com/2008/11/28/business/worldbusiness/28iht-rbs.4.18232236.html; J Treanor, 'RBS Record Losses Raise Prospect of 95% State Ownership', *The Guardian*, 26 February 2009, available at www.guardian.co.uk/business/2009/feb/26/rbs-record-loss.

[92] J Treanor and N Mathiason, 'Government Takes Over Lloyds', *The Guardian*, 7 March 2009, available at http://www.guardian.co.uk/business/2009/mar/07/government-takes-over-lloyds.

[93] AR Sorkin, 'Lehman Files Bankruptcy; Merrill Is Sold', *New York Times*, 14 September 2009, available at www.nytimes.com/2008/09/15/business/15lehman.html; M Wise and S Butler, 'Lehman Brothers Press Release' (15 September 2008), available at www.lehman.com/press/pdf_2008/091508_lbhi_chapter11_announce.pdf, announcing Lehman Brothers' intention to file petition under Chapter 11 of the US Bankruptcy Code with the US Bankruptcy Court for the Southern District of New York.

[94] S Foley, 'Credit Crisis Finally Hits The Real Economy in US', *The Independent*, 9 October 2008, available at www.independent.co.uk/news/business/news/credit-crisis-finally-hits-the-real-economy-in-us-955512.html.

[95] G Gilmore and G Duncan, 'Credit Crisis: The Cracks are Opening in UK's Debt Mountain, The Buy Today and Worry Tomorrow Culture that Has Gripped the Nation in Recent Years Threatens to Make UK Households Particularly Sensitive to the Global Credit Crisis', *Business Times*, 19 March 2008, available at http://business.timesonline.co.uk/tol/business/industry_sectors/banking_and_finance/article3579142.ece.

[96] For a good definition of quantitative easing, see L Elliott, 'Quantitative Easing', *The Guardian*, 8 January 2009, available at www.guardian.co.uk/business/2008/oct/14/businessglossary. Elliott states the straightforward effects of quantitative easing policy as follows: 'Under this policy, the authorities buy up bonds either from banks or from the commercial sector. There are two potential benefits. The first is that the banks get cash in exchange for the gilts they sell back to the government and the increase in the money supply leads to an increased volume of lending.

The second is that decreasing the supply of gilts pushes up their price. When gilt prices go up, gilt yields go down and it is gilt yields that determine long-term interest rates for overdrafts, some fixed-rate mortgage products and most business lending. This policy was first tried in the 1930s and has been dusted off by the Federal Reserve, America's central bank, in an attempt to get the US economy moving again.'

[97] D Oakley, 'German 10-year Bund Auction Fails for Second Successive Time', *Financial Times*, 12 February 2009.

by individual investors, asset-backed securities manufactured to meet the specific demands of institutional investors have become the pump for mass financial destruction.

As of the end of January 2009, the actions of the US government in response to the continuing and deepening financial crisis have been characterised by a series of 'deals' in the fashion of former investment bankers[98] who have not acted for the long-term financial security and stability of the nation but rather in the manner of changing tack whenever they think they can get a better deal by doing exactly the opposite of what was promised before. Note, for example, the US Treasury Secretary Henry Paulson's blunt, unapologetic refusal to apply the main purpose of TARP, which is to clean up the housing, mortgage and mortgage-related industry, six weeks after its official enactment (between 3 October 2008 and 14 November 2008).[99] We do not criticise the then US Treasury Secretary's about face, which was probably heavily influenced by British Prime Minister Brown's international lead to 'recapitalise' major banks with taxpayers' money,[100] but rather theorise that the way out of the credit crisis is something altogether different from what the former US Treasury Secretary and the Prime Minister envisaged as solutions to the credit crisis. Our general theory on how to get out of the credit crisis is also very different from what President Obama and his economic team are proposing as desperate measures to reinflate the US economy with a fiscal stimulus package of $787 billion.[101]

Our proposed solution set, or solution space, as it were, requires us to imagine a world where legal relations inform value and where values may be set by referring to what we term 'legal certainties'. This would include risk symmetric solutions such as that proposed by Thomas Hoenig, president of the Federal Reserve Bank of Kansas City, which 'require firms seeking government assistance to make the taxpayer senior to all shareholders, with the government determining the circumstances for managers and directors'.[102] From a risk symmetric perspective, as Figure 2 tells us, since taxpayers must bear the ultimate risk burden during the period of the Great Unwind, they should be compensated and deemed to have the appropriate risk and return above and beyond that of the shareholders. Moreover, the current pattern of events in terms of government actions in response to the credit crisis could be translated into risk symmetric terms. Through all the accidental details which have absorbed the market players since the beginning of the credit crisis, the government and the markets react and counter-react according to some fairly simple premises (see Figure 5).

---

[98] SM Davidoff and DT Zaring, 'Big Deal, The Government's Response to the Financial Crisis' (24 November 2008), available at http://papers.ssrn.com/sol3/papers.cfm?abstract_id=1306342.

[99] 'Hank Paulson's Latest Response to the Financial Crisis, More Rabbits from the Hat', *The Economist*, 13 November 2008, available at www.economist.com/world/unitedstates/displaystory.cfm?story_id=12597500, stating, 'The [$700 billion TARP] programme passed [ie through Congress and signed by the President on October 3, 2008] but then America's mortgage crisis had become a global panic, dragging down banks and infecting all sorts of debt. No one seemed to care that in a few months the Treasury would be relieving banks of the mortgages that had started all the trouble. So on Wednesday November 12th Mr Paulson unceremoniously buried the idea. Instead he will devote the TARP to recapitalising banks and non-bank financial institutions such as financing arms of America's big car companies (though not, for now, the carmakers themselves). He also disclosed that the Treasury and the Federal Reserve are exploring the creation of a 'liquidity facility' to buy top-rated securities backed by credit-card, car, and student loans, and perhaps mortgages.' This liquidity facility would later be announced on 23 November 2008 as TALF.

[100] N Morris, 'Brown Has a "Good" Crisis as World Follows his Lead', *The Independent*, 13 October 2008, available at www.independent.co.uk/news/uk/politics/brown-has-a-good-crisis-as-world-follows-his-lead-959291.html.

[101] President Obama signed the American Recovery and Reinvestment Act of 2009 on 17 February 2009. The official text can be found at www.opencongress.org/bill/111-h1/text.

[102] T Hoenig, 'Troubled Banks Must Be Allowed a Way to Fail', *Financial Times*, 4 May 2009, 11.

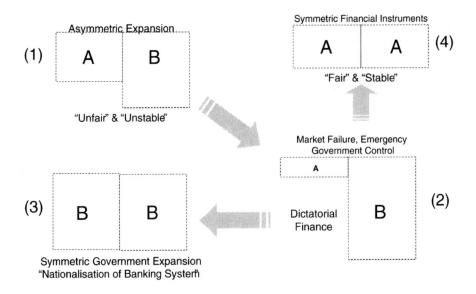

Figure 5. Risk symmetric pathways.

In Figure 5, the diagram in the left top corner recalls the risk symmetries of the pre-default and the Great Unwind which show a world that is both unfair in terms of meeting individual expectations and unstable in terms of global consequences. From this risk asymmetry, there can be an emphasis or exaggeration of the asymmetry such that the 'fair' contracts that are risk symmetric are reduced (represented by the shrinkage of the box marked A in the figure) while there is a concomitant increase in the box marked B, which represents market failure and consequent emergency government control (as in the enactment of TARP in the US or the purchase of financial institution shares). These acts of reduced contractual certainty and enlarged government control are a form of dictatorial finance, in the sense that market mechanisms are replaced by the command-and-control of a central government. Now, under a risk symmetries theory, where risk tends to be 'symmetrised' over time so that the pattern of law and finance phenomena are replicated through time (a form of translational symmetry of risks), we either have a symmetric expansion of government interventions, as in the nationalisation of the banking system, or an expansion of symmetric financial instruments that are fair to individuals and promote financial stability; these instruments would be, for example (as suggested above), in the form of financial innovations aimed at social fairness.

Currently, the governments on both sides of the Atlantic are focused on fighting recession by quantitative easing[103] (code words for the perilous policy of printing money and diplomatic spin for what is exactly to be avoided, which is the destruction of the value of currency[104]). One of the suggestions on the table but not yet enacted in any nation state is the establishment of a 'bad bank', which would resolve to hold and possibly restructure the 'toxic assets' so that they can be sold to long-term investors. The bad bank solution is not likely to be a genuine solution unless it can answer one fundamental question: 'what is

---

[103] See above n 97.

[104] For an especially robust exposure of the effect of quantitative easing, see E Chancellor, 'Beware the Bank of England's Monetary Con Trick', *Financial Times*, 16 March 2009, 13.

the value of the so-called toxic assets?' We can only guess what the final nature of this waste-management-to-recycling institution might be. However, the deep irony of this potential solution is that the investors are either completely new investors or old investors. If they are the latter, then they will more or less fit the profile of the investors in the original financial instruments of the credit crisis—that is, pension funds and insurance companies and other long-term investors looking for value on their long-term portfolios. If they are new investors, then either they fit the profile of the old investors of the original instruments or they are intermediaries, which means they will have the risk-and-return characteristics of the old investment banks. In a very strong sense, the very same class of participants to the securitisation transaction which we described in Part I are exactly the same in any so-called 'new' version of securitisation. *Rien plus change...ou non?*

5. Finale: The Long Term Value of Legal Certainties

One of the deepest problems of the credit crisis is that of value. What is the value of the toxic assets? There are two distinctions which we would like to insert in this debate, and one final solution, which comes from recognising a legal tradition that in many ways is substantively superior to the suggestions posed within the confines of economic mechanics. First, the pattern of long-term value is preserved by laws which have been passed on from generation to generation, which we dub as 'legal certainties'. Secondly, these legal certainties need to be understood in translationally symmetric terms and are renewed, rejuvenated and protected by acts which entail bilateral symmetry (individual and social contracts, as well as by the accepted opinions of the judiciary). For those familiar with symmetry theory, they will recognise the resonance to isometries, where the concept of distance is preserved by translational symmetry, which in turn is composed of bilateral symmetries. For now, let us analogise to a kind of legal distance or legal space where initial certainties are preserved over time and space by individual acts of bilateral symmetry (ie contracts, judicial opinions and legislation[105]) (see Figure 6).

Consider, for example, the ancient right of redemption, which is said to be an inseparable mortgagor's right in the mortgage. The first case cited for the proposition is *Master and Fellows of Emanuel College, Cambridge v Evans*.[106] Halsbury's states:

> From early times, the courts of equity held that until foreclosure by order of the court the mortgagor, by applying within a reasonable time and offering to pay principal and interest and all proper costs, might redeem the estate forfeited at law.[107]

Further, 'any provision inserted in the mortgage to prevent redemption on payment of the debt or performance of the obligation for which the security was given is termed a clog or fetter on the equity of redemption, and is void'.[108] The case law that developed these doctrines was crystallised in the nineteenth century. The right of redemption was a property right that could be sold. And it was a right that

---

[105] Obviously, contracts are bilaterally symmetric with offeror and offeree. Judicial opinions and legislation are bilaterally symmetric in the sense that such opinions and laws are agreed many times by many individuals in a personal one-to-one fashion.

[106] (1625) 1 Rep Ch 18.

[107] 'Mortgagor's Equity of Redemption', *Halsbury's Laws of England*, 4th edn (London, Butterworths, 1999) vol 32, para 307.

[108] Ibid.

The Mortgagor Liberty Act

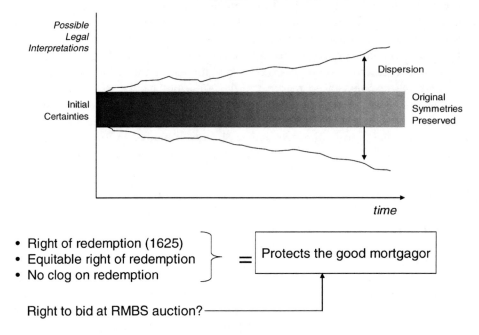

Figure 6. **Translational symmetry of The Mortgagor Liberty Act.**

continues unless and until, by judgment for foreclosure or, in the case of a mortgage of land where the mortgagee is in possession, by the running of time, the mortgagor's title is extinguished or his interest is destroyed by sale either under the process of the court or of a power in the mortgage incident to the security".[109]

Thus, in a recent case, *Horsham Properties*,[110] a power of sale was utilised by the mortgagee when a mortgagor failed to make two payments and the mortgagor was subsequently evicted. However, if the mortgagor is current on all payments, that is, a good mortgagor, then common law appears to be saying that the right of redemption continues until the mortgagor discharges his obligations. We can therefore argue by analogy that the sacrosanct right of redemption in modern twenty-first-century terms translates into the legal power to discharge the full value of the mortgagor's obligation. By this reasoning, the mortgagor should have the right to bid up to the value of his obligation in any auction involving his mortgage.

Our final solution to the credit crisis is to recognise the ancient right of redemption, which confers value on the performance of the good mortgagor. This final solution is actually a fundamental legal certainty that has broad implications on the valuation of asset-backed securities. To make this clear, consider the risk symmetric analysis of TARP in Figure 7.

[109] Ibid.
[110] [2008] WEHC 2327 (Ch).

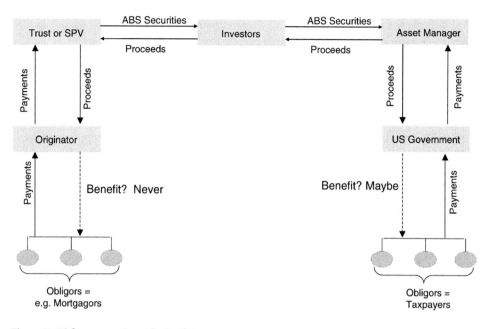

Figure 7. Risk symmetric analysis of TARP.

In Figure 7, we have a risk symmetric representation of a typical RMBS structure juxtaposed against the structure of TARP. One of the formal powers of TARP is that the US government, through the Office of Financial Stability, will be able to appoint asset managers who will be able to bid for poorly performing asset-backed securities, namely, highly discounted RMBS.

It is at this point that we see the potential injustices of the TARP scheme. First, consider the case of the good mortgagor, whom we define as a mortgagor who has currently performed on all his mortgage-loan obligations. Ask this mortgagor what the value of his financial performance is and he is likely to say 'one hundred per cent'. This is obvious because of his recollection, and is evidenced by the receipts he has received from the mortgage-loan servicer and by the records kept by the servicer relating to the performance of his loan repayments. Now consider that the duly appointed asset manager representing the US government under the authority of TARP bids for an RMBS at auction at, say, 60%. If the good mortgagor did not have the opportunity to bid for the value of his mortgage-debt, would he not feel justifiably aggrieved? If the government-controlled or government agency wins the auction at 60% (or, for that matter, at any price less than 100%), from the good mortgagor's perspective he would have been forced out of the opportunity to bid 60% (or, equivalently, at any price less than 100%).

Whatever the technical details of the transaction agreements underlying the RMBS, if the good mortgagor's 100% performance is being used to support the flow of funds of the transaction structure, then the good mortgagor should have the right to bid for up to the full value of his mortgage. In Hohfeldian terms, the good mortgagor not only has the fundamental power to bid but also a claim to do so. The ancient fundamental right of redemption should be accorded its symmetric translation once more in the realms of the rather esoteric complex financial instrument of asset-backed securities, and even more so when an attempted 'clog' in the form of a government action attempts to deracinate this right in the form of a government-sanctioned auction.

Of course, one obvious objection to the good mortgagor's right to bid at the auction is that the auction itself is not about selling the good mortgagor's mortgage-loan but about tranches of the RMBS which are patently different in legal form from the good mortgagor's particular mortgage-loan. We anticipate this argument of 'form over substance' to be made by the holders of the RMBS notes that are being sold at auction. It is precisely here that the argument of the legal certainty of the right of redemption should be applied and extended into the 'virtual' twenty-first-century world of the asset-backed securities transactions. The question of 'what is the value of the asset-backed securities' goes to the valuation of the underlying assets, and here the ancient law provides us with a legal certainty (legal substance, as it were) upon which we can build economic substance. If the counter-argument is that the market players determine the 'value' of the asset-backed securities, it is then important to set the record straight by perhaps enacting legislation which confirms the applicability of the right of redemption, the equitable right of redemption and no clogs on the right of redemption doctrine in residential mortgage-backed securities transactions as well as in any auctions sanctioned by TARP. For those not convinced by this argument, consider the hypothetical situation where individual good mortgagors have transferred their right of redemption into a company which then bids on the individual good mortgagors' behalf up to the value of their putative performance at a TARP auction. Would not this company have rights in precedence over any government fund representing merely the general taxpayers? And what would be the economic effect of such a proposal if instantiated? Would institutional investors wake up to the fact that there are indeed market participants beyond the last resort of the taxpayer-sponsored government agencies who would be most willing to enter into such auctions and who could, in principle, bid up to 100% of the value of their mortgages and thereby restore the AAA-rating of such instruments? One can only hope that, by the swipe of a pen, the madness of regulations may be somewhat subdued.

E.   Conclusion

It is curious that, compared to the scientific disciplines of the twentieth and twenty-first centuries, where symmetry arguments pervade, the social sciences and, especially, the law have almost nothing to say about the theoretical implications of symmetry, let alone risk symmetries. As Van Frassen, the philosopher of science elegantly puts it, symmetry arguments 'carry us forward from an initial position of empirical risk, to a final point with still exactly the same risk [where] the degree of empirical fallibility remains invariant'.[111] In this paper, I have shown how investor rights to rather complex financial instruments, asset-backed securities, appear in a set of rather complex securities regulations in the US (Regulation AB) and the EU (the Prospectus Regulation), and how the theories of information asymmetry of Akerloff have encouraged the production of ever increasingly complex financial instruments. With the unfolding phenomenon of the credit crisis, these complex financial transactions show an asymmetry at a social level which threatens to

---

[111] BC Van Frassen, *Laws and Symmetry* (Oxford, Oxford University Press, 1989) 261.

undermine social cohesion by discrediting the financial system. While the fundamental premises of financial instruments and financial engineering tell us that complex financial instruments may be used to mimic any and all conditions of the real world, the world created by complex financial instruments has not protected the investor in such instruments. Ironically, the credit crisis has shown not only that financial institutions are too big to fail, but that the solutions to the credit crisis are inherent within the financial system if the instruments, whether public or private, are designed consciously to meet risk symmetric criteria. We see that, by rediscovering some of the legal certainties of the past, certain substantive legal rights can be translated with beneficial effect into processes required by current emergency economic legislation. Finally, risk symmetries and risk symmetric analysis, although simple, are powerful tools for helping us see how socially just complex financial instruments are not merely a possibility but a requirement in a world filled with continuous risk and uncertainty.

14

'Corporate Governance' an Oxymoron? The Role of Corporate Governance in the Current Banking Crisis

BLANAID CLARKE[*]

A. Introduction

A number of factors contributed to the current banking crisis. These include the sub-prime mortgage crisis, the property collapse,[1] the liquidity crisis, market volatility and an accommodating accounting and regulatory environment. Martin Lipton has referred to these as 'a perfect storm of economic conditions'.[2] Most commentators also agree that corporate governance failings and in particular the chronic and reckless risk-taking by management played a contributory role. The banks' remuneration policies both created this high-risk environment and rewarded directors for their role in it.[3] Interestingly, the media appears to have singled out directors as the root cause of the current economic turmoil and focused on the level of remuneration. A veritable 'feeding frenzy' has been created, nurtured by vitriolic and belligerent headlines and opinion pieces.[4] Not only have directors been blamed for past wrongs, but in Ireland, more worryingly, they are even being cited as an impediment to political reform and social partnership agreement. 'We

---

[*] Professor, Law School, University College Dublin.

[1] The Financial Regulator confirmed that, although Irish banks did not have exposures to the sub-prime losses and had limited contact with 'toxic products', they were very exposed to the property market, particularly commercial property. As the economic downturn increased, losses on property-related loans increased, and there were increased provisions and write-offs. (Speech by Patrick Neary, Chief Executive, Financial Regulator to Joint Committee Economic and Regulatory Affairs, 14 October 2008, available at www.cahill-printers.ie/Debates/DDebate.aspx?F=ERJ20081014.XML&Ex=All&Page=2 (accessed on 18 August 2009).

[2] M Lipton, S Rosenblum and K Cain, 'Some Thoughts for Boards of Directors in 2009', available at www.wlrk.com/docs/ThoughtsforDirectors2009.pdf (18 August 2009).

[3] See eg C Plath, 'Corporate Governance in the Credit Crisis: Key Considerations for Investors' (20 November 2008), available at www.ssrn.com/abstract=1309707; G Kirkpatrick, 'The Corporate Governance Lessons from the Financial Crisis' (2009/1) 96 *Financial Market Trends* 61, available at www.oecd.org/dataoecd/32/1/42229620.pdf (accessed on 18 August 2009); and Office of the White House, Press Secretary, 'G20 Declaration of the Summit on Financial Markets and the World Economy' (15 November 2008).

[4] See, eg 'Greedy Bank Bosses Whose Blunders Plunged Britain Into A Spiral Of Economic Gloom', *Daily Mirror*, 11 February 2009; 'Reckless Bankers Should Get ASBOs', *Daily Express*, 17 October 2008; 'These Bankers Are Lucky That They Are Not Going To Jail' *The Observer*, 1 March 2009; 'Shoot The Bankers, Nationalise The Banks' *Financial Times*, 19 January 2009; and 'Avarice And Audacity Of Bankers' *The Guardian*, 27 February 2009.

Won't Pay for the Greed of the Bankers' is a common slogan on placards in countrywide protests.

Following the Enron scandal, Alan Greenspan opined in 2002 that 'It is not that humans have become any more greedy than in generations past. It is that the avenues to express greed had grown so enormously.'[5] The role of corporate governance is to provide controls to direct and restrain management and to ensure that these avenues to greed are guarded. This chapter considers how a framework of corporate governance which emphasises the role of independent directors and risk control could have failed so significantly and ponders the implications of these corporate governance failings. There are two questions which governments, regulators, investors and the general public have been asking: 'Why did the system fail?' and 'How can we stop it happening again?' Indeed, a large number of reviews were undertaken at both the macro- and micro-levels to provide answers to these questions. For example, in February 2009, the British Prime Minister asked Sir David Walker to review coprorate governance in UK banks and make recommendations particularly with regard to risk management and boards.[6] In March 2009, the Financial Reporting Council announced a review of the effectiveness of the Combined Code on Corporate Governance.[7] The OECD has also published several reports on the corporate governance failings in the financial crisis.[8] On the micro-level, reviews have been undertaken into failed banks, including HBOS in the UK and Anglo Irish Bank in Ireland. At the time of writing, for example, the latter bank is the subject of four separate external reviews and one internal review.

This paper seeks to provide an overview of the current internal and external corporate governance processes in banking institutions in order to assess their weaknesses and also seeks to make some tentative suggestions as to how these processes are likely to change or be changed. In doing so, I intend to use as a primary case study the Irish registered bank Anglo Irish Bank (Anglo). This company is now synonymous in Ireland with regulatory failures, managerial ineptitude and greed. In the last 12 months of its independent existence the share price had decreased by 98%, and in January 2009 it was nationalised. Any compensation to shareholders is likely to be minimal. Although substantially exposed to the Irish property market, Anglo did not engage in sub-prime lending or possess significant 'toxic assets'. It was regulated by the Irish Financial Regulator pursuant to a principles-led supervisory system. In addition, it appeared to comply with the Combined Code and in some instances seemed to go further than the Combined Code in terms of internal controls. It reported a pre-tax loss of €4.1 billion for the six months to the end of March 2009, precipitating the need for a further €4 billion of capital from the government. Anglo's failure demonstrates in a very stark fashion the governance problems endemic in the banking system.

---

[5] Speech before the US Senate Committee on Banking, Housing, and Urban Affairs, July 2002, available at www.federalreserve.gov/BoardDocs/HH/2002/july/testimony.htm.

[6] HM Treasury Press Release 10/2009. Final recommendations were published in November 2009, available at www.hm-treasury.gov.uk/d/walker-review_261109.pdf.

[7] Financial Reporting Council Press Release FRC PN 258. The review will concentrate on the composition and effectiveness of the board as a whole; the respective roles of the chairman, the executive leadership of the company and the non-executive directors; the board's role in relation to risk management; the role of the remuneration committee; the quality of support and information available to the board and its committees; and the content and effectiveness of Section 2 of the Code, which is addressed to institutional shareholders.

[8] See, for example, Kirkpatrick, above n 3, and A Blundell-Wignall, P Atkinson and S Hoon Lee, 'The Current Financial Crisis: Cases and Policy Issues' (2008/2) 95 *Financial Market Trends* 1.

B. External Controls

For many years, theorists have emphasised the existence of market forces as a stimulant to encourage managers to adopt an optimal governance structure.[9] Competition is often cited as a primary form of external control. Yet competition did not restrict the high-risk behaviour of banks' management as the majority of banks maintained similar risk profiles. Strong investor demand facilitated by an accommodating regulatory framework encouraged many banks to hold assets off their balance sheets and to adopt an 'originate to distribute' model.[10] In Ireland, despite warnings from the Central Bank of the inherent dangers in the banks' property-lending practices,[11] all banks grew their property portfolios. It thus appears that the challenging competitive conditions encouraged rather than restricted management and the herd mentality prevented most institutions from stepping out of line. In July 2008, Chuck Prince, CEO of Citibank, explained that 'When the music stops, in terms of liquidity, things will be complicated. But as long as the music is playing, you've got to get up and dance. We're still dancing.'[12]

A further external control is the market for corporate control. This theory, first proposed by Manne in 1965,[13] suggests that mismanagement is reflected in share prices because shareholders sell their shares rather than replace management. An opportunity thus arises for a bidder to acquire the company cheaply, replace the inefficient managers and turn the company around. The theory suggests that takeovers have a disciplinary effect on managers. Thus, all that regulators must do in such a scenario is to ensure that the takeover market operates freely and without hindrance from the directors themselves. The High-Level Group of Company Law Experts, established by the European Commission under the chairmanship of Jaap Winter (the Winter Group) to examine certain matters relating to takeover bids, cited this theory as one of the justifications for encouraging takeovers and restricting frustrating action in the Takeovers Directive (2004/25).[14]

The following questions must be asked thus: why did the market for corporate control not lead to share price reductions in firms where there was poor risk management and inadequate oversight by the board? Why were these firms not subsequently acquired by buyers who replaced the board and management turning the firms around? Alternatively, why did the fear that this would happen not constitute a sufficient deterrent to prevent poor risk management?

There are a number of reasons why the market for corporate control did not operate as predicted. First, the market for corporate control depends upon the market being efficient.

---

[9] M Jensen and W Meckling, 'Theory of the Firm: Managerial Behaviour, Agency Costs and Ownership Structure' (1976) 3 *Journal of Financial Economics* 305; E Fama, 'Agency Problems and the Theory of the Firm' (1980) 88 *Journal of Political Economy* 288.

[10] A Purnanandam, 'Originate-to-distribute Model and the Sub-prime Mortgage Crisis', unpublished (2009), available at www.ssrn.com/abstract=1167786 (accessed on 18 August 2009).

[11] Central Bank (Ireland), '2007 Stability Report'. However, it should be noted that it expressly stated its opinion that there would be a 'soft rather than a hard landing'.

[12] Interview, *Financial Times*, 9 July 2007. In November 2007, Mr Prince stepped down as chairman and chief executive of Citigroup in the wake of billions of dollars in losses related to sub-prime lending.

[13] H Manne, 'Mergers and the Market for Corporate Control' (1965) 73 *Journal of Political Economy* 110.

[14] European Commission, 'Report of the High Level Group of Company Law Experts on Issues Related to Takeover Bids' (2002) http://ec.europa.eu/internal_market/company/docs/takeoverbids/2002-01-hlg-report_en.pdf (19 August 2009).

Yet the Turner Report noted that 'In the face of the worst financial crisis for a century . . . the assumptions of efficient market theory have been subject to increasingly effective criticism, drawing on both theoretical and empirical arguments'.[15] A fundamental premise underlying the market for corporate control is the existence of a high positive correlation between share price and managerial efficiency.[16] Even if this correlation existed (and there are reasons to doubt it), the risk management policies of the bank do not appear to have been considered as inefficient by the market. Moody's explained the difficulty for investors in appreciating the relevant risks. It noted that '[a]ssessing the quality of risk management practices . . . presents inherent challenges for investors, who are not privy to certain confidential information and who may lack a standard means of company risk management practices among peer groups and across peer industries'.[17]

One might argue, however, that, while this is likely to reflect a correct assessment of individual shareholders, institutional shareholders are in a different position. While they may no longer have access to confidential information, one would expect that they would have sufficient financial expertise and experience to assess risk management practices more accurately. A second problem is that, even if the practices were regarded as risky, they may not have been considered as detrimental to the company and thus may not have impacted upon the share price. Shareholders may have decided not to sell. The Turner Report accepted that all liquid traded markets are capable of acting irrationally, and can be susceptible to self-reinforcing herd and momentum effects.[18] Investors may have considered that, in order to compete, banks had to become less risk averse. It is also possible that investors relied on regulators to determine the level of risk that was acceptable or, rather, was not. They might have assumed that the absence of regulatory intervention implied that risk levels were deemed safe. Finally, even if shareholders correctly identified the inefficient risk-taking, instead of selling they may have decided to take action to remedy matters. They may have exercised their voice[19] to alter corporate strategies. Unfortunately, there is little evidence of shareholders successfully pursuing this course.

A second related reason why the market for corporate control did not operate as predicted is the prevalence of derivative trading in certain securities. Derivatives, unless properly regulated, threaten the market efficiency upon which, as noted above, the market for corporate control theory depends. Ironically, derivatives became increasingly popular post-Sarbanes-Oxley as a means to avoid increasing corporate disclosure and government attention. In the UK, the Financial Services Authority (FSA) has acknowledged that information asymmetries between informed contracts for difference (CfD) holders and uninformed 'ordinary' investors can result in price inefficiency in the market. It noted:

> Uninformed investors may be unable to acquire valuable information because it is held with informed traders. Valuable information in the context of CfDs which could affect pricing of the referenced shares could include information on those holders of large CfD positions who are able either currently or prospectively to exercise ownership rights over the reference shares.[20]

---

[15] Financial Services Authority, 'The Turner Review: A Regulatory Response to the Global Banking Crisis' (2009) 40.

[16] H Manne, 'Mergers and the Market for Corporate Control' (1965) 73 *Journal of Political Economics* 110, 112.

[17] Quoted in C Plath, 'Corporate Governance in the Credit Crisis: Key Considerations for Investors' (20 November 2008) http://ssrn.com/abstract=1309707, 2.

[18] Turner Review, above n 15.

[19] See generally A Hirschman, *Exit, Voice and Loyalty: Responses to Decline in Firms, Organizations, and States* (Cambridge, MA, Harvard University Press, 1970).

[20] FSA, 'Contracts for Difference: Disclosure', Consultation Paper 07/20 (November 2007) para 3.14.

In the case of Anglo, one individual, Sean Quinn (and his family holdings), was estimated to have held a stake of 25% through CfDs. The exact figure is unknown as there was no requirement to disclose this to the market or the Stock Exchange.[21]

It is also argued that CfDs may be used to covertly build stakes in quoted companies without making the normal disclosures.[22] These interests are then converted into direct equity by acquiring the underlying shares from the CfD writer, who holds these shares as a hedge. The problem is that these 'toeholds' could discourage other potential bidders from contesting the takeover, as they would be at a competitive disadvantage relative to a bidder who already has a toehold. This may discourage competitive bidding and reduce corporate contestability to the detriment of the market for corporate control. For example, one might deduce that the existence of this undisclosed 25% CfD position might have reduced liquidity in the market and also made it impossible for another bidder to acquire control without Mr Quinn's approval.

The Winter Group stated that lack of transparency in ownership structure could result in malfunctioning of the market for corporate control. This led to the inclusion of a provision in the Takeover Directive requiring significant direct and indirect shareholdings to be published in annual reports.[23] Overall, the FSA has concluded that uncertainties relating to share ownership can reduce the efficiency of the market for corporate control and dissuade some parties from participation in the market. As a consequence, it introduced a disclosure regime, and the London Takeover Panel introduced disclosure and control amendments to the City Code to deal with derivatives. In Ireland, the Irish Takeover Panel introduced derivatives disclosure rules in 2009,[24] but only limited control rules apply.[25] The importance of disclosure as a means of facilitating the market for corporate control cannot be underestimated. However, this is a complicated area and, as Schouten correctly indicates, 'setting the trigger for disclosure at the appropriate level is key'.[26] This area is currently under review by regulators at a national and international level.

It is also important to note, in the context of derivatives, that there is clear evidence that the share prices of banks were artificially altered by short selling. Again, this affects market efficiency. The International Organization of Securities Commissions (IOSCO) noted that there are circumstances in which short selling can be used as a tool to mislead the market.[27] It can be used in a downward manipulation whereby a manipulator sells the shares of a company short and then spreads inaccurate rumours about a company's negative prospects. (In March 2008, Anglo executives blamed a one-day 19% collapse in the Anglo share price on unidentified short-sellers.) This harms issuers and investors, as

---

[21] Decreasing share prices led to him closing out his position in July 2008 and acquiring a holding of 15% of Anglo. The remaining 10% shareholding was sold to a small group of investors. It has subsequently emerged that the 10 purchasers were former stakeholders in the bank and were given loans of €300m by Anglo in order to purchase the shares.

[22] FSA Consultation Paper, above n 19, para 3.19.

[23] Art 10(1)(c). Of course there may be situations where the company is unaware of the indirect shareholdings.

[24] Prior to this, only very limited rules applied. See the market consultation document.

[25] New Rule amendments dealing with control issues are likely to be introduced this year.

[26] M Schouten, 'The Case for Mandatory Ownership Disclosure', unpublished (2009), available at www.ssrn.com/abstract=1327114 (accessed on 18 August 2009).

[27] IOSCO, 'Technical Committee Members' Initiatives Relating To Restrictions on Short Sales' (2 October 2008).

well as the integrity of the market. This was one of the reasons[28] that led most regulators, including those in the UK and Ireland, to introduce a temporary ban on short selling of securities of listed financial services firms. Indeed, in Australia the ban extended to all listed securities. However, such measures do not represent an ideal solution[29] and many bans have since been lifted.[30] Short selling plays an important role in market liquidity. It provides more efficient price discovery, mitigates market bubbles, increases market liquidity, facilitates hedging and other risk management activities, and limits upward market manipulations. A balance is thus needed.

The third reason why the market for corporate control did not operate as predicted is that the theory assumes that a bidder would be able to buy the shares and reap a sufficient reward from replacing the inefficient directors to be able to afford the acquisition, which in turn assumes that the directors' inefficiency will be significant enough to be reflected in the share price. The share prices of banks remained strong until the crisis crystallised.[31] There did not appear to be opportunities to acquire banks cheaply. By the time the share price of banks began to decrease, it may well have been too late, and there was no guarantee that the situation could be turned around. It has been acknowledged that the market for corporate control is only effective within its limits. As Coffee explained, companies where the level of inefficiency is either 'not extreme enough to justify the necessary premium or so extreme as to surpass the bidder's level of risk aversion' fall outside the range and will not be considered as targets.[32] It has thus been argued that the market for corporate control is 'sufficiently limited that it can serve only as a remedy of last resort for massive managerial failures and not as the principal enforcer of corporate accountability'.[33] Faced with liquidity and solvency challenges, these companies may not have been attractive acquisitions for even the bravest bidder. The RBS takeover of ABN AMRO for €71bn (approximately three times the market value) in 2007 is an example of the dangers of such acquisitions.

Other barriers to the acquisition may take the form of government regulation.[34] Because of the importance of banks in the economy, governments impose additional regulations on banks. As Levine notes, most governments restrict the concentration of bank ownership and the ability of outsiders to purchase a substantial percentage of bank stock without regulatory approval. Of the 107 countries in the Barth, Caprio and Levine database of bank regulation and supervision, 41 have a limit on the percentage of bank capital owned by a single entity that is less than 50% and 38 have limits less than

---

[28] IOSCO noted that short-selling may be particularly problematic in the midst of a loss in market confidence such as occurred in the credit crisis where certain otherwise solvent banks faced liquidity challenges. In such circumstances, the decrease in share prices induced by short-selling led to further credit tightening for the banks in question.

[29] The SEC's office of economic analysis is reported to be evaluating data from the temporary ban on short-selling. Christopher Cox indicated that preliminary findings point to several unintended market consequences and side effects caused by the ban: see www.reuters.com/article/ousivMolt/idUSTRE4BU3FL20081231 (accessed on 18 August 2009).

[30] Whilst the ban on short-selling of financial stocks has been lifted in the UK, it has continued elsewhere. For example, in Australia, ASIC extended the ban until 31 May 2009.

[31] Irish bank shares hit record highs in February 2007, having trebled in value since the start of the decade (Reuters).

[32] J Coffee, 'Regulating the Market for Corporate Control: A Critical Assessment of the Tender Offer's Role in Corporate Governance' (1984) 84 *Columbia Law Review* 1145, 1204.

[33] Ibid, 1153.

[34] R Levine, 'The Corporate Governance of Banks: A Concise Discussion of Concepts and Evidence', World Bank Policy Research Working Paper No 3404 (2004).

25%.[35] Furthermore, in many countries there are constraints on who can own banks (for instance, limits on ownership by non-bank firms). Obtaining regulatory approval can be a long-drawn-out process and this tends to make hostile takeovers in banking rare.[36] Levine also comments on the very large percentage (75%) of not widely held banks and the fact that half of the controlling owners are families. He thus suggests that there exists a situation where regulatory restrictions are not able to limit the family dominance of banks yet restrictions on purchasing equity actually defend the existing owners from competition for control, obstructing this source of corporate governance.

However, studies indicate that government ownership of banks has declined significantly since 1995.[37] A study by Taboada[38] indicates that the average government ownership of banks experienced a 42.7% decline over a 10 year period, dropping from 35.5% in 1995 to 20.3% in 2005. As it decreased, foreign and domestic blockholder ownership of banks increased. The pattern is not consistent throughout Europe, however. A study by Kohler found significant differences between the UK (where the median largest blockholding is 11.09%) and Continental Europe (where it is 47.23%).[39] Clearly, in the UK's dispersed ownership context, it should be relatively easier to acquire control of banks if no defensive tactics exist. However, in the UK, frustrating tactics are prohibited during the course of an offer without the approval of shareholders.[40] In Continental Europe, as a result of concentrated ownership, acquisitions are less likely. This is problematic because even Manne has emphasised that the market for corporate control depends on there being 'a number of voting shares sufficient to guarantee control . . . floating in the open market'.[41]

It seems clear from the foregoing that there are difficulties in relying on the market for corporate control, particularly in the context of the widespread use of derivatives. While certain regulatory changes should improve matters, internal corporate governance controls will remain necessary.

C. Internal Controls

The OECD Steering Group on Corporate Finance concluded that 'the financial crisis can be to an important extent attributed to failures and weaknesses in corporate governance

---

[35] J Barth, G Caprio and R Levine, 'Bank Regulation and Supervision: What Works Best?', NBER Working Paper No W9323 (2002).

[36] S Prowse, 'The Corporate Governance System in Banking: What Do We Know?' (1997) *Banca del Lavoro Quarterly Review* 11.

[37] R La Porta, F Lopez-de-Silanes, and A Shleifer, 'Government Ownership of Banks' (2002) 57 *Journal of Finance* 265. A Taboada, 'Impact of Changes in Government Ownership of Banks on the Allocation of Capital: International Evidence' (2008), available at www.ssrn.com/abstract=1273243 (accessed on 18 August 2009).

[38] AG Taboada, 'Impact of Changes in Government Ownership of Banks on the Allocation of Capital: International Evidence', (1 November 2008), available at www.ssrn.com/abstract=1273243.

[39] M Köhler, 'Blockholdings and Corporate Governance in the EU Banking Sector', ZEW—Centre for European Economic Research Discussion Paper No 08-110 (2009), available at www.ssrn.com/abstract=1338695 (accessed on 18 August 2009).

[40] Rule 21, The City Code on Takeovers and Mergers (The Takeover Panel).

[41] H Manne, 'Corporate Governance—Getting Back to Market Basics' speech to Seminario Consob, 10 November 2008, available at www.consob.it/documenti/Pubblicazioni/Convegni_seminari/seminario_20081110_manne.pdf.

arrangements'.[42] The European High-Level Group on Financial Supervision in the European Union, chaired by Jacques de Larosière, stated that corporate governance 'is one of the most important failures of the present crisis.'[43] In particular, both groups identify failures in risk management systems, incentive structures and board oversight. In the UK and Ireland, the Combined Code is applied to listed companies, supplementing existing statutory requirements. It is applied on a 'comply or explain' basis. The preamble to the Combined Code explains that the flexibility this approach offers is 'valued by company boards and by investors in pursuing better corporate governance'.[44] Whether this flexibility is as valued in the wake of the banking crisis remains to be seen.

1.   The Board's Role in Supervising Risk Management

One of the first of the Combined Code's provisions states that every company should be headed by an 'effective board', which is 'collectively responsible for the success of the company'.[45] The board's role is 'to provide entrepreneurial leadership of the company within a framework of prudent and effective controls which enables risk to be assessed and managed'.[46] The board should include a balance of executive and non-executive directors, and particularly independent non-executive directors.[47] Non-executive directors are charged with scrutinising the performance of management in meeting agreed goals and objectives and monitoring the reporting of performance. They are also required to satisfy themselves on the integrity of financial information and 'that financial controls and systems of risk management are robust and defensible'. The board is charged with conducting at least annually a review of 'the effectiveness of the group's system of internal controls', including 'financial, operational and compliance controls and risk management systems'.[48] The Combined Code recommends the establishment of an audit committee comprising at least three independent non-executive directors, 'at least one of whom should have recent and relevant financial experience'.[49] One of the tasks of this audit committee is 'to review the company's internal financial controls and, unless expressly addressed by a separate board risk committee composed of independent directors, or by the board itself, to review the company's internal control and risk management systems'.[50]

While identifying and assessing relevant risks is a technical matter, the corporate governance dimension involves how such information is used within the organisation including its transmission to the board.[51] The OECD Report on the financial crisis found that corporate governance codes dealt with internal controls related to financial reporting and the need to have external checks and reporting (along the lines of section 404 of

---

[42] Kirkpatrick, above n 3.

[43] 'Report of the High Level Group on Financial Supervision in the European Union' (25 February 2009), available at www.ec.europa.eu/internal_market/finances/docs/de_larosiere_report_en.pdf   (the de Larosière Report).

[44] Financial Reporting Council, 'The Combined Code on Corporate Governance' (June 2008) Preamble, para 2.

[45] Ibid, A.1.

[46] Ibid, A1 supporting principle.

[47] Ibid, A.3.

[48] Ibid, C.2.1.

[49] Ibid, C.3.1.

[50] Ibid, C.3.2.

[51] Organisation for Economic Cooperation and Development, *OECD Principles of Corporate Governance* (Paris, OECD, 2004) 6.

Sarbanes-Oxley) but that not enough emphasis was placed on the broader context of risk management.[52] In this context, boards play a critical oversight role. They are charged with ensuring that a proper risk management framework is in place and then monitoring its application. The former task should include setting the bank's risk appetite and ensuring its fit with corporate strategy.[53] The Turner Report noted:

> While some of the problems could not be identified at firm specific level, and while some well run banks were affected by systemic developments over which they had no influence, there were also many cases where internal risk management was ineffective and where boards failed adequately to identify and constrain excessive risk taking.[54]

The Senior Supervisors Group, assessing a range of risk management practices among major global financial services organisations, identified severe shortfalls both in internal management and in the supervisory role of the board.[55] While nearly all of the banks reviewed failed to anticipate fully the scale of recent market stress, the nature of risk management systems and senior management structures varied greatly. The Group noted:

> Firms that avoided . . . problems demonstrated a comprehensive approach to viewing firm-wide exposures and risk, sharing quantitative and qualitative information more effectively across the firm and engaging in more effective dialogue across the management team. Senior managers in such firms also exercised critical judgement and discipline in how they valued its holdings of complex or potentially illiquid securities both before and after the onset of the market turmoil. They had more adaptive (rather than static) risk measurement processes and systems that could rapidly alter underlying assumptions to reflect current circumstances; management also relied on a wide range of risk measures to gather more information and different perspectives on the same risk exposures and employed more effective stress testing with more use of scenario analysis.[56]

While risk models and stress testing failed due to technical assumptions, the problem from a corporate governance perspective was that this was not part of the dialogue between senior management. Particularly worryingly, the Senior Supervisors Group noted that 'some firms found it challenging before the recent turmoil to persuade senior management and business line management to develop and to pay sufficient attention to the results of forward looking stress scenarios that assumed large price movements'.[57] The OECD referred to evidence which indicated that risk management information was not always available to a board, or in a form corresponding to their monitoring of risks.[58] As a result, bank boards appeared not to understand the risks facing their banks and were not in a position to react quickly enough to the crisis as it emerged.

A number of solutions must be considered. First, boards must be better qualified. The OECD report questioned whether independence might have been prioritised at the expense of qualifications and suitability in the appointment of non-executive directors. It

---

[52] Kirkpatrick, above n 3, 6.

[53] See C Plath, 'Corporate Governance in the Credit Crisis: Key Considerations for Investors' (20 November 2008) http://ssrn.com/abstract=1309707, 2.

[54] Turner Review, above n 15, 92.

[55] Senior Supervisors Group, 'Observations on Risk Management Practices during the Recent Market Turbulence' (6 March 2008), available at www.newyorkfed.org/newsevents/news/banking/2008/rp080306.html. This Group comprised representatives from seven senior financial supervisors from five countries, including the UK's FSA and the SEC.

[56] Ibid, 'Transmittal letter'.

[57] Ibid, 5.

[58] Kirkpatrick, above n 3, 20.

seems that many boards were not sufficiently experienced or versed in the area of risk management.[59] Many directors lacked a thorough understanding of risk management techniques and trends. Banks are different, and corporate governance regulators must appreciate this fact. They have different types of assets, different reporting processes and different risk profiles, and non-executive directors must appreciate this. Indeed, the extreme complexity of large banking groups and the difficulties which non-executive directors face in understanding all the dimensions of the risks being taken may suggest that non-executive directors—and particularly those on audit committees—should have a background in risk or financial management. Unfortunately persons with this type of experience often tend to be ruled out of boards on the basis of potential conflicts of interest. Another possibility is that directors be given specific training and support resources. While the Combined Code currently requires a company 'to provide the necessary resources for developing and updating its directors' knowledge and capabilities', this has clearly not been as extensive as seems to have been required. It is also worth remembering that the boards of many banks such as Northern Rock were composed of qualified and experienced individuals.

Secondly, non-executive directors need to be more diligent in their role. Remedying this problem will involve a significant investment of time, which would normally exceed the time generally made available by non-executive directors. Given the demanding require-ments of committee membership, a strong case could be made for establishing a separate risk committee. One problem to signal at this stage is that finding experienced, independent risk experts with sufficient time on their hands to take on the task and suffi-cient strength of mind to challenge a board will not prove an easy task—particularly in a market the size of Ireland's. It appears that what we are describing are in reality profes-sional non-executive directors, and it is submitted that this may well be the path of choice.[60] To be successful, the risk or audit committees need to communicate and coordinate with the main board. The OECD Report correctly points out that, even if risk management systems are functioning in the technical sense, this will not benefit the company unless the transmission of information is through effective channels.

Thirdly, non-executive directors need to be more assertive. It is a moot point whether unassertiveness can be attributed to a lack of knowledge of the risks or a lack of willingness to confront management. Directors must not only be 'independent' but, as the Cadbury report advised, must 'bring an independent judgement to bear' on board matters. Peter Chambers, Chief Executive of Legal & General Investment Management, stated that his firm had met banking boards on average once a fortnight in 2008 and had interrogated management about their capital needs early in 2008 after the Northern Rock failure. He maintained that too often non-executive directors failed to challenge executives and then blocked investors who asked for checks and balances to be imposed on executives.[61] In similar vein, it was reported that complaints have been made to the FSA from a former government minister, Lord Foulkes of Cumnock, that at least three of the former non-executive directors in RBS may have been intimidated and threatened with dismissal

---

[59] Grant Thornton, 'The Grant Thornton 2008 Corporate Governance Report, Harmony from Discord: Emerging Trends in Governance in the FTSE 350' (2009), available at www.grant-thornton.co.uk/pdf/Corporate-Governance-Review-2008.pdf.

[60] In Ireland, for example, the Financial Regulator has established a new supervisory unit to monitor institutions covered by the scheme which will include attendance at credit, audit and risk committee meetings.

[61] K Burgess and J Macintosh, 'RBS Rebuffed Investor Calls', *Financial Times*, 28 January 2009, 17.

for asking searching questions about its financial affairs.[62] It is acknowledged that boards must be willing to confront management and to take strong independent action when appropriate. However, this insight is not easily translatable into practice. Ensuring that boards act in this way is not easy, and is certainly hard to regulate. The Turner Report reminds us that excessive risk taking, at least at the top management level, 'may be driven more by broad behavioural and cultural factors than by a rational consideration of the precise incentives inherent within remuneration contracts: dominant executive personalities have a strong tendency to believe in their own strategies'.[63]

Finally, the board must place a high priority on risk management in a real sense rather than a superficial sense. In relation to this latter solution, the OECD Report commented that 'in some cases, banks have taken on high levels of risk by following the letter rather than the intent of regulations indicating a box-ticking approach'.[64] It is submitted that Anglo's Annual Reports provide evidence of just such an approach. They indicate that Anglo had a Risk and Compliance Committee, comprising three non-executive directors, with the following role:

> to oversee risk management and compliance. It reviews on behalf of the board, the key risks and compliance issues inherent in the business and the system of internal control necessary to manage them and it presents its findings to the board.[65]

Anglo also appointed a Chief Risks Officer. Yet the following transactions were allowed in this environment. The first relates to the reporting of the full extent of directors' loans of €179 million, which Anglo has subsequently indicated was not identified as a high-risk area.[66] These included a number of significant non-recourse loans to directors. Anglo was forced to acknowledge recently that, as a result of the subsequent permanent deterioration in Anglo's share price, it is likely there will be an impairment provision in respect of these loans. The full extent of this risk would not have been apparent to shareholders. It emerged that over an eight year period the CEO Sean FitzPatrick transferred loans from Anglo off the bank's books before the bank's accounting year-end using short-term loans from another Irish financial institution. Thus, although Mr FitzPatrick took out a total of €129m in loans in 2007, he only disclosed €7m of this to shareholders. The second issue related to a loan by Anglo of €7 billion to Irish Life & Permanent (IL&P) in September 2008, which, in turn, was placed on deposit by an IL&P subsidiary with Anglo. The mechanism used for this very significant transaction enabled Anglo to categorise the deposit as a customer or corporate deposit rather than a short-term 'inter-bank' deposit. This allowed the bank to disguise the heavy loss of customer deposits during the course of September in its annual results presentation in December 2008. One theme, referred to in the introduction to this part of the book, relates to the failure by shareholders to exercise effective control over risk-taking. However, without the relevant knowledge and in the face of substantial agency problems, shareholders in this company were substantially impeded.

There are calls now for greater accountability of non-executive directors to shareholders. The FSA has suggested, for example, that in the future it will be more likely to

---

[62] T Helm, J Doward, P Kelbie, 'Bank Faces Probe over "Threats" to Directors: Peer's Criminal Inquiry Warning on RBS', *The Observer*, 22 March 2009, 1.
[63] Turner Review, above n 15, 81.
[64] Kirkpatrick, above n 3, 11.
[65] Anglo Irish 2008 Annual Report, 26.
[66] Anglo Irish 2008 Annual Report.

hold non-executive directors, as well as the firm and its executives, accountable under its Code of Practice for Approved Persons if there is any evidence to suggest that they have failed to fulfil their duties with competence and/or integrity.[67] Of course, the fault does not lie solely with non-executive directors; the FSA has warned that '[s]hareholders must also take responsibility to be active individually and more importantly, in collaboration with other investors, to engage with senior management and Non-Executive Directors in companies and question the effectiveness of the construct of their boards'.[68]

One of the areas examined in the Walker review of corporate governance was the role of institutional shareholders in engaging effectively with companies and monitoring of boards. It has proposed developing and encouraging adherence to principles of best practice in a stewardship code to be oversen by the Financial Reporting Council.[69] Credit rating agencies and other gatekeepers must also accept some responsibility for their lack of awareness.

2.   Remuneration Policies

A common complaint is that board incentive structures encouraged and rewarded risk taking by senior management. Two separate issues arise. The first relates to concerns surrounding the total level of remuneration paid to executives in banks which have received taxpayer support. For example, in March 2009 AIG announced that it had just distributed more than $160 million in retention payments to members of its Financial Products Subsidiary, the unit of AIG that was principally responsible for the firm's meltdown. This included one payment of more than $6.4 million and payments of 'retention' bonuses of $1 million or more to 11 persons who are no longer employed. This is a legitimate issue of public concern, and one where governments as significant shareholders have crucial roles to play.[70] However, that is beyond the scope of this chapter. What is relevant in this context is whether the structure of remuneration created incentives for excessive risk taking and how the current remuneration processes facilitated this. According to the Turner Report:

> There is a strong prima facie case that inappropriate incentive structures played a role in encouraging behaviour which contributed to the financial crisis . . . [P]ast remuneration policies, acting in combination with capital requirements and accounting rules, have created incentives for some executives and traders to take excessive risks and have resulted in large payments in reward for activities which seemed profit making at the time but subsequently proved harmful to the institution, and in some cases to the entire system.[71]

Similarly, the OECD Report acknowledges:

---

[67] Financial Services Authority, 'The Approved Persons Regime—Significant Influence Function Review', Consultation Paper 08/25 (December 2009). A breach of this Code of Practice by directors can result in action by the FSA under s 66 of the Financial Services and Markets Act (2000).

[68] Speech by Hector Sants, Chief Executive, FSA at the NAPF Investment Conference 2009.

[69] 'A Review of Corporate Governance in UK Banks and Other Financial Industry Entities, Final Recommendations' (HM TReasury, November 2009) ch 5.

[70] See, eg 'Report of the Covered Institutions Remuneration Oversight Committee' (CIROC, 2009), available at www.finance.gov.ie/documents/publications/other/2009/Cirocrept.pdf. It restricts the bonuses which may be paid and sets relative limits for senior management's salaries.

[71] Turner Review, above n 15, 80.

It has often been argued that remuneration and incentive systems have played a key role in influencing not only the sensitivity of financial institutions to the macroeconomic shock occasioned by the downturn of the real estate market but also in causing the development of unsustainable balance sheet positions in the first place.[72]

Remuneration has long been a controversial issue in the corporate governance debate. It is usually the largest cost incurred by firms after funding costs and an obvious area of mismanagement. The so-called 'fat cat salaries' in the 1990s led to calls to link pay to performance.[73] It was felt that this would help to align the interests of shareholders and directors thus reducing agency problems. Changes in disclosure and tax rules also strengthened these links.[74] The Combined Code requires that a remuneration committee composed of at least three independent non-executives should be responsible for developing policy on executive remuneration and for fixing the remuneration packages of individual directors. It provides that a significant proportion of executive directors' remuneration should be structured so as to 'link rewards to corporate and individual performance'. It continues:

> The performance-related elements of remuneration should form a significant proportion of the total remuneration package of executive directors and should be designed to align their interests with those of shareholders and to give these directors keen incentives to perform at the highest levels.[75]

It now appears clear that remuneration became 'a driver for excessive risk-taking'.[76] Many remuneration strategies were inconsistent with sound risk management. One problem was that the balance of risk and reward offered by poor remuneration practices was unequal. Research by the FSA has indicated that 'higher profits translate into higher bonuses for the employee, whereas bonus payments cannot be lower than zero'.[77] The effect of this is that management benefited from risk-taking but any losses were borne by long-term shareholders and society. Regrettably, there are myriad examples of this in the context of the current bank recapitalisations and nationalisations. Often bonuses were based on turnover in the current year which did not encourage a long-term perspective. Risk was not factored into the assessment of remuneration. Bonuses were in effect guaranteed in advance. In Anglo, for example, the annual performance bonus was based on a multiple of base salary and was paid annually in cash once the Group's financial results had been independently audited. A further problem was that cash was the dominant element in variable compensation packages rather than deferred compensation, which might have promoted a greater long-term focus. Deferred compensation adjusted to reflect the future performance of the firm was rare.

In Ireland, up to the year 2000, Irish financial institutions adopted a conservative policy in relation to remuneration. However, that policy began to change and annual bonuses

---

[72] Kirkpatrick, above n 3, 12.

[73] See, eg 'The Director's Remuneration, Report of a Study Group Chaired by Sir Richard Greenbury' (Confederation of British Industry, 1995).

[74] M Jensen, K Murphy and E Wruck, 'Remuneration: Where We've Been, How We Got to Here, What are the Problems, and How to Fix Them', European Corporate Governance Institute—Finance Working Paper No 44/2004.

[75] B.1.1. Interestingly, there is no distinction made in the Code between the company's long term and short term objectives.

[76] FSA Consultation Paper 09/10, 'Reforming Remuneration Practices in Financial Services', para 2.4.

[77] Ibid.

approximately doubled in the last 10 years, influenced by a similar growth in the UK.[78] For example, in 2007 Anglo's CEO David Drumm was paid a total remuneration of €4,656,000, comprising a salary of €956,000 (20%), a performance bonus of €2 million (43%), benefits of €44,000 (1%) and a pension €1,656,000 (36%).[79] The Chairman, Sean Fitzpatrick, received fees of €400,000 and benefits of €40,000. In 2008, while no bonuses were paid, Mr Drumm received a total remuneration of €2,129,000, comprising a salary of €1,150,000 (54%), benefits of €45,000 and a pension of €934,000. The Chairman received fees of €525,000 and benefits of €14,000. That same year, pre-tax profits were €784 million, a 37% decrease from the previous year. Similarly, earnings per share were reported in the 2008 accounts as being down by 34%. Directors held sizeable portions of shares, and the accounts explained 'It is the Group's policy to motivate its executive directors by granting them share options'. The 2008 accounts indicate that Mr Drumm held 1.013million shares and Mr Fitzpatrick (previously CEO) 4.909 million shares.

On 6 March 2009, the Committee of European Banking Supervisors published a consultation paper on remuneration policy.[80] It stated that the key objective of a firm's remuneration policy is 'to adopt an overall remuneration policy that is in line with its business strategy and risk tolerance, objectives, values and long-term interests' and which does not 'encourage excessive risk-taking'. In terms of corporate governance, the recommended statement of principle is not particularly novel. It states:

> The management body, in its supervisory function, should determine the remuneration of the management body, in its management function. In addition it should have oversight of the overall remuneration policy of the firm. The implementation of the remuneration policy should be subject to central and independent review.[81]

Where the pay award is performance related, the Committee recommends that remuneration should be based on a combination of the individual's performance assessment, the performance of the business unit and the overall results of the company or group. When defining the individual performance, it suggests that other factors apart from financial performance should be considered. The measurement of performance, as a basis for bonus awards, should thus include an adjustment for risks and cost of capital. The Committee also recommends that there be a proportionate ratio between base pay and bonus. Where a significant bonus is paid, the bonus should not be a pure upfront cash payment but should contain a flexible, deferred component; it should consider the risk horizon of the underlying performance. (In relation to this latter point, while in the UK there was a strong element of deferral of bonuses, this did not become general practice in Ireland.[82]) It is intended that these principles will be integrated into the Guidelines on Internal

---

[78] CIROC, above n 67.

[79] In relation to his pension, Mr Drumm opted to take this cash allowance (taxable) for pension benefits foregone. CIROC noted that cash allowances were sometimes paid to compensate for the effects of the 'pensions cap' imposed by the Finance Act, 2006. It opined that pension schemes should reflect public policy and tax law and it was unacceptable that arrangements should be put in place which would be inconsistent with the intent of the relevant legislation.

[80] Committee of European Banking Supervisors, 'Draft High-level Principles of Remuneration Policies', Consultation Paper 23 (March 2009), http://www.c-ebs.org/getdoc/c0ce427e-1abe-445a-8619-5c766cb2de81/CP23.aspx (accessed on 19 August 2009).

[81] Ibid, 3.

[82] CIROC, above n 67.

Governance and may lead to the imposition of additional capital charges for incentive structures that encourage risky behaviour.[83]

On 18 March the FSA published a consultation paper 'Reforming Remuneration Practices in Financial Services'.[84] These principles adopt a now common cry to embed risk management considerations in remuneration policy.[85] Firms are required to ensure that their remuneration policies, procedures and practices are consistent with and promote effective risk management. The FSA sets out its expectations for remuneration committees in some detail. These committees should exercise, and be constituted in a way that enables them to exercise, independent judgement and should be responsible for approving and periodically reviewing the remuneration policy and its adequacy and effectiveness. This is consistent with the existing Combined Code requirements. However, the FSA augments this by providing that the committee should be able to demonstrate that its decisions are consistent with a reasonable assessment of the firm's financial situation and future prospects, and that it has the skills and experience to reach an independent judgement on the suitability of the policy, including its implications for risk and risk management. To ensure that this task is taken seriously, the FSA indicates that they may ask a remuneration committee to prepare a statement on the firm's remuneration policy, including the implications of the policy for the firm. This statement should include an assessment of the impact of the firm's policies on its risk profile and employee behaviour. The FSA counsels that, in drawing up this assessment, 'the remuneration committee should exercise its own judgement and not rely solely on the judgement or opinions of others'. It may seek a meeting with members of the remuneration committee to discuss the statement. In terms of the composition of pay, the FSA states that the performance related component of pay should be based primarily on profits rather than turnover and should not be assessed solely on the results of the current financial year but should be adjusted for risk. The measurement of performance for long-term incentive plans, including those based on the performance of shares, should also be risk-adjusted. Finally, it concludes that the majority of any bonuses should be paid in a deferred form with a deferral period which is appropriate to the nature of the business and its risks. Any deferred element of the variable component of remuneration should be linked to the future performance of the firm as well as that of the employee's division or business unit.

It is clear from the FSA Consultation Paper that the FSA envisages a continuing supervisory role. It has also indicated its intention to make adherence to the first overarching principle of the Code an FSA rule, at least for systemically important firms. Furthermore, it suggests that it will integrate assessment of remuneration policies into its standard risk-assessment process with required improvements included in Risk Mitigation Plans. It suggests the possibility of increases in Pillar 2 capital requirements to compensate for incomplete adherence. This is consistent with the measures suggested in the de Larosière Report.[86]

---

[83] 'Guidelines on the Application of the Supervisory Review Process under Pillar 2—CP03 revised' (25 January 2006).

[84] CP09/10.

[85] This is likely also a key element of the Walker report: see http://www.hm-treasury.gov.uk/walker_review_information.htm (accessed on 18 August 2009). See also Institute of International Finance, 'Final Report of the IIF Committee on Market Best Practices' (Washington, IIF, 2008).

[86] High Level Group on Financial Supervision in the European Union, above n 42.

Before we accept the concept of risk adjusted compensation as the panacea to all corporate governance failings, the Turner Report again puts some perspective on this problem by pointing out that, while inappropriate remuneration structures played a role in the credit crisis, they were 'considerably less important than other factors such as the inadequate approaches to capital, accounting, and liquidity'.[87] It also opines that the regulatory responses which will have greatest influence on future remuneration levels will not be the specific remuneration-related policies described above but 'the proposals to increase the capital required against trading book activity which will lead to a reduction in the aggregate scale of trading activity and consequently the aggregate remuneration of people involved in those activities.'[88] The Report also reminds us that excessive risk taking, at least at the top management level, 'may be driven more by broad behavioural and cultural factors than by a rational consideration of the precise incentives inherent within remuneration contracts: dominant executive personalities have a strong tendency to believe in their own strategies'.[89] This again is not something for which one can legislate.

D.   Conclusion

Five years ago, the OECD advised, presciently, if not very successfully, that '[a]s companies play a pivotal role in our economies and we rely increasingly on private sector institutions to manage personal savings and secure retirement incomes, good corporate governance is important to broad and growing segments of the population'.[90]

Unfortunately, the truth of this has been borne out with devastating consequences for the financial markets. The foregoing review of corporate governance failings indicates that myriad different problems may have contributed to the credit crisis. Disparate governance structures and processes were involved. For example, the credit crisis affected companies with dispersed ownership structures, block-holding structures and even privately owned entities. It affected companies caught up in the sub-prime crisis and those which were not. It affected companies with experienced, financially astute directors and those without. This suggests that a monolithic approach to the problem will not work. What also seems certain is that our corporate governance regulations must be specifically designed to deal with banks.

The Turner Report suggests that there is a limit to the extent to which risks can be identified and offset at the level of the individual firm.[91] Most of the proposals stemming from that review thus relate to the redesign of regulation combined with a major shift in supervisory approach (issues which are the subject of other chapters in this book). Furthermore, in many areas, such as the composition of the boards, it would seem that the

---

[87] Turner Review, above n 15, 80.
[88] Ibid.
[89] Ibid, 81.
[90] OECD, above n 50, 3.
[91] Not surprisingly, perhaps, Hector Sants, Chief Executive, FSA has stated 'It also needs to be recognised that the ultimate responsibility for what has happened rests with firms' senior management. In reviewing the recent litany of firm failures in many cases, albeit with hindsight, specific decisions and strategies can be seen to be at the root of those firms' demise' (speech at the NAPF Investment Conference 2009, available at www.FSA.gov.uk/pages/Library/Communication/Speeches/2009/0312_hs.shtml).

principles are in place already but that they need to be implemented in a more complete and unqualified manner. There needs to be in effect a greater 'buy-in' by non-executive directors in particular. However, even the Turner Report does accept that some improvements in the effectiveness of internal risk management and firm governance are also essential.[92]

It is submitted that we should proceed circumspectly with any reform. It seems likely that our experience of this crisis may lead to greater involvement in corporate governance by regulators and more prudential supervision. That said, Sarbanes-Oxley should help focus our minds on the dangers of a legislative knee-jerk reaction.[93] A more considered response is preferable. In the UK, consultation exercises are underway and a number of suggestions have been put forward imposing obligation on companies, boards and regulators. The Irish response appears to have been less measured. For example, the Irish Finance Minister indicated that under new reforms, yet to be published, he would ban bank directors holding other directorships in private companies and bank chief executives would be stopped from becoming chairpersons.[94] In the face of immense public pressure to tackle the banking crisis, perhaps such impetuosity is understandable. There is no doubt that the Irish banking industry has undergone a radical change in the last six months. As noted above, Anglo has been nationalised; two of the three public banks, AIB and Bank of Ireland, have been recapitalised; and the remaining institutions, Irish Life & Permanent, EBS and Irish Nationwide, are the subject of a government guarantee. However, it is important to resist the temptation to play to the public galleries as this risks obfuscating the problem. Such a reaction also runs the risk that 'the variety of legal influences may cause unintentional overlaps and even conflicts, which may frustrate the ability to pursue key corporate governance objectives'.[95]

It is submitted that, in the current economic climate, a complete engagement between regulators, company boards and investors will be crucial to the development of an efficient corporate governance response.

---

[92] Turner Review, above n 15, 92.
[93] R Romano, 'The Sarbanes-Oxley Act and the Making of Quack Corporate Governance', NYU Law and Economics Research Paper No 04-032.
[94] *Financial Times*, 17 March 2009.
[95] OECD, above n 50, I(C) 17.

15

Board Composition and Female Non-executive Directors

SALLY WHEELER*

A.   Introduction

This chapter looks at the issue of board composition, specifically the idea of gender diversity in the context of non-executive directors (NEDs). It examines the numerical picture of the participation of women as NEDs and the reasons suggested for the contours of this picture. The paper attempts to bring together some of the literature in social psychology, gender studies and management studies that looks at the role of gender in board composition and decision making. This literature addresses inter alia the issue of whether the presence of women on corporate boards might alter either the outcome of decisions or the processes by which those decisions are reached. Much of this literature is concerned with women in management generally rather than more specifically in the boardroom. The paper engages with this literature by taking the skills identified by the Higgs Report[1] and the Tyson Report[2] as necessary in NEDs if good governance is to result and grafting them into a discussion based on what the literature tells us about participation, discussion and leadership styles. My interest begins with the observation in the Higgs Report that 'the key to non-executive director effectiveness lies as much in behaviours and relationships as in structures and processes' (paragraph 6.3).

In the inquiry into the financial crisis surrounding Northern Rock and its subsequent nationalisation in February 2008 the Treasury Select Committee found that:

> The non-executive members of the board, and in particular the chairman of the board, the chairman of the risk committee and the senior non-executive director, failed . . . to ensure that it remained liquid as well as solvent, to provide against the risks that it was taking and to act as an effective restraining force on the strategy of the executive members.

One could say that this was the first documented failure of non-executive director monitoring of corporate governance in the post-Higgs Report era. One could then go on

---

* Professor of Law, Queen's University, Belfast.

[1] 'Review of the Role and Effectiveness of Non-Executive Directors' (the Higgs Report) (2003), available at http://www.berr.gov.uk/whatwedo/businesslaw/corp-governance/higgs-tyson/page23342.html (accessed August 2009).

[2] 'The Recruitment and Development of Non-Executive Directors' (the Tyson Report), commissioned by the DTI and published by the London Business School (2003), available at http://www.london.edu/search/search.html?qt=Tyson+report&x=22&y=3 (accessed August 2009).

to wonder whether board composition in terms of the gender dimension would have made any difference to, for example, the way in which risk was viewed, the way in which risk was calculated and the way in which the board decision-making processes were conducted. However, there were two female NEDs on the Northern Rock board. Their presence illustrates rather neatly the difference between treating gender as an essentialist category based upon sex and the idea of feminised practises.[3] This distinction is one which is passed over in much of the literature,[4] yet it is of fundamental importance when considering the implications of token theory,[5] and the importance of situational context on behaviour and perceptions of behaviour.[6] Gender identity theory[7] is the term given to considering gender as distinct from biological sex. Gender identity theory considers biological sex along with instrumental and expressive psychological traits and gender-role theory.

B.   Contextual Background

The background setting for this discussion is the place that questions of board composition have enjoyed in successive reports on corporate governance within the UK's self-regulatory tradition. Beginning with the Cadbury Report,[8] moving through the Hampel Report[9] and onto the Higgs Report, composition has been a key feature of the debates and subsequent reports. The constant presence of board composition on the corporate governance discussion agenda should not be taken to imply that there has been a consistent view on composition from 1992 to 2003. There certainly has not been. In fact, the rollercoaster ride of composition debates exactly matches the rollercoaster ride that the whole arena of corporate governance has gone through. For the Cadbury Report the message was one of ensuring accountability to shareholders as required by agency theory and being seen to make recommendations that would secure this accountability. The control function of NEDs was emphasised through the statements of general principle, eg '[boards of directors] must be free to drive their companies forward, but exercise that

---

[3] Much of this debate can be stylised into a discussion of what exactly it was that Carol Gilligan was saying in her seminal work, *In a Different Voice: Physiological Theory and Women's Development* (Cambridge, MA, Harvard University Press, 1982). Was she setting out a description of women or was she setting out a description of feminine traits? Gilligan spent much of her career post-1982 seeking to answer this question as she was frequently attacked for offering the first when there was intellectual preference amongst feminist scholars for the second. For the contours of the debate see C Greeno and E Maccoby, 'How Different Is the "Different Voice"?' (1986) 11 *Signs* 310; Z Luria, 'A Methodological Critique' (1986) 11 *Signs* 316; C Gilligan, 'Reply' (1986) 11 *Signs* 324.

[4] See, eg V Singh and S Vinnicombe, 'Impression Management, Commitment and Gender: Managing Others' Good Opinions' (2001) 19 *European Journal of Management* 183. For a general discussion of the problem see S Borna and G White, '"Sex" and "Gender": Two Confused and Confusing Concepts in the "Women in Corporate Management" Literature' (2003) 47 *Journal of Business Ethics* 89.

[5] RM Kanter, *Men and Women of the Corporation* (New York, Basic Books, 1977) 210–11.

[6] For the importance of these factors generally see N Weisstein, 'Power, Resistance and Science' [1997] *New Politics* at ww3.wpunj.edu/~newpol/issue22/weisst22.htm and in the context of boardroom cultures see J Wajcman, 'Desperately Seeking Differences: Is Management Style Gendered?' (1996) 34 *British Journal of Industrial Relations* 333 and references therein on the gendering of organisational cultures.

[7] An exploration of this theory in relation to business ethics can be found in A McCabe, R Ingram and M Conway Dato-on, 'The Business of Ethics and Gender' (2006) 64 *Journal of Business Ethics* 101.

[8] 'The Financial Aspects of Corporate Governance' (the Cadbury Report) (December 1992).

[9] 'Committee on Corporate Governance' (the Hampel Committee) (April 1998).

freedom within a framework of effective accountability' (paragraph 1.1), 'non-executive directors have two particularly important contributions to make to the governance process as a consequence of their independence from executive responsibility . . . The first is in reviewing the performance of the board and of the executive' (paragraphs 4.4 and 4.5) and finally 'the emphasis in this report on the control function of non-executive directors is a consequence of our remit' (paragraph 4.10). A minimum number of three NEDs was thought to be necessary by the Cadbury Report to fulfil the tasks it laid out.

The tone in the Hampel Report of 1998 was markedly different. From its first general statement:

> [T]he importance of corporate governance lies in its contribution both to business prosperity and to accountability. In the UK the latter has preoccupied much public debate over the past few years. We would wish to see the balance corrected . . . But the emphasis on accountability has tended to obscure a board's first responsibility—to enhance the prosperity of the business over time (paragraph 1.1)

it was clear that shareholder value was of more importance than efforts towards accountability. Paragraph 3.7 illustrates this neatly: 'the Cadbury committee raised the profile of the nonexecutive director, and this has been very beneficial. An unintended side effect has been to overemphasise the monitoring role.'

Whereas the Cadbury Report worried about whether sufficient NEDs of the required calibre could be found (paragraph 4.17), the Hampel Report was considerably more blasé in the position it took on composition:

> Most non-executive directors are executives or former executives of other companies . . . It was put to us that companies should recruit directors from a greater diversity of backgrounds. We do not favour diversity for its own sake, to give a politically correct appearance to the list of board members or to represent stakeholders (paragraph 3.15).

The mention of 'stakeholders' here is something of a red herring. The Hampel Committee was set up in November 1995 and reported in February 1998. Its immediate political context was the series of speeches in which Tony Blair and other prominent New Labour politicians outlined their concept of the Stakeholder Society and the Third Way as they set out their stall prior to the general election of May 1997 and in the months that followed.[10] Despite New Labour's announced intention to sign the UK into the EU Social Chapter if they were elected, thus ending the Maastricht opt out and opening the way for mandatory works councils,[11] there was never any serious suggestion that taking on board the social chapter would involve corporate boards including employee representatives or that there should be a second-level supervisory board in line with the much earlier suggestions of the Bullock Report[12] and the White Paper[13] that followed

---

[10] T Blair, *Spectator* Lecture, 22 March 1995 at Queen Elizabeth Conference Centre, Tokyo Speech, January 1996; Civil Service Conference Speech, Whitehall London, 13 October 1998.

[11] S Wheeler, 'Works Councils: Towards Stakeholding' (1997) 24 *Journal of Legal Studies* 44.

[12] 'The Bullock Committee' (Committee of Inquiry on Industrial Democracy, 1977, Cmnd 6706) was set up to examine a possible UK response to the draft 5th Directive that there should be pan-EU adoption of the German model of corporate governance—namely two-tier boards. The Bullock Report in fact recommended that there should be three constituencies represented in unitary company boards: employees and shareholders who together made up two-thirds of the board with the remainder of members being drawn from an independent group agreed upon by a majority of the other two constituencies.

[13] 'Industrial Democracy' (1978, Cmnd 7231). The White Paper proposed a two-tier board system that would be adopted voluntarily over time, in order that a flexible and gradual approach to employee participation could be taken.

it.[14] This could be seen as taking a rather cynical reading of the Company Law Review dialogues[15] (see DTI March 1998—the last time in fact that the word 'stakeholder' was mentioned in a document issued in a corporate setting by the DTI or its successor, the Department for Business, Enterprise and Regulatory Reform), but it would seem justified on the basis of ministerial speeches[16] and policy announcements that occurred concurrently with the Review.[17] Rather, the point that the Hampel Report is making is that there is no wider public interest in the idea of accountability through effective corporate governance. Corporate governance exists only to facilitate growth in shareholder value by ensuring that management behaviour is efficient for this purpose; it does not engage in shirking or other opportunistic behaviour envisaged by the matrix of principal-agent theory.[18]

The Cadbury Report was produced in response to the crisis of faith in corporate governance brought on by the high-profile failures in the UK of the late 1980s and early 1990s, principally Maxwell, Polly Peck and BCCI.[19] Consequently it is framed against the backdrop of the 'bad man' scenario, about which I have written on previous occasions,[20] and the (in reality very small) threat of more invasive regulatory intervention by government if a serious attempt was not made by the corporate sector itself to engender political and social legitimacy in corporate governance whilst still maintaining the edifice of principal–agent theory. The Hampel Report had no such constraints. It was a review initiated by the Financial Reporting Council to examine whether the original purpose of the Cadbury Report (which had been to come up with recommendations that would restore investor confidence) was being achieved.[21] The period of time from the Hampel Report to the collapse of Enron, we now know, was the high water mark for Anglo-American corporate governance.[22] In spite of blips, like the bursting of the dot.com bubble, increasing shareholder value continued as the only game in town.[23] There was no pressure to look beyond principal–agent theory or to consider, in any meaningful way,

---

[14] I Jones and M Pollitt, 'Who Influences Debates in Business Ethics? An Investigation into the Development of Corporate Governance in the UK since 1990' in I Jones and M Pollitt (eds), *Understanding How Issues in Business Ethics Develop* (Basingstoke, Palgrave, 2002) 14.

[15] DTI Consultation Document, 'Modern Company Law for a Competitive Economy' (March 1998).

[16] Margaret Beckett, then President of the Board of Trade, speeches to the PIRC Annual Conference, 4 March 1998 and to the CBI Annual Conference, 11 November 1997.

[17] G Wilson, 'Business, State and Community: Responsible Risk Takers, New Labour and the Governance of Corporate Business' (2000) 27 *Journal of Legal Studies* 151.

[18] E Fama, 'Agency Problems and the Theory of the Firm' (1980) 88 *Journal of Political Economy* 288; E Fama and M Jensen, 'Separation of Ownership and Control' (1983) 26 *Journal of Law and Economics* 301; O Williamson, *The Economic Institutions of Capitalism* (New York, Free Press, 1985).

[19] The Cadbury Report inspired a host of other states to look at their corporate governance structures in a similar way; See, eg Canada, 'Where Were The Directors? Guidelines for Improved Corporate Governance in Canada' (The Toronto Report) (Toronto Stock Exchange, December 1994); France, 'The Vienot I Report' (June 1995); and Australia, 'Corporate Practices and Conduct' (the Bosch Report) (1991).

[20] S Wheeler, 'Non-Executive Directors and Corporate Governance' (2009) 60 *Northern Ireland Legal Quarterly* 51.

[21] This is clear from the terms of reference for the Hampel Committee displayed in the annex to the report.

[22] J Parkinson and G Kelly, 'The Combined Code on Corporate Governance' (1999) 70 *Political Quarterly* 101.

[23] The creation of shareholder value in a post-Fordist world has morphed almost seamlessly into the idea of financialisation—the creation of profit through financial channels rather than traditional product based channels: see G Krippner, 'The Financialization of the American Economy' (2005) 3 *Socio-Economic Review* 173; P Ireland, this volume, chapter 6; P Ireland, 'Financialization and Corporate Goverance' (2009) 60 *Northern Ireland Legal Quarterly* 1. For the narrative of financialisation in the context of Enron see J Froud, S Johal, V Papazian and K Williams, 'The Temptation of Houston: A Case Study of Financialization' (2004) 15 *Critical Perspectives on Accounting* 885.

possible public dimensions to corporate existence. Pressure from non-government organsations and supranational bodies such as the EU was dealt with either by capture[24] or by crumbs from the corporate trough in the form of well-publicised, well-designed and relatively costless corporate social responsibility (CSR) interventions.[25]

The Higgs Report, on the other hand, was produced in a similar climate to the Cadbury Report.[26] It was, in effect, the UK response to the Sarbanes-Oxley legislation,[27] along with the Smith Report,[28] on the structure and function of audit committees and listed companies' audit practices. The Higgs Report labels NEDs the 'custodians of the governance process' (paragraph 1.6). The tone is almost apologetic:

> Corporate failure . . . will always be with us. Enterprise creates prosperity but involves risk. No system of governance can . . . protect companies . . . We can, however, reasonably hope that boardroom sins of commission or omission—whether strategy, performance or oversight—are minimised. This Review, by focusing on the quality of non-executive directors and the boardroom climate and behaviours necessary for their success, will I hope help take us towards this goal (paragraph 1.10).

At the base of the spectacular Enron and World Com collapses that triggered the knee-jerk response of the US in the form of the Sarbanes-Oxley legislation was overstated earnings,[29] so it is not surprising that the Higgs Report recommendation is that half the board members should be independent NEDs 'to manage conflicts of interest' (paragraph 9.5). The neo-liberal pomp of shareholder value so evident in the Hampel Report[30] retreated into sentiments about the need to boost 'public and investor confidence' (paragraph 2.10). Just as the Hampel Report rejected the inclusion of a diversity agenda, the Higgs Report was keen to embrace one—prospective NEDs do not need business experience and, moreover, varied and complimentary experiences can improve board performance (paragraph 10.15). In terms that are unfortunately reminiscent of the corporate drive towards high-profile, low-cost CSR interventions in the late 1990s,[31] diversity in board membership is linked to reputational concerns for the corporation around the commitment to equal opportunities (paragraph 10.16).

---

[24] S Eden, 'Greenpeace' (2004) 9 *New Political Economy* 595.

[25] C Smith, 'Corporate Social Responsibility: Whether or How' (2003) 45 *California Management Review* 52.

[26] As Clarke identifies, there is a certain cyclical crisis in corporate governance as the model for wealth accumulation struggles to accommodate the concerns of agency theory in times of corporate growth and stewardship in times of economic recession. This, he explains, is inherent in the nature of markets: see T Clarke, 'Cycles of Crisis and Regulation: the enduring agency and stewardship problems of corporate governance' (2004) 12 *Corporate Governance* 153.

[27] There is a massive literature on this topic, not least of which are some of the contributions to this collection. See generally D Langevoort, 'The Social Construction of Sarbanes-Oxley' (2007) 105 *Michigan Law Review* 1817 and references therein.

[28] 'Audit Committees: Combined Code Guidance' (the Smith Report) (2003).

[29] Ironically, in a period of American economic life that was witnessing large-scale growth, it was the Marxist notion of fictitious capital that proved to be its undoing; see K Ball, 'Death-driven Futures, or You Can't Spell *Deconstruction* Without Enron' (2007) 65 *Cultural Critique* 6.

[30] I Erturk, J Froud, S Johal, A Leaver, D Shammai and K Williams, 'Corporate Governance and Impossibilism' (2008) 1 *Journal of Cultural Economy* 109.

[31] See, eg S Wheeler, *Corporations and the Third Way* (Oxford, Hart Publishing, 2001); J Roberts, 'The Manufacture of Corporate Social Responsibility: Constructing Corporate Sensibility' (2003) 12 *Organization* 249.

C.   Drawing the Participation Picture

The suggestion that there should be a greater diversity on corporate boards by the Higgs Report was unsurprising in the sense that the proposals made demanded a significant number of new recruits to the corporate board and that these recruits should be independent of the corporation, thus a simple rearranging of labels was not going to be possible. In 2005 the consultancy firm Deloittes predicated that an additional 145 NED directors would need to be found if the FTSE 350 was to comply with best practise requirements as set by the Higgs Report recommendations incorporated into the Combined Code. The Female FTSE prepared by the International Centre for Women Leaders at Cranfield University each year since 1998 shows that there has been an increase in female NEDs in the FTSE 100 from 66 (10.82%) in 1999 to 114 (14.9%) in 2008. In the FTSE 250 the percentage of female NEDS dropped from above 9% in 2007 to 8.7% (115) in 2008. Despite the exhortations of the Tyson Report and other initiatives, this remains a depressingly low figure of participation.

This picture is replicated across the world in the more general context of female directorships, both executive and non-executive: Australia,[32] Canada,[33] the US,[34] New Zealand[35] and France,[36] for example, all have low levels. The notable exception is Norway, where there has been legislative intervention to boost the number of female executive directors to 40%.[37] Spain has promised legislation by 2015 if voluntary action has not improved the participation figure. It is not possible to make exact comparisons as appointment cultures differ across jurisdictions: for example, there is a much higher degree of patronage and consequently interlocks in France[38] than elsewhere, and in Italy[39] there is a desire to maintain family control and stability of ownership. Penetration by women in those jurisdictions will be slower as a result.

The boom in required appointments predicated by Deloittes and commented upon by others[40] has failed to lever women into the boardroom in large numbers despite their ever increasing participation in the workforce. The number of women in the workforce has been on an upward trend since the beginning of the 1970s. According to the Labour Force Survey,[41] the employment rate for women in the UK increased from 56% in 1971 to 70%

---

[32] A Ross-Smith and J Bridge, '"Glacial at Best": Women's Progress on Corporate Boards in Australia' in S Vinnicombe et al (eds), *Women on Corporate Boards* (Cheltenham, Edward Elgar, 2008) 67.

[33] B Long and E Morris, 'Beyond Corporate Board Representation: Understanding the Experience of Female Directors in Canada' (2008) *The Workplace Review* 10.

[34] 2008 Catalyst Census of Women Board Directors of the Fortune 500; T Wolfman, 'The Face of Corporate Leadership' (2007) *New England Journal of Public Policy* 37.

[35] J McGregor, 'Girl Power: Double Jeopardy or Diversity in Action behind the Boardroom Doors in New Zealand' (2003) 18 *Women in Management Review* 369.

[36] M Maclean and C Harvey, 'Women on Corporate Boards of Directors: the French Perspective' in Vinnicombe et al, above n 32, 47.

[37] There has also been legislative intervention in Sweden: see S Terjesen and V Singh 'Female Presence on Corporate Boards: a Multi-Country Study of Environmental Context' (2008) 83 *Journal of Business Ethics* 55.

[38] M Maclean, C Harvey and J Press, *Business Elites and Corporate Governance in France and the UK* (Basingstoke, Palgrave, 2006) 164.

[39] M Gamba and A Goldstein, 'The Gender Dimension of Business Elites: Italian Women Directors since 1934' (2009) 14 *Journal of Modern Italian Studies* 199.

[40] J Linck, JS Netter and T Yang, 'The Effects and Unintended Consequences of Sarbanes-Oxley Act on the Supply and Demand for Directors' (2009) 22 *Review of Financial Studies* 3287.

[41] ONS, 'Labour Force Survey' (March 2009).

in December 2008. A similar pattern exists in the US.[42] While these bare figures do not give details of the level of employment that is being undertaken, there is nothing to suggest that the women in employment are involved in low-level work or only involved very peripherally in management positions. In fact, the dedication of the Female FTSE Report 2008 would suggest exactly the opposite: it is dedicated to the 18,877 'women in the pipeline'.[43]

In the UK, particular efforts have been made to encourage women to break through the glass ceiling of senior appointments. One initiative, Opportunity 2000, is interesting in that it made the corporate sector itself responsible for identifying the reasons why women were absent from managerial roles. The idea was that membership of Opportunity 2000 would allow for corporate benchmarking against best practice and the development of gender mainstreaming.[44] The most recent initiative is promoted by a private company— MWM Consulting—and is called 'Women on Board'. It promises to work with female candidates by first identifying them and then finding a mentor for them, while at the same time working with listed companies to find the profile of director they want to appoint. Women on Board was launched in June 2009 to a fanfare of press coverage, both in print and on radio. It remains to be seen whether this initiative produces anything more than an occasional finder's fee for MWM Consulting. While it has laudable aims, it is not particularly different to the FTSE 100 Cross-Company Mentoring Programme, which began in 2004[45] but does not seem to have achieved a breakthrough of any sort, despite setting itself what it described as modest targets.[46] The Programme seeks to offer women working in the FTSE 100, identified by their Chairman or Chief Executive as being in the 'marzipan layer',[47] access to a mentor drawn from one of the FTSE 100 boards. As the specification of the programme dictates that it cannot be used as a poaching device, one wonders what encourages individuals to become mentors, other than maintaining their position within their peer group.

---

[42] A Mosisa and S Hipple, 'Trends in Labor Force Participation in the US' (2006) *Monthly Labor Review* 35. In Table 1 on p 36 the figures for the US female labour market participation are given as 50.1% in 1970, rising to 75.3% in 2005.

[43] The Female FTSE Report in 2007 and again in 2008 developed this concept of the 'pipeline' to demonstrate that there were women of ability waiting to be appointed to directorships, both executive and non-executive, in the FTSE 100 companies. The pipeline is constituted by women serving as executive and non-executive directors in listed companies outside the FTSE 100 and women serving on executive committees and senior teams in all listed companies. See R Sealy et al, 'The Female FTSE Report 2008' (Cranfield University School of Management, 2008) 34; R Sealy et al, 'The Pipeline to the Board finally Opens: Women's Progress on FTSE 100 Boards in the UK' in Vinnicombe et al, above n 32, 37, 42.

[44] For further discussion see E Garnsey and B Rees, 'Discourse and Enactment: Gender Inequality in Text and Context' (1996) 49 *Human Relations* 1014, where the point is made that Opportunity 2000 rather than promoting female participation uses language that reinforces prevailing power structures.

[45] See further P Thompson and J Graham, *A Woman's Place is in the Boardroom* (Basingstoke Palgrave Macmillan, 2008) esp ch 1.

[46] The target figures that the Programme wished to see reached were 10% female executive directors in the FTSE 100 by 2010 and 25% female NEDs in the FTSE 100 by 2010. Both of these figures would seem unobtainable from the baseline of the present position. The target figure for female NEDS has been pushed further away by the redesignation of male executive directors as NEDs since the Higgs Report, which suggests that this is acceptable practice provided that there is also a presence of independent NEDs (para 9.6).

[47] The Tyson Report coined the term 'marzipan' layer to describe the senior management of public limited companies that existed just below board level, and exhorted CEOs to encourage those in the marzipan layer to accept NED appointments in non-competitor companies (see p 14).

D.　The Problem of (Wo)men as (Wo)men

A variety of explanations for the continuing low participation rate of women as both executive and non-executive board members can be gleaned from the literature. What appears to hold the explanations together are two reoccurring themes: the presence of self-replicating male hierarchies and women's self-perception.[48] If we take the second of these themes first, it manifests itself in the literature on self-identity. As Konrad et al[49] explain, gender identities are constructed quite differently from early childhood onwards; the male gender model is focused on such things as dominance, autonomy and provision of material goods, while the female gender model is concerned with nurturing, deference and self abasement. These gender identities have a knock-on effect on career ambitions and career investment.[50] They are reinforced by gatekeepers, who in this context are likely to be male themselves and act true to their own gender self-identity by selecting for training and advancement those whom they perceive as having the characteristics associated with male gender identity.[51]

There is empirical evidence (admittedly quite old now) to the effect that CEOs are reluctant to appoint women who are not already directors of existing companies and also believe that women are fundamentally unqualified to sit in boardrooms.[52] If by 'unqualified' what is meant is measurable intellectual capital, then this is demonstrably not the case; an examination of men and women appointed to their first FTSE 100 corporate board between 2001 and 2004 shows women to be more likely to be in possession of an MBA degree and nearly as likely to have international experience in their career portfolio.[53] While the level of female educational attainment goes some way towards a rejection of self-identity theory and career investment observations, it might indicate that women are victims of status characteristic theory, ie that standards for them as a low status group are higher than those applied to high status groups—in this instance, prospective male appointees.[54] The Cranfield year-on-year study of female directors in the FTSE 100[55] revealed a significant recycling of female appointees supporting the idea that women are more likely to be appointed if they already have board experience. Recycling in this way

---

[48] See the extensive literature review provided by S Terjesen, R Sealy and V Singh, 'Women Directors on Corporate Boards: A Review and Research Agenda' (2009) 17 *Corporate Governance: An International Review* 320.

[49] A Konrad, JE Ritchie, P Lieb and E Corrigall, 'Sex Differences and Similarities in Job Attribute Preferences: A Meta-analysis' (2000) 126 *Psychological Bulletin* 593.

[50] P Tharenou, S Latimer and D Conroy, 'How to Make it to the Top? An Examination of Influences on Women's and Men's Managerial Advancement' 37 (1994) *Academy of Management Journal* 899.

[51] J Oakley, 'Gender-based Barriers to Senior Management Positions: Understanding the Scarcity of Female CEOs' (2000) 27 *Journal of Business Ethics* 321

[52] See R Burke, 'Why Aren't More Women on Corporate Boards?: Views of Women Directors' (1996) 79 *Psychological Reports* 840; B Ragins, B Townsend and M Mattis, 'Gender Gap in the Executive Suite: CEOs and Female Executives Report on Breaking the Glass Ceiling' (1998)12 *Academy of Management Executive* 28; M Mattis 'Women Corporate Directors in the United States' in R Burke and M Mattis (eds), *Women on Corporate Boards of Directors: International Challenges and Opportunities* (Amsterdam, Kluwer, 2000) 43.

[53] V Singh, S Terjesen and S Vinnicombe, 'Newly Appointed Directors in the Boardroom: How do Women and Men Differ?' (2008) 26 *European Management Journal* 48.

[54] M Biernat and D Kobrynowicz, 'Gender and Race-based Standards of Competence: Lower Minimum Standards but Higher Ability Standards for Devalued Groups' (1992) 72 *Journal of Personality and Social Psychology* 544.

[55] The Female FTSE Report 2008, above n 43.

raises the possibility of experienced women becoming gatekeepers[56] through the holding of multiple appointments for inexperienced women and does little to extend female participation.

Self-replicating hierarchies in the context of board appointments refers to the idea that those who, in practice if not in theory,[57] arrange nominations are most likely to want to appoint individuals with characteristics that resemble their own.[58] In contrast to the self-perception explanations considered above, what is being looked at here is the viewpoint of men who already hold positions as directors. According to social identity theory,[59] individuals define their own characteristics, such as gender, educational and class background and occupation, as the characteristics required for the identity of 'director'. Those wishing to become directors who share these characteristics will find it easier to enter the club than those who do not. There is an unearned advantage here brought about by the existence of collusive closure. This closure is triggered by the presence of self-reproducing social constructions that restrict access to those who possess particular social and educational capital.[60] Women may well be seen as having particular demographic profiles (real or imagined) which confine them to roles that conflicts with that of 'director', eg secretary, mother, potential mother. Kanter, exploring the idea of 'token' women on her research site, the Industrial Supply Corporation—one woman or a few women amongst male peers—identified 'role encapsulations' for the women involved. In her view, men assign four roles to women which in their view preserve what they see as familiar social-hetero-normative interactions. The roles are their ideals of traditional femininity and are the mother/Madonna; the seductress or whore; the cute but largely inept pet; and the strong woman/iron maiden.[61]

The idea of path dependency in board structure strikes a similar note: radical restructuring of board composition is unlikely to happen as it signals a loss of confidence in the current board, so only small incremental changes occur. A board is likely to continue with the structure and composition that it historically starts out with, which makes for a rather depressing future for potential female appointments.[62] To this can be added the series of 'small world' or 'interlock studies' that present the argument that the corporate elite is a

[56] The management literature characterises this as the 'Queen Bee' Syndrome; see S Marvin, 'Venus Envy: Problematizing Solidarity Behaviour and Queen Bees' (2006) 21 *Women in Management Review* 264; S Marvin, 'Venus Envy 2' (2006) 21 *Women in Management Review* 349.

[57] In reality, while technically appointed by the shareholders at a general meeting, the appointment of directors, both executive and non-executive, is approved by them, in the overwhelming majority of cases, without any discussion. The board in many ways is a self-perpetuating oligarchy. Its existing members put up new members for election and re-election. Shareholders do not interview directors and rarely even look at their curriculum vitae to determine their suitability. These things are done by existing board members, who 'market' the suitability of new appointees to the shareholders; see GF Davis and GE Robbins, 'Nothing but Net? Networks and Status in Corporate Governance' in K Knorr-Cetina and A Preda (eds), *The Sociology of Financial Markets* (Oxford, Oxford University Press, 2004) 290, 292. Directorships are rarely contested.

[58] R Khurana, 'The Curse of the Superstar CEO' (2002) 80(9) *Harvard Business Review* 60, 64. This short piece is essentially a synopsis of his book *Searching for a Corporate Saviour* (Princeton, NJ, Princeton University Press, 2002).

[59] For an explanation of this in the context of director selection see V Singh and S Vinnicombe, 'Why so few Women Directors in Top UK Boardrooms? Evidence and Theoretical Explanations' (2004) 12 *Corporate Governance* 479.

[60] R Khurana and M Piskorski, 'Sources of Structural Inequality in Managerial Labor Markets' (2004) 21 *Research in Social Stratification and Mobility* 167.

[61] Above n 5, 233–36.

[62] M Lynall, BR Golden, AJ Hillman, 'Board Composition from Adolescence to Maturity: A Multitheoretic View' (2003) 28 *Academy of Management Review* 416.

social network characterised by cross appointments between listed corporations. These cross appointments are facilitated by the members of the network, who recommend fellow network members for vacancies. The latest research on the small world phenomenon in the UK reveals that, while the pattern of the network may be different from earlier studies, it is still extant. NEDs are likely to be retired or existing FTSE 250 executives.[63] Self-replicating hierarchies, path dependency and small worlds all point towards recruitment from a limied tpool of talent, entry into which is restricted. This can lead to the board constituting itself as a cohesive group, which is one of the antecedent conditions for the phenomenon that social psychology calls groupthink.[64] Groupthink results in individuals becoming greater risk takers and less likely to ask questions and request information[65] as the result of a desire to maintain the group rather than perform their individual function. In the context of executive and non-executive board functions, this means that the monitoring part of the NED role is emasculated.[66] Of itself, this is an argument for the need to dilute network ties and challenge stereotypes by encouraging executive directors, in particular CEOs, to look beyond their own replication when recruiting to appointments; it is not an argument that necessarily supports the recruitment of women.[67]

E.   Outside Directors, Diversity Directors and Firm Performance

The question that is explored most often in the literature focusing on NEDs is whether the presence of NEDS and, by extension, 'diversity' improves the performance of the corporation on whose board the appointments are held. In relation to the gender issue, there is a danger that one is read as advancing an economic case only for inclusion rather than pulling together all the evidence to make the argument that there is no practical case for exclusion.[68] The case for inclusion is made at an altogether different level of argument. It is a broad moral and political argument about the place of women in society and the role of the corporate sector in recognising and supporting female ambition.[69] It is a case that is

---

[63] J Froud et al, 'Everything for Sale: How Non-executive Directors Make a Difference' in M Savage and K Williams (eds), *Remembering Elites* (Oxford, Blackwell, 2008) 162, 171.

[64] Groupthink was a concept first illuminated by Irving Janis in his 1972 work, *Victims of Groupthink* (Boston, MA, Houghton Mifflin). It is not an uncontested concept in social psychology and moreover it requires more factors to be present than simply a cohesive group. Cohesion is one of three prior conditions required, so it is easy to overstate the likelihood of the presence of groupthink in situations where there are functional ties between group members.

[65] Sonnenfeld makes the point that the most successful of corporate boards have usually included a dissenting voice, see J Sonnenfeld, 'What Makes Great Boards Great' (2002) 9 *Harvard Business Review* 106.

[66] M O'Connor, 'The Enron Board: The Perils of Groupthink' (2002) 71 *University of Cincinnati Law Review* 1233, 1259–63.

[67] Enron is the obvious case in point here—it is frequently referred to as an example of groupthink, yet there was a female member of the board who herself was one of three board members with what could loosely be termed diverse backgrounds. The most that can be claimed for female appointees in the context of groupthink is that it is less likely to occur as a phenomenon in the presence of diversity, see D Branson, *No Seat at the Table* (New York, New York University Press, 2007) ch 14.

[68] S Brammer, A Millington and S Pavelin, 'Gender and Ethnic Diversity among UK Corporate Boards' (2007) 15 *Corporate Governance* 393, 394–95.

[69] This, in turn, leads to another issue around the nature of the public company. Is it a purely private vehicle to be used by those who can afford to invest in it for wealth accumulation or does it have alongside the status of

already made and embodied in legislative interventions such as the Equal Pay Act 1970 and the Sex Discrimination Act 1975.[70] It is not an argument to be made at the level of corporate financial performance—or, indeed, at the level of any aspect of corporate performance at all. There is evidence to suggest that this moral argument is also endorsed by some institutional investors,[71] if not by all.[72] As explained above, the Higgs Report missed the opportunity to stress and endorse the moral argument for the presence of women and the Hampel Report expressly rejected it. Not even the Tyson Report, with its brief to devise ways of bringing diversity to PLC boards, was prepared to support the moral argument without also emphasising that the presence of women on the board might be attractive to customers and employees. The support of institutional investors for the moral argument has failed to make a significant impact in practical terms on the position of women in relation to board appointments. A strategy that draws attention to the positive contribution women can make to ensuring good and effective governance is required to complement the moral argument if significant progress is to be made in a reasonable timeframe.

Performance in these studies of NED director inclusion is generally taken to mean financial performance, and in fact agency theorists are unable to agree on whether the presence of NEDs does or does not improve a corporation's financial performance.[73] Extant studies provide conflicting conclusions. For example ,while Baysinger and Butler[74] find that it might have a 'mild effect', Kesner and Johnson[75] assert that it has no effect at all. Dalton and Daily[76] use a meta-analysis of 54 studies of board composition and 31 studies of board leadership structure to support Kesner and Johnson by concluding that there is little evidence of a link between a corporation's governance structure and its financial performance. Conflicting empirically based accounts about the effect of the presence of non-executive or outside directors occur throughout the literature on takeover defences, the composition of board committees, the separation of chairman and chief

economic vehicle a wider range of public responsibilities? On one level, this question can be answered by following through the line of debate that comes from the idea that corporate personality is itself a concession of the state, thus tying the corporate form to the actions of a benevolent state; on another level, it can be seen as a vehicle for economic activity the existence of which is tolerated by the state as long as taxation, disclosure and other governing legislation is complied with. There is a huge literature on these issues which is dealt with extensively elsewhere. See, eg J Sara, 'The Gender Implications of Corporate Governance Change' (2002) 1 *Seattle Journal of Social Justice* 457 and references therein.

[70] J Wajcman, *Managing Like a Man* (Cambridge, Polity, 1998) 11–16.

[71] D Bilimoria and J Wheeler, 'Women Corporate Directors: Current Research and Future Directions' (2000) in R Burke and M Mattis (eds), *Women in Management: Current Research Issues*, vol II (London, Sage, 2000) 138; N van der Walt and C Ingley, 'Board Dynamics and the Influence of Professional Background, Gender and Ethnic Diversity of Directors' (2003) 11 *Corporate Governance* 218, 223.

[72] Brammer et al have recently produced a study of corporate reputation (evaluated by selected investment company executives and the directors of the 10 largest PLCs in each industrial sector) and gender diversity at board level. They found a positive correlation between gender diversity and corporate reputation only in companies where there was between product and final consumer; see S Brammer, A Millington and S Pavelin, 'Corporate Reputation and Women on the Board' (2009) 20 *British Journal of Management* 17.

[73] S Zahra and J Pearce, 'Board of Directors and Corporate Financial Performance: A Review and Integrative Model' (1989) 15 *Journal of Management* 291.

[74] B Baysinger and H Butler, 'Corporate Governance and the Board of Directors: Performance Effects of Changes in Board Composition' (1985) 1 *Journal of Law Economics and Organization* 101.

[75] I Kesner and R Johnson, 'An Investigation of the Relationship between Board Composition and Stockholder Suits' (1990) 29 *Strategic Management Journal* 327.

[76] D Dalton and C Daily, 'Meta Analytic Reviews of Board Composition, Leadership Structure and Financial Performance' (1998) 19 *Strategic Management Journal* 269.

executive,[77] executive composition and removal of the chief executive.[78] The same confused picture occurs when the sex of directors is added.[79] The studies that look at the effect of sex in this context do not disaggregate NED appointments from executive appointments because of the low number of female appointments generally. Shrader,[80] using accounting data, finds a negative impact, but Carter, using raw market data, finds a positive one.[81] Francoeur[82] is equivocal about gender impact and, despite using both US and Canadian data over a four year period, makes the point that others have also made about the size of the sample available for analysis; the very low numbers of female directors make all results questionable. Campbell[83] uses Spanish data, which involves drawing upon an even smaller sample to report that firm performance is at worst not impaired.

F.   The Way Forward

The existence of studies that seek to make a business case rather than a moral case for the inclusion of women and the appointment of more women to corporate boards at least have some merit in that they can be taken to have recognised that changing the gender composition of the board might bring additional skills to the boardroom or enhance the skills that are already present there. This is something of a blow for agency theory as it can only look at the structural components of board composition and then only judge them against its assumptions about what motivates opportunistic behaviour[84] and its rather one-dimensional picture of human nature.[85] Rather than embarking on a critique of agency theory, a more instructive way forward is to look at other expansive theories of board behaviour which allow a wider inquiry to take place. The most useful of these in this context is resource dependency theory, or, as it is also termed, relational board theory. This model of board behaviour looks beyond the traditional monitoring function of boards to ask what other resources directors or potential directors can bring to a corporation which will assist it to operate in an uncertain environment. These resources might be linkages

---

[77] C Dalton and D Dalton, 'Boards of Directors: Utilizing Empirical Evidence in Developing Practical Prescriptions' (2005) 16 *British Journal of Management* 91.

[78] M Weisbach, 'Outside Directors and CEO Turnover' (1988) 20 *Journal of Financial Economics* 431; see generally I Filatotchev et al, 'Key Drivers of "Good" Corporate Governance and the Appropriateness of UK Policy Responses' (London, Department of Trade and Industry, 2007).

[79] An extensive review of available studies can be found in N Erhardt and D Werbel, 'Board of Director Diversity and Firm Financial Performance' (2003) 11 *Corporate Governance* 102.

[80] C Shrader, V Blackburn and P Iles, 'Women in Management and Firm Financial Performance: an Exploratory Study' (1997) 9 *Journal of Managerial Issues* 355.

[81] D Carter, BJ Simkins and WG Simpson, 'Corporate Governance, Board Diversity and Firm Value' (2003) 38 *The Financial Review* 38.

[82] C Francoeur, R Labelle and B Sinclair-Desgagné, 'Gender Diversity in Corporate Governance and Top Management' (2008) 81 *Journal of Business Ethics* 83.

[83] K Campbell and A Mínguez-Vera, 'Gender Diversity in the Boardroom and Firm Financial Performance' (2008) 83 *Journal of Business Ethics* 433. They also comment on the available Norwegian, Danish and Scandinavian studies (441).

[84] GF Davis and HR Greve, 'Corporate Elite Networks and Governance Changes in the 1980s' (1997) 103 *American Journal of Sociology* 1.

[85] C Daily, DR Dalton and AA Cannella, 'Corporate Governance: Decades of Dialogue and Data' (2003) 28 *Academy of Management Review* 371.

with outside agencies, legitimacy with internal stakeholders, provision of advice or simply the presence of a different voice.[86] When the function of the board is looked at in this way, the argument for the appointment of women is a strong one. They are likely to bring an as yet untapped resource or an as yet not present relational structure to the boardroom.[87] The requirement to include NEDs in the UK allows that a consideration of resource needs to be made with reasonable frequency, and the requirements of NEDs spelled out by the Higgs Report and the Tyson Report should lead to appointments that will enhance the resource base and relational capabilities of corporate boards.

G.   The Boardroom and the Black Box

The lack of consistency of results between studies that try to link director status (ie executive/insider and outsider/NEDs) or board demographics (gender, race) to firm performance points to there being other factors between input data, ie status or demographic and output data that are not being accounted for or measured. These would appear to be boardroom culture and processes.[88] A legitimate question would be why these studies continue to proliferate if they are failing to account for what occurs inside the 'black box' and look only at inputs and outputs. The answer is that access to conduct observational studies of boardroom interactions is very difficult to obtain, largely because much of what is being discussed amounts to market-sensitive data.

Huse conducted an empirical study of boardroom interactions and has subsequently constructed a process model of boardroom behaviour.[89] Additionally, other qualitative empirical work has been conducted through interviews with executive directors[90] and NEDS,[91] and questionnaire surveys of CEOs,[92] since Pettigrew famously observed in 1992 that the actual work of corporate boards was the most neglected of research topics.[93] From this work, from the knowledge of meeting dynamics drawn from social psychology literature and from ideas about how power, alliances, diversity and sameness are constructed, exercised and constrained within organisations generally, it is possible to set boardroom tasks and deliberations in context.[94] Cohesiveness, openness, generosity, involvement,

[86] L Dallas, 'The Relational Board: Three Theories of Corporate Boards of Directors' (1996) 22 *The Journal of Corporate Law Studies* 2 at 10-13.

[87] C Daily and D Dalton, 'Are Director Equity Policies Exclusionary?' (2003) 13 *Business Ethics Quarterly* 415 at 420.

[88] As Useem puts it, 'what the directors do behind those [closed] doors . . . determines the company's future performance', M Useem, 'Corporate Governance is Directors Making Decisions: Reforming the Outward Foundations for Inside Decision Making' (2003) 7 *Journal of Management and Governance* 241, 251.

[89] M Huse and A Solberg, 'Gender-related Boardroom Dynamics: How Scandinavian Women Make and Can Make Contributions on Corporate Boards' (2006) 21 *Women in Management Review* 113 at 118.

[90] M Huse, ST Nielsen and IM Hagen, 'Women and Employee-elected Board Members, and Their Contributions to Board Control Tasks' (2009) 89 *Journal of Business Ethics* 581.

[91] J Roberts, T McNulty and P Stiles, 'Beyond Agency Conceptions of the Work of the Non-Executive Director: Creating Accountability in the Boardroom' (2005) 16 *British Journal of Management* 5.

[92] A Minichilli, A Zattoni and F Zona, 'Making Boards Effective: An Empirical Examination of Board Task Performance' (2009) 20 *British Journal of Management* 55.

[93] A Pettigrew, 'On Studying Managerial Elites' (1992) 13 *Strategic Management Journal* 163 at 169.

[94] There are two, not necessarily competing, suggestions on how to open the black box. One is that of Forbes and Milliken, who suggest viewing the board as an entity in its own right and using research on cognitive processes to understand what goes on, see D Forbes and F Milliken, 'Cognition and Corporate Governance:

creativity and criticality are all aspects of the decision-making culture that Huse identifies in the boardroom that he studied. This boardroom included both female and employee directors.[95] On Huse's board there were no NEDs as his object of study was a Norwegian company.[96] NEDs have a harder role than executive directors in a strategic sense as they not only have to blend into the social system that is the board but they also have to monitor members of that board. It is at this point that the skills menus for NEDs outlined by the Higgs Report and the Tyson Report become particularly important. These enable a construction of what goes on in boardrooms, or should go on, to be built. This gives a fixed platform on which the contribution of women, with the values and perspectives that are traditionally associated with them, can be placed.

H.   The Realpolitik for NEDs

From the Higgs Report and the Tyson Report we can glean a picture of the characteristics required of NEDs and the functions they are expected to perform. NEDs require integrity and high ethical standards, sound judgement, the ability and willingness to challenge and probe, and strong interpersonal skills to negotiate within the boardroom.[97] What need to be negotiated are issues of power, influence, independence and trust if the board is to be able to function as an effective unit exercising governance tasks, with NEDs also performing their monitoring role. A key question that I have asked elsewhere[98] is whether successful negotiation of these issues is a bar to the accountability function of non-executive directors. In other words, can distant accountability be maintained in the presence of a locally negotiated functionality?

In order to be able to participate in governance tasks, NEDs must be able to display an awareness of how business works in general and be able to assimilate quickly information about how the particular business to which their appointment relates works. They need to be able to understand the dynamics between executive directors. They need to understand how individual strategic decisions will impact on share price, and how strategy is formulated within the organisation and then packaged to those outside the organisation.[99] NEDs need to be able to display sufficient knowledge in these areas to garner the trust of executive directors, thus enabling their comments and views to have an effect, and yet they also need to maintain a sufficient distance so as to avoid capture by executive directors and

Understanding Boards of Directors as Strategic Decision-making Groups' (1999) 24 *Academy of Managment Review* 489; the other is that of Pettigrew, above n 92, who sees the black box as being part of a wider organisational system.

[95] M Huse, A Minichilli and M Schøning, 'The Value of Process-oriented Boardroom Dynamics' (2005) 34 *Organizational Dynamics* 285.

[96] Norwegian corporate governance is a hybrid system in that it separates the roles of the chairman and chief executive, it uses the UK-derived 'comply or explain' system under code governance and gives employees a defined role in relation to the election of directors. It does not require NEDs, but it does require that directors elected by shareholders are independent of management. See the Norwegian Code for Corporate Governance, available at www.ncgb.no.

[97] Tyson Report, above n 2, 4.

[98] S Wheeler, 'Non-executive Directors and Corporate Governance' (2009) 60 *Northern Ireland Legal Quarterly* 51.

[99] P Stiles, 'The Impact of Boards on Strategy: An Empirical Examination' (2001) 38 *Journal of Management Studies* 627.

remain independent. Obviously they will be influenced by the executive voices around them, but they should not be dwarfed by that influence. Trust is a two-way process, as NEDs have to feel able to rely on the extent and quality of information they are given by executive directors in order to perform their monitoring function.[100] Trust and distrust have to coexist[101] but be balanced, as distrust between the two groups splits the board and results in a 'circle of control and counter control' developing.[102]

This would seem to encourage a process-orientated board that goes beyond what would normally be expected of compliance with a code drafted with an agency perspective in mind—that boards should operate in efficient ways to achieve their monitoring task. Codes exist to ensure that the gap between board task expectations and board effectiveness is filled. This results in a decision-orientated culture structured around the demands of finance, which are necessarily short-term.[103] The Higgs Report, though steeped in agency theory and unwilling to advocate a diversity agenda for its own merits alone, moves towards process culture from decision culture by setting out this approach to directorial behaviour which will promote deliberation. It is encouraging the presentation of a different story, the hearing of a different voice and the negotiation of behaviours.

I. What Gender Diversity Can Bring to the Table

There is no given set of rules that defines behaviour as feminine and so more likely to be pursued by women and another set of rules as masculine and so more likely to be encountered in men. Biological sex is only one determinate of behaviour among several. A direction for future research might be the measurement of the presence of masculine and feminine characteristics amongst a sample of NEDs on a Bem scale.[104] In the absence of this, proxy measures have to be used. Just as general social psychology literature has been drawn upon to suggest what processes might take place in board meetings in the absence of empirically derived data, so it is used in the context of the consequences of creating gender diversity in the boardroom. A considerable amount of the literature that is available looks at ethical decision-making and how gender traits and gender role theory interact with decision-making. In this women are seen as more caring and seeking of approval. Much of this research is conducted using questionnaires and mock scenarios, with ethical behaviour measured using a Likert scale. Much of this self-reporting research produces contradictory findings,[105] so to rely on it in the context of boardroom behaviour

---

[100] R Hooghiemstra and J van Manen, 'The Independence Paradox: (Im)possibilities Facing Non-executive Directors in The Netherlands' (2004) 12 *Corporate Governance* 314. On trust more generally within the boardroom see N McInerney-Lacombe et al, 'Championing the Discussion of Tough Issues: How Women Corporate Directors Contribute to Board Deliberations' in Vinnicombe et al, above n 32, 123, 133.

[101] RJ Lewicki, DJ Mcallister and RJ Bies, 'Trust and Distrust: New Relationships and Realities' (1998) 23 *The Academy of Management Review* 438.

[102] P Daudi, *Power in the Organisation* (Oxford, Blackwell, 1986).

[103] M Huse, *Boards, Governance and Value Creation* (Cambridge University Press, 2007) 234.

[104] S Bem, 'Gender Schema Theory: A Cognitive Account of Sex Typing' (1981) 88 *Psychological Review* 354. To date this has only occurred in the US, see J Barnett and M Karson, 'Managers, Values and Executive Decisions: An Exploration of the Role of Gender, Career Stage, Organizational Level, Function, and the Importance of Ethics, Relationships and Results in Managerial Decision-making' (1989) 8 *Journal of Business Ethics* 747.

[105] For a review and summary see D Beu, MR Buckley and MG Harvey, 'Ethical Decision-making: A Multidimensional Construct' (2003) 12 *Business Ethics: A European Review* 88.

would be to suggest incorrectly that the majority of boardroom decisions are ethical in nature and to focus inappropriately on decisions rather than the processes that lead to decisions.

Processes that are undertaken with a diverse membership are more likely to include constructive dissonance and dialogic discussion as the members try to relate to each other. In the context of the boardroom, women, as the more marginal members, are more likely to take the role of the 'tempered radical'.[106] As they look for acceptance and inclusion, their preparation levels are likely to be high,[107] and earlier socialisation patterns for women would suggest that they are likely to be methods orientated rather that result orientated, interested in creating communion rather than extending personal agency and committed to the personal development of others rather than solely task orientated. These differences will result in an alteration of the speed at which decisions are made as process and discussion begins to occupy a higher profile. Discussion might consider the impact of particular decisions on a wider group of people.

Introducing a gender diversity component into what is almost exclusively a male domain—the world of the NED—introduces a different voice: a voice free of network ties and obligations, or least a voice subject to different network ties and obligations. The emphasis here is on difference, and it is at least debatable that introducing a diversity agenda focusing on another group with a different role identity would also bring difference to the boardroom, for example ethnic minorities. The difficulty with assessing precisely what might result from this different voice is that the numbers of female NEDs are so small as to make even in-depth qualitative work difficult even if access could be successfully negotiated. However, it is also the case that a different voice in the boardroom should be seen as an attractive plus, a desirable add-on to boardrooms reflecting the make-up of society and the presence of women as significant players in the labour market.

---

[106] D Meyerson and M Scully, 'Tempered Radicalism and the Politics of Ambivalence and Change' (1995) 6 *Organization Science* 585.
[107] L Carli, 'Gender, Interpersonal Power and Social Influence' (1999) 55 *Journal of Social Issues* 81.

16

Has the Financial Crisis Revealed the Concept of the 'Responsible Owner' to be a Myth?

CHARLOTTE VILLIERS[*]

A. Introduction

In a recently published debate in response to the developing global financial crisis, Catherine Howard asked the following question:

> Are pension funds and other institutional investors simply victims of this financial crisis or, as major market participants, did they actually play some role in precipitating it?[1]

The reply to that question came from James Gifford, executive director of the UN Principles for Responsible Investment:

> Shareholders have to take some responsibility for this, if only because their capital was being used by their agents and investee companies in ways that have clearly caused the meltdown. Clearly they could have been more diligent, supervised these agents better, and ensured that executive remuneration reflected real performance and long-term thinking.[2]

Is Gifford right? Clearly, institutional investors played a role in the drama of the current financial crisis, and in this paper I will explore that role and consider how the contribution of shareholders to corporate governance might be strengthened. Does the concept of responsible ownership offer any potential solutions to the problems identified in the financial crisis? The government's responses to the financial crisis might also provide an opportunity for strengthening the overall corporate governance framework, not least through its creation of a new institutional shareholder body, UK Financial Investments Ltd, to manage its shareholdings in some of the banks that required recapitalisation. In this paper I will first provide a brief overview of the relevant features of the financial crisis. I will then consider the concept of responsible ownership, showing how it has developed on two levels: first, focusing on the role of institutional and other shareholders in corporate governance; and secondly, its growth into a concept related to environmental,

---

[*] Professor of Law, University of Bristol.
[1] C Howarth, 'Desperate Times' in 'Ethical Investors—Are the UN Principles for Responsible Investment Working?' (Ethical Corporation, 4 November 2008), available at www.ethicalcorp.com/content.asp?ContentID=6170&ContTy.
[2] J Gifford, 'Radical Ideas', in 'Ethical Investors—Are the UN Principles for Responsible Investment Working?' (Ethical Corporation, 4 November 2008), available at www.ethicalcorp.com/content.asp?ContentID=6170&ContTy.

social and governance issues. I will then identify some limitations connected with this concept and seek to show how those limitations manifested themselves in the unfolding of the financial crisis. I will consider the UK government's response and how that might impact on the application of the responsible owner concept, and I will suggest how institutional investors might be assisted in their aim to be responsible owners.

B.   The Crisis

Books are already being written on the financial crisis and its causes,[3] and so to provide a description of what happened in this paper is hardly likely to be sufficient. Instead, I will present a brief outline of the significant factors that might relate more specifically to the focus of this paper. In short, the crisis was precipitated by a sub-prime mortgage failure and collapse of a housing bubble in the US, combined with problems of high oil prices and high food prices. These problems led to a crisis among globally interconnected financial institutions in which many commercial and investment banks suffered massive losses and were faced with bankruptcy. The effects of these financial failures within the banking industry have rippled out to other financial sectors and also to retail and manufacturing businesses in all parts of the world, affecting both the western economies and developing economies. Companies are facing liquidity problems because banks are not lending to them and this is affecting their ability to pay suppliers as well as to continue to produce goods. Companies are also facing reduced orders, so their supplies are outweighing demand for their goods and services. The situation is widely regarded as one of a deep recession, with the depth of the economic problems being compared with those of the Great Depression of the 1930s. Individuals are facing financial difficulties as a result of job losses and/or increased debt payments, leading to home repossessions and reduced purchasing power. Falling share prices are also placing their pensions in serious jeopardy. The crisis has required major interventions at state level not least through huge financial bailouts for the failing banks, but also through collective attempts to manage the crisis by leaders across the world. States have incurred massive debts in order to bail out stricken industries, and economic regions such as the EU are facing economic and political crises.

A number of causes for this deep financial crisis have been identified: financial liberalisation[4] through light-touch regulation or deregulation, encouraging regulatory arbitrage via measures such as use of offshore and off-balance-sheet entities; development of innovative and complex financial products, with inadequate transparency about these

---

[3] See, eg G Tett, *Fool's Gold: How Unrestrained Greed Corrupted a Dream, Shattered Global Markets and Unleashed a Catastrophe* (Boston, Little Brown, 2009); R Shiller, *The Sub-prime Solution: How Today's Global Financial Crisis Happened, and What to Do About It* (Princeton NJ, Princeton University Press, 2008); DN Chorafas, *Financial Boom and Gloom: The Credit and Banking Crisis of 2007–2009 and Beyond* (Basingstoke, Palgrave Macmillan, 2009); V Cable, *The Storm: The World Economic Crisis and What it Means* (London, Atlantic, 2009).

[4] CM Reinhart and KS Rogoff, 'Is the 2007 US Sub-prime Financial Crisis So Different? An International Comparison' (2008) 98 *American Economic Review: Papers and Proceedings* 339, 342: 'The majority of historical crises are preceded by financial liberalization . . . While in the case of the US, there has been no striking de jure liberalization, there certainly has been de facto liberalization. New unregulated, or lightly regulated, financial entities have come to play a much larger role in the financial system, undoubtedly enhancing stability against some kinds of shocks, but possibly increasing vulnerabilities against others.'

financial products, which were traded over the counter rather than through exchanges that would have regulated pricing, trading or disclosures; lack of liquidity and inadequate risk premium; a bonus culture that encouraged excessive risk-taking in the financial institutions; and investors seeking high returns through new types of fund and financial product.[5] Martin Wolf, writing in the *Financial Times*, succinctly describes the problems:

> How did the world arrive here? A big part of the answer is that the era of liberalisation contained seeds of its own downfall: this was also a period of massive growth in the scale and profitability of the financial sector, of frenetic financial innovation, of growing macroeconomic imbalances, of huge household borrowing and of bubbles in asset prices.[6]

For a corporate or financial lawyer, these causes suggest fundamental problems in the system of corporate governance. If the corporate governance system were working effectively, the risks might have been identified and management of the risks might have been controlled to avoid the disasters that we have witnessed.

Within any modern system of corporate governance, institutional investors play a crucial role. The Combined Code of Corporate Governance, for example, highlights their participation in the system of monitoring and control of the activities of corporate directors.[7] This approach partly arises from the structure of large companies. While there is a theoretical separation of ownership and control that gives rise to the need for a corporate governance system to protect shareholders from potentially self-interested behaviour on the part of directors and managers, the growth in the proportion of shares held by institutional shareholders gives to them considerable voting power to encourage directors and managers to run the company properly and in their and the company's interests. Yet the current crisis suggests that, at least in the context of innovative financial products, institutional shareholders failed to act as effective corporate governance monitors. As a result, many of the institutional shareholders have suffered major losses in the value of the assets they hold.

Adherence to the concept of responsible ownership in corporate governance debates raises possibilities on at least two levels for institutional investors: applying their responsibilities strictly as corporate governance actors, and thereby engaging with corporate management and exercising their votes; and also, potentially, in the sense of pursuing ethical issues such as the environment and social responsibility, an increasingly recognised version of the concept of responsible ownership. In the next section I will consider the narrower vision of institutional investors in their strict corporate governance role.

C. Institutional Investors as Responsible Owners in Corporate Governance

Company law in the UK, as well as in the US, has traditionally focused on the interests of shareholders. Following the corporate scandal resulting in the collapse of the Maxwell

---

[5] See J Rutterford, 'The Financial Crisis and its Impact on Trusts and Trustees' (2009) *Trusts and Trustees* 1, 1–3.

[6] M Wolf, 'Seeds of its Own Destruction', *Financial Times*, 8 March 2009.

[7] Section 2 of the Code, for example, is devoted specifically to the role of institutional shareholders.

Communication Corporation, the now widely respected Cadbury Report, published in 1992,[8] laid the foundations for the UK's corporate governance system. The Report identifies shareholders as 'owners'. In paragraph 6.1 the Report states: 'the shareholders as owners of the company elect the directors to run the business on their behalf and hold them accountable for its progress'. Paragraph 6.6 makes clear that, since shareholders have delegated their responsibilities as owners to the directors who act as their stewards,

> it is for the shareholders to call the directors to book if they appear to be failing in their steward-ship and *they should use this power*. While they cannot be involved in the direction and management of their company, they can insist on a high standard of corporate governance and good governance is an essential test of the directors' stewardship. The accountability of boards to shareholders will, therefore, be strengthened if shareholders require their companies to comply with the Code. (emphasis added)

It is clear from this statement that the Cadbury Committee did not envisage shareholders behaving passively but rather that they would participate actively in the corporate governance of their companies. Thus the Code made reference to reports and accounts being put to shareholders and for shareholders to comment and ask questions on them, as well as to make use of annual general meetings and other communications with the board to make resolutions and to make use of their votes.

More specifically, the Cadbury Report identified institutional shareholders, given the weight of their votes, as having power that is of fundamental importance for influencing standards of corporate governance. The Report added,

> Their readiness to do this turns on the degree to which they see it as their responsibility as own-ers, and in the interests of those whose money they are investing, to bring about changes in companies when necessary, rather than selling their shares.[9]

Later the Report adds: 'Because of the importance of their collective stake, we look to the institutions in particular . . . to use their influence as owners to ensure that the companies in which they have invested comply with the Code.'[10]

What is clear from the Cadbury Report is that shareholders generally are seen as owners with responsibilities. Viewing shareholders as owners is potentially problematic. Indeed, during the late 1990s there was an academic debate that cast doubt on this identity. Paddy Ireland and John Kay separately pointed out the limitations of the language of ownership in relation to shareholders.[11] Despite their observations, the label has remained in place to a large extent. The media frequently talks about shareholders as owners of the company and more recently the label has been used to underline the responsibilities of share-holders—giving credence to the notion of the 'responsible owner'. In this way, rather than acting as passive share*holders*, a share*owner* role implies a more active role.[12]

---

[8] 'Report of the Committee on the Financial Aspects of Corporate Governance' (Cadbury Report) (London, Gee & Co, 1992).

[9] Ibid, para 6.10.

[10] Ibid, para 6.16.

[11] P Ireland, 'Company Law and the Myth of Shareholder Ownership (1999) 62 *Modern Law Review* 32; J Kay, 'Test of Possession', *Financial Times*, 28 February 1997. See also *Short v Treasury Commissioners* [1948] 1 KB 116, 122 (per Evershed LJ, Court of Appeal): 'shareholders are not, in the eye of the law, part owners of the undertaking'.

[12] C Mallin, 'Institutional Shareholders: Their Role in the Shaping of Corporate Governance' (2008) 1 *International Journal of Corporate Governance* 97, 100.

Institutional shareholders have particular responsibility to seek to influence the board through their collective voting powers arising from the proportion of shares they hold. First, Cadbury recognised the increasing concentration of shares of large companies in the hands of institutional shareholders. At the time of the Cadbury Report institutional shareholders held the 'majority of shares in quoted companies'.[13] Throughout the 1990s institutional shareholders continued to grow and, by the time that the Hampel Committee published the *Combined Code on Corporate Governance* in 1998, institutions held 60% of the shares in UK listed companies.[14] Although the levels have fluctuated and currently domestic institutions such as pension funds and insurance companies hold about a quarter of UK shares, their dominance being challenged by newer owners such as hedge funds and sovereign wealth funds, it is still clear that they 'remain the giants of the investment community'.[15] The foreign investors who now own around 50% of UK shares are predominantly institutional shareholders.[16] The institutions handle enormous sums of money. Tomorrow's Company cites research that shows that the largest 300 pension funds collectively held just over $10 trillion at the end of 2006.[17] Another notable dimension of their potential power is that the institutions, 'by virtue of their size, wide diversification, and tendency to index large portions of their portfolios, the largest of these institutional investors have become *universal owners* as they own a cross section of their national economy'.[18] With such potential influence the institutional shareholders appear to have an obvious role as stewards of the companies whose shares they hold. The Cadbury Committee made this observation clear in its Report.

How might they exercise that role? The Institutional Shareholders' Committee (ISC) was referred to in the Cadbury Report as providing guidance for how the institutional shareholders might perform their ownership responsibilities. In particular, the ISC has periodically updated its Statement of Principles on the Responsibilities of Institutional Shareholders and Agents. The current Statement, updated in 2007, highlights that institutional shareholders will:

— set out their policies on how they will discharge their responsibilities—clarifying the priorities attached to particular issues and when they will take action;
— monitor the performance of, and establish, where necessary, a regular dialogue with investee companies;
— intervene where necessary;
— evaluate the impact of their engagement;
— and report back to clients/beneficial owners.

The Association of British Insurers and the National Association of Pension Funds have also long recognised that shareholders have not only rights but also responsibilities. Thus, not only are boards to be accountable to shareholders, but 'share ownership also gives rise

---

[13] Cadbury Report, above n 8, para 6.9.

[14] Hampel Committee, 'Final Report on Corporate Governance' (London, Gee & Co, 1998) para 5.1.

[15] Tomorrow's Company, *Tomorrow's Owners—Stewardship of Tomorrow's Company* (London, Centre for Tomorrow's Company, 2008) 49.

[16] Mallin, above n 12, 98.

[17] Tomorrow's Company, above n 15, 49, citing 'The World's 300 Largest Pension Funds', Joint Research by Pensions & Investment and Watson Wyatt (2006), available at www.watsonwyatt.com/europe/research/pdf/PI-_300_Analysis_2007.pdf.

[18] JP Hawley and AT Williams, 'Shifting Ground: Emerging Global Corporate-governance Standards and the Rise of Fiduciary Capitalism' (2005) 37 *Environment and Planning* 1995, 1996 (emphasis retained).

to governance responsibilities' and 'institutional investors have an overriding fiduciary responsibility to those on whose behalf they are investing'. They emphasise the role of responsible voting, in particular stating the need to

> exercise their voting policy, in respect of the range of matters on which shareholder decisions are sought, in support of the proper management of companies and directed towards the enhancement of long-term shareholder value and the wider economic benefits which this should also engender.[19]

The Myners Report of 2001 was concerned with the role and responsibility of institutional investors. It made clear that the case for action does not rest on a public interest argument about shareholder responsibility but that institutional investors have a basic duty as managers to do their best for their clients.[20]

A number of institutional shareholder organisations have published their views on the notion of responsible ownership. F&C Investments, for example, recently published a document entitled 'Corporate Governance: Responsible Ownership'[21] that set out its vision of responsible ownership. It suggests that its role is to use its votes and its voice to encourage companies to achieve the key principles of good corporate governance practice, including:

— an empowered and effective board and management team;
— appropriate checks and balances in company management structures;
— effective systems of internal control and risk management covering environmental, social and governance (ESG) issues and all other significant issues;
— a commitment to promoting a 'governance culture' of transparency and accountability that is grounded in sound business ethics; and
— remuneration policies that reward the creation of long-term shareholder value through the achievement of corporate objectives.

The practical expression of responsible ownership according to F&C Investing includes:

— voting in line with its responsible ownership policy;
— communicating its concerns to companies where its votes do not support directors' recommendations;
— engaging in ongoing dialogue with companies on significant matters related to ESG issues, so as to encourage good practice;
— integrating ESG issues into its investment process; and
— reporting on its votes and engagement to clients and for retail funds, to the wider public.

F&C makes reference to a number of international and national codes on corporate governance and on social, ethical and environmental issues, stating that these codes form the basis of its expectations of companies.

---

[19] See 'Responsible Voting—A Joint ABI–NAPF Statement' (Association of British Insurers, National Association of Pension Funds, 19 July 1999).

[20] HM Treasury, 'The Myners Review of Institutional Investment in the UK: Report' (2001) para 57, 13. See further: National Association of Pension Funds, 'Institutional Investment in the UK: Six Years On' (November 2007) and HM Treasury, 'Updating the Myners Principles: a Response to Consultation' (2008).

[21] F&C Investments, 'Corporate Governance: Responsible Ownership' (January 2009), available at www.fandc.com.

It is clear from these documents that institutional shareholders are expected to play a role in corporate governance through engaging with management to let their concerns be known, through voting and monitoring performance, and through maintaining clear audit trails.[22]

During the twenty-first century, the concept of responsible ownership has developed considerably. One of the effects of globalisation has been an increased focus on issues of corporate social responsibility and sustainable development. This trend has led to an expansion of the definition of responsible ownership. This will be the concern of the next section.

D.   Responsible Ownership as an Ethical Concept

Another view of responsible ownership is much broader than that seen through the corporate governance lens. The emphasis on sustainable development, environmental protection and corporate social responsibility brings with it a more widely encompassing potential role for shareholders, in particular the institutional shareholders. Above, I noted that some observers view institutional shareholders as universal owners. Through this identity, '[a] universal owner owns a small, but representative fraction of most of the companies in an economy, and therefore their ability to satisfy their fiduciary duties depend on the economy's overall efficiency and performance'.[23]

As a consequence of this identity, according to Tomorrow's Company, 'universal owners have a natural interest in sustainability because they either receive the benefits of companies managing their external impacts or suffer the negative consequences if they don't'.[24]

Viewing institutional shareholders from this universal ownership perspective involves recognition of the fact that, according to Hawley and Williams, 'maximising shareholder return is not simply a case of summing individual returns on a firm-by-firm basis, but involves the interactions among the whole portfolio'.[25] Hawley and Williams add that recognising this complexity 'becomes one of the foundation blocks for the expanded and expanding definitions of fiduciary obligation'.[26] They also note that with the proliferation of institutional holdings there has been a growth of the corporate governance standards globally, largely promulgated through collective action by institutions. What is noticeable about these standards is that increasingly they focus on long-term considerations rather than on short-term success, reflecting the long-term investment horizons of the institutional shareholders whose investments are also highly diversified.[27] There is also an increasing emphasis on social and environmental impacts. The OECD Principles of Corporate Governance and the Global Compact provide prominent examples, and the more recent UN Principles for Responsible Investment demonstrate a commitment to

---

[22] See also National Association of Pension Funds, 'Pension Funds' Engagement with Companies' (2007).

[23] Tomorrow's Company, above n 15, 51.

[24] Ibid.

[25] Hawley and Williams, above n 18, 1996.

[26] Ibid.

[27] As noted in the 'UN Principles for Responsible Investment' (UNEP Finance Initiative and UN Global Compact, 2006), available at www.unpri.org/principles.

sustainable development through the fulfilment by investors of their fiduciary duty. The latter's stated aim is that 'applying the Principles should not only lead to better long-term financial returns but also a closer alignment between the objectives of institutional investors and those of society at large'. The UN Principles state a belief that ESG issues can affect the performance of investment portfolios and that the Principles may align investors better with broader objectives of society. The participating investors commit, on this basis, where consistent with their fiduciary duties:

— to incorporating ESG issues into investment analysis and decision-making processes;
— to be active owners and incorporate ESG issues into their ownership policies and practices;
— to seek appropriate disclosure on ESG issues by the entities in which they invest;
— to promote acceptance and implementation of the principles within the investment industry;
— to work together to enhance their effectiveness in implementing the Principles;
— and each to report on their activities and progress towards implementing the Principles.

The fact that there are 362 investors who have signed up to the UN Principles[28] reflects the widespread acceptance of this broader notion of responsible ownership.[29] The political power of responsiveness to climate change and to poverty provides strong incentives for companies and investors to pursue ESG policies in their corporate and investment strategies.

It is clear from this and the previous section that responsible ownership is a very real concept that investors are ready to accept. However, the effectiveness of the concept relies on what happens in practice. Whilst the many objectives within the concept appear to be irrefutable, in practice there are limitations and barriers that must be faced. I will seek to identify such obstacles in the following section.

E.   The Limitations of the Responsible Owner

The Principles for Responsible Investment make clear the dual aspects of responsible ownership: active corporate governance participants and emphasis on the ESG issues. This two-layered feature of responsible ownership presents a potential conflict. Although corporate governance is now readily associated with long-term corporate success, such success is still predominantly measured by profit levels. Whilst the business case for CSR is frequently made and recognised, inevitably the CSR issues are bound to conflict with the need to make profit. Indeed, some commentators observe that company law arguably actually mandates profit maximisation and thereby sits in direct conflict with 'any incurrence of uncompensable costs for socially desirable action'.[30] This conflict arises partly as a result of the perceived limitations of the fiduciary duties of institutional investors to their

[28] Howard ,above n 1.
[29] See also National Association of Pension Funds, 'Responsible Investment Guidance' (2009).
[30] J Parkinson, *Corporate Power and Responsibility: Issues in the Theory of Company Law* (Oxford, Oxford University Press, 1993) 260.

clients and a consequent emphasis on short-term financial results.[31] Cadbury and Millstein, for example, highlight the investment horizons of fund managers that focus on quarterly earnings, noting that 'there is simply no avoiding the issue of institutional "short-termism" warping capital markets'.[32] If they too readily pursue a long-term strategy and ESG goals and seek to stay and exercise voice in a failing company this approach may clash with the primary goal of their clients, which is usually interpreted as the maximisation of risk-adjusted returns. Thus it appears difficult to integrate the long-term interests of their beneficiaries into their fiduciary responsibilities and the fund managers are easily put at risk of breaching their fiduciary duty to their beneficiaries.[33] Although broader interpretations of the fiduciary duties of fund managers have been provided which would require them to consider the ESG issues that affect the long-term prospects of their beneficiaries,[34] such interpretations have not yet been tested fully in the courts.

A number of other obstacles to effective responsible ownership have also been identified. Hendry et al, for example, highlight various factors that contribute to investors retaining a 'trader' mentality rather than adopting an ownership identity and taking on the responsibilities that go with ownership. They note that the freedom afforded by a liquid stock market to simply sell shares if things look bad weakens the financial justification for shareholder activism. Furthermore, institutional investors compete with each other, and that reduces the incentive for activism when other investors are likely to free ride. When investors do meet with executives, the purpose is not so much to control or influence management but to use such meetings as a basis for their buying and selling decisions.[35] On the other hand, Hendry et al note that these free-rider problems have been reduced by the reconcentration of share ownership, which also makes it more difficult simply to sell. Engagement then offers the potential to improve returns. In addition, higher voting power and delegated voting rights provide encouragement to be more active. as do the increased opportunities to use votes on matters such as remuneration and reappointment of directors.[36]

Other obstacles include lack of transparency as a result of inadequate information disclosure. This is particularly problematic for effective oversight of CSR and ESG issues, which are usually dealt with in narrative reports and presented more as public relations and reputation-enhancing documents.[37] In addition, the organisational structures of the institutional investors have affected their cultures vis-à-vis socially responsible investment (SRI) matters, and also with regard to shareholder activism more generally. Juravle and Lewis, for example, note that 'organizational culture—comprising organizational artefacts,

---

[31] See, eg Mallin, above n 12, 103.

[32] SA Cadbury and IM Millstein, 'The New Agenda for ICGN', Discussion Paper No 1 for the ICGN 10th Anniversary Conference (London, ICGN, 2005), quoted by Mallin, above n 12, 103.

[33] C Juravle and A Lewis, 'Identifying Impediments to SRI in Europe: A Review of the Practitioner and Academic Literature' (2008) 17 *Business Ethics: A European Review* 285, 288.

[34] Freshfields Bruckhaus Deringer, 'A Legal Framework for the Integration of Environmental, Social and Governance Issues into Institutional Investment' (Geneva, United Nations Environment Programme Finance Initiative, 2005).

[35] J Hendry, P Sanderson, R Barker and J Roberts, 'Responsible Ownership, Shareholder Value and the New Shareholder Activism', BRESE Working Paper No 13 (November 2004) 6, available at www.brunel.ac.u/research/brese/pub/work.htm. See also J Hendry, P Sanderson, R Barker and J Roberts, 'Owners or Traders? Conceptualizations of Institutional Investors and their Relationship with Corporate Managers' (2006) 59 *Human Relations* 1101.

[36] Ibid.

[37] See C Villiers, *Corporate Reporting and Company Law* (Cambridge, Cambridge University Press, 2006) ch 10.

values and underlying beliefs—may be an additional impediment to ESG integration in the core investment decision-making process'.[38] They note the internal environment may be 'dominated by a pull towards short-termism, herding/gravitation towards defensible decisions and a lack of integration of ESG aspects'.[39] Hendry et al note similar problems with regard to more mainstream shareholder engagement.[40]

Corporate social responsibility and ESG matters are also susceptible to contradictions that present obstacles to the objectives of strategic investment policies. The structure of the market economy tends to be based on short-termism, forcing investors to pressurise companies into focusing their efforts on maximising shareholder value and risking the possibility of irresponsible behaviour in order to achieve those shareholder gains.[41] In addition, social responsibility screens operate in relative rather than absolute terms, so that companies given better SR scores are not necessarily responsible but are only better than the worst companies.[42] Companies may also receive good SR scores in some matters but do badly in others. Linda Markovitz provides a number of examples, including companies scoring well on diversity issues yet poorly on treatment of workers or on environmental damage.[43] Effective comparisons are then difficult to achieve.

An important potential obstacle to responsible ownership rests in the corporate law principle of limited liability. The existence of this principle offers little to encourage shareholder activism since the exposure of shareholders to risk is reduced to virtually nothing when applied together with separate personality.[44] The investors' role is then reduced to seeking to maximise shareholder value through short-term speculation.

F.   How Responsibly Did Investors Behave in the Financial Crisis—What Contribution Did They Make to the Crisis?

It is clear that many institutions lost vast amounts of money in this banking crisis. In particular, many who are concerned with SRI were major losers. According to John Entine, SRI funds held far more financial stocks on a percentage basis than did conventional index funds. In the largest 41 US SRI funds, three of the top eight holdings were financials—AIG, Bank of America and Citigroup—all of whom had received praise for various of their CSR credentials.[45] Yet, as Entine remarks, 'the stock price of all three of these companies cratered in part because their loan portfolios were weighed down by securities that even their own accountants could not understand'.[46] This lack of transparency arose as a result of the complexity of the financial products being sold. This problem was exacerbated by the fact that the innovative financial products being sold were

---

[38] Juravle and Lewis, above n 31, 299.
[39] Ibid.
[40] Hendry et al, above n 33.
[41] L Markovitz, 'Can Strategic Investing Transform the Corporation?' (2008) 34 *Critical Sociology* 681, 682.
[42] Ibid.
[43] Ibid, 694–95.
[44] See, eg P Ireland, 'Limited Liability, Shareholder Rights and the Problem of Corporate Irresponsibility' (2008) *Cambridge Journal of Economics* doi:10.1093/cje/ben040.
[45] J Entine, 'Financial Crisis: Social Investment—Crunch Time for Ethical Investing' (2008) *Ethical Corporation* (28 October 2008), available at www.ethicalcorp.com/content_print.asp?ContentID=6159.
[46] Ibid.

not sold through the normal market channels and their complexity made them difficult to understand or to see their limits.[47]

However, it is also possible to argue that socially responsible investing might have added to the problems by distracting the investors from the straightforward corporate governance issues. The research models used for the purpose of socially responsible investing might in fact fail to appreciate the importance of governance structures. Worse, Entine suggests that, not only do critics note that SRI research methodology failed to identify cracks in the mortgage market, 'it may even have encouraged the problem by bypassing market forces and injecting a social agenda into the mix'.[48] Entine cites Dirk Matten, who suggests 'that many social investors have downplayed the actual business of a business . . . while overweighting what he believes are less critical and more symbolic concerns such as announced programmes to combat climate change or targeted philanthropy'.[49]

The suggestion implied in Entine's paper is that the concentration by many investors on the ESG issues caused them to take their eyes off the ball on mainstream corporate governance matters, the nuts-and-bolts practices and the risk management and incentive structures. The written and oral evidence presented to the Treasury Select Committee in the UK appears to support Entine's assertion. Peter Montagnon, for example, who is Director of Investment Affairs at the Association of British Insurers, admitted that the shareholders had not been as effective as they might have been: 'it is right that we are players here and we have to improve our game'.[50] In its written evidence to the Treasury Select Committee, PIRC stated its belief that 'there has been a failure of shareholder engagement in the run-up to the current crisis'.[51] It highlighted the failure of the shareholders to rein in those inappropriate policies on remuneration that led to excessive risk-taking. It noted also that not only are many fund managers lacking in capacity or desire to undertake their responsibility for corporate governance issues, but also a number of large financial institutions have already cut back the resources they dedicate to corporate governance analysis.[52]

The Association of British Insurers (ABI) admitted that analysts tended to place great stress on the impact of short-term developments at the expense of focusing on long-term issues. This stress on the short-term may have encouraged some financial institutions to take excessive risks, which subsequently led to serious losses.[53] This culture needs to change. The ABI also noted the need to improve dialogue between independent directors and shareholders, and to ensure that dialogue appropriately addresses key issues, such as risk management.[54] In turn, the Investment Management Association stated that both exit and engagement strategies were used. However, the engagement was not as effective because it did not achieve the desired results. The barriers to effective engagement it noted

[47] House of Commons (HC) Treasury Committee, 'Banking Crisis: Dealing with the Failure of the UK Banks', Seventh Report of Session 2008–09, HC 416 (London, House of Commons, 2009) para 250.
[48] Entine, above n 43.
[49] Ibid.
[50] HC Treasury Select Committee, 'Banking Crisis—Hedge Funds and Short-selling' (London, House of Commons, 2009) 144-iii, 27 January 2009, Q345.
[51] PIRC, Written Evidence, HC Treasury Select Committee (London, House of Commons, 2009) 287.
[52] Ibid, 288.
[53] Association of British Insurers, Written Evidence, HC Treasury Select Committee (London, House of Commons, 2009) 76.
[54] Ibid.

included restricted information because the shareholders did not have insider status. Nor were the risks on the balance sheets appreciated by the boards and management of financial institutions, though engagement could not have prevented that problem. What seems to come out of the evidence to the Treasury Select Committee was not that the investors were entirely passive but that their activism was not effective. PIRC suggested that this might require a larger role for the state and/or regulators in corporate governance in the future.[55] This leads me to consider the government's response to the crisis and what effect that might have, particularly in relation to responsible ownership.

G.   The Government's Response to the Crisis

As part of the bail-out process, the government has nationalised some banks and part nationalised others by purchasing non-voting shares in them. The government has set up a company, UK Financial Investments Ltd (UKFI), through which it will hold these businesses and shares on a commercial basis and at arm's length. Essentially, UKFI will adopt the role of an institutional shareholder, following the ISC's Statement of Principles. The company is managed by executives from the private sector together with senior officials from the Treasury.[56] The overarching objectives of UKFI will be to protect and create value for the taxpayer as shareholder, with due regard to financial stability and acting in a way that promotes competition. The aim is for UKFI not to hold investments permanently but to develop and execute an investment strategy for disposing of the investments through sale, redemption, buy-back or other means.

According to the Treasury Department, UKFI's role will be to ensure management incentives for banks in which it has shareholdings that are based on maximising long-term value and restricting the potential for rewarding failure. It will also oversee the conditions of the recapitalisation fund, including maintaining, over the next three years, the availability and active marketing of competitively priced lending to homeowners and small businesses at 2007 levels. While it holds investments, UKFI will actively monitor the activities of the investee company's board and engage in open dialogue with the company. Its management activities will include monitoring, intervention when necessary, voting, and evaluating and reporting.[57]

Membership of the UKFI board will comprise a private sector chair, three non-executive private sector members, a chief executive and two senior government officials from HM Treasury, and a shareholder executive. Sir Philip Hampton has agreed to become the UKFI's first chair and John Kingman is the chief executive. UKFI will manage its investments in Northern Rock plc and part of Bradford & Bingley. These companies will continue to have their own independent boards and management teams, determining their own strategies. Importantly, the Treasury Committee highlighted the fact that Mr Kingsman has stressed the need for UKFI Ltd to engage with other institutional

---

[55] PIRC, 'The Limitations of Engagement' (undated), available at www.pirc.co.uk/news/story300.html.
[56] See HM Treasury, 'New Company to Manage Government's Shareholding in Banks', Press Release 114/08 (3 November 2008), www.hm-treasury.gov.uk/press_114_08.htm.
[57] For details see UK Financial Investments Ltd, 'An Introduction: Who We Are, What We Do, And the Framework Document Which Governs the Relationship Between UKFI and HM Treasury' (March 2009).

shareholders.[58] The Treasury Committee also highlighted the need for greater publicity of UKFI's investment mandate and for a clearer definition of the term 'arm's length'.[59]

In addition, the government has begun a consultative review of corporate governance within the banking industry with the remit to examine corporate governance in the UK banking industry and make recommendations, including in the following areas:

— the effectiveness of risk management at board level, including the incentives in remuneration policy to manage risk effectively;
— the balance of skills, experience and independence required on the boards of UK banking institutions;
— the effectiveness of board practices and the performance of audit, risk, remuneration and nomination committees;
— the role of institutional shareholders in engaging effectively with companies and monitoring of boards; and
— whether the UK approach is consistent with international practice, and how national and international best practice can be promulgated.[60]

Obviously it is still early days, and one can only speculate at this stage about the possible effectiveness of the government's response. Already UKFI Ltd has made clear its criticisms of bonuses of certain executives in the high-profile bank failures. For example, UKFI has published its intention to vote against the resolution to approve Royal Bank of Scotland's Remuneration Report because it discloses the decision of former members of the RBS board to treat Sir Fred Goodwin and Johnny Cameron as retiring early, thereby enabling them to take undiscounted pensions, which UKFI considers to be against the company's interests and therefore UKFI's interests as a value-oriented shareholder.[61]

More fundamentally, the government's involvement could lend weight to the universal owner vision of institutional shareholders. The government's intention is to manage its shareholdings at arm's length, and it also sees its shareholder role as temporary. However, its intervention and the involvement of taxpayers' money to deal with the crisis emphasises the responsibility that will fall on the shoulders of the shareholders. If their companies fail, we all lose—as pensioners, as savers, as insurance clients and as taxpayers. The universal owner mandate requires a more effective activism on the part of the shareholders. I will conclude in the next section by highlighting some ways in which their engagement might become more effective.

H.   Possible Solutions

It is clear that the concept of responsible owner is here to stay. Until now it has been taken on board theoretically but less than universally in practice. The definition of responsible

---

[58] HC Treasury Committee, Seventh Report, above n 45, para 213.
[59] Ibid, 83–90.
[60] See Sir David Walker, HM Treasury, 'Independent Review of Corporate Governance of UK Banking Industry', Press Notice 10/09 (9 February 2009), available at www.hm-treasury.gov.uk/press_10_09.htm.
[61] UKFI Ltd press release, 31 March 2009, available at www.ukfi.gov.uk.

owner has been extended and expanded over time, with investors themselves contributing to the development of standards and codes related to the concept.[62]

The financial crisis suggests that there are flaws in the practical application of the concept. Not only is it not universally applied, but, where engagement takes place, it is clear that such engagement has not always been effective, as some institutional investors have themselves admitted. Yet the financial crisis indicates that there is a need for the responsible ownership concept to be put into effect. Reports that institutional investors who fail to comply with the UN Principles for Responsible Investment risk expulsion may show that the signatories actually mean what they say.

The government's intervention is likely to give that argument support because it has brought the whole British economy into play within this arena. The urgency of climate change and alleviation of poverty in the developing world would imply that the ESG aspects will also remain significant.

How might the effectiveness of shareholder engagement be improved? A number of suggestions can be made. First, transparency needs to be improved, and this may require regulatory change. Secondly, there needs perhaps to be better coordination of institutional investors, so that collectively they may be more effective than acting as individual fund managers.[63] They should also be prepared to exercise their right to remove board members more forcefully, so that a genuine threat exists to confront poor management performance. Thirdly, there should be mandatory disclosure requirements for shareholder voting patterns and reports on engagement to clients and other stakeholders. Fourthly, a clear balance between corporate social responsibility and corporate governance strategies needs to be established that identifies clearly how they relate to and affect each other. Fifthly, more resources for effective governance monitoring and engagement are required, as well as a shift of culture away from an emphasis on the short-term issues.

These suggested measures alone are unlikely, however, to result in lasting, deeper changes. More fundamental changes are required to turn the notion of responsible ownership into a more meaningful and convincing strategy. Some structural changes to the corporate law system and corporate cultures are required. A radical step would be to reduce or eradicate altogether the concept of limited liability. That would force shareholders to engage more readily with their boards and to be more prepared to intervene in the activities of their corporations. Of course, there are likely to be practical issues to be answered, not least how shareholders with diversified portfolios can realistically intervene in all the companies in which they hold investments. However, some of these issues already arise for existing company law provisions, so such a step would not necessarily create novel problems. Another approach is required. Emphasising the potential social benefits of companies rather than seeing them only as profit-making entities might provide grounds for encouraging shareholders to engage and act collectively with other corporate constituents to force their boards to direct corporate activities in more positive ways. Shareholders of large companies are not a homogeneous body and so must already balance their different interests for the purposes of effective activism. Working together with other corporate activist groups might bring about an altogether more responsible enterprise.

---

[62] See, eg National Association of Pension Funds, 'Responsible Investment Guidance' (March 2009).
[63] A clear distinction would need to be drawn between collective shareholder engagement and acting in concert.

17

The Institutional Investor's Role in 'Responsible Ownership'

FRANK CURTISS, IDA LEVINE AND JAMES BROWNING*

A. Introduction

The role of institutional investors in the current financial crisis has been brought to the forefront by regulators and the media. Some have voiced the opinion that institutional investors should exert more influence over, and effectively police, the companies in which they are shareholders. This extends not only to broad governance issues, but also to complex industry-specific issues—such as the adequacy of a bank's balance sheet or the extent and nature of its investment in asset-backed securities (ABSs) and other derivatives. Measured against this, institutional investors have been seen by some as having fallen short of their collective responsibilities.

Appealing though this view may be, the reality is far more complicated. Institutional investors are just some of the many 'players' in our global financial system. To name but a few, there are securities and futures exchanges, investment banks, brokers acting for clients and their own account, banks trading their proprietary book, as well as other securities and futures traders. There are also the credit rating agencies and auditors whose role should encompass scrutiny of corporate governance and risk issues in relation to the companies which they review.

Moreover, the term 'institutional investors' embraces both the owners of investment capital, such as pension funds, charities and sovereign wealth funds, and the professional investment management firms they appoint to manage assets on their behalf. This generally creates a two-tier approach in which asset owners set the high-level framework and parameters within which their investment managers then take day-to-day decisions. Asset owners may appoint a wide range of firms with different characteristics and objectives—long-only long-term discretionary asset managers, hedge funds that use leverage and/or hold short positions, managers seeking to match pension fund liabilities, private equity funds taking strategic and/or control positions, and so on.

These institutions operate under many different regulatory frameworks around the globe, each of which may take a jurisdiction-specific approach on issues. So, the global

* Frank Curtiss, RAILPEN Investments; Ida Levine, Capital International Limited; James Browning, Capital International Limited. The opinions expressed in this chapter are entirely the personal views of the authors and are in no way representative of the views held by either RAILPEN Investments or The Capital Group.

picture is nothing if not complicated (arguably, too complicated), and institutional investors are only one part of the puzzle.

While institutional investors as shareholders of public companies may have an important role to play, it would be wrong to suggest that all institutional investors have the same interests, or are able to prevent or provide solutions to the present and future macro-economic crises. Having said this, particularly in the UK, shareholders are provided with a number of tools in law, regulation and 'soft law' that facilitate their engagement with the management and non-executive directors of the companies in which they invest (see section F below). Shareholders should use these responsibly, and with sufficient information and focus to effect positive change where possible. In turn, asset owners should assess the performance of their investment managers in this regard (taking into account the investment manager's mandate).

To understand the role that institutional investors can play in influencing the decisions of companies and the operation of financial markets, it is important to understand the specific legal and commercial background, including the roles and responsibilities of the institutional investor. It is also useful to analyse these roles and responsibilities with reference to two major themes: (i) the role of stock markets as providers of liquidity and opportunities to issuers for capital raising; and (ii) existing legal and regulatory systems that provide opportunities, but also may impose constraints, on institutional investors' influence over companies in which they invest. We examine these aspects in detail below. First, it is important to understand the profile of a typical institutional investor.

B.   Who is the Institutional Investor?

As noted above, there is a wide range of institutional investors with different interests and incentives. However, perhaps one of the largest sources of institutional investment in the global capital markets is pension funds, which have the objective of providing long-term retirement benefits.[1] Given their significant impact on investment in the global public securities markets, we will focus on pension funds and their agents in this chapter with an emphasis on the UK.

The trustees of UK pension funds are asset owners. They are the legal custodians of the assets in pension funds and have a duty to act in the best interests of the fund's beneficiaries. However, in the UK (and, generally, elsewhere) the trustees are not permitted to manage the funds themselves, but are obliged by law to appoint suitably qualified professional investment managers to do so on their behalf.[2] In so doing, trustees must divest themselves of day-to-day investment decisions. This legal requirement is an important safeguard, but it immediately and necessarily distances

---

[1] Pension funds and insurance companies currently account for around 70% of the total assets under management for institutional clients in Europe (in total, €13.5 trillion), with pension funds accounting for 30% and insurance companies accounting for 41%. Source: European Fund and Asset Management Association, 'Annual Asset Management Report: Facts and Figures' (July 2008).

[2] In the UK, this obligation is derived from s 19 of the Financial Services and Markets Act 2000, under which 'regulated activities' can only be carried on by persons appropriately authorised by the Financial Services Authority or exempt persons.

trustees from day-to-day environmental, social and governance (ESG) issues. Indeed, in considering such issues, trustees must be careful that they do not take decisions in relation to matters that, under the various regulatory systems, are the preserve of the professional investment manager.

Instead, trustees' responsibilities lie in choosing suitable investment managers and setting an appropriate framework in which the investment managers must operate, a responsibility which has a significant effect on a manager's approach to ESG issues. A pension fund will tend to be diversified and appoint different types of investment managers. The majority of any such fund's assets will generally be given to managers with mandates to invest in liquid equity and debt securities listed on stock markets or traded in other regulated markets (the primary focus of this chapter), with a much smaller proportion being given to other types of so-called non-traditional investments, such as hedge funds, real estate and private equity investments (in relation to which, see below).

As previously mentioned, institutional investment by pension funds brings with it two key players: (i) trustees, the owners who create the framework for investment; and (ii) investment managers, their agents who make investments and focus on the day-to-day complexities of a portfolio's investments within the framework provided.

C.   Trustees' and Investment Managers' Fiduciary Duties

It is worth noting at this point that trustees are subject to a high duty of care when discharging their obligations and that a breach of trust or fiduciary duty imposes potentially significant personal liability on a trustee up to the full extent of his or her own personal assets. By comparison, the potential liability of (particularly public) shareholders is generally limited to their investment, while that of directors of companies is, save in exceptional circumstances, less acute, with significant protections again being derived from the limited liability nature of companies.

Given that a trustee's overriding responsibility is to act in the best interest of beneficiaries and safeguard the fund's assets, trustees will appoint a range of expert investment managers with wide competencies to invest the pension fund's assets so that the fund can meet its obligations to pay pensions when they fall due, at an acceptable overall level of risk. As the trustees' agent, the appointed investment manager assumes a fiduciary responsibility towards the trustees and the fund, and must manage its mandate within the objectives and guidelines prescribed by trustees.

This informs a trustee's and investment manager's approach to corporate governance and other ESG issues in that any investment decision must generally be driven primarily by financial factors. In the absence of an express objective to the contrary, this is especially so for an investment manager. This includes considering both the level of risk and the return from any investment. Today, the consideration of ESG issues is often integrated into investment managers' decision-making processes. Generally speaking, the weight that ESG factors are attributed depends on the extent to which these issues affect the investment manager's appraisal of the future financial performance and prospects of the company in question. This approach is widely accepted in the context of the legal obligations explained above. The United Nation's report on the legal framework of ESG,[3] led by the law firm Freshfields Bruckhaus Deringer, concludes that:

> the links between ESG factors and financial performance are increasingly becoming recognised. On this basis, integrating ESG considerations into an investment analysis so as to more reliably predict financial performance is clearly permissible and is arguably required in all jurisdictions.[4]

For example, notwithstanding political and public concerns regarding the level of executive pay, an investment manager may approve what might be considered to be a substantial remuneration package provided that, in all the circumstances, it can be justified in terms of the expected return on investment and it aligns the incentives of executives with those of a company's shareholders. It would be inappropriate for shareholders to vote against executive remuneration arrangements on an 'absolute' basis to implement a broader political agenda. The advancement of any broader agenda as to what society considers an acceptable level of executive pay is the responsibility of regulators and legislators, not institutional investors (but see below for further discussion of remuneration and incentives).

In the context of the financial crisis, there has been much commentary on the role that remuneration strategies have had on risk taking, not only for directors but also for individual employees, in particular traders and other employees of investment banks. While it is part of the role of shareholders to concern themselves with the appointment of directors, directors' remuneration and the review of executive remuneration plans put to their advisory vote, it is not their function to scrutinise individual employees' salary and bonus arrangements. Shareholders should not displace management and the human resources function of companies and micro-manage employee remuneration arrangements. They should be able to rely on boards and their remuneration committees to set appropriate remuneration policies and maintain effective internal controls in this area.

For similar reasons, the current emphasis on sustainable development, environmental and corporate social responsibility must be scrutinised in light of a trustee's duties to the pension fund beneficiaries. Where managing and promoting these factors will improve a company's performance (or ignoring them could have a negative effect), these issues become material to investment decisions. However, from an investment perspective, their significance will differ according to circumstances and, again, using pension funds as an example, institutional investors are generally not able to pursue social agendas for their own sakes. Where ESG becomes political or symbolic, it detracts from the core role of an investment manager, which is to assess the fundamental long-term financial performance and prospects of an enterprise. From the perspective of the trustees' fiduciary duties, this has to be the proper approach, given the trustees' responsibility to match pension liabilities as they come due.

---

[3] Asset Management Working Group of the UNEP Finance Initiative (led by Freshfields Bruckhaus Deringer), 'A Legal Framework for the Integration of Environmental, Social and Governance Issues into Institutional Investment' (October 2005).

[4] Ibid, 13.

D.   The Nature and Purpose of Stock Markets

A stock market listing facilitates investment in relatively well-established companies, encouraging expansion and growth. Stock markets achieve this by setting rules, in particular, regarding disclosure of material information on companies' activities, to provide a fair and accessible investing platform. Securities markets also provide liquidity to those investing in listed securities so that available investment capital may move freely. Companies that perform well are able to attract investment on the most attractive terms and continue to prosper, whereas less successful companies find it difficult to do so (or will only be able to do so very expensively). This market mechanism guides investment capital to where it is most valuable.

These aspects of stock markets make listed securities attractive investments for pension funds. Trustees often require their investments to be liquid (to enable them to meet their obligations to pension fund beneficiaries) and investment managers are able to invest on an 'arm's length' basis, knowing that if an investment underperforms they are free to sell their shares and invest elsewhere. This liquid nature of listed stock markets means that any foray into activism by an investment manager must be justified in terms of effort, risk and potential return and should not be pursued for its own sake—the answer to a company that is no longer attractive over the long term is to sell its securities. To invest significant time and resources with one company to try and remedy a discrete business issue in relation to an investment may not serve a fund's beneficiaries well. Moreover, this type of investment crosses over into another asset class, private equity, which is discussed more fully below.

E.   Limits to the Role of Public Shareholders

Allied to the fundamental role of stock markets is the distinction between the roles of a public company's shareholders and its directors. The shareholders own the company, but they have vested the control and responsibility for day-to-day management of the company in the directors and managers.[5] As shareholders, one of the most important roles of institutional investors is to vote for directors with the requisite expertise to successfully manage the businesses of public companies, a task which should be taken very seriously. However, institutional investors should not be expected to have a better understanding of individual business models and specific issues than the companies' directors themselves.

For example, in an arena where neither regulators nor the banks' own board of directors fully anticipated the financial crisis, it is unrealistic to have expected institutional investors to have identified, and in some way directed, the affairs of the companies in which they invested to prevent or confine the crisis. This is particularly unrealistic in complex, less transparent areas such as capital adequacy standards, and permitted lines of business and practices around complex securities and derivatives. The primary responsibility for identifying and controlling banks' risk exposures and setting rules and standards must lie with regulators. It must be responsible regulators who set the yardstick against

---

[5] E Ferran, *Company Law and Corporate Finance* (Oxford, Oxford University Press, 1999) 115.

which performance must be measured. Regulators have superior access to information and detail about companies (particularly banks and other financial institutions), including non-public information, that is not (and should not be) available to public shareholders.

The current financial crisis comes towards the end of the long Basel II and Capital Requirements Directive[6] initiatives to implement more appropriate capital standards for banks across Europe. With hindsight, these initiatives look inadequate. However, in the run up to the financial crisis, institutional investors put their faith in regulatory capital requirements which had evolved through many years of regulatory study and consultation. This turned out to be illusory comfort. However, it was for the regulators to set a higher hurdle in this area, not institutional investors. A key theme of this chapter is that, while institutional investors can engage with the management of companies, an appropriate legal, regulatory and political framework and adequate standards must provide the foundation to make this engagement effective.

F.   Corporate Governance Tools

Having noted some of the background and possible legal and commercial limitations on the institutional investor's role in ESG, it is equally important to note the many tools provided in law, regulation and 'soft law' to enhance the corporate governance of UK public companies, and provide opportunities to shareholders to engage with and exert influence on companies, where they believe that there is a proper investment thesis for doing so. These are especially well developed in the UK financial market, and provide ample opportunity to investors to engage with companies effectively if used in an informed, systematic way. These include the following.

1.   Annual General Meetings

These are perhaps the most important opportunity in a company's calendar for share-holders. Shareholders may consider, and vote on, items on the meeting agenda. In particular, this is an opportunity for institutional investors to vote against director appointments and inappropriate remuneration policies (on an advisory basis). As noted above, the analysis of remuneration policies should not be done mechanically or in a vacuum. They are company specific, and of far more importance than the absolute level of pay is how the structure of pay packages incentivises and affects the level of risk-taking behaviour of company directors. If remuneration is to be used as an industry-wide tool to manage risk, this initiative should come from regulators acting globally on a coordinated basis. Indeed, in this respect we welcome recent initiatives by the UK Financial Services Authority (FSA) to determine, and promulgate, best practice principles in the financial services sector.[7] We also believe that the extent to which a bank's own policies meets the requirements ought to be disclosed in their remuneration reports. It is hoped that an

---

[6] Directive 2006/49/2/EC of the European Parliament and the Council of 14 June 2006 on capital adequacy of investment firms and credit institutions, [2006] OJ L177/201.

[7] FSA Policy Statement 09/10, 'Reforming Remuneration Practices in Financial Services' (August 2009), and FSA Feedback Statement 09/05, 'Reforming Remuneration Practices in Financial Services' (December 2009).

augmented regulatory framework will result in votes against overpaid directors being used more frequently as a sanction where appropriate.

2.   Right to Approve Major Transactions and Pre-emption Rights

Under the UK Listing Authority's Listing Rules, shareholders have the legal right to approve certain major transactions.[8] This is an important right for institutional investors in that it relates to the protection and maintenance of shareholders' capital. It facilitates institutional investors providing input into major transactions proposed by UK listed companies. It is a feature of UK regulation which is not currently replicated in all major financial markets. A related concept is pre-emption rights, which seek to prevent investors' capital being diluted by generally requiring companies to go to existing shareholders first when raising additional capital. Under the UK system, shareholders have significant pre-emption rights, but this is not the case in other jurisdictions, such as the US and the Far East.

3.   Right to Propose a Resolution or Requisition a Meeting

In the UK and a number of other jurisdictions, shareholders have the right to requisition a shareholders meeting to propose shareholders' resolutions. It is wide-ranging and, amongst other things, directors may be appointed or removed via this mechanism. In the UK, shareholders representing at least 10%[9] of the share capital may invoke this right. Although infrequently used, this general power is very important to institutional investors in that a mechanism exists to hold the company to account. The threat of this may underpin discussions between a company and institutional shareholders on matters of concern that would otherwise not be taken seriously.

In addition, 'soft law' and industry initiatives in the UK provide structural and practical support for corporate governance in the UK. The following are some of the most significant.

(a)   The Institutional Shareholders Committee (ISC)

The ISC provides a useful forum at which institutional investors may exchange views and pursue matters of common interest to investors. It initially issued a Statement of Principles for the Responsibilities of Institutional Shareholders and Agents which has recently been developed into the ISC's Code on the Responsibilities of Institutional Investors.[10] The Code is currently voluntary and sets out best corporate governance practices for institutional shareholders in terms of how they monitor and engage companies.[11] This recognises the primacy of financial considerations for institutional investors. The Code only applies in the UK, but, despite this, many managers may adopt the Code (or the relevant parts for

---

[8] UK Listing Authority's Listing Rules, ch 10, Significant Transactions.

[9] UK Companies Act 2006, s 303.

[10] The Institutional Shareholders' Committee, 'Code on The Responsibilities of Institutional Investors' (November 2009).

[11] The Code comprises seven principles, addressing: disclosure of stewardship responsibilities, conflicts of interest, monitoring companies, escalation of activities, collective action, voting policy and reporting.

their businesses) in other markets. The Code is important as it lays down a clear expectation between institutional investors and companies (and between asset owners and asset managers) as to the protocol for corporate governance. Following the Walker Report,[12] it is likely that the Code will be afforded even greater status in the UK because Sir David Walker recommended that it be ratified by the Financial Reporting Council (the regulatory body responsible for the Combined Code—see paragraph (b) below), following which it will become known as the Stewardship Code. This is being consulted on in early 2010 and, if adopted, the Stewardship Code will have a status similar to that of the Combined Code (and, indeed, will replace the existing sections of the Combined Code dealing with engagement), with observance on a 'comply or explain' basis. Common adoption of the Code and its ratification as the Stewardship Code will no doubt force companies to take it seriously. In an era where global mandates are the norm, there could be even greater benefit from codes such as these if they were promulgated on a broader global basis.

(b)   The Combined Code

The Combined Code[13] was adopted in the UK in 1998 and incorporated into the UK Listing Authority's Listing Rules. The Combined Code is the successor to, and brought together, the principles contained in both the Cadbury Code[14] (which focused on corporate governance) and the Greenbury Report[15] (which focused on remuneration). Under the Combined Code, companies are required to disclose how they apply the code and explain any deviations. The Combined Code covers board structures and performance, remuneration, accountability and audit, and relations with shareholders, including institutional shareholders. The Financial Reporting Council (FRC) recently reviewed the Combined Code, a move triggered by the current economic climate, and invited comment on the entirety of the Code. The findings were published in December 2009 and, amongst other things, the opportunity was taken, in the context of bank remuneration issues, to bolster the remuneration aspects of the Code by emphasising the need for performance-related pay to be aligned with the long-term interests of companies. The revised Combined Code will be known as the UK Corporate Governance Code and, when finalised, is intended to come into effect in mid-2010.

(c)   UNPRI

The United Nations Principles for Responsible Investment (UNPRI) also provide a common framework for fiduciaries and their investment managers to integrate ESG issues into their investment portfolios. In early 2005 the then UN Secretary-General Kofi Annan invited a group of the world's largest institutional investors to join a process to develop the Principles. Launched in April 2006, the Principles are a set of global best practice guidelines for responsible investment. They recognise the duty of institutional investors to act in

---

[12] Sir David Walker, 'A Review of Corporate Governance in UK Banks and Other Financial Industry Entities—Final Recommendations' (26 November 2009) Recommendation 17. See chapter 16, 299 for a summary of the scope of the Walker Review.

[13] Financial Reporting Council, 'The Combined Code on Corporate Governance' (June 2008).

[14] Committee on the Financial Aspects of Corporate Governance, 'Report of the Committee on the Financial Aspects of Corporate Governance: The Code of Best Practice' (Cadbury Report) (1 December 1992).

[15] 'Directors' Remuneration: Report of a Study Group Chaired by Sir Richard Greenbury' (17 July 1995).

the best long-term interests of their beneficiaries, but recognise that ESG issues can affect the performance of investment portfolios. Signatories commit to the Principles to the extent consistent with their fiduciary duties—they are given access to examples of good practice from a global network of peers and opportunities to collaborate and network with others, thereby reducing research and implementation costs. By 2009 the number of signatories had grown to 538 institutions, representing US$18 trillion-plus in assets.[16]

G.   Coordinated Action and Transparency

The ISC Code and the UNIPRI initiatives, as well as recent statements from the UK government and the FSA, suggest that coordinated action by institutional investors is an important tool in shaping the activities of public financial institutions and achieving positive outcomes. There are, however, real and perceived legal impediments to investment managers acting together to engage with public companies. This is because of rules regulating the activities of shareholders if they 'act in concert', and additional rules which exist in the EU and other jurisdictions which seek to control the level of ownership or control by entities (or groups of entities) over companies, especially those in regulated sectors such as banks.

In particular, in the UK under the Takeover Code, any person (or group of persons 'acting in concert') must make a bid for a company once their level of control reaches 30%.[17] In the financial services industry, any person (or group of persons acting in concert) must apply to the FSA for pre-approval of any shareholding in a regulated financial services firm that will exceed 10%.[18] These rules are EU-wide and are implemented in all EU Member States pursuant to the Takeover Directive and the Acquisitions Directive.[19] Finally, there are rules in the EU Transparency Directive[20] that require reporting on a consolidated basis by firms acting in concert.

Although each scenario is dependent on its own circumstances, rules such as these may have a 'chilling effect' on collective action by institutional investors. This may mean that, even if a group of institutional investors or investment managers has identified an issue that they feel is significant enough to warrant coordinated action, they must take care to comply with rules regulating investors who are seen to be acting in concert.

The current atmosphere of using regulatory reform to address issues arising from the banking crisis, allied with efforts at the European level to make regulation more harmonious, presents an opportunity for institutional investors to seek an exemption for

---

[16] Annual Report of the PRI Initiative 2009, 6.
[17] The City Code on Takeovers and Mergers, Section F, Rule 9.1.
[18] *The Financial Services Authority's Handbook of Rules, The Supervision Manual,* ch 11.
[19] Directive 2004/25/EC of the European Parliament and of the Council of 21 April 2004 on takeover bids, [2004] OJ L142 and Directive 2007/44/EC of the European Parliament and of the Council of 5 September 2007 amending Council Directive 92/49/EEC and Directives 2002/83/EC, 2004/39/EC, 2005/68/EC as regards procedural rules and evaluation criteria for the prudential assessment of acquisitions and increase of holdings in the financial sector, [2007] OJ L247/1.
[20] Directive 2004/109/EC of the European Parliament and of the Council of 15 December 2004 on the harmonisation of transparency requirements in relation to information about issuers whose securities are admitted to trading on a regulated market and Amending Directive 2001/34/EC, [2004] OJ L390/38. See Chapter 3.

collective action from acting in concert rules that would otherwise apply. This is, perhaps, of most relevance to the Acquisitions Directive, which applies to banks, given that its initial threshold is set at 10%. Although it is only guidance (and not a formal amendment to the law), we welcome the fact that the FSA has, in its recent letter to the Chairman of the ISC,[21] started to engage on this subject and set out where it believes the boundaries lie in the context of market abuse, the Transparency Directive and the Acquisitions Directive. Similarly, the Takeover Panel has also recently issued a Practice Statement on Shareholder Activism[22] offering guidance on the application of the Takeover Code's 'acting in concert' provisions in the context of collective shareholder action. However, these UK initiatives fall short of a formal pan-European 'safe harbour'.

Similarly, insider trading and market abuse regimes have to be considered by an institutional investor considering detailed engagement with an investee company. Insider concerns can mean that institutional investors are simply never made aware of an issue in the first instance, or find it difficult to engage in a candid dialogue with company management. If an institutional investor becomes aware and is willing to engage, the scope of any engagement must be considered very carefully in the context of relevant legal advice.

H.   Private Equity

There are asset classes where control and close engagement with a company are desirable. Indeed, the private equity industry exists to identify companies where private equity firms believe that they can add significant value by working closely with, or changing, a company's management. However, at least initially, private equity investments are generally not listed and the structure of the transactions gives investors many more rights than they would typically have with a listed investment (see below):

— *Board Directors*—Private equity investors generally have board representation taking them from the sphere of owner to manager.
— *Management Information*—In addition to having directors on the board, private equity transactions often contain extensive obligations on investee companies to provide investors with substantial (and confidential) management information, far exceeding the amount of information available to investors in listed companies.
— *Control*—Private equity investors tend to control investee companies, making adopting change much easier. They typically have contractual rights to consider and sometimes veto significant transactions and corporate events. Investment managers investing in listed companies generally do not invest for control, and do not have this measure of influence over the board's stewardship of a company.
— *Transparency*—As private equity investments tend not to be listed, private equity managers need not be as concerned about receiving inside information, or having

---

[21] Letter from the Financial Services Authority to the Chairman of the Institutional Shareholders Committee dated 19 August 2009.
[22] The Takeover Panel, Practice Statement No 26, 'Shareholder Activism' (9 September 2009).

restrictions on buying or selling securities of these companies. This gives them much more access to detailed company information on a day-to-day basis.

This means that private equity investors have much greater flexibility and incentive to improve an investee company's performance through activism and corporate governance. However, this model is not appropriate for, nor can it be replicated in, the listed arena. The limitations of listed investments must be kept in mind, and not confused with the very different private equity arena. Private equity investments are labour intensive for investors, who often take on more of a management role in the companies in which they invest (as reflected in the level of management fee for such funds), and the investments are illiquid. In addition, the investee companies are specifically chosen because of the potential to add value by significant management intervention.

I. The Role of Regulators, Auditors and other Key Players

As we have previously noted, the future of the financial markets and related ESG issues cannot be addressed by institutional investors alone. Instead, the solution must involve the range of actors that shape the financial markets as we know them today. The role of regulators and legislators will, ultimately, have the most profound effect on markets and their participants, and be of far greater significance than institutional investors in providing a framework for our financial services industry that will avoid future financial crises.

With hindsight, there were many regulatory failings that contributed to the financial crisis at all levels. The problems started with the lack of cohesive mortgage selling regulation, particularly in the US, but also in other countries. This was combined with a widespread failure by banks and their regulators to fully appreciate the impact of ABSs and derivatives that were based on them, and the over-reliance of the banks' business models on inter-bank funding to facilitate aggressive mortgage lending and how this affected capital adequacy. All of this was further encouraged by the credit rating agencies, on whom widespread reliance was placed. Although perhaps more fringe players in terms of systemic risk, unregulated hedge funds may have injected further instability into the system. All of this occurred in a political climate that had turned a blind eye to increasing personal debt and house price escalation, and advocated light-touch regulation, not least because of the tax revenues it was producing.

In addition to regulators, auditors and professional bodies responsible for setting accounting standards (such as the International Accounting Standards Board) could have also played a more effective oversight role as the financial crisis unfolded. The external audit function has been described as one of the pillars of good governance and should provide significant reassurance to investors, by whom auditors are nominally appointed, as well as serving the broader public interest. However, with hindsight, the current approach to auditing did not effectively detect or flag the issues leading to the financial crisis. The debate on audit quality has dragged on for many years, with critics claiming that the standard of audit work needs to improve, particularly following Enron and Worldcom in 2001. As with financial services regulation, there also needs to be a high-level focus on accounting standards so that auditors operate within a suitable and properly developed framework. Fair value accounting has been a controversial area during the financial crisis, and auditors and standard-setting bodies need to work together to develop commercially robust standards that are global and suitable for the complexities of the modern financial marketplace.

Perhaps surprisingly, public criticism has not so far focused significantly on auditors and their responsibility for the current crisis. Like regulators, they too have far better access than investors to key financial and other management information, yet, again like regulators, they failed to spot excessive risk taking and certainly did not qualify the accounts of some of their financial services sector clients that went on to fail dramatically.

The audit firms face major conflicts, and the dominance of the 'Big Four' is unhelpful. This is buttressed by inertia on the part of audit committees, as the long tenure of external auditors (which is expressed in decades at many companies) appears to suggest. At the very least there needs to be better disclosure on the process and frequency on the part of audit committees in considering whether to re-tender the external audit contract. In practice, investors have little say in the appointment and retention of auditors, and are not in a position to impose rotation and retendering, or to set limits on non-audit work. Nor is it obvious that auditors really regard themselves as accountable to shareholders rather than management. Much of the solution lies in regulatory and even legislative action, but governments and regulators may have been reluctant to act, partly through competition concerns because they feared that the public interest would not be well served if the 'Big Four' were to be further reduced in number.

In retrospect, an adequate regulatory framework was not in place. Future reforms must focus first and foremost on this aspect. If this is correct, institutional investors will have the framework in which to engage with companies that fall short of the requisite standards, within the parameters of their own ability to act given their role in the system, taking into account their legal and regulatory obligations. This is being clearly recognised at a global level, and recently the OECD has issued a consultation paper on the role of corporate governance in the financial crisis and those areas that are most in need of reform.[23]

In Chapter 18 of this volume Professor Adelman observes that 'the system of regulation is always playing catch up with the new creative forms of abstractly representing wealth and credit',[24] believing that the economic system outgrows any regulatory system put in place to deal with its excesses. As a tendency, this is doubtless true, and, in addition, he advocates developing an early warning system that will signal when the economic system has outgrown the regulatory framework and a response mechanism.

This is a valuable insight—response mechanisms should be the basis of a new type of more adaptable and more responsive regulatory system. If the new systems of regulation are designed to be sensitive to macro-economic conditions and industry-wide business models, there is no reason why they cannot be applied dynamically and keep up with changing economies. In his recent speech summarising his review of the financial crisis,[25]

---

[23] Organisation for Economic Cooperation and Development, 'Public Consultation on Corporate Governance and the Financial Crisis' (Paris, OECD, 18 March 2009).

[24] Chapter 18, 316.

[25] Financial Services Authority, 'The Turner Review Press Conference' (18 March 2009), available at www.fsa.gov.uk/pages/Library/Communication/Speeches/2009/0318_at.shtml.

Lord Turner notes that the analysis of macro-prudential risks fell into a gap and that, 'in future, both the Bank of England and the FSA must be intensively and collaboratively involved in analysing macro-prudential developments'. This may signal the start of a more proactive and practical approach to regulation which is dynamic and able to keep up with changing global markets and the activities of market participants, rather than engaging in a perpetual game of catch-up and risking the disastrous consequences we have seen over the last 18 months.

J.   Conclusion

The institutional investor has an important role to play in terms of corporate governance. In the context of the financial crisis, it is imperative that institutional investors continue to discharge their roles in this regard, and contribute to the debate on where existing practices can be refined or improved. However, the role of the institutional investor is only part of the solution. For the reasons discussed at length in this chapter, institutional investors act within legal and commercial frameworks shaped by law, regulation and 'soft law'. So, while there is some scope for institutional investors to take action, it has to be within this overall framework, which affects the extent to which institutional investors can, or should, 'police' companies in which they invest.

However, institutional investors can bring very real pressure to bear on companies, provided that the framework within which they operate is dynamic and responsive. For this reason, regulatory and government reform must play a key role in ensuring that more stringent standards in relation to matters such as capital adequacy, transparency and remuneration policies are imposed. The roles of other organisations, such as credit rating agencies and auditors, should also be scrutinised to seek ways to improve the quality and effectiveness of their roles. In part, regulation may assist here. For example, there are efforts underway to regulate credit rating agencies and address the conflicts of interest rife in their prior practices which may have contributed to the crisis. The role of auditors seems to be another area that is ripe for review.

These are live issues, and regulatory reform is being considered on many fronts as a matter of urgency. We would also counsel caution in this respect. While regulatory reform is vital, it is important that it is well planned and executed, and coordinated on a global basis, as much as possible. It is important that reform is not rushed through to meet political agendas, as this may result in unintended complications or consequences.

18

Trust and Transparency:
The Need for Early Warning

HOWARD ADELMAN*

A. Introduction

Leonard Cohen, the Canadian poet, singer and songwriter, wrote 'Everybody Knows'.[1] The lyrics of the first verse are as follows:

> Everybody knows that the dice are loaded
> Everybody rolls with their fingers crossed
> Everybody knows that the war is over.
> Everybody knows the good guys lost
> Everybody knows the fight was fixed
> The poor stay poor, the rich get rich
> That's how it goes
> Everybody knows

What Cohen wrote and sang with intensity in his quiet, unadorned, deep but very restrained baritone voice Nick Paumgarten repeated a number of times in an article in *The New Yorker* with respect to the current financial crisis. 'Everybody knows', was the refrain. In his more prosaic form, Paumgarten wrote: 'the precarious arrangement was there all along, for anyone who looked. The dance of revelation and recognition is not well synchronized.'[2] Even more explicitly, he wrote, 'the potential for catastrophe was clear to see, for all who had eyes to see it'.

---

* Professor Emeritus, York University, Toronto, Canada and Adjunct Professor, Key Centre for Ethics, Law, Justice and Governance, Griffith University, Brisbane, Australia. Based on a paper presented at a conference at the University of Glasgow, 30–31 March 2009.

[1] The song, written in collaboration with songwriter and singer, Sharon Robinson, was included in his ninth album in 1988, *I'm Your Man* (Columbia, COL 460642 2), and was on the sound track of the 1990 film, *Pump Up the Volume*.

[2] N Paumgarten, 'Annals of Finance: The Death of Kings', *The New Yorker*, 18 May 2009, 40, 42.

The thesis has several propositions. The evidence of an immanent financial crisis of disastrous proportions was out there. Secondly, everyone could see the evidence—whether in the anecdote of the taxi driver or the cleaning woman betting on stocks and offering tips or in the more sophisticated boardrooms of the capitalist elite. The third proposition offers an explanation of why. If the evidence was overwhelmingly apparent and if everyone had the capacity to see it, why was the immanent disaster not recognised? One answer offered is greed: we were all blindsided by our possessive individualism. Another variation is that we are lemmings who followed the pied piper of promises of greater wealth rather than the prudent prophesiers of doom who recognised that our debt load had become disproportionate to our ability to repay.[3] In other words, most rather than all of us are greedy, and our greed blinded us from reading the signs pointed out by the prudent and the wise. A third explanation is that the titans of finance have the game fixed: the dice are loaded and the captains of finance lie and cheat. That is Cohen's explanation in his poem. Whether the answer is that universal greed that blinds us to the evidence staring right at us or that greed blinds us from seeing the wisdom of the prudent, or whether a rich elite controls the game, the explanation is similar in pointing to the sin of greed as the root cause of the disaster.

Greater transparency and more acute and comprehensive regulation are then postulated to bound our greed and produce either a much more cautious and prudent regime or greater independent governance of the leaders in control. This paper offers a very different account without discounting that greed played a role—for creativity is the necessary condition to allow greed to run loose. Possessive individualists may exist in the state of nature, but until that passion to extend one's being through possessions comes up with the invention of money, there is no way to save up all the grapes we pick. There is a third condition. You need the driving force. You need the invention of an abstract instrument that can represent accumulated wealth in a new way. Greed facilitated by creativity that develops new instruments for expanding credit beyond the established instruments and regulations provide the triumvirate that formed the foundation for the financial crisis that exploded.

Lack of regulation plays a role, not because the capitalist system is intolerant of regulation, but because the system of regulation is always playing catch up with the new creative forms abstractly representing wealth and credit. In other words, the reason the risks are not recognised is because we currently rely on regulatory mechanisms that are designed for what has happened in the past. These mechanisms can only catch up to the destructive potential of creativity when the damage is done and the dangers recognised. Further, regulatory mechanisms are inherently incapable of recognising systemic problems. What is needed is an institutional mechanism specifically tailored to do that job and no other.

---

[3] Gillian Tett, in her otherwise superb account of the history of the debt crisis in *Fool's Gold: How the Bold Dream of a Small Tribe at JP Morgan Was Corrupted by Wall Street Greed and Unleashed a Catastrophe* (New York, Free Press, 2009), holds this view. Fault rested in the mechanisms for institutionalising greed by the banks.

[4] G Scrambler (ed), *Sociology as Applied to Medicine* (Edinburgh, Saunders, 2003).

B.   Underlying Assumptions

There are a number of assumptions underlying this thesis which I will state rather than explicate, let alone argue for, just so the reader may be aware of them.

1.   Hypothesis re Value

A predominant modern classical theory of value is the labour theory of value. Labour is invested in converting what is found in nature to useful artefacts, and the value of the artefact created is equivalent to the amount of labour invested in the conversion process. This concept of value was shared by thinkers as diverse as John Locke and Karl Marx. In a second theory of value, the key variable is not labour or the capital accumulated from past labour, but technologies that create new efficiencies for transferring labour into nature to create artefacts. Thus, innovation is the key component in the creation of wealth through improving efficiencies, productivity, quality and, as I argue in this essay, the most funda-mental innovation of all, creating tools to represent future risk. In a third view, value is that which we attribute to something independent of anything underlying it. There is no reality referent. It is the belief that creates the value, a belief that others in the future will recognise that value. So the phenomenal is emphasised as having value in and for itself; appearances determine value—what one wears and drives at its most superficial. The artefacts themselves, the products of marketing that continually raise the bar for indebt-edness and then 'invent' the psychotropic drugs needed to handle the additional stress,[4] are the two sides of the faith in the simulacrum itself.[5] In this version, an elite consciously distracts the public with endless superficial entertainments in a compelling cornucopia of distractions complemented by a plausible simulacrum of justice, equality of opportunity and good governance to foster a sense of identity in a celebrity-consuming culture where outward appearance is seen as providing meaning in wearing the right labels and driving a 'cool' car.[6] This chapter believes that all three presumptions of value are at work, with different ones taking precedence as bubbles begin, when they are being inflated and when they reach their bursting point.

---

[5] *Cf* C Schinckus, 'The Financial Simulacrum: The Consequences of the Symbolization and the Computer-ization of the Financial Market' (2008) 37 *Journal of Socio-Economics* 1076. Schinckus argues in the tradition of Jean Baudrillard (*Simulacra and Simulations—VI. The Beaubourg Effect: Implosion and Deterrence*, trans Sheila Faria Glaser) that the innovations in financial markets transformed the world of finance into a supersensible world of abstract hyper-reality that itself allowed a multiplicity of representations and interpretations of what was happening. See also JJ Chung, 'Money as a Simulacrum: The Legal Nature and Reality of Money' (2009) 5 *Hastings Business Law Journal* 109.

[6] There is a long tradition of such interpretations: *cf* T Veblen, *The Theory of the Leisure Class: an Economic Study of Institutions* (1899), esp ch 4 on conspicuous consumption, available at http://xroads.virginia.edu/~HYPER/VEBLEN/chap04.html; J Ellul, *Propaganda: The Formation of Men's Attitudes* (New York, Vintage Books, 1973); A Pratkanis and E Aronson, *Age of Propaganda: The Everyday Use and Abuse of Persuasion* (New York, Henry Holt & Co, 2001).

2.   Hypothesis re the Nature of Money

A.   Money as a veil indicating an underlying reality.
B.   Money as a force in its own right.
C.   Money as a simulacrum in which the sign is the reality.

According to John Locke, man in the state of nature was always a possessive individualist. However, there were natural boundaries to his striving to extend his material being in the form of material possessions because there was no means to save up the figs or bananas he picked from the trees; they simply rotted. When money was invented, though, man's possessive individualism was released, for humans now had a mechanism for representing accumulated capital in an abstract way. Money, in this formulation, is an artefact that represents the value of labour beneath. Money represents past accumulated productivity. Secondly, money becomes recognised as a force in its own right when it is freed up from any natural measure, such as a gold standard, and recognised itself as the most fundamental innovation of all, one that connects past accumulated value with future faith in the preservation and enhancement of that value. Thirdly, money is the ultimate simulacrum, for it is the tool in terms of which the values of all other simulacra are denominated. Money thereby gets freed up from any connection to past productivity and, instead, represents the degree of faith in the amount of future wealth that can and will be created.

3.   Destructive and Creative Capitalism

Joseph Schumpeter[7] was an advocate of Werner Sombart's thesis of creative destruction, that is, that radical innovation is the essence of capitalism that transforms and leaves behind the old order. Thus, the key player is the entrepreneur and innovator—in German, the *Unternehmergeist*, the entrepreneurial spirit that, in its corporate form, becomes an investment in research and development. The most recent contributor to the debate over capitalism as a creative enterprise has been Bill Gates, but what he offers is merely a warmed over version of corporate social responsibility.[8] The argument is that the corporation is not only beholden to its shareholders but has a more general responsibility, the benefit of society as a whole. Some profit should be sacrificed as a form of charity for that purpose. It is the economic equivalent of the international political doctrine of the Responsibility to Protect or, on the domestic level, the Swedish model of the corporation as a partner in the welfare state that can be traced to Bismarck. This is a normative sense of creativity because the definition defines how corporations ought to behave and, further, that, in behaving that way, they best benefit both their shareholders and everyone else in a positive sum game.

---

[7] *Cf* JA Schumpeter (trans R Opie), *The Theory of Economic Development: an Inquiry into Profits, Capital, Credit, Interest, and the Business Cycle* (New York, Oxford University Press, 1961 English edn). See also A Greenspan, *The Age of Turbulence: Adventures of a New World* (New York, Penguin, 2007); TK McCraw, *Prophet of Innovation: Joseph Schumpeter and Creative Destruction* (Cambridge MA, Belknap Press, 2007); EG Carayannis and C Ziemnowicz, *Rediscovering Schumpeter* (New York, Palgrave Macmillan, 2007).

[8] John Mackey, head of Whole Foods, also takes this position. See his 2005 debate, 'Rethinking the Social Responsibility of Business,' with Milton Friedman; TJ Rogers, the CEO of Cypress Semiconductors, 'A Reason Debate' (October 2005), available at www.reason.com/news/show/32239.html.

But capitalism is not charity, even if such an accidental feature might marginally benefit both the world and the respect and recognition of the capitalist enterprise. Innovation is the key in the formula of the creative destructive process of capitalism, for innovation not only adds new wealth but has to make up for the diminishing returns of capital and labour invested in nature to produce artefacts. Capital (diminishing returns) + Labour (diminishing returns) + Innovation (greater than the diminishing returns of capital and labour) together produce a positive sum game. This productivity paradox was popularised in a widely cited 1993 article by Erik Brynjolfsson, who identified four possible explanations for the collective enterprise of capitalism veering out of control: mismeasurement of the benefits, redistribution, time lags and mismanagement, especially as applied to the communication revolution that just preceded the financial revolution.[9]

The lessons learned from this immediately preceding revolution are instructive. The first point suggests that the productivity benefits of computers are overestimated. Computers may perform a variety of tasks, but only do the old tasks faster rather than in any particularly new or efficient manner. That advantage is often offset by the fact that the mastery of computers requires time, the scarcest complementary human input. Further, the 'productivity revenues' are hidden by data; the ratios for input and output, and, therefore, the revenue benefits, are almost impossible to parse, particularly in the service sector.[10] Related to the first explanation is a second: the net benefit of the incorporation of computers into the productivity process may not even be noticeable because their introduction will accelerate the diminishing returns of capital and labour, resulting in losses in other divisions/departments of the company. The mismeasurement and displacement factors are compounded by a third element—the time lag. Productivity gains of computers are realised only after a lag period because complementary forms of capital investment must be developed to allow computers to be used to their full potential. Even if computers increase productivity by 50%, because of the time lag for their introduction, the capital input may offset the benefit in the short run. Finally, even several decades into the information revolution, we do not have the data to either confirm or deny any of these hypotheses. It is not surprising, therefore, that, in this 'veil of ignorance', managers mismanage and cannot determine when and where to invest capital in communications technology. In the end, there may be a systemic problem: we lack the measures for calculating the increases in productivity due to computers, especially if the productivity gains are reflected in quality changes and new products.

---

[9] E Brynjolfsson, 'The Productivity Paradox of Information Technology' (1993) 36(12) *Communications of the ACM* 67. See also E Brynjolfsson and H Mendelson, 'Information Systems and the Organization of Modern Enterprise' (1993) 3 *Journal of Organizational Computing* 245. Brynjolfsson's more recent articles focus on how one can invest in new communication innovations that both offset the propensity of capital and labour to decline while offsetting the advantages of competitors. See A McAfee and E Brynjolfsson 'Investing in the IT that Makes a Competitive Difference' (2008) 86(7/8) *Harvard Business Review* 98.

[10] For example, some applications of computer technology—as in word processing—have relatively little impact at first compared to the offset of the inefficiencies of using typewriters, especially in the beginning when the two technologies are employed in parallel and we find a technology alignment problem with poor user interfaces and mutual recognition issues, inadequate hardware and perplexing software prone to create almost as many problems as those solved, leading to a compounding of problems as new software has to be introduced rapidly to supersede the old. See SD Oliner, DE Sichel and KJ Stroh 'Explaining a Productive Decade', Federal Reserve Board Working Paper No 2007-63 (December 2007).

Now if these difficulties remain several decades into the information revolution, one must be more modest about offering simplistic explanations that everybody knows to account for the disarray that resulted in the much more recent financial revolution..

C.   Financial Entrepreneurs: Swaps, Credit Defaults, Securitisation and Tranching

When Jamie Dimon, CEO of JP Morgan, and his 'mafia' invented the 'credit default swap' in 1994, Felix Rohatyn warned derivatives were 'financial hydrogen bombs built on personal computers by 26-year-olds with MBAs'.[11] Ten years later, an economist at the Bank for International Settlement, Claudio Borio, assisted by the acute analysis of data of Bill White, challenged the belief that financial innovation was an unadulterated good.[12] Ignoring these warnings and the accumulating black clouds, the European Securitisation Forum, at its annual meeting entitled 'Global Asset Backed Securitisation: Towards a New Dawn!' on 11 June 2007 in Barcelona, celebrated the most profitable year in history for investment banks. The next day, Bear Stearns began to unravel and was eventually bought at a bargain price by JP Morgan Chase. Fifteen years after the pool party where his team came up with the idea of the credit default swap, Jamie Dimon held another party at the World Economic Forum in Davos, Switzerland, not to celebrate the fifteenth anniversary of that revolutionary innovation, but to hail the hundredth anniversary of J Pierpont Morgan as the saviour of the financial system in 1907.

Were these financial innovations the forerunners of doom and gloom or the creative innovations that allowed the total capitalisation in the world to expand enormously and thus finance new and unprecedented investments in productivity? This paper argues that entrepreneurship depends on playful creativity to try to see how to use existing rules in new ways to provide for future capital growth and accumulation rooted in our creative playful imagination. The idea may be terrific, but unless it can be managed in terms of a recognisable set of rules, outsiders cannot trust the players. After a bubble of confidence

---

[11] This is perhaps the most quoted sentence in many books in the current financial crisis so that the frequency of its repetition hides its original source. *Cf*, eg RJ Teweles and ES Bradley, *The Stock Market* (New York, John Wiley & Sons, 1998) 471; P Jorion, *Value at Risk: The Benchmark for Controlling Market Risk Scandals* (New York, Prometheus Books, 2000) 31; SB MacDonald and JE Hughes, *Separating Fools from their Money: A History of American Financial Scandals* (New York, John Wiley & Sons, 2007) 165. There is also a host of articles and blogs, eg M Renner, 'Treasury Secretary Tim Geithner: Actual Bailout Mat Exceed $10 Trillion' (13 May 2009), available at www.antemedius.com/category/tags/treasury;-secretary-tim-geithner.

[12] C Borio, 'Change and Constancy in the Financial System: Implications for Financial Distress and Policy' (Bank for International Settlements, 2003); *cf* D Duffe, 'Innovations in Credit Risk Transfer: Implications for Financial Stability', BIS Working Paper No 255 (July 2008), one of the papers that followed in the series.

has burst, the key and central problem remains how to restore faith in our material god—in this case, the very lifeblood and circulatory basis of the system itself, the financial sector. How was that to be accomplished? Apply government regulation to the new sectors of hedge fund financing. Regulate hedge funds and derivative markets. How? By new self-policing systems, by independent systems or by creating new barriers for financial institutions, new red lines that cannot be crossed? The solutions proliferated, as did the debates. How were we to deal with this dangerous breach of public confidence in our materialist religion? What measures were needed to restore people's faith?

The core rules may be simple, but their application to specific situations at specific times and places varies. The propensity of any entrepreneur will be to adapt the rules to favour his or her own style of play. Thus, there is an inherent tension between the referee obligated to uphold the existing rules and the entrepreneur driven to adapt and alter rules to facilitate play. There never will be or can be a stable set of fixed rules, for the very nature of entrepreneurship as creative play will mean challenging and adapting the rules themselves. There will always be a tension between ensuring the rules are not utilised for either nefarious purposes or for products and ideas that are beyond the elasticity of the system to handle. There is a need to adjust rules to allow for creativity and new situations. So how does society govern such an unstable system in flux without destroying its dynamic character and reifying the process?

Let us first focus on the forces that favour set rules over play and the propensity to literally deform the system. There are many ways in which the dialectic of play and the rules of the game may be deformed. One conservative way entails upping the equity requirements before building for the future; this strategy inherently stunts growth. The system is deformed in the direction of the preservation of the past rather than in favour of a creative approach to the future. In the 1997 financial crisis in the Third World that led to at least one very positive outcome—the freeing of East Timor from Indonesian control—cronyism, corruption and nepotism in a system of predatory capitalism tended to favour those players in the know or who knew someone rather than entrepreneurs. The system can be deformed beyond conservatism towards a reactionary form of finance common in the medieval period and so well illustrated in Shakespeare's *Merchant of Venice*. The game was fixed to favour the few. Reform required moving from an interpersonal model of playing favourites to a detached impersonal, technocratic, apolitical model of regulation or refereeing by an independent agency with powers of enforcement. But this just shifted the problem and did not resolve it. Either the referees were too literal and inhibited creativity in favour of bureaucratic processing or the referees were brought into the crony system and given a cut so that regulation, though strong on paper, was weak in practice.

Cronyism based on family loyalty and friendship is a historic foundation for trust. A depersonalised system must earn its reputation to counteract this natural trust. Further, traditional systems will have developed vested interests resistant to displacement by an impersonal system. In the case of local systems that deal with pressures from international agencies, a system of mock compliance may be put in place that actually operates underneath according to crony norms.

The new system involved a number of key components. The first step was put in place in the early eighties with the institutionalising of the 'swap' by Salomon Brothers that involved trading obligations and rewards without the necessity of transferring the underlying security itself.[13] When Jamie Dimon, CEO of JP Morgan, held his intense brainstorming session in 1994 with his 'mafia' beside a pool in Boca Raton, swaps had grown into a twelve trillion dollar business. In their quest for new tools and new sources of profit in what had become a highly competitive business, the team came up with the idea of swapping the risk rather than the interest rate obligations of loans. Instead of arranging a loan to secure the debt, securing the risk itself required a fraction of the amount of the loan, thereby drastically reducing the cash that needed to be held in reserve and enormously increasing the credit supply. The mechanism came to be known as the 'credit default swap'.[14]

The third step in the development of this new mechanism of increasing the money supply and the amount of credit available was based on securitisation, bundling together different debts and, based on the law of averages, selling the risk of the bundled securities rather than that of a single loan, thereby ostensibly reducing the risk if a single loan failed. The fourth invention involved 'tranching', that is, dividing the bundled securities into different slices and paying interest according to the degree of risk of that slice of the bundled securities. Safer tranches paid less interest and highly risky tranches paid more. In this fourth step, an offshore company—a 'special purposes vehicle'—was created to handle all the transactions involved in the tranching of these credit default swaps. The fifth step involved getting the rating agencies to go along with the risk analysis of this new mechanism of synthetic 'collateralised debt obligations' (CDOs), which Moody's did for JP Morgan in 1997. However, the really large profits could only come when the whole process was streamlined and industrialised. This was the sixth necessary step.

This took place when a simple algorithm was created to calculate the risk.[15] However, the biggest threat to breakdown does not come from the overhang of old systems of trust, but from situations in which trust is based on the most impersonal of systems, a

---

[13] See Tett, above n 3.

[14] Blythe Masters is credited with inventing the credit swap in 1995; cf A Kohler, 'Credit default swap vertigo', *Business Spectator* (28 February 2008), available at www.businessspectator.com.au/bs.nsf/Article/Credit default-swap-vertigo- C3S5W?OpenDocument. Cf Masters's testimony before the Senate Subcommittee, 24 July 2007, available at epw.senate.gov/public/index.cfm?FuseAction=Files.View&FileStore_id=7b637e60-0d4d-4982-ae01-6a2f4f304288.

[15] See F Salmon, 'Recipe for Disaster: The Formula that Killed Wall Street,' *Wired Magazine*, 23 February 2009; also F Salmon, K Ryssdal, 'Did Math Formula Cause Financial Crisis?' *Marketplace*, 24 February 2009, available at marketplace.publicradio.org/display/web/2009/02/24/pm_stock_formula_q/. David Li was the creator of applying the Gaussian copula function to financial risk applications:

$$C_\rho(u, v) = F_\rho\,(\Phi^{-1}(u), \Phi^{-1}(v))$$

Based on his research work on loss modelling applied to insurance at the University of Waterloo (after he graduated and when he was already a partner in JP Morgan's Risk Metrics unit), he adapted the formula in 2000 to enable a new generation of risk-based securities to be leveraged. See D Li, 'On Default Correlation: A Copula Function Approach' [March 2000] *The Journal of Fixed Income* 43. As Cathal Kelly wrote in 'Meet the Canadian Whose Big Idea Felled Wall Street', *The Toronto Star*, 18 March 2009, A1, A17, 'Li's model sidestepped the problem of trying to correlate all the variables that determine risk. Instead it based its assumptions of the historic dips and swells of the market itself. In essence, *Li used the past to map the future*' (emphasis added). In the formula, the correlation 'P' of disparate variants, where each variant has a maximum correlation of 100% or

mathematical formula. It is misplaced trust—as has been proven to be the case—when the mathematical model developed is a positivist one based on extending past experience into the future without taking into account the fact that the new model itself, let alone other new factors, confronts principles of indeterminacy and the effects of cumulative chance factors to alter or even invert previous patterns.

The formula allowed investors to buy credit default swaps as a form of insurance against failure. The algorithm allowed a far larger investment pool to be created than the underlying securities; investors were not directly investing in bonds but in the probability of the bonds going belly up. They were betting on the formula rather than investing directly in a security. A system had been created with an enormous range but one which did not and could not take into account systemic failure when batches of credit default swaps could themselves be combined into collateralised debt obligations (CDOs) without the necessity of purchasing bonds at all. Based on historic patterns, investors were betting on a group of players winning at a casino and banks were selling and trading these CDOs and significantly increasing their sources of profit. The insurance system had been turned into a lottery and the lottery became an item for investment, but an item that did not include the possibility of the casino burning down or the workers in the casino going on strike. Further, rating companies no longer had to do their homework but began to rely on the formula.

A simple practical model had been created based on past patterns for predicting future ones. Many believe that the banking sector behaved irresponsibly in creating enormous new risks in the 'overexpansion of credit' through over-engineering credit and risk. I argue that the problem did not rest in creating the new tool but in basing that new tool on old-fashioned probability theorems that could not factor in systemic risk. We have not developed and do not use mathematical models for predicting international and national financial data based on fuzzy logic. When positivist algorithms go wrong on a global scale, they go spectacularly wrong because they are based on a conservative doctrine of preserving and reifying the past and projecting that past into the future. The formulas, rather than their use, are then blamed. Investment banks retreat back to making income on spreads, brokerage fees and underwriting; they reject proprietary trading, securitised packaged products and structured financial deals. I predict that this will be a tactical retreat and that those initiatives will once again come to the fore in a more regulated universe.

The problem of herd patterning, the weakness of projecting results based on past patterns rather than actual performance and the inability to create trajectories for many possible worlds rather than just an extension of the existing one doomed the model to producing both a bubble and a burst. In addition, there is the propensity of regulatory norms to stifle creativity as they are imposed indifferent to local conditions. There is also

---

>1, is a multiple standard normal cumulative distribution function multiplied by these variable risks combined in a common formula, though one not based on independent assessments of risk but on historical patterns. The algorithm linked and correlated different disparate risks, that is, formulated a multivariant distribution (a copula) representing different degrees of interconnectedness to estimate probabilities of future occurrences of a bundled group of separate risk items based on traditional patterns. The bundling was supposed to reduce risk because of linking different degrees of risk. The formula explicitly did not reduce the risk of a single occurrence and was not applicable where risks were systemic and applied to the whole system. By 2005, Li warned that the model was limited in its application for it could not predict what would happen in extreme economic environments: M Whitehouse, 'Slice of Risk', *Wall Street Journal*, 12 September 2005.

the tension between the world we trust and the impersonal world of referees, between the natural propensities of trust based on nepotism and cronyism (without the use of the loaded language) and detached 'objective' evaluation. Systems of adaptation use mock compliance to bolster local practices. The same mistrust of that type of corruption needs to be applied to positivist algorithms. We also need to develop algorithms based on fuzzy logic and principles of indeterminacy. Instead, no regulatory regime governed this new class of investments. No global gambling tsar was in place to police the system and take into account all the new variables in constructing a strengthened rules-based international order. Since we have loaded onto the system other responsibilities, such as concerns for climate change, energy security, alternative sources of energy and human rights, in addition to transparency and accountability, the difficulties multiplied.

There are other complications. Assume you want to reduce risk by introducing mortgage insurance—ether voluntary or compulsory—say at an extra quarter per cent interest charge on the value of the mortgage. One result is moral hazard in which there develops a propensity to increase risk than would otherwise be the case without the insurance. Further, as with deposit insurance schemes, the more generous the insurance, the greater the fragility there will be in the system.[16] Not only will the mortgagee tend to take a higher risk, but so will the mortgagor as well as the mortgage brokers, appraisers and lawyers, because it is in each of their interests to promote mortgage financing. The compensation of these professionals is directly proportional to their ability to persuade a consumer to assume more debt to acquire a good or service. That does not mean that mortgage brokers, appraisers and lawyers want to intentionally overburden the consumers with too much debt. Rather, they are just doing their jobs and helping a consumer achieve his or her goals. Because of the reinforcing action, however, the risk grows exponentially, as does the degree of moral hazard.

Others argue that this representation of an interlocking system of non-conscious actors misrepresents reality because there are conscious actors, both the plutocrats who allegedly manipulate the system and the soothsayers who warn the multitude of the wayward direction in which everyone is headed. The plutocrats shape our experience with myths, incentives and assumptions into a politically pliable complacency to induce somnolence, allowing them to continue their privileged lives without questioning what they are doing. When they are caught, they still manage to convince the political leadership to bail them out lest the economic benefits for everyone suffer more drastically.[17]

I clearly cannot delve into all of these issues, or even any one of them, with any degree of depth. However, I will sketch the overall problem and then focus a bit on the issue of transparency[18] with respect to financing of construction, an old tried and true economic endeavour and one with which almost everyone has some acquaintance since ownership of a home is the most common and important form of accumulating capital for the vast

---

[16] This is the same pattern as in deposit insurance: JR Barth, G Caprio Jr and R Levine, *Rethinking Bank Regulation: Till Angels Govern* (Cambridge, Cambridge University Press, 2006) 13.

[17] R Bitner, *Greed, Fraud and Ignorance: A Subprime Insider's Look at the Mortgage Collapse* (London, Palgrave Macmillan, 2008); F Partnoy, *Fiasco: The Inside Story of a Wall Street Trader* (New York, Penguin, 1999).

[18] The issue of transparency permeates public as well as private and corporate use of credit. 'The lack of transparency in governmental derivatives trading has resulted in the loss of billions of tax dollars in a string of mishaps spanning a decade. The largest municipal bankruptcy in US history ($1.6 billion) occurred in Orange County, California, in December 1994, when the county treasurer used derivatives to bet that interest rates would stay low': G Calalhan and G Kaza, 'In Defence of Derivatives', *reasononline* (February 2004), available at www.reason.com/news/show/29033.html. Only Michigan State mandated full transparency for municipalities.

majority of people. The issue is: how can one expand the potential of ownership for most people without putting the financial system at risk? By understanding the issue in this way rather than focusing on sub-prime mortgages as themselves at fault, I want to shift the debate to the issue of transparency and the importance of initiating an early warning system.

D.   Transparency in Plato's Cave

Plato's story of the cave in chapter VII of *Republic* can be understood as an allegory concerning transparency. In the tale, people are sitting on a log in a cave and confined in such a way that they are unable to turn their heads and understand the source of the projected images on the walls of the cave. They take those illuminated images on the cave wall coming from a projector to be reality. What appears bright and transparent as two-dimensional reflected figures on the cave wall are anything but. Without the ability to turn and explore the sources of the images, our imagination becomes transfixed with the imagery without being able to discover the real source. In contemporary society, individuals work and consume in this same peculiar state of unawareness, ignorant even of the fact that they are unaware and of what they do not know, let alone the incentives, drivers and consequences of their 'seemingly conscious' choices.

This is how I would characterise the sub-prime mortgage crisis, not as one rooted in providing homeowners with 100% mortgage financing without properly assessing the ability of the homeowners to repay. This was in fact the least important element in the scheme, for the same sub-prime mortgage system had allowed individuals with very little capital and income to acquire property for a number of years. We tend to focus on the losers in the scheme rather than the winners who would not have been allowed to win under the old rules.

The ones who least understood the situation were the bankers charged with managing the rules of the system but who could not understand the reality under the scheme of collateralised and packaged mortgages with an insurance scheme vested in an insurance company that was also full of actuaries mind-blinded by the sheer brightness of the images on those cave walls. And what was the source of the illumination that so blinded these eminent professionals? The very mathematics that Plato saw as the ultimate source of illumination that provided the route out of the cave. For mathematics went beyond common sense (which Plato distrusted intensely) and customary sources of light. In fact, the new generation of financiers and managers bought into these predictive algorithms that allowed institutions like Countrywide Mortgage in the US to collapse and be taken over by Bank of America at a bargain basement price and the American International Group (AIG) to be bailed out with billions of dollars in government loans. Eddy Liddy, the current CEO of AIG, copied the pattern of blaming the new-fangled technocrats in the AIG Financial Products unit that induced AIG to stray from the straight and narrow to create a company too complex and opaque for even its custodians to understand.[19]

Most commentators have accused these new wunderkinder of abandoning the old tried

[19] 'Mistakes were made at AIG, and on a scale that few could have imagined possible. The most egregious of those began in 1987, when the company strayed from its core insurance competencies to launch a credit

and true ways of testing the creditworthiness of a client, not by employing an algorithm, but by using established credit rating agencies to assess the credit worthiness of a client. The system required directly assessing whether the client could repay the loans by evaluating and interpreting that data according to simple formulas that determined the veracity of the claims on the application of clients, past record and history. Those factors had to demonstrate the character and ability to repay the loan as agreed. In other words, it was a simple common sense and directly intuitive method, but one identical in substance to the complicated positivist predictive algorithms of the sophisticated analysts in the high echelons of the financial world. The past was used to predict the future. The manipulators of collateralised mortgages, however sophisticated, still used an old base of a formula projecting the past into the future, a formula inapplicable in a situation of dramatic flux and indeterminacy where fuzzy rather than lineal logic is more appropriate in making risk assessments.

This is the context in which the issue of transparency must be understood. Transparency is usually taken to mean the availability of reliable, comprehensive and timely information and the elimination of opaque barriers to accessing the data. However, the information that the managers of these sophisticated financial packages had was in some sense reliable but in another sense not, in some sense comprehensive and in another sense not, and in some sense timely and in another sense not. The information was certainly accessible but usually its meaning was not, and the implications went beyond the ability of most so-called sophisticated analysts, let alone lay people, to decipher.

The sophisticated managers detached from the local scene operated with similar attitudes to traditional mortgage company and bank managers. Nothing has changed other than the apparent complicatedness of the images on the walls of the cave.[20] The critics of sophistication in favour of the more primitive forms of assessment extant 40

---

default-swaps portfolio, which eventually became subject to massive collateral calls that created a liquidity crisis for AIG. Its missteps have exacted a high price, not only for the company and its employees, but for the American taxpayer, the federal government's finances and the global economy. These missteps brought AIG to the brink of collapse and to the government for help': EM Liddy, 'Our Mission at AIG: Repairs and Repayment', *Washington Post*, 18 March 2009, A13. Ironically, when the populace copied this pattern of scapegoating in resentment of the $165 million in bonus payments and the politicians magnified those voices a hundredfold, Joseph Brusuelas, a director at Moody's Economy.com in West Chester, Pennsylvania, correctly noted that, 'An instinct exists among members of our political class to convene show trials to make up for their own shortcomings. This is on the verge of damaging the real progress made by the Federal Reserve in addressing the financial crisis': E Kaiser and C Daly, 'AIG CEO Asks Employees to Repay some Bonus Money', *Reuters*, 18 March 2009, available at ca.news.yahoo.com/s/reuters/090318/us/politics_us_financial_aig.

[20] Cf Emmanuel Salta, 'Variance Reduction Techniques in Pricing Financial Derivatives', PhD thesis in mathematics (Florida State University, 2008). For example, at 73, Salta discusses Glasserman and Staum's estimators for knock-down barrier options, that is, a barrier that triggers an automatic call when a stock reaches a certain price in accordance with a formula that minimises risks of loss and provides for offsets to minimize those risks further, but all according to accumulated records of past performance without taking into account how the insertion of these formulae for managing risk will increase moral hazard and raise the overall prices that cumulatively will literally 'break the bank' and cause the whole edifice on which records of past performance on which the predictive models were developed to collapse. For the developers of these mathematical formulae, the intent was to arrive at more sophisticated techniques that could substitute for the crude ones currently in use to more accurately assess where it is best to set the barrier to trigger the call. The thesis that evaluated Monte Carlo estimates and its own estimators for pricing financial derivatives from the perspective of variance reduction ended up showing that the complicated formulae were only marginally better for prediction than an unsophisticated raw simulation effort. For a general reference, see S Das, *Derivative Products & Pricing* (New York, Wiley Finance, 2005) and SM Ross, *An Introduction to Mathematical Finance Options and Other Topics* (Cambridge, Cambridge University Press, 1999).

years ago just miss the point, for the same elements were in play well before computer scanners and formulas for predicting the odds of repayment became common. To repeat, the problem was NOT in the formulas used to predict repayment odds and the development of credit scoring systems (or credit default swaps), in contrast to a reliance on common sense and traditional values to predict worthiness, but on the fixation with images on the cave wall, however they are produced, without the loan officers understanding the sources, and, more fundamentally, on the assumption that the past is a predictor of the future. The basic tenets of play and entrepreneurship challenge that presumption.

Eddy Liddy, CEO of AIG, whether he actually believed what he was saying or was simply providing a cover for the public explosion of anger over the bonuses paid to AIG executives in the AIG Financial Products division that was being wound down, explained that the company had to retain the executives as the unit was wound down and so had to pay them the $165 million in bonuses that were promised in order to dispose properly of the $2.7 trillion in derivative positions that the company had on its books. Since the explanation was coming from a $1-a-year man, he hoped, in the old-fashioned way, that he would be taken at his word. Of course, what was offered was a non-explanation; we did not learn the contents of those retention contracts, who received the bonuses or the size of the bonus, nor why the bonuses were not held back until the unit was totally wound down and the executives left. We just had far more questions. Liddy therefore had to go deeper and provide a structural scapegoat.

What lesson did Liddy learn? 'There must be safeguards against the systemic consequences of failures of large, interconnected financial institutions. Where safeguards are lacking, such companies need to be restructured or scaled back so they no longer come close to posing a systemic risk.'[21] To translate that into English, this insurance executive provided an answer standard to all insurers—buy more insurance, in this case in the form of barriers to growth or actual insurance for systemic failures on a grand scale.

Rules are not barriers. They are common operational standards of conduct that are open to anyone. They require a system to adjudicate and tell whether the rules are being followed. The real problem emerges, though, when new creative entrepreneurs in the world use the rules to go outside the standard game and begin to play without rules, with the old rules themselves being made part of the playful enterprise. To repeat, the issue is not to squash playful creativity in the name of the past, for the mistakes that were made were the projection of that past as if it foretold the future. The system demonstrably did not do what it said it would. The question is why not? Moving backwards may be necessary to restore the reputation of AIG, but do not look on that as a formula to deal with the systemic issue.

The problem is always how to build rules of a game when the rules are being managed by jokers and there is a need to extend those rules in new ways and in new areas where a regulatory mechanism is not yet in place. Play is inherently reckless in the literal sense. The Canadian Prime Minister, Stephen Harper, a conservative and an economist, blamed reckless US consumers and investors who believed they could borrow without consequences rather than the custodians of the financial system.[22] However, the very nature of

---

[21] Liddy, above n 19, A13.

[22] D Akin, 'Reckless US consumers caused recession: Harper', *Canwest News Services* (12 March 2009).

play is to introduce a degree of heedlessness of consequences and a lack of care and prudence as we allow our imaginations to go beyond existing boundaries. Everyone had become part of the new playful spirit—investors, consumers, custodians, government officials, politicians and prime ministers. Playing the blame game and pinning the tale on the donkey is a contest played with blindfolds and simply puts us back on the log in Plato's cave.

The issue is one of timing. How do we expand the rules of the game to new areas and create new regulatory mechanisms on the heels of players who invent new ways of mortgaging futures to allow for present creativity? We do not do so by heeding Liddy's advice, and certainly not by listening to Prime Minster Harper indulge in the old tried and true Canadian sport of blaming Americans. Why not blame the Icelanders?

E.   Accountability and Early Warning

How do we create new rules and new regulatory mechanisms on the heels of creative enterprise? The issue is anticipation as a precondition of regulation and accountability. We have to be able to ascertain when and how the creativity is getting onto dangerous ground, just as we have to anticipate when weather systems threaten storms and when low-level conflicts can become violent. What is needed is not an effort to stuff the burst bubble back into an old container—and there are plenty around for everyone to have their favourite pick. The bubble has burst. It burst not because a few particular people were engaged in venality—though there were plenty of Madoffs around who could hide as the bubble was inflating, though most were not on Madoff's scale; the very area of play attracts the venal and the crooked who share with creative entrepreneurs a disdain for confining rules. Bubbles burst because the elasticity of the container is inflated beyond its inherent capacity, where elasticity at its most basic means the percentage change in quantity in relation to the percentage change in price. How do we ensure that expansion follows some inherent natural laws at the very same time that we are increasing elasticity by inventing new forms for expanding credit? One cannot expand capacity and attract investments in virtual products ad infinitum. The principle of inelasticity comes into play.

In physical laws of elasticity, such as Hooke's law, the extension of a spring is in direct proportion to the load. In 2008, the debt load became far too heavy for the springs to respond and the sleeping arrangements collapsed, waking everyone up. In economics, specifically in reference to the laws of supply and demand, elasticity is a central concept correlating supply and demand with other independent variables often expressed as a percentage change relative to another variable. The degree of change permissible and likely in relation to other factors introduced over time, along with the response of supply and demand to those various factors, become part of the calculus. In the case of the loan swap bundled derivatives, the quantity demanded or supplied when the price changed did not matter as much as the precipitous drop in demand so that holders of those CDOs could not sell them. They had lost their liquidity and the elasticity of the bubble had been stretched so far that the bubble burst. When the demand drops to zero and the supply is enormous, the elasticity of the system also plunges to zero and the result is a vertical line rather than a curve matching supply and price.

As the inelasticity percolated through the whole market system, the demand for goods and services dropped precipitously. Auto workers and others were pressured to reduce their actual incomes and not just their demands. Fewer and fewer people could afford to buy goods and services at previous prices. Elasticity in relation to variables other than price can also be considered. As income dropped, fear set in and the fall in demand was multiplied by the fear factor. Buyers of property turned into tyre kickers, reluctant to buy lest they overpay in a declining market, thereby propelling the market downward even further and putting more properties underwater relative to the liabilities for which the property served as securities. The cross elasticity of demand in an interrelated system had fallen and the demand for new appliances, furniture and drapes declined as the prices of properties declined.

All these shifts can be accommodated in a normal market. However, with an absolute loss of faith, trust in all parts of the system collapses and the value of almost everything begins to fall precipitously. The problem has gone far beyond regulation. The public had built a golden calf and had projected a virtual divine reality onto a concrete object. Instead of a system of faith or trust, everyone had been into idolatry, but the idol was inert and could not perform the magic expected of it. So, instead of the market moving to equilibrium, it fell over the edge of a metaphorical Niagara Falls. Now we all know that markets, even in normal times, take time to adjust and do not move to equilibrium easily. However, there were plenty of indicators available—as Li recognised in 2005—to suggest that the system was heading to its maximum tensile strength. Unfortunately there was no institutionalised mechanism of early warning and response to allow the system to move gradually back from the brink.

There is always asymmetry in a system relative to inadequate information. This was demonstrated in the Rwanda genocide:[23] there was plenty of information in different areas well before the genocide, but that information had not been systematically collected, correlated and analysed to anticipate the mass slaughter. The disaggregated information that was available at the highest echelons had not been communicated. The same was true of the disaster that just took place in the global credit system. Plenty of evidence existed well before the credit bubble reached its bursting point,[24] just as there had been many signals forewarning of the stock market bubble at the beginning of the twenty-first century,[25] only an independent early warning agency had not been developed that could correlate the factors and demonstrate that the pressure within the bubble was increasing so that the bubble could not sustain the pressure. Rating agencies were complicit in the system and only rated individual offerings. They are not early warning mechanisms. The information was there to anticipate that the apocalypse was nigh, but we lacked an institutionalised information collection and analysis system to warn clearly and unequivocally of

---

[23] H Adelman and A Suhrke, *The International Response to Conflict and Genocide: Lessons from the Rwanda Experience, vol 2. Early Warning and Conflict Management* (Copenhagen, DANIDA, 1996).

[24] As early as January 2002, Howard Davies, chairman of the UK Financial Services Authority, quoted a source that described derivatives as 'the most toxic element of the financial markets today'. In his 2002 Berkshire Hathaway annual report, Warren Buffett, whose reputation has become somewhat tarnished recently, characterised derivatives as the atomic bombs of the economic system and viewed them 'as time bombs, both for the parties that deal in them and the economic system'.

[25] This is a reference to three of the six largest bankruptcies in the USA—WorldCom, Enron and Global Crossing—that triggered a stock market decline in which stocks lost almost a quarter of their value on average. Similar prognostications were available before the October 1987 market crash, the early 1990 savings and loans scandals, and the international state bond crisis of the late 1990s.

the danger. An early warning system has to have no vested interest in growth and must possess only a warning mandate. Without a recognised early warning system in the most sophisticated of economic systems, we rely on trial and error and sometimes avoid catastrophe,[26] but usually make increasingly more catastrophic errors.

In sum, my plea is not for a new regulatory global regime—which is on the way now to set forth the new rules of the game, the entrepreneurs having stretched the old rules beyond their residual elasticity—but for an early warning system that can spot and measure the degree of danger in the system as a whole. My plea is for creating an independent institutionalised economic warning system funded by a tiny cost on all financial transactions that would be tasked with the job of measuring when the joyful players in some new area start to create tulip speculation, dotcom stocks' inflated values or debt derivatives married to bundled swaps, or whatever the next phase of financial innovation brings forth. Creative players will once again put the whole system at risk in ways we currently cannot imagine and which will make our current crisis look like a simple wayward and hazardous trip but one which allowed us to eventually resume our journey. The problem is not the derivatives themselves but the lack of transparency and the absence of a monitoring system that looks at the system as a whole. Demand and supply in the form of price action is not an early warning system but a late signal that disaster is underway.

I anticipate that if an early warning system is not created and we simply rely on a new regulatory system with a global reach covering the new mechanisms and institutions for dealing with money and credit, we will have gone through this dramatic foreshadowing for nothing and we will face a true apocalypse the next time round. Supply and demand curves are inadequate predictors when the system itself is put at risk. As the artist Vanessa Beecroft makes evident, the act of observing the self-images created are at the core of art. This applies to the economic art of making money and wealth out of future beliefs, and we need a system of reflective self-consciousness in the creative world of economics that puts those objects on naked display in the same shocking manner that Beecroft displays her nude women. We may be disgusted or appalled at the result, but it is better to see it coming in a virtual form on the wall of the cave than before the dreadful reality strikes home and we are drowned by the rush of water through the cave opening.

---

[26] For conservative critics of the catastrophe, Bill Demchak is held out as an example of someone who had detected what was wrong early on, bowed out of the game and lived to thrive. Demchak had been with Morgan Stanley, led the pioneering effort to develop credit derivatives, marry them to securitisation and slice them up into tranches relative to risk, and created the team that adopted David Li's formula and marketed the method of financing detached from the risk of a specific loan defaulting. The system expanded into almost $60 trillion in credit contracts. Demchuk left JP Morgan in 2002 to rescue PNC Financial, which spurned new debt instruments to recover its shattered reputation by avoiding any questionable debt altogether and did not get involved in lending money and repackaging the loans for resale, for such loans were inherently bound to be riskier than a debt that a bank had assumed for itself, since the tranches it retained on its own books were the riskiest slices. Many very thin slices of high-risk tranches are as dangerous as one high-risk loan, especially when there is systemic failure. See J Eisinger, 'The $58 Trillion Elephant in the Room', *Condé Nast*, available at www.portfolio.com/views/columns/wall-street/2008/10/15/Credit-Derivatives-Role-in-Crash?page=4#page=4.

19

Regulation, Ethics and Collective Investments

PAMELA F HANRAHAN*

A. Introduction

The theme of this collection is the future of financial regulation; its aim is to explore what regulation might or should look like in the aftermath of the global financial crisis (GFC).

To date, governmental responses to the GFC have concentrated on immediate priorities: restoring confidence and liquidity in international banking; addressing the pressing threat of recession through fiscal, monetary and other measures; and addressing, through international bodies such as the G-20, the Financial Stability Board and the International Organization of Securities Commissions (IOSCO), specific regulatory gaps, for example in relation to credit rating agencies and unregulated products and markets (including securitisation). The broader project of reassessing financial regulation—its goals, its methods and its operation—in light of the GFC lies ahead. The purpose of this paper is to contribute to that project through a discussion of the role of regulation in signalling the ethical character of the relationship between financial intermediaries and investors. Its particular focus is the relationship between the operators of collective investment schemes (CIS) and the investors in those schemes.

A defining characteristic of financial markets in recent years has been the widespread 'engineering' of financial and other assets to create new financial products. Assets such as shares in business corporations, government and semi-government bonds, corporate and personal debt obligations, derivatives, real estate, infrastructure assets and commodities have been packaged up (or in some cases disaggregated) to create new instruments that can be sold on to investors. CIS are the most longstanding and established of these engineered financial products. The more recent variations are what Paul McCulley from PIMCO memorably described in September 2007 as 'the whole alphabet soup of levered up non-bank investment conduits, vehicles and structures',[1] including securitisations and structured products like residential mortgage-backed securities, commercial mortgage-backed securities and collateralised debt obligations.

What distinguishes these structures from the traditional bank-based financial intermediation is that the vehicles for holding assets typically sit outside the balance sheet of the

---

* Associate Professor of Law, Melbourne Law School, the University of Melbourne, Australia, and Senior Executive Leader, Investment Managers, Australian Securities and Investments Commission (ASIC). The views expressed in this paper are the author's own and not those of ASIC.
[1] http://www.pimco.com/LeftNav/Featured+Market+Commentary/FF/2007/GCBF+August-+September+2007.htm (accessed on 21 August 2009).

issuing entity. The maturity transformation function performed by banks—at its simplest, borrowing short and lending long—occurs on the bank's balance sheet, and the bank's capacity to meet its obligations is the subject of prudential regulation. In contrast, in CIS and other engineered structures the underlying assets typically sit is a pool or trust that is operated on a 'best endeavours' basis. Importantly, the legal or regulatory frameworks within which these structures operate generally require the operator to act in the interests of the investors in the structure in administering it. In many cases, this obligation is said to give rise to a fiduciary relationship between the operator and the investors.

This paper argues that, to the extent that legal or regulatory requirements assume or create a fiduciary relationship between the parties in these structures, they are signalling that the relationship has a particular ethical character that differs from the arm's-length ethics of the market.

The paper is structured as follows. Part B begins with a discussion of the role and prospects of financial regulation in defining the ethical paradigm for financial market transactions, suggesting a broader understanding of the role of financial regulation that is not limited to (or by) economic rationales. Part C explains CIS and the transnational principles, developed by IOSCO, that guide their regulation. Part D discusses the nature of the 'fiduciary duty' referred to by IOSCO, the ethical paradigm of the fiduciary and the aptness of this model for CIS.

B.   Financial Regulation and Ethics

What is the function of financial regulation, and what principles guide its design? Australian regulation provides a unique insight into these questions, because the system has been entirely reshaped over the last decade. In 1996, the Australian government launched an inquiry (the Financial System Inquiry or FSI)[2] into the financial system that was asked to make recommendations 'on the nature of the regulatory arrangements that will best ensure an efficient, responsive, competitive and flexible financial system to underpin stronger economic performance, consistent with financial stability, prudence, integrity and fairness'.[3] Its Final Report led to wholesale reform of financial regulation in Australia, albeit within the international framework of the Basel Core Principles for Effective Banking Supervision, the Insurance Core Principles, the IOSCO Objectives and Principles of Securities Regulation, and the CPSS[4] Core Principles for Systematically Important Payment Systems.

This context and the timing of the FSI are significant for two reasons: first, it involved the wholesale redesign of an already mature regulatory system; and secondly, it took place in the boom, rather than the bust, phase of the economic cycle.[5]

Following the FSI, Australia implemented what is often described as the 'twin peaks' regulatory model. The Australian Prudential Regulation Authority (APRA) is primarily

---

[2] Its Final Report is often referred to as the Wallis Report, after its chairman, Stan Wallis.
[3] Commonwealth of Australia, 'Financial System Inquiry Final Report' (March 1997) vii.
[4] The Bank for International Settlements Committee on Payment Systems and Settlement.
[5] This is unusual. Most major regulatory reform takes place in the aftermath of a bust—witness the Bubble Act of 1720, the US federal securities laws of the 1930s and the Australian securities laws of the 1970s.

responsible for prudential regulation, while the Australian Securities and Investments Commission (ASIC) is responsible for consumer protection and market integrity regulation.[6] These two Commonwealth agencies operate alongside the Reserve Bank of Australia, which is Australia's central bank, and the Australian Competition and Consumer Commission, which regulates anti-competitive behaviour across the economy, including in the financial sector.

APRA's enabling legislation states that it is established

> for the purpose of regulating bodies in the financial sector in accordance with other laws of the Commonwealth that provide for prudential regulation or for retirement income standards, and for developing the administrative practices and procedures to be applied in performing that regulatory role.

Its regulatory responsibilities cover authorised deposit-taking institutions (that is, banks, building societies and credit unions), general insurers, life insurance companies, friendly societies and superannuation trustees. Its legislation provides that, 'in performing and exercising its functions and powers, APRA is to balance the objectives of financial safety and efficiency, competition, contestability and competitive neutrality and, in balancing these objectives, is to promote financial system stability in Australia'.

ASIC performs several distinct regulatory functions. It is the registrar of companies, and it administers and enforces Australia's company and securities laws. Within the financial sector it regulates (through licensing) financial services providers such as CIS operators, broker/dealers and advisers, as well as the operators of financial markets and clearing and settlement facilities. It administers and enforces the governance laws for CIS, and the disclosure laws that apply to issuers of financial products. More broadly, it has the function of monitoring and promoting market integrity and consumer protection in relation to the Australian financial system and the payments system. In performing its functions, ASIC is required by its enabling statute to strive to 'maintain, facilitate and improve the performance of the financial system and the entities within that system in the interests of commercial certainty, reducing business costs, and the efficiency and development of the economy' and to 'promote the confident and informed participation of investors and consumers in the financial system'.[7]

The particulars of the Australian regulatory system are, needless to say, endlessly fascinating to Australians, and are perhaps also of interest to those who wonder why the Australian financial system has fared better, on all measures, than many others in developed economies. What is relevant for the present discussion, though, is the statutory language that establishes the mandates of the relevant agencies. The key drivers are: for APRA, financial safety and systemic stability; and for ASIC, market integrity and consumer protection.

Ethical behaviour by regulated entities and the people who run them is necessary if regulation is to achieve these goals. Rules, particularly legal rules, cannot cover the whole field of conduct—like a net, there are gaps between them. A person who is unethical will

---

[6] Jeremy Cooper, Deputy Chairman of ASIC, 'The Integration of Financial Regulatory Authorities—the Australian Experience', speech to Comissão de Valores Mobiliários, 4–5 September 2006, Brazil, available at www.asic.gov.au (accessed on 21 August 2009).

[7] For a more comprehensive discussion of the Australian model, see P Hanrahan 'Improving the Process of Change in Australian Financial Sector Regulation' [June 2008] *Economic Papers* special edition 6; University of Melbourne Legal Studies Research Paper No 348, available at SSRN: http://ssrn.com/abstract=1184463.

try to fit through those gaps, rather than treat the net as being designed to mark out the boundary between permissible and impermissible conduct.

Ethical behaviour involves, of course, people acting in accordance with the rules or standards for right conduct or practice in the context. Regulation has an important role to play in signalling what is right conduct or practice in a particular context. What is appropriate between friends, for example, might not be appropriate between spouses. This is because the ethical character of the relationship between friends is different from that between spouses. Marriage signals that difference. Regulation—in particular, the parts of regulation that deal with conduct—can serve a similar signalling function.

However, the language of regulatory change rarely speaks about the role of regulation in marking out the ethical nature of the relationship between the regulated entity, its customers and counterparties, and the broader market. Debates about regulatory change are conducted in the language of economics, not ethics. For example, the Australian Office of Best Practice Regulation recognises a need for regulation

> where there is a monopoly and potential abuse of market power; where there is incomplete information or there are information asymmetries between buyers and sellers; where goods or services are 'public goods'; and where there are impacts (externalities or spillovers) on third parties that are not reflected in market prices.[8]

There is an emphasis on risk-based approach to regulation, which entail 'the use of technical risk-based tools, emerging out of economics (cost–benefit approaches) and science (risk assessment techniques)' which reflect a 'cost–benefit analysis culture' that 'moves away from informal qualitatively based standard setting towards a more calculative and formalised approach'.[9]

Recognising the signalling function of regulation, particularly regulation directed at governance, opens up the possibility of more nuanced discussion of how regulation should or might work (and perhaps a whole new world of influence for Kantian scholars, which can be only for the good).[10]

C.   CIS and their Regulation

I now turn to consider what regulation signals about the ethical character of the relationship between a CIS operator and its investors.

CIS are central to what is sometimes termed the 'third stage' of capitalism. In 1981 Professor Robert Clark (later Dean of the Harvard Law School) described four stages of capitalism—characterised by the dominance of, in the first stage, the entrepreneur; in the second, the professional business manager; in the third, the portfolio manager; and in the fourth, the savings planner. He characterised the third stage as being:

---

[8] Australian Government *Best Practice Regulation Handbook* (Canberra, AGPS, 2007) 60.

[9] B Hutter, 'The Attractions of Risk-based Regulation: Accounting for the Emergence of Risk Ideas in Regulation' Discussion Paper No 33, ESRC Centre for the Analysis of Risk and Regulation, London School of Economics (2005), available at www.lse.ac.uk/collections/CARR/.

[10] See, eg JM Lipshaw 'Sarbanes-Oxley, Jurisprudence, Game Theory, Insurance and Kant: Toward a Moral Theory of Good Governance' (2004) 50 *Wayne Law Review* 1083, available at SSRN: http://ssrn.com/abstract=576761.

the age of the portfolio manager, and its characteristic institution is the institutional investor, or financial intermediary. As the second stage split entrepreneurship into ownership and control, and professionalised the latter, so the third stage split ownership into capital supplying and investment, and professionalised the latter.[11]

A typical or orthodox CIS is a pool of (usually exchange traded) financial assets that is selected (either actively or by reference to an index) and held by the CIS operator for the benefit of investors who have contributed to the scheme. Most CIS are structured either as investment funds, established as a trust or contract with individual investors; or as investment companies, established as a corporation in which investors are the share-holders.[12] They include arrangements such as mutual funds, investment trusts and funds, and managed investment schemes, operated by entities referred to in different markets as fund managers, asset managers, investment managers, mutual fund advisers or, in Australia, responsible entities.[13] Internationally, CIS currently hold over USD $18 trillion in net assets under management.[14]

In many jurisdictions, restrictions or requirements are imposed on the commercial features of CIS offered to retail investors. These may relate to the nature of the underlying investments, the spread or diversification of those investments, the obligation of the operator to redeem or repurchase investors' interests, the level of borrowing or the use of derivatives by the scheme. In others (including Australia) there are few such restrictions, and CIS are used as vehicles to hold a range of highly geared or specialist assets for retail, as well as institutional, investors.[15]

In all major jurisdictions, the structure and governance of CIS offered to retail investors are subject to varying degrees of governance regulation. Typically this regulation sits alongside mandatory disclosure requirements intended to ensure that investors can under-stand and assess the commercial merits and risks of the CIS offering. IOSCO has identified five different approaches to governance regulation[16]—the unifying principle from

---

[11] RC Clark, 'The Four Stages of Capitalism' (1981) 94 *Harvard Law Review* 561. Perhaps the fourth stage of capitalism has turned out to be the age of the 'structurers'—the investment banks and other financial engineers who take real economy financial assets and recut, reassemble and hedge them to produce new instruments for investment by retail and institutional investors.

[12] IOSCO, 'Summary of Responses to the Questionnaire on Principles and Best Practice Standards on Infrastructure for Decision Making for CIS Operators' (May 2000) 1.

[13] Not included in this discussion are superannuation or pension funds, because of the specialist regulatory requirements that typically apply to such arrangements. However, privately operated defined contribution funds share many of the features of a typical CIS.

[14] The Investment Company Institute (which is the umbrella industry body for US investment companies) calculates worldwide mutual fund net assets for Q1 2009 at USD $18,151,541 million. This is divided into: Americas, $10,220,885 million; Europe, $5,880,216 million; Asia Pacific, $1,973,094 million; and Africa, $77,347 million. The four largest domicile jurisdictions are: US, $9,234,558 million; Luxembourg, $1,742,219 million; France, $1,538,409 million; and Australia, $808,175 million. See http://www.ici.org/pdf/ww_03_09_sup_tables.pdf.

[15] CIS is a term that is generally understood to cover schemes for portfolio-style investment in financial assets such as shares, debentures, bonds and derivatives. These underlying investments may be exchange traded, traded in OTC markets or illiquid (such as early-stage equity held in venture capital or private equity funds). In contrast to conglomerates, CIS do not take a controlling position in the underlying assets. This type of CIS spans the risk spectrum from cash management trusts and money market funds at one end to highly leveraged hedge funds at the other. However, in some jurisdictions, including Australia, collective investment vehicles are used to hold other classes of investments, including real property (in REITs and other property trusts), property loans (in mortgage funds), infrastructure assets, and forestry and other agribusiness assets.

[16] CIS in the various jurisdictions adopt a contractual form, a corporate form or a hybrid form. Contractual form CIS are further subdivided into those where independent oversight of the conduct of the CIS operator is in the hands of a depository (contractual model 1) or a trustee (contractual model 2). Corporate form CIS are

IOSCO's point of view is that the CIS must be operated in the interest of investors, rather than the interests of CIS insiders (including the operator itself). This principle is set out in the June 2006 report on CIS governance prepared by IOSCO's Technical Committee in the following terms:

> Many [IOSCO Standing Committee 5] jurisdictions impose a fiduciary duty on CIS Operators to act in the CIS Investors' best interests. Independently of the form or model under which a CIS is organised, CIS Operators should always be subject to the fiduciary duty of acting for CIS Investors in the best possible way. The respect for this duty constitutes a core fundamental principle of CIS management.[17]

For the purposes of this paper I describe the fiduciary duty referred to by IOSCO as a duty of loyalty to the investors' interests.

D.   The CIS Operator as a Fiduciary

IOSCO's reference to the 'fiduciary duty of acting for CIS investors in the best possible way' sounds odd to Australian lawyers. First, to us, fiduciary principles are principles of equity—it is hard to imagine how they might apply in civil law jurisdictions.[18] The traditional precepts of equity—loyalty, confidence and good faith—that are reflected in the fiduciary principle are qualitatively different from the core (common law) principles for commercial dealing—honesty, careful conduct and the keeping of promises.[19] Secondly, we tend to speak in terms of fiduciary relationships which carry with them certain proscriptions, rather than prescriptive fiduciary duties. [20] However, in other jurisdictions,

---

subdivided into those where independent oversight is in the hands of a board of directors (corporate model 1) or a depository (corporate model 2). In hybrid form CIS, independent oversight is the responsibility of a supervisory board or compliance committee. The structures adopted by IOSCO member jurisdictions are: Australia, hybrid; Brazil, corporate model 2 and contractual model 1; Canada, hybrid; France, corporate model 2 and contractual model 1; Germany, corporate model 2 and contractual model 1, Hong Kong, contractual model 2; Ireland, corporate model 2 and contractual model 1; Italy, corporate model 2 and contractual model 1; Japan, corporate model 1 and contractual model 2; Jersey, corporate model 2 and contractual model 2; Luxembourg, corporate model 1 and contractual model 1; Mexico, corporate model 1; Netherlands, corporate model 2 and contractual model 1; Portugal, contractual model 1; Spain, corporate model 2 and contractual model 1; Switzerland, corporate model 2 and contractual model 1; UK, corporate model 2 and contractual model 2; and USA, corporate model 1 and contractual model 2. See 'Examination of Governance for Collective Investment Schemes: Final Report Part 1', Report of the Technical Committee of the International Organization of Securities Commissions (June 2006) 10.

[17] IOSCO Report, above n 12, 11. Standing Committee 5 is the IOSCO working group on CIS.

[18] Of course, such concepts are applied in civil law jurisdictions. See, eg the discussion of 'trusts without equity' by Professor Michael Bryan in 'Reflections on Some Commercial Applications of the Trust' in IM Ramsay (ed), *Key Developments in Corporate Law and Trusts Law: Essays in Honour of Professor Harold Ford* (Sydney, LexisNexis, 2002) 205–26.

[19] See Lord Millet's foreword to J McGhee *Snell's Equity*, 30th edn (London, Sweet & Maxwell, 2000).

[20] Under Australian law, a person is treated as a fiduciary in certain circumstances, including where the person is a trustee or has otherwise undertaken or agreed 'to act for or on behalf of or in the interests of another person in the exercise of a power or discretion which will affect the interests of that other person in a legal or practical sense': *Hospital Products Ltd v United States Surgical Corporation* (1984) 156 CLR 41, 96–97, per Mason J. In these circumstances, equity imposes certain proscriptions on the person—often referred to as the 'no conflict' and 'no profit' rules. These are: that the fiduciary must not be in a position where there is a real, sensible possibility of conflict between its own interests (or its duty to another person) and its obligation to act in the interests of the other; and that it must not use its position, or knowledge or opportunity arising from it, to benefit itself (even where the benefit is not at the expense of the other person).

including the US and Canada, there are positive obligations described as fiduciary duties, including obligations of diligence and prudence.[21]

1.   A Duty of Loyalty to Investors' Interests

The 'fiduciary duty' to which the IOSCO report refers is, broadly, an obligation on the operator of the CIS to act in the best interests of the investors in carrying out the scheme. This is fundamentally an obligation of loyalty—that is, a positive obligation to put the interests of the investors first in making decisions relating to the scheme, with a corresponding negative duty to avoid conflicts. The distinguishing characteristic of a fiduciary relationship is 'that its essence, or purpose, is to serve exclusively the interests of a person or group of persons; or, to put it negatively, it is a relationship in which the parties are not free to pursue their separate interests'.[22] This is reflected in the regulatory principle articulated by IOSCO.

In a CIS or other investment vehicle structured as a trust, the relationship between the CIS operator and the investors necessarily carries with it this obligation of loyalty. It is part of what has been described in England as the 'irreducible core of obligations owed by trustees to beneficiaries and enforceable by them which is fundamental to the concept of a trust',[23] and what in the US has been called 'the implicit norm that the trust must be for the benefit of the beneficiaries'.[24] In other forms of CIS, the obligation to conduct the scheme for the benefit of, and in the interests of, investors is imposed by law or as a term of the scheme's contract or charter. For example, in Australia, the obligation arises under section 601FC(1)(c) of the Corporations Act 2001 (Cth), which provides that the operator of an Australian registered managed investment scheme must 'act in the best interests of the members [of the scheme] and, if there is a conflict between the members' interests and its own interests, give priority to the members' interests'.

The positive obligation of loyalty is to exercise the powers and discretions conferred on the CIS operator in its operation of the scheme having primary regard to the interests of the investors, rather than those of the CIS operator or other insiders. This obligation gives rise to corollary negative duties in the CIS operator, not to obtain any unauthorised benefit from the relationship and not to be in a position of, or act in circumstances of, conflict. These negative duties are, recognisably, the proscriptive fiduciary duties in Australian (and English) law. The effect of the proscriptions is that the fiduciary must account

> for any benefit or gain (i) which has been obtained or received in circumstances where a conflict or significant possibility of conflict existed between his fiduciary duty and his personal interest in

---

[21] In *Breen v Williams* (1996) 186 CLR 71, 113, the High Court held that 'the Canadian cases also tend to reveal a tendency to view fiduciary obligations as both proscriptive and prescriptive. However Australian courts only recognise proscriptive fiduciary duties . . . In this country fiduciary obligations arise because a person has come under an obligation to act in another's interests. As a result, equity imposes on the fiduciary proscriptive fiduciary obligations—not to obtain any unauthorised benefit from the relationship and not to be in a position of conflict. If these obligations are breached, the fiduciary must account for any profits and make good any loss arising from the breach. But the law in this country does not otherwise impose positive legal duties on the fiduciary to act in the interests of the person to whom the duty is owed.'

[22] RP Meagher, JD Heydon and MJ Leeming, *Meagher Gummow & Lehane's Equity: Doctrines and Remedies*, 4th edn (Sydney, LexisNexis, 2002) [5-020].

[23] *Armitage v Nurse* [1997] 2 All ER 705, 713 per Millet LJ.

[24] J Langbein, 'The Contractarian Basis of the Law of Trusts' (1995) 105 *Yale Law Journal* 625.

the pursuit or possible receipt of such a benefit or gain; or (ii) where it was obtained or received by use of or by reason of his position or of opportunity or knowledge relating to it.[25]

In some jurisdictions these proscriptions are reflected in explicit restrictions on self-dealing[26] and on other types of conduct where pursuit by the operator of its own interests might come into conflict with its duty to operate the CIS in the interests of the investors.

2.   The Ethical Model for CIS

What ethical model underpins the fiduciary principle? If we look, we can see different ethical models in different legal and regulatory relationships. There is the 'arm's length' model that underpins, for example, much of contract law—under which each party is entitled to pursue its own interests (to the limits of the law, including misrepresentation and unconscionability) without special regard to the impact of that pursuit on the other party. There is the 'even up' model that is evident in consumer law, which adjusts for the relative disadvantage of one party to a dealing (for example, by mandating disclosure or implying certain contractual terms). The ethical character of the fiduciary relationship is different. The proposition explored below is that, for a fiduciary to behave ethically, the fiduciary must act selflessly, by putting the interests of the other party ahead of its own.

In *Meinhard v Salmon*,[27] Cardozo CJ famously observed that:

> Many forms of conduct permissible in a workaday world for those acting at arm's length, are forbidden to those bound by fiduciary ties. A trustee is held to something stricter than the morals of the market place. Not honesty alone, but the punctilio of an honor the most sensitive, is then the standard of behaviour.

The fiduciary principle evolved outside the commercial world—its genesis is in the ameliorative jurisdiction of equity. However, many of the established categories of fiduciary relationships—between commercial trustee and beneficiary, broker and client, director and company, agent and principal, and partners—are commercial in character.[28] The key consideration in applying the fiduciary principle in commercial contexts is recognising equity's ability to be pragmatic and flexible.[29] The fiduciary principle adapts to, and operates in the context of, the commercial relationship from which it arises.[30] For example, it does not preclude the payment of fees to the CIS operator (so long as they are disclosed) but it would prohibit the operator deriving collateral advantages from its position without the express consent of the members of the scheme. The underlying

---

[25] *Chan v Zacharia* (1984) 154 CLR 178, 194 per Deane J (HCA).

[26] Eg in s 17 of the US Investment Company Act of 1940.

[27] 249 NY 458; 164 NE 545 (1928).

[28] There is a wealth of literature on commercial fiduciary relationships, and the challenges they present for the law. See, eg D DeMott, *Fiduciary Obligation, Agency and Partnership: Duties in Ongoing Business Relationships* (1991); D Heyton (ed), *Extending the Boundaries of Trusts and Similar Ring-Fenced Funds* (Kluwer, The Hague, 2002).

[29] In *Mills v Mills* (1938) 60 CLR 150, 164, Sir John Latham observed, in the application of fiduciary principles to company directors, that directors are 'not, in my opinion, required by the law to live in an unreal region of detached altruism and to act in a vague mood of ideal abstraction from obvious facts which must be present to the mind of any honest and intelligent man when he exercises his powers as a director'.

[30] See P Hanrahan, *Funds Management in Australia: Officers' Duties and Liabilities* (Sydney, LexisNexis, 2007) [2.74]–[2.77].

ethical character of the relationship is that, within and in the carrying out of that relationship, the fiduciary must act with regard to and be solicitous of the interests of the other person.

Writing in Australia in 1989, Professor (now Justice) Finn said of the circumstances in which a fiduciary relationship will arise in equity that:

> What must be shown, in the writer's view, is that the actual circumstances of the relationship are such that one party is entitled to expect that the other will act in his interests in and for the purposes of the relationship. Ascendency, influence, vulnerability, trust, confidence or dependence will doubtless be of importance in making this out. But they will be important only to the extent that they evidence a relationship suggesting that entitlement. The critical matter in the end is the role that the alleged fiduciary has, or should be taken to have, in the relationship. It must so implicate the party in the other's affairs or so align him with the protection or advancement of the other's interest that foundation exists for the fiduciary expectation. A person will be a fiduciary in his relationship with another when and insofar as that other is entitled to expect that he will act in that other's or their joint interests to the exclusion of his own several interest.[31]

In my view, by imposing fiduciary duties on CIS operators, the various regulatory systems are signalling to the operator, the investors and the market what is ethical (as distinct from merely legal) in the operator's dealings with investors. By imposing a legal duty on a CIS operator to act in the interests of the investors, the regulatory system invites us to 'fill in the gaps' between specific legal rules by reference to a particular ethical model. This is important function of regulation.

What character does the imposition of fiduciary duties give the ethical relationship between CIS operators and investors? By that I mean, what does it say about how the parties are to treat each other, and expect from each other, in their dealings? The language used by Professor Finn and others suggests that the ethical model underpinning fiduciary obligation is one of 'selflessness'. Under such a model, while the interests of the parties to the arrangement are aligned, both can be pursued, but when they diverge, the interests of the fiduciary must yield.

An alternative, although less compelling, view is that the ethical model is 'professionalism', at least where commercial fiduciaries are concerned. This view may resonate more fully in North America than in Australia, as in Australia members of the professions (other than solicitors) are not fiduciaries per se.[32] The ethical obligation of a member of a profession is to apply their special skill and expertise in carrying out the project for which they have been retained by the client, in the interests of the client and in accordance the standards and values of that profession. What distinguishes the professional ethic is that a person dealing with a member of a profession expects that the professional will be paid, and will have other clients whose interests may not coincide perfectly with their own.

Either way, the ethical model signalled by the fiduciary duty is not the arm's length model of contract and the market.

---

[31] PD Finn, 'The Fiduciary Principle' in TG Youdan (ed), *Equity, Fiduciaries and Trusts* (Toronto, Carswell, 1989) 46–47.

[32] In Australia, the relationship between solicitor and client is fiduciary in character. For a discussion of the circumstances in which financial intermediaries have been treated as fiduciaries by Australian courts, see R Baxt, A Black and P Hanrahan, *Securities and Financial Services Law*, 7th edn (Sydney, LexisNexis, 2008) ch 15.

3.   The Aptness of the Ethical Model

Is the ethical model that underpins fiduciary obligation the correct one for CIS? That depends on what we mean by 'correct'. It may be that the ideal of a disinterested CIS operator is attractive in a normative sense, but that as a practical matter it is difficult to realise in the context of CIS. I have argued elsewhere that the fiduciary model may not be the most useful or robust for securities intermediaries,[33] having regard to (among other things) the difficulties faced by the Australian regulator in characterising as a fiduciary an investment bank advising a client in relation to a takeover.[34] The utility of the fiduciary concept as an organising principle for the regulation of securities intermediaries can be questioned, given that a divergence of commercial interest between the intermediary and its client may in many cases be inevitable.

CIS involve the creation (out of other assets) of new financial instruments that can be sold to investors for the profit of the CIS operator, typically through ongoing management fees that increase as the CIS grows in size. As Langevoort has observed in relation to US mutual funds:

> Once the mutual fund is viewed as a product to be marketed within liberal societal expectations as to fair advertising like any other, then any notion that the producer is a 'fiduciary' is awkward and disorienting. The transaction is instead simply embedded in the morals of the marketplace. To be sure, the adviser *is* deemed a fiduciary to the fund and its investors. From a business stand-point, however, the law's move makes little sense.[35]

If there is, as Langevoort suggests, a real 'disconnect' between the ethical character of the relationship and the commercial reality of the arrangement, something has to give. Either the commercial features of CIS must be brought more closely in line with the hoped-for ethical model or the true arm's-length nature of the arrangement should be made clearer to investors.

---

[33] P Hanrahan, 'Fiduciary Duty and the Market: Private Law and the Public Good', paper presented at Obligations IV, 23 July 2008, Singapore, available at http://ssrn.com/abstract=1184443.

[34] *Australian Securities and Investments Commission v Citigroup Global Markets Australia Pty Ltd* (No. 4) (2007) 160 FCR 35; 62 ACSR 427 (Federal Court of Australia).

[35] DC Langevoort, 'Private Litigation to Enforce Fiduciary Duties in Mutual Funds: Derivative Suits, Disinterested Directors and the Ideology of Investor Sovereignty', European Corporate Governance Institute Working Paper 61/2006 (February 2006). Available at http://ssrn.com/abstract=885970.

20

Financial Crisis and Economist Pretensions: A Critical Theological Approach

WERNER G JEANROND[*]

A. Introduction

The present crisis, often referred to in terms of 'financial crisis', 'credit crunch', 'banking crisis' or 'market crisis', is in reality a much larger crisis. It concerns the whole fabric of our culture: how do we organise economic relations in our globalised world? What ethos supports these relations today? Who are the subjects in this globalised economy and what kind of human self-understanding guides their actions? Hence it seems appropriate to explore some of the dimensions and the range of this crisis before considering moves toward a new economic ethos and related frameworks of financial regulation. In this article I wish to offer first some reflections on the connection of the present crisis of trust and the religious pretensions of economism. Secondly, I shall outline the theological task of criticising the apotheosis of certain capitalist structures. Thereafter, I wish to retrieve some of the concerns of enlightenment economic theory and consider proposals for a new ethos for our globalised world. I shall conclude my discussion with some thoughts on the relationship between such a new ethos and the future of financial regulation.

B. The Crisis of Trust and the Religious Pretensions of Economism

At present we are confronted with a debate in the media on who has the proper grasp of this crisis, who owns the crisis, who is best equipped to interpret it, who is to blame for it and who decides on the most adequate horizon for approaching it. From whatever angle one approaches the present crisis, it is a crisis of trust. Our trust in the financial institutions and the regulatory institutions has been betrayed and would need to be restored as a first step toward tackling the crisis. But how can this be achieved in the absence of a clear

[*] Professor of Divinity, University of Glasgow. I am grateful to Jakob Jeanrond, European University Institute at Florence, and to my colleague Julie Clague, University of Glasgow, for constructive comments on this article.

and public identification of the people responsible for this crisis? Who is responsible: just a few super-agents in the economy or our culture as a whole, including our political leadership and our media? Who has welcomed, supported and promoted the narrow business ethos for which money remained the sole criterion of success?

Moreover, this crisis has produced a deep uncertainty about the changing roles of the state and of economic agency, as well as their mutually critical coordination. During recent decades most of the representatives of the so-called market forces have proclaimed that a decrease in state intervention and public control stands in proportion to an increase in market activity and success. Freedom from the kind of omnipresent control that charac-terises all other aspects of our personal and public existence today should have automatically led to a flourishing development of all the blessings which we human beings are rightfully to expect from a properly functioning market. The invisible hand of the market shall govern and order everything for the best of society, both in the local and the global spheres of our existence. Thus, what we have been urged to do, and what we also did, was to continuously increase our trust in the market's own absolute mechanisms, to free the market's own dynamics, to grow in faith in the coming blessings of the market (first for us and eventually even for poorer societies) and to hand over our future to the competent hands of our financial agents. The market thus assumed control of and power over our destiny. The dialectics between market and cultural critique was sublated in favour of an absolute market.

Parallels to systems of religious belief are evident: as ordinary believers, we have developed a faith in the autonomous logic of economism, a belief in the banking and finance hierarchy whose priests and high priests on their own and without any functioning control worth its name have administered and transformed our money and assets, but also our cultural approach to the market. We have believed in this act of trans-formation and in the system's own mysterious power and dynamics. Even entire states have shared this belief. As a result, we have been encouraged by our states to hand over parts or all of our pension investment to the market's miraculous dynamics. In many of our cultures economism has taken on the role of a state religion, ie of an established religion. This religion's particular form of organisation and its highly specialised priesthood have increasingly been worshipped as a kind of guarantee for the friction-free flow of the market system and the delivery of its salvific promises. The less we understand the system, the better it will work. Ultimately, the clever handling, wrapping and packaging of risks, eg in so-called derivatives, has only further strengthened our trust in the working of risk management. Finally, the risks were considered negligible. At the same time, financial regulatory systems have become all the more fragile, incompetent and partial to the very mechanisms which they were to control.

At this point it is important to recall that this trust in the mysterious and miraculous power of the market was itself based on the deeply rooted belief in money and in its complex essence and dynamics. Jochen Hörisch, who has explored this connection in greater depth, sums up:

> Money is at the same time an exchange medium, a unit of calculation, and a means to store val-ues. Moreover, money continues the magic of transubstantiation of the Eucharist in the most profane way: whoever gives away a monetary sign receives in turn a really real value. In God we trust, in money we trust. We trust that money affords us access to that which we call 'real values', yes, that it can transubstantiate itself into these real values. Money, like previously the host, is

what pious philosophers and theologians of the Middle Ages called 'ens realissimum', the most real being.[1]

As long as the system functioned, that is, as long as the system helped some of its agents to increase their profits and yields, no critique of the system was taken seriously. However, now that the system has collapsed, the widespread trust in the market has also withered, ie in its autonomy, hierarchy, invisible hand and autodynamics, internal and external control mechanisms, claims to salvific blessings, and trust in the substantial relationship between money and the real world.[2]

Moreover, banking and finance agents have stopped trusting each other and each other's aims and working habits. People in these branches know only too well that their respective attempts to maximise profits through fusing businesses and banks on a global scale, to increase shares, yields and bonuses for company directors, and to reduce the visible risks of financial transactions through ever more intricate packaging have now been discovered, exposed and condemned. Suddenly the public has awoken from its slumbers to a gloomy reality of destroyed values, empty promises, overly clear risk factors and catastrophic bankruptcies, with resulting unemployment and personal as well as social misery. Not only has the public, thus shaken, now lost its faith in the autodynamics of this economistic religion and its financial promises, but even the financial priesthood itself has lost faith in its own religion. What remains is the heartfelt cry that the state ought to intervene in this very system which had so pervasively insisted that it was able to function best autonomously, ie without this very intervention. What we are witnessing now, therefore, is not only some passing weakness of the system; rather, we are witnessing the death of economism as a religion and the resulting lack of orientation in the very culture that had been so concerned to let economism flourish.[3]

Every crisis contains the potential for renewal and improved development,[4] but at the same time it seems to invite certain people to engage in acts of simplification and new forms of instrumentalisation. In the heat of the present financial crisis populists have emerged that promise to create a new sense of order if only we now offer them our trust, a trust so deeply shaken and betrayed in recent times. A number of politicians on both sides of the Atlantic have quickly indicated that they would be committed to solving the problems of the economistic order with the help of gigantic salvaging, investment and incentive programmes. The task of these programmes is to re-establish trust both in the system's goodness and in the ability of our politicians to succeed with urgent and complex crisis management. However, so far efforts to re-establish trust between the banks themselves have failed. Bankers continue to mistrust each other.

Apart from measures to refloat the banking system, gigantic investment programmes

---

[1] J Hörisch, *Gott, Geld, Medien: Studien zu den Medien, die die Welt im Innersten zusammenhalten* (Frankfurt am Main, Suhrkamp, 2004) 13 (my translation).

[2] For an insightful discussion of the role of trust both in religion and in our money economy see M Petzold, 'Geld-Gegenstand christlicher Kritik?' in S Beyerle and M Roth (eds), *Geld als bestimmender Faktor menschlicher Existenz* (Leipzig, Evangelische Verlagsanstalt, 2006) 121–44.

[3] See also M Bunting, 'Faith. Belief. Trust. This Economic Orthodoxy Was Built on Superstition', *The Guardian*, 6 October 2008, 31.

[4] See N Hertz, 'Abschied vom Gucci-Kapitalismus', *Handelsblatt*, 17 February 2009, available at www.handelsblatt.com/politik/gastbeitraege/abschied-vom-gucci-kapitalismus;2157956. Hertz is optimistic that an increasing insight into the worldwide need to reform the capitalist order will motivate a radical reform of the financial order. In this respect she stresses that there is now a real opportunity to create a better regulated and balanced economic system, but she emphasises that 'a global industry cannot be regulated with national means' (my translation).

are intended to renew our trust in the market forces through stimulating consumption and production. This means that we are expected to overcome our lack of trust in the market forces by allowing ourselves to be lifted onto a new level of consumption. Hence, we are offered a new status as consumers. We are not respected as free subjects and responsible citizens; rather, once more, we are functionalised within this system as consumers.

This development contains much political explosiveness: incredible sums of money are made available in order to save the banks from death, to refloat the broken financial market and to stimulate consumption. Suddenly we realise that earlier attempts to solve relatively small social, existential, ecological, peace enhancing, developmental and research projects and activities, which at the height of the economic boom were judged to be unrealistic, would have cost only a tiny fraction of those sums which are now pumped into the market in order to save the shaken system and its underlying economistic religion. Our political culture is unlikely to accept this very obvious disparity: with our taxes we are to save the banks that have been ruined by egoistical agents claiming to do best when acting without appropriate control, transparency and responsibility.

C.   Criticising the Apotheosis of the Market

Faith is a phenomenon that has engaged theologians at all times and in all religions. Faith in God and in God's creative and reconciling project in our universe has inspired many generations of Jews, Christians and Muslims to develop personal and communal patterns of orientation. Religious faith can be a constructive force for shaping, changing, reforming and criticising ways of life in this universe. Faith has freed strong energies in order to meet life's many challenges. But, like all human phenomena, religious faith is both pluralistic and ambiguous: it can be developed for good and bad, for emancipatory and for oppressive purposes. Theology knows that religious faith must be examined, interpreted and exposed to a radical critique of ideology.

For quite some time voices in church and theology have been criticising the apotheosis of the market and its forces.[5] These voices have stressed the radical difference between, on the one hand, faith in the loving God who continues her creating and reconciling project in our universe and who invites all human beings to a rich and happy life in the network of mutual love relations,[6] and on the other hand, faith in the magic and promises of the market economy.

From a theological perspective, the market itself needs to be de-ideologised in the first place. The market is not a power of destiny, but a mere instrument to shape and order an important part of human relationships. Theology rejects all attempts to declare market mechanisms as god-given or as predestined. Faith in God can never approve of any sort of market religion or market ideology. 'You shall not have other gods before me.'[7] The market does not require some kind of priesthood; rather, it needs adequately educated, competent

---

[5] See, eg the contributions by the Roman Catholic Church to rethinking the purpose of economic order in RA Sirico and M Zieba OP (eds), *The Social Agenda of the Catholic Church: A Collection of Magisterial Texts* (London, Burns & Oates, 2000) 103–29.

[6] For an in-depth analysis of the potential of love see WG Jeanrond, *A Theology of Love* (London, T&T Clark/Continuum, 2010).

[7] Exodus 20:3.

and self-critical people who understand their work also as a service to humankind. The market and the financial 'services' must be humanised, that is, they have to be returned to their proper function in and for human life in a sustainable universe. These systems are to serve human beings, not human beings these systems. Every human person is called to become a fulfilled, responsible and engaged subject together with other human beings in a sustainable universe. Therefore a human being must never be content with being assigned the status of a mere consumer. According to Abrahamic faith, human beings are created by God for freedom, love and solidarity. This human dignity must never be compromised by financial and other market forces. Faith in God excludes all systems that threaten the dignity of women, men and children as free and interrelated subjects.

The biblical traditions inspire the establishment of such an order for our market that is built on freedom, respect, love, trust, development and justice. Thus, in this tradition, poor, handicapped, isolated and oppressed women, men and children must be the ultimate measure for judging whether or not any particular financial and market system serves human beings and their development. The option for the poor and oppressed will disclose all efforts to instrumentalise the eternal dignity of a human being. Therefore a critical and self-critical theology can never accept any economistic claim to dominating the economic logic of our time. Naturally, theology is happy to participate in the multidisciplinary effort to civilise and improve capitalism, but theology can never accept the totalitarian aspirations of economism.[8]

Theologians, of course, are not alone in demanding a clear commitment to a humanising agenda in economic theory and praxis; nor are they the first group of intellectuals to do so. Economic philosophers and economic ethicists have richly contributed to the debate on the orientation and purpose of the market economy.

D.   Towards an Enlightened Economics

In 2009, the 250th anniversary of the publication of Adam Smith's book *The Theory of Moral Sentiments* is being celebrated in and beyond the University of Glasgow. Smith's book is an integrated part of his wide-ranging economic theory. However, it has often been neglected when Smith's theory of capitalism has been discussed, celebrated or rejected. A fair assessment of Smith's proposal for an economic order must, however, acknowledge that this Scottish enlightenment thinker always understood his economic theory in terms of contributing to the enhancement of the common good.

In our time, many commentators agree that only a holistic view of Smith's trilogy (*The Theory of Moral Sentiments* of 1759, *An Inquiry into the Nature and Causes of the Wealth of Nations* of 1776, and *Essays on Philosophical Subjects*, published posthumously in 1795) allows for an adequate assessment of the interconnectedness of his moral, economic and political theories.[9] For Smith, it was impossible to reflect on economics and the market

---

[8] *Cf* also the pertinent contribution by the Archbishop of Canterbury to the debate on the necessary renewal of our economic order: R Williams, 'Ethics, Economics and Global Justice', *The Guardian*, 9 March 2009, available at www.guardian.co.uk/world/2009/mar/09/rowan-williams-lecture-full-text/print.

[9] See, eg HC Recktenwald, 'Adam Smith (1723–1790)' in J Starbatty (ed), *Klassiker des ökonomischen Denkens*, Teil 1 und 2 in einer Gesamtausgabe (Hamburg, Nikol, 2008), 134–55.

without at the same time considering their moral foundation and orientation.[10] Human freedom was a decisive factor for Smith. Human striving for a happy life must never be reduced to mere material aspirations.

Smith was concerned with exploring the ground, the order and the principles according to which both individuals and society are trying to secure existence and well-being. He recognised the individual person's natural concern to improve his situation, that is, to secure his existence, to increase his (at times only imagined) comforts, to gain the acknowledgement and respect of his environment, and to augment his time for leisure. When Smith reflected on human self-interest he distinguished carefully between self-love, on the one hand, and selfish love or egoism, on the other hand.[11] According to Smith, human self-interest in terms of feeling, affect or motif is innate. Like sympathy, this interest is part of human nature. However, this relation to the self must not be confused with survival instinct. Rather, human self-interest can be interpreted as a natural striving that characterises the human being in all his periods of life.[12]

Smith considered this natural striving to be a positive moral force which is of significance for society as a whole. Such personal aspiration is at the centre of Smith's entire system. However, as Smith observed, this force can become a liability if it mutates into self-centredness or egoism. That is why Smith demanded different correctives that help human beings to civilise this personal ambition and striving. Hence, it would be wrong to accuse Smith of having favoured some sort of laissez-faire capitalism. Rather, the opposite is the case: every society requires a clear moral and legal framework in which the free economic subject can act. In this respect, Smith's category of sympathy is of significant interest. He devoted a large part of the first chapter in *The Theory of Moral Sentiments* to a discussion of sympathy.[13] His economic outlook is always already anchored in 'our fellow-feeling' with other human beings.[14]

Of course, Smith's economic theory cannot be explored and applied in today's situation and crisis without significant alterations and corrections. However, it still seems appropriate to reflect on how human nature influences and challenges all attempts to develop economic systems. It is not possible to maintain an economic system against the natural constitution of human beings. Totalitarian forms of collectivism, forms of egoism and ideological distortions of human freedom are incompatible with the freedom-aspiring self-interests of human beings and therefore they will sooner or later collapse. In this respect, Adam Smith also implicitly challenges Christian theologies of love that do not attach sufficient importance to the human vocation to love oneself and instead demand both a total annihilation of the self and a total sacrifice to God and the neighbour.[15]

Smith developed his theory with reference to independent states, whereas today we need economic models for a globalised world. He did not know of our massive ecological problems and challenges. Economic theories today need to respond to this ecological crisis and consider necessary actions for sustainable development in a universe of limited

[10] *Cf* A Broadie, 'Sympathy and the Impartial Spectator', in K Haakonssen (ed), *The Cambridge Companion to Adam Smith* (Cambridge, Cambridge University Press, 2006) 158–88, esp 164–65.

[11] *Cf* A Smith, *The Theory of Moral Sentiments*, K Haakonssen (ed) (Cambridge, Cambridge University Press, 2002) 158.

[12] *Cf* Recktenwald above n 9, 153–55.

[13] Smith, above n 11, 11–17; and A Smith (ed K Sutherland), *An Inquiry into the Nature and Causes of the Wealth of Nations. A Selected Edition* (Oxford, Oxford University Press, 2008) 22.

[14] Smith, above n 11, 13. On Smith's concept of sympathy see also Broadie, above n 10, 163–70.

[15] *Cf* Smith, above n 11, 30.

resources. Moreover, Smith worked in the long androcentric tradition of the west that considered the free man to be the economic subject par excellence. This male-centred view of economics and its related patriarchal structures of domination must be exposed, criticised, dismantled and replaced by a holistic approach to economics that promotes human dignity, freedom, equality, development, participation, mutual cooperation and justice for all women and men—for present and coming generations.

E.   Developing a Global Ethos for a Global Economy

For some time, a number of Christian voices have been warning against the illusion of unlimited economic growth and the related costs for human beings and the universe as a whole.[16] However, the present crisis has made the ears of a wider population and of the media more receptive to such critical voices and their respective proposals for alternative ways of living human life in this universe. Moreover, constructive proposals even from religious and theological bodies are receiving greater attention today. Fortunately, there are a number of long-term projects and conversations available now for our reflection on how we might wish to reshape global approaches to ethics at a time of global challenges and crisis.[17]

The Swiss-German theologian Hans Küng, working at the University of Tübingen, has been one of the major promoters of a debate on global responsibility and on the related potential of religious traditions to work together with all women and men of good will toward the development of a global ethos for our time.[18]

In the framework of the discussion of aspects of such a global ethos, the St Gallen business ethicist Peter Ulrich contributed a perspective on an ethics of economy in 1998.[19] In his perspective, building on the humanist concern of all major ethos traditions, Ulrich distils an at once both culture specific and transcultural normative logic of interpersonality. Moreover, Ulrich sees no necessary opposition between Hans Küng's espousal of a shared religious vision of human dignity, value and vocation (what Küng calls the '*Humanum*'[20]) on the one hand, and the normative logic of interpersonality which is based on an ethics of reason and mutuality, on the other hand.[21] Rather, Ulrich wishes to combine an emphasis on personal virtue development with an emphasis on the development of formal principles for the just living together of free, mature and responsible citizens in a well-ordered society.[22] Therefore, he calls for a basic consensus that safeguards

---

[16] See, eg J Gerlach, *Ethik und Wirtschaftstheorie: Modelle ökonomischer Wirtschaftsethik in theologischer Analyse* (Gütersloh, Chr Kaiser/Gütersloher Verlagshaus, 2002); H-S Haas, *Theologie und Ökonomie: Ein Beitrag zu einem diakonierelevanten Diskurs* (Gütersloh, Gütersloher Verlagshaus, 2006) 161–245. For a discussion of Roman Catholic Social Teaching see RG Simons, *Competing Gospels: Public Theology and Economic Theory* (Alexandria, AJ Dwyer, 1995) 105–23.

[17] See, eg Canadian Conference of Catholic Bishops, 'Ethical Reflections on the Economic Crisis' in K Aman (ed), *Border Regions of Faith: An Anthology of Religion and Social Change* (Maryknoll, Orbis, 1987) 486–93.

[18] H Küng (trans J Bowden), *Global Responsibility: In Search of a New World Ethic* (London, SCM Press, 1991); *cf* also H Küng, *Weltethos für Weltpolitik und Weltwirtschaft* (Munich/Zurich, Piper, 1997).

[19] P Ulrich, 'Weltethos und Weltwirtschaft—eine wirtschaftsethische Perspektive' in H Küng and K-J Kuschel (eds) *Wissenschaft und Weltethos* (Munich/Zurich, Piper, 1998) 40–60.

[20] Küng, above n 18, 89–93.

[21] Ulrich, above n 19, 43.

[22] Ibid, 45.

the pluralist interaction of cultural identities and forms of life. 'Such an intercultural neutral basic consensus first of all constitutes the political basic order of an open, just and peaceful (global) society.'[23]

Within this philosophical and religious context, Ulrich considers the radical critique of economism as the most important task of a contemporary business ethics. He stresses the need for an enlightened economic ethos which abandons the economistic metaphysics of the market and instead recognises the priority of the normative logic of interpersonality over the logic of the market.[24] Hence, a global world economic order is to be shaped primarily by concerns for the ethical–practical values of the good life and the just living together between people and peoples. Because it values service to life as the overriding principle of economic order, such an approach is opposed to reducing concerns for economic order to the politics of competition.

This approach has three important implications for the development of regulative mechanisms: first, the primacy of politics for the development of future global economic order has to be restored; secondly, the development of a global citizenship of women and men needs to be promoted on the basis of personal ethical maturity and responsibility; and thirdly, we also need to develop models of a corporate ethics that explore the wider spectrum of corporate maturity and global responsibility.[25]

A coordinated view of these three dimensions of a new global ethos for a global economy frees us from populist shortcuts in the ongoing debate on how to master the present crisis. New forms of regulation, however desirable and necessary, can never replace the need for the development of moral agents—personal, political and corporate. In this respect, religious traditions potentially have much to offer, not just in terms of moral theory, but also in terms of moral praxis.

F.   Conclusion: A New Ethos and the Future of Financial Regulation

Approaches to financial regulation in our globalised world must go hand in hand with approaches to a global ethos. Regulation does not lead to moral convictions; rather, moral convictions allow regulations to function. An essential part of any emancipatory ethos in our world is the understanding of what constitutes both a free and responsible human subject and inter-human relations in a sustainable ecology. Hence, no forms of global financial regulation will ever succeed if they do not take this basic insight into account. Moreover, financial regulation is in the service of humankind, not vice versa. Thus, such models of regulation will have to be developed and considered that both enhance the common good of a global humanity and promote the development of human agency in freedom, equality and justice.

---

[23] Ibid (my translation).
[24] Ibid, 51.
[25] See also C Döpfner and J Hoffmann, 'Mit gutem Gewissen Rendite erwirtschaften! Corporate Responsibility-Unternehmensbewertungen für ethisch-ökologisch und kulturell 'saubere' Geldanlagen' in P Biehl et al (eds) *Gott und Geld: Jahrbuch der Religionspädagogik* vol 17 (Neukirchen-Vluyn, Neukirchener Verlag, 2001) 65–75.

Trust is a fragile good in human relationships. It will take much time and effort to rebuild trust in our economic systems. However, it is not only patience that is required here, but also honesty by all agents in the emerging global cultural framework. It makes no sense to participate in a pseudo-religious economistic system while at the same time criticising only its leadership. The rebuilding of inter-human and inter-cultural trust requires critical and self-critical attention to all issues concerning the common good. Economic relations are vital for human beings, but they form only one part of human relationships. Therefore, totalitarian approaches to economic relations must be rejected in the name of humanity's wider cultural aspirations.

Economic theory needs to be brought back to the larger multi-disciplinary discussion on the nature and aspirations of women, men and children in this universe. It has much to contribute to, and much to learn from, this global conversation on what makes life in this universe meaningful, and on the rules and regulations that are required to support both this conversation and the future shape of a pluralist and free global humanity.

21

Dealing Fairly with the Costs to the Poor of the Global Financial Crisis

CHRISTIAN BARRY AND MATT PETERSON[*]

A. Introduction

It has become a commonplace that the costs of the current global financial crisis are massive. In 2009, the world's combined economies are predicted to shrink by almost 3%—the first global contraction in 60 years. Although the bulk of that decline in income is concentrated in affluent countries, developing countries other than India and China are expected to shrink by 1.6%.[1]

While the scope of the financial crisis has been global, the policy response to it has not been. The recent international summit convened by the UN General Assembly to address the effects of the financial crisis on developing countries is instructive in this regard. An initial draft of the summit's outcome document boldly called for a $3 trillion 'Global Stimulus for Restructuring and Survival'.[2] However, the notion of a global stimulus ultimately disappeared completely; the world's governments promised, rather vaguely, to 'work in solidarity on a vigorous, coordinated and comprehensive global response to the crisis in accordance with our respective abilities and responsibilities'. How this is to be achieved is not spelled out, beyond that 'each country has primary responsibility for its own economic and social development'.[3]

Given the failure to agree on a collective response, national policymakers need guidance on how the costs of responding to the crisis should be allocated. In this essay, we will sketch out some possible answers to the question of how to address one particular type of cost that the crisis is engendering: severe shortfalls that persons are likely suffer in their

[*] Senior Research Fellow, Centre for Applied Philosophy & Public Ethics (CAPPE), Australian National University and Postgraduate Fellow, Yale University.

[1] India and China should grow, but at a considerably slower pace. World Bank, 'Global Development Finance: Charting a Global Recovery: I: Review, Analysis and Outlook' (Washington, DC, 2009) xi, available at http://siteresources.worldbank.org/INTGDF2009/Resources/gdf_combined_web.pdf (accessed on 26 August 2009).

[2] President of the General Assembly, 'Draft Outcome Document for the United Nations Conference on the World Financial and Economic Crisis and Its Impact on Development' (8 May 2009), available at http://www.un.org/ga/president/63/interactive/financialcrisis/outcomedoc80509.pdf (accessed on 26 August 2009).

[3] United Nations, 'Outcome of the United Nations Conference on the World Financial and Economic Crisis and Its Impact on Development', A/CONF.214/3 (22 June 2009) para 10, available at http://www.un.org/ga/search/view_doc.asp?symbol=A/CONF.214/3&Lang=E (accessed on 26 August 2009).

health, civic status or standard of living relative to the ordinary needs and require-ments—food, drink, shelter, minimal health protection—of human beings.[4] Of course, there is a great deal of severe deprivation in our world that cannot in any way be attributed to this crisis. We want to ask who, morally speaking, should bear the costs of trying to alleviate or at least mitigate the additional deprivations that will be engendered by the crisis. Recent estimates suggest that these deprivations will be substantial. The Interna-tional Labor Organization estimates that some 40 million people may lose their lobs in developing countries as a result of the crisis—more than twice the number of job losses expected in developed countries.[5] In China alone, 20 million migrant workers have lost their jobs already.[6] Per capita income in sub-Saharan Africa may decline by 20%.[7] Predictably, this loss of income by the world's most vulnerable people will produce immense suffering—an additional 1.4–2.8 million infants will die over the next six years as a result of the financial crisis.[8]

A.   Choosing the Right Comparison

Many policymakers and commentators have reached outside of the realm of finance to frame our understanding of the crisis. It has been likened to (amongst other things) the sinking of the Titanic (by Brazilian president Lula da Silva),[9] a car wreck (by numerous media commentators),[10] a shipwreck (by French president Nicholas Sarkozy)[11] and a tsunami (by former US Federal Reserve chairman Alan Greenspan).[12] Our choice of analogy is significant, since, as we argue, they each express different attitudes toward the nature of the costs and the responsibilities of the various actors involved. None of the analogies are perfect, but the first and last seem clearly to be the least apt. The world economy is (unlike the Titanic) still afloat despite the recent downturn, and (unlike a

---

[4] We refer to these shortfalls from a minimally adequate standard of living simply as 'severe deprivations'.

[5] International Labour Organization, 'Global Employment Trends: May 2009 Update' (Geneva, International Labour Office, 2009) table B2, 27, available at http://www.ilo.org/wcmsp5/groups/public/—-dgreports/—-dcomm/documents/publication/wcms_106504.pdf (accessed on 26 August 2009).

[6] Chi-Chu Tschang, 'A Tough Year for China's Migrant Workers', *BusinessWeek*, 4 February 2009, available at http://www.businessweek.com/globalbiz/content/feb2009/gb2009024_357998.htm (accessed on 26 August 2009).

[7] UNESCO press release, 'Global Crisis Hits Most Vulnerable', 3 March 2009, available at http://portal.unesco.org/en/ev.php-URL_ID=44687&URL_DO=DO_TOPIC&URL_SECTION=201.html (accessed on 26 August 2009).

[8] World Bank, 'Swimming Against the Tide: How Developing Countries are Coping with the Global Crisis' (March 2009), available at http://www-wds.worldbank.org/.../477800WP0swimm10Box338866B01PUBLIC1.pdf (accessed on 26 August 2009), p 10.

[9] D Francis, 'World Is Titanic without Paddle—Lula', *National Post*, 15 April 2009, available at http://network.nationalpost.com/np/blogs/francis/archive/2009/04/15/world-is-titanic-without-paddle-lula.aspx (accessed on 26 August 2009).

[10] Among many others, see P Thomasch, 'Zelnick: Welcome to the Emergency Room', *Reuters*, 4 December 2008, available at http://blogs.reuters.com/summits/2008/12/04/zelnick-welcome-to-the-emergency-room (accessed on 26 August 2009); and E Simon, 'Financial Crisis: Is It Time to Invest', *Daily Telegraph*, 19 September 2008, available at http://www.telegraph.co.uk/finance/newsbysector/banksandfinance/2992018/Financial-crisis-is-it-time-to-invest.html (accessed on 26 August 2009).

[11] L Marlowe, 'Sarkozy Calls for Capitalism with a Dose of Morality', *Irish Times*, 26 September 2008, available at http://www.irishtimes.com/newspaper/world/2008/0926/1222374595726.html (accessed on 26 August 2009).

[12] 'Financial Crisis "Like a Tsunami"', *BBC News*, 23 October 2008, available at http://news.bbc.co.uk/2/hi/business/7687101.stm (accessed on 26 August 2009).

tsunami) the crisis and the costs it have engendered are clearly man-made, rather than the handiwork of Mother Nature. The same goes for the shipwreck analogy—although the movements of financial markets are often as unpredictable as the ocean, they are at least in principle subject to the controls of human agency. A car wreck, on the other hand, involves, as the crisis does, interactions between human beings using powerful vehicles that lead to significant damage. And, just as in the aftermath of a car wreck, it is sensible to ask who if anyone is at fault for its occurrence, and who should pay the damages. A car accident would involve costs to the cars and motorists involved, and perhaps also to third parties, and the question would be whether these costs should be left to fall on these people or shifted (partially or in whole) to others.

To make things more concrete, let's focus in on just one of the many ways that the financial crisis may contribute to severe deprivations—it may create a financing gap and make the debts of many countries unserviceable.[13] The International Monetary Fund (IMF) projects that the poorest 38 countries will need to borrow some $216 billion dollars to meet their national and international obligations this year.[14] This figure assumes that development aid flows will remain unchanged, however, which is doubtful given the recent track record of the affluent in meeting their existing aid targets.[15] The World Bank suggests that developing countries as a whole will need some $700 billion in additional financing.[16] High debt levels and financing gaps can limit the capacities of countries' governments to provide the social services necessary to ensure even a minimally adequate standard of living for their people, and to divert resources and energy from the pursuit of short- and long-term strategies that further their peoples' well-being. This effect is particularly acute in the poorest countries and is magnified by exchange rate volatility, since poor countries often borrow in foreign currencies.

In the late 1980s, economists began to caution against 'debt overhang'—the build-up of large debts, which creates a climate of permanent financial fragility in a country, leaving that country in a financial and economic slump, without domestic revenue to pay for current expenditures. Because of its financial instability, the country is deemed to be high-risk from an investment perspective.[17] Creditors demand a higher interest rate on investment finance—if willing to lend at all—since many of them may have substantial outstanding debt claims on the country.[18] Financial crises and the debts that often engender them can also lead the crisis countries to increased dependence on international institutions such as the IMF, which arguably limits the capabilities of their citizens to exercise meaningful control over their policies and institutions.

---

[13] This is not, of course, the only way that the crisis may produce deprivation. As consumption slows in net-importing countries like the US, the volume of international trade will decline, and high-income export-production jobs will disappear in export-oriented countries. Similarly, the flow of remittances—a critical income support for many in developing countries—will also diminish. To the extent that these sources of income are taxed, government revenues will decline, with a consequent decrease in the provision of social services. These consequences, and others, are reviewed in the World Bank's 'Swimming against the Tide' report, above n 8.

[14] International Monetary Fund, 'The Implications of the Global Financial Crisis for Low-Income Countries' (March 2009), available at http://www.imf.org/external/pubs/ft/books/2009/globalfin/globalfin.pdf (accessed on 26 August 2009), p. 34.

[15] V Walt, 'Why Wealthy Nations Are Stiffing Africa', *Time*, 12 June 2009, available at http://www.time.com/time/business/article/0,8599,1904339,00.html (accessed on 26 August 2009).

[16] World Bank, above n 8, 6.

[17] T Palley, 'Sovereign Debt Restructuring Proposals: A Comparative Look' (2003) 17(2) *Ethics & International Affairs* 26.

[18] Ibid.

Suppose that some country becomes heavily indebted, and that its government can, as a result of decreased resources resulting from the crisis, service its contractually defined debt obligations only by severely cutting back on expenditures on education, health and security. Suppose further that these cutbacks will predictably lead to severe deprivations in its population. We would then be faced with the question of whether the government (and, ultimately, the population) of this country ought to bear the costs of the country's earlier decision to borrow—or whether these costs ought to be pushed (in part or as a whole) onto others.

C.   Principles of Cost Allocation

What principles would we appeal to in determining who is responsible for the costs in the case just imagined? The answer to this question has seemed plainly obvious to some advocates of human rights and poverty relief. They deny that we can reasonably demand that a country repay its debts or fulfil other contractual obligations when repayment will predictably lead to deprivations for its population, especially since others (such as wealthy countries or financial institutions) could arguably bear the financial costs of nonrepayment of these debts in a way that would not lead to comparably regrettable outcomes. The Austrian economist Kunibert Raffer has argued, for example, that 'one must not be forced to fulfill contracts if that leads to inhumane distress, endangers one's life or health, or violates human dignity. Civilized laws give unconditional preference to human rights and human dignity.'[19] This view is endorsed by many others, including advocates of the Fair and Transparent Arbitration Process (FTAP), developed by Raffer and modelled on chapter 9 of the US Bankruptcy Code, which governs the bankruptcy of municipalities. The FTAP would ensure that the basic human rights (somehow under-stood) of citizens of debtor countries are given higher priority than creditors' rights in the management of debt crises.[20] Those who favour such initiatives appeal to what David Miller aptly calls the capacity principle, which requires that those who can alleviate acute deprivations most easily must do so regardless of their connection to them.[21]

On this view, those with access to funds ought to spend them in ways to help those at most risk of suffering severe deprivation. Such actors need not be governments: the head of the UN Conference on Trade and Development recently called on the IMF to provide debt relief to developing countries that have diminished foreign reserves due to the crisis.[22] The IMF in fact responded by reducing interest rates to zero until 2011 for some of its loans. The Fund is financing this move by selling off some of its substantial gold reserves.[23] Were those with the greatest capacity to avert severe deprivation to do so, one would

[19] K Raffer, 'Risks of Lending and Liability of Lenders' (2006) 21(1) *Ethics & International Affairs* 93.

[20] See, eg Erlassjahr, 'A Fair and Transparent Arbitration Process for Indebted Southern Countries', updated submission to Financing for Development, September 2001, available at www.erlassjahr.de/content/languages/englisch/dokumente/ftap_englisch_rz.pdf (accessed on 26 August 2009).

[21] D Miller, 'Distributing Responsibilities' (2001) 9(4) *Journal of Political Philosophy* 453.

[22] 'Poor Nations Need Temporary Debt Relief Amid Economic Crisis—Senior UN Official'. *UN News Service*, 30 April 2009, available at http://www.un.org/apps/news/story.asp?NewsID=30643&Cr=Financial&Cr1=crisis (accessed on 26 August 2009).

[23] 'IMF Backs New Package to Support World's Poorest During Crisis', *IMF Survey*, 29 July 2009, available at http://www.imf.org/external/pubs/ft/survey/so/2009/POL072909A.htm (accessed on 26 August 2009).

expect much more aggressive measures by wealthy countries. The thought is not that market participants should not generally bear the risks of their decisions—no market system could function well without doing this—but that certain extremely bad outcomes should not be allowed to stand when they can be averted at relatively small cost.

The capacity principle holds that the provision of assistance should depend on how heavily burdened the population of a country would be in absolute and relative terms were that country to pay its debts or absorb the full burden of its financial losses and how costly it would be for others to offset the costs that it would otherwise face. It might plausibly be argued, however, that whichever claims take precedence ought to depend not only on this, but also upon how the country became heavily indebted, or economically vulnerable, in the first place. Miller himself, for example, has recently argued that 'If people have poor or otherwise inadequate lives because of decisions or actions for which they are responsible, then outsiders have no obligation of justice to intervene'.[24] There, we would justify departures from the capacity-based allocation of costs by appeal to what might be called the principle of contributory fault.

The principle of contributory fault sharply limits the conditions under which those who suffer hardships can disrupt others' plans and shift the costs of alleviating their deprivations onto those third parties. It is worth pausing to explore this principle and to examine its possible application to different agents involved in sovereign borrowing and lending. Drawing on the car accident analogy, we can look to tort law for guidance. Standards of tort liability generally demand that an agent bear the costs of her harmful conduct when it can be shown that:

1. she has causally contributed to them;
2. the harmful outcome was her fault; and
3. the faulty aspect of her conduct (and not merely her conduct as a whole) was causally relevant to the outcome (for example, to show that some driver is liable for the injuries of another person, it must not merely be shown that the driver was negligent and that she caused the accident, but that the injuries resulted from her negligence).[25]

Theorists of the law of torts differ over how these conditions should be understood, but there are some elements that are common to nearly all accounts of them. First, the notion of fault operates with some notion of a 'standard of care'. That is, agents are at fault for some harmful outcome, and thus can be held liable for bearing its cost, when they have not lived up to an objectively defined normative standard.[26] When an agent fails to live up to this standard, she is deemed to be 'negligent', and thus at fault for any harmful outcome of her conduct. Secondly, the normative standard that is invoked for the purpose of determining negligence depends on some conception of what a 'reasonable person' could be expected to have done in the situation given what was foreseeable in the context in which the agent acted. If the agent acted in the way a reasonable person could have been expected to act in the circumstances, then that agent did not act negligently and is thus not at fault

---

[24] D Miller, 'Justice and Global Inequality' in A Hurrell and N Woods (eds), *Inequality, Globalization and World Politics* (Oxford, Oxford University Press, 1999) 187–210.

[25] For a discussion, see RW Wright, 'The Grounds and Extent of Legal Responsibility,' (2003) 40 *San Diego Law Review,* available at SSRN: http://ssrn.com/abstract=438640.

[26] These notions are described well in A Ripstein, *Equality, Responsibility, and the Law* (Cambridge, Cambridge University Press, 1999).

for the costs engendered by her conduct. Consequently, such an agent should not be made to bear these costs, even if her conduct is causally relevant to bringing them about. If, when driving at normal speeds and obeying all traffic signals, I swerve my car to avoid hitting a child dashing across the street and smash into a parked car, I am not at fault for the damage done to the parked car, and thus not liable in tort for bearing the costs of its repairs.

The contributory fault principle might also be thought to apply to countries.[27] If a country has acted negligently, either through severe imprudence or recklessness, it might therefore be argued that the costs resulting from this cannot fairly be pushed onto others, no matter how severe they may be, even if the country can now shoulder these costs only with great difficulty and at significant sacrifice. To be plausible, this type of argument would require a compelling account of how a standard of care can be defined to apply to collective agents like countries—and this, in turn, will depend on a convincing account of what a reasonable country would do under various sets of circumstances.

However challenging it may be to develop a plausible conception of the contributory fault principle for countries, some principle of this kind is likely to hold quite significant intuitive appeal, not least because failing to hold countries responsible for their irresponsible conduct may provide very poor incentives for the future. It is also difficult to deny that some of the damages of the current crisis have resulted from countries' failures to exercise reasonable care in the management of their financial affairs. For instance, under General Pervez Musharraf Pakistan borrowed heavily and spent its foreign reserves on imports, only to find itself unable to repay its debts as its currency collapsed last autumn.[28] The same pattern of excessive borrowing and inability to repay is visible in a number of other developing and emerging economies, including Ukraine, where paralysing political infighting has prevented economic reform for years, and Latvia, which directed foreign capital toward now much diminished real estate and mortgage lending.[29] All three—among others—have turned to the IMF for emergency loans to cover their foreign obligations.

It seems extremely unlikely, however, that any conception of the contributory fault principle would provide grounds for concluding that the burdens resulting from the financial crisis more generally should be borne solely or even mostly by the populations of the poorer countries. This is so for several reasons. First, a great deal of the damage resulting from this crisis cannot plausibly be characterised as resulting from the imprudence or recklessness of poorer countries. The unstable global environment in which they operate produces many changes to the circumstances of these countries; these changes are not only impossible for them to control, but also quite difficult or impossible to foresee.[30] The present financial crisis is only the most recent and vivid example of such instability.

[27] Miller's own view on how such an idea might be extended to nations: see D Miller, 'National Responsibility and International Justice' in D Chatterjee (ed), *The Ethics of Assistance: Morality and the Distant Needy* (Cambridge, Cambridge University Press, 2004).

[28] S Mufti, 'Cash-strapped Pakistan Finds Few Friends in Time of Economic Need', *Christian Science Monitor*, 23 October 2008, available at http:// www.csmonitor.com/2008/1023/p04s01-wosc.html.

[29] D Stern, 'Economic Crisis Sweeps Eastern Ukraine' (8 April 2009), available at http:// www.nytimes.com/2009/04/08/world/europe/08ukraine.html (accessed on 26 August 2009); O Ryan, "Latvia's Dramatic Fall from Grace," *BBC News*, 8 June 2009, available at http://news.bbc.co.uk/go/pr/fr/-/2/hi/ business/8085007.stm (accessed on 26 August 2009).

[30] For an illuminating discussion by a policymaker about why so few foresaw the crisis, see D Gruen, 'Reflections on the Global Financial Crisis', Keynote Address at the Sydney Institute, 19 June 2009, available at http://www.treasury.gov.au/documents/1564/PDF/Sydney_Institute_Address.pdf (accessed on 26 August 2009).

In response to this, it may be argued that these are simply the risks of activities like borrowing money and other economic activities. That is, while specific circumstances are impossible to foresee, any borrower is aware (or at least should be aware) that there are general risks that accompany economic activities like borrowing money, which include the risks of financial crises and natural disasters. It is a common feature of contracts that those who engage in them are usually supposed to assume the risk that fulfilling the conduct that is required of them will turn out to be more difficult, and perhaps much more difficult, than anticipated.[31] Critically, however, the law also acknowledges that there are contexts in which this supposition no longer holds. For example, if an unanticipated tsunami of unprecedented ferocity wreaks havoc on some country's economy, this event should not be viewed as part of the 'normal' background risks that agents ought to have considered when entering into contracts or in making other financial decisions. Indeed, contract law and the law of torts has made legally relevant the distinction between ordinary and extraordinary events that lead to the non-performance of contracts or damages. When extraordinary events—including so-called acts of god—lead to non-performance of contracts, the duty to perform them is excused in many legal systems and the contract is viewed as 'impracticable'.[32] When the performance of a contract becomes impossible for reasons other than the negligence of the contracting parties, it is typically treated as void under the doctrine of frustration.[33]

This analysis suggests that there are some respects in which the financial crisis was like a tsunami after all. Although made-made—the critical difference—the financial crisis was (with a few exceptions) unforeseen, and, from the perspective of under-resourced developing countries, unpredictable.[34] For policymakers in developing countries, the collapse of Lehman Brothers and its consequences for financial markets, for example, would have been very similar to the deadly tsunami of 26 December 2004. Without a warning system in place, few would have known that the damage was occurring until much of it was already irreversible.

In addition, in those cases where countries have clearly conducted themselves irresponsibly, it often does not seem plausible that the vast majority of their present and future people should bear the full cost of this conduct. There are several reasons for this. First, on any plausible reading of the contributory fault principle, it will not follow from the mere fact that some agent's negligence or misconduct has been a cause of some harm that he should bear the full cost of that harm. This is especially true when the negligence or misconduct of other agents were also causes of it. Imagine that a pedestrian crosses a busy street against a red light without paying attention to the passing cars, and is hit by a driver

---

[31] See PS Atiyah, *Introduction to the Law of Contract*, 5th edn (Oxford, Oxford University Press, 1995), esp 212–15, for discussion.

[32] The US Uniform Commercial Code, §2-615, for example, excuses a party from delivering goods specified in a contract when the reason for their failure to do so results from events such as 'acts of god', whose absence was a 'basic assumption' of the contract, whether or not such exclusion is specifically stated in the contract. For detailed discussion of the jurisprudence and justification of these measures, see AO Sykes, 'The Doctrine of Commercial Impracticability in a Second-Best World' (1990) 19(1) *Journal of Legal Studies* 43; RA Posner and AM Rosenfield, 'Impossibility and Related Doctrines in Contract Law: An Economic Analysis' (1977) 6(1) *Journal of Legal Studies* 83.

[33] For a discussion see Atiyah, above n 31, 229–44.

[34] Tellingly, the NYU economist Nouriel Roubini, now famous for having predicted the crisis, was profiled dismissively by Prakash Lougani in the IMF's in-house newsletter in 2006 under the headline 'Meet Dr Doom' (*IMF Survey*, 16 October 2006, 308, available at www.imf.org/external/pubs/ft/survey/2006/101606.pdf (accessed on 26 August 2009)).

who does not see the pedestrian because the driver is talking on his cell phone. In this scenario, most modern law will allocate the liability for the pedestrian's injuries between the driver and the pedestrian to the extent of their fault. This seems reasonable—why, after all, should the cost that results from the negligence of one actor be borne entirely by someone else, even when this second person has also acted negligently?

This consideration may be particularly relevant when there is a clear connection between the negligence of one actor and another, such that the negligence of one agent can plausibly be viewed as encouraging (and thus significantly raising the risk of) negligent conduct by the other. If we lend a car to our teenage niece and she drives it into a tree after drinking several cocktails, then she has clearly acted negligently and can reasonably be expected to bear at least some of the cost of the harms her conduct creates. The extent to which she should bear the cost of harms, however, will also depend on other factors, such as whether her acquiring the alcohol involved the negligence of other actors. If a liquor store clerk served her without requesting proper identification, then this clerk (and perhaps also his employer) can be held partially liable for the costs of the accident. And if we have acted negligently by buying liquor for her, it can reasonably be questioned whether we retain any claim whatsoever to compensation for the damages to our car that ensue from her conduct, or, indeed, whether we should escape from full liability for the harms her conduct inflicts on others.

These considerations are particularly relevant in the context of assessing responsibility for the costs to poorer countries that are the result of the present financial crisis. While the negligence of poorer countries may have played some role in creating these costs, the negligent conduct of other countries seems also to have contributed causally to them. Indeed, regulators in the US and the UK have admitted as much. In March 2009, Verena Ross, director of strategy and risk at the UK's Financial Services Authority (FSA), laid blame at the feet of the FSA and other major regulators for a 'failure to identify that the whole system was subject to market-wide, systemic risk'.[35] In the US, chairman of the Security and Exchange Commission (SEC) Christopher Cox—while resisting broad claims of responsibility—acknowledged that the SEC's programme to regulate Wall Street investment banks was 'fundamentally flawed from the beginning', a failure which in turn contributed to the financial crisis.[36] The SEC seems to have been particularly negligent as a regulator. Under the Bush administration, the SEC was 'missing in action' and simply failed to regulate according to its mandate, not to mention its failure to act when tipped off to Bernard Madoff's Ponzi scheme.[37] The US Federal Reserve has also been a focal point of criticism. Its formerly unimpeachable ex-chairman, Alan Greenspan, admitted in a Congressional hearing that his deregulatory ideology was flawed and had contributed to

---

[35] V Ross, 'Lessons from the Financial Crisis', speech to the Chatham House conference on Global Financial Regulation, London, 24 March 2009, available at http://www.fsa.gov.uk/pages/Library/Communication/Speeches/2009/0324_vr.shtml (accessed on 26 August 2009).

[36] S Labaton, 'SEC Concedes Oversight Flaws Fueled Collapse', *New York Times*, 27 September 2009, available at http://www.nytimes.com/2008/09/27/business/27sec.html.

[37] J Westbrook and R Schmidt, 'Cox "Asleep at Switch" as Paulson, Bernanke Encroach,' *Bloomberg*, 22 September 2008, http://www.bloomberg.com/apps/news?pid=20601109&sid=aoM0mju1ARQo&refer=home (accessed on 26 August 2009); A Blumberg, 'Now You SEC Me, Now You Don't', *This American Life*, 12 September 2008, available at http://www.thisamericanlife.org/Radio_Episode.aspx?sched=1260; J Westbrook, D Scheer and M Pittman, 'Madoff Tipster Markopolos Cites SEC's "Ineptitude"', *Bloomberg*, 4 February 2009, available at http://www.bloomberg.com/apps/news?pid=20601103&sid=axvJfch6PDjs& (accessed on 26 August 2009).

the current crisis.[38] Many critics, such as economist Jeffrey Sachs, go further, arguing that Greenspan's decision to keep US interests rates low after 9/11 recklessly encouraged the kind of excessive borrowing that Pakistan, Ukraine and many other countries engaged in.[39]

Furthermore, the widespread official practice of guaranteeing the 'political risk' faced by lenders—the promise to the lender by its government that the latter will bail out the former and take over its claims in case the debtor government declines for whatever reason to honour an obligation—creates a double moral hazard in the international lending system. On the one hand, more capital will flow to reckless governments, which will tend to be willing to borrow more than would be prudent from the standpoint of their population; on the other hand, since creditors will have incentives to lend more, the greater their exposure, the greater the likelihood their government will need to bail them out in order to prevent losses to domestic stockholders. This practice shifts a great deal of the risk to the population of the borrower government, which will have to repay or otherwise make other concessions to the government of the lender. For example, in the 1970s US private banks lent to Indonesia's national oil company Pertamina, even as the US Senate Committee on Foreign Relations declared that the company's debt was uncontrollable and the IMF had put a cap on the loans that should be made available to the country. Nevertheless banks lent above the IMF ceiling and, when the crisis broke out, the US government stepped in to bail them out and assumed Indonesia's obligations.[40] It hardly needs mentioning that the same kind of moral hazard is at work in the numerous corporate bailouts enacted by affluent governments.[41] The current system is not one in which all market participants are expected to bear the risks of their choices.

In practice, debtor countries are often in so vulnerable a condition that refraining from entering into debt contracts with creditors (even particular creditors) is not a reasonable option for them. Faced with the choice of making a loan that it knows will be difficult to repay and forgoing funds needed to maintain basic services and governmental functions, it seems likely that any reasonable government would borrow. In domestic legal contexts of this kind, contracts are often viewed as non-binding, either because they were entered into under severe duress or because enforcing them would be unconscionable.[42]

Even when (unlike in this case) it seems appropriate to attribute the costs of crises entirely or mainly to the negligent conduct of a country, it may be implausible to hold the

---

[38] K Scannell and S Reddy, 'Greenspan Admits Errors to Hostile House Panel', *Wall Street Journal*, 24 October 2008, available at http://online.wsj.com/article/SB122476545437862295.html?mod=todays_us_page_one (accessed on 26 August 2009).

[39] J Sachs, 'The Roots of Crisis', *The Guardian*, 21 March 2008, available at http://www.guardian.co.uk/commentisfree/2008/mar/21/therootsofcrisis (accessed on 26 August 2009). For an insightful overview of the relationship between low interests rates and the financial crisis, see 'The Giant Pool of Money', *This American Life*, 9 May 2008, available at http://www.thislife.org/radio_episode.aspx?episode=355 (accessed on 26 August 2009).

[40] For a discussion of this example and the (in)operation of risk in international lending, see K Raffer, 'Risk of Lending and Liability of Lenders' (2007) 21(1) *Ethics and International Affairs* 85. For a more extended discussion of the various ways that the international lending system encourages problematic borrowing and lending, see C Barry and L Tomitova, 'Fairness in Sovereign Debt' (2006) *Social Research* 74.

[41] For details of US bailouts, see 'History of US Bailouts', *Pro Publica*, 15 April 2009, available at http://www.propublica.org/special/government-bailouts; 'Adding Up the Government's Total Bailout Tab', *New York Times*, 4 February 2009, available at http://www.nytimes.com/interactive/2009/02/04/business/20090205-bailout-totals-graphic.html (accessed on 26 August 2009).

[42] It is worth noting that the domestic law of many countries has traditionally regarded with great suspicion loans to poor persons in distress, such as by payday lenders or check cashers. For discussion see J Cartwright, *Unequal Bargaining: A Study of Vitiating Factors in the Formation of Contracts* (Oxford, Clarendon Press, 1991).

vast majority of the country's present and future people solely, mainly and, in some cases, even partially responsible for shouldering the costs that such crises engender, especially with respect to severe deprivation. One main reason for this relates to the fact that those agents who take out a loan or make financial decisions and those who are obliged to repay it are different. It is the finance ministers and other public officials of a country's government who make borrowing decisions in the name of the country, while it is the present and future citizens and other subjects taxable by the government who are asked to do the repaying. Of course, this is not in itself necessarily problematic. Indeed, when a creditor's claims on individual agents, for example, result from decisions or policies that have been adopted by the agent's political community, and where she either played some role in choosing the policy or at least had her interests given adequate weight by those making the decision, there is at least a prima facie case for taking her to be obliged to honour them.[43] The present and/or past governments of many vulnerable countries, however, are not even minimally representative of the interests of those they rule, failing to give due consideration to the interests of its people in both the making of decisions and in the decisions themselves.

D.   Determining Responsibility in the Real World

In the real world, it is often difficult, if not impossible, to determine with much confidence whether and to what extent different individual and collective agents (a person, a development bank, a firm, a national government, and so on) have individually and collectively contributed through their negligent conduct to severe deprivations. It is thus unclear whether those who grant substantial weight to the principle of contributory fault should take these agents to have responsibilities to remedy them, or how weighty they ought to hold them to be. This problem can only be fruitfully addressed by examining the appropriateness of different standards—which we call standards of application—that might be appealed to for determining agents' responsibilities in such contexts.[44] Let us imagine the following case: a relatively poor developing country (DC), asserts that a rich country (RC) has undertaken a set of policies (P) that have contributed to severe deprivations among DC's citizens.

Because of this, DC argues, RC has strong contributory-fault-based reasons to undertake efforts to alleviate these problems and to avert further deprivations that RC's past conduct would otherwise cause in the future. Evaluating DC's compensation claim in contexts in which substantial factual uncertainties of this kind are present will require us to distinguish three different standards of application for the contributory fault principle:

1.   The burden of proof: who has the burden of proof in this case? Must DC (or some other agent) show that P contributed to the deprivations in question? Or must RC show that it has not done so?

---

[43] As argued in D Miller, *National Responsibility and International Justice* (Oxford, Oxford University Press, 2007).

[44] This section draws on discussions of these themes in C Barry, 'Understanding and Evaluating the Contribution Principle' in A Follesdall and T Pogge (eds), *Real World Justice* (Dordrecht, Kluwer, 2005) 103–37 and 'Applying the Contribution Principle' (2005) 36(1–2) *Metaphilosophy* 210.

2. The standard of proof: what evidential threshold must be reached for it to count as proven that P did or did not contribute to deprivations amongst DC's people?

3. The constraints on admissible evidence: what kinds of evidence may be employed to corroborate the thesis that P has contributed to deprivations amongst DC's people?

How each of the standards of application identified above is specified will often be quite consequential. But how can we determine whether any particular way of specifying these standards is fair? The first thing to note is that there is no obviously correct answer to this question, nor is there any neutral or natural way of specifying these standards that can serve as a default. It clearly depends upon the context of the inquiry and the goals of the practice within which it is undertaken. For example, the appropriateness of different standards of application for establishing a causal connection between some chemical substance and a medical condition may vary, depending upon whether we are engaged in scientific inquiry, criminal or civil legal proceedings, or ethical reflection. Consider some agent A, who operates a factory that is alleged to release chemical agents that are harmful to children. In a criminal trial in which A is accused of causing serious health problems to children in a neighbouring school, most would insist that high evidential thresholds be employed for determining the causal links between the substance and the harm, and that the burden of proof be placed with the prosecution. We might further insist on very strict constraints on admissible evidence, perhaps allowing only epidemiological studies conducted using methodologies sanctioned by highly regarded professionals to count as evidence of causation. We might also demand only what Judith Thomson has called 'individualized' evidence, which is 'in an appropriate way causally connected with the (putative) fact that the defendant caused the harm', rather than 'probabilistic' evidence that the chemical was causally relevant to the harm.[45]

In a civil trial in which some agent A is being tried for a similar offence, however, establishing a 'preponderance of evidence'—that is, it is more likely than not—that the chemical released by A has contributed to the children's health problems might provide adequate grounds for assigning liability to him. We might also allow a broader range of evidence (such as studies of the effects of the chemical on animals), or merely probabilistic evidence. If the question is whether further such chemical releases should be legally permitted, it is not implausible that even slight evidence that these releases harm children should suffice to disallow them, at least until further study of their effects can be undertaken.[46]

When we engage in ethical reflection about what the correct policy response should be, meanwhile, the mere suspicion that one may have contributed to some acute deprivation often provides sufficient reason to act to address it. If, for example, A suspects that the chemical she has released may have contributed to children's health problems, she might reasonably take herself to have an ethical responsibility (although not a legal or enforceable one) to contribute towards meeting the costs of the treatment of their problems—or at least more reason to do so than she would have in the absence of her suspicion that she may have contributed to their condition. This may also be true where it

---

[45] J Thomson, 'Liability and individualized evidence' (1986) 49(3) *Law and Contemporary Problems* 199, 203.

[46] For a discussion of the standards relevant for determining the toxicity of substances in basic scientific research and governmental regulation see C Cranor, *Regulating Toxic Substances: A Philosophy of Science and the Law* (New York, Oxford University Press, 2007).

is impossible to determine whether the preponderance standard is met, or even when we know that it has not been met.

Different standards of application will result in different probabilities of these types of errors. In characterising any such set of standards, then, some view must be taken of the relative costs of these types of errors. Stringent standards of proof and restrictions on admissible evidence in criminal proceedings, for example, reflect a strong aversion to Type 1 errors,[47] expressing the conviction that falsely criminalising the innocent is more costly than allowing many crimes to go unpunished. The preponderance standard in civil procedures also expresses an aversion to Type 1 errors, reflecting a willingness to err on the side of failing to allocate resources to those who have been injured by inordinately risky conduct or products. However, it is much less stringent than the standard of application for criminal trials, and it foreseeably engenders both a higher probability of Type 1 errors and a lower probability of Type 2 errors.

Returning to our imagined case, if we believe that the cost of Type 1 errors to RC is substantially less than the potential cost of Type 2 errors to DC, for example, then we ought strongly to consider adopting standards of application that are far more tolerant of Type 1 than of Type 2 errors in assessing claims of contributory fault, and vice versa.

But what are the relative costs of Type 1 and Type 2 errors in the case of RC and DC? Consider first the cost of a Type 1 error to respondents such as RC if the claim of contributory fault is falsely found to be true. This cost will depend on how well off RC is, how badly off the claimants are (for example, the deprived parties in DC) and how much it will cost for RC to alleviate their deprivations. These costs may be monetary, involving the transfer of resources, but they might also involve the extension of special privileges and rights to DC, such as tariff-free access to RC's markets, or perhaps RC's efforts to increase the quantity of funds available to DC at lower rates of interest. In practice, these costs seem manageable. If, for instance, the US wrongly assumed that it had harmed some group of developing countries and gave away 0.7% of its stimulus package—as proposed by the president of the World Bank—it would have lost only some $4.9 billion.[48] That is the cost of about 11 days of war in Iraq, or about 3% of the American International Group (AIG) bailout.[49]

But what of the costs of Type 2 errors to the subjects that might wrongfully go uncompensated—in this case, the deprived parties in DC? Since, by hypothesis, DC is a poor country, those who suffer from severe deprivations within its territory will likely remain very badly off if they do not receive the funds. This, of course, depends on the assumption that the world that RC and DC inhabit is one like our own, and does not possess formal mechanisms (such as a global system of social insurance) or informal arrangements (such as a generally known and complied-with norm of providing assistance to the severely deprived) that reliably meet the costs of addressing severe deprivations within DC. (Recall that we should expect per capita income in sub-Saharan Africa to decline by one-fifth this year.)

[47] For an explanation of type 1 and type 2 errors see http://www.stats.gla.ac.uk/steps/glossary/hypothesis_testing.html (accessed on 26 August 2009).

[48] R Zoellick, 'A Stimulus Package for the World', *New York Times*, 22 January 2009, available at http://www.nytimes.com/2009/01/23/opinion/23zoellick.html (accessed on 26 August 2009).

[49] D Goldman, "Iraq War Could Cost Taxpayers $2.7 Trillion," *CNNMoney*, 12 June 2008, available at http://money.cnn.com/2008/06/11/news/economy/iraq_war_hearing/index.htm (accessed on 26 August 2009); 'American International Group, Inc', *New York Times*, 13 May 2009, available at http://topics.nytimes.com/top/news/business/companies/american_international_group/index.html (accessed on 26 August 2009).

Given the relative costs to RC and DC of Type 1 and Type 2 errors, we conclude that there is a strong prima facie case for specifying standards of application for applying the principle of contribution that expresses a willingness to err in favour of the severely deprived subjects, whether they are the party alleging that they have been harmed or the party against which such claims have been made. In other writings,[50] one of us has called this norm the 'vulnerability presumption principle'. While implausible as a principle for specifying standards of application in a criminal legal context (and most likely in most civil legal contexts), or as a principle for assessing ethical responsibilities more generally, the vulnerability presumption principle seems clearly superior to stringent standards of proof and evidence with respect to the determination of ethical responsibilities to address severe deprivations.

E.   Conclusion: Implications for Policy Orientation

The international response to the financial crisis's devastating effects on developing countries has been extremely limited so far. There has been no global stimulus, despite calls from the UN and the IMF, nor has there been a great outpouring of development aid—perhaps more aptly termed humanitarian aid in this case. The meeting of the Group of 20 in April was trumpeted as good news for the poor, but resulted only in increased funding for IMF loans. Some countries have balked at the application of traditional IMF conditionality to these loans. Ukraine, for instance, argued that it would have had to reduce social spending in order to be eligible for additional IMF funding. While a detailed analysis of the human impacts of IMF conditionality is beyond the scope of this chapter, our analysis above gives us some reason to question this method—conditional IMF loans—as a means for responding to the crisis.

Although there would not be enough evidence to hold Alan Greenspan and other regulators responsible in a criminal—or even civil—court for the harm their policies have caused to developing countries (along with the damages caused to their own and other developed countries, of course), as we have argued, the standards here are different. When the livelihoods of the world's poorest people are at stake, as they are here, we ought to construct standards that err in their favour. We suggest that any plausible specification of those standards would hold the world's financial giants, especially the US and UK, morally liable for contributing to harm in the developing world. The admissions of guilt by key regulators reviewed above indicate as much. As such, these countries have contributory fault-based duties to ameliorate the damage done, and to ensure that they will not cause further harm in the future. Simply increasing the indebtedness of developing countries would not discharge these duties.

What would a more appropriate policy response look like? To start, governments that are implementing fiscal stimulus should consider designing their policies so that they advantage rather than disadvantage developing countries. This guideline would lead not only to disallowing provisions like the notorious "Buy American" clause in the US stimulus package, it could also lead policymakers to consider supporting domestic

---

[50] Barry, above n 44.

industries that have strong connections with other countries. For instance, the decline in the US construction industry has led to a decrease in remittances to Latin American countries, whose emigrants often man construction sites.[51]

In addition, affluent governments should give no-strings-attached development aid, in the form of grants rather than loans where possible, insofar as it seems likely that doing so would benefit the recipient populations.[52]

Consider that the US government has given $150 billion in loans to the thoroughly discredited AIG and $97 billion to the US auto industry.[53] It is extremely unlikely that these loans will be recouped in full. In contrast, all developed countries combined gave a total of $12.2 billion in aid for basic social services in 2007, the last year for which data is available.[54] Assisting developing countries in balancing the budgets that the affluent have broken would be cheap in comparison. To return to our analogy, the world's affluent governments are currently speeding away from the scene of an accident. It is not too late for them to turn around and help to offset the costs of this accident for those least able to bear them.

---

[51] D Ratha, S Mohapatra and A Silwal, 'Outlook for Remittance Flows 2009-2011: Remittances Expected to Fall By 7–10 Percent in 2009', Migration and Development Brief 10 (World Bank, 13 July 2009), available at http://siteresources.worldbank.org/INTPROSPECTS/Resources/334934-1110315015165/Migration&DevelopmentBrief10.pdf (accessed on 26 August 2009).

[52] Injecting more resources into a very poorly governed society or one with a corrupt government would not, obviously, meet this requirement.

[53] 'American International Group', above n 46; J Hyde, 'Bottom Line: US Auto Industry Says It needs $97.4 Billion to Live', *Detroit Free Press*, 19 February 2009, available at http://www.freep.com/article/20090219/BUSINESS01/902190486/1210/BUSINESS/Bottom+line++US+auto+industry+says+it+needs+$97.4+billion+to+live (accessed on 26 August 2009).

[54] United Nations, 'Millennium Development Goals Indicators, 2009', available at http://unstats.un.org/unsd/mdg/Data.aspx (accessed on 23 July 2009).

22

Professions, Integrity and the Regulatory Relationship: Defending and Reconceptualising Principles-based Regulation and Associational Democracy

KEN MCPHAIL*

A.   Introduction

During a recent Treasury Select Committee[1] review of the banking crisis in the UK, one committee member asked Sir Fred Goodwin, ex-director of the Royal Bank of Scotland,

> Sir Fred, in the public eye, in the media, you are perhaps taking a much harder hit than anyone on this. This is not actually to get to you—I am interested in the culture. Is it that you are an aberration? Is it that you are someone with a different moral compass in terms of what motivates you; or, in your view, are your integrity and ethics representative of the trade and profession of bankers?

While much of the discussion surrounding the financial crisis has focused on the failure of global regulatory systems and the collapse of the wholesale money markets, another key area of concern is the failure of specific individuals within the banking and finance sector, and in particular a perceived lack in their integrity. Will Hutton,[2] columnist for *The Observer* newspaper, expresses this concern over the attitudes of those professionals at the heart of our financial systems, as follows,

> [This] is a crisis of a particular capitalism that has set aside respect for trust, integrity and fairness as fuddy-duddy obstacles to 'wealth generation'. What we are re-learning is that without trust and fairness, capitalism risks its own sustainability . . . London's money markets froze because of a trust collapse . . . Trust matters.

To date, much of the discussion in the UK has focused on the Financial Services Authority (FSA) as the primary regulator of the financial services sector. However, the regulatory

---

* Professor of Social and Ethical Accounting, University of Glasgow.
[1] The Treasury Committee is one of a number of Select Committees tasked by the House of Commons to independently scrutinise the policy and practice of Government departments. The remit of the Treasury Committee covers the Treasury, Her Majesty's Revenue and Customs and other related public bodies, like the Bank of England and the Financial Services Authority.
[2] W Hutton, 'I've Watched the Economy for 30 Years. Now I'm Truly Scared', *The Observer*, 28 September 2008.

functions and failings of professional bodies and trade associations like the British Bankers Association, the institutes of chartered bankers (the Institute of Financial Services and the Chartered Institute of Bankers in Scotland) and the institutes of charters accountants (for example the Institute of Chartered Accountants in England and Wales and the Institute of Chartered Accountants in Scotland) have been relatively overlooked. It has been professionals—members of professional bodies—who have 'set aside respect for trust, integrity and fairness as fuddy-duddy obstacles to "wealth generation"', an observation which once again raises questions about the function of professional bodies in society and their claims to have the public interest, as opposed to their own interests or those of their members, at heart.[3]

In an attempt to stimulate a wider debate on the future of financial regulation, this chapter presents some thoughts on professions and integrity. Specifically, the chapter does two things. First, it endeavours to open up the discussion on the role of professional bodies as voluntary associations within the broader regulation of financial systems; and secondly, it presents some thoughts on how a different conceptualisation of integrity might lead to a case for a stronger role for the market for values in relation to the regulation of the financial services sector. Through an attempt to combine professional and private notions of integrity, the chapter promotes both a principles-led approach to regulation and an associationalist view of democracy. By adopting this position, the chapter therefore takes an opposing view to that increasingly espoused by the FSA in response to the financial crisis.

The chapter therefore explores the idea of the regulatory function of professional bodies, and the subsequent regulation of the self by professionals that a notion of professional integrity might entail. However, both the idea of professional integrity and the legitimacy of professional bodies are problematic.

The difficulty is that, while most would agree with Will Hutton that 'integrity matters', exactly what we mean by integrity is quite difficult to pin down. Historically, within the professions this idea was construed in terms of ensuring that individuals entering the profession were of appropriate character. In accountancy, the profession's primary claim in relation to serving the public interest was construed narrowly in terms of ensuring both the character and competence of those entering the profession. Character was defined by reference to gender and the ability to pay exam dues, and competence was understood in narrow technical terms. So, while we might be able to reach some consensus that integrity matters, it is more difficult to determine exactly what we mean by integrity.

John Mann's questioning of Sir Fred Goodwin in relation to the integrity of the profession of bankers should sound familiar. The glut of corporate scandals around the turn of the last century resulted in a renewed focus on the function of professional bodies and the notion of professional integrity by academics,[4] big audit firms[5] and professional accountancy bodies.[6] The International Federation of Accountants IFAC),[7] for example,

---

[3] Sir Fred Goodwin, for example, was a member of the Institute of Chartered Accountants in Scotland.

[4] J Fuller and MC Jensen, 'What's A Director To Do?' in T Brown and R Heller (eds), *Best Practices: Ideas and Insights from the World's Foremost Business Thinkers* (Cambridge MA, Perseus Publishing, 2003).

[5] SA DiPiazza and RG Eccles, *Building Public Trust—The Future of Corporate Reporting* (New York, John Wiley & Sons, 2002).

[6] The Institute of Chartered Accountants in England and Wales, *Information for Better Markets, Reporting with Integrity* (London, Institute of Chartered Accountants in England and Wales, 2007).

[7] A global association of professional accounting bodies. The organisation develops standards on auditing practice, ethics and education.

concluded that, 'Failure to recognise the primacy of integrity has been a major contributor to the financial scandals of recent years'.[8] Consequently, there have been a number of attempts to ensure greater integrity through new regulation (see, for example, the US Sarbanes-Oxley Act of 2002 and the EU's 2006 Statutory Audit Directive).

Many of the accounting professional bodies have also developed new ethical education programmes in response to IFAC's criticisms. For example, both the Institute of Chartered Accountants of Scotland and the Association of Chartered Certified Accountants now have a mandatory ethics module. For the past few years, the Association of Chartered Certified Accountants has also been attempting to develop an enhanced ethical culture around the notion of professional values. However, as Stephen Cohen comments in relation to the implementation of Sarbanes-Oxley,[9] 'the question for accountants, "How can we remedy the ethical problems?" was replaced by the question "What does it take to satisfy the specific prescriptions of the new legislation?"' The current financial crisis has therefore occurred against a backdrop of supposedly greater focus on professional integrity more generally.

However, concern with professional integrity extends beyond just the financial services professions—it seems endemic to the professions in general. Concern has long been expressed within the medical profession that the focus on the transmission of technical skills and scientific knowledge marginalises ethics[10] and dehumanises medicine.[11] Hafferty and Franks[12] conclude that the professional culture of medics has become 'ethically compromised'. A review of the legal education journals also reveals a considerable level of concern about the ethical predispositions of lawyers over a significant period of time. Lieberman,[13] Kronman,[14] Smith[15] and Webb[16] have all expressed concern at the unethical behaviour of lawyers.[17] Smith,[18] for example, is worried that being a lawyer 'inevitably corrupts lawyers' characters'. The ethical status of the legal profession in the UK has also been the subject of major institutional scrutiny in the past. The Lord Chancellor's Advisory Committee's (ACLEC) First Report,[19] for example, represents an early attempt to address the ethical problems of the legal profession.[20]

---

[8] International Federation of Accountants *Rebuilding Public Confidence in Financial Reporting: An International Perspective* (New York, IFAC, 2003)

[9] S Cohen, 'Management, Ethics, Accountability and Responsibility' in SR Clegg and C Rhodes (eds), *Management Ethics: Contemporary Contexts* (New York, Routledge, 2006) 118.

[10] FW Hafferty and F Franks, 'The Hidden Curriculum, Ethics Teaching and the Structure of Medical Education' (1994) 69 *Academic Medicine* 861. See also M Parker, 'Autonomy, Problem-based Learning and the Teaching of Medical Ethics' (1995) 21 *Journal of Medical Ethics* 305.

[11] SH Miles, LW Lane, J Bickle, RM Walker and CK Cassel, 'Medical Ethics Education: Coming of Age' (1989) 64 *Academic Medicine* 705. See also B Green, PD Miller and CP Routh, 'Teaching Ethics in Psychiatry: A One-day Workshop for Clinical Students' (1995) 21 *Journal of Medical Ethics* 234.

[12] Above n 10.

[13] JK Lieberman, 'Moral Choices: Ethics And Values in the 80s Putting Law into Ethics' (1979) 65 *Liberal Education* 259.

[14] A Kronman, *The Last Lawyer* (Cambridge MA, Belknap Press, 1993).

[15] MBE Smith, 'Should Lawyers Listen to Philosophers about Legal Ethics?' (1990) 9 *Law and Philosophy* 67.

[16] J Webb, 'Inventing The Good: A Prospectus For Clinical Education and the Teaching of Legal Ethics in England,' (1996) 30 *The Law Teacher* 270.

[17] This concern is being expressed both within and outside the profession. See Smith, above n 15.

[18] Ibid.

[19] ACLEC produced two reports in 1996 following a four year comprehensive review of legal education in England and Wales: 'First Report on Legal Education and Training' (London, ACLEC, 1996) and 'Continuing Professional Development for Solicitors and Barristers' (London, ACLEC, 1996). The committee was superseded by the Legal Services Consultative Panel in 1999.

[20] Webb, above n 16.

Banking is therefore not the only profession whose members are coming under increasing ethical scrutiny, and this change in attitude towards the professions is reflective of broader societal shifts. While Giddens[21] suggests that a shift in trust from persons to institutions is a characteristic of modernity,[22] postmodernity is reflective of a broader demise in trust in institutions, including professional bodies. This shift in trust is also associated with a questioning of the function of professional bodies within society. It seems strange, therefore, that the crisis in financial regulation is not being connected to the broader crisis within the regulatory function of professional bodies more generally.[23] This chapter therefore explores the issues of integrity and the professions within a context where both notions are problematic and contested.

The chapter is split into four sections. The following section provides some introductory comments on the regulation of the financial services sector in the UK. It provides a very sketchy outline of the historical development of the FSA and its response to the present crisis. Section C provides a brief introduction to integrity, the professions and the regulatory process. It also introduces a brief Foucauldian analysis of the relationship between the professional's regulation of the self and professional bodies. Section D provides some thoughts on re-imagining the relationship between integrity and professional ethics, and the final section provides some concluding remarks.

B.   The Financial Services Authority, Integrity and Regulation

Much of the discussion in the UK has focused on the FSA as the primary regulator of the financial services sector. The Financial Services and Markets Act (2000) established the FSA as the principal regulator for the financial services sector, a move that may be seen partly as a response to prior regulatory failures represented by the collapse of BCCI and Barings in the 1990s. The FSA is part of a tripartite model (with the Treasury and the Bank of England) of regulation in the UK and is effectively a state regulatory body. This section provides a brief historical overview of the FSA's regulatory approach, along with the emerging discussion of the perceived failings of that approach.

1.   Historical Development

In the opening address of the 2000 Annual European Business Ethics Network Conference, Howard Davies, then chairman of the FSA, commented:

---

[21] A Giddens, *Modernity and Self-Identity: Self and Society in the Late Modern Age* (Cambridge, Polity Press, 1991)

[22] CJ Cowton, 'Integrity, Responsibility and Affinity: Three Aspects of Ethics in Banking' (2002) 11 *Business Ethics: A European Review* 393.

[23] See K McPhail, 'Professional Anxiety, Deliberative Democracy and Ethics Education' (2007) 4 *Journal of Business Ethics Education* 127. It also seems strange that there are not more interdisciplinary perspectives on regulation, a point that seems well made from the composition of this edited volume. There has been a renewed interest in the sociology of the professions recently and it would seem strange that this development has not been applied more specifically to the current financial crisis.

Compliance is not sufficient; for the system to work there needs to be an ethical culture at the level of the organisation, and a commitment to integrity on the part of those who work in the sector. The Financial Services Authority aims to work with the industry to build individual and corporate responsibility.[24]

From its inception, therefore, the FSA promoted a principles-based approach to regulation, and one of the key principles it sought to promote was integrity. In an outline of its thinking at the time, David Jackman,[25] the FSA's Business Ethics Advisor, commented, 'The FSA, mindful of the limitations of a highly detailed bureaucratic framework, is developing an approach sometimes described as "values-led" regulation'. He went on to explain, 'By placing emphasis on the principles rather than detailed rules, the expectation was that people within the industry would think, "even harder than before about what integrity is"'.[26] Cowton[27] suggests the intention was that firms would 'work out what integrity means in their context, rather than merely seek a rule to follow'.

The FSA's values-led approach was supported by an ethical framework published in October 2002. The framework stated that the FSA wanted 'to establish a clear and explicit, shared understanding about what integrity means in practice'. While there was some suggestion that the priorities outlined in the ethical framework would be incorporated into educational programmes, the financial press were less than convinced about the mechanisms in place for fostering this shared understanding. The *Financial Times*,[28] for example, commented:

> A laminated sheet inscribed with advice from the Financial Services Authority (FSA), will be sent to financial firms as part of an effort to raise ethical standards of City of London people. The sheets, suitable for sticking in walls, are meant to serve as a reminder to workers of such abstract values as openness, responsibility and fairness.

In their public documents and pronouncements at least, the FSA clearly espoused a principles-based approach to regulation, and in particular stressed the importance of integrity as a key functional characteristic of financial systems. Yet, regardless of the clarity with which the FSA articulated its regulatory approach, this framework still had to be both implemented by the FSA and translated by those whom it was intended to supervise. There is certainly some evidence to suggest that the implementation of the FSA's approach was rather weak, a fact evidenced by the perception both within the FSA and within the city that a principles-based approach equated to a 'soft' and 'light touch'.[29] What the FSA may have said publicly seems to have been construed both internally and by the financial sector as signifying something quite different. Either the meaning of a principles-based approach was lost in translation and the financial institutions did not understand what a principles-based approach to regulation required or they understood that it really meant a light touch. There is a suggestion that the banks' interpretation might have been

---

[24] Reported in H Davies, 'Ethics in Regulation' (2001) 10 *Business Ethics, A European Review* 280.

[25] D Jackman, 'Values-led Regulation' in C Moon and C Bonny (eds), *Business Ethics: Facing Up to the Issues* (London, Economist Books, 2001).

[26] Ibid.

[27] Above n 22.

[28] J Mawson and T Tassell, 'FSA Aims to Raise Standards in the Square Mile', *Financial Times*, 31 October 2002, 4.

[29] J Pickard, 'FSA under Attack on Regulation in Boom', *Financial Times*, 17 April 2009, 1.

influenced by an inferred government tone that it did not want an overbearing regulator or overbearing regulation to get in the way of city business.[30]

While no doubt there are many explanations for why the government wanted a light-touch approach to the regulation of the city, theoretically at least, it might be possible that this approach was understood or justified in terms of the state's role in the regulation not only of financial markets but also the function of the state in relation to democratic regulation in general. Over and above the adoption of a principles approach, the regulatory strategy espoused by the FSA may have been influenced by an associationalist model of democratic regulation.[31] In her review of Labour's Third Way, for example, Newman[32] highlights a tension between Labour's attempts to re-imagine the relationship between the state and the citizen and promote civil society on the one hand and the tendency to centralise on the other. She explains:

> Labour attempted to respond to the challenges of governing a complex and differentiated society in the aftermath of two decades of neo-liberal reforms. At the centre of its response to these challenges was an attempt to transform the policy process and to modernise the public sector . . . These changes can be set in the context of deeper shifts in governance based on the re-imagination of the relationship between the state and citizen, a new emphasis on the values of community and the role of civil society, the remaking of key areas of social policy, and the introduction of fundamental changes in the state itself through constitutional reform.[33]

Despite this focus on civil society, however, Newman also comments that the government 'Became increasingly frustrated by its power to make things happen and engaged in a struggle to exert tighter control from the centre'.

The associationalist model, with its opposition to both free-market individualism and state collectivism, is based very much on trust, civic engagement and social capital.[34] From this theoretical perspective, the state adopts a secondary role in supporting the development of voluntary self-organising associations, including professional bodies, thus maintaining the conditions or forms of social organisation under which regulatory mechanisms emerge. Hirst[35] contends that this kind of model of representative democracy construes the state as the guardian of democratic processes as opposed to a service provider.[36]

The financial crisis and ensuing debate therefore bring into question not only the effectiveness of principles-based regulation, but also associationalist models of government. Certainly, recent comments from the FSA indicate a reversion to a more state interventionist rules-based model.

---

[30] Ibid.

[31] S Meredith and P Catney, 'New Labour and Associative Democracy: Old Debates in New Times?' (2007) 2 *British Politics* 347.

[32] J Newman, *Modernizing Government, New Labour Policy and Society* (London, Sage Publications, 2001).

[33] Ibid, vii.

[34] The associationalist model resonates with Braithwaite's model of responsive regulation. See, eg J Braithwaite, 'Responsive Regulation and Developing Economies' (2006) 34 *World Development* 884.

[35] P Hirst, 'Renewing Democracy through Associations' (2002) 73 *The Political Quarterly* 409. See also P Hirst and VM Badner, *Associative Democracy: The Real Third Way* (Abingdon, Routledge, 2001).

[36] L Baccaro, 'Civil Society Meets the State: Towards Associational Democracy?' (2006) 4 *Socio-Economic Review* 185.

2. Failings and the Future

The FSA's initial public pronouncements laid the blame for the crisis on its underlying theoretical approach, on the banking system and on bankers themselves, and hinted at changes in all three areas.

First, the FSA changed its position on the principles-based model, suggesting that it was limited and hinting that a more disciplinary approach would be required in the future. Hector Sants indicated on a number of occasions that the FSA would take a much tougher and more intrusive approach to regulation,[37] commenting, for example, that 'People should be very frightened of the FSA . . . not only is this what society now expects regulators to be doing, it was what they thought we were doing'.[38]

The failings of a principles-based approach and the requirement to take a tougher stance was attributed to a failure of the bankers themselves. As Sants commented, 'A principles based approach will not work with individuals who have no principles'. In response to this perception, the FSA hinted that they would take a tougher approach to ensuring that traders are 'fit and proper persons'. Sants also commented that 'the FSA will judge managers—and if necessary, correct them'. There also seemed to be some indication that the idea of a fit and proper person may be primarily construed in terms of technical competence rather than moral rectitude, particularly in relation to the global financial system. Sants said it is a 'mistake to judge senior bank appointments on a candidates probity and not their competence'.[39]

From this very sketchy outline of some of the initial responses to the crisis, a number of issues are worth noting. First, it seemed that the balance between principles and rules would shift more in the direction of rules,[40] and secondly, it seemed that the associationalist model might give way to a more interventionist attitude. Finally, in conjunction with a focus on the integrity of individuals, the FSA hinted at a renewed focus on the technical competence of bankers.

Following on from these initial comments, the Turner Review[41] provides some further elaboration on the FSA's thinking.[42] It provides an analysis of the systemic failings that led to the financial crisis and, as such, offers a relatively technical and mechanical explanation of where the global system failed. Both the explanation and the proposed reforms are narrated overwhelmingly in terms of 'systemic risk'.[43] The review also proposes a new Supervisory Enhancement Programme that would see the FSA's limited resources being apportioned based on a risk assessment approach that would 'focus on technical skills as well as probity of approved persons'. Lord Turner also suggests that the Bank of England needs to be involved in more 'macro-prudential analysis' and the identification of policy

---

[37] A Hill, 'FSA Removes Velvet Glove and Tries Iron Fist', *Financial Times*, 12 March 2009.

[38] Ibid.

[39] Ibid.

[40] The FSA has always had an extensive rules handbook; however, the discourse surrounding their approach is changing.

[41] Financial Services Authority, 'The Turner Review: A Regulatory Response to the Global Banking Crisis' (London, 2009).

[42] Specifically, the report calls for greater capital adequacy and accounting disclosure requirements, and intimates that the FSA will extend its regulatory reach into areas that were previously unregulated. The review also recognises that the role of non-executive directors needs to be reassessed and outlines a new Code for remuneration.

[43] Lord Turner, for example, employs the term 'risk' 376 times. By way of contrast, the report contains no reference to the terms 'integrity', 'education' or 'ethics'.

measures in order to offset risk. From this very schematic review of the emerging discussion of what has gone wrong and the emerging response from the FSA, a number of themes seem to be worth noting.

First, the criticisms levelled at the principles-based approach must be set against the comparative lack of a supporting structure. Before passing judgement on a principles-based approach, it is important to reflect on the lack of resources and mechanisms that underpinned and facilitated this strategy, and the way in which it was interpreted by the City, a point made by the Institute of Chartered Accountants in England and Wales's chief executive Michael Izza: 'Whilst we welcome Lord Turner's emphasis on effective regulatory supervision, we believe that this should be achieved within a robust principles-based system.'[44] It is also important not to forget that the focus on a principles-based approach has emerged as a consequence of prior failings (notably within the accounting profession) in a rule-based regulatory system.

Secondly, as with the original ethical framework, while the review suggests that the FSA will ensure the probity of individuals working in the financial services sector, this objective seems aspirational, with little substance being conveyed about how this might actually be accomplished, beyond the inferred link with remuneration packages. Put somewhat crudely, the way to ensure probity is to align remuneration packages with desired behaviour in an instrumentalist fashion.

Finally, much of the emerging discussion seems to focus on the failings of the current regulatory environment in relation to its ability to identify broader systemic risk. The Turner Review therefore calls for greater technical competence, primarily in relation to 'macro-prudential analysis'. It also advocates a broader system view, in the sense that the utility of individuals' behaviour requires a certain competency in understanding the broader banking system.

C.   Integrity, The Professions and Regulation

The discussion above has introduced the primary institutions responsible for regulating the financial services sector in the UK. However, the tripartite model only captures a part of the regulatory environment. Many of the individuals who work within the financial services sector are also members of professional associations, and these bodies have traditionally been viewed as performing a broad regulatory function within society. In relation to the associationalist model, they can be seen to form part of the broad range of institutions promoting specific interests, primarily the interests of their members but also, in theory at least, the broader public interest. Professional bodies can perform a useful oversight function in relation to the power of the state. Post-Enron, the accounting profession faced the threat of a move towards a corporatist model with the state exercising much more control over the business reporting and auditing functions. Yet, from a political economy perspective, many commentators who were uncomfortable with the level of power of the profession nevertheless argued that the interests of democracy could

---

[44] M Izza, 'ICAEW Urges Lord Turner Not to Lose Sight of Principles-based Regulation' (2009), available at www.icaew.com/index.cfm/route/164338/icaew_ga/en/Home/Press_and_policy/Press_releases/ICAEW_urges_Lord_Turner_not_to_lose_sight_of_principles_based_regulation (accessed on 27 August 2009).

be served better by a strong and independent group of professions. Although many are rightly sceptical of the potential role of professions within society, others contend that they do, or at least could, serve an important regulatory function. Indeed, there has been a renaissance in interest in the sociology of the professions in the past few years as we have become increasingly aware of the important function that they perform in society.

Although there is no definitive set of 'professional characteristics', most sociological studies suggest that professions are characterised by a body of expert knowledge; a commitment to public service; self regulation; independence; a disciplinary function; and a common set of values. Of course, these characteristics are ideals, and there are many examples of professional bodies promoting the interests of their members over the general public interest. However, despite their failings, professional bodies quite obviously serve an important regulatory function. They act as gatekeepers to what are perceived to be socially important practices. They ensure the competence of individual practitioners and they also present themselves as having some concern for the character of those entering the profession. The remainder of this section will focus on the relationship between professional bodies, ethics and regulation.

In his seminal study of the professions, Abbot[45] suggested that one way that professional bodies attempt to regulate professional conduct is via a code of ethics. These codes may be aspirational and based on broad principles or take the form of enforceable rules.[46] An example of a broad principle can be found in the ACCA's requirement that accountants, 'refrain from . . . misconduct which . . . [is] likely to bring discredit to themselves, the association or the accountancy profession'.[47] This distinction between rules and principles resonates with the discussion above. Both types of code, however, serve an obvious regulatory function. Ruland and Lindblom[48] convey a related distinction when they discuss the difference between implicit and explicit expectations. They define explicit rules as those outlined in professional codes of conduct. Implicit rules, by comparison, are derived societal expectations in relation to the professional's role in society.

From a regulatory perspective, then, professional bodies not only have the potential to perform an important function within an associationalist model, they also play an important disciplinary role, a function which would seem to resonate with the FSA's concern to ensure the probity and competence of individuals working within the financial services sector. In relation to the aspirational nature of some of the discussion surrounding professional ethics, the regulatory function of broader notions of professionalism has been conceptualised as part of the mechanisms or architecture that contributes towards the regulation of the self, over and above simple financial utility models that underpin the focus on bankers' remuneration packages. Drawing on work of the French historian of ideas Michel Foucault, this regulatory function is often construed in terms of the self's disciplining of the self. Briefly stated, Foucault's later work on ethics presents a

---

[45] A Abbott, *System of Professions: An Essay on the Division of Expert Labour* (Chicago, IL, University of Chicago Press, 1988). See also A Abbott, 'Professional Ethics' (1983) 88 *American Journal of Sociology* 855.

[46] MS Frankel, 'Professional Codes: Why, How and With What Impact?' (1989) 8 *Journal of Business Ethics* 109. See also GA Claypool, DF Fetyko and MA Pearson, 'Reactions to Ethical Dilemmas: A Study Pertaining to Certified Public Accountants' (1990) 9 *Journal of Business Ethics* 699.

[47] See AM Fleming, 'Ethics and Accounting Education in the UK—A Professional Approach?' (1996) 5 *Accounting Education* 207.

[48] RG Ruland and CK Lindblom, 'Ethics and Disclosure: An Analysis of Conflicting Duties' (1992) 3 *Critical Perspectives on Accounting* 259.

four-component model that captures the way in which individuals regulate themselves in relation to some notion of the good person.[49] These elements are as follows.

1. *The means by which we change ourselves in order to become ethical subjects:* the self's disciplining of the self.
2. *The telos:* the type of person we aspire to be when we behave morally.
3. *Ethical substance:* the parts of our lives where ethical judgment is relevant.
4. *The mode of subjection:* the way in which individuals are incited to recognise their moral obligations. For example, by religious invocation, social convention or reasoned analysis.

Much of the emerging debate in relation to the regulation of bankers has already taken place in relation to the regulation of accountants. Post-Enron, the ICAEW has been trying to reconceptualise what it does around the notion of integrity, saying that, 'for integrity to live in organisations, it is necessary to embed the concept in everyday discussions, decisions and actions. Integrity needs to be internalised in an organisation in both words and deeds'.[50] The Institute of Chartered Accountants in Scotland also embarked on a programme designed to 'take ethics to heart'.[51]

Much of this focus on integrity within the accounting profession may be seen as an attempt to clarify the rather nebulous and unspecified notion of character (or probity in the case of the banking discourse) that historically was associated with the individual's class status, gender and ability to pay professional dues as indicated above. A review of the accounting profession's response to crisis, however, would seem to indicate that the notion of character has been replaced by an equally nebulous notion of integrity.

The question nevertheless remains whether the idea of the professions and the notion of integrity are in anyway potentially useful concepts for helping us to understand the present banking crisis and begin to formulate a response.

D.   Re-imagining the Regulatory Relationship

The previous sections have introduced the idea of integrity in relation to financial regulation and professionalism. However, it has also been suggested that professional bodies are trying to figure out both what integrity means and what their regulatory function should be in the twenty-first century.

This section provides some thoughts on how we might begin to re-imagine the idea of integrity and the function that such a notion might play in re-imagining the current regulatory relationship. It commences by introducing some alternative conceptualisations of integrity, then, based on these ideas, some thoughts are presented on how they might lead to different types of regulatory models.

---

[49] KJ McPhail, 'The Threat of Ethical Accountants: An Application of Foucault's Concept of Ethics to Accounting Education and Some Thoughts on Ethically Educating For The Other' (1999) 10 *Critical Perspectives on Accounting* 833.

[50] The Institute of Chartered Accountants in England and Wales, 'Information for Better Markets: Reporting with Integrity' (2007) 59.

[51] J Bebbington and C Helliar, *Taking Ethics to Heart* (Edinburgh, Institute of Chartered Accountants of Scotland, 2004).

1. Re-imagining Integrity

Around the time of the banking crisis the press carried another discussion about integrity. Writing in the obituary column, one journalist commented, 'he kept his looks but he also kept his integrity'. The journalist was referring to the actor Paul Newman.[52] Some of the obituaries and comments about the famous actor stand in contradistinction to the discussion of the financial crisis. One columnist said 'For me, Cool Hand Luke was his greatest performance: he was the archetypal outsider, determined to be true to himself against the most awful oppression and unfairness'.

It is this idea of integrity as being true to oneself that provides the starting point for the observations in this section. What might the idea of being true to oneself mean if applied to the issue of financial regulation?

Paul Newman's obituaries present quite a different perspective on integrity from that found in contemporary discussions about the integrity of bankers. In this latter discourse, the idea of integrity is associated with particular kinds of moral qualities or character traits like honesty, competence and compliance. The emerging discussion in relation to tougher rules, macro-prudential analysis and fit and proper individuals seem to connect integrity with the capacity to play by the rules. While historically some of these rules have been implicit, the current crisis has led to calls for their codification, with the FSA inferring that more rules, more compliance and tougher sanctions all equate to more integrity.

Integrity is therefore construed as an individual virtue and, reflective of the Turner Report's relatively mechanistic analysis of the banking sector, it is also often viewed in instrumentalist terms. Will Hutton[53] sums up this perspective when he says,

> Even in the dog-eat-dog financial markets, trust and integrity are matters of self-interest. However amoral you may be, it is in your interest to care about your reputation, because if you behave badly you will not do business with me—or others—on favourable terms again.

However, as Bernard Williams has argued in his famous example of 'Jim and the Indians',[54] this instrumentalist view of integrity is quite problematic. He says,

> It is often suspected that utilitarianism, at least in its direct forms, makes integrity as a value more or less unintelligible . . . Of course, even if that is correct, it would not necessarily follow that we should reject utilitarianism; perhaps as utilitarian's sometimes suggest, we should just forget about integrity, in favor of such things as concern for the general good. However, if I am right, we cannot merely do that, since the reason why utilitarianism cannot understand integrity is that it cannot coherently describe the relations between a man's projects and his actions.

Simply encouraging traders to see that short-term bonuses are neither in their long-term interests nor in those of the institutions for which they work does not seem like a very satisfactory interpretation of the idea of integrity.

The remainder of this section develops Bernhard Williams's contention that the utilitarian view of integrity is problematic because it cannot help us understand the relationship between the project of society and the projects that constitute the individual.

---

[52] The American actor Paul Newman is perhaps best known for his performances as Butch Cassidy in *Butch Cassidy and the Sundance Kid*, Luke Jackson in *Cool Hand Luke* and Gondorff in *The Sting*.

[53] Hutton, above n 2.

[54] B Williams, 'Jim and the Indians' in P Singer (ed), *Ethics* (Oxford, Oxford University Press, 1994) 339.

The notion of being true to oneself carries with it a different kind of conceptualisation of integrity. It includes the idea of being whole, entire or undiminished, that quality or condition of being undivided; of being complete. Integrity, certainly in this second sense, is a different kind of word; it is more slippery and because of that slightly unsettling. Indeed, translated into the second definition, the issue of integrity in professional life takes on an entirely different complexion. The question becomes, how can finance professionals maintain their completeness at work?

2.   Professional and Personal Integrity

Bernard Williams's contention therefore sets up a tension between what we might call professional integrity and personal integrity. There are many different ways in which individuals might discover that they are not being true to their self. In some instances this challenge might come in the form of pressure to do something that is patently illegal or dishonest. However, in other circumstances the challenge to the completeness of and wholeness of one's self comes from different sources. For example, after the Civil Partnerships Act was passed in 2005, Judge Alexander McClintock requested that he be excused from presiding over cases involving adoption by homosexual couples due to his religious beliefs. However, an Employee Tribunal in Sheffield concluded that, despite his religious beliefs, he may not so be excused. The tribunal's ruling says that 'If a judge personally has particular views on any subject, he or she must put those views to the back of his or her mind when applying the law of the land impartially'. Consider also the case of Police Constable Alexander Omar Basha, a member of the Metropolitan Police's Diplomatic Protection Group, who asked to be excused from guarding the Israeli embassy in Kensington, West London on moral grounds. PC Basha, a Muslim, told his superiors he objected to the Israeli bombing campaign against Hizbullah in south Lebanon.

These examples suggest that commitments to ideas profoundly affect both our individual sense of identity and also our sense of completeness. Thus, sometimes work disrupts those ideals, that sense of integrity or undividedness.

Much of the discussion about integrity within the financial services sector therefore is about an important, though rather narrow, form of integrity that we might call 'professional integrity'. Mike Martin, in his thoughts on meaningful work, talks about the distinction between professional integrity and what he calls overall integrity. Martin introduces the distinction as follows.[55]

> According to the consensus paradigm, burnout and family life are either irrelevant to understanding professional integrity or pose threats to it. The consensus paradigm limits professional ethics . . . to the duties accepted as a consensus within a profession and incumbent upon all its members. These duties are specified as independent of family situations. Should family or other personal matters conflict with codified duties, it is assumed that the latter alone specify one's duty as a professional. In turn, this duty is taken to be what one ought to do, all things considered, in professional contexts. Family considerations are either irrelevant or a threat to that duty.

Much of the discussion in relation to the regulation of the financial services sector since the inception of the FSA has focused on either codes or principles, but in both instances

---

[55] M Martin, *Meaningful Work: Rethinking Professional Ethics* (New York, Oxford University Press, 2003).

they still seem to be subsumed within the boundary of professionalism. Martin labels this 'role integrity'. The point here is that to talk in terms of professional integrity is somewhat paradoxical. If integrity does have something to do with completeness and undividedness, then professional integrity is a misnomer, because integrity should not be subject to fragmentation. In a section that echoes Bernard Williams's comments above, Martin says 'Integrity provokes us to seek wider unities. If we establish a framework for connecting professional with other major dimensions of life, we need to attend to a professional's wider integrity'.[56]

This overall integrity involves a unity between professional commitments peculiar to members of the profession and wider personal commitments specific to each individual. He explains how overall integrity considers 'all of the individual's central commitments, including those to family and to oneself'.[57] Martin's contribution to the debate is therefore that professional ethics or work ethics should really involve a discussion about how to integrate all the major dimensions of one's life, or central commitments. Again, this seems to resonate with Bernard Williams when he asked,[58]

> What projects does a utilitarian agent have? As a utilitarian, he has the general project of bringing about maximally desirable outcomes; how he is to do this at any given moment is a question of what causal levers, so to speak, are at that moment within reach. The desirable outcomes however do not just consist of agents carrying out that project; there must be more basic or lower-order projects which he and the other agents have, and the desirable outcomes are going to consist, in part, of maximally harmonious realizations of those projects . . . The vital question is . . . whether it and similar projects are to count among the projects whose classification is to be included in the maximizing sum and correspondingly as contributing towards the agent's happiness . . . Among the things that make people happy is not only making other people happy, but being taken up or involved in any of a vast range of projects.

Of course, this will generate a healthy amount of disruption and anxiety, along with the requirement to negotiate a set of competing and conflicting commitments. It is here that Martin draws on Carol Gilligan for some advice: 'Gilligan's approach to moral reasoning envisions integrity as the search to maintain all moral relationships relevant to particular contexts. What is needed is not the absolute ranking of principles, but skill in reconciling competing legitimate demands.'[59]

Integrity here is defined not in terms of the contravention of a code but rather in terms of the consistency of one's life. Martin says,

> maintaining integrity is an ongoing process rather than a final achievement. In addition to effort and self-control, it requires habits of moral reasoning in discerning possibilities, setting desirable priorities, and appreciating the need for compromises. This reasoning implies struggling to see one's life in its entirety.[60]

The question, then, is where individuals get the opportunity and space to reflect on and struggle with one's life in its entirety—or, indeed, where they are equipped with the competencies to be able to do this. Where are these institutional spaces, and in what sense

[56] Ibid, 203.
[57] Ibid.
[58] Above n 54, 339.
[59] Above n 55, 213.
[60] Ibid, 210–11.

might these struggles lead to new forms of institutional practices which constitute part of the broader circle of regulation?[61]

3.   Integrity and Practices

Thus far this chapter has focused on the integrity of professionals, and in particular the integrity of bankers. The following discussion shifts the focus of attention onto the integrity of the practice of banking, and in particular whether the idea of the personal overall integrity of individual bankers introduced above represents a threat to the integrity of the practice of banking.

It is possible to construe the integrity of the practice of banking in a number of different ways. Cowton,[62] for example, comments on how 'integrity is important in banking, helping to generate the trust that is vital for a financial system to flourish'. Here the integrity of the practice of banking is linked to the common notion of honest individuals introduced above. However, from an alternative perspective, the actions of the policeman and the judge discussed earlier may be construed as representing a threat to the integrity of, respectively, the judging and policing system. If individuals do not play by the rules of the game, if they do not do what might reasonably be expected of them in their capacity as a policeman or a judge, then it might not be possible to play the game of policing or judging at all.[63]

The point here is that, if one introduces a broader notion of the complete integrity of individuals into the division of expert labour in general and the banking system in particular, then we might find that individuals end up questioning the integrity of the practice of banking. Take, for example, the case not of a Muslim policeman, but of a Muslim banker. For that banker, a broader view of integrity might result in a conflict between the charging of interest and his or her individual religious beliefs, for example. The issue here is that we might display a great amount of integrity in performing a particular action although we might, from a different standpoint, think that the action should not be performed at all.

The important point to note here is not just that some individuals might end up rejecting a particular form of practice that is inconsistent with their broader view of the world, but that other systems of practice emerge as alternatives. So, for example, Islamic banking practices emerge, as do other forms of ethical banking systems, like the Co-operative and Triados banks. Chris Cowton refers to this form of banking as affinity banking.[64] Of course, the development of alternative forms of values-based financing also cater for the integrity of individual depositors.

As we noted above, the Turner Review encourages a broader view of global systemic risk, yet there seems to be comparatively little critical discussion of the extent to which the provision of financial services in general is misaligned with the central commitments that constitute us as individual selves. The point that seems important to make here is that the

---

[61] Braithwaite, above n 34, 884. See also P Drahos and J Braithwaite, 'The Globalization of Regulation' (2001) 9 *Journal of Political Philosophy* 103; and J Braithwaite, 'Rules and Principles: A Theory of Legal Certainty' (2002) 27 *Australian Journal of Legal Philosophy* 47.

[62] Above n 22, 395.

[63] J Hooker, 'Professional Ethics: Does It Matter Which Hat We Wear?' (2007) 4 *Journal of Teaching Business Ethics* 103.

[64] Above n 22.

regulatory environment that impinges upon the financial services sector extends far beyond the traditional tripartite model of the FSA, the Treasury and the Bank of England, and also the professional institutions. The market for different types of banking generates different types of regulatory pressure on the types of banking that will grow and flourish. However, the development of these different kinds of practice is related to, and in some way dependent upon, professional competence. It also requires the development of an environment where values can be aligned. This alignment has occurred in relation to pension and charity funds only relatively recently. From this perspective, a key aspect of re-envisioning the regulatory relationship might involve a policy agenda that makes the development of these values-based systems easier. Part of the response must and no doubt will come in the form of a market response, but the conditions of possibility for these markets may rest with the state.

Braithwaite's responsive regulation model[65] envisions a broader array of different regulatory institutions and mechanisms all contributing towards systems of regulatory oversight. He specifically talks about the key role of the state not in directly regulating, but rather creating the possibility for the emergence of, regulatory systems. He comments that the function of the state is to ensure that a healthy civil society can emerge, that a strong civil society emerges with non-government organisations and other forms of associations combining with more state-based regulatory bodies, forming circles of regulation in which disparate bodies check each other. What I am proposing here is some further reflection on the potential role of the state in creating the possibility for values-based market alternatives to emerge.

It is here that we come to the issue of whether the financial crisis undermines the potential of associationalist theory to provide an effective model for regulating the financial services sector. There is undoubtedly some truth in the observation that the crisis represents further evidence that the individualising nature of developed global capital systems undermines the possibility of society, yet formulating a response solely in terms of a reversion to state intervention in the form of aggressive deterrents would seem rather simplistic. Instead of rejecting the associationalist model out of hand, perhaps more analysis is required into the failings of professional associations and how the notions of professional competence, integrity and professional education could be reformulated in order to serve an associationalist model better, by providing individuals with the space, opportunity and competence to reflect on all their projects and commitments. Examples like the Co-operative bank also indicate that, while punitive state regulation is important, values-based market innovations also have a role to play in maintaining a strong liberal democracy.[66] The state, the market and civil society all have a role to play.

E.   Conclusion

This chapter has attempted to contribute to the debate on how to re-imagine the regulatory relationship in the wake of the current financial crisis. It has done this in three ways. First, it has raised the issue of the function of professional bodies in connection

---

[65] Braithwaite (2002, 2006) above n 61, 34.
[66] E Cox, 'The Functional Value of Social Capital' (2007) 42 *Australian Journal of Social Issues* 503.

with the regulation of financial practitioners; secondly, it has contributed towards a re-imagining of the meaning of integrity within the context of professional work-life; and finally, it has endeavoured to open up some discussion on the broader meaning of the integrity of the banking system by reference to the development of ethical or affinity banking.

The chapter implicitly defends a principles-based approach to regulation, despite the position being adopted by the FSA. However, it is contended that a principles-led approach requires a structured system of networks and educational commitment to make it work. These systems were not implemented by the FSA or the professional bodies associated with the financial sector. The chapter also defends the associational model in light of calls for greater state intervention in the regulatory relationship. Although the chapter supports a strong state involvement, it has been suggested that there is a clear role for the market and voluntary associations, like the professional bodies.

Instead of rejecting the associationalist model out of hand, the chapter calls for more critical reflection on the historical failings of professional associations and whether the notions of the expert division of labour, integrity and professional education might have a role to play in re-envisioning the future of financial regulation.

23

Financial Services Providers, Reputation and the Virtuous Triangle

SEUMAS MILLER*

A. Introduction: Ethical Failures and Reputational Risks

It is universally agreed that the current global financial crisis is the worst since the Great Depression. The main aspects of the problem include frozen credit markets, the sub-prime mortgage crisis, slow and inconsistent policy responses, and an unfolding global recession. The crisis has involved major corporate investment and mortgage banking collapses and bailouts in the US (Lehmans, Freddie Mac and Fannie Mae), UK (Northern Rock), Europe (Fortis, Hypo) and elsewhere, and it is having a devastating effect on homeowners who cannot pay their mortgages (foreclosures), retirees whose pension funds have plummeted in value, employees whose jobs are at risk in the developing recession and taxpayers whose money is being injected into the banking system in vast quantities to rescue it (eg trillions of dollars by the US government).

Unethical and imprudent individual and collective practices and processes have been identified as being among the principal causes of the crisis.[1] These practices and processes include:

1. reckless and predatory lending by banks;
2. the growth of highly leveraged investment banks;
3. the selling of toxic financial products—notably non-transparent packaged bundles of mortgages, including sub-prime mortgages;
4. failure to avoid or adequately manage structural conflicts of interest, including ratings agencies assessing the non-transparent toxic financial products mentioned above as high quality because the investment banks that packaged them—and who fund the ratings agencies—allegedly had good risk assessment processes;
5. massive frauds, eg Bernard Madoff's Ponzi scheme
6. excessive executive remuneration that in numerous cases has in effect rewarded

---

* Foundation Professor of Philosophy at Charles Sturt University, Australia, Foundation Director of the Centre for Applied Philosophy and Public Ethics (an Australian Research Council Special Research Centre), Professor of Philosophy at the Australian National University and Senior Research Fellow at the 3TU Centre for Ethics and Technology, Delft University of Technology.

[1] P Krugman, *The Return of Depression Economics and the Crisis of 2008* (New York, Norton & Co, 2009); J O'Brien, *Engineering a Financial Bloodbath* (London, Imperial College of London Press, 2009).

management failure, eg in the case of the failed investment banks and the giant insurer, AIG;

7.   the unconstrained and unwarranted growth of the financial sector (Wall Street) ultimately to the detriment of, rather than in the service of, the productive business sectors (Main Street);

8.   the growth of unsustainable debt by governments and, indeed, whole economies (eg the US overseas debt accumulated in 2006 alone was $850 billion); and

9.   the negligence and/or ideologically based complicity of legislators and regulators regarding all of the above.[2]

Self-evidently, these developments have been extraordinarily damaging economically and in human terms. Moreover, it has become apparent that these corporate collapses and corruption scandals in the overall context of a massive, global, speculative boom/bust are symptomatic of underlying systemic deficiencies. These deficiencies evidently exist in all three fundamental institutional dimensions,[3] namely:

1.   structure, eg corporate governance and regulation;
2.   culture, eg predatory and reckless lending; and
3.   purpose, eg regulatory negligence in ensuring that the 'invisible hand' mechanisms of competitive markets actually do their work of serving the greater, long-term, collective interests of whole communities (rather than the immediate financial interests of powerful, individual market actors).[4]

The global financial crisis has rightly and reasonably focused attention on regulatory deficiencies. A number of regulatory gaps have been identified, eg innovative financial products, the so-called 'shadow banking system' of non-depository banks,[5] the hedge fund industry[6] and private equity firms. In some cases there is arguably under-regulation by virtue of, for example, inadequate capital holding requirements for some kinds of banking institutions, or the absence of disclosure requirements for various kinds of business and financial institutions.[7] In other cases there is a need to revisit the regulation of specific ethical problems, eg conflicts of interest, perverse incentive structures.

Other identified regulatory inadequacies include complexity, inconsistency and a lack of coordination between regulators. The President of the Federal Reserve Bank of New York has conceded that the US regulatory system

> has evolved into a confusing mix of diffused accountability, regulatory competition, an enormously complex web of rules that create perverse incentives and leave huge opportunities for arbitrage and evasion, and creates the risk of large gaps in our knowledge and authority.[8]

---

[2] O'Brien, ibid, 85–88.

[3] S Miller, 'Social Institutions' in E Zalta (ed), *Stanford Encyclopedia of Philosophy* (online winter edition, 2005), available at plato.stanford.edu/.

[4] S Miller, *The Moral Foundations of Social Institutions: A Study in Applied Philosophy* (New York, Cambridge University Press, 2009) ch 2.

[5] Krugman, above n 1, 160.

[6] International Organisation of Securities Commissions, 'Report on Hedge Funds' (Madrid, 2009).

[7] O'Brien, above n 1, 59–60.

[8] T Geithner, 'The Current Financial Challenges: Policy and Regulatory Implications', speech delivered at Council on Foreign Relations Corporate Conference, New York, 6 March 2008, available at www.newyorkfed.org/newsevents/speeches/2008/gei080306.html.

Moreover, the allegedly superior responsive principles-based regulatory regime in the UK has proved to be equally inadequate.[9]

In the case of the global financial sector, regulation and integrity assurance are ultimately in the hands of national governments; this goes for the regulation of financial products and securitisation processes as well as other elements of the sector. However, national governments—and their regulatory authorities—are not simply umpires, they are also players in the financial—and, more generally, corporate—'game'. For example, the UK government, and its financial regulator the Financial Services Authority, cannot be expected to regulate entirely impartially in the interests of ethical ends and principles, given the substantial interest the UK government has in ensuring that the UK corporate and financial sector retains and increases the benefits accruing to it from global financial markets. Hence there is a need to address the issue of impartiality in the design of the global regulatory system.[10]

There is a range of occupational groups involved in the financial services sector. Investment bankers, financial advisors, lawyers and auditors have gate-keeping roles in relation to the provision of loans, and the production and selling of a wide range of financial products. And there is a host of other financial services providers who facilitate the workings of the market in relation to these financial products and processes, including fund managers, broker/dealers, securities analysts, credit rating professionals and asset consultants. Most, if not all, of these groups are causally, if not morally, implicated (directly or indirectly) in the global financial meltdown. However, let us consider briefly only a few of these groups, albeit important ones.

Auditors are charged with specific duties, including independent attestation of corporate disclosures on financial position and performance. However, in a number of cases auditors and accounting firms have prioritised the proximate goal of economic self-interest over independent adjudication. Indeed, it has been argued that some accountancy firms have (perhaps unconsciously) sought to mask these market influences on the auditing profession—and limit their exposure to civil litigation—by taking refuge in compliance with technical procedural requirements.[11] There is a risk that privileging technical requirements through creative compliance over a commitment to substantive ethical principles, such as the provision of a true and fair record, weakens the reputation of both the profession and its corporate clients more generally. To this extent an important element in the integrity system has been weakened. It should also be noted that a good deal of critical reflection has taken place recently within the audit profession in relation to the importance for the profession of inculcating the ethical virtues in practitioners, not least because of the reputational risks of not doing so. It is well understood that if an auditing firm loses its reputation for honesty, accuracy, independence and so forth then all may well be lost; consider the collapse of the large accounting firm Arthur Anderson in the wake of its role in the Enron scandal.

Lawyers are another important professional group in the finance sector, and a group currently experiencing a process of institutional change. The advent of incorporated legal

---

[9] A Turner, 'A Regulatory Response to the Global Banking Crisis' (London, Financial Services Authority, 2009).

[10] Miller above n 4; J O'Brien, *Redesigning Financial Regulation* (Chichester, Wiley, 2007) 174–205.

[11] FL Clarke, GW Dean and KG Oliver, *Corporate Collapse: Accounting, Regulatory and Ethical Failure* (Cambridge, Cambridge University Press, 2003) 319; D McBarnet, 'Compliance, Ethics and Responsibility: Emergent Governance Strategies in the US and UK' in J O'Brien (ed), *Private Equity, Corporate Governance and the Dynamics of Capital Market Regulation* (London, Imperial College Press, 2007).

practices, which, increasingly, are also multi-disciplinary, represents the response of both the profession and the legislature to the changing legal services market. These practices offer (potentially) greater profit to those who own them. However, they also generate new and more complex forms of ethical problems for the profession and its regulators.[12] Arguably, a corporation's primary duty is to enhance shareholder value. (This might be so even on a corporate social responsibility model of the corporation.[13]) This is usually interpreted as an obligation to return maximum profit within market regulations and norms. However, it seems that these emerging corporate and multi-disciplinary settings are exacerbating existing ethical problems and generating new ones. What counts as legal work for the purposes of holding accountable an incorporated multi-disciplinary practice staffed, on the one hand, by solicitors offering 'legal advice on tax laws' (supposedly within the solicitors' framework of strict professional accountability) and, on the other hand, by tax experts offering 'tax advice in the context of current tax laws' (outside the solicitors' framework)? If the lines of accountability have become blurred and/or unenforceable, what are the consequences for ethical responsibility? There are well-defined and very strict requirements imposed on lawyers to maintain client confidentiality. However, non-legal members of a multi-disciplinary practice may have no such responsibility. More generally, these developments raise questions in relation to the ability of lawyers to perform their duties to the court in organisational settings in which there is enormous pressure to prioritise commercial organisational imperatives. It is self-evident that public trust in the judicial system depends in part on lawyers not only discharging their duties to the court, but being seen to do so. So the ethical failures referred to above constitute a reputational risk that can translate into a lack of public trust not only in the legal practitioners and their corporate employers, but also in (relevant parts of) the judicial system itself.

Investment bankers provide a range of services, including securities underwriting, due diligence investigations associated with initial public offerings, the provision of analytical reports for affiliated retail brokerage facilities or wider market dissemination, private client money management, private equity financing and proprietary trading.[14] There is a range of ethical concerns in this area, including failure to discharge fiduciary duties (insofar as they apply to investment bankers) and conflicts of interest.[15] In the context of the global failure of investment banks and their partial nationalisation in many jurisdictions, conflicts of interest issues have come to the fore, notably with respect to relationships with rating agencies. Credit rating agencies have a key role in relation to the ethical health of the financial system, a role which has recently been compromised in the case of securitisation processes.[16] This role hinges on their capacity to enhance or diminish the reputation of financial actors. The key notion here is deserved reputation. Reputation ought to track actual financial health, and the credit rating agencies are crucial here. Perceived conflicts of interest in particular, are obviously a key reputational risk.

---

[12] S Marks and G Cowdroy, 'Incorporated Legal Practices—A New Era in the Provision of Legal Services in the State of New South Wales' (2004) 22 *Pennsylvania State International Law Review* 671; S Miller and M Ward, 'Complaints and Self-assessment Data Analysis in Relation to Incorporated Legal Practices', report for the Office of the Legal Services Commissioner (2006).

[13] R Audi, *Business Ethics and Ethical Business* (Oxford, Oxford University Press, 2009).

[14] O'Brien, above n 1.

[15] PF Hanrahan, '*ASIC v Citigroup*: Investment Banks, Conflicts of Interest and Chinese Walls' in O'Brien, above n 11.

[16] T Sinclair, *The New Masters of Capital* (Ithaca, Cornell University Press, 2005); International Organisation of Securities Commissions, 'Report on Credit Ratings Agencies' (Madrid, 2009).

B. Integrity Systems

So-called integrity systems are arguably the primary institutional vehicle available to reduce ethical misconduct, to combat crime and corruption, and to promote institutional virtues. Integrity systems include aspects of legal or regulatory systems, but they are not to be identified with these. Integrity systems include both reactive mechanisms (eg police agencies, corporate fraud investigation units) and preventative means (eg ethics education, elimination of perverse incentives).[17] Integrity systems exist at the occupational, organisational and industrial levels, and also at the national and global levels.[18]

The term 'integrity', as used in the expression 'integrity system', appropriates a moral notion normally used to describe individual human agents and applies it to organisations and other large groups of individuals. Roughly speaking, individual human persons have integrity if: (i) they possess the full array of central moral virtues, such as honesty, loyalty and trustworthiness; and (ii) they exercise rational and morally informed judgement in their adherence to any given virtue, including when the requirements of different virtues might seem to come into conflict. In contrast with the notion of an individual person's integrity, there is the integrity of an occupational group, organisation or industry sector, ie of institutional entities. Examples of elements of institutional integrity systems include agencies such as the representative bodies of professional groups (eg the Institute of Chartered Accountants) and industry regulators (eg the Australian Securities and Investments Commission, the US Securities and Exchange Commission).

The integrity of an occupation, organisation or industry is in large part dependent on the individual integrity of its members, and therefore an integrity system is in large part focused on developing and maintaining the individual integrity of these members. Nevertheless, these occupational groups, organisations and industries are not simply the sum of their members, and so determining the integrity levels for them is not simply a matter of summing the levels of integrity of the individual members. For one thing, the required virtues of specific occupational groups can differ from that of ordinary citizens, eg the numerical exactitude of good auditors. For another, the ethical risks of market actors are different from that of ordinary citizens, eg of traders in large volumes of shares. More generally, the causes of ethical failure are often at the institutional—or, indeed, macro-institutional (eg global)—level; it is not simply a matter of inadequate general ethics education in a population or of targeting a few individual rotten apples by means of increased enforcement (although these measures have their place). This is the case with the current ethical failures in global financial markets. Accordingly, the solutions are largely to be found at the institutional and macro-institutional levels.

As noted above, integrity systems can be thought of as being either predominantly reactive or predominantly preventive.[19] Naturally, the distinction is somewhat artificial, since there is a need for both reactive elements (eg criminal investigation units, a complaints and discipline system) and preventive elements (eg occupation-based ethics training, transparency of organisational processes, independent boards of directors)[20] in

---

[17] S Miller, P Roberts and E Spence, *Corruption and Anti-corruption* (Saddle River NJ, Pearson, 2005).

[18] A Alexandra and S Miller, *Integrity Systems for Occupations* (Aldershot, Ashgate, 2009).

[19] Miller et al. above n 17.

[20] P MacAvoy and I Millstein, *The Recurrent Crisis in Corporate Governance* (Stanford, CA, Stanford University Press, 2004).

any adequate integrity system. At any rate, integrity systems can be considered under the two broad headings: reactive and preventive.

1.   Reactive Integrity Systems

The reactive way of dealing with ethical misconduct and corruption is the one that first comes to mind. The logic is direct: an activity is defined as one that is not acceptable; an individual engages in that activity and therefore, as a direct result, should be held to account for the misconduct and, if found guilty, disciplined in some way. The rationale for the reactive response for dealing with unethical behaviour, including criminality and corruption, is threefold: offenders are held to account for their actions; offenders get their just deserts; and potential offenders are deterred from future offences. Reactive mechanisms are fundamentally linear and generally take the following form: setting out a series of offences (usually in legislation or regulations); waiting for an individual to transgress; then investigating, adjudicating and finally taking punitive action. The criminal justice system, the investigative arms of regulatory agencies and the internal complaints and discipline systems are basically reactive institutional mechanisms.

Reactive mechanisms are necessary; moreover, a high level of intensity of enforcement is often entirely appropriate. Nevertheless, over-reliance on the reactive approach is problematic. One obvious weakness is the passivity of the approach; by the time the investigators swing into action, the damage has been done already. Consider the situation in relation to fraudsters such as Bernard Madoff in the current financial crisis. Another problem stems from the fact that corrupt behaviour such as insider trading and bribery is often by its nature secretive and can remain so if corporations and professional associations choose to 'close ranks' to protect the reputation of the offending organisation or group. A further problem stems from the inadequacy of the resources to investigate and successfully prosecute; investigation and prosecution are resource intensive. Many fraudulent schemes, for example, are not adequately investigated due to lack of police and other resources. Again, heavy-handed overuse of reactive methods can alienate even those who believe in compliance with regulations and ethical standards. Consider the responses to the apparent or threatened overuse of negotiated prosecutions in the US in the aftermath of the Enron scandal.[21] Finally, if the chances of being caught or complained about are relatively slight for whatever reason (eg under-resourcing, regulatory negligence, lack of political will, an unwarranted belief in the ability of the market to 'self-regulate'), the deterrent effect is undermined, which in turn means there are an even larger number of offences and offenders for investigators to deal with.

Of course, the effectiveness of a reactive approach requires that significant detection mechanisms are available. If so, then those who engage in corrupt or unethical conduct have at least two good reasons to fear exposure: first, detection may lead to legal, regulatory, organisational or associational sanctions, such as imprisonment, fines, suspension or expulsion from the industry; and secondly, it may lead to morally based reputational loss in the eyes of superiors, subordinates, peers, colleagues, clients, customers, the community, friends and/or relatives.

---

[21] O'Brien, above n 1.

There are a number of sources of information in relation to most forms of ethical misconduct and corruption. One of the most important is fellow workers, who may report such conduct or suspicious activity to superiors, to confidential helplines or to watchdog agencies, or even blow the whistle by going to the media.

2. Preventive Integrity Systems

A preventive integrity system will typically embrace, or act in tandem with, a reactive integrity system. However, we can consider preventive mechanisms for dealing with ethical misconduct independent of any reactive elements. If we do so, we see that they can be divided into three categories:

1. Institutional mechanisms for promoting an environment in which integrity is specified and rewarded while unethical behaviour is specified and discouraged, eg by developing codes of ethics/conduct and ethics training programmes, by establishing transparent and fair promotions, remuneration and other reward processes, by mobilising reputation in the service of self-interest (see next section). The focus of these mechanisms is on reducing the desire or motivation to act unethically, so that even when opportunities for unethical behaviour arise they are not pursued or taken.

2. Institutional mechanisms which limit (or eliminate) the opportunity for unethical behaviour. Such mechanisms include corporate governance mechanisms, such as establishing genuinely independent boards of directors, segregating commercial from investment banks, separating the roles of receiving accounts and paying accounts to reduce the opportunity for fraud, and eliminating structural conflicts of interest.

3. Institutional mechanisms which act to expose unethical behaviour, so that the organisation, occupational association or community can deal with them, eg complaints systems, helplines, mandatory reporting requirements, ombudsmen, financial audits, ethics audits, research instruments such as ethical attitude surveys and quantitative complaints, data-gathering and analysis.[22] The term 'transparency' may be used to characterise these mechanisms.

I accept that this threefold distinction is somewhat artificial, and that some institutional mechanisms will in fact come under more than one heading; indeed, some, eg regulations, codes of conduct, ethics and compliance offices,[23] and organisational fraud units, have both a reactive and a preventive role.

3. Holistic Integrity Systems

I suggest that holistic integrity systems can be looked at in relation to three axes, namely, the reactive–preventive axis, the internal–external axis and the self-interest–ethical attitude axis. Thus far in the analysis of integrity systems, I have looked at integrity systems and

---

[22] Miller and Ward, above n 12.

[23] Ethics and Compliance Officer Association Foundation, *The Ethics Compliance Handbook: A Practical Guide from Leading Organisations* (Waltham MA, ECOAF, 2008).

mechanisms under the headings of reactive systems and preventive systems. It is evident that in most societies, jurisdictions and, indeed, organisations the attempt to combat unethical behaviour involves both of the above. That is, integrity-building strategies involve reactive systems as well as preventive systems, and within the preventive systems are mechanisms that promote ethical attitudes, mechanisms that reduce opportunities for criminality, corruption and other forms of unethical behaviour, and various transparency mechanisms.

It seems clear that an adequate integrity system cannot afford to do without reactive as well as preventive systems, and that preventive systems need to have all three kinds of elements detailed above. This suggests that there are two important issues. The first is the adequacy of each of the elements of the above systems. How adequate are the complaints and discipline processes, including the investigations? How effective are the mechanisms of transparency? The second issue pertains to the level of integration and congruence between the reactive and the preventive systems, and the elements of these systems. To what extent do they act together to mutually reinforce one another?

In this connection, it is also worth noting the distinction between internal and external integrity mechanisms. Many large corporations have an array of internal integrity mechanisms, both reactive and preventive, eg ethics and compliance offices.[24] However, many jurisdictions also have external 'watchdog' agencies, including regulatory authorities. Such bodies are established by statutes that also define a range of offences, and have powers to investigate and refer matters to the courts for prosecution. However, it is notable that these watchdog agencies also often involve themselves in prevention programmes involving the development of preventive mechanisms; they do not necessarily see their role as merely that of a reactive agency. The key point for our purposes here is that in a holistic integrity system these internal and external mechanisms ought to complement and mutually reinforce one another. Both types are necessary, and they ought not to be seen as in competition—hence the sterility of some of the debates between, for example, advocates of external regulation and proponents of self-regulation.

A third important axis around which the concept of a holistic integrity system rotates pertains to motivational attitudes: specifically, self-interest and ethical attitudes. Here we need first to remind ourselves what is presupposed by an integrity system, namely, shared ethical attitudes.

There are at least two aspects of these shared ethical attitudes. On the one hand, and most obviously, there must be some shared moral values in relation to the moral unacceptability of specific forms of behaviour and in relation to the moral desirability of other specific forms of behaviour, eg market actors must actually believe that bribery is wrong. That is, there needs to be a framework of accepted social norms and a means for inculcating these norms, eg via ethics training programmes or by ethical leadership. On the other hand, there also needs to be a shared ethical conception in relation to what institutional and other measures ought to be taken to minimise corruption, criminality and unethical behaviour more generally; very harsh penalties and other draconian measures, for example, may simply alienate reasonable, ethical people.

Holistic integrity systems rely on both self-interest and ethical attitudes. As we have just seen, integrity systems presuppose ethical attitudes. However, they also obviously rely on

---

[24] Ibid.

self-interest. For example, they seek to deter wrongdoing by investigating and punishing offenders. They also seek to promote compliance with laws and regulations by providing incentives and removing disincentives and perverse incentives, eg forms of remuneration that instil a habit of taking undue risks with other people's money. A further element of self-interest that holistic integrity systems should make use of is the desire for good reputation. It is this element that I now want to focus on. I note that, as was the case with reactive and preventive mechanisms, and with internal and external mechanisms, holistic integrity systems seek to utilise both self-interest and ethical attitudes in the design of integrity systems, and do so in a manner such that these different motivations end up mutually reinforcing the integrity systems in question.

C.   The Virtuous Triangle

1.   Professional and Corporate Reputation

A key element in the establishment of effective integrity systems for occupational groups, organisations and industries in general, and corporations and professional groups in particular, is the mobilisation of reputation. Naturally, some groups and organisations are more sensitive to reputational loss (and the possibility of reputational gain) than others. Corporations and professional groups in the financial services sector, including bankers and auditors, are very sensitive to reputational loss. Those entrusted to make prudent decisions with other people's money are inevitably heavily dependent on a good reputation, as are those entrusted to provide independent adjudications in relation to financial health.

When a high professional reputation is much sought after by members of an occupational group or organisation and a low one is to be avoided at all costs, there is an opportunity to mobilise this reputational desire in the service of promoting ethical standards. Here the aim is to ensure that reputation aligns with actual ethical practice, that is, that the high or low reputation of an organisation, group or individual is deserved. The way to achieve this is by designing appropriate integrity systems. As we have seen above, key elements of an integrity system track compliance with regulations; for example, accountability mechanisms ensure compliance (or, at least, expose non-compliance) with regulations. The additional thought here is that key elements of an integrity system should track features of organisations and occupational groups that determine, or should determine, reputation. More explicitly, a reputational index could be constructed whereby an ethics audit awards scores in relation to specific ethical standards. In what remains of this chapter I will sketch the broad outlines of such a reputational index.

Deserved reputation can provide an important nexus between the self-interest of corporations and professional groups, on the one hand, and appropriate ethical behaviour towards consumers, clients and the public more generally, on the other. More specifically, the deserved reputation of financial services providers, be they corporations or professional groups, can provide such a nexus. Here there are three elements in play: (i) reputation; (ii) self-interest; and (iii) ethical standards, such as compliance with technical accounting standards and avoidance of specific conflicts of interest, but also more general desiderata such as client/consumer protection. The idea is that these three elements need to interlock in what might be called a virtuous triangle.

First, reputation needs to be linked to self-interest; this is obviously already the case—individuals, groups and organisations desire high reputation, and benefit materially and in other ways from it. Secondly, reputation needs to be linked to ethics, in that reputation ought to be deserved; as already mentioned, the integrity systems are the means to achieve this. Thirdly, and as a consequence of the two already mentioned links, self-interest is linked to ethics; given robust integrity systems that mobilise reputational concerns, it is in the self-interest of individuals, groups and firms to comply with ethical standards (that are also professional standards). Here I reassert that self-interest is not the only or necessarily the ultimate motivation for human action; the desire to do the right thing is also a powerful motivator for many, if not most, people. Accordingly, the triangle is further strengthened by the motivation to do right.

In recent years the notion of a reputation index has gained currency in a number of contexts, especially in business and academic circles. The term seems to have a number of different senses. Sometimes it is used to describe a way of measuring the reputation that an organisation actually has. Since reputation exists, so to speak, in the eye of the beholder, actual reputation does not always match deserved reputation. Accordingly, sometimes the term is used to describe a way of calculating the performance of an organisation on the basis of which its reputation should be founded.

The first step in the process is to determine a way of accurately measuring the ethical performance of individual or organisational members of occupational and industry groups. This is an ethics audit. Here I stress the importance of objective measures of ethical performance. These might include such things as: results of consumer satisfaction surveys; gross numbers and trends in warranted complaints; numbers of disciplinary matters and their outcomes; and outcomes of financial and health and safety audits (for example, regarding electronic crime and corruption vulnerabilities). They would also include the existence of institutional processes established to assure compliance with ethical standards, eg codes of ethics and conduct, financial and other audit processes, ethics committees, complaints and disciplinary systems, fraud and ethics units, ethical risk assessment processes, ethics and compliance officers, and professional development programmes in ethics.

I note that, while some of these institutional systems and processes might be legally required—and, indeed, some are under section 406 of the Sarbanes-Oxley Act—this is by no means the case for all them.[25] In short, while reputational indexes include some indicators of compliance with those ethical standards (and associated processes of assurance) that are enshrined in law, they also include indicators of adherence to ethical standards that are above and beyond what is legally required. This is important, given that: (i) laws and regulation inevitably play 'catch up' in relation to new and emerging ethical problems (including loopholes that are exploited by 'creative' accountants and 'legal engineers'[26]); (ii) it is both impractical and undesirable for all ethical standards and virtues to be embodied in laws and regulations (aspirational ethical goals are a case in point); and (iii) ethical behaviour and attitudes cannot simply be regulated into existence.

---

[25] O'Brien, above n 10, 27–54.
[26] See McBarnet, chapter 4 in this volume.

In addition to the ethics audit itself, there is a need for a process that engages with ethical reputation. Since ethical reputation should reflect the findings of the ethics audit, an ethical reputation audit should drive the relationship between de facto ethical performance (in effect, the deserved reputation) and actual reputation for ethical performance. The way to achieve this is by the participation of as many occupational members and industry organisations as possible in ethics audits, and by the widespread promulgation of the results of their de facto ethical performance (as determined by the ethics audit), including in the media. Naturally, the results promulgated could be more or less detailed; they could, for example, simply consist in an overall rating as opposed to a complete description of the ethics audit results.

Reputational indexes give rise to a number of problems. There is the problem of devising acceptable, objective measures of ethical performance. While ethical performance in a general sense is a somewhat nebulous notion, determining minimum ethical standards—that are, nevertheless, above and beyond legal requirements—and levels of compliance with them is doable. Indeed, criminal justice and regulatory systems are devised in large part to prescribe objectively specifiable, pre-existing, minimum ethical standards—for example, do not defraud or bribe. Reputational indexes of minimum ethical standards simply take this process further by, so to speak, raising the ethical bar.

A greater problem is participation: what means are available to ensure the participation of occupational groups and organisations in reputational indexes? (Of course, in the case of those indexes that simply measure compliance with legal requirements, there is no need to secure 'participation'; the compliance failure is already in the public domain and reputational indexes simply provide additional and more targeted publicity.) In relation to the problem of non-participation, there is a variety of responses ranging from the mandatory use of reputational indexes by members of professional or industry groups (on pain of exclusion from the relevant professional or industry association) through to the provision of various kinds of incentive. The Professional Standards Council (PSC) in Australia provides one kind of example for occupational groups: it offers capped liability as an incentive to occupational groups to participate in its ethico-professional standards schemes.

A third, and still greater, problem is effectiveness. The use of reputational indexes can easily reduce into 'tick-the-box' processes on the part of clever, well-resourced organisations seeking to avoid actual compliance with ethical standards in favour of engaging in elaborate exercises in window-dressing. Hence the need for meaningful ethical audits conducted by independent, adequately resourced and professionally trained ethics auditors.

2. Professional Standards Council of Australia

Organisations such as the PSC are important participants in this process of ethico-professionalisation; indeed, this is arguably the *raison d'être* of the PSC. Moreover, the conferring of good reputation is central to the PSC's role.[27] The PSC offers capped

---

[27] A Alexandra, T Campbell, D Cocking and S Miller, 'Professionalisation, Ethics and Integrity Systems: The Promotion of Professional Ethical Standards, and the Protection of Clients and Consumers', report for the Professional Standards Council (Parramatta NSW, Professional Standards Council, 2006).

liability to occupational groups in exchange for their establishment of integrity systems; accordingly, there is a financial incentive to occupational groups to join a scheme and thereby reduce their insurance premiums. However, the PSC also offers a kind of ethical accreditation to occupational groups via its Cover of Excellence® scheme; groups establishing an appropriate integrity system are awarded a Cover of Excellence®. Indeed, the central instrument of the PSC in its effort to promote ethical standards is arguably not so much the capped liability provision but, rather, its de facto ethical accreditation of occupational groups—an accreditation that confers good ethical reputation on these groups.

As shown above, having a good reputation can be made to depend primarily on possession of an effective integrity system, because an effective integrity system is one that maintains and promotes compliance with high ethical standards and, therefore, provides an assurance that a good reputation is deserved. Accordingly, the PSC has an important role: to establish and reinforce the dependence between good reputation and possession of an effective integrity system.

This is, in effect, what the PSC is doing by approving its Cover of Excellence® schemes for those occupational associations that have put in place appropriate integrity systems— or, at least, significant components of integrity systems, eg codes of ethics, complaints and discipline processes. Moreover, the PSC, and like organisations, could do more to strengthen this dependence between good reputation and possession of an effective integrity system by mobilising the desire on the part of occupational groups to gain a high reputation and avoid a low reputation. For example, an integrity system that includes reputational indexes for members of an occupational group, and corresponding ethics audits, directly connects the desire for a high reputation on the part of a member of an occupational group to the maintenance and promotion of ethical standards. To this extent the integrity system in question is more effective than it would otherwise have been.

Naturally this whole process is predicated on the reputation of occupational groups and firms actually being deserved. Good reputation that is undeserved is not an ethical good; it does not benefit consumers or clients, and it does not serve the public interest. It is also important to stress that the credibility of the PSC is also on the line: its approval of a Cover of Excellence® scheme must be seen to be warranted.

Integrity systems for different groups may vary in the weight they give certain considerations over others. So, for instance, anti-competitive concerns or claims to professional autonomy with respect to a body of knowledge may be more relevant to some groups than others. Accordingly, deserved reputation will track such differences. It will, for instance, be more significant to the overall deserved good reputation of, say, a real estate agent to establish that she does well in relation to anti-competitive and market norms than it will be for most doctors. That is, such an integrity system provides the reputational indexes against which reputation may be assessed and so 'good' reputation may be shown to be deserved or otherwise.

The PSC's instruments aimed at enhancing integrity systems for occupations, and which provide such reputational indexes, are:

— the development of effective codes of ethics, conduct or practice, in collaboration with occupational associations;
— complaints and discipline procedures; and
— professional development and ethical education programmes.

3.   Ethical Reputation Indexes

If reputation is to be mobilised in the service of raising ethical standards, then the following steps need to be taken.

1.   For each occupation or organisation, it needs to be determined what the appropriate ethical standards are: for example, avoidance of specific kinds of conflicts of interest, compliance with technical accounting standards, compliance with health and safety standards, compliance with market norms of fair competition.

2.   An integrity system for these ethical standards needs to be developed comprised of various elements: for example, code of conduct, ethical risk assessment process (in relation to conflicts of interest, breaches of confidentiality, etc), complaints and discipline system, ethics and compliance office, fraud unit, self-assessment process.

3.   Objective indices need to be worked out in relation to what counts as compliance with ethical standards and in respect of such integrity systems and their workings: for example, number and type of complaints, success rate of investigations, responses to identified ethical risks.

4.   An applicable reputational index (composed in part by a set of appropriate indices) needs to be developed and accepted by the occupational group or industry organisations in question.

5.   There is a need for the actual participation of a reasonably large cross-section of the occupational group or industry organisations in question. So there is a need to provide some kind of incentive to participate (or disincentive to non-participation). It is likely that, at a certain threshold of participation, non-participants will suffer reputational loss simply by failing to participate.

6.   An independent entity needs to be established to conduct the actual process of assessing members of the occupational group or industry organisations in question (that is, applying the reputational index).

7.   The results need to be presented in a suitable form for public promulgation, and then promulgated.

Reputational indexes can be developed and used to measure a variety of different kinds of entity. Thus, members of an occupational group can be rated as a whole or against one another, as can firms in a given industry. Here I note that what is made publicly available is not necessarily a ranking of members of an occupational group or set of organisations; rather, there could be simply the statement that the minimum threshold of ethical standards had been met, eg by way of a 'certificate of ethical health' or perhaps a 'badge of excellence'. Alternatively, there might be, say, a five-star ratings system, in which more than one practitioner or firm could get a five-star rating. And there are other possible systems.

D.   Conclusion

In this chapter I have outlined the important role that integrity systems play in maintaining ethical standards in occupations and organisations, including financial services providers. Moreover, I have argued for what I have termed holistic integrity systems. I have further suggested that financial services providers have a high degree of sensitivity to reputational loss (and to the possibility of reputational gain) and that, therefore, greater use could be made of reputational indexes in current integrity systems in this area. I have also outlined the general features of reputational indexes. However, I have not undertaken the more difficult task of actually constructing a reputational index for any given occupational group or organisational sector within the financial services area. That important task, or set of tasks, remains to be done.

24

Toward A 'Responsible' Future: Reframing and Reforming the Governance of Financial Markets

A. Introduction

On 17 June 2009, the White House officially launched its proposals for reforming the federal government's approach to reform oversight of the banking industry and financial markets.[1] It promised to be the most significant overhaul of any US regulatory system in nearly 80 years, and involved structural and jurisdictional changes that (if passed and implemented) would transform the way both government and the entire financial sector conducted business in the US and globally.

Reflecting the strategic and politically pragmatic orientation of the Obama Administration, this was no mere 'pie-in-the-sky' plan that could be easily blocked and dismissed by the powerful forces in and around Congress that typically find ways to emasculate—if not effectively pre-empt—such schemes. The concerns and/or displeasure of potential opponents from most quarters had been considered, and few if any of the main players complained that they had not been consulted or their ideas not given serious consideration. As one measure of how well the Administration had designed the plan for a soft landing on the political runway, Wall Street indicators such as the Dow Jones average barely registered an impact that day despite the transformational nature of what the White House had put on the table.

Although many of the specifics of the Obama plan for reform are likely to be modified as proposals wend their way through the policy-making process, few doubt or challenge the basic premise of the effort: the regulatory system focused on the financial sector in the US is broken to the extent that it requires major repairs. It demanded a regulatory system overhaul that will prevent a recurrence of a situation that had developed over the years and came to a critical head the previous fall with the collapse of several major firms and a 'freeze' of the credit markets that effectively converted an emerging recession into what

* Professor of Political Science, University of New Hampshire.
[1] US Department of the Treasury, 'Financial Regulatory Reform: A New Foundation' (2009).

many analysts term an economic depression.[2] In this chapter I argue that this attempt at reform will not, in fact, achieve that objective, but not for the reasons most of its critics offer. Among the critics, the proposals either go too far or do not go far enough in the changes they will bring about. In contrast, I contend that the problems facing these reforms are not a matter of too much or too little reform, but rather an unfocused (and misfocused) approach to reform.

The current efforts to design relevant reforms of the troubled financial markets both in the US and abroad are preoccupied with repairing a fundamentally flawed set of policies. There will no doubt be some initial sense of accomplishment as regulatory jurisdictions are reorganised and regulatory agencies are created and or shuffled about in a reform scheme that seems radical on the surface, but is in fact superficial.

After a brief consideration of the dynamics of the 'blame game' that is generating and shaping most of the reform agenda in Washington, London and elsewhere, I make the case for an approach that goes beyond mere tinkering with traditional regulatory mechanisms and instead focuses on the need to reform the 'governance' of the financial sector. This perspective requires that we shift and raise our sights from the arena of institutions and regulatory mechanisms to the domain of governance regimes. Further, I make the case for the existence of two interrelated regimes that require attention if we are to make any headway in the design of relevant and effective reforms. One of those regimes—the regulatory, which focuses on governance through control—has already received considerable attention from analysts, and I highlight one effort (by Hood, Rothstein and Baldwin (HRB), referred to in more detail below) at framing the elements of that regime. The other regime—accountability, which fosters governance through responsibility—requires more analytic attention, and I offer the foundations for a framework the seeks to emulate the HRB effort. I conclude by offering some basic 'design principles' that need to be kept in mind as we deal with the future of financial market governance.

B.   Random Fishing in the Accountability Stream

'It isn't that they can't see the solution. It is that they can't see the problem' (GK Chesterton)

Developing long-term and appropriate solutions to the current financial crisis requires a thorough assessment of the problems that generated the situation. Given the complexity of domestic and global financial markets, even the most knowledgeable minds of the era find the analytic challenge overwhelming.[3]

In lieu of some consensus on credible paradigmatic framing of the crisis, policymakers have found other means for filling the 'problem definition gap'.[4] Thus, although one would

---

[2] At the start of the crisis there was considerable debate about whether the US economy was technically in a 'recession'—a debate nurtured by the rather formal process put in place for declaring that condition. Once that hurdle was completed, the term 'depression' was put into play by analysts and commentators. See 'Diagnosing Depression; Economics Focus 2009', *The Economist*, 1 March 2009, 57; see also RA Posner, *A Failure of Capitalism: The Crisis of '08 and the Descent into Depression* (Cambridge, MA, Harvard University Press, 2009).

[3] Economists and other analysts were similarly perplexed during the initial stages of the Great Depression. Keynes drew so much attention because his perspective seemed to fill a void created by the failure of extant theories and models.

[4] On the nature and dynamics of problem definition, see D Dery, *Problem Definition in Policy Analysis* (Lawrence KS, University Press of Kansas, 1984); R Hoppe, 'Cultures of Public Policy Problems' (2002) 4 *Journal*

hope for a more rational approach to designing policies that might prevent any future recurrence of the current problems, we are currently engaged in multiple 'blame games' that will invariably influence the shape of government regulation of financial markets for the foreseeable future.

Beyond the well-studied dynamics of political blame avoidance,[5] driving the emergence of 'blame games' during times of crisis is the pressure policymakers feel as they attempt to fill the gap created by ignorance or uncertainty about the problematic situation they are facing.[6]

To make matters more complicated, those who assume the task of designing policy responses face a range of ontological choices. At one extreme is the assumption that the universe generates problems (eg crises, disasters) randomly—that is, 'stuff happens' without any explicable explanation and the best we can do collectively is prepare for those eventualities that seem to have a greater probability of occurring. A second extreme position—let us call it the 'acts of god(s)' perspective—views the universe as subject to the whims and unfathomable logic of some supernatural beings or forces that cannot be subjected to our powers of understanding. The best we can do under such assumed circumstances is prepare for any eventuality and engage in considerable praying or perhaps some ritual sacrifices.

Modern policy designers (at least those who accept the basic premises of the Enlightenment) assume some position between those two extremes, which ideally requires a careful analysis of a problematic condition so as to determine those causal factors which can be addressed by policy actions—or at minimum those factors that can be addressed by policies designed to ameliorate the consequences or prevent a recurrence.[7] For students of the policy design process, the fact that the universe provides few opportunities for applying objective analysis leads to a fall-back position relying on the social construction of problematic realities that can be subjected to some policy fix. Even here, however, uncertainty (and thus controversy) rules unless there exists some 'theory' or 'model' powerful enough to preclude or direct debates over those factors that policies need to address. Here is where the 'blame game' typically enters the picture.

of Comparative Policy Analysis 305; DR Rochefort and RW Cobb (eds), *The Politics of Problem Definition: Shaping the Policy Agenda* (Lawrence, KS, University Press of Kansas, 1994).

[5] See, eg C Hood, 'The Risk Game and the Blame Game' (2002) 37 *Government and Opposition* 15; DL Weimer, 'The Puzzle of Private Rulemaking: Expertise, Flexibility, and Blame Avoidance in US Regulation' (2006) 66 *Public Administration Review* 569; R Ellis, *Presidential Lightning Rods: The Politics of Blame Avoidance Studies in Government and Public Policy* (Lawrence, KS, University Press of Kansas, 1994); KM McGraw, 'Managing Blame: An Experimental Test of the Effects of Political Accounts' (1991) 85 *American Political Science Review* 1133; KM McGraw, 'Avoiding Blame: An Experimental Investigation of Political Excuses and Justifications' (1990) 20 *British Journal of Political Science* 119.

[6] Studies of the blame game and similar concepts (eg hindsight causal analysis, attribution, issue responsibility) include S Iyengar, *Is Anyone Responsible? How Television Frames Political Issues* (Chicago, IL, University of Chicago Press, 1991); S Iyengar, 'Framing Responsibility for Political Issues' (1996) 546 *Annals of the American Academy of Political and Social Science* 59; JJ Strange and CC Leung, 'How Anecdotal Accounts in News and in Fiction Can Influence Judgments of a Social Problem's Urgency, Causes, and Cures' (1999) 25 *Personality and Social Psychology Bulletin* 436; S Knobloch-Westerwick and LD Taylor, 'The Blame Game: Elements of Causal Attribution and Its Impact on Siding with Agents in the News' (2008) 35 *Communication Research* 723. See also DA Kysar and TO McGarity, 'Did NEPA Drown New Orleans? The Levees, the Blame Game, and the Hazards of Hindsight' (2006) 56 *Duke Law Journal* 179.

[7] For a positive expression of this agenda, see D Lerner and HD Lasswell (eds), *The Policy Sciences; Recent Developments in Scope and Method* (Stanford, CA, Stanford University Press, 1951) and Y Dror, *Design for Policy Sciences* (New York, American Elsevier, 1971); Y Dror, 'Prolegomena to Policy Sciences' (1970) 1 *Policy Sciences* 135.

The 'games' themselves are part of a cultural phenomenon basic to modern societies fixated on determining and dealing with the causes of our collective ills. At least in the realm of public policy, secularisation and 'scientism' have for the most part deposed most forms of fatalism and replaced them with a pragmatic belief that public problems can be analysed and ameliorated, if not actually 'fixed'.

Put otherwise, the salience of these games reflects an inherent bias in our policy-making process that seeks out a causal factor that can be acted upon. The urge to take collective (policy) action to deal with a public problem reflects the perceived possibility of taking effective action—and this, in turn, requires some sense of a link between some factor that can be acted upon and the problem. Deborah Stone[8] provides a simple but insightful view of options offered in her four types of 'causal theories' underlying public policies (see Figure 1). Assuming some degree of consensus among policymakers regarding who or what 'caused' (ie is to blame for) the problem at hand, these 'theories' can have considerable impact on the form and content of resulting decisions. Blame games emerge where such a consensus is lacking, the result being a political struggle to define the cause and (eventually) policy choices that reflect the competition among conflicting views.

In the current debate over the financial meltdown, these 'games' have taken a variety of forms—from well thought out studies to blogger rants to Oxford-style debates—and not surprisingly are leading to the conclusion that both everyone and no one has some causal responsibility to bear. Was it Wall Street's fault for taking advantage of newly created instruments and schemes to create a bubble that would eventually burst, or was it Washington's (or London's or Paris's) fault for letting down its regulatory guard allowing the banks to run bullishly through the markets? Or perhaps it was the fault of the Main Street folks who let themselves be conned into believing that home values would rise

Actions:	Consequences:	
	Intended	Unintended
Unguided	*Mechanical cause* intervening agent machines trained animals brainwashed people	*Accidental cause* nature weather earthquakes machines run amok
Purposeful	*Intentional cause* assault oppression conspiracies that work programs that work	*Inadvertent cause* intervening conditions unforeseen side effects neglect carelessness omission

Figure 1. Stone's types of causal theories.

[8] DA Stone, *Policy Paradox: The Art of Political Decision Making*, 2nd edn (New York, WW Norton, 1997) 285.

forever and that there were no risks in taking on the debt obligations of a new mortgage or ever higher credit card balances. A convincing argument has also been made for placing the blame at the systemic level where the interconnectedness of globalised financial markets made the entire network vulnerable to collapse once a critical link (in this case, most point to the US housing market) weakened.

Whatever one can conclude from these various finger-pointing exercises, the significance of these blame games in shaping the causal theories (that will, in turn, shape future policy) might be substantial. Without a consensus view or coherent framing of what caused the present crisis, we should not be surprised to see the emergence of a 'hodge podge' set of proposals that reflect political bargaining and compromise rather than what economists regard as an effective and coherent package of solutions.[9]

That noted, the resulting 'hodge podge' is not without its common thread. If one were to focus on the rhetoric used to rationalise proposals put forth by the White House and others, it would be clear that solutions proffered by a variety of politicians and experts rely on actions designed to improve accountability. The underlying logic is simple and sensible on its face: once we determine (correctly or incorrectly) that someone or some agency or some process is to blame, the steps taken to prevent or mitigate a future recurrence must necessarily include some account-giving mechanisms.

But here, too, the lack of a more developed framing logic proves problematic for designing policy solutions. The issue of which accountability mechanisms are relevant to the current financial crisis remains an open question. What does it mean to demand 'greater accountability' of the various actors in the financial services industry? The typical responses to that question generate a plethora of 'usual suspects'. We want those involved—whether bankers or regulators or customers—to assume greater 'responsibility' for their actions. At the same time, we desire that each be 'answerable' to their respective principals—shareholders for the bankers and the public for the regulators. For bankers and others in the corporate sector of this domain, we require that they live up to the fiduciary 'obligations' they assumed when taking on their respective positions. As for the regulators, we assume they will be 'responsive' to the concerns and complaints brought before them. And for those bankers or regulators or customers who might attempt to circumvent or undermine the mechanisms established for those various purposes, we want them to be 'liable' for the consequences of their possible mis/malfeasances.

The argument I offer here is that, without some effort to define the problems being addressed in a clear and coherent way, reforming the financial services industry by establishing greater accountability will prove difficult at best. The general rhetoric of reform, however, has not fostered any such clarity. 'Make them [more] accountable' is the clarion call from all corners of the policy-making world. And, at least to this point in the crisis, that rhetorical theme has trumped any effort to focus attention on exactly what it is we wish to accomplish by declaring our desire for more accountability.

For many students of the public policy-making process, the present situation confirms the growing popularity of what is called the 'garbage can model' (GCM) of decision-making. Originally articulated as a model to explain decision-making in

---

[9] By the spring of 2009, the main discussion among economists had moved from the academic journals to editorial op-ed pages, the internet and comments made on podcasts and mass media business news shows. Despite criticisms of government proposals that emerged from the blame game, many of the same experts contributed to the cacophony that generated the many and varied proposals.

'organised anarchies' such as universities,[10] GCM has been transformed into a widely used model of the complex policy-making process in the US which has features resembling anarchical arrangements. Perhaps the best known of these GCMs was developed by John Kingdon,[11] who described the process as involving three independent 'streams': a 'problem' stream, representing the current flow of issues of potential interest to policy-makers; a 'policy' stream of possible solutions, many seeking a problem to deal with; and a 'political' stream of various actors whose interests and activities vary over time. For Kingdon and others who use this model, the adoption of a policy involves a fortuitous convergence of these three streams during a 'window of opportunity' when all three happen to flow together.

Applied within a particular 'policy domain' such as the reform of financial markets, this multiple streams model helps us make sense of the current situation where the ongoing blame game is generating multiple problems (related to a range of accountability deficiencies) to be 'solved', with policymakers responding by throwing various account-ability-based solutions at those situations that seem to be the most salient at a given moment.

Perhaps the most obvious example was the flare-up involving the infamous 'retention bonuses' at AIG. In the midst of a major effort to design a reasonable and feasible plan for relieving banks of their 'toxic assets' (which was itself filled with many different account-ability-related challenges), the primary policy actors had to contend with a media-fed public outrage by attempting to hold AIG 'to account' for what many (incorrectly, as it turned out) perceived as a violation of the public trust and treasure. Executive compensation restrictions had in fact been part of the ongoing deliberation of how to design the troubled asset-relief programme (TARP) from the outset, but the issue was plucked from a problem stream filled with many more (and less) significant issues, and the resulting 'crisis' generated a frenzied search for a quick-fix response from among those found in the stream of policy instruments that would satisfy the whirlwind that brought turbulence to the political stream.[12]

While the AIG episode may prove to be exceptional in light of the attention it received and the extreme nature of the policy responses it drew, there is nothing in the public record to indicate that a more reasoned (non-GCM-like) process is being applied in response to other issues in this policy domain. Faced with specific issues related to a particular aspect of the financial crisis, policymakers will respond with accountability mechanisms pulled from the policy stream that seems the best fit to deal with the narrowly defined problem.

Put another way, the ambiguous nature of the rhetorical calls for 'greater account-ability' are producing the expected response (at least under the GCM): an ad hoc

---

[10] For the original version of the model, see MD Cohen, JG March and JP Olsen, 'A Garbage Can Model of Organizational Choice' (1972) 17 *Administrative Science Quarterly* 1; see also JG March and JP Olsen (eds), *Ambiguity and Choice in Organizations* (Bergen, Universitetsforlaget, 1976); MD Cohen and JG March, *Leadership and Ambiguity: The American College President*, 2nd edn (Boston, MA, Harvard Business School Press, 1986).

[11] JW Kingdon, *Agendas, Alternatives, and Public Policies* (Boston, MA, Little Brown, 1984); see also G Mucciaroni, 'The Garbage Can Model and the Study of Policy Making: A Critique' (1992) 24 *Polity* 459.

[12] See B Webel, 'Ongoing Government Assistance for American International Group (AIG)', Congressional Report (Washington, Library of Congress Congressional Research Service, 1992); LG Thatcher, 'Executive Compensation Restrictions under the American Recovery and Reinvestment Act of 2009' (2009) 41(3) *Compensation Benefits Review* 20.

proliferation of policy proposals that are incoherent and inconsistent at best. In some instances we have reforms designed (intentionally or not) to strengthen oversight and control—of both the regulated and the regulators! At the same time, demands for greater 'transparency' and open deliberations are made of all parties. In other cases we find accountability mechanisms aimed at ensuring that the internal decision processes (again, of both the regulated banking community and the regulators) follow a certain pattern and that the targeted decision makers behave in an 'ethical' or appropriate way. Still other responses impose 'high stakes' performance standards and measures designed to direct and 'motivate' the various agents and agencies involved.

Each of these policy responses makes sense in light of the narrow and specific nature of the problems drawn from the stream at a given time. The more general question is whether, when taken together and assessed in their entirety, they can constitute an effective effort to deal with the need for 'greater accountability' in the financial services domain.

C.   Framing the Design Problem

If we are to develop solutions to the current financial crisis, we need to begin by articulating and framing the problem, and here we can start with a basic assumption about the corporatised market that has been accepted by both political scientists and economists since at least the 1930s: the central problems are those of creating and sustaining 'good governance'.[13]

As with all terms that are part of the common parlance of political dialogue (eg power, sovereignty), reference to the concept of governance requires some analytic clarity. Among those engaged in the analysis of government, however, the focus of attention is so wide ranging that any study must assume an arbitrary position regarding the concept. So, for many, governance is 'what governments do'—the tasks and functions they carry out as the legitimate controllers of the machinery of the modern state.[14] At the other extreme are those who regard governance as 'socio-cybernetic systems' and 'self-organising networks' which emerge as authoritative sources of control within and among all forms of organised life—from the family unit to the modern state and global networks.[15] Taking a somewhat middle course are analysts such as Oliver E Williamson, who traces the study of

---

[13] The use of the phrase 'good governance' may be troublesome for some, not merely for its obvious normative implications, but also due to its association with 'neo-liberal' policies of the World Bank and International Monetary Fund. See, eg LS Finkelstein, 'What Is Global Governance?' (1995) 1 *Global Governance* 367; CH de Alcántara, 'Uses and Abuses of the Concept of Governance' (1998) 50 *International Social Science Journal* 105; TG Weiss, 'Governance, Good Governance and Global Governance: Conceptual and Actual Challenges' (2000) 21 *Third World Quarterly* 795; M Doornbos, '"Good Governance": The Rise and Decline of a Policy Metaphor?' (2001) 37 *Journal of Development Studies* 93; RV Aguilera and A Cuervo-Cazurra, 'Codes of Good Governance Worldwide: What Is the Trigger?' (2004) 25 *Organization Studies* 415; P Bourdieu, *The Social Structures of the Economy* (Malden MA, Polity, 2005), 10–12. In the analytic exercise that follows I attempt to circumvent both the normative and ideological implications of the concept.

[14] See, eg R Rose, 'On the Priorities of Government: A Developmental Analysis of Public Policies' (1976) 4 *European Journal of Political Research* 247.

[15] RAW Rhodes, 'The New Governance: Governing without Government' (1996) 44 *Political Studies* 652; see also G Stoker, 'Governance as Theory: Five Propositions' (1998) 50 *International Social Science Journal* 17.

governance to the work of John Commons and Ronald Coase, and defines it as the examination 'of good order and workable arrangements'.[16]

For present purposes we will follow that 'middle road' definition and assume that the focus of our policy design task is to articulate reforms that can be made to enhance the 'good order and workable arrangements' that 'govern' the form and operations of today's financial markets.

Another central tool for this design task is that of 'regimes', a concept often used by students of governance, whether they are focusing on states, networks or formal organisations. In conventional discussions about politics, the term 'regime' is loosely applied to types of political systems or styles of governance (eg democratic regimes, authoritarian regimes, Stalinist regimes), or the government of a country that has been ruled by some person or party for an extended period (eg the Castro regime, the Communist regime).[17]

Among scholars who study governance, the term 'regime' is typically assigned to those politically relevant social and economic arrangements that endure over time to form the setting within which governments (and political systems in general) operate. More specifically, what the term 'regime' means analytically depends on the scope, breadth and depth of the domain of governance action to which it is being applied. For some, regimes constitute the basic moral order or (in Charles Taylor's phrase) social imaginary[18] that influences the form, direction and force of governance. In Taylor's sweeping historical analysis and critique of the modern 'secular' age, for example, the term regime is synonymous with the underlying 'moral order' of a society, and he regards changes and shift in regimes (ie social imaginaries) to be rare and revolutionary.

For others, regimes are reflected in the patterns of governance that emerge within settings where the traditional structures and mechanisms of government are not available. Students of world politics have paid growing attention to the role that both formal and informal international regimes have played (and continue to play) in transnational relationships and the development of the global economy.[19] Another group of scholars, many of whom are associated with the public choice perspective that spans economics and political science, regard a regime as the 'logic' of governance (eg Madisonian, Weberian)

---

[16] OE Williamson, 'Visible and Invisible Governance' (1994) 84 *American Economic Review* 323; OE Williamson, 'The Institutions of Governance' (1994) 88 *American Economic Review* 75; OE Williamson, 'The Economics of Governance' (1998) 95 *American Economic Review* 1; see also JR Commons, 'The Problem of Correlating Law, Economics and Ethics' (1932) 8 *Wisconsin Law Review* 3; RH Coase, 'The Nature of the Firm' (1937) 4 *Economica* 386.

[17] There is notably a negative, judgemental sense implied in the popular use of the word 'regime' evidenced by the fact that the concept is rarely applied to US regimes (typically labelled 'administrations') or many parliamentary regimes (which are noted as 'governments' in the media).

[18] C Taylor, *Modern Social Imaginaries* (Durham, NC, Duke University Press, 2004); C Taylor, *A Secular Age* (Cambridge, MA, Belknap Press of Harvard University Press, 2007).

[19] Eg OR Young, 'Review: International Regimes: Toward a New Theory of Institutions' (1987) 39 *World Politics* 104; OR Young, 'Regime Dynamics: The Rise and Fall of International Regimes' (1982) 36 *International Organization* 277; OR Young, 'International Regimes: Problems of Concept Formation' 32 *World Politics* 331, SD Krasner, 'Structural Causes and Regime Consequences: Regimes as Intervening Variables' (1982) 36 *International Organization* 185; SD Krasner, 'Regimes and the Limits of Realism: Regimes as Autonomous Variables' (1982) 36 *International Organization* 497; JG Ruggie, 'Reconstituting the Global Public Domain—Issues, Actors, and Practices' (2004) 10 *European Journal of International Relations* 499; JG Ruggie, 'International Regimes, Transactions, and Change: Embedded Liberalism in the Postwar Economic Order' (1982) 36 *International Organization* 379; EB Haas, 'Words Can Hurt You; or, Who Said What to Whom About Regimes' (1982) 36 *International Organization* 207.

that develops within a constitutional ordering of political and social relationships.[20] At an even more specific level, students of regulatory policy apply the term regimes to the range of strategic approaches used within a particular policy arena (eg utility pricing, telecommunications).[21]

For present purposes, the concept of regime will be applied to the two governance arrangements that are most salient in the reform of the financial services sector. A regulatory regime involves arrangements of institutions, norms, values and relationships intended primarily to exercise some degree of control over the governed acts and actors. It is somewhat synonymous with Jessop's 'regulation approach' view of capitalist economies, involving 'economic and extra-economic institutions and practices which help to secure, if only temporarily and always in specific economic spaces, a certain stability and predictability in accumulation—despite fundamental contradictions and conflicts generated by the very dynamic of capital itself'.[22]

A regulatory regime can take an explicit form, as manifested in legal and bureaucratic frameworks that generate and enforce laws and rules,[23] or it can take a more implicit form in the development of a Foucauldian 'governmentality' that (in its most extreme) fosters a sense of panoptic oversight and monitoring.[24]

Among the most useful, design-relevant explications of regulatory regimes is that offered by Hood, Rotherstein and Baldwin (HRB) in their watershed book, *The Government of Risk*.[25] Although their study directly addresses social risk policies in the UK, their framework has a broader applicability through its focus on the variations of means and mechanisms used to control individual and collective risk behaviour across several different policy domains, including related to the domestic and global marketplace. Central to the HRB construct (see Figure 2) are three core forms of 'control components' used to deal with risk within an examined domain: information gathering; standard setting; and behaviour modification. These are then explicated in terms of the context (type of risk, public attitudes, organised interests) and content (size, structure and style of regulatory effort). The result is an analytic frame developed to describe (for heuristic purposes) and empirically examine (for research and theory development/testing

---

[20] See E Ostrom, *Governing the Commons: The Evolution of Institutions for Collective Action* (Cambridge, Cambridge University Press, 1990); see also E Schlager and E Ostrom, 'Property-rights Regimes and Natural Resources: A Conceptual Analysis' (1992) 68 *Land Economics* 249. A classic expression of the public choice perspective does not rely on the concept of 'regime,' but implies it in considering American public administration from both a Madisonian and Weberian ('Wilsonian') paradigm; see V Ostrom, *The Intellectual Crisis in American Public Administration*, rev edn (Tuscaloosa, AL, University of Alabama Press, 1974).

[21] Eg R Schmalensee, 'Good Regulatory Regimes' (1989) 20 *Rand Journal of Economics* 417; DL Weisman, 'Superior Regulatory Regimes in Theory and Practice' (1993) 5 *Journal of Regulatory Economics* 355; J Rust and G Rothwell, 'Optimal Response to a Shift in Regulatory Regime: The Case of the US Nuclear Power Industry' (1995) 10 *Journal of Applied Econometrics* S75.

[22] B Jessop, 'Survey Article: The Regulation Approach' (1997) 5 *Journal of Political Philosophy* 287, 288.

[23] The 'regulatory state' concept that reflects this view is found in G Majone, 'From the Positive to the Regulatory State: Causes and Consequences of Changes in the Mode of Governance' (1997) 17 *Journal of Public Policy* 139; G Majone, 'The Regulatory State and Its Legitimacy Problems' (1999) 22 *West European Politics* 1; G Majone, 'Regulation in Comparative Perspective' (1999) 1 *Journal of Comparative Policy Analysis* 309; see also M Moran, 'The Rise of the Regulatory State in Britain' (2001) 54 *Parliamentary Affairs* 19.

[24] See N Rose and P Miller, 'Political Power Beyond the State: Problematics of Government' (1992) 43 *British Journal of Sociology* 173; N Rose, 'Government and Control' (2000) 40 *British Journal of Criminology* 321; NS Rose, *Powers of Freedom: Reframing Political Thought* (Cambridge, Cambridge University Press, 1999).

[25] C Hood, H Rothstein and R Baldwin, *The Government of Risk: Understanding Risk Regulation Regimes* (Oxford, Oxford University Press, 2001).

	Control components:		
	Information gathering	**Standard setting**	**Behaviour modification**
Context: eg type and level of risk being tackled, nature of public media attitudes, configuration of lobbies and organized interests	Example: risks individuals can assess at low cost v risks assessable only by professionals or at high cost	Example: risks involving high stakes for organised groups v risks with no lobby groups	Example: risks where mass public opinion resist state control v regulation 'with the grain'
Content: eg regulatory stance, organisational structure, operating conventions and regulator attitudes	Example: active v passive information-seeking by regulators	Example: cost–benefit v technical feasibility approaches to goal setting	Example: price signals v command approaches to control

Figure 2. HRB's control components and regulatory regime content and context.

purposes)[26] regulatory regimes aimed at risk. In addition, the dimensions used in the framework can be articulated in forms that facilitate at least comparative (if not even more systematic) assessment. As significant, those interested in generating solutions to problems plaguing a particular policy domain can certainly find value in the design elements implied in the HRB analytic scheme.[27]

Within the governance setting there is a second and quite necessary complement to the regulatory regime that fosters a sense of responsibility and obligation among actors in the domain. This accountability regime involves arrangements and 'assemblages'[28] of institutions, norms, values and relationships related to the fact that governance involves more than a web of control components and associated mechanisms; governance is based as much on some normative order—a 'moral community' context or 'accountability space' within which the governed population (of acts and actors) necessarily operates. It is within that regime space that standards of appropriate and ethical behaviour—in very general terms, expectations of responsible behaviour—are established and sustained, and where trust can be nurtured.

---

[26] See C Hood and H Rothstein, 'Risk Regulation under Pressure: Problem Solving or Blame Shifting?' (2001) 33 *Administration & Society* 21.

[27] D Levi-Flaur, 'Regulatory Capitalism: The Dynamics of Change Beyond Telecoms and Electricity' (2006) 19 *Governance* 497.

[28] See S Sassen, 'Neither Global nor National: Novel Assemblages of Territory, Authority and Rights' (2008) 1 *Ethics & Global Politics* 61.

Seen from a domain perspective, governance primarily (but not exclusively)[29] involves both the control of risk and the management of expectations. A governance effort involves both, and an effective ('good') governance effort (which is the assumed goal of policy reform) is one that treats the regimes that address these two functions as complementary.

Applying this two-regime perspective to the current efforts to reform the financial services market, it can be argued that almost all reform efforts have been focused on the regulatory aspects of the general governance problem. In part, this contention reflects the 'blame game' approach that has dominated explanations of what went wrong in the financial sector; in the aftermath of a crisis, when all or most systems have failed or seem in disarray, the regulatory mechanisms (and regulators) provide easy targets for blame gamers. In addition, the concentration on regulatory regime reforms reflects the fact that (re)designing control regimes seems less challenging than designing accountability regimes.

A more fundamental view of the problem is conceptual. The difficulty with designing reforms for the accountability regimes of governance can be traced to our inability to understand and appreciate what this important area of governance entails. In the remainder of this chapter I explore the nature of the accountability regime with the intent of constructing a preliminary framework for the design of reform policies that can offer a more effective approach to solving the governance issues that plague that arena. While the goal is an analytic frame of utility and power equal to the HRB scheme, what follows should be regarded as foundational at best.

D.   Mechanisms and Moral Standards

Despite the drawbacks of following the conventional blame gaming approach to determining the problems of a policy domain in crisis, there are some insights to be gained by examining the resulting political rhetoric and policy responses—especially their common focus on the need for 'greater accountability'.

In the talk about reform, accountability emerges in two very different but interrelated conversations. In one conversation, accountability (or the lack thereof) is being discussed as a key factor in bringing about the 'meltdown' of economic relationships built around the high-flying financial services industry. Accountability, in some form or another, is viewed by the participants as a problem—perhaps the problem—that needs addressing.

The other conversation (occurring almost simultaneously) is focused on solutions rather than problems. The major refrain here—repeated constantly in more rhetorical settings—is the need for 'greater' and 'more' accountability as a (if not the) solution to that very same crisis.

This observation about the role of accountability as both problem and solution—cause and cure—begs for clarification if we are to make some sense of the accountability regime's place and role in governance. What does accountability mean to those engaged in

---

[29] Governance, of course, serves many other purposes. See, eg R Rose, *What Is Governing? Purpose and Policy in Washington* (Englewood Cliffs, NJ, Prentice Hall, 1978); R Rose, 'Models of Governing' (1973) 5 *Comparative Politics* 465; BG Peters, *The Future of Governing: Four Emerging Models* (Lawrence, KS, University Press of Kansas, 1996); BG Peters and J Pierre, 'Governance without Government? Rethinking Public Administration' (1998) 8 *Journal of Public Administration Research and Theory* 223.

these searches for causes and cures, and in what way(s) do various views of accountability impact on our understanding of the financial crisis and/or our responses to it?

Interestingly, the myopic obsession with regulatory control comes into play at this juncture. In discussions dealing with the search for causes of the crisis (ie the 'blame game'), the failure of accountability is typically (if not always) articulated in terms of some specific institutional mechanism or policy instrument failure. The list of suspected culprits ranges from the insufficiency of basic managerial controls and internal corporate governance mechanisms to the lack of transparency and due diligence, the lax enforcement of banking and securities regulations, and the absence of effective oversight of regulators by executive, legislative or judicial officials. Shortcomings abound in all these assessments of the problems—shortcomings in the sense that the regulator or regulated party is just not living up to expectations. Regulatory regime control components overlap with—perhaps are actually embedded in[30]—the accountability regime. Each and all are regarded as part of an accountability infrastructure composed of various tools (eg oversight, audits, inspections, investigations, chains of command) that share a defining characteristic that distinguished them from other control components: each operates by establishing account-giving relationships among at least two parties in an organised effort that addresses the need to deal with unaddressed or unfulfilled expectations.[31]

Viewed narrowly as account-giving mechanisms or instruments, accountability is a means for the management of expectations and takes on the characteristics of a technical feature of the financial marketplace, a functional (often institutionalised) part of the economic, political and social relationships that comprise this sector. It follows that when the focus turns to failures of accountability (that is, these 'mechanisms') as the cause of the current crisis, attention necessarily turns to the absence or breakdown of social relationships and expectations. The 'cure' implied in that analysis most often finds expression in proposals to repair or replace the failed or damaged mechanisms.

However, such mechanisms must be regarded as only part of the accountability regime construct. An alternative dimension of accountability is also at work in the cause/cure discussions, one that regards accountability as playing more of a normative role than a technical one. Here the talk is not about the failure of mechanisms or instruments of account-giving, but rather the failure of more amorphous conditions that foster

---

[30] M Granovetter, 'Economic Institutions as Social Constructions: A Framework for Analysis' (1992) 35 *Acta Sociologica* 3; M Granovetter, 'Economic Action and Social Structure: The Problem of Embeddedness' (1986) 91 *American Journal of Sociology* 481.

[31] The idea of an 'account-giving relationship' demands some clarification at this juncture in regard to four points. The first is to highlight that we are dealing with social relationships, and therefore these have to be understood as fundamentally social mechanisms despite the fact that we often perceive them too narrowly in strictly formal or legalistic terms. Secondly, although frequently associated with the logic of principal-agent relations (especially when operationalised in academic models), such relationships do not necessarily involve hierarchical or super/subordinate arrangements. At least in theory (and, more often than is acknowledged, in practice), account-giving relations can be horizontal as well as vertical, bottom-up as well as top-down—and even circular in form (eg the 'reflective' practitioner). Thirdly, these relationships are based as much (if not more) on expectations as they are in actions. Often it is the anticipation of claims on one's account-giving capacity that determines the effectiveness of an accountability mechanism. Anxiety about who might seek an account, what action one might be held to account for and when one might be called to account—all play major roles in shaping the relevant relationships. For more on this point, see SL Darwall, *The Second-person Standpoint: Morality, Respect, and Accountability* (Cambridge MA, Harvard University Press, 2006). Finally, these account-giving relationships cannot be viewed in isolation from other social relations, including other account-giving claims. The existence of multiple, diverse and potentially conflicting expectations is itself to be expected in the world of accountability mechanisms.

expectation management, such as a moral sense of responsibility, fiduciary obligations, responsiveness and liabilityetc. These reflect the idea of accountability as providing the moral, normative setting for the operation of financial markets. The emphasis here is on the premise that any set of social relationships—especially those involving complex inter-actions and transaction such as those found in global financial markets—requires some commitment to a functional and effective set of expectations in the form of rules, norms and mores. Among those conversing from this perspective, it is the absence or ineffec-tiveness or collapse of these normative (that is, 'moral') standards that is at the heart of the current crisis. The implied 'cure' would be whatever policies might restore or reconstruct that normative infrastructure.[32]

Figure 3 attempts to summarise the implications of this distinction (simplified as accountability-as-mechanism and accountability-as-setting) for the discussions about the causes and cures of the present crisis. The implications of this framework for designing policy responses to the financial crisis will be discussed in the next section, but there are two additional observations that require attention before moving to that point.

First is the extent to which one of the perspectives dominates the most important of the conversations about the financial crisis. Where those conversations really 'matter'—in those venues where policymakers talk about 'causes and cures'—the mechanism per-spective drowns out the normative infrastructure (setting) view. In this and other areas where the issue is the breakdown of an ongoing system, 'technical' explanations usually hold sway, and not necessarily because they are more credible or convincing. Rather, as complements to the regulatory control regime, they tend to be 'easier' to grasp concep-tually and have the benefit of generating relatively quick solutions. If the problem is determined to be lax enforcement of banking regulations, then enhance the enforcement power of regulators and back it with more funding. If the 'problem' is lack of transparency in the operations of hedge funds or private equity firms, then require more reporting and openness. In both examples, there is a clear sense that regulatory control will be enhanced, but only a vague hope for the more responsible behaviour on the part of the regulated parties. Nevertheless, such reforms are proffered as having enhanced accountability.

Perspective:	Focus on:	
	Cause	**Cure**
Accountability-as-mechanism (ie control)	Failure of instrument	Reform, replace, repair the instrument
Accountability-as-setting (ie normative infrastructure)	Absence or collapse of norms, mores, standards	Re-establishing, rebuilding moral community based on effective norms/standards

Figure 3. Accountability as cause/cure.

[32] *Cf* J-E Lane, *Public Sector Reform: Rationale, Trends and Problems* (London, Sage Publications, 1997); also PJ May, 'Regulation and Compliance Motivations: Examining Different Approaches' (2005) 65 *Public Adminis-tration Review* 31; PJ May, 'Regulatory Regimes and Accountability' (2007) 1 *Regulation and Governance* 8.

Whether they actually do have (that is, whether they foster more responsible behaviour) is an empirical question.

This leads to my second point, namely the ironic tendency of policymakers to rely on the rhetoric of accountability in their rhetorical rationalisations for mechanism-focused policy decisions. The justification for undertaking regulatory-based reforms is to create a 'more responsible' market or to make certain actors 'answerable' and 'liable' for their actions. There is an assumed effective link between the exercise of control and the enhancement of responsible behaviour—a link that has rarely been tested in the governance context let alone empirically proved. Each of these rhetorical flourishes at minimum implies the existence of that connection and begs the question about the need for some moral community that provides a normative understanding of what constitutes (ir)responsible and (in)appropriate behaviour.

To summarise briefly, when it comes to accountability regime issues raised by the current financial crisis, (i) there are at least two conversations taking place, one focused on the role of accountability (or lack thereof) in creating the crisis (the 'cause' conversation) and the other positing accountability as a major part of the solution (the 'cure' conversation); (ii) beneath the surface of these conversations are two very different perspectives on accountability, one perspective viewing it as social mechanisms and policy instruments rooted in 'account-giving' relationships (accountability-as-mechanism) and the other seeing accountability as providing the moral setting for the market (accountability-as-normative infrastructure); (iii) among policymakers (the conversations that really matter), the mechanism view prevails as they seek to match control-based technical solutions to technical problems perceived as regulatory; but (iv) the rhetoric of accountability-based reform remains normative-based and is tied to a sense that what is needed is behaviour that is more responsible, responsive, answerable, etc among market actors.

Underlying the present effort is the belief that there is a more substantial case to be made for taking the accountability-as-setting (normative infrastructure) view seriously, not only as part of a more general theory of policy domain governance, but also as the basis for policies that can have a real impact on the future operations of global and national financial markets. Putting that belief to work, however, requires that we develop an HRB-like analytic frame that can do more than help us appreciate the importance of the accountability regime as part of governance. We need a framing that allows us to focus on those elements that comprise the accountability setting in order to facilitate efforts to describe the regime, assess its effectiveness and (where possible) assist in the design of solutions to the broader governance problems.

E.   Articulating Design Options

An effort to emulate the HRB framework for accountability regimes runs into an immediate problem, for the core components of accountability (as imagined here) encompass normative settings as well as 'mechanisms'. While contextual factors play a role in the HRB scheme, they do so as independent or intervening variables affecting the form and content of the core control-components. But, as noted below, in accountability arrangements many aspects of the setting are themselves core components of the regime.

Beyond including those setting factors as core components, our framing should meet two additional, interrelated criteria. First, it should be empirically inclusive and capable of encompassing the range of actionable options that are proposed to deal with the problematic conditions 'greater accountability' is intended to address. Secondly, the options it includes should be problem relevant and expressly aimed at dealing with the causes and/or conditions of the problematic situation. Excluded under this framing scheme would be pseudo-proposals that amount to mere symbolic expressions of the need for reforms and those designed to solve problems outside the scope of policy problems. While symbolic gestures such as a rhetorical call for making the financial system more accountable may serve important political purposes (eg for the mobilisation or acquiescence of publics),[33] they would fall outside our frame unless accompanied by some articulated agenda for reform. Similarly, options aimed at more fundamental changes (eg changing human nature or radically altering the general economic system) would be outside the scope of the framing, given its 'practical' focus.

There are two major efforts to frame accountability regimes, the first relating to reforms that reshape the context and conduct of accounting, auditing and other financial management operations,[34] and the second (more recent) examining the increasingly complex arena of nonprofits operating in a global context.[35] Almost all treat accountability as a variant of regulation and control, and not surprisingly are preoccupied with viewing it in 'mechanism' terms. As such, they fail to stress the distinction between the different roles that such mechanisms play in regimes of control and regimes of managed expectations (that is, responsibility). The task here is to construct a framework that stresses that distinction.[36]

Turning specifically to the core components of the accountability regime, the range of options for 'greater accountability' reforms can be usefully framed by focusing on two common features of most proposals: (i) the extent to which they seek to specify the activity and actions of those being held accountable; and (ii) the degree to which the accountable agent is given some degree of discretion to act (ie autonomy).

[33] M Edelman, *The Symbolic Uses of Politics* (Urbana, IL, University of Illinois Press, 1964); M Edelman, *Politics as Symbolic Action: Mass Arousal and Quiescence* (Chicago, IL, Markham Publishing, 1971)

[34] The major work in this area is attributable to James Guthrie and Linda English at the University of Sydney. See L English and J Guthrie, 'Public Sector Auditing: A Case of Contested Accountability Regimes' (1991) 50 *Australian Journal of Public Administration* 347; J Guthrie, 'Critical Issues in Public Sector Auditing' (1992) 7(4) *Managerial Auditing Journal* 27; J Guthrie, 'Australian Public Business Enterprises: Analysis of Changing Accounting, Auditing and Accountability Regimes' (1993) 9 *Financial Accountability and Management* 101; LD Parker and J Guthrie, 'The Australian Public Sector in the 1990s: New Accountability Regimes in Motion' (1993) 2 *Journal of International Accounting, Auditing and Taxation* 59; see also J Broadbent and J Guthrie, 'Changes in the Public Sector: A Review of Recent 'Alternative' Accounting Research' (1992) 5(2) *Accounting, Auditing and Accountability Journal* 3.

[35] See the work of Alnoor Ebrahim and his colleagues: A Ebrahim, 'Making Sense of Accountability: Conceptual Perspectives for Northern and Southern Nonprofits' (2003) 14 *Nonprofit Management and Leadership* 191; A Ebrahim, 'Accountability in Practice: Mechanisms for NGOs' (2003) 31 *World Development* 813; A Ebrahim and S Heerz, ;Accountability in Complex Organizations: World Bank Responses to Civil Society;, KSG Working Paper No RWP 07-060 (John F Kennedy School of Government, Harvard University, 2008), available at papers.ssrn.com/sol3/papers.cfm?abstract_id=963135; A Ebrahim, 'Placing the Normative Logics of Accountability In "Thick" Perspective' (2009) 52 *American Behavioural Scientist* 885. See also L Jordan and PV Tuijl (eds), *NGO Accountability: Politics, Principles and Innovations* (Sterling, VA, Earthscan, 2006); A Ebrahim and E Weisband (eds), *Global Accountabilities: Participation, Pluralism, and Public Ethics* (New York, Cambridge University Press, 2007).

[36] Cf JL Mashaw, 'Accountability and Institutional Design: Some Thoughts on the Grammar of Governance' in MD Dowdle (ed), *Public Accountability : Designs, Dilemmas and Experiences* (Cambridge, Cambridge University Press, 2006).

		Specificity of accountable activity	
		Low	High
Autonomy of accountable agent	High	*Constitutive* Creation of 'accountable space' of internalised norms and standards	*Managerial* Set 'what' agent is accountable for (objective or standard), allow agent to determine 'how'
	Low	*Regulative* Creation and externalised oversight of actions of agent within 'accountable space'	*Performative* Set 'what' agent is accountable for and 'how' to proceed

Figure 4. Accountability regime's core component types.

Of the four resulting core component types, the performative accountability reforms are the most closely associated with the accountability-as-mechanism perspective. Here the assumption is that greater accountability requires the specification of certain actions and behaviours which are to be mandated and enforced, typically by a governing authority outside the organisation. These reforms stress the control functions of accountability, and they are not uncommon in the banking industry. They are so pervasive, in fact, that many view them as the very definition of accountability. Nevertheless, what differentiates these account-giving performatives from controls is the underlying intent that the performance (conducting an audit, publishing the results, etc) will lead to responsible behaviour. Here there is an implied link between a required behaviour and the sense of responsibility that it is assumed to generate or awaken in the target population. The strength of this assumed link is very high, and therefore clearly stated and strictly enforced reporting requirements by a variety of regulatory and other oversight agencies are regarded as part of the necessary infrastructure for conducting business in many of the world's jurisdictions.[37]

Reforms based on the logic of managerial accountability differ from the performative in allowing greater discretion to the accountable agent while at the same time holding it accountable to meeting a specified objective or standard. Reflecting the growing cultural acceptance of managerialism,[38] it is based on the assumption[39] that those 'professionals'

---

[37] R Ball, 'Infrastructure Requirements for an Economically Efficient System of Public Financial Reporting and Disclosure', Brookings–Wharton Papers on Financial Services No 1 (Washington, DC, Brookings Institution, 2001).

[38] The logic of this approach in the corporate world was first described by Berle and Means when they presented their classic exposition of the transformation of the modern corporation into a professionally managed organisation. 'A management may well insist on as free a managerial hand as possible as to how it shall run its business,' they observed. 'Nor has anyone grudged managements this group of powers, not only in law but in ideology. No better principle in carrying on business has yet been worked out than to find able men and give them the completest latitude possible in handling the enterprise': AA Berle and GC Means, *The Modern Corporation and Private Property* (New Brunswick, NJ, Transaction Publishers, 1932) 60. See also ES Mason, 'The Apologetics Of 'Managerialism'' (1958) 31 *Journal of Business* 1; LE Preston and JE Post, 'The Third Managerial Revolution' (1974) 17 *Academy of Management Journal* 476; P Miller and T O'Leary, 'Hierarchies and American Ideals, 1900-1940' (1989) 14 *Academy of Management Review* 250.

[39] Although this assumption originated in the private sector, it has been critically examined most often with public sector contexts. On the private history of managerialism, the classics are J Burnham, *The Managerial*

who operate regulated organisations are by definition (after all, they are professionals) predisposed to responsible behaviour once provided with guidance regarding the ends to be achieved. A law or regulatory body might require, for example, that a bank chartered to operate within a state or community commit at least *x* per cent of its loan portfolio to local businesses or individuals. The standard for conducting business is set, but how they go about doing so is left to the bank and its management. This form of accountability assumes that those professionals who manage the financial institution will act, as Berle argued in 1932, 'more as princes and ministers than as promoters or merchants'.[40]

While the mechanism perspective characterises both performative and managerial accountability approaches, the regulative and constitutive forms rely more on what can be termed an 'accountable space' perspective. Here accountability is viewed more as a general context or setting—what Bourdieu terms a 'field'[41]—within which relationships occur rather than as a specific relationship per se. These accountable spaces can be characterised by both their structure and substance.

Structurally, they exist as arrangements within parameters set by a range of normative constraints in the form of general roles and rules that shape the relationships that take place within that space.[42] Constitutive accountability reforms[43] focus on the establishment and adjustment of those parameters, effectively constituting (or reconstituting, as the case may be) the environment within which accountable behaviour occurs. Again, we find these types of reforms to be familiar in the financial markets. The roles and rules required by accountability 'regimes' for financial institutions vary depending on the 'constitutional

Revolution (Bloomington IN, Indiana University Press, 1960) and AD Chandler Jr, *The Visible Hand: The Managerial Revolution in American Business* (Cambridge MA, Belknap Press of the Harvard University Press, 1977). The classic expression of a positive view of public sector managerialism was found in CJ Friedrich, 'Public Policy and the Nature of Administrative Responsibility' in CJ Friedrich and ES Mason (eds), *Public Policy: A Yearbook of the Graduate School of Public Administration of Public Administration, Harvard University* (Cambridge MA, Harvard University Press, 1940). The recent new public management reforms that took root in New Zealand, Australia, the UK and Canada had a strong managerial accountability component; see C Pollitt, *Managerialism and the Public Services: Cuts or Cultural Change in the 1990s?*, 2nd edn (Oxford, Blackwell Business, 1993); C Pollitt and G Bouckaert, *Public Management Reform: A Comparative Analysis* (Oxford, Oxford University Press, 2000), A Cochrane, 'From Financial Control to Strategic Management: The Changing Faces of Accountability in British Local Government' (1993) 6 *Accounting, Auditing and Accountability Journal* 30; C Campbell, 'Does Reinvention Need Reinvention? Lessons from Truncated Managerialism in Britain' (1995) 8 *Governance* 479; C Hood, 'Public Service Managerialism: Onwards and Upwards, or "Trobriand Cricket" Again?' (2001) 72 *Political Quarterly* 300.

[40] AA Berle Jr, 'For Whom Corporate Managers Are Trustees: A Note' (1932) 45 *Harvard Law Review* 1365, 1366–67. In the same publication (1377) he offers the following: 'Most students of corporation finance dream of a time when corporate administration will be held to a high degree of required responsibility—a responsibility conceived not merely in terms of stockholders' rights, but in terms of economic government satisfying the respective needs of investors, workers, customers, and the aggregated community. Indications, indeed, are not wanting that without such readjustment the corporate system will involve itself in successive cataclysms perhaps leading to its ultimate downfall.'

[41] P Bourdieu, 'The Social Space and the Genesis of Groups' (1985) 14 *Theory and Society* 723; P Bourdieu and LJD Wacquant, *An Invitation to Reflexive Sociology* (Chicago, IL, University of Chicago Press, 1992).

[42] N Fligstein, *The Architecture of Markets: An Economic Sociology of Twenty-First-Century Capitalist Societies* (Princeton, NJ, Princeton University Press, 2001), esp ch 4; see also A Preda, *Framing Finance: The Boundaries of Markets and Modern Capitalism* (Chicago, IL, University of Chicago Press, 2009); GF Davis, *Managed by the Markets: How Finance Reshaped America* (New York, Oxford University Press, 2009).

[43] Perhaps the most relevant and useful approaches to analysing these types of reform is found in the work of Elinor Ostrom and her colleagues, whose work has focused on solutions to the common pool resource problem. See E Ostrom, *Understanding Institutional Diversity* (Princeton, NJ, Princeton University Press, 2005); T Dietz, E Ostrom and PC Stern, 'The Struggle to Govern the Commons' (2003) 302 *Science* 1907; Ostrom, *Governing the Commons*, above n 20.

setting' within which they operate. With both deregulation and liberalisation of banking laws over the past several decades, the number of such settings has multiplied. This has created opportunities for banks to 'shop around' for what they regard as more suitable accountability regimes both domestically and globally.

Regulative accountability comes into play when the substance of those roles and rules is determined to call for the active monitoring and oversight of an accountable agent. The logic is drawn from the regulatory regime, but the design premise is different. The assumption here is that the target population will be more 'responsible' in exercising discretionary behaviour knowing that there is a regulatory agent overseeing what is taking place in the accountability space. Parker uses the term 'responsive regulation' to capture this approach:

> Simple deterrence will often fail to produce compliance commitment because it does not directly address business perceptions of the morality of regulated behaviour—it merely puts a price on noncompliance, and the ability of that price to deter misconduct will depend on the operation of the deterrence trap. Responsive regulation, by contrast, seeks to build moral commitment to compliance with the law.[44]

For example, the proposal to establish a consumer protection agency with jurisdiction over credit products is in part designed to enforce 'control' provisions of the law. However, the agency is also intended well to monitor complaints about credit providers from consumers and even rate card services, thereby giving the financial institutions reason to consider a more responsible ('customer friendly') approach to doing business.

As the core components of accountability regimes, each of these stresses the need to establish and foster responsibility (that is, expectations management) over the demand for control. Even the form that comes the closest to a control mechanism—performative accountability—differs in purpose (if not in content) from the behaviour modification mechanisms represented in the HRB frame. Consider, for example, the requirement in section 302 of the 2002 Sarbanes-Oxley Act[45] that corporate CEOs and CFOs attach their signatures to mandated audit reports that essentially certifies the 'appropriateness of the financial statements and disclosures contained in the periodic report, and that those financial statements and disclosures fairly present, in all material respects, the operations and financial condition of the issuer'. Contrast that requirement with a provision in section 401 that specifies the 'annual and quarterly financial report . . . shall disclose all material off-balance sheet transactions' and 'other relationships' with entities that can materially have an impact on the financial condition of the issuer. The latter is an explicit instruction seeking a behavioural change, while the former is at best an indirect attempt to foster a more responsible approach to the way corporate executives do their jobs.

Of course, that type of distinction is often blurred by the fact that the two regimes overlap in the overall scheme of governance. Recently imposed provisions to control compensation received by executives in US banks that received 'bailout' funding from the TARP can be regarded as driven by both regulatory and accountability drivers. The regulatory aspects stress a combination of both standard setting and behaviour

---

[44] C Parker, 'The "Compliance" Trap: The Moral Message in Responsive Regulatory Enforcement' (2006) 40 *Law & Society Review* 591, 592; see also I Ayres and J Braithwaite, *Responsive Regulation: Transcending the Deregulation Debate* (New York, Oxford University Press, 1992).

[45] For an examination of the role of accountability in provisions of Sarbanes-Oxley, see MJ Dubnick, 'Sarbanes-Oxley and the Search for Accountable Corporate Governance' in J O'Brien (ed), *Private Equity, Corporate Governance and the Dynamics of Capital Market Regulation* (London, Imperial College Press, 2007).

modification by the subject firms, but implied in the action is the message that those executives who are assumed to have played a role in the policy-precipitating crisis need to learn their lesson and act more responsibly in the future.[46]

With the core components of the accountability regime established, and continuing in the attempt to emulate the HRB approach, we now turn to those factors that lead to variations in accountability regimes across and within policy domains. As reflected in Figure 5, there are three likely sources that determine such variation: content, context and conditions.

Regarding content, as conceptualised here, accountability regimes are primarily about the management of expectations, thus making variations of expectations extremely important in the description, assessment and design (and reform) of domain governance. Approaching expectations analytically is no simple task,[47] given its sometimes implicit nature. For example, while it might be possible to articulate some legal requirements and general standards of behaviour that we expect from domain actors (eg that they perform their tasks with 'due diligence'), there is also a more general, often unarticulated sense of 'responsible' and 'appropriate' behaviour that plays an important role in accountability regimes.[48] For present purposes, those more amorphous standards can be shifted to the 'context' factor category, leaving 'content' to reflect expectations that have an explicit presence in the regime.

Having put aside the unarticulated expectations, getting a useful analytic handle on the expectations content of accountability regimes is still quite challenging. Expectations can vary from very specific requirements, often laid out in laws and regulations, to those such as due diligence and fiduciary that involve very general standards (with real consequences for actions) applied from case to case. Beyond their specificity, other dimensions of expectations that come into consideration include (in no particular order):

	Performative	Managerial	Regulative	Constitutive
Content				
Context				
Conditions				

Figure 5. Framing the accountability regime.

---

[46] There is a sense of collective indignation and retribution also associated with those efforts.

[47] Eg MJ Dubnick and BS Romzek, 'Accountability and the Centrality of Expectations in American Public Administration' in JL Perry (ed) *Research in Public Administration* (Greenwich, CT, JAI Press, 1993).

[48] The 'logic of appropriateness' factor in choice is likely to play a significant role in the further development of this scheme; see JG March and JP Olsen, 'The Logic of Appropriateness', ARENA Working Papers WP 04/September (2004) 28, reprinted in M Moran, M Rein and RE Goodin (eds), *Oxford Handbook of Public Policy* (Oxford, Oxford University Press, 2006); JG March and JP Olsen, *Democratic Governance* (New York, Free Press, 1995).

— the scope of their coverage: for example, does the expectation for transparency apply to all behaviour within the domain or are some (for example, proprietary information) exempted?

— the distribution of expectations within the domain: does it apply to the entire population of targeted actors in a domain (eg all commercial banks) or only to those that are 'too big to fail'?

— the salience of a given expectation or set of expectations within the domain: just how important is the standard among the range of expectations applied in the domain?

— the stability of the expectation over time: is the standard expressed in an expectation going to endure over time, or does it shift from circumstance to circumstance—and, if so, is there a pattern to that 'shifting'?

— the source(s) of the expectation or standard: does it emerge from within the domain or is it imposed from outside, etc?

— the purpose or intended function of the expectation: is it regarded as a means for promoting integrity and trust among domain actors or is it focused on enhancing the efficiency or fairness of domain actor actions?

While not exhaustive, this list of content factors indicates how complicated accountability regimes can be—and how challenging the design task is likely to be as well. The situation is complicated further by the fact that context matters as much as content when it comes to accountability. For present purposes, we will differentiate between the more general (that is, background) context from the immediate circumstances having an impact on the operations of the regime (see the discussion of 'conditions' that follows).

There are a number of relevant analytic approaches to the context of accountability regimes that can be applied for this framing project. The 'group-grid matrix' typology developed initially by Mary Douglas and extended by Aaron Wildavsky and others[49] highlights the variation in expectations that emerges from five cultural orientations that emerge from differences along two dimensions: the extent to which one perceives the world from a vantage point that stresses a collective (high group) or individual (low group) approach to problems, and the extent to which one regards oneself as constrained (high grid) or allowed discretion to act (low grid) by the demands of society. The four major types of actors that emerge from this framework relate to expectations differently, ranging from the egalitarian, whose expectations are shaped by a strong identity with group values and a high sense of efficacy, to the fatalist, whose expectations are neither coherently organised nor actively pursued. Between the two extremes are the cultures of the market (individualist) and the organisation (hierarchist).

Alternatively, Pierre Boudieu's view of social contexts as 'fields' of often competing 'forces' can provide significant insights into the factors that shape expectations and shape/drive the accountability regime. In his examination of economic markets, for

---

[49] M Douglas, *Risk and Blame: Essays in Cultural Theory* (London, Routledge, 1992); M Douglas, 'Four Cultures: The Evolution of a Parsimonious Model' (1999) 47 *Geojournal* 411; RJ Ellis and M Thompson (eds), *Culture Matters: Essays in Honor of Aaron Wildavsky* (Boulder CO, Westview Press, 1997); A Wildavsky, 'Cultural Theory of Responsibility' in J-E Lane (ed), *Bureaucracy and Public Choice* (London, Sage, 1987); A Wildavsky, 'A Cultural Theory of Budgeting' (1988) 11 *International Journal of Public Administration* 651; A Wildavsky, 'A Cultural Theory of Leadership' in B Swedlow (ed), *Cultural Analysis. Volume 1. Politics, Public Law and Administration* (New Brunswick NJ, Transaction, 2006); see also C Hood, *The Art of the State: Culture, Rhetoric, and Public Management* (Oxford, Clarendon Press, 1998). For an excellent overview, see V Mamadouh, 'Grid-group Cultural Theory: An Introduction' (1999) 47 *Geojournal* 395.

example, he attributes the decisions of various actors to their 'positions' within the fields as well as their 'dispositions' (which he often terms 'tastes', but which can be treated as expectations) related to the choices and options before them.[50]

Which of these (or other)[51] models of context variations will prove most useful within this regime framework awaits further exploration. What needs to be emphasised is that any framework for designing financial market reforms must take into account the variability of accountability regimes across different cultures.

The same holds true for 'conditional' factors—the more immediate political, economic and social circumstances—in which reforms would be implemented. The HRB framing of regulatory regime context is relevant here. Among the factors they highlight are three major sources of 'pressure' at work within risk regulation regimes: market-failure pressures, which generate demands for pre-emptive or corrective policies; opinion-response pressures emanating from the general public; and interest-driven pressures, which reflect stakeholder demands.[52] In addition, the current forms and styles of policy-making styles in different countries are an essential set of factors that require attention.[53]

Of course, what is provided here is merely a preliminary framing that requires further elaboration and application to current accountability regimes. Only through enhancing our capacity to describe the elements of accountability regimes can the design of effective reforms progress to the next stage.

F.   Working on Design Principles

That 'next stage' is a critical one, for, having established the conceptual foundations for understanding the design of governance and its associated regimes, we face the task of articulating design principles that can guide the policy reform effort. Some of those principles are already implied in the governance approach and regime frameworks themselves, but others require further articulation and testing before they can prove useful.

The very idea of 'design' used here is both analogical and metaphorical. Analogically, we are engaged in a process not unlike that undertaken by designers in a number of fields—from the artist and craftsperson to the architect and engineer. For them, as for us, the task is to develop a plan for putting the material and nonmaterial elements at our

---

[50] P Bourdieu, *Outline of a Theory of Practice* (Cambridge, Cambridge University Press, 1977); Bourdieu, above n 41; P Bourdieu, *The Logic of Practice* (Stanford CA, Stanford University Press, 1990); Bourdieu, above n 13.

[51] Eg Y Wiener, 'Forms of Value Systems: A Focus on Organizational Effectiveness and Cultural Change and Maintenance' (1988) 13 *Academy of Management Review* 534; G Hofstede, 'The Cultural Relativity of Organizational Practices and Theories' (1983) 14(2) *Journal of International Business Studies* 75; G Hofstede, 'Cultural Constraints in Management Theories' (1993) 7 *Academy of Management Executive* 81; G Hofstede, 'Attitudes, Values and Organizational Culture: Disentangling the Concepts' (1998) 19 *Organization Studies* 477; MJ Dubnick, 'Public Service Ethics and the Cultures of Blame', Fifth International Conference of Ethics in the Public Service, Brisbane, Australia (1996).

[52] Hood et al, above n 25, 61–67.

[53] RE Löfstedtand and D Vogel, 'The Changing Character of Regulation: A Comparison of Europe and the United States' (2001) 21 *Risk Analysis* 399, especially the contribution by Renn.

disposal to work to achieve some preconceived 'notion' in the form of a sculpture, product, house or bridge. Our notions take the form of public policies.

'Policies are the first expressions and guiding images of normative thinking and action,' noted Eric Jantsch. 'In other words, they are the spiritual agents of change—change not only in the ways and means by which bureaucracies and technocracies operate, but change in the very institutions and norms which form their homes and castles.'[54] In that sense, design is an appropriate metaphor for the creative act—the development of 'spiritual agents of change'—that the process involves. This is captured by the very concept of policy analysis as a 'design science',[55] which seems oxymoronic at first. What bridges the art and science are those principles that guide the design project.

For present purposes, design principles are of three types: logical, conceptual and strategic. The principles related to the logic of policy reform are reflected in the governance perspective offered earlier in this chapter. Reform of a policy domain such as the financial markets can be approached through a variety of logics, each reflecting a general theoretical perspective that might be regarded as little more than a particular (albeit more structured and formalised) view of some participants in the blame game.[56] From economists we have a plethora of such logics (for example, drawn from basic market failure[57] and rational expectation theories[58] to those stressing more popular insights regarding 'animal spirits'[59] and irrational exuberance[60]). From the world of political science emerges the logic of various 'regulatory capture' and other 'government failure' theories.[61] The perspective offered here focuses on the notions of governance (mostly drawn from the study of public management reform) and regimes (from the study of international organisations), but also relies on the work of economic sociologists and critical theorists who emphasise the importance of governmentality (from the work of Michel Foucault)[62] and embeddedness (initially articulated by Karl Polanyi).[63]

---

[54] E Jantsch, 'From Forecasting and Planning to Policy Sciences' (1970) 1 *Policy Sciences* 31, 32.

[55] HD Lasswell, 'The Emerging Conception of the Policy Sciences' (1970) 1 *Policy Sciences* 3; Dror, above n 7.

[56] Cf PC Light, *The Tides of Reform: Making Government Work, 1945–1995* (New Haven, CT, Yale University Press, 1997).

[57] FM Bator, 'The Anatomy of Market Failure' (1958) 72 *The Quarterly Journal of Economics* 351; JR Davis and JR Hulett, *An Analysis of Market Failure: Externalities, Public Goods, and Mixed Goods* (Gainesville, FL, University Presses of Florida, 1977); however, see RO Zerbe Jr and HE McCurdy, 'The Failure of Market Failure' (1999) 18 *Journal of Policy Analysis and Management* 558; RO Zerbe Jr and H McCurdy, 'The End of Market Failure' (2000) 23(2) *Regulation* 10.

[58] JF Muth, 'Rational Expectations and the Theory of Price Movements' (1961) 29 *Econometrica* 315; G Corsetti, P Pesenti and N Roubini, 'Paper Tigers?: A Model of the Asian Crisis' (1999) 43 *European Economic Review* 1211.

[59] GA Akerlof and RJ Shiller, *Animal Spirits: How Human Psychology Drives the Economy, and Why It Matters for Global Capitalism* (Princeton, NJ, Princeton University Press, 2009).

[60] RJ Shiller, *Irrational Exuberance*, 2nd edn (Princeton, NJ, Princeton University Press, 2005).

[61] BM Mitnick, *The Political Economy of Regulation: Creating, Designing, and Removing Regulatory Forms* (New York, Columbia University Press, 1980); J Le Grand, 'The Theory of Government Failure' (1991) 21 *British Journal of Political Science* 423; G Tullock, A Seldon and GL Brady, *Government Failure: A Primer in Public Choice* (Washington DC, Cato Institute, 2002).

[62] G Burchell, C Gordon and P Miller (eds), *The Foucault Effect: Studies in Governmentality: With Two Lectures by and an Interview with Michel Foucault* (Chicago, IL, University of Chicago Press, 1991); M Foucault, 'Governmentality' in G Burchell, C Gordon and P Miller (eds), *The Foucault Effect: Studies in Governmentality: With Two Lectures by and an Interview with Michel Foucault* (Chicago, IL, University of Chicago Press, 1991); M Bevir, 'Foucault, Power, and Institutions' (1999) 47 *Political Studies* 345; Rose (1999), above n 24; OJ Sending and IB Neumann, 'Governance to Governmentality: Analyzing NGOs, States, and Power' (2006) 50 *International Studies Quarterly* 651.

[63] K Polanyi, *The Great Transformation: The Political and Economic Origins of Our Time* (Boston, MA, Beacon Press, 1944). A considerable body of work—some previously cited—has been constructed around the notion of

Although the logic of governance reform was generally touched upon here, much of this chapter has been explicitly devoted to dealing with the conceptual 'principles' that emerged from the framing of the regimes. By positing an alternative conceptualisation of accountability as a regime, I am (by implication) offering a normative reordering of what constitutes the operations of governance of (and through) responsible action within the policy domain.

Despite seeming more like firm directives, the strategic aspects of policy design principles are perhaps best regarded as working hypotheses—ideally in the form of testable assumptions—that attempt to apply the logic and conceptual elements of the reform effort to the problematic domain. Design principles applicable exclusively to the regulatory regime have been presented in a variety of forms depending on the goal of the presenter. For some it is a matter of designing policies that are more likely to pass muster with policymakers. The guidance they offer is addressed to the rule-designing staff of regulatory agencies and is typically more oriented to meeting political requirements than to developing effective solutions to governance problems. For them, the design principles include

— clarity and precision of legislation;
— adherence to the general objects and spirit of the empowering legislation;
— not unduly trespassing on personal rights and liberties;
— not reversing the onus of proof in criminal proceedings; and
— ensuring protection from self-incrimination.[64]

Policy analysts who take a less politically sensitive approach to regulatory design typically work within some variation of the following principles:

— setting down different types of 'regulation';
— considering if and when governments should regulate;
— deciding what forms of government action might best be adopted; and
— examining features that characterise poor or ineffective regulation.[65]

More common among economists who approach the design problem as policy analysis but with a focus on what will work for the regulated (as opposed to the politicos) are principles similar to the following offered by Sappington for designing 'incentive'-based regulations:

1. Use incentive regulation to employ the firm's superior information better.
2. Prioritise regulatory goals and design incentive regulation to achieve stated goals.
3. Link the firm's compensation to sensitive measures of its unobserved activities.
4. Avoid basing the firm's compensation on performance measures with excessive variability.
5. Limit the firm's financial responsibility for factors beyond its control.

embeddedness; see Granovetter (1986), above n 30; JK Frenzen and HL Davis, 'Purchasing Behaviour in Embedded Markets' (1990) 17 *Journal of Consumer Research* 1; Granovetter (1992), above n 30; J Lie, 'Sociology of Markets' (1997) 23 *Annual Review of Sociology* 341; GR Krippner, 'The Elusive Market: Embeddedness and the Paradigm of Economic Sociology' (2001) 30 *Theory and Society* 775; G Krippnerand et al, 'Polanyi Symposium: A Conversation on Embeddedness' (2004) 2 *Socio-Economic Review* 109.

[64] P Coghlan, 'The Principles of Good Regulation' in A Sidorenko and CC Findlay (eds), *Regulation and Market Access* (Canberra, Asia Pacific Press, 2003) 16.
[65] Ibid.

6. Adopt broad-based performance measures where possible, unless their variability is excessive.

7. Choose exogenous performance benchmarks.

8. Allow the firm to choose among regulatory options, while recognising the interdependencies among the regulatory options that are offered to the firm.

9. Promise only what can be delivered, and deliver whatever is promised.

10. Plan for the rare, unforeseen event, but minimise after-the-fact adjustments to the announced regulatory policy.[66]

Proffered as advice to policymakers, these design principles are stated in simple terms, but underlying them are difficult challenges reflecting the complex combination of logics, concepts and strategic norms. Some of these principles can be translated and transposed to the task of formulating policy options to change the accountability regime, but not without some conceptual and theoretical costs. Care must be taken in developing design principles relevant to the reform of accountability.

While this project is not at the stage where design principles can be summarised pithily in short bullet point statements or sentences, some basic points have emerged that are indicative of the kinds of principles which are likely to emerge. Here are offered three examples:

Example 1: Reforms of global financial markets must address problems of governance within and across relevant policy domains.

This principle can easily be transformed into a question: does the proposed policy address governance problems associated with the challenges of control and responsibility? The importance and necessity of this principle becomes obvious at a number of points. It is not uncommon for those engaged in the policy design process to find themselves enthralled with a particular policy approach or instrument to the point that he or she might lose sight of the policy objective. It is also within the nature of the policy-making and policy-legitimation processes that compromises intended to guarantee passage can effectively divert or replace key elements of the reform proposal. A demand for greater discretion by the target population might be necessary for getting the policy adopted, but the policy should be designed to prevent that provision from emasculating the reform effort. Critics of both the recent bank bailouts and the economic stimulus packages have noted the conflicts and flaws that emerged over time with both policies, but that is to be expected of such emergency measures. However, in a highly fragmented policy-making system such as the US, where partisan divides remain strong, adhering to this design principle is likely to prove difficult at best.

Example 2: Governance involves two interrelated functions: establishing control and facilitating responsible action within the policy domain. The efforts made to fulfil both functions are manifest in governance regimes. The operations of the two regimes should be regarded as complementary.

This principle combines logical, conceptual and strategic guidance. The 'bottom line' is highlighting the complementarity of the two regimes. This point emerges from the lessons of more myopic governance reforms in financial markets over the past three decades

---

[66] DEM Sappington, 'Designing Incentive Regulation' (1992) 9 *Review of Industrial Organization* 245, 269.

which, in turn, can be related to the current crisis. From the early 1980s, banking reforms in the US and abroad have been characterised as 'deregulatory' when seen from the narrow perspective of the regulation regime side of governance. The term 'deregulation' is, in fact, a misnomer,[67] for what occurred was a reform of the governance arrangements under which banks operated. What took place has been more appropriately termed a 'liberalisation' and/or harmonisation of the regulatory regime that governed the financial sector.[68] The results were a slow but thorough loosening of the control features of domestic, transnational and international regulatory regimes.

Under the governance perspective offered here, one can argue that the lack of complementary adjustments in relevant accountability regimes has proven central to creating the current depression. Good governance does not necessarily require an optimal balance between control and responsibility, but too great a gap between the two regimes created by ill-advised reforms can certainly generate systematic dysfunctions similar to those we now endure.

Example 3: The values guiding the two regimes can differ. While regulatory control has primarily instrumental value, the facilitation of responsibility fostered by the accountability regime can have both instrumental and intrinsic value.

There are cases where the exercise of control over the financial sector has been undertaken for purposes other than the need for more effective governance of that domain, but rarely is regulatory control assumed to hold some intrinsic value. Expropriation of banks for the purpose of fulfilling an ideological or nationalistic programme[69] notwithstanding, regulatory regime actions should be described and assessed according to their instrumental value.

In contrast, while accountability regimes serve instrumental purposes, their role in governance may be for intrinsic value. Thus, a policy that seemingly has no substantial instrumental value at all, such as the required restrictions on executive pay, plays a role in enhancing the public perception of a more accountable banking sector, and therefore indirectly achieves an objective of governance reform, such as increasing confidence in the banking sector. Or consider the value of policies insuring bank deposits, which play an instrumental role in the regulatory regime as a means for assuring bank solvency while being valued for enhancing accountability and an accompanying sense of bank security and integrity. While critics of the policy note moral hazards created by the insurance (and

[67] Similarly, the term 're-regulation' would not suffice since it implies a deregulation effort preceding it.
[68] GRD Underhill, 'Markets Beyond Politics? The State and the Internationalisation of Financial Markets' (1991) 19 *European Journal of Political Research* 197; S Claessens, GRD Underhill and X Zhang, 'The Political Economy of Basle II: The Costs for Poor Countries' (2008) 31 *World Economy* 313; GRD Underhill and X Zhang, 'Setting the Rules: Private Power, Political Underpinnings, and Legitimacy in Global Monetary and Financial Governance' (2008) 84 *International Affairs* 535; BA Simmons, 'The International Politics of Harmonization: The Case of Capital Market Regulation' (2001) 55 *International Organization* 589; EJ Pan, 'Harmonization of US–EU Securities Regulation: The Case for a Single European Securities Regulator' (2003) 34 *Law and Policy in International Business* 499; G Majone, 'Liberalization, Re-regulation, and Mutual Recognition: Lessons from Three Decades of EU Experience', Second Biennial Conference of the European Consortium for Political Research, Standing Group on Regulatory Governance, Utrecht, 5–7 June 2008; A Abiad and A Mody, 'Financial Reform: What Shakes It? What Shapes It?' (2005) 95 *American Economic Review* 66; M Giannetti, 'Financial Liberalization and Banking Crises: The Role of Capital Inflows and Lack of Transparency' (2007) 16 *Journal of Financial Intermediation* 32.
[69] MC Lewis, 'International Bank Expropriations: The Need for a Level Playing Field' (1985) 4 *Annual Review of Banking Law* 237; L Trotsky, *The Transitional Program* (London, Workers' Revolutionary Party, 1938).

thus question its instrumental value),[70] their concerns are determined to be more than offset by the benefits generated by the assumed enhancement of integrity fostered by responsible behaviour of the insured bank.

G.   Concluding Comments

The task that initiated this project was to address the current financial crisis as a policy design problem, and the intent was to develop some reasoned and reasonable paths to reform. 'What is to be done?' is the question of the hour, and most responses have unfortunately relied on the usual bag of policy tricks that many regard as merely spot repairs that will keep the system going for long enough to get to the next crisis. As noted earlier, it is a good example of the 'garbage can model' at work: streams of problems, policy solutions and political demands converge at some point and some form of policy emerges from the mix. At times we get lucky and the process works—producing policies that satisfy our needs for at least a short-term resolution. If we are really fortunate, that solution sticks for an extended period.

That seems to be the situation we face at the moment concerning reform of the financial services market. At present, policymakers are relying on the advice given by analysts who specialise in policy repairs and quick fixes rather than policy design. The reasons are many, but they certainly include significant time pressures as well as the dynamics of the blame game, which offers up all sorts of targets for so-called reform policies.

To engage in a more substantial policy design effort under crisis conditions might be regarded as a waste of time and energy. Significant policy design requires a critical rethinking of how we approach the collapse of the financial markets, the subsequent damage it caused to economic stability and the possibility of economic growth. In the earliest stages of the design effort, description and theorising about the problem take priority over when the primary goal is to establish an understanding of the domain and its problems. At this point, it is difficult to pull back from the demands for more than mere analysis. Richard Posner, the polymath who combines his full-time position as a major American jurist with his work as a well-known public intellectual, published a careful and thoughtful examination of the crisis in the spring of 2009 and maintained an ongoing discussion of his views on a widely read blog.[71] Pushed to suggest long-term solutions, he steadfastly refused, noting that it is too early to make suggestions that match his assessment that there is something fundamentally wrong with the US economy. He is, in that sense, the model policy designer.

I approach the present project with a similar perspective, engaging in a critical (and time-consuming) rethinking of the way we approach the problems of the financial markets and attempting to construct a framework that might prove useful in developing a long-term strategy for reform of that sector. What I have provided here is a perspective

---

[70] DC Wheelock and SC Kumbhakar, 'Which Banks Choose Deposit Insurance? Evidence of Adverse Selection and Moral Hazard in a Voluntary Insurance System' (1995) 27 *Journal of Money, Credit & Banking* 186; GPJ O'Driscoll, 'Bank Failures: The Deposit Insurance Connection' (1988) 6(2) *Contemporary Policy Issues* 1.

[71] Richard Posner; the blog is located at correspondents.theatlantic.com/richard_posner/.

emphasising the central role that governance plays in this policy domain, and an attempt to make the case for a more balanced approach to governance that encompasses the need for greater accountability as well as more regulatory control. Emulating the work of Hood, Rothstein and Baldwin on regulatory regimes, I have presented the basic framing for understanding accountability regimes. Although that part of the project remains to be completed, I have also addressed the need for policy design principles that reflect the complex nature of the governance arrangements that are in need of major reform.

More work remains to be done.

25

Re-regulating Wall Street: Substantive Change or the Politics of Symbolism Revisited?

JUSTIN O'BRIEN[*]

A. Introduction

The gap between the rhetoric and reality of the market is pronounced in the very architecture of the New York Stock Exchange, where, as the cultural commentator Simon Fraser has noted, above the inscription of 'Business Integrity Protecting the Industries of Man', 'integrity', personified as a woman, dominates the neo-Grecian façade, with 'her outstretched arms hovered protectively over sculptured figures frozen in a choreography of productive labor; to her left, Agriculture and Mining; on her right, Science, Industry, and Invention. Beneath Integrity's solicitous gaze, a harmonious Commerce reigned'.[1] This benign vision has long been questioned in popular culture, most recently in the movie *Wall Street* (1987), Tom Wolfe's biting satire *Bonfire of the Vanities* (1987) and *The Daily Show*, John Stewart's vehicle for defenestrating the excess of financial markets on the cable network Comedy Central. In sharp contrast, political support for market-based solutions to corporate and regulatory failure has remained remarkably constant. This has substantially reduced capacity to engage in a sustained preemptive discussion with industry over what constitutes or should constitute integrity. It has also meant that the political support for regulatory enforcement is contingent and, in the main, short-lived. It is no coincidence that the excesses that accompanied the securitisation bubble took place against a background in which regulatory agencies were defenestrated over the cost of compliance.[2]

[*] Professor of Law, University of New South Wales, Sydney.
[1] S Fraser, *Wall Street, A Cultural History* (New York, Oxford University Press, 2007) 221 (further noting that 'Wall Street, once a scarlet woman, a disreputable habitueé of capitalism's badlands, was here miraculously beautified': 221–22). The interpretation of Wall Street mirrors that of Galbraith, who argued its 'supreme accomplishment is as a harlot', see JK Galbraith, *The Great Crash* (London, Penguin, 1954) 48.
[2] See R Romano, 'Sarbanes-Oxley and the Making of Quack Corporate Governance' (2005) 114 *Yale Law Journal* 1521 (condemning the flawed empirical justification); D Langevoort, 'The Social Construction of Sarbanes-Oxley' (2007) 105 *Michigan Law Review* 1817 (arguing that the Act was designed to achieve a much more coherent objective but that its legitimacy is undermined by the dominance of the ill-conceived panic discourse). The Department of Justice in the US has been particularly susceptible to the rise of a (partially justified) meta-narrative, see J O'Brien, 'Accounting and Accountability Failure: The Implications of the Kaplan Ruling on Corporate Enforcement Strategies' (2006) 1 *Compliance and Regulatory Journal* 28.

Moreover, the assertion by practitioners that the financial crisis was the result of the confluence of factors none could have predicted mirrors claims during the conflicts of interest investigations that accompanied the collapse of Enron, WorldCom and Tyco at the turn of the millennium.[3] This reflects a continuing failure to put in place and monitor—on an ongoing basis—proper mechanisms for the transmission of institutional memory.[4] More problematically, it suggests that regulatory solutions based on internal governance reform will be insufficient. This chapter critiques the response of the US to the crisis. It argues that, despite President Obama's claim that fundamental reform is required, his administration's continued reliance on failed models of oversight make the claim an exercise in political symbolism.[5]

B.   Bringing the State back in

As with fall-out from the Enron-related financial reporting scandals, policymakers in Washington sought to benefit from (or insulate themselves against) an increasingly irate American public, scandalised at the excesses of Wall Street and the desultory failure of executive agencies and political oversight. The provision of a lifeline to those responsible for generating the crisis at a time of record foreclosures and increased economic uncertainty was always going to be a difficult sell.[6] At a series of hearings, the nation's financial custodians claimed that failure to provide emergency funding through a Troubled Assets Relief Program (TARP) would prompt catastrophe.[7] The decision to advocate a $700 billion solution was accompanied by belated and half-hearted recognition that the policy choices heretofore adopted were, at best, based on an optimistic, if not naive, reading of what was fast becoming a global financial crisis. At each stage they had maintained that the credit crunch was contained and containable, that markets were stable, that institutions were viable and that the existing regulatory structures were sufficiently robust. With the credit markets paralysed, systemically important financial institutions falling and contagion spreading, this was not, they argued, a time for recrimination

---

[3] Newspaper profiles were also used to again deflect responsibility, see E Dash and J Creswell, 'Citigroup Saw No Red Flags Even As It Made Bolder Bets', *New York Times*, 23 November 2008, A1 (quoting an April 2008 interview in which Rubin argued 'In hindsight, there are a lot of things we'd do differently. But in the context of the facts as I knew them and my role, I'm inclined to think probably not'). This reprised an argument made in his autobiography on the financial reporting scandals at the turn of the millennium; see R Rubin, *In An Uncertain World* (2003) 337 ('The great bull market masked many sins, or created powerful incentives not to dwell on problems when all seemed to be going well—a natural human inclination').

[4] See P Moore, 'Memo to Treasury Select Committee', Westminster, 10 February 2009, in which he states 'my personal experience of being on the inside [of British bank HBOS] as a risk and compliance manager has shown me is that, whatever the very specific, final and direct causes of the financial crisis, I strongly believe that the real underlying cause of all the problems was simply this—a total failure of all key aspects of governance. In my view and from my personal experience at HBOS, all the other specific failures stem from this one primary cause.'

[5] M Edelman, 'Symbols and Political Quiescence' (1960) 54 *American Political Science Review* 695.

[6] It also prompted concern, particularly on the left, of a democratic deficit; see W Greider, 'Economic Free Fall', *The Nation*, 18 August 2008, 18 (arguing that Washington's selective generosity for influential financial losers is deforming democracy and opening the path to an awesomely powerful corporate state: at 20).

[7] See J Toobin, 'Barney's Great Adventure', *The New Yorker*, 12 January 2009, 37 (reporting an emergency meeting called by the Treasury Secretary with senior congressional Democrats to secure support for the bailout legislation. The House Speaker, Nancy Pelosi, is quoted as saying that the meeting—held on Thursday 18 September just after the collapse of Lehman Brothers and the emergency rescue of AIG —was necessary because Paulson claimed 'if we don't act now we may not have an economy on Monday night': 44).

or reflecting on the moral hazard of providing bailouts to those guilty of reckless disintermediation; necessity required providing the Treasury with what amounted to a blank cheque.[8] The Federal Reserve Chairman, Ben Bernanke, accepted the need for a more far-reaching reorganisation of regulatory structure and purpose, but argued: 'at this juncture, in light of the fast-moving developments in financial markets, it is essential to deal with the crisis at hand'. The Treasury Secretary, Henry Paulson, was even more direct: 'I am convinced that this bold approach will cost American families far less than the alternative—a continuing series of financial institution failures and frozen credit markets unable to fund everyday needs and economic expansion'.[9]

The initial plan contained a range of flaws, most notable of which was a total lack of accountability. The draft contained a provision that precluded judicial review. Once given authority, the Treasury embarked on a series of contradictory strategies, which were never adequately explained. As a consequence, public confidence in the integrity of TARP and the accountability of the Treasury Department was compromised, a fact accepted by Timothy Geithner, the incoming Treasury Secretary, at the confirmation hearing. Acknowledging past failure and designing credible programmes that have the capacity to engineer meaningful change in corporate and regulatory governance are, however, very different things. The evidence to date is that confusion and incoherence still inform regulatory responses in the US.

Examining the provisions of a bill that transmogrified from a three-and-a-half-page imperial command into a 451-page Act is exceptionally revealing of the regulatory dynamics in the US. First, earmarks—distinctly American legislative adornments that incorporate stunningly unrelated measures—were required to secure passage.[10] These included the provision of $192 billion in rebates to rum producers in Puerto Rico[11] and the US Virgin Islands, and tax incentives of $478 million to film and television producers to use domestic locations in upcoming productions.[12] Secondly, as with the first incarnation, the legislation's purpose is 'to immediately provide authority and facilities that the Secretary of the Treasury can use to restore liquidity and stability to the financial system of the US'. This is to be achieved by a series of potentially conflicting imperatives. As the lead agency, the Treasury is asked to ensure that such authority and such facilities are used in a manner that: (i) protects home values, college funds, retirement accounts and life savings; (ii) preserves homeownership and promotes jobs and economic growth; (iii) maximises

---

[8] For a compelling overview of the decisions taken by the Federal Reserve see J Cassidy, 'Anatomy of a Meltdown', *New Yorker*, 1 December 2008, 49; for an examination of the role played by the Treasury, see Government Accountability Office, 'Troubled Asset Relief Program', GAO-09-61 (Washington, DC, December 2008); Congressional Oversight Panel for Economic Stabilization, 'Questions About the $700 Billion Emergency Economic Stabilization Funds' (Washington, DC, 10 December 2008).

[9] Evidence from B Bernanke and H Paulson to Senate Committee on Banking, Housing, and Urban Affairs, Washington, DC, 23 September 2008.

[10] If not corruption, earmarking is certainly corrupting of public life. Opposition to the practice played a pivotal role in Senator John McCain's presidential campaign. Before the Senate vote, the Republican candidate stated categorically that 'it is completely unacceptable for any kind of earmarks to be included in this bill. It would be outrageous for legislators and lobbyists to pack this rescue plan with taxpayer money for favored companies. This simply cannot happen.' In the event, Senator McCain and Senator Obama both voted in favour of the legislation; neither queried the earmarks involved. A spokesperson for the McCain campaign said a national emergency overcame principle; see M Shear, 'With Bailout Vote, McCain Voted For Earmarks', *Washington Post*, 3 October 2008 (online edition); P Abrams, 'Loopholes v Earmarks', *Huffington Post*, 6 October 2008 (online edition).

[11] *Emergency Economic Stabilization Act* (2008), s 502.

[12] S 308.

overall returns to the taxpayers of the US; and (iv) provides public accountability for the exercise of such authority.[13] The manner in which the Treasury acquiesced in allowing leading banks to exit early congressional oversight suggests disproportionate exercise in authority that raises profound legitimacy questions.

The Treasury Secretary is mandated to provide guidelines outlining the criteria and mechanisms for purchasing and pricing assets and procedures for hiring asset managers within two days of the first purchase (or 45 days after enactment).[14] In addition, a Financial Stability Oversight Board is to be established. The board is to meet monthly and report to Congress every six months. It is made up of the chairman of the Federal Reserve, the Director of the Federal Home Finance Agency, the Chair of the SEC and the Secretary of Housing, along with the Secretary of the Treasury, who is precluded from serving as chair.[15] The reporting mechanism specifically calls for congressional notification within seven days of expenditure reaching $50 billion trigger intervals. This reporting requires

> a description of all of the transactions made during the reporting period; (b) a description of the pricing mechanism for the transactions; (c) a justification of the price paid for and other financial terms associated with the transactions; (d) a description of the impact of the exercise of such authority on the financial system, supported, to the extent possible, by specific data; (e) a description of challenges that remain in the financial system, including any bench marks yet to be achieved; and (f) an estimate of additional actions under the authority provided under this Act that may be necessary to address such challenges.[16]

The plan bore an uncanny resemblance to proposals first mooted the previous northern autumn when major banks, including Citigroup, began posting colossal losses. Those plans, which were ultimately rejected by the market, involved establishing what was termed a master liquidity enhancement conduit. As with the current plan, its aim was to allow the banks most exposed to progressively unwind their positions. Despite the passage of time, there is no indication that policymakers at the Treasury are going to be any more effective in divining actual prices. Moreover, a close reading of the legislation suggests that claims of fettered discretion are somewhat overblown.

The Secretary is mandated to make 'such purchases at the lowest price that the Secretary determines to be consistent with the purposes of this Act through mechanisms such as reverse auctions'.[17] When making direct purchases, the Secretary is given discretion subject only to undefined 'additional measures to ensure that prices paid for assets are reasonable and reflect the underlying value of the asset'.[18] This creates, in turn, two further interlinked policy dilemmas. First, forcing the banks to sell the assets at market prices could have the effect of worsening the solvency problem. Secondly, it potentially legitimises retrospectively the abdication of responsibility that saw investment bankers create conduits to introduce and disseminate toxicity with careless disdain for the consequences. Furthermore, the Treasury Secretary has the right to request non-voting or preferred stock warrants but not an obligation to demand them if

---

[13] S 2.
[14] S 101(d).
[15] S 104(b–e).
[16] S 105(b)(1).
[17] S 113(b).
[18] S 113(b).

the cumulative total of investment is less than $100 billion.[19] Indeed, the evidence to date is that it has overpaid already.[20]

The criteria for corporate governance and executive compensation are equally nebulous. Corporations taking advantage of the scheme to offload toxic products are required to meet 'appropriate standards'.[21] These include:

> (a) limits on compensation that exclude incentives for executive officers of a financial institution to take unnecessary and excessive risks that threaten the value of the financial institution during the period that the Secretary holds an equity or debt position in the financial institution; (b) a provision for the recovery by the financial institution of any bonus or incentive compensation paid to a senior executive officer based on statements of earnings, gains, or other criteria that are later proven to be materially inaccurate; and (c) a prohibition on the financial institution making any golden parachute payment to its senior executive officer during the period that the Secretary holds an equity or debt position in the financial institution.[22]

It is far from clear that the Treasury has used its power to ensure that the banks will change practice. Indeed, its lack of consistency has enhanced the power of the banks to thwart further intervention.

On 13 October 2008, the Treasury announced that $250 billion would be invested in preferred stock. On 12 November, the Treasury Secretary noted that the $700 billion fund would not, in fact, be used to purchase asset-backed securities directly. Yet less than two weeks later the Treasury, along with the Federal Reserve, approved a rescue package for Citigroup, which had the effect of providing backing for $306 billion in loans and securities. Under the terms of the agreement, Citigroup is liable for only the first $29 billion in losses. After that, the government will assume 90% of future liabilities. No time-limitation has been imposed. The following day, the Treasury changed tack again. It offered financing to private investors willing to purchase (allegedly) highly rated asset-backed securities, while continuing to invest directly into the banks through the Capital Purchase Program. The Capital Purchase Program has now invested $115 billion in senior preferred shares of eight of the largest financial institutions and a further $139 million in smaller banks. The Government Accountability Office (GAO) noted, however, that the Treasury had not instituted robust oversight and monitoring functions. As a result, it argued, 'Treasury's ability to help ensure an appropriate level of accountability and transparency will be limited'.[23]

A further damning report was released by the Congressional Oversight Panel, which was established to provide a further layer of accountability.[24] The Panel—chaired by Elizabeth Warren, a professor at Harvard Law School—demanded that the Treasury 'articulate its vision of the problem, its overall strategy to address that problem, and how its

---

[19] S 113(d).

[20] The chair of the Congressional Oversight Panel, Elizabeth Warren, told a Senate Banking Committee that the price differential was significant, see M Crittenden and D Solomon, 'Watchdog Says US Overpaid For Troubled Assets', *Wall Street Journal*, 6 February 2009, C3 (reporting Warren's assertion that Treasury paid $254 billion for preference shares and warrants that had a market value of $176 million).

[21] S 111(b)(1).

[22] S 111(b)(2). It is hard to see, in the absence of direct involvement in the development and execution of a risk management system, how the Treasury could second-guess management on what constitutes 'unnecessary and excessive risk'.

[23] GAO, above n 8, 7.

[24] S 125.

strategic shifts since September 2008 fit into that strategy'.[25] In other words, the Panel saw no vision, no strategy and no coherence.

According to the Panel,

> Congress provided substantial flexibility in the use of funds so Treasury could react to the fluid and changing nature of the financial markets. With these powers goes a responsibility to explain the reason for the uses made of them. With these monies goes a responsibility to ensure that the support to the economy from each dollar spent is maximized consistent with the purposes of the Act.[26]

The Panel found, however, that the Treasury has not conducted a detailed audit of the impact of the $254 billion already disbursed through the Capital Purchase Program nor had it been 'seeking to monitor the use of funds provided to specific financial institutions'. As with the GAO, the Panel found the Treasury's reliance on general economic indicators unacceptable. For the Panel, 'using general metrics could be a substitute for using no metrics at all, thus committing taxpayer resources with no meaningful oversight'.[27]

A major part of the perceived legitimacy problem is that little action has been taken on the rise of foreclosures. The provisions on foreclosure reduction are, at best, optimistic. The Treasury is mandated

> to implement a plan that *seeks to maximize* assistance for homeowners and use the authority of the Secretary *to encourage* the servicers of the underlying mortgages . . . to minimize foreclosures. In addition, the Secretary *may* use loan guarantees and credit enhancements to facilitate loan modifications to prevent avoidable foreclosures.[28]

Evidence to the Senate Banking Committee in the closing days of the Bush presidency opened fissures between the Treasury and the Federal Deposit Insurance Corporation (FDIC) on how to proceed. The Treasury representative wanted to give the banks latitude. He maintained that it was not in society's interest to micro-manage these institutions.[29] The chair of the FDIC, Sheila Blair, was much more forthright. 'We need to act quickly and we need to act dramatically.'[30] This, she claimed, may involve economic incentives for the banks to modify loans to reduce foreclosure rates, which had risen by over 70% since the crisis began. The Treasury representative would not commit the Department to this course of action, although, with unemployment levels exceeding 9.4%, it may have to revisit this reticence.[31] The Congressional Oversight Panel is exceptionally critical of Treasury's actions to date, most notably its failure to make funding conditional on foreclosure relief for existing borrowers and apparent opposition to proposals put forward

---

[25] Congressional Oversight Panel, above n 8, 13. For insight into the views of the chairman, see E Warren and A Warren Tyagi, 'Protect Financial Consumers', *Harpers*, November 2008, 39 (arguing for the need for a Consumer Product Safety Commission). After early success in setting the agenda, the work of the Panel has begun to come under intense scrutiny, particularly over the age and lack of experience of staffers and what was been termed Warren's reputation as 'a sharp-elbowed ideological infighter', see S Schmidt, 'Policing TARP Proves Tricky', *Wall Street Journal*, 20 February 2009 (online edition).

[26] Congressional Oversight Panel, above n 8, 13.

[27] Ibid, 20; see also GAO, above n 8, 10, 25. For initial Treasury response, see GAO, above n 8, 64–65.

[28] S 109(a) (emphasis added).

[29] See J Politi, 'Senators Question Bank Oversight Plan', *Financial Times*, 24 October 2008, 6 (reporting derision with this caution from Senator Charles Schumer of New York, who charged that the Treasury was 'leaning too far in giving them desert and not enough in making them eat their vegetables').

[30] Ibid.

[31] J Politti, 'US Grapples With Shift of Mood in Jobs Markets', *Financial Times*, 24 October 2008, 6.

by the FDIC. It asks 'the Department to explain how its broad authority reflects the purposes of the Act'.[32]

Similar problems have now become apparent in the ongoing regulatory arbitrage between the US and other key jurisdictions. The legislation allows the Treasury to buy securities from foreign-owned banks and explicitly calls for coordination to work toward the establishment of similar programmes.[33] What is also clear, however, is that regulatory arbitrage remains a significant risk. Following the British decision to inject capital directly into its banks, the then US Treasury Secretary partially followed suit. Hank Paulson summoned representatives of nine of the most important banks to a meeting in Washington and demanded that each accept government funding.[34] The funding, however, was offered at substantially less punitive rates than those imposed by the British government. The Congressional Oversight Panel noted that while 'the Act provides the Treasury with broad authority to set the conditions under which companies may receive aid . . . the public has a right to know to what extent conditions have been imposed on financial institutions receiving public funds, and if not, why not.'[35] The Panel concluded by arguing that the policies lack strategic direction and impose nowhere near the changes demanded by the London government.

> It is critical for Congress and the public, including participants in the banking industry, to under-stand exactly what the criteria are for receiving money under the TARP programs, what the strategic intentions of the criteria are, if any, what the strategic effects of the criteria are, and how the criteria advance the purposes of the Act.[36]

The failure to engage in more invasive monitoring highlighted the continued power of the banking lobby in the US. It also foregrounds the risk that international coordination will be much more difficult to achieve than previously understood.

The report, along with the publication of the GAO findings, prompted extremely hostile questioning to the Treasury Under Secretary, Neel Kashkari, from members of the House Financial Services Committee, including its chairman, Barney Frank, who condemned the

> blatant refusal [by the Treasury] to enforce any lending obligations on individual institutions, the continued policy of ignoring the clear intent of the EESA to aid in the reduction of foreclosures put the Treasury perilously close to a breach [of] faith with those who responded to the Bush Administration's request to establish the program.[37]

The problems intensified with the publication of the Congressional Oversight Panel's second report in January 2009. The Panel found that a lack of consistency and coherence still animated the Treasury decision-making process, a situation that was exacerbated because of the failure to provide a detailed analysis of the causes of the crisis.

---

[32] Congressional Oversight Panel, above n 8, 18–19.
[33] S 112.
[34] For detailed accounts, see D Paletta, J Hilsenrath and D Solomon, 'At Moment of Truth, US Forced Big Bankers to Blink', *Wall Street Journal*, 15 October 2008 (online edition); M Landler and E Dash, 'Drama Behind a $250 Billion Banking Deal', *New York Times*, 15 October 2008 (online edition).
[35] Congressional Oversight Panel, above n 8, 27–28.
[36] Ibid, 30.
[37] B Frank press release, 'Statement on GAO TARP Report', 3 December 2008.

> For the Panel, it was important for the Treasury and our financial services regulators to have an analysis of the causes and nature of the financial crisis to be able to craft a strategy for addressing the sources, and not solely the symptoms, of the problem or problems.[38]

Foremost among them is the issue of executive pay.

The Obama administration has promised significant action to strengthen oversight and reduce contestation over the payment of bonuses to executives in banks that avail of the bailout. On 4 February 2009, President Obama announced that pay would be capped at $500,000 for the most senior executives in any corporation that received exceptional assistance in the future, with share incentives paid only after the government has been repaid in full. He described the payment of bonuses totalling $18.4 billion in 2007 (itself a reduction of 44% on the 2007 round) as a 'shameful' practice. The changes were not, however, to be applied retrospectively. Senior Democrats called for and managed to legislate further action. The chairman of the Senate Banking Committee, Christopher Dodd, tabled an amendment to the TARP through the American Recovery and Reinvestment Act (2009) that mandates the Treasury Secretary

> to review bonus awards paid to executives of TARP recipients to determine whether any payments were excessive, inconsistent with the purposes of the Act or the TARP, or otherwise contrary to public interest and, if so, to seek to negotiate with the recipient and the subject employee for appropriate reimbursement to the Government.[39]

It underscores the extent of popular revulsion with bailing out Wall Street and demonstrates just why the planned redesign of the TARP, announced by the Treasury Secretary the previous week, proved so disappointing to markets and politicians on the left alike.

On 10 February 2009, Timothy Geithner unveiled what he termed, rather grandiosely, a new Financial Stability Plan. This was necessary, he argued, because of the failure of piecemeal attempts to reform the financial system.[40] Geithner argued that it was necessary for comprehensive, forceful and sustained intervention to prevent an intensification of the financial crisis. He made clear that 'access to public support is a privilege not a right' and that 'government support must come with strong conditions to protect the taxpayer and with transparency that allows the American people to see the impact of those investments'. The Secretary further argued that, In the future, 'polices must be designed to mobilize and leverage private capital, not to supplant or discourage private capital'. The plan has four major components. First, a comprehensive stress test is to be conducted to evaluate the health of specific banks and 'initiate a more consistent, realistic, and forward looking assessment about the risk on balance sheets, and we're going to introduce new measures to improve disclosure'. No further detail was provided as to how this intervention will ensure greater lending.

Secondly, the Treasury is to set up a Public Private Investment Fund to target legacy loans and stalled securitisation markets.[41] Here again, however, no detail was provided

---

[38] Congressional Oversight Panel, 'Accountability for the Troubled Asset Relief Program', Second Report (Washington, DC, 9 January 2009) 9. The passage of time has not reduced the perceived accountability and transparency deficit, see M Crittenden, 'TARP Watchdogs Criticize Treasury Over Transparency', *Wall Street Journal*, 22 July 2009, C1.

[39] Senate Committee on Banking, Housing and Urban Affairs press release, 'Dodd Commends Administration's Announcement on Executive Pay', 4 February 2009.

[40] T Geithner, 'Remarks Introducing the Financial Stability Plan', speech delivered at US Department of the Treasury, Washington, DC, 10 February 2009.

[41] Ibid.

about how the mechanism would work, the proportion of public to private contribution or whether the investment would come from traditional investors or Sovereign Wealth Funds—and, if the latter, whether this injection would require legislative change. Moreover, the policy framework suggests that the critical question is one of illiquidity born of panic rather than a systemic solvency problem. As a consequence, the plan suggests that government intends prop up 'zombie' banks and serves to undermine Obama administration's claim to inculcate change we can believe in.[42] Senior Senate Democrats, including Chris Dodd, the influential Chairman of the Senate Banking Committee, however, have indicated that nationalisation may be necessary, suggesting fissures within the party.

The third component of the plan was to commit up to $1 trillion to support what was termed a Consumer and Business Lending Initiative, designed to jumpstart the securitisation markers for small business lending, consumer and auto finance, and commercial mortgages. Again, no detail was provided, nor was any provided on how the government plans to bring down mortgage payments and reduce default rates. Moreover, the fourth component, the expansion of the TARP to the automotive industry, raises enormous exit problems for the government in the future. Providing emergency funding helped stave off the risk of an unruly bankruptcy for Chrysler and General Motors. It also opened a range of questions about what should be the purpose and limits of government intervention.

C.   A New Paradigm for Financial Regulation

Despite the severity of the problems facing both the auto industry and the wider credit markets, it is also clear that a unique window of opportunity has opened to reconfigure the debate about what should constitute the boundaries of corporate governance. Rhetorically at least, the President has recognised the opportunity.

> In many ways, our financial system reflects us. In the aggregate of countless independent decisions, we see the potential for creativity—and the potential for abuse. We see the capacity for innovations that make our economy stronger—and for innovations that exploit our economy's weaknesses. We are called upon to put in place those reforms that allow our best qualities to flourish—while keeping those worst traits in check. We're called upon to recognize that the free market is the most powerful generative force for our prosperity—but it is not a free license to ignore the consequences of our actions.[43]

It is questionable whether the policy choices adopted match the power of the soaring rhetoric. In announcing his nominations for the chairmanship of the Securities and Exchange Commission (Mary Shapiro) and the Chicago-based Commodity Futures Trading Commission (Gary Gensler), Barack Obama commented that financial regulatory

---

[42] See M Wolf, 'Why Obama's New Tarp Will Fail to Rescue the Banks', *Financial Times*, 11 February 2009, 13 (suggesting that by imposing 'three arbitrary self-imposed constraints: no nationalisation; no losses for bondholders; and no more money from Congress' the administration has acted with 'timidity' and is taking a 'huge gamble'). The editorial writers are even more forthright; see Editorial, 'Son of Tarp Follows in Father's Footsteps', *Financial Times*, 11 February 2009, 12 ('Saving the financial system will take more money and a greater degree of public control than the government is yet willing to admit').
[43] Speech delivered at the White House, Washington, DC, 17 June 2009.

reform 'will be one of the top legislative priorities of my Administration'. He noted that the approach needed to be informed by

> common-sense rules of the road that will protect investors, consumers, and our entire economy from fraud and manipulation by an irresponsible few. These rules will reward the industriousness and entrepreneurial spirit that's always been the engine of our prosperity, and crack down on the culture of greed and scheming that has led us to this day of reckoning. Instead of allowing interests to put their thumbs on the economic scales and CEOs run off with excessive golden parachutes, we'll ensure openness, accountability, and transparency in our markets so that people can trust the value of the financial product they're buying.[44]

The critical question is not whether the appointees have the experience to undertake the task, but rather whether they have a track record in aggressive enforcement, the necessary degree of independence and the willingness to accept that previously held positions were instrumental in exacerbating the crisis. Both nominees have significant track records and are firm supporters of self-regulation and the use of principles rather than invasive and prescriptive rules. Such an approach is clearly deficient in dealing with the global financial crisis in either the domestic US or the international dimension. Prior to her nomination, Shapiro was the head of the Financial Industry Regulatory Authority, which combines the enforcement arm of the National Association of Securities Dealers and the regulatory component of the New York Stock Exchange. It is the peak body responsible for monitoring self-policing. In confirmation hearings in January 2009, Shapiro quoted with approval the remarks made by the foundation chair, Joseph Kennedy, in 1934 that 'the Commission will make war without quarter on any who sell securities by fraud or misrepresentation' and promised that she would 'move aggressively to reinvigorate enforcement'.[45] As the chair of the Senate confirmation panel put it, the Securities and Exchange Commission (SEC) must address significant market and regulatory failures to oversee critical issues. In such circumstances

> it is absolutely critical that the Chairman and the Commissioners [of the SEC] make an extraordinary effort to pursue these issues fairly and independently—free from political considerations and from the industries which formerly employed them. That is always true—but particularly so today.[46]

While the SEC has made much of its decision to prosecute Bank of America over the payment of bonuses to Merrill Lynch, a New York judge has criticised the timidity of the settlement and the lack of information provided.[47]

At a broader level, the policy challenge ahead is to address incoherence in regulatory structures and purpose. The US Treasury Secretary, Timothy Geithner, for example, has conceded that the regulatory system there

---

[44] 'President-elect Obama Names Key Regulatory Appointments', Press Conference, Chicago, IL, 18 December 2008.

[45] Prepared Statement by SEC Chairman Designate (M Shapiro), Senate Banking, Housing and Urban Affairs, Washington, DC, 15 January 2009.

[46] Opening Statement (C Dodd), Hearing on Nominees for SEC, CEA, and Fed, Washington, DC, 15 January 2009; see also Editorial, 'Starting the Regulatory Work', *New York Times*, 7 January 2009, A14 (noting that the nomination for the chair of the CFTC, Gary Gensler, a former Goldman Sachs banker who as Treasury Under Secretary in 2000 oversaw the legislation that exempted derivatives from regulation, was 'troubling . . . It could be that the people whose actions contributed to the mess are best equipped to clean it up. That remains to be seen. But it would be tragic if Wall Street concludes from Mr. Obama's choices that it need not worry about the world changing in ways that would fundamentally alter its pursuit of profits.')

[47] C Bray, 'BofA Judge Seeks More Data on SEC Bonus Deal', *Wall Street Journal*, 9 August 2009, C1.

has evolved into a confusing mix of diffused accountability, regulatory competition, an enormously complex web of rules that create perverse incentives and leave huge opportunities for arbitrage and evasion, and creates the risk of large gaps in our knowledge and authority.[48]

In announcing a blueprint for overhauling the regulatory system, however, Geithner stepped back from fundamental reform. The lack of cohesion reinforces a reactive, piecemeal approach to functional regulation that is clearly unsustainable, particularly where innovation has left, by design or by default, large swathes of the financial services market either unregulated or under-regulated. Moreover, despite suggestions that oversight would be strengthened, transparency enhanced and accountability embedded, the administration has continued to adopt a policy of creative ambiguity.

This is most apparent in the thorny issue of how to wean the banking sector off its addiction to irresponsible and unsustainable lending and trading practices. Treatment options were clarified with the release on 7 May 2009 of stress tests conducted by the Federal Reserve in conjunction with the Department of Treasury into 19 of the most important banks. Not surprisingly, given the extensive media management that preceded publication, prognosis was favourable. As widely reported, the Charlotte-based Bank of America is the most exposed. The bank is required to enhance capital reserves by $34 billion. Citigroup, by contrast, one of the weakest major banks, requires only $5.5 billion. The former investment banks Morgan Stanley and Goldman Sachs have fared much better. Morgan Stanley has been cautioned to raise just $1.5 billion. Goldman is regarded as adequately capitalised, as is JP Morgan Chase, which has managed the integration of Bear Stearns much more successfully than the hapless management at Bank of America, where empire building led to the disastrous acquisition of Merrill Lynch and Countrywide at the peak of the crisis. Remarkably, this exercise in regulatory oversight did not identify the need to change senior management. Indeed, the overall picture presented was of relative strength, not weakness. In total, only $75 billion was deemed necessary to insulate the banking sector. It presented a benign picture; investors should now be reassured that all losses were accounted for and that entrenched management was credible. The suggestion overstates the case.

The content and conduct of the tests and the way in which the results were disseminated leave huge questions about the ultimate purpose and who will stand to gain most of all from this exercise in managing expectations. There are a number of profound methodological flaws. The tests used worst-case scenario baselines that have already been proved optimistic. More problematically, the banks were able to negotiate privately with the government over how the latter interpreted the results. None of this gives confidence in the veracity of claims that the banking sector as a whole is adequately capitalised, or would remain so if explicit and implicit guarantees were removed. What is clear, however, is that a process of differentiation has begun. The perceived stronger banks have already extricated themselves from congressionally imposed remuneration caps and trading

---

[48] T Geithner, 'The Current Financial Challenges: Policy and Regulatory Implications', speech delivered at Council on Foreign Relations, New York, 6 March 2008; H Pitt, 'Bringing Financial Services Regulation into the Twenty-first Century' (2008) 25 *Yale Journal on Regulation* 315; see also Evidence from S Bartlett, President of Financial Services Roundtable, to House Committee on Financial Services, Washington, DC, 21 October 2008. Bartlett complains, with cause, that federal and state financial regulators lack a common set of regulatory objectives.

restrictions.[49] Weaker entities face unpalatable options. They can offload prize assets at bargain-basement prices or convert government stakes, which take the form of preferred stock, into common equity. This raises a profoundly difficult policy option that the Treasury is, for now, evading. Preferred stock provides the government with the privileges of repayment over holders of common equity. It also attracts a guaranteed interest premium and a lower risk profile. Common equity, on the other hand, forces the government to articulate a vision of how it will exercise its ownership rights and for what purpose. As noted above, for the moment, economic policymakers appear to favour creative ambiguity. This involves the creation of the mandatory convertible preferred share (MCPS). The MCPS is designed for conversion into common equity only when required. Crucially, it does not dilute further existing shareholders. It also delays the need for an articulation of what kind of banking sector the federal government would like to see estab-lished. This has clear short-term benefits. First, it staves off the immediate need for partial or total nationalisation, a policy option that is anathema to leading economic advisors. Secondly, it quells, partially, investor fear of expropriation just as the government suggested a pragmatic revoking of decades of precedent in bankruptcy law. Its contro-versial support for the Chrysler reorganisation saw the UAW trades union retirement fund privileged over bondholders, who were pressured to accept a payment of just 30 cents in the dollar. Crucially, the plan gained the support of the major banks, many of which had a vested interest in not being seen to contradict the government. It is not a good idea to alienate the body that is to decide your viability just days before adjudication. Bondholders outside this US version of a tarnished golden circle rejected the deal on the ground that liquidation would generate a fairer outcome. President Obama dismissed their under-standable concerns as the greed of speculators who failed to put America first.

The Obama administration is playing a very dangerous game here. Already the Treasury and Federal Reserve stand accused of attempting to coerce Bank of America into its ill-starred acquisition of Merrill Lynch. The Obama administration clearly thrives on its can do attitude. Such strategies risk tarnishing the administration with the oxidisation of Chicago-style politics, a messy brand of compromise inconsistent with the mantra that we can and should expect change we can believe in. The potential saving of a single American institution, even one as storied as Chrysler, is an enormous price to pay if it reduces capacity to engineer broader change in the operation of the banking sector.

D.   Conclusion

There can be no doubt that the presentation of policy has improved significantly since the debacle that accompanied the announcement of what was billed, rather grandiloquently, a comprehensive plan for economic reform in February 2009. The lack of detail undermined already weak confidence. A reformulated plan to kickstart lending by offloading 'legacy assets' to public–private partnerships in which the downside risk was disproportionately held by the taxpayer proved more palatable to the market. Despite the remarkably

---

[49] See Crittenden, above n 38 (reporting calls from the GAO for Treasury to disclose additional information on the price paid by banks for repurchasing warrants and the calculation of the COP that the taxpayer stands to lose $2.7 billion on warrants repurchased by 11 smaller banks as of July 10 2009).

generous terms, the programe remains stalled. This can be traced to the failure to resolve two intractable issues. First, the banks were not prepared to relinquish 'legacy assets' at prices the markets are prepared to offer. Note here the subtle but deliberate change in terminology. The lexicological illusion is to transform what remain exceptionally suspect financial products of questionable value into something of intrinsic value. Alchemy, it appears, is not confined to the securitisation process itself. Secondly, the stated policy position that no major bank would be allowed to fail reduced the pressure to disinvest. Washington, scared and scarred by the Lehman debacle, was mindful of the unintended consequences of addressing questions of moral hazard.

The release of the stress tests only partially changes this dynamic. At the same time, dismissing bondholders as amoral speculators risks undermining the stated policy goal of engaging in public–private partnerships. While much has been made of plans to regulate the over-the-counter derivatives market and impose more stringent caps on executive pay, neither initiative offers fundamental change. The first provides more transparency, but does not necessarily deliver on more effective risk management. The second focus on executive remuneration, while laudable, derives from imperatives imposed by Congress rather than the White House, which had initially argued that such policies were too invasive. What makes matters even more problematic is that the conditions to allow banks to exit Congressional oversight are remarkably lax. Suggesting that the marketplace is somehow cleansed and chastened by the experience is naive. There is simply no evidence of the Pauline conversion that the Obama administration is suggesting has occurred. Far from controlling Wall Street, the government's policy is likely to increase its capacity at precisely the same time as the economic crisis hits Main Street with increasing force. While the rhetoric has improved dramatically, the policy choices remain remarkably consistent. The opportunity to engage in a sustained and sustainable conversation about the parameters of integrity has been missed by policymakers thankful that markets are beginning to stabilise. There is little of substance behind the façade. As with the illusion of integrity made manifest on the walls of the New York Stock Exchange, so too with the policy responses from the Obama administration.

26

Banking Crisis:
Regulation and Supervision

KERN ALEXANDER[*]

A. Introduction

The credit and financial crisis has exposed major weaknesses in UK banking supervision and regulation. This paper elaborates further on the issues discussed at the Treasury Select Committee's hearing on 23 June 2009. Specifically, it will address the recommendations set forth in the Turner Review with respect to capital and liquidity regulation and the supervisory responsibilities of the Financial Services Authority (FSA) for cross-border banks that operate in the EU. Further, it will address the regulation of the shadow banking sector, and the meaning of macro-prudential regulation and how it should fit into the UK's reformed regulatory framework.

B. The Need for Macro-prudential Regulation

UK financial regulation will need to expand its focus to include not only individual financial institutions and investor and depositor protection, but also the broader financial system. This means that UK supervisors will have to manage and control systemic risk in the financial system by monitoring the aggregate levels of leverage in the financial system and by adjusting micro-prudential regulation of individual firms to take account of macro-economic factors. One of the major failures in UK regulation over the last 10 years was that prudential regulation was too market-sensitive; it focused on the individual institution and did not take into account the level of risk or leverage building up in the whole financial system. The FSA thought that, if individual firms were managing their risk appropriately, then the financial system would be stable. This failed to take into account the fallacy of composition that what appears for individual firms to be rational and prudent actions in managing their risk exposures under certain circumstances can, if followed by all firms, potentially produce imprudent or sub-optimal outcomes for the

[*] Professorial Chair of Banking and Financial Market Law, University of Zurich Law Faculty and Senior Research Fellow in International Financial Regulation, the Centre for Financial Analysis and Policy, University of Cambridge. This paper was given as supplemental written evidence to Professor Alexander's oral evidence submitted on 23 June 2009 to the UK Parliament's Treasury Select Committee.

whole financial system. The challenge now is to link micro-prudential regulation of individual firms within a robust macro-prudential framework.

C.   Counter-cyclical Capital Adequacy Rules

Capital adequacy regulation will need to become more rules-based. The main aim of Basel II and the Capital Requirements Directive (CRD) is to make bank regulatory capital more sensitive to the economic risks that individual banks face, while ignoring the larger social risks that bank risk-taking poses to the financial system. Indeed, the FSA has adhered to the Basel II approach by permitting banks to use their own economic capital models to measure credit, market and operational risk, and to estimate lower levels of regulatory capital than regulatory rules would normally require. An important weakness of the CRD/Basel II is that it fails to address liquidity risk, which precipitated the present credit crisis and allows banks to hold lower levels of regulatory capital for assets which banks securitise through special purpose vehicles in the wholesale debt markets.

Another weakness of Basel II/CRD is that it is procyclical because regulatory capital calculations are based on the riskiness of assets on the banks' balance sheets. Rather, regulatory rules should impose counter-cyclical capital requirements, such as higher capital charges during an asset price boom and lower charges during a market downturn. The experience of using counter-cyclical capital rules—or dynamic provisioning—in Europe has generally been positive. Spain had counter-cyclical capital rules that led to their banks having more capital than other banks in Europe. They were therefore able to withstand the crisis much better. Spanish banks did not receive bailouts from the Spanish Central Bank. The FSA and the regulatory authorities of other EU Member States should adopt counter-cyclical rules as well. These need to be somewhat formulaic, but there should be some regulatory discretion to adjust their application to changing market structures and financial innovations.

D.   Rules versus Discretion in Capital Regulation

It is necessary to have a rules-based capital adequacy regime in order to bind the regulator's actions so that they do not acquiesce to political pressure by failing to apply counter-cyclical capital rules. A rules-based regulatory regime is also necessary in the EU, where many Member State regulators are, by law, required to have more rules-based regulatory regimes and the regulators are not allowed so much discretion as, say, the FSA has. This is because of constitutional law principles of due process and equal protection under the law. Nevertheless, efficient capital adequacy requirements need to provide regulators with a combination of rules and discretion, and the rules need to provide reference points or guidelines for regulators. This means that there needs to be a balance between rules and discretion. However, a rules-based capital adequacy regime needs some supervisory discretion to provide flexibility for the regulator to adopt different rules and practices when market conditions change. This allows regulators to learn to adapt their supervisory practices to evolving markets and to adjust to innovations in the market.

E.   What Type of Regulatory Capital?

The definition of 'core tier one capital' should be made more precise to include any financial instrument that can fully absorb losses on the bank's balance sheet. Core tier one capital should constitute most of a bank's regulatory capital and should be included as tier one only if it can absorb losses fully. Under this more limited definition, tier one capital will mainly include common equity shares. If preferred shares or subordinated debt are also included, these types of capital will have a more limited ability to absorb losses, because they are essentially debt claims. Capital regulation should focus not necessarily on having higher capital charges, but instead on ensuring that regulatory capital consists of equity shares and similar instruments that have the ability to absorb losses for the bank, and that this core tier one capital should constitute most of the bank's regulatory capital. Tier two capital—subordinated debt, preferred shares and other hybrid instruments—should be relied on less as a regulatory requirement for banks to demonstrate adequate capital. In the EU, the lack of a harmonised and meaningful definition of tier one capital under the CRD has led to an unbalanced playing field across EU states because there are different definitions of what comprises regulatory capital and in particular tier one capital. The main point is that the definition of 'regulatory capital' should be linked to its ability to absorb losses.

F.   Bank Size and Interconnectedness of Financial Firms

A bank's or financial institution's regulatory capital level should be linked, in part, to its size and interconnectedness in the financial system. Larger banks pose a larger systemic risk to the financial system and therefore should pay a tax or a higher capital charge to reflect that; smaller banks perhaps do not need such high capital charges as they pose less systemic risk. Interconnectedness brings us to the capital markets and how they have certainly become complex. The crisis demonstrates how liquidity risk can arise in the wholesale capital markets, not necessarily with individual banks. Securities regulation has traditionally focused on conduct of business rules and the segregation and protection of client account money, but the crisis shows that securities regulators should focus much more than they have in the past on systemic risk in capital markets.

G.   Regulating Liquidity Risk

Before the credit crisis, there was an under-appreciation of liquidity risks in the financial system. Much of the policy debate, and thus many of the academic models, had analysed financial stability issues from the perspective of market risk and credit risk. In fact, Alan Greenspan praised credit risk transfer and securitisation as spreading and smoothing risk in the financial system, and said that this had enhanced liquidity in financial markets. Indeed, Dr Greenspan's view was that securitisation and other types of credit risk transfer financial instruments had spread risk and thus had enhanced financial stability. As a result of this conventional wisdom, there was no appreciation that liquidity risk could arise in these inter-connected and highly leveraged financial markets. The academic and bank models, and the regulatory frameworks, were built upon the fact that credit risk transfer was promoting liquidity, but what we did not count on was the fact that liquidity could suddenly evaporate in the wholesale funding markets. In the summer of 2007 institutional investors in the wholesale debt markets suddenly refused to roll over their short-term investments, thus causing liquidity to dry up. That was something that was not foreseen, and was a major failing on the part of the academics, policymakers, regulators and, of course, the risk managers in the banks and investment firms who failed to appreciate this. Therefore, regulation should address the maturity mismatches which special purpose entities and structured investment vehicles have in the wholesale funding markets, and should control and limit these exposures; it should also require banks to hold some regulatory capital against these exposures, even though they have been swept off their balance sheets.

H.   The European Dimension of UK Regulation

UK prudential regulation should take account of the cross-border risks that UK financial institutions pose to other countries—especially in the EU. The UK financial crisis, with the collapse of the Royal Bank of Scotland, demonstrated how the risk-taking of UK banks can generate cross-border externalities to other countries and financial systems. Banks have exposure to each other throughout Europe in the money markets through a variety of risk exposures, and European policy-making needs to begin to have better surveillance of the systemic risk posed by certain banking groups and financial institutions that operate in Europe. It does not mean that EU regulation and oversight should displace national regulators; it simply means that member state regulators, at the national level, must have more accountability to committees of supervisors at the EU level in order to carry out more efficiently cross-border supervision of the largest forty or so of Europe's banks that have extensive cross-border operations. The De Larosiere Committee's proposal for a European Systemic Risk Council and for a European System of Financial Supervision, consisting of the three Lamfalussy 3 committees is an appropriate institutional step to developing a more accountable and efficient EU regulatory structure.

I.   Who Should Regulate Systemic Risk?

The Bank of England has broad powers over macro-economic policy, interest rates and managing the currency, but in the recent crisis it was shown that systemic risk can arise not only from individual financial institutions, but also from the broader wholesale capital markets and in the over-the-counter derivatives markets. Indeed, the failure of AIG demonstrated that a non-banking financial firm can have huge counter-party exposures in the credit derivatives market that can put the whole financial system at serious risk. The regulation of the structure of the financial system—in particular clearing and settlement—is another source of systemic concern. The FSA is the primary regulator of wholesale capital markets and the post-trading system in capital markets. The FSA has the data not only for supervising individual institutions, but also for regulating the clearing and settlement system and the exchanges, which is where much of the systemic risk in the recent financial crisis arose. That is why the FSA is well positioned to exercise supervision over these systemically important areas of the financial system. By possessing market intelligence, the FSA is well positioned to supervise and control systemic risk as it occurs in the broader capital markets and trading systems. Nevertheless, there should be improved operational linkages with the Bank of England regarding the FSA's regulation of systemic risk in the capital markets and its relationship to macro-prudential regulatory policy.

J.   Banks' Business Models and Corporate Governance

Effective supervision and regulation require banks to have robust corporate governance arrangements that incentivise bank management and owners to understand the risks they are taking and to price risk efficiently in order to cover both the private costs that such risk-taking poses to bank shareholders and the social costs for the broader economy if the bank fails.[1] Corporate governance plays an important role in achieving this in two ways: to align the incentives of bank owners and managers so that managers seek wealth maximisation for owners, while not jeopardising the bank's franchise value through excessive risk-taking; and to incentivise bank management to price financial risk in a way that covers its social costs. The latter objective is what distinguishes bank corporate governance from other areas of corporate governance because of the potential social costs that banking can have on the broader economy.[2]

Major weaknesses in UK bank corporate governance have not only resulted in substantial shareholder losses, but have also contributed significantly to the significant contraction of the UK economy, which has, among other things, led to massive layoffs in the financial services industry and related economic sectors, and dramatically curtailed the availability of credit to individuals and businesses. Most UK bank senior managers and board members did not understand the risky business models that drove UK bank lending and which led to much higher levels of leverage in deposit banks and investment banks. Moreover, they failed to grasp the true risks which their banks' risk managers had approved based on faulty value-at-risk models that were used to determine credit default risk and market risk. Equally important, they allowed irresponsible compensation packages to be awarded to bankers which incentivised them to book short-term profits

---

[1] H Mehran, 'Critical Themes in Corporate Governance' (April, 2003) *FRBNY Economic Policy Review*; see also J Macey and M O'Hara, 'The Corporate Governance of Banks' (2003) *FRBNY Economic Policy Review*, 91–107.

[2] Moreover, it should be noted that regulatory intervention is necessary to address the social costs of bank risk-taking because the regulator is uniquely situated to assert the varied interests of other stakeholders in society and to balance those interests according to the public interest.

based on excessively risky behaviour which increased systemic risk in the financial system and weakened the medium and long-term prospects and profitability of the bank. Moreover, weak governance and risky business models contributed to the poor performance of banks and in some cases to their failure and bailout or nationalisation by the government.

The UK regulatory regime should establish new corporate governance standards that cover most areas of bank management, including controls on remuneration that are linked to the long-term profitability of the bank, while foregoing short-term bonuses. The FSA should exercise the power to approve bank director appointments and ensure that bank directors have the knowledge and training to understand the bank's business and risk models and its financial implications not only for the bank's shareholders, but for the broader economy. Bank management should be required to understand the technical aspects of stress-testing, which the regulator should require to be done on a much more frequent basis than what was done prior to the crisis. Essentially bank corporate governance regulation should focus not only on aligning the incentives of bank shareholders and managers, but also on aligning the broader stakeholder interests in society with those of bank managers.

K.   Regulating Off-balance Sheet Structures

Structured investment vehicles (SIVs) and special purpose vehicles are important elements in financial innovation, and these structures largely were responsible for allowing securitisation to thrive and to provide increased liquidity in the financial system. However, these structures were also a type of regulatory arbitrage that allowed banks to reduce their regulatory capital requirements and to lower the costs of managing their balance sheets. Excesses occurred in the use of these off-balance sheet structures that allowed leverage to grow unchecked. Nevertheless, securitisation is an important component of our financial system and we should not prohibit banks from using it and other off-balance sheet operations to generate liquidity and to manage more effectively their balance sheets. Regulators should understand better the systemic risks which securitisation structures pose to the financial system and impose efficient regulatory charges on firms which transfer assets off their balance sheets through such structures and on the risk traders who invest in these risky assets. The real regulatory challenge will be how to require the market participants to internalise the costs of the risks they create in these structures. If we properly regulate securitisation, SIVs and the various conduit funding mechanisms that banks have been using, then they will provide appropriate and economically beneficial ways to raise capital. They are a part of financial innovation, which we should not curtail, though we have to understand that the funding through SIVs is short-term and that it can disappear quickly, and we have to think about how to regulate that by devising pricing mechanisms that require issuers and investors to internalise the social costs of these risks.

L.   The UK Tripartite System

The UK Tripartite System was established by a legally non-binding Memorandum of Understanding in 1998 that was designed to provide flexibility to the FSA, the Bank of England and the Treasury to coordinate their regulatory interventions and systemic oversight in times of crisis. Although the Chancellor chaired the tripartite bodies and exercised ultimate decision-making authority, there was no clear delineation of responsibilities between the three for acting in a financial crisis. The FSA, the Bank and the Treasury had only committed themselves to consult, and there was no clear procedure for determining how the bodies would act in a banking or financial crisis and who would take what decisions. The Tripartite Arrangement failed to work effectively in the summer of 2007, when Northern Rock failed, and had continuing difficulties in its operations until the Banking Act 2008 was adopted, which established stronger legal grounds and procedural rules for the Tripartite system's operations. Presently, the Banking Act 2009 reinforces many of the reforms that were made to the Tripartite System's operations in 2008. One weakness, however, that should be remedied is the Banking Act's creation of a Financial Stability Committee, which is chaired by the Governor of the Bank of England. Membership of the committee is composed of two of the Bank's deputy governors and representatives from the Treasury, but there is no representation from the Financial Services Authority on the Committee. It is necessary to have the FSA as a member of the committee for the oversight of systemic risk because we have learned in the credit crisis that systemic risk can arise not only from individual banks (which the FSA regulates), but also from the broader wholesale capital markets and over-the-counter (OTC) derivative markets (which the FSA also regulates). Therefore, the FSA should be given statutory authority to supervise both individual institutions and to oversee the broader financial system (ie wholesale capital and OTC markets) to ensure against systemic risk and other threats to financial stability.

M.   Macro-prudential Regulation and Principles-based Regulation

Macro-prudential regulation will change in important respects the nature of principles-based regulation. The FSA's principles-based regulation (PBR) approach was focused on individual firm outcomes and allowed firms to experiment with different risk management practices so long as they achieved satisfactory firm outcomes that were measured by shareholder prices and so long as the 11 high-level FSA principles were being achieved (ie treating customers fairly). The FSA's PBR approach did not take into account the aggregate effect of firms' performance on the financial system in terms of leverage generated and overall systemic risks and liquidity risk exposures. To address adequately these macro-prudential risks in the future, principles-based regulation will necessarily become more rules-based at the level of the firm and at the level of the financial system. The Turner Review supports the creation of a macro-prudential regulatory regime that is directly linked to the micro-prudential oversight of individual firms. Macro-prudential regulation will change regulation for individual banks in two main areas: (i) the regulation of individual firms must take into account both firm level practices and broader macro-economic developments in determining how regulatory requirements will be applied to firm risk-taking (ie the relationship of the growth of asset prices and GDP with contra-cyclical bank reserves and liquidity ratios); and (ii) bank innovation in the types of financial products offered will be constrained by controls on the overall levels of risk-taking and leverage at the level of the financial system (ie limits on loan-to-value and loan-to-income ratios). If adopted, macro-prudential regulation will require that principles-based regulation become more rules-based because tighter ex ante constraints will need to be applied to the risk exposures of individual firms (ie leverage ratios and limits on maturity mismatches in wholesale funding). FSA regulation will gradually become more rules-based in order to achieve macro-prudential regulatory objectives. The FSA's PBR regime that focuses on individual firm outcomes will become much less relevant to achieving macro-prudential objectives. The FSA will need to adopt a new PBR approach based on macro and micro rule-based controls which will dramatically change the nature of FSA supervisory practices and potentially lead to new regulatory risks that will arise because of the responses of market participants, who will undoubtedly seek to avoid these regulatory controls by adopting innovative financial instruments and structures. This will be the main challenge for the FSA and its PBR approach in the future.

27

Macro-prudential Regulation

AVINASH PERSAUD*

A.   Introduction

This is not the first international banking crisis the world has seen, though the previous ones occurred without credit default swaps, special investment vehicles or even credit ratings. While we cannot hope to prevent them, we can perhaps make crises fewer and milder, by adopting and implementing better regulation—in particular, more macro-prudential regulation.

There is a widely held view that the current financial crisis resulted from an insufficient reach of regulation and that the solution is to take existing regulation and spread it, without gaps, across institutions and jurisdictions. If this were to be the main policy response, it would be a mistake for several reasons, the most important of which is that at the heart of the crisis lay highly regulated institutions in sophisticated jurisdictions—Northern Rock, IKB, Fortis, Royal Bank of Scotland, UBS, Citigroup. Even if there had been no mortgage fraud, no tax secrecy and no conflicts of interest, a crisis would still have occurred. And while risk did shift outside the capital adequacy regime, the special investment vehicles were not secret and supervisors had the discretion to look at how regulated institutions were managing risks and to respond if necessary.

As noted, this is not the first international banking crisis the world has seen. Some estimates put it as the eighty-fifth.[1] If crises keep repeating themselves, it seems reasonable to argue that policymakers need to carefully consider what they are doing and not just 'double-up'. It also means that policymakers should not superficially react to the characters and colours of the current crisis. The last 84 crises occurred without credit default swaps and special investment vehicles. The last eighty-something had nothing to do with credit ratings. The solution to the crisis is not more regulation, though more comprehensive regulation may be required in some areas. Instead, it is better regulation—in particular, regulation with a greater macro-prudential orientation, as recommended by numerous recent official reports.[2]

---

* Avinash Persaud (avinash@intelligence-capital.com) is Chairman of Intelligence Capital Limited, Member of the UN Commission of Experts on Financial Reform and Emeritus Professor of Gresham College in London.

[1] For a discussion on the history of financial crises see C Reinhart and K Rogoff, 'This Time Is Different: A Panoramic View of Eight Centuries of Financial Crises', NBER Working Paper 13882 (Cambridge MA, National Bureau of Economic Research, 2008).

[2] These include the 2 April 2009 communiqué of the G-20 leaders; the Turner Review: UK Financial Services Authority, 'The Turner Review: A Regulatory Response to the Global Banking Crisis' (London, 2009); the G-30

B.   What is Macro-prudential Regulation?

It seems banal today to point out that the reason we try to prevent financial crises is that the costs to society are invariably enormous and exceed the private cost to individual financial institutions. We regulate to internalise these externalities in the behaviour of such institutions. One of the main tools regulators use to do this is capital adequacy requirements. However, the current approach to capital adequacy is too narrow. Capital adequacy levels are set on the implicit assumption that we can make the system as a whole safe by ensuring that individual banks are safe. This represents a fallacy of composition. In trying to make themselves safer, banks and other highly leveraged financial intermediaries can behave in ways that collectively undermine the system. This is in essence what differentiates macro-prudential from micro-prudential concerns.

Here is an example of a macro-prudential concern. Selling an asset when it appears to be risky may be considered a prudent response for an individual bank and is supported by much current regulation. However, if many banks do this, the asset price will collapse, forcing risk-averse institutions to sell more and leading to general declines in asset prices, higher correlations and volatility across markets, spiralling losses, and collapsing liquidity. Micro-prudential behaviour can cause or worsen systemic risks. A macro-prudential approach to an increase in risk is to consider systemic behaviour in the management of that risk: who should hold it, and do they have the incentive to do so? If it is liquidity risk, is it in the interests of the system if all institutions, regardless of their liquidity conditions, sell the same asset at the same time? Risk in a financial system is more than an aggregation of risks in individual institutions; it is also about endogenous risks that arise as a result of the collective behaviour of institutions.

Macro-prudential regulation is concerned with the stability of the financial system as a whole. By contrast, micro-prudential regulation, consisting of such measures as the certification of those working in the financial sector and rules on how financial institutions operate, is concern with the stability of individual entities and the protection of individuals. Micro-prudential regulation examines the responses of an individual bank to exogenous risks. By construction, it does not incorporate endogenous risk. It also ignores the systemic importance of individual institutions resulting from such factors as size, degree of leverage and interconnectedness with the rest of the system.

The existing framework of banking regulation was insufficiently macro-prudential, and had been recognised as such by commentators for some time.[3] Moreover, the emphasis on micro-prudential regulation may have contributed to the build-up of some macro-risks.

report: Group of Thirty, 'Financial Reform—A Framework for Financial Stability' (Washington DC, 2009); de Larosiere Group, 'Report of the High-Level Group on Financial Supervision in the EU' (Brussels, 2009); the UN Commission of Experts on Reforms of the International Monetary and Financial System, 'Recommendations' (New York, United Nations, 2009); and the 11th Geneva Report: M Brunnermeier, A Crockett, CAE Goodhart, AD Persaud and H Shin, 'The Fundamental Principles of Financial Regulation', Geneva Report on the World Economy 11 (Geneva, International Center for Monetary and Banking Studies; London, Centre for Economic Policy Research, 2009).

[3] C Borio, 'Monetary and Financial Stability: So Close and Yet So Far' (2005) 192 *National Institute Economic Review* 84; C Borio and W White, 'Whither Monetary and Financial Stability? The Implications of Evolving Policy Regimes', BIS Working Paper 147 (Basel, Bank for International Settlements, 2004); A Persaud, 'Sending the Herd off the Cliff Edge: The Disturbing Interaction between Herding and Market-sensitive Risk Management Systems', First Prize Essay, Jacques de Larosiere Award in Global Finance (Washington, Institute of International Finance, 2000).

Through many avenues, some regulatory and some not, and often in the name of prudence, transparency and sensitivity to risk, the growing influence of current market prices has intensified homogeneous behaviour in financial systems. These avenues include mark-to-market valuation of assets; regulator-mandated market-based measures of risk, such as the use of credit spreads in internal credit models or price volatility in market risk models; and the increasing use of credit ratings, where the signals are slower moving but positively correlated with financial markets. Where measured risk is based on market prices, or on variables correlated with market prices, it can contribute to systemic risk as market participants herd into areas that appear to be safe.[4] Measured risk can also be highly procyclical, because it falls in the build-up to a boom and rises in volatile busts.

C.   Macro-prudential Regulation and the Cycle

The economic cycle is a major source of homogeneous behaviour, so addressing it is a critical macro-prudential concern. In the up phase of the cycle, price-based measures of asset values rise, price-based measures of risk fall and competition to increase bank profits grows. Most financial institutions respond spontaneously by expanding their balance sheets to take advantage of the fixed costs of banking franchises and regulation, trying to lower the cost of funding by using short-term funding from money markets, and increasing leverage. Those that do not do so are seen as under-leveraging their equity and are punished by stock markets. In the prosaic words of Chuck Prince, former CEO of Citigroup, during an interview with the *Financial Times* in July 2007, 'when the music is playing, you have to get up and dance'.[5] By contrast, when the boom ends, asset prices begin to fall and short-term funding to institutions with impaired and uncertain assets or high leverage dries up. Forced sales of assets drive up their measured risk, and the boom inevitably turns to bust.

One of the key lessons of this crisis is that market discipline is little defence against the macro-prudential risks that come with the economic cycle. The institutions that have been most resilient to the crisis, such as HSBC and JP Morgan, had lower equity 'ratings' (lower price–earnings ratios) than those that proved to be less resilient, such as Northern Rock, Bear Stearns, Fortis and Lehman Brothers. Market discipline has an important role to play in the efficiency of the financial sector, but it cannot be on the front line of defence against crises.

One reason that market discipline was seen as such an important pillar in the pre-crisis approach to banking regulation was the implicit model that regulators had in mind: financial crashes occur randomly as a result of a bad institution failing and that failure becomes systemic. The historical experience is rather different. Crashes follow booms. In the boom almost all financial institutions look good, and in the bust almost all look bad. Differentiation is poor. The current crisis is another instance of this all too familiar cycle. If crises continue to repeat themselves and follow booms, banning the products, players

---

[4] See Persaud, ibid, for a discussion on how, through the financial sector's use of value-at-risk models, 'the observation of safety creates risk and the observation of risk creates safety'. The late economist Hyman Minsky also argued in more general terms, and long before the advent of value-at-risk models, that risks are born in periods of stability.

[5] H Kaufman, 'Watch Your Step in the Liquidity Polka', *Financial Times*, 31 July 2007, 1.

and jurisdictions that were merely the symptoms of the latest boom will do little to prevent the next one.

The notion that some financial products are safe and some are not, and that the use of unsafe products is the problem, also looks suspect in a boom–bust world. The booms are often a result of things appearing to be safer than they really are. Securitisation was viewed as a way of making banks safer. Diversified portfolios of sub-prime mortgages were viewed as having low delinquency rates. Micro-prudential regulation is necessary to weed out the truly reckless institutions and behaviour, but it needs to be supplemented with macro-prudential regulation aimed in part at acting as a countervailing force against the decline of measured risk in a boom (and thus excessive levels and interconnectivity of risk taking) and against the rise of measured risk in the subsequent collapse.

Supervisors have plenty of discretion, but they find it hard to use because of the politics of booms. Almost everyone wants a boom to last. Politicians want to reap electoral benefit from the sense of well-being and prosperity during a boom. Policy officials convince themselves, and try to convince others, that the boom is not an unsustainable credit binge but the positive result of structural reforms that they have put into place. Booms have social benefits. They are associated with a greater appetite for risk and a perception that risks have fallen, and this often means greater access to finance for the previously unbanked and underinsured. Booms are not quite a conspiracy of silence, but there are few who gain from their early demise. Booms thus tend to be explained away, excused and accommodated, allowing them to grow larger and larger and thus to cause more damage when they eventually collapse.

1.   Countercyclical Charges and Buffers

In light of the observations above, there is a growing consensus around three ideas: (i) capital requirements need to have a counter-cyclical element in order to, in the words of the G-20 communiqué on 2 April 2009, 'dampen rather than amplify the financial and economic cycle' by 'requiring buffers of resources to be built up in good times';[6] (ii) there should be greater emphasis on rules rather than supervisory discretion to counterbalance the political pressures on supervisors; and (iii) these rules should include leverage limits and liquidity buffers.

The references in the G-20 communiqué echo a statement by the Basel Committee on Banking Supervision following its March 2009 meeting, recommending the 'introduction of standards to promote the build-up of capital buffers that can be drawn down in periods of stress'.[7] These statements by the G-20 and the Basel Committee, coupled with similar conclusions by other official reports, suggest that the argument in favour of macro-prudential regulation has been won. How counter-cyclical capital charges and liquidity buffers are to be implemented, however, has not yet been addressed in great detail. Given the politics of booms, the 'how' is almost as important as the 'whether'.

---

[6] 'The Global Plan for Recovery and Reform', statement issued by the G-20 leaders, 2 April 2009, available at www.number10.gov.uk/Page18914.

[7] Basel Committee on Banking Supervision, 'Basel II: International Convergence of Capital Measurement and Capital Standards: A Revised Framework' (Bank for International Settlements, June 2004), available at www.bis.org/publ/bcbsca.htm.

In practical terms, Goodhart and Persaud have recommended that regulators increase the existing or base capital adequacy requirements (based on an assessment of inherent risks) by two multiples calculated using a few simple, transparent rules.[8] The first multiple would be a function of the growth of credit and leverage. Regulators should meet with monetary policy officials (where they are separate) in a financial stability committee. This meeting would produce a forecast of the growth of aggregate bank assets that is consistent with the central bank's target for inflation (or other macroeconomic nominal target). The forecast would have a reasonable band around it reflecting uncertainty. If a bank's assets grow above this band, the bank would have to put aside a higher multiple of its capital for this new lending. If its assets grow less than the lower boundary, it may put aside a lower multiple.

For example, suppose that the financial stability committee concluded that growth in aggregate bank assets of between 7.5 and 12.5% was consistent with its inflation target of 3%. Growth in a bank's assets by 25%, or twice the upper range, may lead to a doubling of the minimum capital adequacy level from 8 to 16% of risk-weighted assets. A related approach is to have one minimum capital adequacy requirement for 'bad' times and one that is twice that level for 'good' times, with good and bad times being determined by bank profitability. It is, of course, impossible to ascertain whether these capital levels would have made the system safe, but the consensus today is that they would have at least made it safer.

Financial stability committees exist in many countries, but they generally work poorly because their deliberations have no consequence. Requiring such committees to agree on a sustainable level of growth in bank assets could make their work more penetrating and action oriented.

The second multiple on capital requirements would be related to the mismatch in the maturity of bank assets and liabilities. One significant lesson of the crisis is that the risk of an asset is determined largely by the maturity of its funding. Northern Rock and other casualties of the crash might well have survived with the same assets if the average maturity of their funding had been longer. The liquidity of banks' assets has fallen far more than the credit quality of those assets.

If regulators make little distinction on how assets are funded, however, financial institutions will rely on cheaper, short-term funding, which increases systemic fragility and interconnectedness. This private incentive to create systemic risk can be offset through new capital or reserve requirements. It is partly this notion that the G-20 communiqué refers to when stating that the G-20 leaders have agreed to introduce measures 'to reduce the reliance on inappropriately risky sources of funding'. Liquidity buffers, with their size related to maturity mismatches between assets and liabilities, would have similar effect. Once again, however, there is little discussion of methodology and implementation. Measuring the true maturity of bank assets and liabilities is not a straightforward exercise.

In the framework set out in the Geneva Report,[9] assets that cannot be posted at the central bank for liquidity can be assumed to have a minimum maturity of two years or more. If a pool of these assets was funded by a pool of two-year term deposits, there would be no liquidity risk and no liquidity charge. If, however, the pool of funding had a

---

[8] The original ideas were published in CAE Goodhart and AD Persaud, 'How to Avoid the Next Crash', *Financial Times*, 30 January 2008; CAE Goodhart and AD Persaud, 'A Party Pooper's Guide to Financial Stability', *Financial Times*, 5 June 2008; and expanded by Brunnermeier et al, above n 2.

[9] Brunnermeier et al, ibid.

maturity of one month and so had to be rolled over every month, the liquidity multiple on the base capital charge would be near its maximum—say two—so the minimum capital adequacy requirement would rise from 8 to 16%.

In a boom in which the first counter-cyclical multiple is also two, the final capital adequacy requirement would be 32% of risk-weighted assets (8% × 2 × 2). Liquidity multiples would make lending costlier, since banks traditionally fund themselves short and lend long, but the liquidity multiples would also give banks an incentive to find longer-term funding and, where they could not do so, a liquidity buffer or liquidity reserve that could be drawn down in times of stress would buy time for institutions to deal with a liquidity problem.

2.   Can the Cycle be Measured?

Many people, most notably former US Federal Reserve Chairman Alan Greenspan, have voiced the concern that it is very hard to know when we are in a boom. Of course, measuring the cycle is what inflation-targeting central banks do on a daily basis—but this misses the point. If the purpose of counter-cyclical capital charges were to end boom–bust cycles, we would need to be more confident about the calibration of booms than we are today. If the purpose were to lean against the wind, however, our calibrations could be less precise.

Recall that, without counter-cyclical charges, the natural inclination in a boom is to lend even more because measured risks fall. The pre-crisis regulatory approach took the economic cycle and amplified it. The goal instead should be to moderate the worst excesses of the cycle, not to kill it. Indeed, the cycle is an important source of creative destruction in our economic system.

3.   Valuation and Mark-to-Funding Accounting

Many commentators consider accounting issues to be central in the crisis. They argue that the use of fair-value accounting has added to the spiral of sales—but suspending fair-value accounting is not helpful in an environment made worse by uncertainty. Instead, financial institutions should complement mark-to-market accounting with mark-to-funding valuations.[10]

Under mark-to-funding valuations there are essentially two alternative prices for an asset: today's market price and the discounted present value of the future earnings stream. In normal times these two prices are nearly the same, but in a liquidity crisis the market price falls substantially below the present value. If an institution has short-term funding, the realistic price to use is the market price. If it has long-term funding, the present-value price is a better measure of the risks faced by the institution. A mark-to-funding accounting framework would use a weighted average of the market price and present-value price, whose weights would depend on the weighted average maturity of the institution's funding. The combination of liquidity charges and mark-to-funding value accounting would create incentives for institutions to seek longer-term funding and would encourage a tendency for illiquid assets to be owned by institutions with longer-term funding.

[10] Ibid.

At first sight, mark-to-funding would not appear to alleviate the problem facing banks today—in fact, it could make matters worse—because they have short-term funding. However, this proposal would have had two ameliorating effects in the crisis. First, many of the bank-owned special investment vehicles that managed assets that were still performing from a credit point of view but had become highly illiquid had long-term funding. In the absence of fair-value accounting standards, they would not have joined the selling frenzy that compounded the crisis. Secondly, without the mark-to-market volatility, institutions with long-term funding would have been more willing to buy these assets. That would have provided greater price support, limiting the spiral of losses that endangered so many banking institutions.

4.   Compensation

In the G-20 communiqué and elsewhere, great attention was placed on dealing with the incentives of individual bankers and traders. However, there are clear limits to how much governments should be involved in private firms' decisions on executive pay. While measures to lengthen bankers' horizons are necessary, greater hopes should be placed in macro-prudential regulation pushing banks to develop incentive packages that promote through-the-cycle behaviour better. If that failed, however, regulators should certainly do more to address the important issue of incentives.

D.   Macro-prudential Regulation beyond the Cycle

The other dimension of macro-prudential regulation is the cross-sectional one, namely, how to manage the build-up of risks arising from the structure of the financial system.

1.   Risk Assignment

Requiring the banking system to hold more capital on average will not improve the resilience of the financial system as a whole unless there is also a better match of risk taking to risk capacity. Indeed, piling up capital requirements may act as an anticompetitive barrier, reinforcing the spectre of a few banks holding a government hostage because they are too big to fail.

Micro-prudential regulation has often been accompanied by a misguided view of risk as an absolute, constant property of an asset that can be measured, sliced, diced and transferred. This is an elegant view of risk and has the merit of allowing banks to build highly complex valuation models and to sell highly complex risk management products to handle and distribute risk. It is also an artificial construct that has little bearing on the nature of risk.

In reality, there is not one constant risk. The three broad financial risks—credit risk, liquidity risk, and market risk—are very different. Moreover, the potential spillover risk from someone holding an asset depends as much on who is holding the asset as on what it is. Different holders have different capacities for different risks. The distinction between "safe" and "risky" assets is deceptive: one can do a lot of damage with a simple mortgage, for example.

The capacity for holding a risk is best assessed by considering how that risk is hedged. Liquidity risk—the risk that an immediate sale would lead to a large discount in the price—is best hedged over time and is best held by institutions that do not need to respond to an immediate fall in price. A bank funded with short-term money market deposits has little capacity for liquidity risk. Credit risk—the risk that someone holding a loan will default—is not hedged by having more time for the default to happen but by having offsetting credit risks. Banks, with access to a wide range of credits, have a far greater capacity than most to diversify and hedge credit risks.

The way to reduce systemic risk is to encourage individual risks to flow to where there is a capacity for them. Unintentionally, much micro-prudential regulation did the opposite. By not requiring firms to put aside capital for maturity mismatches and by encouraging mark-to-market valuation and daily risk management of assets by everyone, regulators encouraged liquidity risk to flow to banks even though they had little capacity for it. By requiring banks to hold capital against credit risks, regulators encouraged credit risk to flow to those who were seeking the extra yield, were not required to set aside capital for credit risks and had limited capacity to hedge that risk. No reasonable amount of capital can remedy a system that inadvertently leads to risk-bearing assets being held by those without a capacity to hold them.

So what can regulators do? They need to differentiate institutions less by what they are called and more by how they are funded. They should require more capital to be set aside for risks where there is no natural hedging capacity. This will draw risks to where they can be absorbed best. They must also work to make value accounting and risk management techniques sensitive to funding and risk capacity. However, under the current system, the natural risk absorbers behave like risk traders, selling and buying when everyone else is doing so.

Capital requirements encouraging those with a capacity to absorb a type of risk to hold that risk will not only make the system safer without destroying the risk taking that is vital for economic prosperity, they will also introduce new players with risk capacities. This should both strengthen the resilience of the financial system and reduce our dependence in a crisis on the few banks that appeared to be well capitalised during the previous boom.

2.   Systemic Institutions

Not all financial institutions pose systemic risks. Regulation should acknowledge that some banks are systemically important and others less so. In each country supervisors establish a list of systemically important institutions that receive closer scrutiny and require greater containment of behaviour. Critical factors that determine systemic importance for an institution, instrument or trade are size of exposures, especially with respect to the core banking system and retail consumers; degree of leverage and maturity mismatches; and correlation or interconnectivity with the financial system.

In the past, interconnectivity has been understood to include issues such as payment and settlement systems, and these remain vital. Today, interconnectivity may also include institutions that behave in a highly correlated manner even if individually they appear small relative to the size of the financial system.

Goodhart and Persaud, as members of the UN Commission of Experts on Reforms of the International Monetary and Financial System, have urged the commission to recommend establishing a list of systemically important instruments.[11] Where instruments are declared systemically important because of their volume, link to leverage or interconnectivity, they recommend requiring that the instruments be registered and, where appropriate, exchange traded and centrally cleared.

E.   Host and Home Country Regulation

A gathering view is that financial institutions are global and so financial regulation needs to be global, but reality does not rhyme so easily. The crisis would not have been averted by more international meetings, and it has taught us that there is much that needs to be done at the national level to strengthen regulation. Countercyclical and liquidity charges cannot be set or implemented globally but need to be handled nationally in accordance with national cycles.

Although there is a clear need for cross-border sharing of information and coordination of regulatory actions and principles (particularly in micro-prudential regulation), the setting of capital rules and banking supervision is likely to switch back from 'home country' to 'host country'. This should not be resisted because it would have two additional benefits, particularly for emerging economies. First, if foreign banks were required to set up their local presence as independent subsidiaries that could withstand the default of an international parent, it would reduce exposure to lax jurisdictions more effectively than trying to force everyone to follow a standard that could be inappropriate and would in any case be enforced with different degrees of intensity. Secondly, nationally set counter-cyclical charges could give common-currency areas or countries with fixed or managed exchange rates a much-needed additional policy instrument—one that could provide a more differentiated response than a single interest rate could to a boom in one member state and deflation in another. This policy instrument may also be important in emerging economies, where, perhaps as a result of the absence of developed bond and currency markets, interest rates are not an effective regulator of the economic cycle.

F.   Conclusion

Warren Buffett famously remarked that you see who is swimming naked only when the tide runs out. By this, he probably means that, while fraud and unethical practices are going on all the time, they become visible only when the veil of rising market prices is removed. They are not the cause of the tide going out; they are merely revealed by it. We must continue to clamp down on fraud and ethical abuses and promote transparency, but this is not enough to avoid crises. We cannot avoid crises without avoiding the booms—booms that are always underpinned by a good story explaining why it is prudent

---

[11] Above n 2.

for individual institutions to lend more. Micro-prudential regulation is not enough; it must be supplemented by macro-prudential regulation that catches the systemic consequences of all institutions acting in a similar manner. While we cannot hope to prevent crises, we can perhaps make them fewer and milder by adopting and implementing better regulation—in particular, more macro-prudential regulation.

The Regulatory Cycle: From Boom to Bust

JEREMY COOPER[*]

A. Introduction

While attempting to stay ahead of the market might be the sole objective of the average investor, regulators are often challenged in their endeavour to do likewise. This is because regulators are typically most challenged, and therefore most active, right in the middle of a bust.[1] When regulators should be trying to look over the horizon and anticipate future regulatory challenges, the political and social imperative is often directed at mopping up the immediate problems of the past. This means regulators, themselves, are entwined in the very cycle that they seek to beat.

It is also said that regulators are often at their best in explaining in infinite detail how the last crisis might have been averted or ameliorated. This is because they spend a lot of time picking through the causes and casualties of a particular crisis and learn a great deal about what to do if something like it were ever to happen again. The difficulty is that no two crises are ever the same.

There is also the phenomenon which could be called the 'politics of boom'. Booms are great for politicians. Voters' house prices go up, they feel better off, the tax base and tax revenue increase, unemployment falls and so on. In fact, there is almost nothing adverse about a boom from a political perspective—except, of course, the timing and severity of its ending. Commentators have observed just how much this was a factor in the way regulators in the US were caught short and perhaps made less able to respond to the crisis as it unfolded.

Politics aside, regulators are challenged in executing their function by the particular economic circumstances of the time; by the scope of their own mandate; and, most crucially, by the market and the unpredictability of market participant behaviour.

This chapter considers the role of investor behaviour in economic policy, regulatory levers that can influence investor behaviour and challenges posed for regulators in trying to influence behaviour. The Australian perspective is considered, as well as current developments internationally. It concludes by arguing that arming regulators with the necessary tools to influence investor behaviour is key to developing a regulatory system less likely to be affected by the vagaries of market gyrations. However, just as important is ensuring

---

[*] Deputy Chairman, Australian Securities and Investments Commission (ASIC). The views expressed in this paper are strictly personal and are not necessarily those of ASIC, nor the Australian Government.
[1] R Rajan, 'Cycle-proof Regulation', *The Economist*, 11 April 2009, 70.

that, in times of economic crisis, regulators stop and consider which regulatory tools to employ, or regulatory levers to pull next, rather than succumbing to the urge to just 'do something'.

B.   The Australian Regulatory Environment

In the current cycle, Australia has lived up to its reputation as 'the lucky country' by remaining relatively unaffected by the worst of the global financial crisis. This is due to a number of factors: an extremely strong economic position leading into the downturn; a smaller market with less incentive for financial institutions to pursue excessive risk taking; and key financial institutions with limited exposure to toxic assets.

That said, it should be emphasised that the general health of Australia's financial system is only strong when compared to countries like the US and the UK. Australia is in a recession, or at least on the verge of one.[2] Unemployment has increased[3] and the federal government, like many others, has been forced to pour billions into stimulus packages to help sustain momentum in the domestic economy.[4]

However, Australia is nonetheless the envy of many countries that have been hit by the global financial crisis. It is not just its resources boom, or the 'Four Pillars' banking policy,[5] that set Australia up so well to weather the global financial storm; it is also Australia's regulatory settings, which have received much international attention,[6] that set Australia apart.

Australia's financial system regulatory structure is similar to the tripartite model proposed by the US Treasury in March 2008.[7] The Reserve Bank of Australia handles monetary policy and stability across the financial system, the Australian Prudential Regulation Authority prudentially supervises systemically important financial institutions, and the Australian Securities and Investments Commission (ASIC) regulates the financial markets and corporate conduct and protects investors.

While ASIC works together with the other regulators in the tripartite structure, ASIC is not a prudential regulator; nor is it responsible for financial stability or monetary policy. Therefore, the structural design of the Australian regulatory system is one way in which ASIC, in particular, can be bound up in the boom to bust cycle itself—simply because it has fewer counter-cyclical tools at its disposal.

---

[2] G Stevens, 'Road to Recovery', address to the Australian Institute of Company Directors, Adelaide, 21 April 2009, available at www.rba.gov.au/Speeches/2009/sp_gov_210409.html.

[3] Australian Bureau of Statistics, 'Labour Force Data—Australia: March 2009', Catalogue No 6202.0, (Canberra, ABS, 2009), available at www.abs.gov.au/ausstats/abs@.nsf/mf/6202.0.

[4] Prime Minister of Australia, '$42 Billion Nation Building and Jobs Plan', media release, 3 February 2009, available at www.pm.gov.au/media/Release/2009/media_release_0784.cfm.

[5] The Four Pillars policy is an Australian government policy that there should be no fewer than four major banks to maintain appropriate levels of competition in the banking sector. This policy has been credited by some as ensuring the relative strength of Australia's banking system in the current crisis. See, eg C Yates, 'Four Pillars Policy Saved Us: Macfarlane' *Sydney Morning Herald*, 3 March 2009, 19.

[6] Group of Thirty, 'The Structure of Financial Supervision: Approaches and Challenges in a Global Marketplace' (2008) 12, available at www.group30.org/pubs/GRP30_FRS_ExecSumm.pdf.

[7] US Department of the Treasury, 'Blueprint for a Modernized Financial Regulatory Structure' (March 2008), available at www.treas.gov/press/releases/reports/Blueprint.pdf.

This is particularly challenging because, following a bust, there is often a regulatory backlash leading to new and tighter rules for regulators to enforce. This contrasts with the attitude in boom times, when there is often a push towards deregulation or business-friendly application of existing rules. It is paradoxical that, while the role of the regulator might well be to 'take away the punchbowl just when the party starts getting interesting', the reality is that the punchbowl is only willingly ceded up when the party is well and truly over. This syndrome fuels what has been called a cycle of decay and growth of regulation.[8]

The current crisis has played out true to form in this respect, and there is now a concern globally that there will be a heavy-handed regulatory response to the current crisis.[9] A recent example of what has been perceived as a 'heavy-handed' approach is the Sarbanes-Oxley Act (SOX).[10] SOX was a political response to a series of very severe corporate governance and 'gatekeeper' failures in the US (eg Enron, WorldCom and Arthur Andersen). At the time, many market participants viewed SOX as an alarming and unwelcome development. The legislation was seen as stifling risk taking, having an enormous financial cost and encouraging regulatory arbitrage, where companies would choose to base themselves in the jurisdiction with the lightest regulatory touch—an outcome that would give a competitive advantage to non-US companies.

Some of these concerns played out. However, of greater significance is that only a few years after SOX there was a massive boom and bust in the shape of the sub-prime crisis leading to the global financial crisis. This time, the massive frauds that led to SOX were absent from the heart of the crisis, though the underlying ingredients were the same: excessive risk taking, complexity and lack of transparency, and conflicts of interest. Yet, while SOX failed to prevent this most recent economic crisis, commentators and market stakeholders have also found fault with a lighter-touch regulatory model. For example, the much lauded 'principles-based' or 'light-touch' regulatory approach, most famously espoused by the UK's Financial Services Authority, has also been found to be wanting in the current economic crisis and now risks being, if not jettisoned, at least modified.[11]

All of this simply illustrates the challenge governments and regulators face at a time of economic crisis, in terms of the structural design of a regulatory system and the appropriate content of that regulation. In the face of such critical choices, it can be useful to revert to first principles and, in this case, focus again on those whom regulators and government seek to both protect and control: investors.

C. Role of Behaviour in Economic Policy

The role of investor behaviour in shaping economic policy cannot be underestimated. Benjamin Graham understood that better than most when he formulated the 'Mr Market' parable. This oft-cited parable describes the affable, but hypothetical, Mr Market, who

---

[8] E Gerding, 'The Next Epidemic: Bubbles and the Growth and Decay of Securities Regulation' (2006) 38 *Connecticut Law Review* 393.

[9] See, eg F Gelber, 'Over-regulation Can Be Just as Bad as Under-regulation', *The Australian*, 23 April 2009, available at www.theaustralian.news.com.au/story/0,25197,25371759-30538,00.html.

[10] Pub L No 107-204, 116 Stat 745 (2002).

[11] PT Larsen, 'Gloves to Come Off as FSA Ends "Light Touch" Era', *Financial Times*, 13 March 2009, 17.

goes to work each day with an offer to his fellow partner to buy or sell his share of the equity in their business. Sometimes his valuations seem plausible; on other days, Mr Market seems wildly optimistic or overly pessimistic about the business. Mr Market is a very human investor.

Graham's point was that if the offeree (that is, the partner in the business) thinks what Mr Market proposes is in their interests, then they should transact with him; otherwise they would do best to ignore him. The Mr Market tale is, of course, an allegory for the stock market, but it is also a salutary reminder of how strongly investor behaviour will affect notions of value.

In their recent book *Animal Spirits*, George Akerlof and Robert Shiller explain in detail how markets routinely (but not predictably) move from euphoria to pessimism (and back again) and that effective macroeconomic policy must take this into account.[12] Regulators need to assume that investors will often not behave as if they were rational economists, or 'Econs', with a perfect information set.

So, if it is accepted that Mr Market and animal spirits are here to stay and will continue to cause booms and busts, what does this tell policymakers about the role of regulation in financial markets?

D.   Regulatory Levers to Influence Investor Behaviour

There are many regulatory levers that a conduct regulator like ASIC uses to influence investor behaviour: a rigorous disclosure regime and an investor protection and financial literacy mandate; an ability to give signals to the market (such as through enforcement actions aimed at deterring certain types of behaviour); and what might be called 'architecture solutions'.

1.   Disclosure

All markets need 'systemic' disclosure—that is, disclosure that fully explains the products trading in the relevant market to the 'system'. The 'system' here includes wholesale participants, regulators, analysts and retail investors. However, the proposition that disclosure is sufficient for investors (even sophisticated ones) to understand complex products or financial decisions, or that they will necessarily take the time to read any such disclosure, can be difficult to sustain.

Cigarette packets in the US have required written warnings on them since 1966.[13] This means that for more than 40 years consumer have had express, written disclosure about the harms of smoking cigarettes. While governments have employed a range of other measures to combat cigarette smoking, it is still incontrovertible that disclosure alone, and sometimes very graphic and shocking disclosure (far exceeding the granularity of financial disclosure), has been of limited efficacy in reducing cigarette smoking. Similar examples

---

[12] G Akerlof and R Shiller, *Animal Spirits: How Human Psychology Drives the Economy, and Why it Matters for Global Capitalism* (Princeton, NJ, Princeton University Press, 2009).
[13] Federal Cigarette Labeling and Advertising Act of 1966 15 USC §1331.

abound in the context of financial disclosure. For example, Australian law requires issuers of financial products to accompany them with product disclosure statements (PDS)—prospectus-like documents intended to disclose to the average retail investor the information they need in order to decide whether or not to invest in a particular financial product.[14] However, so concerned are issuers to discharge this obligation of disclosure that a complex, dense and lengthy document, where risk after risk is embedded in the fine print, has become the industry standard. This has rendered such disclosure far less useful than intended by legislators and regulators alike. The standard PDS is now so opaque that one consumer involved in a research study on their efficacy complained that the sample document was like reading 'Shakespeare for dogs'.[15]

All of this suggests the system is informed, but not necessarily the individual consumer. Why is this? People are moved by other, more basic, drives when they make decisions about investments, not necessarily the fine print. Take, for example, the dotcom boom in the late 1990s. Most people invested on the basis of the 'story' of the internet and the confidence they had that 'things were different this time' and that a new era of prosperity had emerged that they definitely should not miss out on. This might be an extreme example, but this type of investor behaviour is far more prevalent in many investment decisions than regulatory settings suggest.

2. Behaviour Management—Signals to the Market

Signals that a regulator gives to a market, be they in the form of policy pronouncements, media statements or enforcement actions, can be powerful behaviour management tools. This is core business for markets regulators. Opinions differ, but in some respects the prosecution or law enforcement tool can be the most effective. However, there is an argument that enforcement (or deterrence, as we now call it) is inherently pro-cyclical. It was Warren Buffett who said that it was only when the tide went out that you could tell who had been swimming naked.[16] There are parallels for law enforcement in financial markets. While there are breaches in a boom that can be, and are, regularly detected by regulators, it is often the deeper and more serious types of misconduct that only come to light just as the boom reaches its peak or is already in descent.[17]

The response to this is, of course, that regulators need to be more vigilant in a boom to find out who is swimming naked; but this is a big task. The impetus of the animal spirits driving a boom puts a lot of pressure on the resources of a regulator seeking to use the enforcement tool to be overtly counter-cyclical. Large risks are involved in tackling deep-pocketed participants at the height of a boom and making predictions about where their conduct might be heading. Regulators do this, but it is, to use an Australian phrase, 'Hard Yakka'. Conduct regulators also look for deterrence actions that can be taken quickly so that a signal is sent to the market while the targeted misconduct is still relevant—that is,

---

[14] Corporations Act 2001 (Cth), Part 7.9 Division 2.

[15] Susan Bell and Associates, 'The Provision of Consumer Research Regarding Financial Product Disclosure Documents', unpublished research for the Australian Treasury Department's Financial Services Working Group (December 2008).

[16] W Buffett, 'Berkshire Hathaway—Chairman's Letter to Shareholders' (2001), available at www.berkshirehathaway.com/2001ar/2001letter.html.

[17] The Madoff scandal is a good example.

while the behaviour in question is still potentially attractive to participants. This sort of intervention is counter-cyclical, albeit modestly.

3.   Information Tools such as Financial Literacy

A commitment to financial literacy is an essential part of any advanced economy. Credit and other financial products have been well and truly democratised, and it follows that the populace must have the tools to make informed decisions about them. ASIC, for example, has devoted a significant amount of time to financial literacy issues and sees this as a priority for the future. In addressing this issue, ASIC recognises that both the message and the means by which that message is communicated (eg letters, speeches, online, email, social networking sites) are of equal importance. To bring the idea that different types of investment carry different risks to the consciousness of everyday Australians, ASIC is using an image recognisable throughout the country: 'swimming between the flags'.[18]

This initiative is aimed at ensuring investors understand when they are 'swimming between the flags' and so in 'patrolled waters' and when they are 'outside the flags' and so swimming in potentially unsupervised water. At its simplest, this translates to the difference between investing in bank deposits, diversified blue-chip shares, vanilla managed funds and other investments with known risks or with professional advice, and investing in riskier and more complex investments that may encompass unregulated investments and scams.

It follows that if investors can ask themselves whether they might be swimming outside the flags, then they are in a position to decide their next course of action. This might be to swim back to within the flags, get a stronger swimmer to go with them (that is, obtain independent advice) or simply take the risk. Taking the risk means accepting the potential consequences: at best, an enjoyable day at the beach; at worst, being eaten by a shark.

It must be emphasised, however, that financial literacy is not a panacea and is a very long-term, incremental and aspirational proposition. It is also painstakingly difficult to measure progress. Measurement must be carried out longitudinally and over relatively lengthy periods. Also, financial literacy measures are inevitably retrospective, constantly lagging behind the emergence of ever more innovative and complex products. It is like a seesaw: the more complex the choices that have to be made by the participant, the greater the pressure on financial literacy to redress the informational asymmetry created by the complexity. It follows that financial literacy alone is not the answer.

Lauren Willis, Visiting Associate Professor, University of Pennsylvania Law School, has argued that the financial literacy model is flawed because it relies on a standard of education of consumers that is simply not achievable.[19] Instead, she argues that governments should focus on making more direct routes to welfare-enhancing choices or at least on making it easier for consumers to navigate.

Similarly, Kevin Davis, Director, Melbourne Centre for Financial Studies, University of Melbourne, has suggested that, since deregulation has increasingly shifted the burden of financial risk from governments to households, policy incentive settings should assist

---

[18] The area of a beach patrolled by life savers which is demarcated by two yellow and red flags.
[19] L Willis, 'Against Financial Literacy Education' (2008) 94 *Iowa Law Review* 197.

consumers to make complex financial decisions.[20] What both academics are advocating for is another type of regulatory lever: architecture solutions.

4. Architecture Solutions

Architecture solutions assume that both humans and markets are going to misbehave (that is, that there are going to be booms and busts) or suffer other informational and behavioural failures, but seek to ameliorate those factors by better design.

Bad design characterises quite a few of the failures that presented themselves in the global financial crisis. These include some markets (for example, credit default swaps), features of regulatory systems (for example, parts of the US regime) and products themselves (for example, collateralised debt obligations).

In Australia, the development of financial product innovation has focused on the adaptation of wholesale products for the retail market with generally positive outcomes. For example, the cash management trust[21] gave retail investors exposure to securities and rates of return that were previously not available to them on a small scale. However, this migration of products from wholesale to retail is not always foolproof, particularly where care is not taken to adjust the product for retail participation. Recent examples, in Australia, include taking the wholesale stock lending model to the retail space (as in the case of Opes Prime)[22] or margin lending for retail investors (as in the case of Storm Financial).[23] In addition, ASIC has seen many 'black-box' type products that have behaved in unexpected and unpleasant ways in the hands of retail investors. As was famously said by Peter Lynch, who ran Fidelity's Magellan Fund for many years, 'Never invest in an idea you can't illustrate with a crayon'.[24]

In this, the impact of skewed incentives (skewed incentives being another category of bad design) becomes apparent. Incentives, after all, are the key to much of the behaviour in the financial system. If the incentives are designed badly, then there will be sub-optimal outcomes. For example, financial advisers who are remunerated in a particular way might have more incentive to advocate what might be inappropriate products for a retail investor. Likewise, the current rhetoric around executive remuneration can be seen as more of a design problem than a quantum problem.

Certainly, many people find the amount of compensation paid to corporate executives hard to accept, but it is actually the design that is the real issue. In other words, what behaviour does it drive? Which parts are payable under what circumstances? What bias does the package create? A 'golden parachute' is an example of a payment that might be objectionable purely by reason of its design (that is, a payment ex post facto).

At least some of the solutions to the global financial crisis have to come from better design. More attention needs to be paid to how things work. It is a fair point that more time and effort seem to be expended on ensuring a toaster is safe from catching fire than is

---

[20] K Davis, 'Increasing Household Financial Risk—An Increasing Social Risk?' (2007) 26 *Dialogue* 1.

[21] A cash management trust is very similar to a money market fund.

[22] Australian Securities and Investments Commission, 'Opes Prime: Proposed Settlement and ANZ Enforceable Undertaking', Media Release 09-37 (6 March 2009), available at www.asic.gov.au/asic/asic.nsf/byheadline/MR09-37+Opes+Prime%3A+proposed+settlement+and+ANZ+enforceable+undertaking.

[23] Australian Securities and Investments Commission, 'Storm Financial', Advisory 08-89 (24 December 2008), available at www.asic.gov.au/asic/asic.nsf/byheadline/AD08-89+Storm+financial.

[24] P Lynch, *Beating the Street* (New York, Simon & Schuster, 1994).

the case with many financial products.[25] Many systems have tolerated relatively dangerous financial toasters, so long as the risks of incineration are disclosed.

There is an argument for building safer and simpler financial products, creating defaults and soft-compulsion options where good design seeks to compensate for poor investor behaviour. Such an example of product design that seeks to build out poor investor behaviour is the pension product in the US known as the 'target date retirement fund'. This product works on a person's projected retirement date and automatically adjusts the asset allocation and corresponding risk/return profile as that person ages. The person makes no decisions other than to join the fund and when they wish to retire. All their tendencies to panic, chase past performance, switch their investment option to what the neighbour mentioned over the fence last week (and so on) are engineered out of the product. Although some free market advocates will argue that this line of thinking is too paternalistic, it is also cognitively efficient. Do consumers need so many bewildering choices with basic products like mortgages and insurance? Or are well made defaults a better option?

Fifty years ago, buying and owning a car had a big advice/disclosure component. There was a big owner's manual and lots of tools in the garage. You had to know where to put the oil, tyre pressures and so on. Today, all you need is the key—all the 'advice' and 'disclosure' has been 'embedded' in the car. This is a realistic metaphor for financial products.

5.   Challenges in Trying to Influence Behaviour

There are several challenges regulators face in trying to influence behaviour: unintended consequences, short-term thinking, policy use-by dates and moral hazards, such as 'looting'.

(a)   Unintended Consequences

The first problem that policymakers and regulators encounter in trying to influence behaviour is that people might respond, though not in the way that was intended—which, when it is deliberate, we call 'gaming'. For example, in 1993, President Bill Clinton tried to restrain executive remuneration by denying tax deductibility for that part of an executive's salary over US$1 million, unless certain performance standards were met.[26] The result was that corporations soon learned that they could reward their executives with stock options, and so circumvent the ban (which focused on cash remuneration). The excesses and distortions this created are well-documented and far exceeded the problem sought to be solved, ultimately ending in various controversies, including the US Financial Accounting Standards Board (FASB) requiring the grant of executive stock options to be expensed in the P&L and the options backdating scandal.[27]

In a similar vein, who could forget the unintended consequences of the interventions after the crash of Wall Street in 1929? First, there was fiscal and monetary austerity; secondly, too many banks were allowed to fail; thirdly, tariff barriers were raised; fourthly, international cooperation was eschewed. No wonder the Great Depression followed.

---

[25] E Warren, 'Unsafe At Any Rate' (2007) 8 *Democracy: A Journal of Ideas* 8.

[26] Omnibus Budget Reconciliation Act of 1993, Pub L No 103-66, §13211(b), 107 Stat 312, 471.

[27] C Cox, testimony concerning options backdating, before the US Senate Committee on Banking, Housing and Urban Affairs, 6 September 2006, available at www.sec.gov/news/testimony/2006/ts090606cc.htm.

With efforts by government to restrain executive remuneration in the banking sector currently underway,[28] these unintended outcomes and consequences of well-intentioned government regulation have never been more topical. History might be set to repeat itself unless the lessons of the past are heeded, a fact which remains to be seen.

(b) Pro-cyclical Policy Driven by Short-term Thinking

Basel II has been criticised as pro-cyclical in encouraging financial institutions to increase capital in response to greater risks, which might lead banks to lend less in a downturn, but not necessarily store more capital in an upturn.[29] Similarly, International Financial Reporting Standards and fair value accounting can also be seen as pro-cyclical. This is because banks can be forced to write down assets to levels that are beyond what might be regarded as realistic, simply by reason of the market dislocations. This further exacerbates the downturn.

However, some of these policies are now being reassessed. For example, the Financial Accounting Standards Board has recently said that if there is no active market and there is distressed selling, rather than marking to market, holders can mark to 'model' instead.[30] Claudio Borio, Craig Furfine and Phillip Lowe argue that this pro-cyclicality has been driven by short-term thinking.[31] Risk is overestimated in the bad times and underestimated in the good times; not enough is set aside in the good times, meaning it is necessary to overcompensate in the bad times. Borio, Furfine and Lowe suggest that risk should be assessed over a longer term and provisions and capital ratios should be increased in the boom times so that there is a cushion effect in bad times.

(c) Policy 'Use-by Dates'

Regulatory interventions generally create a bias or incentive for market participants to behave in a particular way. This is based on the view that behaviour is most affected by incentives (either positive or negative). Such interventions are aimed at solving a particular problem or encouraging behaviour that is thought to be beneficial.

The question for policymakers and regulators is whether an intervention needs to be permanent (or at least as permanent as such things can be) or linked to the likely duration of the problem, or perhaps to the economic cycle itself. The problem is that most regulation is merely imposed without regard to its likely 'use-by date' and without a dedicated system for testing or revisiting its effectiveness. Certainly, the political process itself will detect repugnant or totally unworkable regulation, and there have been other attempts, such as the 'sunset' clause approach, for giving regulation a finite life, but these are blunt and imperfect tools.

An interesting aspect of the sub-prime crisis, as it unfolded in the US, was the

---

[28] Assistant Treasurer and Minister for Competition Policy and Consumer Affairs and Minister for Superannuation and Corporate Law, 'Productivity Commission and Allan Fels to Examine Executive Remuneration', Media Release 025 (18 March 2009).

[29] Financial Services Authority, 'The Turner Review: A Regulatory Response to the Global Banking Crisis' (London, 2009), available at www.fsa.gov.uk/pubs/other/turner_review.pdf.

[30] Financial Accounting Standards Board , 'FASB Issues Final Staff Positions to Improve Guidance and Disclosures on Fair Value Measurements and Impairments', media release, 4 April 2009, available at www.fasb.org/news/nr040909.shtml.

[31] C Borio, C Furfine and P Lowe, 'Procyclicality of the Financial System and Financial Stability: Issues and Policy Options' (2001) 1 *Bank for International Settlements Paper* 1.

surprising role that post-Depression era regulation (that was, by that time, around 70 years old) played in 'turbo-charging' the problems. These post-Depression interventions had apparently been seen as permanent.

The first example was the way in which home mortgages work in certain North American States. In the relevant States, a home loan is customarily secured by a mortgage, but the loan is without recourse to the borrower. This is a hangover from the Great Depression and flows from the so-called 'anti-deficiency' statutes in those States that prevent a lender from pursuing a defaulting borrower for the difference between the balance owing and the value of the mortgaged home (ie the deficiency). This regime exists in a minority of States (relevantly in California and Florida where the property and lending booms were among the worst), but this difference in the risk profile of the transaction (ie if it goes wrong the borrower just walks away) was a key contributor to excessive borrowing and the bubble in the real estate market.

The second example is Fannie Mae, which was set up as a government agency in 1938 to provide liquidity for aspiring homeowners and their related mortgages.[32] Prior to that time, there was only limited, short-term finance available for homebuyers. In 1968, the agency became a private enterprise and its role in the sub-prime crisis and subsequent events is well known.

Both of these interventions were a good idea at the time, but later caused distortions, or perhaps the distortions they were always intended to create became problematic as time passed. It is illustrative of the fact that sometimes the potential distortions of government intervention create even greater hazards.

(d)   Looting and Moral Hazards

US economists George Akerlof and Paul Romer suggested over 15 years ago that a number of financial collapses and crises in the 1980s involved investors taking irrational risks in the knowledge that the government would be forced to bail them out.[33] In the language of the authors, they 'looted' the public purse. This issue, as relevant now as it was then, is therefore how to prevent market participants from what US Federal Reserve Chairman, Ben Bernanke, recently called 'excessive risk taking'?[34] This will be a big theme going forward as financial institutions are taken off the life support of government bailouts consisting of explicit guarantees, toxic asset purchases, equity injections and semi-nationalisations. These events will take a long time to erase from the memories of participants, even in light of the old saying that there is no memory in the finance industry.

D.   Flexible Settings—Dynamic Regulation

These potential pitfalls suggest that financial regulation needs to be more dynamic, with a means of being refocused to meet the changing conditions of the market. For example, Borio, Furfine and Lowe suggest that authorities should be able to make discretionary

---

[32] K Pickert, 'A Brief History of Fannie Mae and Freddie Mac', *Time*, 14 July 2008, available at http://www.time.com/time/business/article/0,8599,1822766,00.html.

[33] G Akerlof and P Romer, 'Looting: The Economic Underworld of Bankruptcy for Profit', Brookings Paper on Economic Activity 2 (Washington, DC, Brookings Institution, 1993) 1.

adjustments.[35] These adjustments could be to reassess changes to capital provisioning periodically or to lower property loan-to-value ratios where there are signs of a bubble. To avoid moral hazard, these adjustments could be linked to objective assessments of risk—for example, stress tests.

The challenges here are, of course, immense. First, regulators would need to get ahead of the curve to spot the distortions in the first place. Secondly, they would need to manage the market's expectations of certainty. Thirdly, they would need to overcome the influence of short-term political cycles. Perhaps the key to flexibility is giving regulators rule-making powers or principles-based regimes that can be adjusted to suit market conditions and evolving products and practices (and, particularly, different stages of the boom and bust parts of the cycle).

As noted above, principles-based regimes have been criticised recently, with the chief executive of the UK Financial Services Authority, Hector Sants, observing that 'a principles-based approach does not work with participants who have no principles'.[36] However, it is not inherent in the concept of a principles-based regime that it is necessarily ineffectual or weak. In theory, there is no reason why the penalties for failure under a principles-based regime should be soft. If the principles are accepted and capable of recognition, then those who breach them should readily accept firm sanctions. In jurisprudential terms, if the principles are easier to understand than complex black-letter rules, it would seem equitable to punish at least as forcefully for breach of them. It is only where the principles themselves are questionable or too ephemeral, or the logic of compliance with the principles is not accepted unquestionably, that problems emerge. It is therefore too early to condemn principles-based regulation. A rule-making power allows a regulator to be accountable for a progressive agenda of market-focused regulation and this flexibility is a key advantage over legislation.

1. New Risk Assessors or Oversight Bodies?

Another option being discussed is an independent oversight body able to warn about potential global systemic risks.[37] Some suggest that it needs to be independent of existing policymakers, lending institutions, international financial institutions and countries that might contribute to further instability (for example G8 nations).[38]

Federal Reserve Chairman, Ben Bernanke, has said it is necessary to review policies and accounting rules to assess whether there is excessive pro-cyclicality. He believes some level of 'macro-prudential regulation' is required where there is holistic oversight of the whole financial system, not just prudential supervision of banks. Again, this raises questions of which regulatory body should play this role, should this be one body; and should it be one global body?

A key proposal in Lord Turner's review of the FSA was the establishment of a

---

[34] B Bernanke, 'Financial Reform to Address Systemic Risk', address to the Council on Foreign Relations, Washington, DC, 10 March 2009, available at www.federalreserve.gov/newsevents/speech/bernanke20090310a.htm.

[35] Borio et al, above n 31.

[36] Larsen, above n 11, 17.

[37] See, eg S Davis, J Lukomnik and D Pitt-Watson, 'Towards an Accountable Capitalism' (March 2009), available at www.ippr.org.uk/publicationsandreports/publication.asp?id=652.

[38] N Stern, 'The World Needs an Unbiased Risk Assessor', *Financial Times*, 24 March 2009, available at www.ft.com/cms/s/0/4dbf6ae2-1894-11de-bec8-0000779fd2ac.html.

pan-European body to focus on cross-border supervision and standard setting.[39] This would mean that there is more focus on utility banking and less on 'casino' banking, lower margins and lower risks. Although higher capital requirements can mean higher borrowing costs and possibly lower macroeconomic growth, these costs are justifiable if the result is avoiding a repeat of the global financial crisis.

In determining which oversight body could play this role, numerous issues arise, particularly in relation to the potentially conflicting regulatory responsibilities of different authorities. It will be necessary to exercise caution and not create a moral hazard where private institutions depend on policy settings established by the oversight body as a proxy for risk, similar to the way credit ratings were relied on by participants leading up to the current crisis. There is also a strong body of opinion urging that stronger national regulation is the solution and that a system that respects national diversity is preferable.[40]

2.   Financial Product Safety Commission Idea

Professor Elizabeth Warren's suggestion of a financial product safety commission is also worthy of further exploration.[41] Professor Warren suggests an independent oversight body that could protect financial consumers from dangerous financial products.[42] A commission like this would serve as an advocate and ombudsman and source of information about financial product safety, and could also impose regulations aimed at making products safer.

Not all regulators are well placed to perform this role, largely because their other day-to-day obligations conflict with the role suggested by Professor Warren, that is, an independent agency that analyses and expresses views on financial products. If we look at the recent carnage, there are many examples where such a commission might have been able to fire some early warning shots: sub-prime mortgages turned into collateralised debt obligations, auction-rate securities, many of the activities of investment banks, 'black box'-type products, 'mini-bonds', insurance wraps and so on.

A product safety commission could not be too 'noisy' lest its message become diluted in a regulatory equivalent of the boy who cried wolf. Also, it is interesting to consider how much it would cost to establish and maintain such an organisation. It would not necessarily have to be a regulatory behemoth but could start quite modestly, focusing on a menu of particular products and methodically work its way across the investment landscape. There are also two ways such a body might approach its work: the opaque route, where all issuers have to assume that their products are being scrutinised; or the transparent route, where issuers get a specific warning that particular types of products will be the subject of scrutiny. Both approaches have their merits. It is possible, also, that such a commission could have a 'cardboard policeman' effect (that is, the mere existence of such a body could have an impact on issuers' appetite for distributing dangerous products).

[39] Turner Review, above n 29.
[40] D Rodrik, 'A Plan B for Global Finance', *The Economist*, 14 March 2009, available at www.economist.com/finance/displaystory.cfm?story_id=13278147.
[41] See generally Warren, above n 25.
[42] Ibid, 17.

While a financial product safety commission could hover above (or be subsumed in) the tripartite model put forward by the US Treasury last March,[43] to be truly effective, it should sit beside the day-to-day regulators involved in authorising and facilitating the distribution of financial products. The difficulty with turning a market conduct regulator into a financial product safety commission is that those regulators are at the coalface. New products are created every day, and need to be processed quickly as part of an efficient and competitive market. These regulators often have their responsibilities split between consumer protection on the one hand and efficient capital formation on the other. There is not the luxury of taking time to study trends, test new products in a 'laboratory' atmosphere and challenge established nostrums and practices. For this reason, an independent financial product safety commission seems like a good idea.

E.   Conclusion

The Governor of the Bank of England, Mervyn King, was recently quoted as saying that 'there is no hurry to choose among [the competing suggestions for financial regulatory reform]'.[44] And, of course, he might be right. The point Mr King was making is that banks will be so risk averse for the next few years that they will hardly need new draconian and restrictive regulation. The post-crisis problem has been, and will continue to be, the need to get banks to take risks by resuming the ordinary business of lending and taking on credit risk. On the other hand, governments and regulators are keen to be doing something to restore confidence. This is a difficult balancing act. Mr King recognised this challenge when he noted that when the crisis abates it will be time to toughen financial regulation and to prevent banks, which he called 'dangerous institutions', from amplifying the natural economic cycle.[45] 'Regulation', Mr King said, 'should aim to be simple and robust', and he criticised complex measures of risk as 'rarely robust to developments that are neither easy to anticipate nor calibrate'.[46] He also suggested that if the sort of regime of stiffer regulation had been imposed in the past, it would have imposed constraints on the growth and profitability of bank balance sheets and would have operated as a form of tax on the success of investment banking and the City of London more generally.

It is clear that regulators need to take time to consider which levers to pull next, rather than falling foul of 'activity bias': the only too human urge to do something. At the crux of regulatory reform, it should be recognised that the objective is to influence behaviour. If it is accepted that it is imperative to influence the behaviour of investors (and all the other relevant actors in the system) in all the changing manifestations of that behaviour at difference stages of the 'fear and greed' cycle, it is clear that there is no simple regulatory 'set and forget'. The mechanisms and incentives to reassess and adapt regulatory policy need to be rigorous and operate regularly enough to ensure that whatever behaviour-modifying regulation was thought to be important enough to be imposed in the first place is still both necessary and has the outcome that was originally intended.

[43] US Department of the Treasury, above n 7.
[44] C Giles, 'No Hurry over Regulation, Says UK Bank Chief', *Financial Times*, 18 March 2009, 18.
[45] Ibid.
[46] Ibid.

Index